Peter Bogason
NATO and the Baltic Approaches 1949–1989

De Gruyter Studies in Military History

Edited by
Jörg Echternkamp and Adam Seipp

Volume 7

Peter Bogason

NATO and the Baltic Approaches 1949–1989

—

When Perception was Reality

DE GRUYTER
OLDENBOURG

ISBN 978-3-11-221532-6
e-ISBN (PDF) 978-3-11-123575-2
e-ISBN (EPUB) 978-3-11-123576-9
ISSN 2701-5629

Library of Congress Control Number: 2023941775

Bibliographic information published by the Deutsche Nationalbibliothek
The Deutsche Nationalbibliothek lists this publication in the Deutsche Nationalbibliografie;
detailed bibliographic data are available on the internet at http://dnb.dnb.de.

© 2025 Walter de Gruyter GmbH, Berlin/Boston
This volume is text- and page-identical with the hardback published in 2023.
The publication is supported by the VELUX FOUNDATION
Cover image: USS IOWA in BALTOPS exercise 1985 in the Baltic (Forsvarsgalleriet)
Typesetting: Integra Software Services Pvt. Ltd.
Printing and binding: CPI books GmbH, Leck

www.degruyter.com

Foreword

The defence of the Baltic Approaches during the Cold War is a large theme, and I have not attempted to include everything. My main focus concerns the two navies which in my opinion had the core roles, but I have not forgotten that defending that area is a task across the traditional three military forces. So army and air force are included, but mainly in a skeleton version.

I have had great help from the national archives, but reader be warned: there is a huge NATO archive which is still classified, and the message from NATO is that declassifying papers will take years, and finding them takes years before such declassification. Therefore, the BALTAP archives are not included in my research. So the narratives in the book are mainly based on declassified documents in national archives and those papers NATO has already declassified and made accessible on the internet.

I have also used a quite large part of the existing literature, but preferably so that my archival sources add to the knowledge from that literature which therefore is not repeated in depth. With a few exceptions I have refrained from initiating a who-is-right discussion.

The NATO organisation uses a deluge of abbreviations for organisations, commanders and various activities, and the most common ones are used here, too. A list of abbreviations located after this foreword will help the reader who is not familiar with that terminology.

During the Cold War there were two countries called Germany – East and West. I use the word Germany and Germans for West Germany; if East is meant, it is spelled out. I also use miles frequently, meaning nautical miles (1852 meters).

Geographical names have mostly been spelled in the native language.

No book is created by one person alone, at least not when I am the author. I have been heavily dependent on access to archives in Copenhagen, Freiburg and Mons, three institutions whose personnel have been very helpful along the way. The Royal Danish Defence College provided me with a security clearance that led the way to certain classified documents. The Zentrum für Militärgeschichte und Sozialwissenschaften der Bundeswehr in Berlin gave me access to office space in the Freiburg Archive. I thank all of the above institutions.

The people listed below have – in quite various ways – helped my progress in a large research field:

Steen Bornholdt Andersen, Jens Bisgaard-Frantzen, Heiko Biehl, Iben Bjørnsson, Gitte Brinkbæk, Sebastian Bruns, Jørgen Bæk-Mikkelsen, Jens Ole Christensen, Kurt Lundholm Christoffersen, Michael H. Clemmesen, Robert Dalsjö, Ineke Deserno, Steen Ole Dyrmose, Per Fischer, Cynthia Flohr, Thomas Wegener Friis, Hans-Ove Görtz, Claus Haas, Peer Henrik Hansen, Steen Hartov, Janec Helsted, Beatrice Heuser,

Jesper Thestrup Henriksen, Kjeld Hillingsøe, Mikael Holmström, Ian Hope, Martin Jespersen, Tim Sloth Jørgensen, Jonas Körtner, Peter M. Legêne, Fredi Von Essen Müller, Jens Perch Nielsen, Søren Nørby, Konstantinos Panapoulos, Thomas Tram Pedersen, Peter Hertel Rasmussen, Poul Villaume, Ulrik Wesche and Lars Wille-Jørgensen.

Of course, they have no responsibility for my mistakes.

Finally, I want to thank De Gruyter Verlag and its editors for accepting the book for publication; special thanks go to Rabea Rittgerodt and Jana Fritsche for taking the responsibility to coordinate the complexities of publishing and dealing with an often quite impatient author who keeps forgetting that *omnia tempus habent*.

The Velux Foundation has generously supported the publication of the book. Thank you very much!

Copenhagen August 2023
Peter Bogason

Logistics: NATO storage in Denmark —— 152
Offensive operations in the Baltic? —— 155
Stationary forts or mobile batteries? —— 158
US aircraft stationed in Denmark? —— 159
Integrated air defence in Europe —— 173
Summing up: Trouble spots in military policy in the 1950s —— 179

Chapter 7
NATO's New Approach and The Danish "No" to nuclear weapon: A Janus Head? —— 183

Nuclear tactical warfare – A primer —— 184
MC 48 and the "New Approach" —— 187
The analysis – objectives and campaigns —— 189
    Objectives —— 190
    Campaigns —— 191
The New Approach: Danish general strategy —— 195
The New Approach: Control of warheads —— 198
Danish first reactions to nuclear warheads —— 199
    The military chiefs —— 199
    The politicians: A policy of not rocking the boat —— 204
Nuclear warheads: A formalized "no" —— 205
New SACEUR and the stockpiling of nuclear weapons —— 207
MC 70 – facing the economic facts —— 208
    New features in MC 70 —— 209
    Consequences for the Baltic approaches —— 210
    Strong criticism —— 212
The military make-do —— 215
A "no" turned into a "maybe"? —— 219
Summing up: More becomes less —— 222

Chapter 8
West Germany's rearmament —— 227

Initial conceptions of German rearmament —— 228
Army: Bundesheer —— 229
Air force: Luftwaffe —— 232
Navy: Bundesmarine —— 237
Admiral Ruge's forward defence in the Baltic Approaches —— 245
Navy tactics: Conceptual analyses —— 250
Destroyers, frigates and FPBs —— 251
    Submarines —— 254

Mine laying —— 257
Mine sweeping —— 259
Amphibious forces —— 261
Naval air arm —— 263
The emerging threat: Ship-to-ship missiles —— 266
Nuclear weapon platforms under German control —— 269
Exercises —— 274
Summing up —— 278

Chapter 9
The Creation of Baltap —— 281
First step: Discussions of the border —— 283
Second step: Naval integration? —— 287
Third step: Integrated naval command —— 297
Planning issues —— 299
Command over naval aircraft – AFNORTH or AFCENT? —— 305
SACEUR intervenes —— 309
Fourth step: Public discussions and a political solution —— 312
Fifth step: Final negotiations —— 318
The Soviets react —— 322
Summing up: Eight years of bureaucratic and symbolic politics —— 324

Chapter 10
The Warsaw Pact and its Tactics – as seen by NATO —— 328
Organising the Warsaw Pact —— 328
NATO's perceptions at the command level —— 330
Danish Intelligence sources —— 331
Routine reports —— 332
Special reports —— 336
Special themes —— 338
Exercises —— 341
Summing up: information from exercises —— 350

Chapter 11
The 1961 Berlin crisis —— 352
Live Oak 1958–59 —— 352
Berlin crisis summer 1961 —— 353
Denmark —— 355
West Germany —— 361
NATO and Live Oak —— 362

BERCON DELTA: Problems of legality —— 364
　　West German considerations —— 365
　　AFNORTH implementation of BERCON —— 367
And the Warsaw pact? —— 368
Summing up: Close to a stalemate —— 370

Chapter 12
Making BALTAP operational: Organising for WAPA threats —— 371
　　The threat picture: SG 161, Danish intelligence and a Polish plan —— 372
　　　　SG 161/15 —— 372
　　　　A Danish report —— 373
　　　　A polish plan for attacking the Baltic Approaches —— 379
　　Status 1962: Annual review and combat effectiveness —— 381
　　　　Annual review —— 382
　　　　Combat effectiveness —— 383
　　Organizing BALTAP —— 387
　　Strategy —— 389
　　Sweden —— 392
　　　　The changes in 1958 —— 392
　　　　Contacts withering away —— 396
　　Summing up: Protecting the Baltic Approaches by 1962 —— 399

Chapter 13
Making BALTAP operational: Naval tactics in the 1960s —— 401
　　The general NAVBALTAP perspective —— 402
　　　　Denmark —— 403
　　　　Germany —— 409
　　Danish-German cooperation in Denmark: Exercise DALGAS —— 416
　　Modernisation of the two navies —— 419
　　　　Self-evaluation of the Danish navy 1962 —— 420
　　　　A modernised Danish navy —— 423
　　　　Modernisation problems in the German navy —— 425
　　Summing up: Caution in the Baltic —— 450

Chapter 14
Towards flexible response and new NATO bodies —— 452
　　Strategy under stress —— 453
　　Flexible response elements —— 455
　　The increased importance of surveillance —— 460
　　Danish considerations —— 463

German consequences —— **464**
Tactical nuclear weapons —— **468**
  Denmark —— **468**
  Germany —— **470**
Summing up: Flexible response complexity —— **472**

Chapter 15
NATO-reinforcements —— 474
What to do if tension arises? —— **475**
AMF: SACEUR's task force reinforcements —— **477**
Reinforcements by surface vessels and aircraft carriers —— **478**
Flexible response for the flanks and the UKMF —— **481**
Reinforcement options in the 1970s —— **483**
The AMF —— **487**
Reinforcements in the 1980s —— **490**
Summing up: Reinforce management taking its time —— **492**

Chapter 16
Crises in the 1960s —— 494
The Cuban missile crisis —— **494**
The 1968 Czech crisis —— **502**
  Confusion in the NATO HQ —— **502**
  Disagreements at the Danish top level —— **503**
Summing up: Crises with little alarm —— **507**

Chapter 17
Towards NATO missiles in the 1970s —— 508
Status 1969: A German "head count" —— **508**
The tactical operations of an amphibious WAPA assault —— **514**
  Closing in on the landing areas —— **515**
  The landing process —— **517**
The missile threat in the Baltic and NATO's response —— **520**
  WAPA missiles —— **520**
  Developing NATO missiles —— **522**
  Missiles in the Danish navy —— **525**
  Missiles in the German navy —— **529**
Danish defence policy under review —— **532**
Modernising the navies in the Baltic Approaches —— **535**

Contents

Foreword —— V

Abbreviations —— XV

Chapter 1
Introduction —— 1
    The approach of the book and its position within the literature on NATO —— 3
    The Baltic Approaches and littoral warfare —— 6
    Military sufficiency and reinforcements —— 10
    Three levels of analysis —— 12
    NATO's overall strategy: A brief overview —— 15
        MC 14 —— 15
        MC 14/1 —— 15
        MC 14/2 —— 16
        MC 14/3 —— 17
    The structure of the book —— 18

Chapter 2
Initial ideas for defending the Baltic Approaches —— 20
    1948–49: The Scandinavian Defence Alliance —— 22
    Danish strategic considerations based on German thoughts —— 25
    1949–50: NATO's organisation and first strategy —— 30
    Sweden's defence —— 34
    Swedish cooperation with NATO? —— 36
    Summing up: The strategic steps towards NATO —— 39

Chapter 3
NATO's military organisation and initial plans —— 41
    Making DC-13 operational (1): Organisation —— 41
    Making DC-13 operational (2): Strategic & tactical guidance —— 45
    The Russian threat as perceived by NATO's standing group —— 47
    The first defence plans for AFNORTH —— 52
        Land —— 53
        Sea —— 54
        Air —— 55
    A British critique —— 56
    A British plan for nuclear attack on Baltic and Northern targets —— 57

SACLANT and AFNORTH strategy & cooperation —— 62
Operation MAINBRACE —— 64
    Initial situation —— 66
    What happened —— 68
    Evaluation —— 69
Summing up: Towards NATO's War plans and tactics —— 72

Chapter 4
NATO in control: Annual Review and intelligence reporting —— 76

Towards the Annual Review —— 76
Annual Review 1952 —— 78
Combat effectiveness —— 83
Annual review 1957 —— 84
    Denmark —— 86
    West Germany —— 87
Combat effectiveness 1957 —— 88
    Denmark —— 88
    West Germany —— 89
The enemy: Intelligence reporting to the standing group —— 90
Summing up: NATO's instruments of information and control —— 95

Chapter 5
Denmark almost alone —— 97

Denmark's weak defence in 1949–50 —— 97
Danish defence principles in the early 1950s —— 101
    The Danish Army —— 101
    The Danish Navy —— 104
    The Danish Air Force —— 109
Counter-offensive attacks in the 1950s —— 110
Cooperation between the Danish navy and air force —— 114
Cooperation with the Norwegian and British navies —— 116
Exercise brown jug 1957 —— 118
Integrating Danish Defence into NATO —— 130
Squeezing the Danish military budget 1955–60 —— 132
Summing up: A weak defence of the Baltic Approaches —— 136

Chapter 6
NATO Policy and Danish military issues in the 1950s —— 139

Soviet uses of the Bornholm agreement —— 139
The territorial defence of Schleswig-Holstein 1949–62 —— 144

    The Danish navy: Plan "1982" —— 536
    Plans for the German navy —— 539
    Summing up: The modernised NATO navies —— 555

Chapter 18
NATO and the Baltic Approaches in the 1980s —— 557
    NATO strategy for the 1980s: CONMAROPS —— 558
    WAPA risks —— 560
        Poland 1981 —— 560
        Denmark —— 561
        Germany —— 565
    Operational plans in the Baltic Approaches —— 567
        NATO and communication —— 569
        Danish naval tactics —— 571
        German naval tactics —— 575
        Operation HURRICANE —— 578
    Replacement plans in the navies —— 580
        Denmark —— 580
        Germany —— 582
    WAPA Tactics —— 589
        Units in the Baltic —— 589
    Exercises —— 592
    WAPA use of nuclear warheads? —— 596
    1989 – the end? —— 598
    Summing up: NATO and the WAPA in the 1980s —— 600

Chapter 19
Conclusions —— 602
    The short, general answers —— 602
    Military capabilities in littoral warfare —— 604
    Negotiating the defence of the Baltic Approaches —— 607
    Perceptions and realities —— 612

Sources and References —— 615

Abbreviations

2. ATAF	2nd Allied Tactical Air Force
AA	Anti-Aircraft (guns/missiles)
AFNORTH	Allied Forces Northern Europe
AFCENT	Allied Forces Central Europe
AMF	Allied Command Mobile Force
ASW	Anti Submarine Warfare
ASP	Atomic Strike Plan
BALTAP	Allied Forces Baltic Approaches
CINCLANT	Chief Atlantic Forces
CINCNORTH	Chief Allied Forces North
CINCENT	Chief Allied Forces Centre
COMTAFDEN	Commander, Tactical Air Force, Denmark
DC	Defence Committee (NATO)
D-day	Day of initiation of hostilities (+ yy indicates D-day plus yy days)
EDC	European Defence Community
ECM	Electronic Counter Measures
FOD	Flag Officer Denmark
FOG	Flag Officer Germany
FPB	Fast Patrol Boat
FSS	Forsvarsstyrelsen – The Danish Joint Chiefs of Staff
GIUK	gap – waters between Greenland, Iceland and the UK
GTB	Gas Turbine Boat
Helo	Helicopter
HQ	Head Quarter
IFF	Identify Friend and Foe
LOC	Line of communication – transport corridor
MC	Military Council (of NATO)
Miles –	always nautical miles, 1.852 km.
MTB	Motor Torpedo Boat
M-day	Day of Mobilisation (+ yy indicates M-day plus yy days)
NAVNORTH	Naval Command AFNORTH
NCS	Naval control of Shipping
POL	Petroleum, oil and lubricants
Recce	Reconnaissance
SACEUR	Supreme Allied Commander Europe
SACLANT	Supreme Commander Atlantic
SAR	Sea-air-rescue operations
SG	NATO's Standing Group
SHAPE	Supreme Headquarters Allied Powers Europe
STANAVFORLANT	Standing Naval Force Atlantic
TCC	Temporary Council Committee

UKMF	United Kingdom Mobile Force
WAPA	Warsaw Pact
WEU	West European Union
WWI	World War I
WWII	World War II

Chapter 1
Introduction

This book analyses NATO's defence plans for the narrow sea exits from the Baltic to the North Sea, called the Baltic Approaches, in the time period from 1949 to 1990 – commonly named "The Cold War". It is not a story of NATO as such, the perspective limits the analysis to those segments of NATO that dealt with the Baltic Approaches. Why such a theme? Because the military story of the defence of the Baltic Approaches during the Cold War has never been written in one treatise. This book takes important steps, but even then it is lacking in the sense that its primary focus is on the role of the navies.

Originally, the NATO commands for the Baltic Approaches were Allied Forces Northern Europe, AFNORTH, and a small portion of Allied Forces Central Europe, AFCENT. The military forces were, by and large, from Denmark, West Germany and, over time less and less, Great Britain and (Southern) Norway. Since they were controlling AFNORTH, some other NATO bodies must be included in the analysis: Supreme Allied Commander Europe, SACEUR and the main governing bodies of NATO.

The book is not a narrative praising or rebuking the various regional commanders of AFNORTH and their staffs. The focus is less on individual officers and the politics of their organisation. The focus is more on what they stood for: the military policies and military wishes for a particular setup which, hardly surprisingly, clashed with political goals now and then.

So our questions regard what the purposes were of the military organisations, what military instruments they were meant to organise, how they organised cooperation with one another in order to create a military alliance among units from sovereign states and how they tested the military capabilities of the organisations. All of this is on the basis of how the military leaders perceived the goals of the stated enemy, the Soviet Union, and its allies.

Five easy questions? Well, as we shall see, things quickly got complicated, and the result was the creation of a large, bureaucratic military organisation which constantly channelled complex communications among its parts and to its political masters. In all organisations one will find agreements and disagreements among persons and sections, creating factions which must negotiate compromises in order to move on.[1] NATO, a military command organisation, was no exception from this rule.

---

[1] Peters, B. Guy. *The Politics of Bureaucracy*. London: Routledge, 2000.

The stories told in this book exemplify the perceptions of the military leaders, not some abstract or objective truth. What the "real" size of the enemy troops was does not matter; it is the attempts by the actors to create some vision of that phenomenon, interpret it, communicate this perception on to other actors, be they military or political, and subsequently negotiate the consequences of the interpretations with those other actors.

This is mirrored in the subtitle of the book: perception became reality.

The NATO organisation was build to create such visions. NATO was created in 1949 as a defence organisation and initially only had military defence against any attacker stated as its object. But after six months, the generic defence concepts were sharpened into a more precise understanding of what the defence was aimed at – curbing Soviet intentions of World dominance:

> The ultimate objective of Soviet policy is the establishment of Communist regimes, directed from Moscow, throughout the world. The Soviet leaders will appreciate that this objective can only be attained through the collapse of the main bastions of democratic power . . . The USSR would seek first to complete the domination of Europe and Asia and to defeat the United Kingdom followed by the integration of the economic and industrial resources of the Eurasian land mass, so as to place the Soviet Union in an impregnable position, from which North America could be attacked ultimately by military forces. (MC 14, paragraph 7, 14-3-1950)

We shall probably never know if this statement was mirroring any actual plan in the East, we only know that it never materialised. But it expressed the basic belief system for NATO during the Cold War. And the Soviet Union had similar concepts regarding NATO's intentions, seen with Marshall Gretschko after an exercise in May 1961:

> (In the West) we find an aggressive state like West Germany . . . NATO's war industry is in a high state of alert, in West Germany a mass army is being set up. . . . NATO has plans for a surprise attack on the socialist camp. Especially their exercises in the Fall of 1960 point to the fact that they are testing their plans.[2]

We shall see that over time both perceptions of the future became less and less likely. Ultimately they had to be changed, and NATO changed focus.

The Soviets never attacked any NATO country, nor did NATO attack the Soviet Union and its protective territorial belt of East European countries. NATO's plans were all formulated as reactions to an attack from the East, but contained comprehensive attacks in the Soviet Union, far from an initial battle field in Middle Europe. The military plans of the Soviet Union (and its allies) that we know of all

---

2 Nielsen, Harald. *Die DDR und die Kernwaffen – Die nukleare Rolle der National Volksarmee im Warschauer Pakt*, 30. Baden-Baden: Nomos Verlagsgesellschaft, 1998.

stated that the strategy and tactics were defensive, not aggressive. Nonetheless, the plans were purely formed as attacks until the mid-1980s – formulated as responses to a NATO attack.

The approach of the book and its position within the literature on NATO

We shall not pursue the above political themes at their somewhat abstract level of thought. This is not a history of international politics, the political systems and their policy-making. Traditionally, that has been the theme of many analyses of NATO. Some have concerned international politics and the East-West confrontations by political leaders – the Cuban missile crisis being one lucid example.[3] Others have analysed the political game of defence policy – Danish defence policy, international politics and NATO come to mind with comprehensive analyses of both political parties and foreign policy offices.[4]

Recently NATO has been of increasing interest for academic analysts. Using an institutional approach by conceptualising NATO as an international institution, Seth Johnston has analysed its ability to adapt to changing circumstances in "critical junctures" or crises in its environment.[5] NATO and its role in maintaining nations as democratic institutions has been analysed by Sayle.[6] Susan Colbourn has analysed various processes involving NATO, NATO member countries, the Soviet Union and various anti-missile groups during the "Euromissile Crisis" in the early 1980s, based on a conception of fear: the reactions of various actors when faced with the threats of missiles in Europe.[7]

These analyses tell the reader about various political processes in NATO's top, among the national political actors of the member states and their relations to outside interests. Important as they are, we do not ignore such political discussions and analyses, but in this book there is no independent analysis of those processes; we use existing publications for the purpose of creating the political background as

---

3 Allison, Graham T. *Essence of Decision*. Boston: Little, Brown & Co, 1971.
4 Villaume, Poul. *Allieret med forbehold*. København: Eirene, 1995; Dansk Institut for Internationale Studier. *Danmark under den kolde krig. Den sikkerhedspolitiske situation 1945–1991. Bind 1: 1945–1962*. København: Dansk Institut for Internationale Studier, 2005a.
5 Johnston, Seth. *How NATO Adapts: Strategy and Organization in the Atlantic Alliance Since 1950*. Baltimore: John Hopkins University Press, 2017.
6 Sayle, Timothy Andrews. *Enduring Alliance: A History of NATO and the Postwar Global Order*. Ithaca: Cornell University Press, 2019.
7 Colbourn, Susan. *Euromissiles: The Nuclear Weapons That Nearly Destroyed NATO*. Ithaca: Cornell University Press, 2022.

time passes. Our focus and use of primary sources concern the military side: the ideas of the military decision-makers and the games of constructing and implementing defence policies based on those perspectives – in continuous interaction with their political masters, of course. Communication between military top officers and ministers is thus included.

In broad theoretical terms this book carries out an institutional analysis, focusing on actors performing roles within a series of organisational constraints understood as norms and rules, creating a temporary balance among various interests in a complicated process involving (mostly) many actors.[8] We follow various actors interacting with other actors within the institutional constraints of their organisations which may be military, administrative or political. The constraints may, however, be interpreted variously over time, and they may be changed as a result of the processes among those actors. The interaction takes place on the basis of a policy problem the actors wish to change (or maintain unaltered) – in this book the various ways of letting military forces prepare for action.

However, the institutional framework is only that – a way of organising a large number of actors and incidents into order for the analyst. It makes traditional explanatory factors like personalities less relevant; we do not pursue the personal whims of e.g. General Montgomery or Eisenhower, but we do take note of the expressions of their policy principles. Thus the primary ordering principle of the analysis comes from the problem the actors address. The general theme is the defence of the Baltic Approaches, but in this analysis it is subdivided into various issues; examples are the creation of BALTAP, the issue of having American aircraft stationed on Danish soil or the defence of Schleswig-Holstein before West Germany took over, or the introduction of missiles on NATO warships. The second ordering principle is the way the actors express their policy positions vis-à-vis other actors – found in documents in the various archives – and reach an understanding of the solution to the problem. That solution may and may not be sustainable over time; if not, the issue will in most cases come back on the agenda sooner of later. As we shall see later, the issue of stationing American aircraft on Danish soil is exemplary in this respect: it was never solved according to its original formulations, but was replaced by a system of reinforcement.

This book is unique in its approach to the defence of the Baltic Approaches, but analyses having comparable elements and interests in their empirical approach would be Lemke's narrative of the AMF,[9] Grove's analysis of NATO exer-

---

[8] Bogason, Peter. *Public Policy and Local Governance: Institutions in Postmodern Society.* New Horizons in Public Policy. Cheltenham: Edward Elgar, 2000.
[9] Lemke, Bernd. *Die Allied Mobile Force.* München: De Gruyter, 2011.

cises in Norwegian waters[10] and a series of analyses of NATO exercises.[11] They all include the operational and tactical levels of military activities, but differ in many other ways.

Not all military perspectives are included. The book does not analyse strategic warfare, i.e. the use of inter-continental bombers and missiles – land or submarine based – aimed at key military command centres and metropolitan and industrial centres. These strategic weapons, of course, were key in the NATO deterrence policies, and they may have been the determining factors in preventing war. But they are outside the scope of our analysis *per se*; we do, however, include supporting and escorting engagements for the strategic plans from local forces. And eliminating this sort of strategic warfare does not keep us from analysing the more localised strategy of the countries around the Baltic Approaches.

The bulk of the analysis, then, concerns what may be termed the operational level, i.e. the building up of the military command organisations and the forces available for them, and the processes of preparing, constructing and exercising war plans.[12] Tactical nuclear weapons are included as part of operational and tactical activities in NATO.

We shall return to these perspectives below. But it must be stated from the outset that due to the lack of declassification of the NATO regional command archives, including the BALTAP, and facing the fact that specific demands for declassification take long time and are difficult because one can not really identify relevant papers, many perspectives simply cannot be researched. Fortunately, the Danish and German archives have many relevant NATO documents in stock.

This book has less interest in the weaponry or "military hardware" *per se*. Of course, we cannot eschew an understanding of the technological development which determines much of military capability, but the reader will find no detailed discussions of the technical pros and cons of various types of guns, tanks, missiles, aircraft and warships of NATO and its adversary in the East. There is a vast literature on military weapons for those who want to pursue that interest. We do, however, analyse in some detail the tactical pros and cons which the military leaders had to ponder, e.g. when choosing among systems of weapons.

---

10 Grove, Eric. *Battle for the Fiørds*. London: Ian Allan Ltd, 1991.
11 Heuser, Beatrice, Tormod Heier, and Guillaume Lasconjarias, eds. *Military Exercises: Political Messaging and Strategic Impact*. Rome: NATO Defense College. Forum Paper 26., 2018.
12 Vego, Milan. *Operational Warfare at Sea. Theory and Practice*. New York: Routledge, 2009.

The Baltic Approaches and littoral warfare

Geography determines many of the limits for our analysis. The Baltic Approaches are the waters connecting the Baltic Sea with the North Sea, and throughout the Cold War most of the area was Danish national waters within a distance of three nautical miles. The easterly coastal waters between Denmark and Sweden are Swedish national waters, and to the North, Skagerrak's coastal waters are Danish, Swedish and Norwegian. To the South, The European mainland formed the coast line of the Middle and West Baltic with Poland, East Germany and West Germany as territorial proprietors.

Much of the waters, however, was international sea and therefore freely accessible, guaranteed by international law. But as the map indicates, any ship wanting to go to the North Sea from the Baltic or wanting to enter the Baltic must pass though the Danish and Swedish narrows. Consequently, Denmark and Sweden have the possibility of acting as a choke point (see below) and prevent such passage. However, international law defines the narrows (less than six nautical miles broad) in Øresund and Storebælt as international waters for peaceful passage. Nonetheless, in times of war passage of the narrows may be controlled by the nation adjacent to the strait if the security of the nation is at risk.

Seen from the Soviet Union, the passage area was important for several reasons. First, if war broke out, and the Soviet Union wanted to attack NATO's lines of communication (LOCs) – transports of war supplies – from the USA to Europe, Soviet submarines slated for that role and stationed in the Baltic had to pass the narrows in order to get out to the North Sea and from there to the Atlantic, exactly as the Germans did during the Second World War. Warships also needed to come back from the North Sea or the Atlantic for repair and supplies in the Baltic harbours. Second, the area as such was of interest because of the airfields which formed bases for NATO's tactical attacks towards the east, and they would form excellent bases for Soviet attacks towards the west, if they were captured. Third, the area also was a possible base resource for other types of naval military activity. Fourth, if the area was conquered, the NATO threat against the flank of Soviet operations in Central Europe was diminished, and NATO was prevented from letting warships pass into the Baltic and disturb Soviet sea LOCs – whereas it would take five days with 2,000 vehicles along the roads to move a division 800 kilometres along the Baltic coast, it would take two days on ships to an East German harbour, so naval transport had many advantages if the Soviets wanted reinforcements brought towards the west.[13]

---

13 Diedrich, Torsten. "Zur Rolle der Nationalen Volksarmee der DDR." In *Die Streitkräfte der DDR und Polens in der Operationsplanung des Warschauer Paktes*, edited by Rüdiger Wenke, 26. Potsdam: Militärgeschichtliches Forschungsamt, 2011.

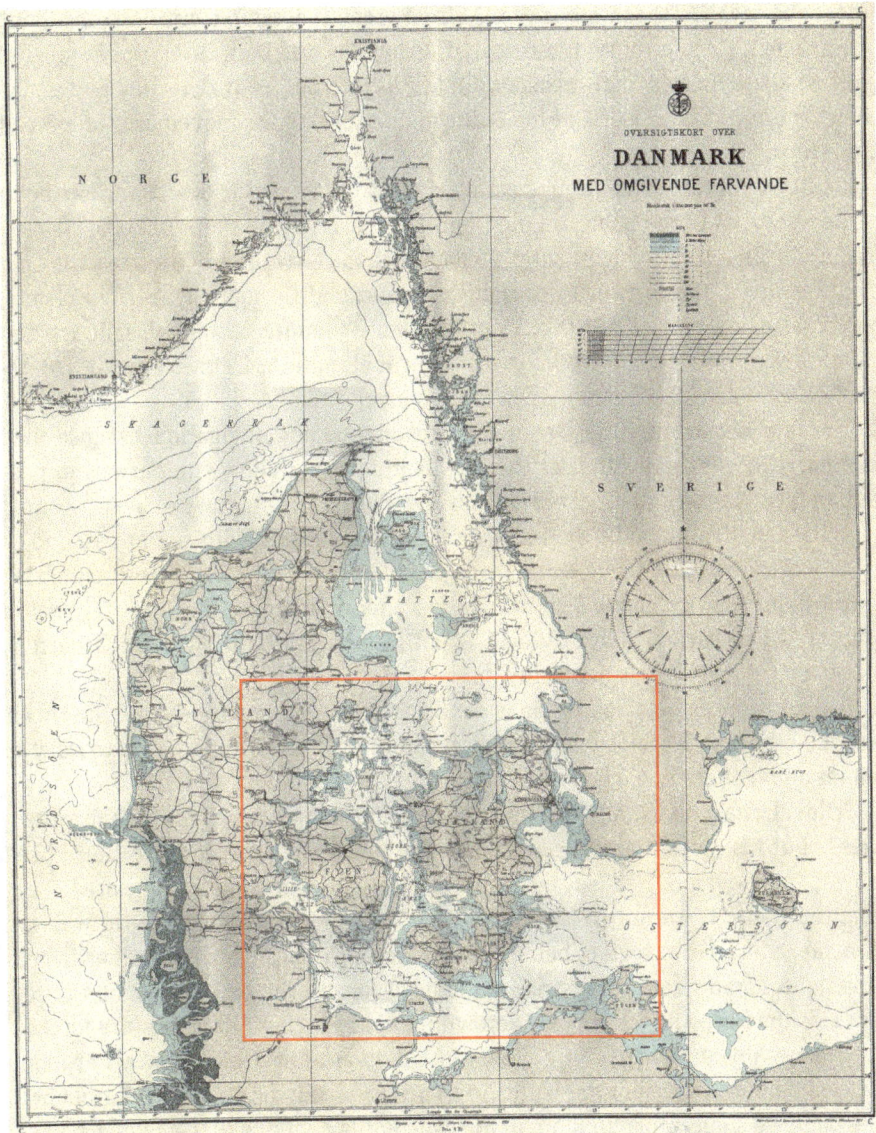

Figure 1.1: The Baltic Approaches. There are three straits: Øresund (East), Storebælt (middle) and Lillebælt (West). To the north Kattegat and Skagerrak (leading to the North Sea), to the south and east the Baltic. Shallow waters dominate the narrows, demanding very careful navigation. Map source: Forsvarsgalleriet.

Consequently, NATO as well as WAPA had a great interest in controlling the Baltic Approaches. Furthermore, the island of Bornholm was Danish territory and situated so far to the east that it was useful as an electronic hub, detecting and analysing communication traffic in the Baltic and observing the movements of aircraft and ships.

In geographic terms the focus therefore is on the Baltic Sea from Bornholm and westwards in the Baltic, on the Danish-Swedish narrows and Kattegat. Skagerrak is only included intermittently. Included are the territories of the area, the *Cimbric Peninsula*, the territories of Danish Jutland and German Schleswig-Holstein, which all were part of AFNORTH but also have common historical, military and cultural roots as elements of the Danish Kingdom until 1864. Other parts of the AFNORTH area are included when the sources involve them.

A ship negotiating the straits requires meticulous navigation because they are narrow with many shoals. The low depths do not allow submarines to pass submerged; very small u-boats may, however, be successful in Storebælt.

The low depths make the narrows ideal for blocking with sea mines, and in both world wars the Germans and the Danes controlled passage with extensive mine fields – the Germans to hinder the enemy entering the Baltic (Winston Churchill had such a plan in World War II, Operation Catherine, see Osborn[14]), the Danes to guard their neutrality.

The distances between Denmark and Eastern Germany are short, both by air and by sea, and therefore careful observation around the clock is necessary to maintain an overview of activities in the area.

Naval analysts usually discuss strategy and tactics based on Mahan's theories.[15] But his ideas mainly concerned large fleets and the concentration of sea power, "blue water" strategies. Narrow straits, low waters and semi-closed areas like the Baltic were not in his focus. Vego uses the concept of littoral warfare (warfare in a coastal region; being close to the shore) for naval operations in confined and narrow seas;[16] he stresses the need for fast action and reaction at sea, but also the necessity for cooperation with other branches of the military forces.

The main analytical components of conducting littoral warfare[17] are condensed below, adapted to the Baltic Approaches during the Cold War. Throughout the book we shall return to them in the concluding analyses of the chapters.

---

14 Osborn, Patrick R. *Operation Pike: Britain Versus the Soviet Union, 1939–1941*. London: Greenwood, 2000.
15 Mahan, Alfred Thayer. *The Influence of Sea Power Upon History: 1660–1783*. Boston: Little, Brown and Company, 1890.
16 Vego, Milan. "On Littoral Warfare." *Naval War College Review* 68, no. 2, Article 4 (2015).
17 Ibid.

- The geography often creates choke points, narrow passages which are easy to block for passage by sea mines and other obstacles, mostly bolstered by coastal batteries. The Danish narrows are examples of choke points for ships entering or exiting the Baltic. Navigation is complicated due to shallow waters with shifting depths, often many islands and inlets, as can be seen from the map of the Baltic Approaches above. A special issue is that the easternmost Baltic Approaches strait, Øresund, has Sweden as its eastern coast, and Sweden was a neutral country until 2022.
- For the defender of choke points, the goal is to obtain sea control and consequently create sea denial for the enemy. The denial in principle only refers to the passage of the narrows, but the consequence is sea denial beyond the narrows if the enemy has no other way of getting there. But the attacker will also desire to deny the defence access by sea to protect their own areas, and in the Baltic area distances are relatively short – from the former East Germany to Denmark there were only a few hours sailing time, and by aircraft the travel took minutes.
- The navigational challenges make the use of large ships questionable. Aircraft carriers need much space to operate safely and they are vulnerable to attacks by enemy airplanes. Cruisers also may face difficulties in shallow waters, and submarines need considerable depth to operate safely – in the Cold War their operation areas were east of Bornholm. Mini submarines may, however, become handy. Destroyers are probably the largest units applicable. Areas with many islands and inlets invite the use of small sea craft such as FPBs and corvettes armed with guns, missiles and torpedoes. Mine laying capabilities are indispensable, and (mobile) shore batteries may protect the mine fields once laid. The short distances in the area favour the use of helicopters and fighter-bombers which can quickly be deployed and redeployed.
- One can therefore expect actions involving more than one force type, typically navy and air force, and if the landing of troops is expected, also the army. Consequently, command and control requires integrated staffs across the traditional single-force organisations, and the top commander must have a thorough understanding of the operating conditions of the other branches. The communication procedures and hardware must be founded on the same system. In may cases, mission command should be applied, giving the commander considerable liberty to adapt and act as necessary in the situation. Force integration of the staff then is a must.
- Advanced reconnaissance and information systems are desirable to give the commanders at all levels a graphical depiction of the movements of the enemy as well as their own forces under and on water and in the air. It goes without saying that an integration of weapon direction systems with that sys-

tem is warranted. The specific combination of systems will depend on the tasks of the commander in question; there are different needs at the very top (overview) and at the action levels (tactical information and weapon direction). Care must be taken not to feed so much information that the systems get clogged. Furthermore, the meteorological conditions in littoral waters may inhibit electronic interaction, making such systems inoperable.
- In a wider context, littoral waters may form the border for the flank of ground forces; this was the case for the Baltic Approaches which formed transport corridors for the northernmost WAPA forces along the border between East and West Germany (and likewise for NATO forces in Schleswig-Holstein). This created an interest for NATO – as a defence measure for their own ground forces outside the approaches – to attack WAPA ships along the Baltic coast.

We have strong emphasis on naval operations, but we also have to include army and particularly air force operations to understand the complex military task of controlling the Baltic Approaches. In NATO, this necessity induced the creation of a particular command, the BALTAP which created close cooperation and coordination among the three military branches.

Military sufficiency and reinforcements

Why a military defence? Until about one year after World War II, Danish foreign policy was one of being neutral in any military standoff; this had been successful in WWI, less so in WWII when the Germans occupied the country in April 1940. After the creation of the United Nations, Denmark was neutral under its principled protective umbrella, but as the West European countries increasingly perceived a military as well as political threat from the Soviet Union, the neutrality of a small nation increasingly lost its credibility. Realising both a political threat from communists of a takeover of the state apparatus and at the same time a military risk because of its geo-political position with the Baltic Approaches, Danish politicians (excepting the Communist Party) in 1948 started a process of, first, seeking to preserve neutrality by bonding with neighbouring Scandinavian countries, and – when this possibility withered away – second, in 1949 to engage in a non-neutral military and political cooperation with a large number of western countries.

So from 1949, Danish neutrality was history and instead Denmark actively participated in building up a defence against military action by the Soviet Union. NATO was explicitly formed as a defence union, but the Soviets could hardly avoid looking at the NATO military build-up as a threat against the Soviet Union, which they did.

Militarily, the defence of the Baltic Approaches was complicated, requiring intimate cooperation among army, navy and air force in a diverse geographical setting, as we saw above. However, the crux of the matter of defending Denmark and the Baltic Approaches was that Denmark could not by itself muster a military defence force which could fend off Soviet forces for a long time. The defence of the Baltic Approaches heavily depended on military assistance from other NATO members within a relatively short time horizon. The military history of defence of the area therefore is a history of, first, NATO urging Danish political and military decision-makers to strengthen Danish military forces as much as possible and, second, Danish and NATO decision-makers working to achieve sizeable military reinforcements from other countries as soon as possible: preferably before a military attack by the Soviet Union was seen to be under implementation. If not, immediately after.

Such interactions about their own national defence and international reinforcement were complicated in military as well as political terms. Regarding Danish national military forces, we can state from the outset that military decision-makers, as one might expect, pressed for voluminous resources, and political decision-makers reacted with many reservations, referring to the (poor) state of the national economy and in some cases also political belief systems of specific political parties. NATO officials also prompted for more resources and, in addition, for specific military technical solutions to perceived weaknesses in the defence; for instance, the length of time served for conscripted soldiers. From 1956, similar discussions took place in West Germany in a somewhat different political and military setting.

Regarding reinforcements, the general story is complicated. There were many ways to carry out reinforcements. First, by creating access to military supporting features:
- by participating in military investments in base facilities and storage for common NATO use – e.g. airfields, harbours, ammunition stores;
- by participating in communication infrastructures to support the exchange of information among NATO countries – e.g. radar information relay systems.

Second, by bringing in military forces to participate in defence activities by sending in:
- active force components from another location – e.g. a mobile force already under command like the naval standing force STANAVFORLANT or the (mainly) army AMF (Allied Mobile Force);
- amphibious forces which bring along all equipment as they travel – e.g. the US Marine Corps or an aircraft carrier strike fleet;
- forces which are earmarked and trained for particular action, mostly prepared by packed storage on-the-spot – e.g. aircraft squadrons to specific airfields;
- strategic reserve forces which need some time to prepare for transfer and then train for specific action.

Furthermore, support could come as attacks at source – destroying military bases and lines of communication east of the Iron Curtain – which could prevent or reduce the use of enemy military means in the Baltic Approaches.

Most of these forms of reinforcements and supporting strikes were in play for the Baltic Approaches during the whole Cold War period. Documents on attacks at source, however, are difficult to find in the archives, so reinforcements dominate the analysis. Apart from interventions by 24/7 active force components like STANAVFORLANT, reinforcement was a complicated process, both in the process of moving the forces to the desired location and in the ensuing logistic processes of getting supplies to them. Certain earmarked forces, though, had supplies stored beforehand.

We shall go through many discussions and points of view on reinforcements. There were, however, differences between political and military spheres.

In Denmark, the political debates for many years were played out in a setting formed by the experiences from the German occupation, creating a quite intense atmosphere of protest against any foreign military presence on Danish soil. In West Germany, the political debate also was rooted in WWII and the subsequent partitioning of Germany, but understandably with quite different experiences and lessons learned.

In military terms, after the first years there were only a few discrepancies between Danish and West German officers; all parties agreed on the military needs for cooperation in general, although differences might be found within particular issues.

So the military goals for the defence of the Baltic Approaches were complicated to express, given the multi-faceted military defence technology in a cooperation between army, navy and air force segments, and given the need for negotiation and cooperation between several nations to build up the NATO forces necessary for solving the task if war broke out.

Three levels of analysis

Military organisation and action is a complex topic, so a brief discussion of the concepts one may use to organise it will follow. We are concerned with three levels of analysis: strategy, operational art and tactics. Most of the analysis in this book will deal with the operational and tactical levels, but we cannot ignore strategy.

The first conceptual level concerns strategy. Duffield distinguishes between four components:[18] first, the general political-military objectives which the strategy should fulfil; second, an estimate of the threats making the use of military means necessary to obtain the goals; third, a statement of the military responses that are deemed effective or appropriate to address the threats; and fourth, an indication of the types and numbers of forces that are required to implement the strategy.

A strategy, then, is an instrument at a fairly abstract level in the sense that it only indicates what to obtain and the aggregate military means to do this. It says nothing of how to organise those forces and how to conduct a military confrontation with an adversary.

In NATO, the NATO Council dealt primarily with strategy: what were the overall threats from the enemy, what were the goals for the military commanders to counter those threats and what resources were available at the general level to counter any attack. In this book, we discuss strategy now and then, particularly in the formation years of 1948–50, but also in the mid-1950s when nuclear warheads became part of NATO's weaponry.

The second conceptual level is operational art which comprises how to organise the military forces for action: planning, preparing, conducting and sustaining major operations and campaigns.[19] This is, broadly speaking, how to organise for action so that the military forces are brought together to maximise their capability. This level is often ignored conceptually by analysts and conflated with either strategy or tactics, but that is at the peril of the observer. The practitioner must deal with operational art – take as an example a case where logistics is ignored. No military force can sustain actions without access to resources supplanting those used. Napoleon, Hitler and lately Putin have learned that lesson the hard way.

In NATO, the composition of the forces were important elements in operational activities. How many armoured vehicles should an army infantry division preferably have? How many destroyers should operate in the Baltic? Were they to coordinate attacks with aircraft? With MTBs? In what areas should minefields be placed, and when? Logistics also was an important element in making the strategy operational. One had to prepare for action by those forces which were to immediately counter any attack, but given the short time available if the attack came without warning, resources had to be available to re-supply units at the front. This had to be planned, taking the geography and the general infrastruc-

---

18 Duffield, John S. *Power Rules. The Evolution of Nato's Conventional Force Posture*, 10–12. Stanford, CA: Stanford University Press, 1995.
19 Vego, *Operational warfare at sea. Theory and practice.*, 1–2.

ture of the supposed front area into consideration. If the Danish troops in the Jutland area were to be moved to defend the Kiel Canal, how were they to be transported, and how would they get supplies? If mine fields were to be laid in the Baltic approaches, what would the best locations for storing those mines be? And how were they to be transported to a harbour? NATO had planned the use of resources for 30, 60 and 90 days of fighting; the 30-day plans were those of greatest importance.

The NATO regional commands and their sub-commands played a strong role in planning the operational activities of the organisation. They planned the military infrastructure and allocated resources (units) for action. They monitored the military status and quality of the forces involved and the level of supplies available on an annual basis. However, the national C-in-Cs were those responsible for the nitty-gritty details of making the forces operational, and comprehensive reporting was made nationally; in addition, frequent personal contacts were necessary to deal with present problems, past mistakes and future wishes for resources.

The third conceptual level is tactics: how to manoeuvre military forces in such a way that the opponent's forces are destroyed, withdrawn or surrendered while one's own forces are damaged the least possible – or until it makes military sense to withdraw or surrender. Tactics concern the military action minute-by-minute: who does what, when and how, taking into account the overall goals for military action.[20]

In NATO, tactics were to be decided upon when the alert level came close to general alert. Such decisions would be based on intelligence reports about the location and composition of enemy forces. Over the years, forces had been through a large number of exercises where tactical decisions were made day by day, even hour by hour, taking the situation and available resources into consideration. The overall distribution of resources was decided by the NATO subcommands, but the detailed decisions regarding operations were made by the commanders of the fighting units. In various narratives about exercises in this book, the tactics used by the local commanders come to the fore.

In empirical terms, these three conceptual levels do not have strict boundaries, they overlap and should not be exaggerated as means for military conduct. But they are useful instruments for understanding the many aspects of military action.

---

20 Ibid., 17.

NATO's overall strategy: A brief overview

Our focus is on NATO's military build-up. Its organisation was developed step by step over three years from 1949, from a principled political system to a military command system based on a strategic vision, to be implemented by more specific plans. Four documents from the Military Committee ("MC") stand out as general strategic principles, first formulated in 1950 and until 1967 revised three times. We review them briefly below because they created the strategic framework for this book.

MC 14

Initially, NATO did not integrate the forces of the individual countries into a coherent military apparatus. The document MC 14, approved in March 1950, was a general strategic plan based on piecemeal military responses at military key points, each to be taken care of by national forces. In addition, it indicated a broad defence line along the rivers Rhine and Ijsel in Central Europe – the Soviets were not to go further towards the west. MC 14 was not backed up by any general strategic striking force against the Soviet Union; it just met the enemy where they decided to attack.

NATO developed its organisation and a strategy over a few years in the early 1950s, followed by more operational plans on how to counter Soviet attacks, and set up goals for military strength in the regional commands and their sub-commands. Soon major military exercises were carried out to test the principles of the plans.

MC 14/1

Greece and Turkey joined NATO in early 1952, and the desirable sizes of military forces within NATO were agreed on in Lisbon in February. By December 1952, NATO changed MC 14 into MC 14/1 which was based on the regional NATO commands and therefore permitted steps toward military, integrated or coordinated action, still with the Rhine as a stop-point. A strategic group of American and British bombers now backed NATO as a deterrence against Soviet assaults by attacking targets behind the front line, particularly in the Soviet Union. In addition, American and British bombers were available for tactical strikes along and closely behind the front from British airfields. From 1953, NATO began planning the use of nuclear warheads.

The two states of West Germany (German Federal Republic) and East Germany (German Democratic Republic) were created in 1949. It soon became clear to the major European members of NATO that if they wanted to defend West Germany, the country had to be rearmed. A series of negotiations created a sketch of the EDC, the European Defence Community, a supra national military treaty to include the Benelux countries, France and West Germany. But the EDC foundered in 1954 because the French parliament would not approve the scheme.

The other countries involved, however, realised that engaging West Germany in the defence was a must. So one year later, West Germany (and Italy) became members of the Brussels Treaty, and subsequently West Germany also became a member of NATO. As a reaction, the Warsaw Treaty was signed in May 1955 between the USSR and Albania, Bulgaria, Czechoslovakia, East Germany, Hungary, Poland and Romania to defend those countries against aggression from NATO.

MC 14/2

In 1957, NATO had completed plans for the use of nuclear warheads, and a period based on strategic "massive retaliation" began with the approval of MC 14/2 which was based on a more integrated military system with a number of military corps each having responsibility for a part of West Germany, the so-called layer cake. The resistance point now was moved east from Rhine/Ijsel to the rivers Lech and Weser, supported by tactical nuclear warheads from bombers stationed in Britain and various missile and gun platforms in Central Europe. The strategic nuclear coverage was improved with missiles from submarines and land-based platforms.

The Soviets had detonated their first atomic bomb in 1949, and the launch of the Soviet satellite Sputnik in 1957 opened the possibility that the Russians could hit American soil with nuclear warheads carried by missiles, and the satellite opened new possibilities for watching activities on the ground.

As we shall see, the MC 14/2 and its massive retaliation strategy was from day one nearly under attack from various members of NATO for being too blunt an instrument, and the American Kennedy administration, which took over in 1961, worked piecemeal for a change of that strategy towards a more flexible response. Formally it did not happen until 1967 with MC 14/3.

MC 14/3

In 1967, after the French left the integrated military system of NATO, the decision of rescinding the massive retaliation and instead using what was called a strategy of Flexible Response was put on paper in MC 14/3. This opened up the possibility of a non-nuclear response to a Soviet attack. But small steps towards that had been taken in the first half of the 1960s: in 1963, the forward defence line was moved to the border between East and West Germany, and various possibilities of non-nuclear response were analysed. Capacity for bringing American conventional reinforcements in from the USA was expanded. In the early 1970s, NATO declared itself not to be a first user of nuclear warheads. But the middle range missile capacity in Europe was increased with cruise missiles from 1983. Strategic missile capacity was also increased by American and British submarines.

One addition of strategy took place later. From the start, NATO did not have a comprehensive naval strategy; the organisation had in principle relied on the various navies each to take care of the tasks in their area, coordinated by the relevant NATO command. But in the light of the fast growth of the Soviet navy, now threatening to dominate the seas in large proportions of NATO-waters, a strategy became desirable, and in 1981 the Concept of Maritime Operations, CONMAROPS, was decided, linking naval forces together from the Mediterranean to the Norwegian Sea.

The creation of the strategies are outside the scope of this book. But a few issues must be mentioned. Several political discussions took place to reduce the number of intercontinental missiles – SALT and ABM – and in Europe a system of controlling the tensions between West and East started with the Conference on Security and Co-operation in Europe (CSCE) which resulted in an agreement on security and peace in Helsinki in 1975. CSCE developed into quite an active forum for military reductions.

However, a few years later, a major disagreement between NATO and WAPA regarding weapons in Europe started with Soviet SS-20 missiles being deployed to Eastern Europe. In 1979 NATO retorted that the Soviets would have four years to take them away, and if they did not do so NATO would deploy 572 middle distance missiles in Western Europe. The Soviets did not comply, and therefore the so-called double-track decision was implemented with the NATO missiles being deployed, particularly in West Germany.

In the early 1980s, President Reagan reversed a policy of detente which President Carter had initiated in 1987. Reagen ordered a massive military buildup especially focusing on the navy and the air force. After the Soviets declined to remove the SS-20 missiles, he supported the deployment of Pershing missiles in West Germany. When Gorbachev became leader of the Soviet Union, Reagan shifted pressure to diplomacy, and four subsequent meetings between the two leaders led to the agreement to abolish all nuclear weapons.

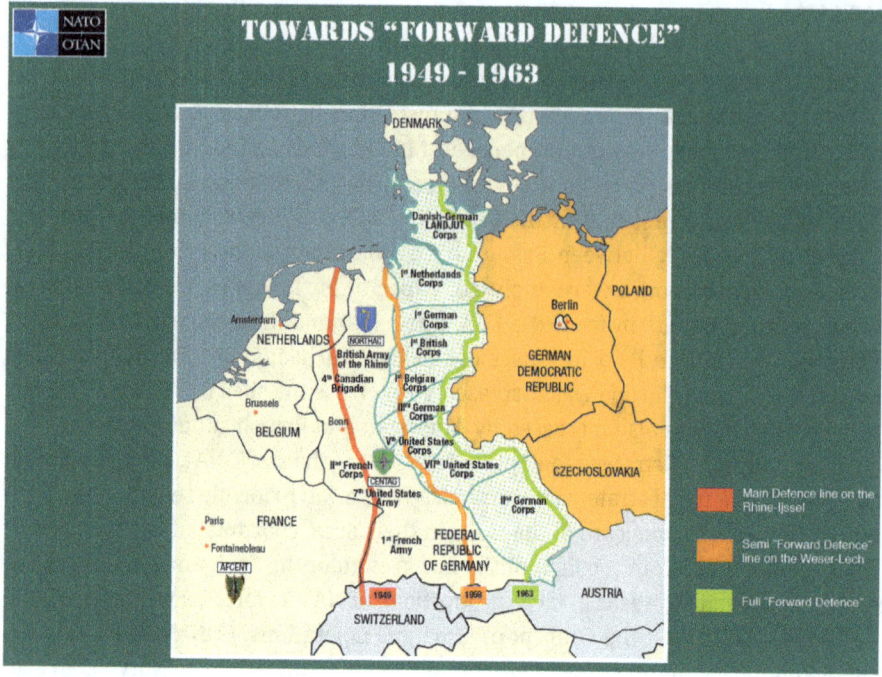

Figure 1.2: The map shows three defence lines for NATO during the various MC 14s: first the Rhine/Ijsel line from 1949, then the Weser/Lech line from 1958 and finally the full forward line at the border to Eastern Europe from 1963.
Source: the NATO seminar of December 2013.

This was what initiated the end of the Cold War – the Soviet Union could not go on expanding the military, and anyway there was a general liberalisation of economic, social and political affairs in the Soviet Union which meant that the traditional iron grip on the nations in Eastern Europe could not be upheld. The ideological foundation for the Cold War also withered away, and the fall of the Berlin Wall was the signifier to the rest of the world of the end of the Cold War.

The structure of the book

The organisation of the defence of the Baltic Approaches was under the auspices of AFNORTH, but there were quite strong, albeit somewhat diverging pressures to create a sub-command, integrating military NATO-actions in that area. A compromise was reached in late 1961, and the BALTAP command was initiated in 1962.

The first ten chapters after this introduction deal with the defence of the Baltic Approaches until 1962 and the difficult processes of creating the militarily sound solution to integrated action in littoral warfare, namely the BALTAP. The remaining six chapters analyse the organisation created to fulfil this role: BALTAP's organisation, planning and exercises in the 1960s, 1970s and 1980s to make possible the integration or rather a very close cooperation of the forces of two nations and their three military branches – plus reinforcements from other countries.

Chapter 2
Initial ideas for defending the Baltic Approaches

Before World War II the Scandinavian countries were neutral and therefore strategy was limited to preparing forces to counter threats against their neutrality. There was no larger context to take into account apart from using foreign policy activities to support neutrality and reject any foreign endeavours at undermining the neutrality.

After the war all three Scandinavian countries went back to neutral status under the auspices of the United Nations. Denmark and Norway initiated rearmament. The Norwegian fighting units returned to Norway and formed the foundation for reconstructing Norway's defence. The World War had left Denmark fairly intact, compared with the rest of Europe, but given that the navy had sunk its ships in 1943, and the occupying Germans had taken all that was left of equipment of the armed forces, it was back to square one.

At that time, a large part of the Soviet navy was stationed in the Baltic and therefore it was crucial to have control of the Baltic Approaches, both for those who wanted to attack eastwards and for those who wanted to attack westwards. The Soviet bases in the Murmansk and Kola areas were only starting to assume significance, but as time went by they became more important – especially for submarines to attack NATO lines of communications. From 1953 to 1960 the number of large attack submarines in Murmansk grew from 26 to 132, or 47 per cent of that type in the Soviet navy.[1]

During the Cold War, the same strategic understanding was voiced time and again. The following themes persist throughout the Cold War, albeit with minor differences and shifting importance, and we shall not repeat these details throughout this book:

- Denmark was a possible base area for operations in the Baltic and parts of Northern Europe. If it was conquered by the Soviets, it could be a base area for submarines, surface craft and air crafts in operations against the West allies. Seen from the East, the area likewise was important as a NATO-base for attacks against the Baltic and North-Eastern Germany. Therefore, NATO had to be sure to hold airports and other infrastructures.
- The military goals included both general defence of the area and plans to keep control of particularly vital areas or key spots in each country. Regard-

---

[1] Berdal, Mats. *The United States, Norway and the Cold War, 1954–60*, 64. London: Macmillan, 1997.

ing the South, NATO had to do its utmost to keep control of the territory along the Baltic Coast from the border to Eastern Germany to South Jutland, conceptualised as a bridgehead. This would prevent the Soviets from using it for supplies and communication lines, and the area with its airfields and harbours was preserved for NATO.
- The Baltic Approaches were the key area for passage from the Baltic to the Atlantic, and it was important to prevent Soviet navy from passing into the Atlantic. One had to control all straits, construct their own minefields and prevent the enemy from entering the waters and set up mine sweeping for mines laid from the air. The navies had to protect their own shipping, e.g. by establishing systems of convoy, and escorts should have anti-submarine weapon systems.
- Danish forces were small and difficult to move around because of many islands. Early warning therefore was essential, but one had to expect that the Soviets depended on surprise attacks. Forces therefore had to be dislocated to the right places, and when an attack struck, flexibility would be important. This was even true after West Germany joined NATO.
- Counter-operations were desirable against Soviet airports to give NATO superior air control. Comprehensive air bombardments of bases, airports and ships would be necessary. One had to sever Soviet lines of communication at sea, using submarines and surface craft. Laying mines from ships and aircraft was also possible.

In this chapter we shall go through several policy discussions which illustrate the political and military settings for the defence of the Baltic Approaches which became important for NATO's strategy: the attempt at creating a Scandinavian Defence Alliance in 1948–49; the strategic thoughts in Denmark in 1949–50 after entering NATO; NATO's initial strategy which was developed in five committees at a rather general level in 1949–50; and finally the thoughts on military cooperation between Sweden and NATO in the Baltic Approaches.

We should realise a number of societal limitations of that time. There were severe confines on mobility, particularly in Scandinavia and the Baltics: the roads were narrow and often winding; four-lane freeways were almost non-existent and lorries were small and therefore railroads and ships were quite important in transport; there were few bridges to connect islands with the mainland, and instead one had to use ferries; sea transport was the major means of transportation of goods where possible; air transport was expensive and supply limited. Most infantry actually moved by walking. Furthermore, communication was slow and the faster channels like telephone and telegraph were limited and expensive. Dissemination of information was slow, as was manipulation of data: most computation was done by hand and brain. Indeed, another world.

1948-49: The Scandinavian Defence Alliance

The three Scandinavian countries were neutral when World War II broke out, but they had vastly different experiences from then on. Sweden remained neutral and was never attacked by the Germans. The country mobilised its forces and was considered a major military segment in the Baltic. Norway and Denmark were attacked by the Germans on 9 April 1940. Norway resisted militarily and had support from Great Britain and France with an expeditionary corps landing in Northern Norway, but had to give up in June 1940. Norway was then occupied by the Germans. The Norwegian Government did not capitulate, however, it sought exile in London, and some Norwegian forces escaped to Britain and continued fighting throughout the war. Denmark capitulated after a few hours of resistance and was occupied by the Germans. In 1943, the Danish forces were disarmed by the Germans; they were dissolved and all equipment was taken over by the Germans; most of the navy was scuttled by own crews; a few ships escaped to Sweden.

In the first years after 1945, Denmark and Norway re-established their position as neutral states under the auspices of the United Nations. However, the Soviet Union was perceived in an increasingly aggressive role towards the Capitalistic West, and the coup d'etat in Prague in March 1948, soon to be followed by the first Berlin crisis, created a real scare among politicians. In September 1948 the three countries initiated a series of negotiations about the creation of a military alliance. A special committee dug into the military issues and wrote a white paper describing the three countries' military in detail and analysing a number of ways the Soviet Union might attack one or more of the countries. The report also specified how they might assist one another during specified attack situations. Given the many military details, the report remained Top Secret until the 1990s.

The Scandinavian Defence Union report[2] formed the basis for political negotiations in December-January 1948-49. It demonstrated that Sweden was quite strong in military terms, and Norway and particularly Denmark were quite weak. Therefore, Norway wanted to keep a relationship with the USA for getting military equipment; Denmark had a similar interest. Sweden, however, wanted a

---

2 Marinestaben: V. Den skandinaviske Forsvarskomité (1948–1949) 1: Den skandinaviske Forsvarskomite 1948 – Den skandinaviske Forsvarskomite 1949.

purely neutral alliance. But the Americans informally indicated that a neutral alliance would have least priority in subsequent military aid (Marshall Aid etc.), and thus a priority for the Norwegians was crushed. In February 1949 it became obvious that a compromise was impossible to reach, and Norway deflected to the USA to become part of the negotiations on NATO. Denmark soon followed.

What were the military insights of the Scandinavian committee, related to the defence of the Baltic Approaches? A map of Scandinavia indicates that an attack from the Soviet Union of any significance for the approaches would strike the Southern part of Sweden and the Danish islands of Bornholm, Lolland, Falster and Zealand. The Danish narrows and the Southern Baltic were obvious waters to deny to the enemy. In a Scandinavian Alliance, the defence of the territories proper would be left to the individual countries, and the evident areas for cooperation between Denmark and Sweden therefore would involve the two navies in the Southern Baltic, Øresund and Kattegat. Furthermore, the location of (new) coastal batteries could be coordinated in the Øresund area. In addition, cooperation might be desirable between the two armies in the case of the need for reinforcement to or withdrawal from either country across the Øresund. Finally, the use of air forces could be coordinated all over the territories.

Successful cooperation would presuppose common signal- and communication systems, free access to each other's bases and full sharing of intelligence information. There were then different tasks for the three forces.

The armies would take care of business on own territory. But there might be situations that necessitated a move of forces to the other country, most likely in cases of a Danish withdrawal; the towns of Helsingborg (Sweden) and Helsingør (Denmark) are only four kilometres apart across the Øresund. Swedish troops withdrawing from southern Skaane would most likely stay in Sweden, with the next "natural" defence line north of Helsingborg.

The air forces were flexible in use, and it would be easy to create concentrated actions against land and sea targets. Therefore, pilots should train the use of airfields across the countries. Command systems, then, must be common and interchangeable without loss of time. Reconnaissance reporting systems must also be common.

The two navies had many possibilities for cooperation. Submarines could coordinate actions in the Baltic, attacking amphibious forces as well as transport ships and larger naval vessels. Surface units could likewise operate in the Baltic, attacking any ship of the enemy's navy and supply ships, and laying minefields. In order to create freedom of operation, it would be wise to divide the Baltic into separate fields of operation for each navy, and share all information about minefields and other obstacles for free navigation. In the strait of Øresund, close cooperation was required in all aspects: coastal batteries, mine fields and actions by surface vessels – it was not possible to operate with submarines in the shallow waters. Likewise, operations in Kattegat required coordination in most aspects, and systems of convoying must be set up. Coastal mine sweeping would be a national task.

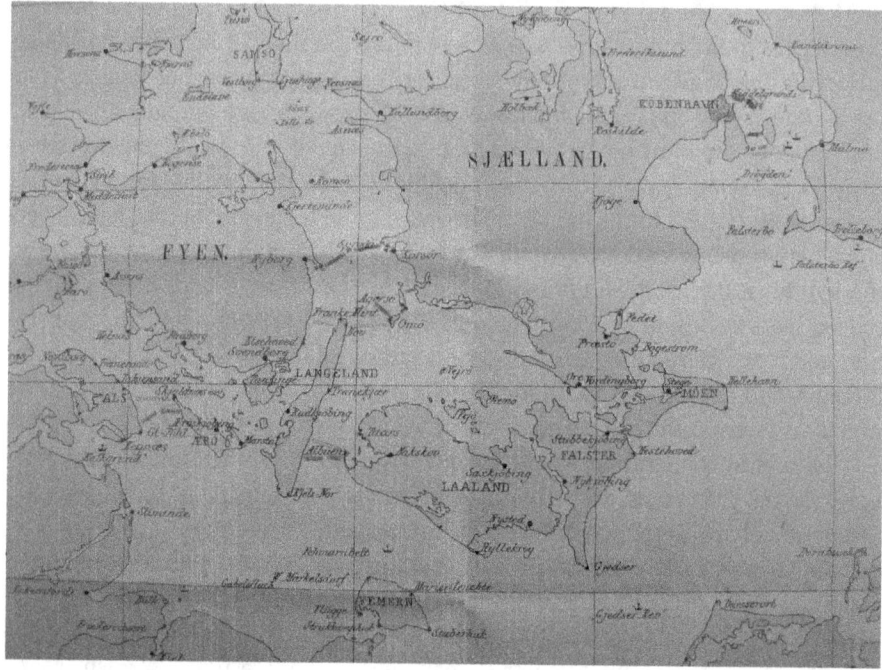

Figure 2.1: Possible mine fields in the Baltic Approaches. The blue and red fields are minefields from First and Second World War. The green mine fields are possible new fields under the Scandinavian alliance. Source: Rigsarkivet.

The Scandinavian Defence Alliance never came beyond the paper processing stage, but the comprehensive exchanges of military information and analytical discussions of strategy and tactics put military officers in a unique position to analyse defence possibilities after Denmark and Norway joined NATO. In addition, staff officers had learned how to cooperate and had become well acquainted with the forces and plans for military development in the two countries. They had learned to contemplate military strategy as well as tactics in a larger perspective than the narrow national interest.

Danish strategic considerations based on German thoughts

We shall now leave Sweden and Norway aside. Sweden remained neutral (but no one could deny the possibility that Sweden might be drawn into a comprehensive war). Norway had no direct defence role in the Baltic Approaches – but it had a strong interest in the approaches being held as a first defence line against the Russians.

Joining NATO completely changed the military visions for the Danes. They now were part of a large defence union and had to define their roles in a much larger perspective – from setting up military forces for their own defence to being part of a division of labour and thus create military instruments that could prevent damage in other areas. The case in point, of course, was the Baltic approaches. Denmark could prevent Russian attacks on other countries by blocking the straits for passage and keep the enemy away from bases and airfields. In the comprehension of the NATO treaty paragraph five, this was "one for all". But of course, the Danes also could expect the "all for one" clause by getting assistance in performing the role.

Readers of the twenty-first century should keep in mind that in 1949–50 the military weaponry and capabilities for action were radically different from only 10 years later. The weapons were conventional, much like WWII. There were no missiles; communication and electronic devices were quite cumbersome; and no tactical nuclear weapons existed. USA had strategic nuclear weapons, and the Soviet Union tested its first bomb in August 1949, but the future role of nuclear weapons was still in the haze. Therefore, the main strength of the Soviet Union lay in a formidable conventional army which – contrary to the Western powers – had not been reduced after 1945. The air force and the navy were not so strong, but still to be considered, particularly in the Baltic.

NATO's first strategy was developed in a setting of regional committees. Parallel with that, analyses took place nationally. If we want to understand how the Danish top military viewed the strategic situation around 1949–50, a set of papers written by Germans will be a good starting point. In Bremerhaven, a group of ex-German naval officers worked for the Americans in a small organisation, the Naval Historical Team (1949–52), whose task formally was to analyse the war at sea during WWII, but actually the members wrote analyses on how the navy of the Soviet Union was operating, and how to fight it. Thus they analysed the strategic and tactical principles to be used for a future West German navy.[3] One of the

---

3 Pfeifer, Douglas. "Forerunners to the West German Bundesmarine: The Klose Fast Patrol Group, the Naval Historical Team Bremerhaven, and the U.S. Navy's Labor Service Unit (B)." *International Journal of Naval History* 1, no. 1 (2002).

members, Friedrich Ruge, became the first C-in-C (Inspector) of the new navy, the Bundesmarine, in 1956.

In the Spring of 1949, the intelligence section of the Danish navy started cooperating with a former German vice admiral, Hellmuth Heye.[4] In the last year of the war, Heye had been chief of small naval combat forces, which included mini-submarines, combat divers, etc. He knew the conditions of the Baltic as an area for littoral warfare quite well. He was convinced that large ships were at a disadvantage in the shallow waters, and, therefore, small, fast craft together with submarines and mines would form a superior defence group. A large number of these ships was more important than size. Permanent bases should be avoided, and workshops, repair facilities etc. had to be mobile.

Task-oriented communication with Heye started after Denmark joined NATO in 1949. By then, he was member of the Naval Historical Team and wrote several papers on strategy. Although a former admiral, he did not analyse naval affairs solely; he underlined the need for all three forces to operate in a coordinated fashion – a theme that became quintessence later in the negotiations about BALTAP. We shall digest some of the main thoughts regarding a strategy for the Atlantic alliance, NATO.

In a note on the role of the Baltic[5] Heye criticised that the main interests of the NATO planners apparently concerned the armies in Central Europe. The role of naval power was only discussed regarding the Mediterranean and the Atlantic, and Heye commented that a few Russian submarines hardly could wrestle the sea power from NATO. But the importance of the Baltic apparently escaped the visions of the NATO planners who failed to observe the following:

- Having sea power in the Baltic had severe consequences for a war in Central and Northern Europe. Gaining power, however, required all three forces – army, navy and air force, to work together in a common strategic framework, somewhat like how the USA operated in the Pacific during WWII. NATO should not allow the three forces to operate independently of one another.
- It was noteworthy that in the Soviet military system, the navy was mostly regarded as a means for the army, e.g. by securing supplies from one harbour to another, as the army needs arose. Likewise, it was desirable that the navy attacked the communication lines of the enemy, first of all by submarines,

---

4 Unless otherwise noted, sources in this section are in Forsvarets Efterretningstjeneste: V. Diverse sager (afklass.) (1940–1966) 4: Diverse 1942–1966, Heye. Heye's role is also discussed from a more political perspective by Henriksen, Jesper Thestrup. "Side om side i det kommende Europa." *Sønderjyske Årbøger*, 2016 2016, 95–120.
5 "Die Bedeutung der Ostsee fuer die sowjetische Kriegsfuehrung", probably written by Hellmuth Heye on an non-German typewriter. HEM.

denying their army necessary supplies. Therefore, the Soviet navy was relatively weak regarding surface crafts. NATO had strong navies which should be used as indicated below.
- For the Soviet Union, the Baltic coast area contained important harbours, industry and shipyards and hence the area was key to creating, handling and transporting (by sea) supplies to an army operating in Northern and Middle Germany. Furthermore, the Soviet navy had important bases and about 50 per cent of its navy there. Consequently, the Soviets must secure their lines of communication by getting control over the Baltic approaches, i.e. the Danish Straits and the adjacent territory. Furthermore, Sweden must be kept neutral so that the West could not use its bases and airfields. The Russians might be expected to make use of a large number of small ships, able to navigate close to land under the protection of batteries, and hardly worth the use of a torpedo from submarines. Loss of such a small craft was bearable, loss of large ships less so.
- The task for NATO, then, was to control the approaches, block the LOCs of the Soviet Union, and build up a strong amphibious force based on navy, army and air force, capable of landing a strike force anywhere along the Baltic coast. We shall return to this in chapter 6
- If such an operation force was not possible, there should be a minimum force ready for action if war broke out, consisting of a strong air force able to do surveillance, attack various targets and protect their own ships; mid-sized submarines (350 t.) able to lay mines, attack merchant ships and guard mine fields; midget submarines for shallow waters; mine layers; small submarine chasers and MTBs. In addition, the Danish Baltic Approaches must be protected with minefields with coastal batteries, preferably mobile. Ships operating in that area should include mine sweepers and convoy escorts equipped as submarine chasers and having anti-aircraft gunnery. Finally, a comprehensive system of surveillance (radar) and reporting should be set up to disclose all Soviet movements in the Baltic.
- The above forces could not solely be set up by Denmark; it was a NATO task, and the USA had to take a strong role, particularly in building the necessary ships and submarines in large numbers. In addition, it would be necessary to involve Germany – people from its former navy had the knowledge and experience to fulfil the tasks.

Heye, then, understood the strategic parameters set up above and the conditions for littoral warfare (though he did not coin that term): creating choke points, denying a strong enemy passage by cheap means, using small craft at sea, creating cooperation among army, air force and navy and establishing a strong recce system. As we shall see later, Heye's observations were to some degree what SACEUR Eisenhower had in mind, and the new Bundesmarine developed considerable amphibious powers. Later papers from the Danish navy staff also reflected much of the above.

Denmark was not alone in using former German officers for military preparation. In the summer of 1949, a group of German ex-top officers visited Oslo, and in a heavily guarded hotel they discussed strategy and tactics and played war games with Norwegian officers. One of the lessons learned was that the defence of Southern Norway began in the Danish Straits – as we shall see, this became the received view in NATO, too, but initially the Norwegians were somewhat taken aback by that conclusion.

Heye wrote a skeleton plan for naval development within NATO. In his opinion, only two countries – Britain and USA – had navies large enough to be balanced (had all types of ships), and their role would be to create sea power for NATO in the Atlantic and the Mediterranean. Other navies then would have to specialise and be assigned particular roles according to a general plan.

Heye's plan mirrored his ideas of using small craft in the Baltic. His starting point was that prevention would be better than war. Therefore, one had to create images in the minds of the Soviet decision-makers and see to it that they were permanently in doubt about what the West might do. NATO also had to create good knowledge of what went on in the East, and Heye complained about the inefficient British and American systems of intelligence. The Danes soon realised that by creating a state-of-the-art intelligence system based on radar and radio listening techniques, Denmark would have a strong role within the soon-to-come NATO early warning system.

Heye pointed out that the West was stronger than the East in naval and air forces, vice versa on the ground. Therefore, the Baltic and its approaches were important scenes. Denmark and Norway would have substantial roles in attacking the Northern flank of a Russian attack in Western Europe. Historically, the Russian armies had weak flanks, and the Russians were aware of this. Therefore, it was important to strengthen the flanks of NATO and hopefully scare the Russians from attacking in Central Europe. It was also important to resist fiercely in the first weeks of the war while NATO was mobilising its reserves. NATO could win, but mobilisation took time. The Russians would be eager to earn some easy victories in the start to support the policy points of the Communist parties in the West.

Denmark's role would be to block the Baltic Approaches with mines to prevent Russian submarines and other ships from getting out into the Atlantic. This, however, presupposed that air and ground forces were effective in preventing Russian forces from landing by sea or air. The ships of the navy must be mobi-

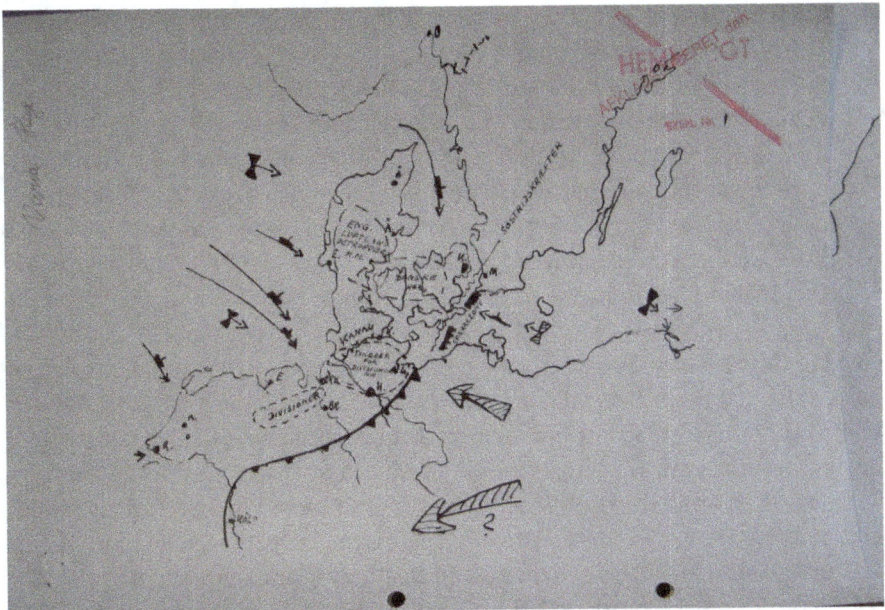

Figure 2.2: Admiral Heye's map of threats and counter moves. Source: Rigsarkivet.

lised with very short notice, and a large number of mines had to be ready in storage. The navy would need small mine layers, fast patrol craft and submarines – mid-size (350t.) as well as very small (20t.). Mobile coastal batteries – not stationary, they were too easy to destroy – could yield support. The navy also needed a dedicated air force during the first days of a war, and a fast and efficient intelligence section. Britain and France were supposed to assist with fast small craft, submarine chasers and mine sweepers. British air forces should take over roles for aircraft in the Baltic, if necessary from own air fields.

Heye also analysed the role of Norwegian and Swedish defence forces in the overall plan:
- Norway's main role would be in the North Atlantic with fast patrol craft, submarine chasers and mine layers also capable of acting as mine sweepers. Submarines large enough to navigate in the Atlantic and dedicated naval air forces would be necessary. The need for destroyers and other relatively large ships had to be analysed. Britain and France were supposed to be ready to assist in the North with cruisers, submarine chasers and submarines to control Russian harbours and lines of communication, make minefields etc. Air forces for surveillance of Russian harbours and support nodes were also present. Use of aircraft carriers as floating airfields was to be analysed.

- Sweden, of course, was not a member of NATO, but in military terms its presence in the area was real and challenging for a prospective aggressor. History had shown Sweden's ability to keep its territory and waters outside war and, if challenged, its participation in a war would be a real threat to the Russians in the Baltic. According to Heye, fast small crafts and submarines could challenge the enemy together with potent air forces which also would secure the larger ships of the navy, but actually the large ships would not be necessary if the air forces were brought to good use. As we shall see, the Swedes followed that line of thought ten years later.

Some of Heye's ideas, particularly the heavy reliance on submarines in the deeper parts of the Baltic, probably did not please the top of the Danish navy. In 1949, the Danish admirals wanted a balanced navy (below cruiser size, though) and, in particular, destroyers to work together with MTBs in attack groups in the Baltic. In addition, they wanted two new stationary coastal batteries covering the straits; mobile batteries were too expensive. But his strategic perspective on the Baltic was most welcome and soon found use in Denmark's strategic papers to NATO. A new Danish C-in-C was appointed in October 1950; he was an admiral who had been informed about Heye's papers along the way by the chief of the Naval Intelligence Office. We shall return to the Danish plans in chapter 5

1949–50: NATO's organisation and first strategy

The NATO treaty was signed in April 1949 and approved by the national parliaments in the subsequent months. During the first year, the NATO members created a skeleton for an organisation. The North Atlantic Council was established in the founding document paragraph 9. At its first meeting in September 1949, it founded the Defence Committee (DC), created to develop and oversee the capacity of the NATO countries to resist armed attack. Furthermore, the DC created as a subcommittee the MC, the Military Committee, with the top brass of the member countries. The MC had the SG, the Standing group of three members, whose task was to function as an executive committee. The limited membership of the SG created tensions within the alliance, and after a few years the Military Representative Committee with members from all countries ensured proper representation to all meetings.

Finally, five planning groups for five regions were set up to analyse military problems and plan accordingly: Northern Europe, Western Europe, Southern Europe/Western Mediterranean, United States/Canada and the North Atlantic Ocean.

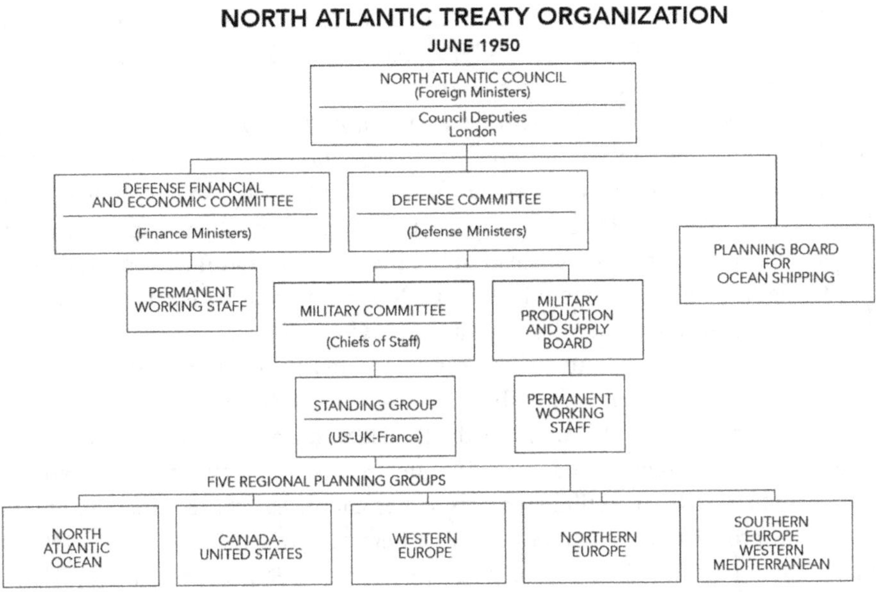

NORTH ATLANTIC TREATY ORGANIZATION
JUNE 1950

```
                    NORTH ATLANTIC COUNCIL
                       (Foreign Ministers)
                    ─────────────────────────
                        Council Deputies
                            London

  DEFENSE FINANCIAL          DEFENSE COMMITTEE
  AND ECONOMIC COMMITTEE                                    PLANNING BOARD
                                                            FOR
     (Finance Ministers)      (Defense Ministers)           OCEAN SHIPPING

      PERMANENT                              MILITARY
      WORKING STAFF    MILITARY COMMITTEE    PRODUCTION
                                             AND SUPPLY
                        (Chiefs of Staff)    BOARD

                                             PERMANENT
                         STANDING GROUP      WORKING
                                             STAFF
                         (US-UK-France)

                   FIVE REGIONAL PLANNING GROUPS

                                                         SOUTHERN
    NORTH       CANADA-        WESTERN      NORTHERN     EUROPE
    ATLANTIC    UNITED STATES  EUROPE       EUROPE       WESTERN
    OCEAN                                                MEDITERRANEAN
```

Figure 2.3: NATO's organisation June 1950.[6]

So in the beginning there was no military organisation in the normal sense of the word – no command-control system with a top executive and staff to make the organisation able to gain, process and proceed the information necessary for fulfilling the tasks. It took several years to get that far (see chapter 3).

NATO was created as an instrument to be used in an emergency, reacting to threats of war in Europe caused by attacks from the Soviet Union. Therefore, there were initially no over-arching principles of a strategy, directing tactical military movements if or when Soviet troops crossed the border. There was no clear understanding in the West about the intentions of the Soviet leadership. There only was agreement that the Russians appeared menacing, and that the changes in government systems in Eastern Europe towards Communist rule were clear indicators of similar changes to be expected if some or all countries of Western Europe were occupied by the Russians.

The changes in the East had taken place country by country, but the Musketeer oath of the NATO countries made a similar change pattern in the West impossible. If one country was attacked, a response would come from all. Consequently,

---

6 Pedlow, Gregory W. *NATO Strategy Documents 1949–1969*, xii. Bruxelles: Supreme Headquarters Allied Powers Europe, 1997.

NATO prepared for a massive Russian attack with conventional weapons over a broad front in Western Europe. Still, the defence was based on the plans of the military forces of each individual country.

Be that as it may, let it be clear from the outset that for many years American politicians and the military top brass had severe doubts about the possibility to withstand a Soviet attack on West Europe.[7] If you look at a map of Europe, the first "natural" defence line seen from the East is the Rhine River and its distributary arm leading north to the ocean in the Netherlands, and it became known as the Rhine/Ijssel defence line which in reality left Northern Germany and Denmark open to intruders (see the map in the previous chapter).

Danish, Norwegian and British forces located in Schleswig-Holstein were slated to stop a Soviet invasion, but they were few and only armed with light weaponry (see chapter 6). Therefore, the Danish military quickly realised that the only way to strengthen the defence of Denmark (Jutland) would be to allow West Germany to reinstall its military forces. Other countries realised this too, but an American proposal in 1950 to re-arm West Germany under the auspices of NATO did not win support of the majority who preferred a European solution, if any. Over several years, the negotiations of the European Defence Community (see chapter 1) seemed promising to that end. As EDC failed, NATO took over by including West Germany and planning for a much stronger defence of Schleswig-Holstein.

Until 1953, the Danish military and political actors never spelled out their worries about the realities – possibilities – of NATO-support to Denmark in public, and in the interaction between themselves and NATO the problems were only discussed in terms of military techniques – force evaluations, projections into the future etc. – which were hardly comprehensible to the lay man.

The first rather loose strategic principles were set up by the Military Committee in the fall of 1949 while the five planning groups worked on issues in their regions. Step by step these papers were integrated by the Standing Group[8] into the first comprehensive strategic document for NATO, an aggregate result named DC 13, which from April 1950 formed the basis for more detailed work in the five planning committees. It was often referred to as the *Medium Term Defence Plan*, MTDP.

The DC-13 was a comprehensive document, analysing political, economic and military developments since WWII, and estimating the political goals of the Soviet

---

7 Villaume, Poul. "Mulig fjende – nødvendig allieret?" In *Danmark, Norden og NATO 1948–1962*, Carsten Due Nielsen, Johan peder Noack, and Nikolaj Petersen, 147–90. København: Jurist- og Økonomforbundets Forlag, 1991.
8 The details and specific documents are found in Pedlow, op. cit.

Union: Communism all over the world under direction from Moscow. It was foreseen that if the Soviets chose to act in 1954, they would initiate an attack against Western sea lines of communication, and a comprehensive military campaign against Western Europe, Scandinavia, the Iberian peninsula, Italy and Yogoslavia. The British isles, USA and Canada would be attacked from the air. Other areas might also be attacked, but Western Europe would be the main target.

DC-13 first had a broad and very general description of the military processes, followed by a more specific description of what might take place in the five regions. The Northern European Region, which is our subject, consisted of Norway, Denmark and Schleswig-Holstein. In strategic terms, DC-13 followed the goals set up first in this chapter, not to be repeated here.

Regarding attacks, there were two possibilities – an attack on Denmark and Norway, or an attack on all three Scandinavian countries.

In the first case, the attack on Denmark was expected to be carried out by land operations against Jutland through Northern Germany, coordinated with the attack on Western Europe and accompanied by air and seaborne operations against the Danish Islands, especially Zealand. Simultaneously, Norway would be attacked, probably by an amphibious and airborne operation striking at the Norwegian Skagerrak coast and the Oslo area initially, and extending mainly along the railroads and highways leading to Trondheim, Bergen and Stavanger. A secondary and probably simultaneous operation would presumably start from Murmansk and strike towards Narvik from the sea, combined with crossing of the Northern frontiers by road. The forces would strike south as far as the nature of the country and logistic conditions permitted.

In the second case, the main Soviet effort would still start from the South, with a secondary effort being made in the North as described above, and through Finland. Only in the South could an assault be provided with land based air cover from across the Baltic. In the interior, communications were very limited, and operations against Norway would be restricted to the routes leading toward Oslo and Trondheim.

The recommendations for defence in DC-13 were quite abstractly formulated. The general task was to defend as far to the East as possible and to keep control of key points supporting own forces.

- For the armies, not much was said concretely beyond the need for offensive-defensive acts; more anti-tank weapons would be essential, and the enemy should be met so that they would have to send in relatively more forces than the defenders.
- The air forces were to establish air superiority to allow forces on the ground to operate safely; one important means would be to bomb enemy airports and aircraft on the ground, and to attack fuel installations, aircraft, storage

depots and the like. Effective air action should protect one's own lines of communication and vital administrative centres and centres of population by using interceptor fighter forces and anti-aircraft defences. Radar warning and control facilities must maximise effectiveness. Intruder operations should be planned.
- The naval forces were to protect their own merchant shipping, ports and bases. Coastal waters and narrows should be protected, mine sweeping carried out and defensive mines laid where appropriate. Areas suitable for enemy submarines or surface ships operations should be sealed off. On the offensive side, enemy shipping, enemy forces and facilities should be attacked; own land forces attacking should be supported from the sea if possible, and commando operations carried out against bases and various forms of coastal facilities. Finally, convoy systems should be planned, and widespread actions against Russian submarines planned and coordinated among the regions. One's own harbours and communication lines should be protected against mines, and offensive mine laying carried out at enemy harbours.

How NATO made the strategic principles of DC-13 operational is the topic for the next chapter.

Sweden's defence

The defence of the Eastern part of the Baltic Approaches was dependent on Sweden because the Eastern coast of Øresund was Swedish territory. The landscape there is much like the Danish, farm country with a few hills and accessible beaches. But Sweden is a large country, about 1,600 kilometres in length, and much of the terrain further to the North is mountains and forests. The urban centres are in the South and South-East, but even there open country or forest dominate. The coast is rocky in many places.

The defence plans for Sweden were based on a series of comprehensive analyses of Sweden's position in international politics as a neutral state and the risk of war – understood as an attack by the Soviet Union.

The main tenet was that Sweden could not win such a war; the task therefore was to resist attacks for so long that military help from the outside – i.e. the West, maybe under the auspices of the newly created United Nations – could come and join the fight. Accordingly, a strategic defensive approach was created, protecting a number of vital strategic areas within a "tough" in-depth system of defence – thus delaying the enemy, waiting for military assistance from the West (through Norwegian territory).

This strategic concept endured for 20 years, but maybe more as a principle than an actual directive; the operational war plans mainly dealt with a quite vigorous periphery defence at the borders in the North and along the coast lines in the South; it was supposed that the Russians did not possess the naval strength to attack the coast at Stockholm. This actual doctrine – as opposed to the principled one – was decided by the parliament.[9]

The Swedes were not without means for defence. In 1949,

- The air force had 551 fighters in 33 squadrons; 278 bombers in 12 squadrons and 132 recce airplanes in 5 squadrons; a total of 961. It was the fourth largest air force in Europe and kept its strength throughout the 1950s.[10]
- The navy had three obsolete monitors, four cruisers (one obsolete), 29 destroyers (10 or more obsolete), 26 submarines, 21 FPBs, and 50 mine sweepers. In the 1950s many obsolete ships were scrapped, and the main force now consisted of two battle groups headed by the two cruisers. There were eight new destroyers, cooperating with about 45 FPBs in attack groups, plus about 20 submarines; most were built after the war.[11] In addition there were many coastal batteries.
- The army had ten divisions, subdivided into 37 brigades, some of them tank brigades; the annual number of conscripts trained was about 40,000; the army could mobilise up to 6–800,000, but not all with modern equipment.[12] In addition there was a home guard of about 100,000.

The Plan for defending Southern Sweden, and hence the Swedish part of the Baltic Approaches, operated with four army divisions with two armoured brigades and one motorised infantry brigade in the South of Sweden.[13] They constituted 40 per cent of the Swedish army. The navy would patrol the Southern coast with destroyers, FPBs and submarines. The air force would support the army and the navy and keep watch and defend the Eastern part of Sweden.

---

9 Wallerfelt, Bengt. *Den hemliga svenska krigsplanen*, 112. Stockholm: Medströms Bokforlag, 2016.
10 Wennerholm, Bertil. *Fjärde Flygvapnet i Världen?* 155–58. Stockholm: Försvarshögskolan, 2006.
11 https://www.naval-encyclopedia.com/cold-war/swedish-navy.
12 Gustafsson, Bengt. *Det kalla kriget – några reflexioner*, 15. Stockholm: Försvarshögskolan, 2006.
13 Wallerfelt, op. cit., pp. 97–101.

Swedish cooperation with NATO?

The Swedish government firmly believed that Sweden should stay neutral, so no matter what the British and the Swedish military top thought and did, the government stayed on that course. Nonetheless, the cabinet accepted a minimum of military contact to NATO in order to be prepared for close cooperation in war time. They thought that Sweden could avoid a Soviet attack, but they knew very well that if attacked, Sweden could not resist for more than a few weeks, and then reinforcement from the West would be necessary.[14]

Over the years, there had been many rumours of secret cooperation between NATO and Sweden. In the Scandinavian negotiations on a Defence Union, the location of mine fields was discussed, as we saw above. After the collapse of the negotiations, the Swedish cabinet approved a number of contacts between the Swedish top military and their counter numbers in Norway and Denmark.[15] The contacts regarded coordination of air surveillance, control of fighters, SAR and

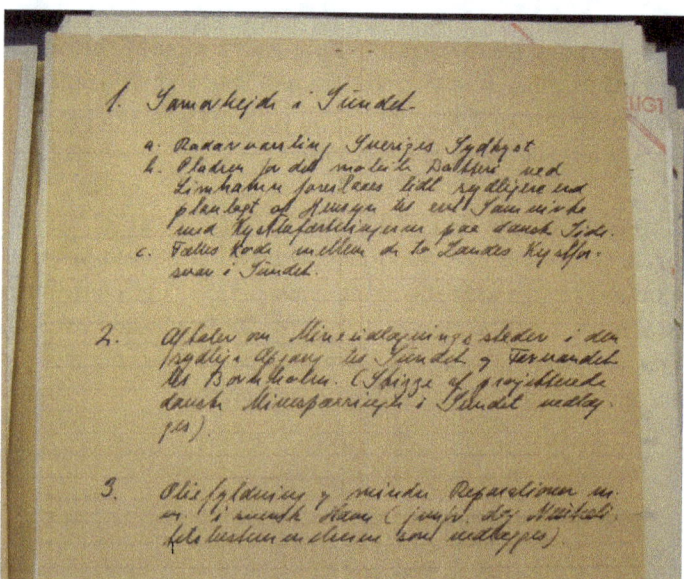

Figure 2.4: Handwritten note from the Archive of the Danish navy regarding cooperation with the Swedes in the Sound. Source: Rigsarkivet.

---

14 Neutralitetspolitikkommissionen. *Om Kriget Kommit*, 295, 301. Stockholm: Statens Offentliga Utredningar 1994:11, 1994.
15 Ibid., 17.

military weather reporting. Suggestions of more direct cooperation within specific issues like mine laying in the Baltic and escorting in Skagerrak, and land defence in areas adjacent to Norway, did not win support from the politicians.

In the Danish archival files on future cooperation with Norway,[16] there is one hand-written draft note – see figure 2.4. – which reads:
1. Cooperation in the Sound
   a. Radar watch (from) the Southern coast of Sweden
   b. We suggest that the location of the mobile battery at Limhamn is moved slightly more towards the South than planned to ease potential cooperation with the Danish coastal fortresses.
   c. Common code between the coastal defence of the two countries.
2. Agreement on the location of mine fields in the Southern approach to the Sound and the waters at Bornholm (sketch of planned Danish minefields attached).
3. Oil replenishment and small repairs etc. in Swedish harbours (but see the attached rules on neutrality).

Clearly, the note addresses Swedish affairs. It turns out that these were points for discussion (by someone else, probably a superior, PB) with the Swedes; the (Danish) reader is informed of the present plans for Danish minefields, and he is asked to adhere to the rules of neutrality – which prevent long stays in neutral harbours by belligerent warships. Actually, these points were discussed with the Swedes in January 1950; they are reflected exactly in the same order in the diary of the Swedish C-in-C and found as a note in the archives of the Swedish Prime minister from January 1950.[17]

It appears, however, that the Swedish cabinet denied permission to pursue the "Øresund issues" later in 1950. Nonetheless, some evidence points in the direction of a substantive cooperation of how to lay mines in the Sound.[18]

In the 1950s, several cooperative measures were planned for by the Swedes – as contingencies. On the West Coast, two bases were planned to be used, if necessary, by allied warships and for laying up merchant ships. Stores were to service the warships with oil, water, food and smaller repair services; therefore, the stores were planned to have 50 per cent more capacity than would be normal for sustaining only one's own forces. It was not foreseen that warships would call on a permanent basis, but if a system of convoys along the coast from Norway was

---

16 Marinestaben: V. Atlantpagten (1949–1951) 1: Atlantpagten 1949 – Atlantpagten 1951. This section is based on a series of documents from June 1949 to July 1950.
17 Ibid., 233.
18 Ibid., 152, 230.

set up, some visits for stores and service were anticipated by ships up to destroyer size.[19]

In Øresund, the Swedes planned two alternative minefields. If there was a threatening situation or if Denmark and the Soviet Union initiated war, the minefields were to be laid in Swedish waters only. If Sweden got involved in the war, the minefields were to be expanded into the international waters and coordinated with the Danes so that Øresund was completely mined at the Island of Saltholm. But there is no evidence that these plans were discussed with the Danes.[20]

Control of the air space of the Scandinavian countries was negotiated several times after the breakdown of the Scandinavian Defence Union discussions. A general common wish was to coordinate air rescue; this could be accomplished without involving any military tactics. But the military defence was also discussed, and early on Sweden and Norway reached several agreements, and a plan for possible cooperation within air defence between Denmark and Sweden was signed in June 1955.[21] In indicated procedures for reporting every three minutes the progress of aircraft within 250 kilometres of the main control stations in Skaane, East Denmark, Gothenburg and West Denmark: data on position, course, type, nationality, number, altitude, speed and supposed task. Some signal particulars were included in a "Signal Plan Denmark-Sweden" (which was revised in 1957[22]). The air defence plan was extremely secret; its existence was to be told only orally to key personnel, and the plan itself was to be "put into an envelope which until further notice is kept in the HQ of the two countries". The plan was signed, but its operational significance is unknown.

How much detail did they have about one another?
In November 1960 the Danish Chief of Defence Staff, Air Force General Major Erik Rasmussen, visited his Swedish colleague. He left after some days, very well informed about the state of the Swedish defence:

> On the first day Rasmussen got information about plans for new material and for our management. He also was informed by the three chiefs of the army, air force and navy. The strategic basics for East Middle Sweden were presented, and the regional chiefs told quite detailed about their special arrangements in peace and war. Peyron (major general, chief of Air Force Section E 3) was particularly frank about the war organisation of his forces and their dislocation, the air defence system and the war control system with the radar stations and the cabled con-

---

19 Ibid., 226.
20 Ibid., 233–34.
21 Görtz, Hans-Ove. *Skandinavisk försvarsutredning 1948–1949 – uppstarten och dess inverkan under kalla kriget*, 54. Försvarets Historiska Telesamlingar Flygvapnet, 2020b.
22 Ibid., 58.

nections. On a field visit in the E 3 area the Air Force representatives were particularly candid. The guests were allowed to follow the activities at a large modern radar and air control system (English PS 08) and got the opportunity themselves to control a group DRAKEN fighters, attacking a group of airplanes which had crossed the border at the island of Gotland. The Danes also got a briefing on the defence intelligence system and the daily preparedness, and the forms and scope of collecting intelligence by air over the Eastern Baltic. They also visited the mountain works of Wing F 13 and were briefed on the setup of the air defence central of Norrköbing.[23]

We may conclude, then, that at least in the minds of the Swedish military, Sweden was ready to support NATO forces and get support in return. Some politicians wanted to have an idea what the defence plans of NATO were about, so that in case of a Soviet attack they were somewhat prepared for action. But there were very few concrete discussions and next to no straight decisions on cooperation – submarines being one exception along very broad lines plus concrete cooperation about warning and emergency procedures. And one should take note that all agreements were made between the nations of Denmark and Sweden, not NATO and Sweden.

Summing up: The strategic steps towards NATO

In 1948, the three Scandinavian countries tried to maintain their neutrality by engaging in a defence union. Their focus was not particularly the Baltic Approaches, but the region as such and the possible channels for a Soviet attack. The Approaches were one, and the Swedes and Danes analysed the ways their navies might cooperate there, using their capabilities to create choke points in the narrows by minefields (jointly in Øresund), supported by coastal batteries. The navies also could cooperate in protecting own LOCs and denying access for amphibious forces.

The defence union did not materialise; Norway and Denmark gave up neutrality and joined NATO in April 1949 while Sweden stayed neutral. From then on, the Baltic Approaches became a key area for defence against the Soviet Union, and strategic NATO-goals were formulated; roughly, they stayed the same for the entire Cold War:
- Denmark was a key area to defend for its airfields and naval bases;
- NATO wanted a general defence of the area and of key points;
- NATO had to prevent the Soviet navy from passing the approaches into the North Sea and then Atlantic; mine fields were to be planned;

---

23 Ibid., 63.

- Early warning was essential by regular monitoring; the Soviets were expected to use surprise attacks;
- Counter-operations were desirable against Soviet bases and airfields in the Baltic area at the earliest time possible to give NATO air control and to sever Soviet lines of communication.

The first Danish strategic and tactical visions from 1949 were based on the ideas of a former German admiral, Heye, who drew up plans for defending the Baltic Approaches, but also for attacking Soviet LOCs in the Baltic; his strategic ideas turned out to be close to those of the first NATO commander, SACEUR Eisenhower, and his flank perspective. Heye had a very good understanding of the conditions for littoral warfare: He recommended a navy of relatively small craft – small destroyers and FPBs supported from the air – and submarines (to operate in the deep parts of the Baltic Sea), as well as amphibious forces to attack along the Baltic coast. The approaches were to be choke points blocked by mine fields and coastal batteries, and cooperation among army, air force and navy was a must. One proposal ran counter to his general approach: he suggested NATO might prepare a strike fleet with large units to enter the Baltic when appropriate – i.e. not early in a combat. Heye saw the defence of the Baltic approaches as important in that NATO could threaten the Northern flank of a Soviet attack in Central Europe so much that they refrained from attacking.

NATO took some time to develop a command structure; in the first year the national commands were the only ones to fight a war. Five regional committees worked on strategic goals, and in the years 1950–51 a skeleton was developed under the so-called DC-13 strategy for the years until 1954 – along the lines indicated above. They were quite general in scope and first of all mirrored the scare of Soviet submarines escaping to the Atlantic. A primary goal was thus to create choke points by minefields, preventing Soviet passage. A second goal was to attack the enemy's LOCs while protecting own shipping from attacks.

The Swedes had tacit talks and coordination with some NATO countries in the early 1950s, but over time the contacts dried out except for some coordination of air traffic with Denmark and Norway. Sweden had several plans for countering a Soviet attack, but the aim really was to buy time for support from the Western Allied. Formally, Sweden remained neutral.

Chapter 3
NATO's military organisation and initial plans

This chapter first discusses the development of NATO in general and then regarding the Baltic approaches. Much of it concerns the operational art level of military planning, but we also take a look at a major exercise.

We focus on the military side of NATO, but of course the politicians had a role to play, first of all in the NATO Council which met quite frequently in the first years. The ninth meeting was held in Lisbon in February 1952, and it became very important because a number of far-reaching decisions were made there: the so-called Lisbon goals for the development of NATO's military forces and the introduction of a civil Secretary General to supervise the whole of NATO's organisation; the first incumbent became the British Lord Ismay. The problems and subsequent changes of the top organisation are analysed by Pedlow.[1] The description below aims at creating an understanding of the NATO commands related to the Baltic Approaches – meaning the organisation of Northern Europe, Central Europe and the Atlantic. Southern Europe and the Channel area will by and large be neglected.

The two first sections of the chapter describe how the first command organisations were set up and what their war planning was about. Then we deal with NATO's Standing Group's perception of the Soviet threats, and section four analyses the first defence plan which comprised the Baltic Approaches. Then follows an analysis of The British Joint Chiefs of Staff's severe critique and their response – a rather comprehensive nuclear bombing plan of the Baltics. Section seven goes through negotiations between AFNORTH and SACLANT about organisation and strategy, and the last section deals with the major exercise MAINBRACE in 1952 to test the general flank strategy.

Chapter 5 will go more into detail with what military actions were planned and exercised in the Baltic Approaches.

Making DC-13 operational (1): Organisation

In the previous chapter we saw the creation of the DC-13, NATO's first strategic plan. It indicated some ways to go, but the regional planning groups were not in a position to make the principles operational. The personnel of the groups worked

---

[1] Pedlow, Gregory W. "The Politics of NATO Command, 1950–1962." In *U:S: Miliitary Forces in Europe. The Early Years*, eds Simon W. Duke and Wolfgang Krieger, 15–42. Boulder, CO: Westview Press, 1993.

for and reported to their respective national C-in-Cs, and hence did not have the necessary international perspective regarding the organisation of activities that crossed the national borders.²

The war in Korea soon made NATO members realise that an integrated and international, not national, command organisation for NATO was necessary, if NATO were to prevent and, if necessary, meet and stop a Soviet attack on one or all of the member states. So in September 1950, one year after the first meeting, the NATO Council, an integrated command for land, sea and air, was created: the Supreme Headquarters Allied Powers Europe, SHAPE, located in Paris and directed by the Supreme Allied Commander EURope, SACEUR. General Dwight Eisenhower was named for that position, to start in April 1951.

The Atlantic got its own planning group in 1949, and it formed the basis for a separate command on equal footing with SACEUR, the Supreme Allied Commander Atlantic, SACLANT, located in Norfolk, Virginia. A third command, Allied Commander Channel, ACHAN, was set up and located in Portsmouth for the seas around the English Channel, to be led by a British admiral, CINCHAN.

Major NATO Commanders, 1952-1991

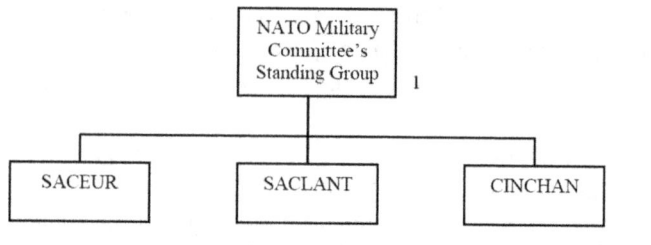

[1] The Standing Group – made up of representatives from France, the United States, and the United Kingdom - was abolished during the major reform of 1967 that resulted from France's departure from the Integrated Military Command Structure.

Figure 3.1: NATO's three commands 1953.³

NATO thus ended up with three commands under the Standing Group. Without doubt, SACEUR was the largest and most influential command, and since he was

---

2 SHAPE. *SHAPE History Volume I*, 154. Versailles: SHAPE, 1953.
3 Pedlow, Gregory. *The Evolution of NATO's Command Structure 1951–2009*, 4. Brussels: NATO, n.d.

also permanent member of the Standing Group, he was difficult to circumvent in almost any case.

Eisenhower's basic strategic idea was to build up a defence system of strong army components in Central Europe and strong naval and air components on the flanks. The army forces did not have to be as strong on the flank; hammering by air and naval forces would suffice: "Our purpose should be to make Norway, Denmark and Holland hedgehogs – all supported by a large naval and air force commanding the North Sea and surrounding waters."[4]

A similar build-up was to be made in Southern Europe. If the Russians attacked the European centre, they were to be hit "awfully hard from both flanks", to the north from air bases in Britain and Scandinavia and to the south from bases in Italy, North Africa, and the Near East. So one task was to create the air powers to be used in the two flanks. This perception of Europe was maintained – in various versions, though – throughout the Cold War.

In one year, SACEUR Eisenhower organised SHAPE into five subcommands – two integrated commands for north (AFNORTH) and south (AFSOUTH) Europe, roughly based on two of the previous planning groups. Eisenhower decided to take command himself in Central Europe and created three subcommands for sea, air and land, respectively, In 1953, the new SACEUR, General Ridgeway, created an integrated command for Central Europe, AFCENT, so he had three main sub-commands for north, center and south.

The Baltic Approaches were part of the area of AFNORTH which was set up in London in June 1951, and shortly after moved to Oslo, Norway. It had four subcommands, one for air forces, one for naval forces and two for land forces for Norway and Denmark, respectively. The air and naval command each had their operational staff in Oslo, but the two army commands were located in their respective countries and therefore, a small advisory army staff was set up in AFNORTH.

Given that the two army commands were national in Denmark and Norway, respectively, and given that the two army forces would operate only within the national borders (plus Schleswig-Holstein with Danish and Norwegian troops, see chapter 6), Eisenhower's strategic ideas perceived AFNORTH as a command mainly handling sea and air forces which might quickly include reinforcements from several nations, operating across large areas. The naval command would have two operational sub-commands, one for each navy with headquarters in each country. The air command likewise would get national sub-commands. The

---

[4] Davis, Robert Thomas. *The Dilemma of NATO Strategy, 1949–1968*, 60. Athens, OH: Ohio University, 2008.

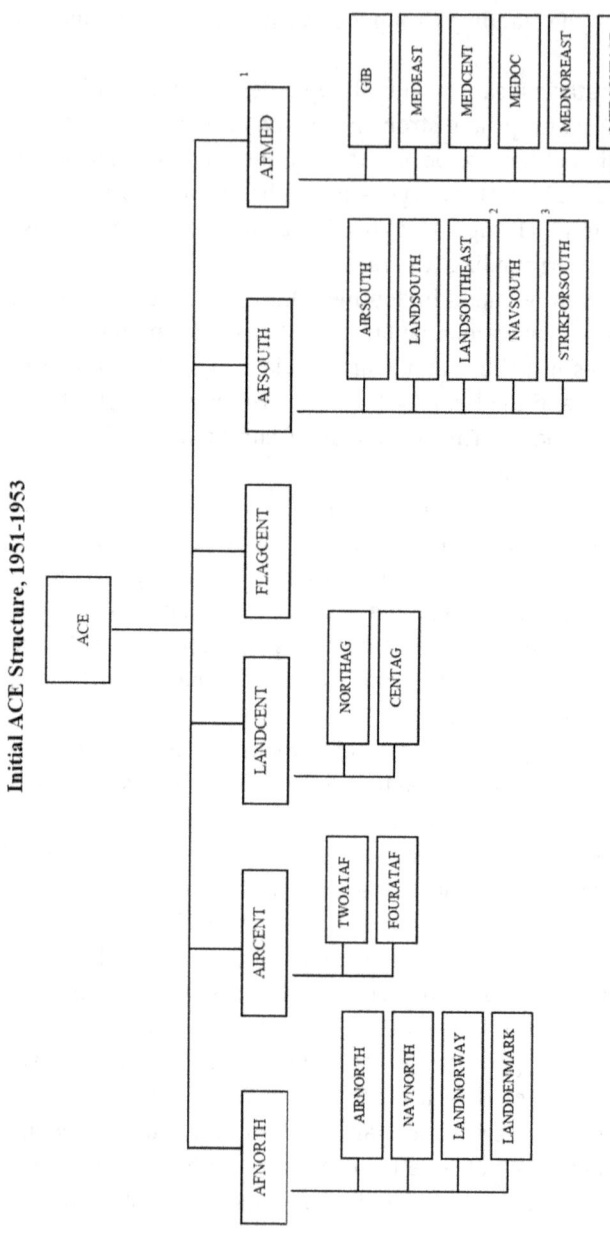

[1] Established in March 1953.
[2] Disestablished in March 1953 when AFMED came into existence.
[3] Established in March 1953 after NAVSOUTH was disestablished.

Figure 3.2: Organisation of European Command 1953.[5]

---

5 Pedlow, Gregory, op. cit., p. 5.

first CINCNORTH became the British Admiral Brind who chose to take the position as naval commander himself.⁶

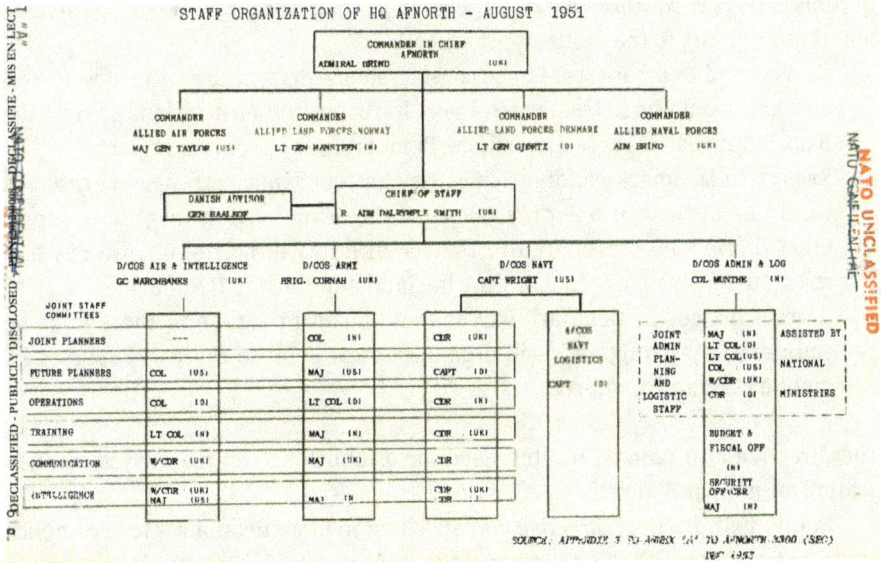

Figure 3.3: Organisation of AFNORTH.⁷

Making DC-13 operational (2): Strategic & tactical guidance

The interim organisation had begun working on important topics already before SACEUR Eisenhower formally started his work in April 1951, and among them DC-13, which step by step became more operational. In May 1951, *Strategic Guidance no 1* was launched.⁸ It saw Europe divided into three areas, in accordance with the supreme commander's organisation. The European centre had the largest role, and the Northern and southern parts were planned as strong flanks, creating sea power and air superiority with a series of strongholds, securing the links within the flanks. AFNORTH's main role was to:
- Hold base areas in Denmark and Norway for offensive and counter-attack operations;

---

6 More details of the creation of the AFNORTH organisation are found in SHAPE's history SHAPE, op. cit., pp. 159–63.
7 SHAPE, op. cit., p. 161.
8 Ibid., 208–9.

- Close the Baltic Approaches;
- After stabilisation of any Russian attack, destroy enemy forces in the region.

In June 1951, *Tactical Directive no 1* specified a few parameters of which we mention those relating to the Baltic Approaches:[9]
- Norway and Denmark were to be considered one defence area; the most important task would be to keep control over harbours and airfields and to close the Baltic approaches. Therefore, holding Denmark was of greatest importance.
- Regarding Denmark, holding Schleswig-Holstein against strong enemy attack would be difficult if one only relied on the Scandinavian Brigade Group. It must therefore be prepared to fight a withdrawal battle northwards to a strong defensive position guarding the land approach to Denmark.
- A great danger in Denmark was sea and airborne landings; these must be countered by strong and well organised local defence forces, supported by mobile regular army forces.

The directive also pointed out the need for establishing command systems integrating air and land forces.

In July 1951, *Tactical Directive no 2* specified in more detail how to accomplish a number of factors.[10] The directive made it clear that NATO had planned to use its air powers immediately to counter-attack Soviet tactical air forces and airfields, combat stockpiles, ports and submarine facilities and lines of communication, employing all available weapons and special operations. Priority in these operations would be given to Soviet airfields and lines of communication. Airplanes from aircraft carriers could be expected to become involved.

A number of general tasks were listed, such as the establishment of an adequate air defence system, creating an intelligence network to warn against preparations of airborne or amphibious operations; protection of lines of communication, port areas, air facilities, transportation systems and other key targets; plans for the redeployment of allied naval and air forces as required; and preparation of detailed offensive and defensive plans prior to the outbreak of hostilities.

Regarding the Baltic and the Baltic Approaches, a number of tasks were stipulated:
- tactical air reconnaissance for land forces, and long range reconnaissance within the southern region of the Baltic.
- plans for anti-invasion minefields in the Baltic exits, particularly Danish and Norwegian waters.

---

9 Ibid., 349–51.
10 Ibid., 352–57.

- maximum utilisation of surface and submarine mine laying resources in order to free air forces for other vital tasks. NATO aircraft would only be used for mine laying in enemy waters.
- air bases would be developed in Denmark to provide adequate air support for armies operating in the area. Consideration must be given to redeployment and reinforcement from other areas. Such forward airfields in Denmark should be developed to minimum operating standards only.
- provision should be made for the detection of submarines attempting pre-D-day transit out of the Baltic.
- close coordination with SACLANT and British Home Command in covering the exits from the Baltic, supporting operations against seaborne invasion of Norway and Denmark, and securing lines of communication from the UK and Channel ports to Norwegian and Danish ports.

These 1951-tasks remained relevant and were pursued throughout the Cold War. As we shall see, the issue of planning the use of non-national air power became dominant in the years to come because both Denmark and Norway were hesitant to allow any stationing of foreign forces in peace time (see chapter 6). As to aircraft carriers, we shall return to them below.

The Russian threat as perceived by NATO's standing group

During Winter 1951–52 the Standing Group wrote up an intelligence estimate, SG 176,[11] assessing the risk of an attack by Russia and the military extent of the threat. The final version was ready on 17 March 1952.

In this analysis, the SACEUR planners clearly had Norway and even Sweden as the main elements of Soviet interest in Scandinavia. For an observer of NATO and the Baltic approaches it is somewhat dissuading to see that the Baltic approaches were not mentioned at all in the document. Denmark was – as a part of Western Europe – mentioned, first, as an element in a "secondary attack" (as opposed to the primary attack towards the Channel and then France) with a "thrust into Denmark". A chart illustrated the directions by broad arrows, one pointing through Schleswig-Holstein up to the Danish southern border of Jutland.

The second mention of Denmark was linked to an attack on Southern Norway with an amphibious and airborne operation striking at Oslo from Denmark and

---

11 Report by the Intelligence Committee to the Standing Group COSMIC SG 176/1 17-3-52 (First version, SG 176, is from 17-12-51).

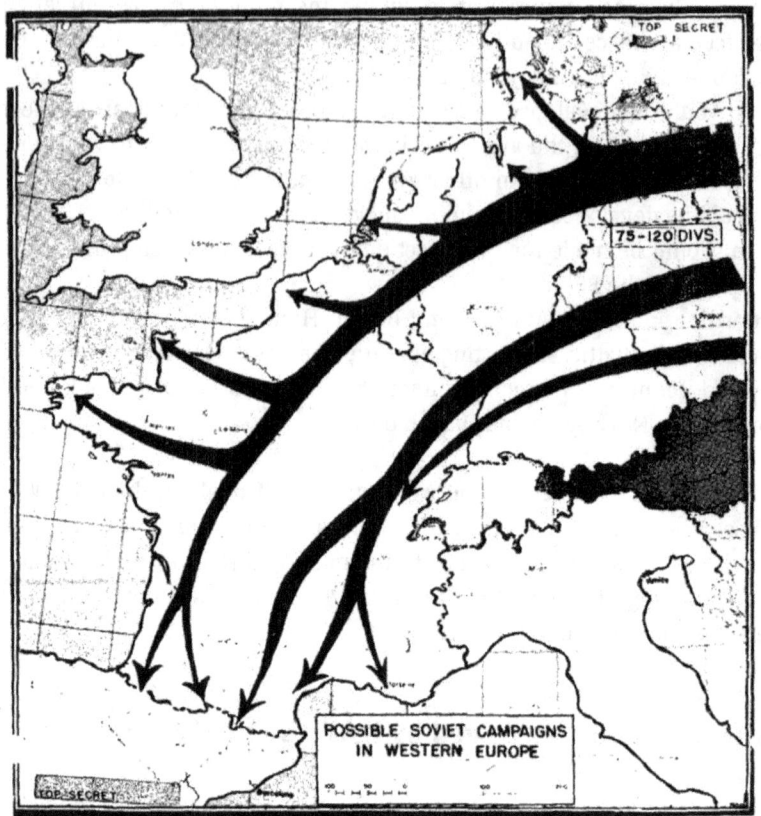

Figure 3.4: Map of possible attacks on Europe by Soviet forces (SG 176, 52).

Germany. The third discussion of Denmark foresaw an attack on both Norway and Sweden, mainly from the south. It could be "mounted from Denmark and Germany to assault the southern Swedish beaches, and/or Norway with one thrust toward Oslo and with the principal effort made toward Stockholm".

In a section called "Campaign against Norway and, if necessary, Sweden" Norway was the possibility for the Soviets to get direct access to the Atlantic; Sweden was a pass-through to Norway, but also a direct opponent in war. Denmark was put in as a stepping stone northwards from Germany. First mention of an attack against Denmark came as part of a section on Western Europe.[12] A second mention came as part of a section on Scandinavia, focusing on Norway and Sweden.[13]

---

12 SG 176 48–52.
13 SG 176 53–59.

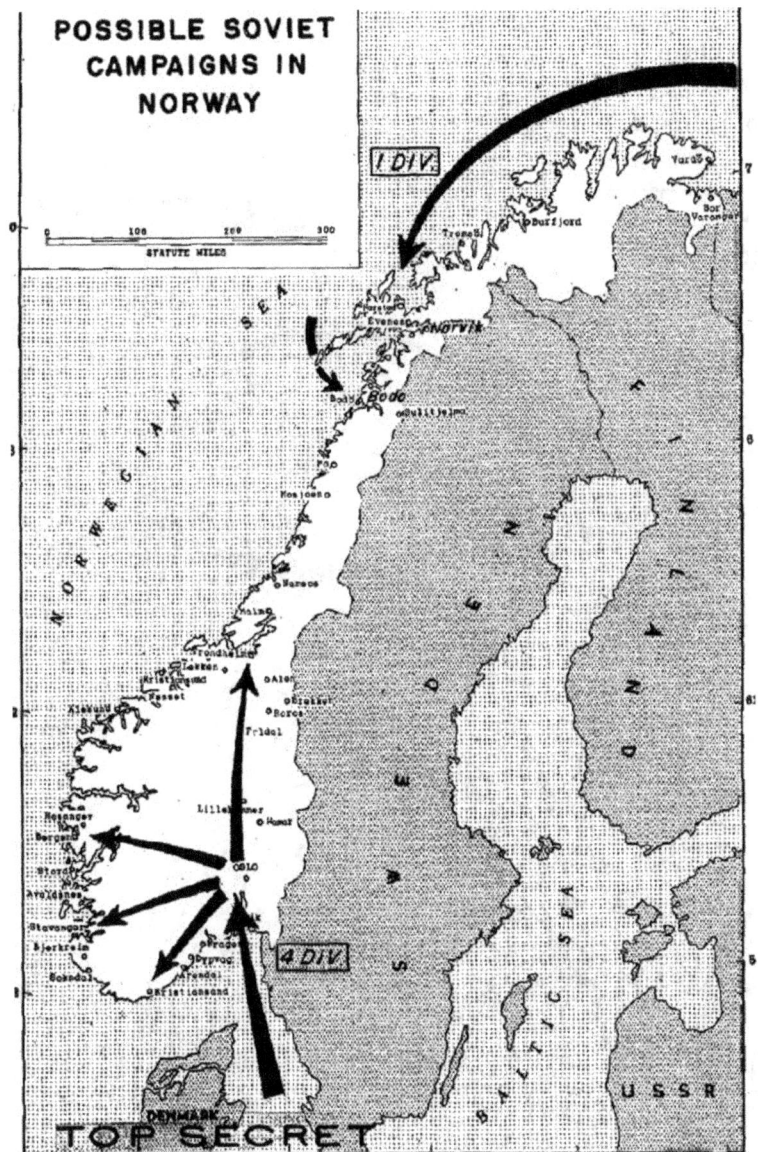

Figure 3.5: Map of Soviet possible attacks on Norway (SG 176, 58).

As the maps show, the analysis of attacks against Norway and Sweden included other directions from the north and across the Mid-Baltic, but we shall not go into details with those parts (see chapter 2 for Sweden's own defence plans). What concerns us is the rather awkward discussion of Denmark and the Baltic approaches.

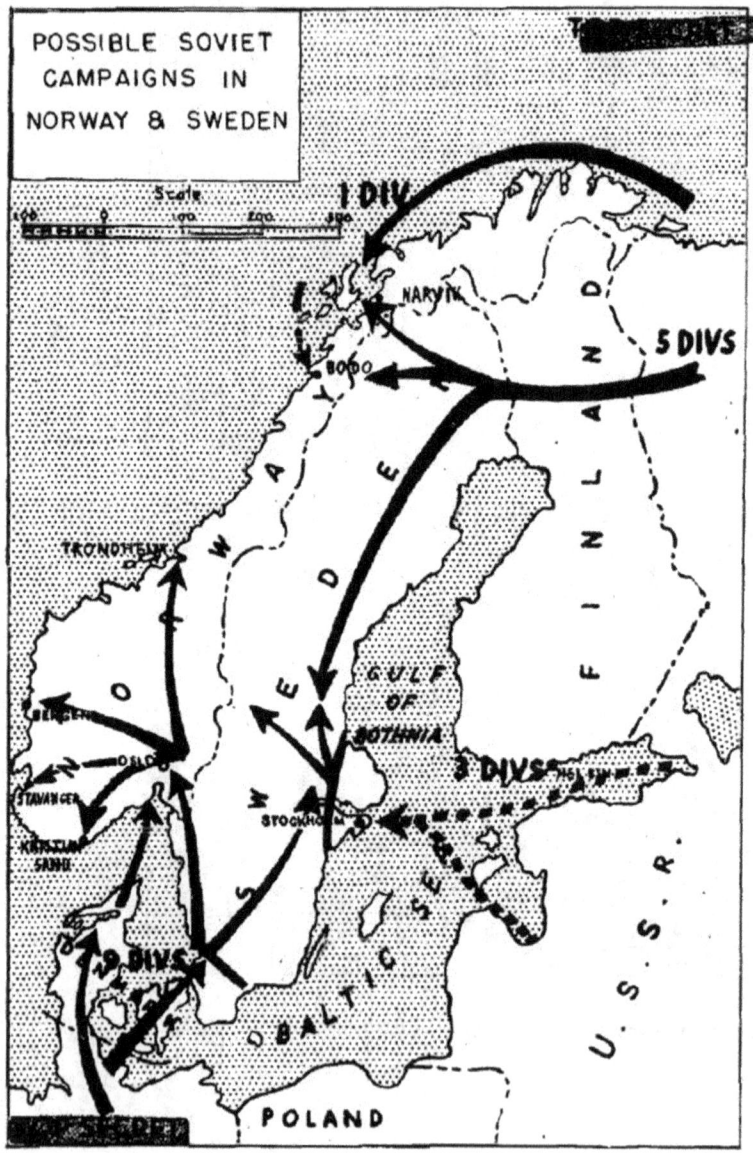

Figure 3.6: Map of Soviet attacks on Scandinavia (SG 176, 59).

A draft version of SG 176 had been circulated among the member states for comments, but apparently not to much avail. The Danish C-in-C had expressed a number of worries regarding the first days of a war.[14] From his perspective, the NATO planners did not understand the geography of the Baltic approaches, in particular the fact that if one wanted to control those waters, one also had to have control of the whole territory of Denmark. Therefore, if the goal of the Russian submarines to pass through to the North Sea and the Atlantic were to be reached, the Russians had to get such control. This was not even mentioned in the draft.

But the main worry of the C-in-C was that NATO-planners did not sufficiently stress the role of Denmark blocking the Baltic Approaches – the cork in the bottle, so to say. In addition, Denmark should be analysed as a part of Scandinavia in the cases of the Russians attacking Norway and possibly Sweden. The draft paper did not understand the most likely Russian form of action, namely an attack against Jutland through Northern Germany and simultaneously an amphibious attack across the Baltic against the Zealand islands – precisely to get the required control of the approaches and the adjacent airfields and from there attack Norway and/or Sweden and eliminate the threat to the Russian flank. Finally, the options for offensive NATO operations in the Baltic to disturb the Russian lines of communication were not adequately recognised (see chapter 6 on offensive operations in the Baltic).

In the final version of SG 176 his comments were, by and large, neglected. The NATO planners of the Standing Group were mainly interested in listing the numbers of army divisions and aircraft. The tricky problems of passing the Baltic approaches as well as blocking them and the difficulties in bringing army troops to Sweden from Denmark had no ears in that particular group.

Given the fact that the both the two SACEUR directives of June 1951 and the AFNORTH Defence Plan 1954 (as we shall see below) – all of which were written before this analysis – did analyse the role of the Baltic approaches in some detail, it seems clear that the different parts of NATO did not work in a synchronised manner, or maybe they competed for influence.

SG 176 was not reissued. Until 1966, its contents were updated annually and expanded in another annual report, SG 161 – and comments did assume influence, as time went by. In 1953, Denmark and the problems of the Baltic Approaches were included in the section on Scandinavia, now under the heading "Campaign against Denmark, Norway and, if necessary, Denmark, Norway and Sweden". And Denmark now got its own subsection discussing the control of the

---

14 Letter HEM Forsvarschefen C.401/0. 222 19-1-52 to the Ministry of Defence.

outlets from the Baltic and the possibilities for getting naval and air bases. We shall return to some of those annual versions in later chapters.

The first defence plans for AFNORTH

As SACEUR's regional subcommands became ready, they started writing plans for their area, specifying the general NATO-directives in more local operational plans. Initially, two types of plans were written – one emergency plan for immediate use in case of an attack; and aother plan with a three-year time horizon, describing the desired state of the defence three years ahead. When the Annual Review process (see chapter 4) became routinised, the three year plans were abandoned. The emergency plans were reviewed every year and adapted to what was actually available.

We shall take a look at the first three-year plan which was ready in late 1951 and described the planned NATO defence by 1954.[15] We also use a later Emergency Plan 1953, which laid bare some tactical principles which showed the militarily rather weak foundation of the whole plan.[16] The plans were not operational, but the overall sizes of necessary military forces were stated; their allocation for specific tasks then was for the four sub-commanders to decide.

The overall pattern followed the strategic goals we have presented earlier: NATO should protect the northern flank, initiate counter operations, deny submarines passage, create depth in the defence and fight for air supremacy. The Soviet interest in the area was obvious: to get bases for aircraft and submarines to attack the NATO lines of communication; airstrips in Denmark and Southern Norway would ease bombing in Western Europe and alleviate protection of submarines using the Baltic approaches; and finally Russian air defence would gain significant depth.

Sweden formed a sort of bulwark, securing the eastern flank of the AFNORTH region, and Russia supposedly regarded Swedish forces as a threat against its bases and lines of communication in the Baltic and in the White Sea, as well as the White Sea Channel.

Nonetheless, NATO-planners concluded that the most likely outcome would be a simultaneous attack on all three countries, following the first NATO plan by the Northern European Regional Group from 1949–50 in which the planners

---

15 Letter HEM to Minister of Defence 02-11-51 C 6/0 4662. The plan is reviewed, the original plan (which was only in one copy) was burned in the ministry by mistake.
16 Notat om det militære planlægningsarbejde inden for NATO, HEM Forsvarsministeriet 11. kontor 10-11-53 313/52-68.

chose to comprise Sweden.[17] The planners saw Sweden as a stepping stone to Denmark as well as Norway, and the lack of coordination between NATO and Sweden was considered an asset for the Russians. Once Southern Sweden was conquered, its naval and air bases could be used for operations against Denmark and Southern Norway. Last, not least, the NATO planners thought that Sweden could not accept Russia surrounding Sweden militarily and therefore would initiate attacks.

Of course, it was not possible to include any details of Swedish military action in the plan beyond a more or less educated guess to the effect that, time and again, the plan only regarded attacks on Denmark and Norway. The plan covered land, sea and air defence but only analysed a first phase, that of resisting a Russian attack. Phase two, counterattack, was presumed, but not discussed and planned for. But offensive air and naval attacks should be directed towards enemy bases and lines of communication in the Baltic area and Northern Germany to prevent invasion and disturb supplies.

We discuss land, sea and air force plans separately below and compare them with forces actually available, that is, the NATO D-day goals for Norway and Denmark January 1952.[18]

Land

Denmark and Southern Sweden were the closest and easiest areas to attack, hence Denmark had to be on full strength, mobilised from day one. The enemy was expected to deploy nine divisions towards Schleswig-Holstein, planning to move up through the Jutland peninsula with fast armoured vehicles as spearheads, and then let three division turn east towards Fyn and possibly Zealand. The NATO forces actually available made a general defence of the whole area unlikely, and help from AFCENT was improbable, as those forces were slated to go west to specified defence posts, not north, during initial battles. Consequently, only certain key military points were to be defended. The enemy should be hindered in moving forward as much as possible, troops be eliminated and equipment be destroyed as far to the south as possible. One's own forces should be kept intact and preserved until full strength was obtained.

The main defence forces would be in Jutland and Schleswig-Holstein and include Norwegian and British forces: on the south side of the Kiel Canal three in-

---

17 Aunesluoma, Juhana. *Britain, Sweden and the Cold War, 1945–54*, 91. Oxford: Palgrave Macmillan, 2003.
18 SHAPE, op. Cit., pp. 212–16.

fantry divisions and 2/3 armoured division; on the north side 2 infantry divisions and 1/3 armoured division; north of the border 1/3 infantry division and one armoured battalion.

They were to be deployed as far to the south into Schleswig-Holstein as possible and impose maximum delay on enemy forces trying to cross the Kiel Canal or River Eider by demolition of bridges and other crossings. In addition, the Kiel Canal should be destroyed as a waterway. If withdrawal through Jutland became necessary, actions should be delayed by all possible means. Vendsyssel (the area north of Limfjorden) should be held as long as possible.

On Zealand and Bornholm the plan required two 1/3 infantry divisions and 1/3 armoured division. These forces were NATO forces. On Zealand, troops should prepare to counter airborne forces and amphibious landings. Possibly up to three enemy divisions might be transported from harbours in the Baltic, to land in the Bays of Køge and Faxe.

In addition, the plan operated – for the whole country – with 24 battalions infantry and 11 artillery batteries for local defence, plus various other defence measures such as 37 heavy and 96 light air artillery batteries.

Those were the plans. The realities differed significantly. The plan operated with something between eight and nine divisions, but Denmark had no more than three, maybe four, and the Norwegians and British only delivered a brigade and a regiment, respectively, to the Baltic Approaches. Norway had nearly all forces located in Norway. The nearly four divisions south of the Kiel Canal were wishes never to come true.

Sea

In 1951, NATO feared a Russian naval attack force, but two years later no major attacks were expected from the Russian Baltic fleet, although one could not deny the possibility of amphibious attacks. The main role of the navy would be to protect one's own lines of communication and support army movements on land, but various Soviet raids could be expected. Few Russian ships were expected to operate outside the reach of own air forces. After laying defensive mines in the straits, the NATO task was to initiate offensive operations to destroy enemy bases and lines of communication and shipping with naval forces in combination with air forces. SACLANT was expected to protect convoys from the west.

Enemy submarines were expected to have left the Baltic before hostilities were initiated, and hence threats against lines of communication from submarines were to be expected from day one at all coastal areas. In the Baltic, offensive NATO naval operations were limited to submarines, destroyers and MTBs (with air support in daylight), and offensive mine laying by aircraft and said ships. These tasks required six submarines, four destroyers and 16 MTBs.

The NATO naval invasion defence was concentrated in the Baltic approaches (with a forward base on Bornholm) and required eight destroyers, 40 MTBs, three submarines, 12 patrol craft and two repair ships for MTBs and subs, in addition to 24 mine sweepers. This force also provided the army forces in Jutland with support for their eastern flank. Protection of the western flank (to the North Sea) would be provided from a reserve of ships organised by the Norwegian navy.

A significant number of minefields was required in order to prevent the Russian navy from breaking out to the North Sea and the Atlantic via the Baltic approaches.

However, Denmark and Norway were nowhere near to having eight destroyers and 40 MTBs in the Baltic, so all capacity for forward defence was in thin air.

Air

The Russians were expected to have about 1,000 fighters and 900 light bombers in the region. The planners did not have enough aircraft and regretted the Danish decision of not allowing allied aircraft in Jutland in peace time (see chapter 6).

The role of the air force was to protect the military key points in the area and help defend the Central European sector applying a forward strategy (i.e. attack key points towards the east). But as long as only Danish and Norwegian forces were available, local defence had first priority. The Russians had airfields all the way along the Baltic coast and Northern Germany with fighters, fighter-bombers and light bombers, which could all reach Denmark and Southern Sweden; Southern Norway could only be reached by light bombers.

The NATO tasks were: to defend vital areas against air attacks; to maintain such air power that ground and naval forces could move relatively freely; support said forces; attack enemy ground installations to stop progress; assist in closing the Baltic approaches; fight enemy shipping and support mine laying operations; perform reconnaissance; and attack enemy strategic bombers. These tasks required Southern Norway and Denmark to have 695 fighters, 135 light bombers and 64 aircraft for naval support plus a number of other aircraft. In Denmark, the plan required 394 fighters and fighter-bombers, 28 night fighters and 18 reconnaissance aircraft.

The actual number available in the two countries by 1952 was 89 fighters, 47 fighter-bombers, six recce and 10 transport aircraft, but no night fighters. As with army and navy, the two countries were nowhere near the desired number of aircraft. Therefore came the suggestions for stationing aircraft in peace time, to which we shall return in chapter 6.

A British critique

The British did not trust the AFNORTH 1954 plan. In particular, the British Chiefs of Staff had severe doubts that the Baltic Approaches could be held with the forces available in the plans of SACEUR and AFNORTH and made a study of the situation in 1953.[19] The immediate future looked bleak (as confirmed with the figures above): "The forces at present available to CINCNORTH for his task of controlling the western exits from the Baltic, together with the assistance that could be expected from outside Commands, are totally inadequate . . .".

Grave consequences followed: CINCNORTH would have to give up the Kiel Canal and Schleswig-Holstein. The canal therefore had to be obstructed before the withdrawal, and there were hardly forces available to do the job.

The regional commander could do no more than fight a delaying action on his main defence line between Esbjerg and Kolding in Southern Jutland. Control of the Sound and Belts would depend on NATO's ability to hold Zealand and Fyn which were likely to be attacked at the same time as Jutland. Reinforcement of the Danish Islands from Jutland was hardly practicable in these circumstances. Evacuation of forces from Jutland would therefore have to go to Southern Norway.

Unless Sweden were committed to giving planned and practical assistance from the outbreak of war, the chances of holding Zealand would be remote. Even with Swedish assistance it was unlikely that NATO would be able to deploy and maintain sufficient forces to hold these islands for long. But any time gained by the defence of Zealand would enable NATO to use Øresund for light naval forces which could interfere with the Soviet attack on Sweden, and would help NATO to carry out a mining campaign in the narrows and Kattegat.

When forced to evacuate Jutland and the Danish islands, NATO would have to rely on further mining of the Kattegat, and on sea and air patrols from bases in Southern Norway and possibly Sweden, for controlling the Skagerrak.

In other words, the state of the defence of the Baltic Approaches was alarmingly poor in 1953. In the long run, i.e. after West German forces became available, the British thought it would be possible to maintain control over the Baltic Approaches by, first, protecting Jutland by holding the Kiel Canal, but this required six army divisions and 28 squadrons aircraft. Second, control could be maintained of the passages if NATO forces had the Zealand islands. This required, however, four army divisions plus troops in Jutland as well as considerable air and some naval forces. The logistic difficulties of supporting forces in these islands would be considerable. Expenditure would also be required now (in 1953)

---

19 Controlling the exits from the Baltic. Annex to J.P. (53) 83 Final, 24-9-53 Top Secret.

to build up adequate airfields, beach and coast defences, radar cover, mining and demolition stores and other similar resources.

If Sweden could be induced to abandon her neutrality, the Allied use of air and naval bases on Swedish soil would be of great value and the gap in defences caused by Swedish territorial waters would be eliminated. This, of course, could only be solved by a political decision which appeared unlikely to be taken.

However, the British felt, based on informal conversations with a broad range of military and diplomatic sources in all Scandinavian countries, that strategically, the Swedes were approaching the west because they realised that in the case of war, they were almost bound to be attacked by the Soviet Union.[20] The Russians would very quickly take Zealand, and as soon as Zealand fell, the fate of Sweden would be sealed. According to Buzzard, the Swedish military top hoped that facing this military risk, the Swedish politicians would join forces with NATO when east-West tensions worsened.

But from 1954, the military planning circumstances changed because it became clear that in a few years West Germany would be rearmed and create a counter force to the Soviets which made Sweden less important in military terms. This fact became part of NATO planning, and indeed the planners stopped taking the Swedes into their documents as partners.

A British plan for nuclear attack on Baltic and Northern targets

The worries of the British Chiefs of Staff about the Soviet threat against British and NATO lines of communication in the North Sea and the Atlantic concerned the traffic from the USA to Europe bringing supplies in war time.[21] The Baltic was regarded as vital to the protection of sea communications on which the U.K. and Allied operations in Western Europe and Scandinavia depended; it was the key to Southern Scandinavia which was of utmost importance to the strategic air campaign; and it was an important factor in the Western European land campaign.

They had expressed dissatisfaction with SACEUR's treatment of the Baltic approaches in his war planning and wrote an analysis of the issues.[22] Like the Danes, the British found that it was of utmost importance to retain control of the Baltic exits in order: a) to deny egress of Russian warships and shipping from the

---

20 Aunesluoma, op. cit., pp. 146–53.
21 C.O.S. (53) 172 8-4-53 Note: Closing the exits from the Baltic. Top secret.
22 C.O.S.(52)164th Meeting: Minutes of meeting held on 2-12-52. Top secret.

Baltic; b) to enable the Allies to threaten or attack with warships the Russian Baltic communications leading to their western front and/or relating to their seaborne operations against Sweden; and c) to support Sweden and encourage her to join the allies before she was cut off.

As quoted above, the Chiefs of Staff found the forces available to CINCNORTH now and in the near future completely inadequate. The defence of Southern Sweden, which would be of great value, required coordination with Allied plans. They decided to carry out an analysis of the military issues and informally informed the regional commander of this.

Although the British from the outset in April acknowledged that the Baltic Approaches were the responsibility of SACEUR and CINCNORTH in cooperation with SACLANT, the study was purely a British endeavour and did not include any NATO officers in the making. There were, however, thoughts of sharing it with the Americans at a later stage.

The plan illustrates the complexity of a comprehensive military plan. The analysis included threats from Northern Russia.[23] The overall issue was how to reduce the risk for Russian break-out of submarines and/or getting access to airfields in Western Denmark and Norway. This was to be prevented by carrying out attacks "at source" (destroying bases, airfields etc.) by the end of 1954 in the Baltic and in Northern Russia at the White Sea.

The analysis mainly concerned actions which would have an effect within the first two months of a war, but a few more long term actions also were considered. The target types of interest were:
- medium and light bombers on airfields and under construction, and the airfields they planned to use;
- submarines in their bases and under construction in yards; bases used by submarines and mineable areas on submarine routes;
- surface vessels in their bases, possible bases and mineable areas on surface vessel routes:
- communication lines such as the Kiel Canal; the Danish narrows; the Trave-Elbe Canal and the Baltic-White Sea Canal;
- oil production

There was a fear that the Russians would try to secure the Baltic Approaches by amphibious attacks on the Danish islands, Sweden and subsequently Norway. These attacks would be launched from ports in the Baltic. Therefore, all forces

---

23 J.P. (53) 18 (Final) 24-8-53, Attack at source to reduce the threat to sea communications in a war beginning in December 1954. Top secret.

moving to concentrate at embarkation points in that area must be considered for destruction. Finally, attacks might be necessary upon fleet units, submarines and depot ships dispersed from their bases.

Three assumptions were made in setting the priorities for attacks: the two canals in Northern Germany would be temporarily blocked by demolition or other methods; the majority of the large submarines would be based on Northern ports and would be at sea on D-day; and submarines and surface ships not at sea would be dispersed from their bases.

Medium bombers and their airfields were not selected for inclusion in the plan because they were expected to be destroyed by NATO's strategic air force. Light (naval) bombers were targets.

On that basis, the following groups of targets were set. Most of the actions were to be carried out by land- or carrier-based aircraft; which ones would actually be used would depend on the tactical situation and availability in each case. However, whereas carrier-borne aircraft could reach a number of inland targets, it was doubtful whether their navigation and radar equipment were adequate for pinpointing certain targets. Mining operations would in most cases be carried out by ships, but air mining would also be possible. Most attacks would be done by atomic bombs, either 10 kilotons or 30 kilotons, and about 75 bombs would be necessary. For each sortie of a plane with an atomic bomb, 5 simultaneous sorties would be necessary for escort or diversion.

First priority targets were
- destruction of 10 Baltic bases for surface ships and submarines with 15 to 20 10 kiloton atom bombs, requiring 90 to 120 sorties – alternatively conventional bombing with 400 tons in 520 sorties;
- destruction of any amphibious forces seen concentrating in up to 12 Baltic ports with 18 to 24 30 kiloton atomic bombs, requiring 108 to 144 sorties – alternatively 1,600 tons conventional bombing from 2500 sorties;
- mining of the Danish narrows (to be done by CINCNORTH) and if the fall of Denmark was imminent, Kattegat with 1,150 mines and (if demolition was unsuccessful) the approaches to the Kiel Canal with 200 mines. If Denmark was overrun, 500 aerial mines had to be laid weekly in the Sound and the straits.
- destruction of naval aircraft and their seven airfields in the Baltic with 11 to 14 10 kiloton atomic bombs and 66 to 84 sorties – alternatively conventional bombing with 380 tons from 346 sorties;
- destruction of nine bases for surface forces and submarines in the north with 14 to 18 10 kiloton atomic bombs and between 84 and 108 sorties – alternatively conventional bombing with 400 tons from 468 sorties; and

– destruction of certain locks of the Baltic-White Sea Canal by conventional bombing with 62 "tall-boys" and 124 sorties by especially trained crews – alternatively 42 1,000 pounds bombs from low-level glide bombers with 14 sorties.

We shall not detail the rest of the priorities, just mention the targets. Second priority would be submarines and surface vessels dispersed from their bases, attacked individually from aircraft carriers, and destruction of naval aircraft and airfields with 10 kiloton atomic bombs in the North. Third priority would be mining of the approaches to the Baltic shipping ports by aerial mining and to the Northern ports by submarines mining. Fourth priority would be destruction of submarine yards, aircraft factories and oil production centres. However, the consequences of such an attack would not be felt in the first months thereafter and, therefore, fourth priority targets were not planned for.

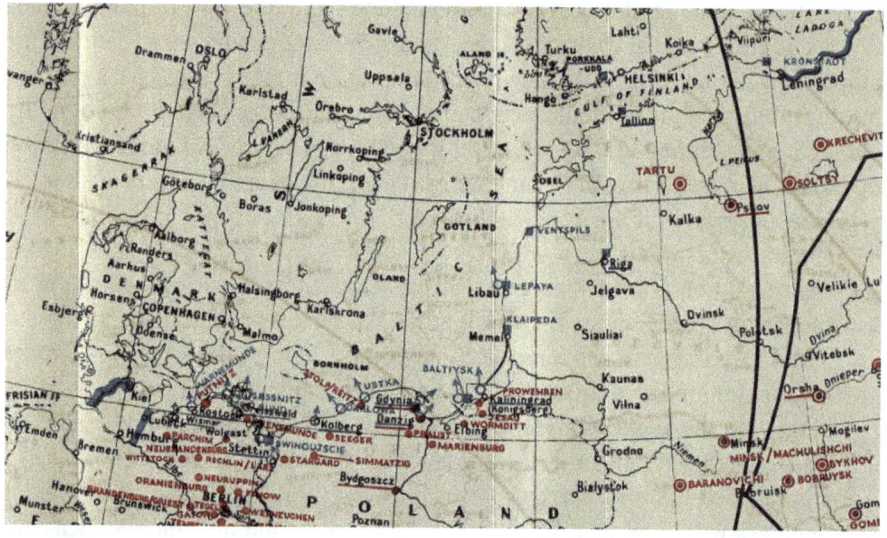

Figure 3.7: Map of Baltic area and the targets. Source: COS J.P. (53) 18 (final).

Detailed planning. For each type of target listed above, details were listed in terms of the types of bombs and their consequences for conventional as well as atomic bombs. The following sections concern such details regarding an attack on ports to be used for amphibious attacks on the Baltic approaches.
– The amount of shipping likely to be concentrated in any one of the ports on the list when an assault is imminent would be of the order of 20 ships, in addition to large numbers of coasters, large barges and landing craft. The object

of the attack would be to prevent an invasion of Scandinavia by the destruction of at least three-quarters of the ships and craft.
- Conventional bombing. All the Baltic invasion ports were within range of carrier aircraft and of piston-engined and jet medium bombers based in Britain. They were suitable for radar or visual attack. To achieve a 75 per cent destruction of invasion shipping would require between 400 and 1,600 tons of high explosives for each port, depending on the concentration of shipping. To attack all 12 ports would require from 624 to 2,496 sorties.
- Atomic bombing. One large airburst atomic bomb would, on average, disable 55 per cent of shipping, a smaller airburst atomic bomb 35 per cent. Against these targets the large atomic bomb appears to be preferable. Wherever a waterburst bomb could be dropped in fifty or more feet of water within one mile of the target, it would be more effective than an airburst bomb of similar size, since ships and installations could not be used for a considerable time afterwards, however ruthless the Russians were in expenditure of human life [sic]. Only the most adverse weather conditions would preclude the effective use of waterburst bombs. The requirement would be for between 18 and 24 atomic bombs and between 108 and 144 aircraft sorties.

What happened to this plan? The Chiefs of Staff discussed it during a meeting on 20 October 1953.[24] They agreed that the plan was premature and not feasible by 1954, but three years later the outlook might "be rosier". Cooperation with the Americans would be necessary, and in order to become a worthy partner, Britain would have to strengthen its air force. Furthermore, the plan must be coordinated with another study of British air defence. So at a later point of time it might be discussed with the American Joint Chiefs of Staff with the year 1956 as target year.

But in December 1953 the Chiefs of Staff decided not to take the case further and not to approach SACEUR in this matter per se. However, they found the land defence of Schleswig-Holstein very weak and therefore advised the British Command in Germany to approach the supreme commander for preparing – "chambering" – the canals in the area for demolishing, but got a reply that he found such a measure politically not feasible at this point of time.[25] And given the British cut-backs on defence in the subsequent years and the change in aircraft carrier deployment to mainly east of Suez after 1957,[26] it is not likely that the Americans ever got involved. The plan remained a drawer plan, but still it is in-

---

[24] Response to a COS letter 19-12-53. Minutes from C.O.S. (53) 119th Meeting October 20, 1953.
[25] C.O.S. (54) 310 21-9-54.
[26] Berdal, Mats. *The United States, Norway and the Cold War, 1954–60*, 86. London: Macmillan, 1997.

dicative of the massive use of nuclear weapons in the minds of the military planners.

In American and in CINCNORTH's war plans, however, strikes at Soviet sources with nuclear warheads soon were included, maybe inspired by the British drawer plan. In 1956 they were aimed at shore-based naval potential in the Baltic and in the north and in addition some targeted cruisers of the SVERDLOV-class if they attempted to escape from the Baltic into the North Sea (plan Jutland Charlie).[27]

NATO's New Approach, first aired in 1954 (see chapter 7) was contingent on such heavy bombing at source. So important aspects of the British thoughts from 1953 became NATO realities as plans from the mid-1950s.

SACLANT and AFNORTH strategy & cooperation

In 1952, SACLANT finally was organised, and the work on a strategy continued. The Korean war had renewed the interest in naval aircraft, and therefore the USA increased its investments in aircraft carriers. SACEUR Eisenhower used the interest in these carriers to call for a new role for naval power in Europe's defence. He wanted to use carrier air power in a manner which was neither a strategic air offensive nor a traditional sea control mission:[28] since ground forces were scarce and difficult to support in the Northern Flank, one should mainly use naval and air forces there. So the term Carrier Strike Fleet (Force) was coined; its roots were in the old type of strike force, typically based on battleships, but now aircraft carriers were the core units.

While battleships mainly had rendered sea control because they could not attack land targets beyond the coastal area, the aircraft from carriers had a much longer span, attacking inland or sea targets on the other side of a land stretch – e.g. targets in the Baltic attacked from the Norwegian Sea (flying across Norway and Sweden) or from the North Sea (crossing Denmark, Germany or Southern Sweden). Such use of carriers meant that AFNORTH got a strong interest in what SACLANT could offer by allocating a carrier strike force, not only as support at sea, but actually as a principal instrument for fulfilling the goals of AFNORTH, particularly in Northern Norway, but also in the Baltic Approaches, covered by carriers in the North Sea.

These ideas were advocated by Britain and the USA, providing ships as well as aircraft from carriers. The Royal Navy even foresaw British carriers as the

---

27 Ibid., 76.
28 Davis, op. cit., p. 60.

main operators during the first 15 days of a conflict, until American carriers could reach the eastern side of the Atlantic.

This novel use of carriers spurred a renewed interest in the cooperation possibilities, and a series of discussions between SACLANT and AFNORTH now determined the principles for their cooperation during war.[29]

CINCLANT in principle accepted a responsibility to assist the defence of the Northern flank. In the years to come, there would be an immediate need for assistance by aircraft-carrier based forces in Denmark and possibly Southern Norway. The carriers would stay in the North Sea (operating an aircraft carrier and its support group successfully in war times in the shallow and/or narrow Danish waters is nearly unthinkable, PB) and yield counter measures like bombing enemy air and naval bases in the Baltic area. But given the fact that the operational range of carrier aircraft at that time was 300 miles – i.e. maybe 50 miles east of the border between Eastern Germany and Poland – there were limits to such attacks at source. So CINCLANT also acknowledged the need for direct maritime air support, primarily to naval operations in the Danish narrows. This probably would allow the carriers to stay further out in the North Sea, outside the reach of enemy aircraft.

The Royal Navy created a maritime Atlantic strategy for using naval air power to support the landward flanks. The bearing principle was to let carriers operate in groups of four with about 350 combat aircraft per group. Eisenhower had indicated that most of the 26 American aircraft carriers would be allocated to SACEUR for his flank operations. This would allow for two American carrier groups for the North and south, respectively. Eisenhower hoped to "get an agreement of the British Admiralty to provide, in operational emergency, naval strength to support Norway and Denmark". The Royal Navy established strike groups similar to the American ones. They also wanted to prevent Russia from establishing submarine bases in Northern Norway, e.g. in the wake of an atomic exchange.[30]

But this soon became unlikely. In April 1957 a White Paper was published, giving the British defence system an overhaul in the light of a financial squeeze. The gist of it was a reduction of conventional forces in Europe and an increased dependence on the deterrence created by atomic weapons. This policy pushed the Royal Navy to give up the fleet of large carriers for the Northern Flank and move them to the areas east of Suez where atomic capabilities were not part of the mili-

---

29 Notat om grænse i Nordsøen mellem CINCNORTH og CINCEASTLANT, HEM Forsvarsministeriet 11. kontor 11-6-52 and Bemærkninger om samtaler med admiral Mc Cormick under besøg i Olso, 6-8 marts 1952, YHM Forsvarsministeriet 11. kontor 29-5-52.
30 Berdal, Mats. *British Naval Policy and Norwegian Security. Maritime Power in Transition, 1951–60*, 10–12. Oslo: Institutt for forsvarsstudier, 1992.

tary forces. Light carriers, however, were maintained in the north for ASW purposes.

As a consequence, the roles and importance of the American Carrier Fleet grew. But after 1960, no carriers were preplanned for the North Sea and the Baltic Approaches, and as the years passed there was less and less enthusiasm in using carriers close to the Baltic approaches.[31]

Operation MAINBRACE

Exercise MAINBRACE[32] was designed as a test of Eisenhower's flank strategy; it took place during September 14–25, 1952. It was NATO's largest exercise to date and it was meant to demonstrate that Denmark and Norway – in spite of being somewhat isolated from Central Europe with its large NATO forces – could be helped by modern navies with their air, amphibious and surface components, all commanded in cooperation between SACLANT and AFNORTH.[33] In addition to the advanced training of the forces involved, command relationships, logistics and communications facilities were to be tested. Exercise missions were broadly in accord with wartime missions. SACLANT was to control the sea lines of communication within his command and to support the sea, land and air battles in Northern Europe. CINCNORTH was to withstand the initial enemy thrusts into Norway and Denmark and seal the exits from the Baltic.

At sea, the exercise had five phases.[34] First, a carrier force would sail from Britain to Northern Norway to support ground forces there. Then the carriers would sail south, replenishing at sea. Third, convoys from and to Scandinavia would be protected by surface and carrier forces and land-based air forces. Fourth, an amphibious force would sail from Britain to land forces at Northern Jutland. This group was to reinforce Danish and British troops already there, and they would bring their own air support. Finally, light Danish, British and Norwegian forces would operate in Kattegat and the Baltic Approaches to chase submarines and protect the Danish shores. Carrier-based aircraft would attack a number of railroad junctions and bridges, among those the important bridge across Lillebælt, five ferry harbours and three airfields.

---

31 Berdal, *The United States, Norway and the cold war, 1954–60*, 75.
32 Sometimes (and in this book) spelled MAINBRACE, sometimes MAIN BRACE.
33 Unless otherwise stated, this presentation of the exercise is based on the MAINBRACE sections of the report to the Standing Group 21-11-52 SG 207-3.
34 Note HEM Forsvarsministeriet 1. kontor 11-8-52, 981.239-27/52.

The Baltic part of the exercise had come under heavy critique by the Soviet Union – but we shall not pursue that theme which is analysed elsewhere.[35] During the preparation phase, the Danish C-in-C was very dissatisfied with the naval part of the exercise because apart from a few FPBs, no American or British naval vessels would enter Danish waters and the Baltic; consequently, there would be no lessons learned for the two navies about the possibilities and dangers of sailing in the Baltic approaches. This was not in accordance with the original conceptualisation of the exercise.[36] The hesitation to include a larger component probably stemmed from the British government, which reacted to the Soviet critique and expressed doubts about the naval presence in the Baltic. The Danish government also expressed hesitations and in August was assured that the foreign FPBs would not bunker at the island of Bornholm; in fact, they would stay 25 miles west of the island. Thus the Danish C-in-C came into quite a disagreement with his political masters.

The NATO forces participating in MAINBRACE
NATO naval forces were provided by Belgium, Canada, Denmark, France, Netherlands, Norway, UK and U.S. and maritime and patrol aircraft by the UK and U.S.

Table 3.1: Naval Forces – Operation Mainbrace, 1952.

NATO member	Air Carr	BattleS	Cruiser	Destr.	Minel.	Sub	MTB	Other	Total
United States	6	1	3	40	—	9	—	—	59
UK	3	1	2	31	—	17	4	8+	66
Canada	1	—	1	5	—	—	—	—	7
France	—	—	—	7	11	—	—	2	20
Denmark	—	—	—	3	2	2	—	—	7
Norway	—	—	—	2	16	2	3	3	26
Portugal	—	—	—	3	—	—	—	—	3
Netherlands	—	—	—	5	—	3	—	5	13
Belgium	—	—	—	—	2	—	—	—	2
TOTALS:	10	2	6	96	31	33	7	18	203

Source: Wikipedia.

---

35 Dansk Institut for Internationale Studier. *Danmark under den kolde krig. Den sikkerhedspolitiske situation 1945–1991. Bind 1: 1945–1962*, 236–40. København: Dansk Institut for Internationale Studier, 2005a.
36 This becomes very clear from the C-in-C's amendments to the minutes of the AFNE C-in-C meeting 25-4-52; C.C. 621/A 2152 (in error dated 6-4-52).

They were organised in two carrier striking forces with a carrier support force, a logistic support force (oilers etc.), an amphibious force; furthermore, there were convoys and escorts, mine sweeping groups and maritime and patrol aircraft based at Trondheim, Norway.

Enemy Orange forces were: Danish, Netherlands, Norwegian and U.K. submarines supported by French, Netherlands and U.K. reconnaissance aircraft. RAF and RN shore bases air acted as enemy strike aircraft against the forces at sea. A cruiser and a fast mine layer acted as surface raiders; mines were laid by ships, submarines and aircraft. Norwegian and Danish aircraft provided limited air opposition during the air support actions.

The Danish forces participating were:[37] army: the Danish forces in Schleswig-Holstein, reinforced to a regiment, and local defence forces; navy: two frigates, two coastal destroyers, two depot ships, two submarines, eight MTBs, two mine layers and three mine sweepers; air force: 4–6 recce, 24 METEOR and 16 F-84 fighter bombers.

Initial situation

The NATO countries were presumed to now have been at war with a Continental Eurasian Power for 30 days. Sweden had remained neutral but Finland had been occupied. The following situations were assumed at the commencement of the exercise:

a. Land. South of Denmark the enemy was being held at bay with difficulty at the Kiel Canal-Eider River Line and was expected to launch amphibious assaults against Zealand and/or Jutland. In Northern Norway the enemy had advanced westward through Finmark although Allied forces were holding the Lyngen Line (simulated in the Narvik area). A naval force, believed to contain troops, was at sea presumably endeavouring to outflank the Lyngen Line.

b. Sea. A Carrier Strike Force was replenishing in a U.K. port. A Carrier Hunter Killer Force was operating in the Northern Approaches to the U.K., acting in support of a Logistic Support Force. An Amphibious Force was in the U.K. and an important U.K./Scandinavian convoy covered by a Carrier Support Group was due to sail. Maritime and patrol aircraft were operating from U.K. and Norway. It was estimated that 15 to 20 enemy submarines, supported by reconnaissance aircraft are in the area, were close to Britain, apparently concentrating on mining and shipping attacks. Although the Baltic exits were not closed, neither submarines nor surface vessels could exit undetected. An enemy cruiser at Narvik was expected to attempt a breakout into the Atlantic.

---

37 Letter FTR to the Danish C-in-C Forsvarsministeriet 1. kontor 19-7-52, 981.239-27/52.

c. Air. Enemy tactical air forces, far larger in number, were supporting the land battles. Enemy medium and heavy bombers were operating over the Norwegian Sea, the North Sea and the East Atlantic.

Figure 3.8: Gun crew on 40 mm anti-aircraft gun – hand controlled WW2-style, with the metal scaffold to prevent the gunner from firing on the ship's superstructure. Danish Frigate HOLGER DANSKE during MAINBRACE 1952. Source: Forsvarsgalleriet.

CINCNORTH appreciated that he could not fulfil his mission with the forces at his disposal. Through SACEUR he requested maximum support from SACLANT, particularly with carrier air support in North Norway (Lyngen Line), and by placing an amphibious force at immediate readiness. SACLANT agreed, ordered his East Atlantic commander to provide the required support, and passed to him the operational control of the Striking Fleet.

CINCNORTH stated that he required immediate disruption of the hostile forces advancing south from Narvik and close air support for his forces deployed between Narvik and Bodo. He further advised that the situation in Denmark was deteriorating and that additional support might soon be required in that area.

What happened

The first half of MAINBRACE covered the start, transit north, anti-raider action, replenishment and support operations by the Striking Fleets passage of the convoy from UK to Norway and return and A/S operations and reconnaissance by maritime and patrol aircraft. We shall skip those details.

When the situation in the north had been stabilised, CINCNORTH requested aid in the form of amphibious troops landed in Jutland and carrier air support for his land forces in Southern Denmark because reinforcements could not be expected from AFCENT. This portion of the exercise covered the transit south, replenishment and support operations by the Striking Fleets; Carrier Hunter Killer operations in support of the Fleet and the Logistic Support Force; the transit from the UK and unopposed landing in Jutland of the Marine assault force and A/S operations and reconnaissance by maritime and patrol aircraft.

For the Baltic Approaches, two elements of the exercise were particularly important: an amphibious landing of supporting Marine troops and operations in the Baltic by Danish, Norwegian and British FPBs.

The amphibious landing took place on 22 September[38] but had to be changed from the west coast to the east coast of Jutland due to adverse weather conditions. The operation was initiated by air attacks on the airfields of Orange forces. Six carriers operated about 100 miles west of Jutland in the North Sea in gusty winds and high sea, 15 to 18 feet waves, giving the escorting destroyers a challenge, but the carriers did well. The allied planes caught the enemy with most of the planes on the ground or just taking off and thus won the first struggle for air superiority which had been thought to be near impossible because the enemy outnumbered the allies. The surprise and power of the morning attacks demonstrated the flexibility and power of a carrier striking force and its ability to implement the old military principle of concentrating your forces. Nonetheless, the operations raised doubt as to the feasibility of large scale carrier operations in the North Sea due to risk of mines, limited space for manoeuvring for large carriers and frequently bad weather. One solution might be to use smaller carriers which should operate in groups of three to four to create a strong group for own defence.

Low visibility hampered supporting flights from land airfields, cancelling one of two days' support operations. This meant that planned air attacks on the advancing enemy ground troops in Schleswig-Holstein had to be cancelled.

---

38 The narrative is based on New York Times 23-9-52 and 26-9-52.

Figure 3.9: Landing craft on the beach at Skagen, Denmark. Source: Forsvarsgalleriet.

Evaluation

NATO command relationships involving SACLANT, SACEUR and several of their major subordinate commanders turned out to work well in spite of the well-known difficulties that always arise in cross-command relations. It became apparent that priority must be given to the establishment of a single headquarter if operations were to be conducted with the maximum efficiency.

Enemy operations – orange forces – were met as follows. Submarines by and large operated as they would during war. They achieved their greatest success in focal areas and on known convoy routes where they could operate as weapons of position. Their air reconnaissance provided good information of force movements. But advanced intelligence from other sources became superior to air reconnaissance, since the latter can seldom be acted upon in time to effect interception. The enemy did succeed to establish air opposition to the carrier aircraft encountered over Norway and Denmark, but only to a very limited degree. Therefore, enemy aircraft was mainly confined to attack forces at sea. In general, aircraft attacking from medium and high level were tracked and countered by aircraft and AA gunfire. It would appear that the low flying enemy aircraft were in many cases able to attack either undetected or not intercepted, particularly against lightly defended forces.

The main activities for blue forces are spelled out below:

Strike fleet. Operations were hampered by bad weather. The carriers encountered severe storms for three days whilst operating off North Norway. One half day of air operations was completed off Bodo, and one full day off Denmark. However, had this been during war, the necessary peace time safety measures would have been waived and air operations (somewhat curtailed) could have been carried out on both bad weather days off North Norway and Denmark.

Operational control of the Striking Fleet was vested in the Area Commander, CINCNORTH. Various deficiencies, including communications difficulties, produced situations whereby the Area Commander was, for considerable periods, unaware of the position, actions and future intentions of the Striking Fleet. This naturally caused concern and difficulties in arranging shore-based air operations.

Enemy raids. NATO air reconnaissance found and tracked the raiders breaking out from Narvik into the North Atlantic and from the Baltic into the North Sea. They were subsequently engaged by surface action groups and considered sunk by naval gunfire. The major lesson here would appear to be the disproportionate effort in ships and aircraft that is required to locate and destroy a single enemy surface raider.

Amphibious operations. The amphibious operation, although it was an unopposed landing in friendly territory which did not exercise supporting arms in the roles they would play under war conditions, provided some excellent training. As the landing was unopposed, no new lessons were learned once the exercise had started. The necessity for detailed planning beforehand was emphasised by the fact that the beach had to be changed at the last minute due to weather conditions.

Airborne early warning. The results achieved by recce aircraft were most encouraging. They were employed to search for and track raiders, as barrier patrols to locate attacking aircraft, and also to work as an advanced picket for the Carrier Striking Force, and the aircraft could be employed in the best manner to meet changing situations.

Communication. MAINBRACE gave NATO Communications doctrine a gruelling test. Much went right, much was put right after a shaky start, and the suspected unsatisfactory nature of various aspects was fully confirmed. Planning was hampered by the incompleteness of the NATO general communications plan. As a result the communications orders had to be very extensive; there were too many messages which often were poorly drafted and too long. Many messages were addressed to too many authorities. The effect of this was that the whole communications system was clogged, particularly the Broadcast (to ships).

As expected, the existing NATO crypto system proved far too slow. It was the major factor in communications delays, and forced the Strike Fleet to use plain language to an extent which would have been suicidal in the face of an efficient enemy intelligence organisation. It was clear that the implementation of an improved crypto system should be given high priority, if operations were not to be seriously hampered and forces needlessly imperilled.

There were many complaints of the inexperience of much communications personnel due to the short service system which reduced the number of experienced personnel.

SACLANT concluded: the difficulties in MAINBRACE were caused by adverse weather, by deficiencies in communications and by general lack of experience in working together. No evaluation of the effect of hostile action against the carrier task force can be made. In war, the probable scale and type of enemy attack must be taken into account in planning such an operation. On the other hand, we should never minimise the tremendous defensive capability and mobility of this type of task force.

SACEUR more or less agreed and saw the carrier forces on his northern flank as indispensable to his mission. The exercise thus validated new US Navy expenditures for powerful carrier forces at a key moment.

However, the British Chiefs of Staff did not agree that MAINBRACE in general was a success.[39] In terms of aerial support to AFNORTH it was rather a failure; only one fifth of planned sorties were carried out. Four out of five British bomber attacks on the carriers were successful – under two attacks, the carriers were not able to launch their planes. Furthermore, in some situations, failure to launch expected fighter support created a "very unsatisfactory situation for land and air force commanders who, while constantly encouraged to expect powerful carrier-borne air support, can never count on it either in planning or in an emergency." Also, the British did not agree that an important task for aircraft carriers was to intercept enemy troop convoys in the Baltic.

As to the Baltic Approaches in MAINBRACE, the Danish Joint Chiefs of Staff had a meeting with the chairman of the Standing Group on 31 July 1953 and expressed a general satisfaction with MAINBRACE.[40] At the command level, the cooperation between all three forces gave good lessons and worked well. For the navy, training communication between ships from different countries was valuable. For the air force, cooperation between carrier based and land based aircraft went better than expected, but, seen from the command level, it was clear that

---

[39] Annex III to C.O.S. (52)630 2-12-52: S.G. 207/3 N.A.T.O. exercises 1952.
[40] Minutes in SGM 1666-53 6-11-53.

carrier forces might not be available all the time. Therefore, it was best that demands for immediate operations be fulfilled with land based aircraft, and pre-planned operations with carrier based airplanes. The army had similar experiences. The question was raised whether war plans permitted air carriers to move into Skagerrak to get close enough to the war theatres in Denmark; present plans positioned the carriers west of Norway in the Atlantic. The Danish C-in-C recommended them to operate in Skagerrak which had adequate depth for such operations, the only risk possibly stemming from submarines.

Problems in MAINBRACE

The American magazine *Air Force* spelled out the weaknesses of the carrier strike force in MAINBRACE (*Air Force*, December 1952: 27)

- Vulnerability to submarine attacks: although the enemy only had ten submarines, indications were that they seriously crippled the fleet
- Vulnerability to air attacks: the task force was attacked successfully several times, both from high and low altitudes
- Weather: 400 of 500 sorties were cancelled in the first two days and half in the last days due to the weather
- Need for frequent refuelling forced the fleet to withdraw after two days of support to the land battle even though only 20 per cent of the planned sorties had been executed
- Excessive costs relative to firepower delivered. Dozens of ships were needed to protect the group, yet only one third of the aircraft were over the battlefield at one time.
- Poor endurance. A carrier group could only operate two, maybe three days in a row, then it had to withdraw for replenishment. But this meant that if the group was sent to support ground forces, they would be left in limbo.

The magazine stated that four aircraft carriers needed a support group of two battleships, four cruisers, 30 destroyers, four submarines, eight oilers and five other support ships. It therefore concluded that in view of the costs to the taxpayer, carrier strike fleets were not panacea, particularly not regarding the mobility the navy had claimed.

Summing up: Towards NATO's War plans and tactics

In 1950–51 a series of documents laid the basis for NATO's operations throughout the Cold War. Military commands were organised and staffed with General Eisenhower as head of Europe, SACEUR. The Baltic Approaches became part of a Northern command, AFNORTH, which relied heavily on national commands – subordinate, of course – to carry out the actual military operations. Therefore, AFNORTH was in daily life a staff agency having oversight with planning and training of the military forces. Eisenhower perceived AFNORTH as a flank organisation, threatening a possible Soviet enemy in Central Europe with cutting off resources and attacking (weaker) flank forces.

In the summer of 1951, the strategic goals for AFNORTH were ready for operational implementation. They remained relevant for the whole Cold War. Denmark was a key area with its bases and airfields, protecting the Baltic Approaches and keeping the Soviets stuck in the Baltic. An integrated approach among the three forces would be necessary to prevent Soviet forces from landing on the islands; a weak spot was the defence of Schleswig-Holstein as an entry to Jutland. In general, the defence was dependent on early counter-attacks in the Baltic area to crush bases and airfields – possibly partly done by forces from aircraft carriers. To do this, early warning and intelligence gathering was very important. AFNORTH was to prepare air reconnaissance, prepare mine fields – preferably by the navy – and prepare for getting reinforcements from Britain. In particular, it was important to prepare for receiving foreign air squadrons at various (else dormant) airfields. A special task was to prevent Soviet submarines from exiting the Baltic. Close cooperation with SACLANT and the British Home Command was necessary on all counts.

Although the first NATO planning directives had stressed the need to close the Baltic Approaches for the Soviets and the danger of amphibious attacks on the Zealand islands, a first intelligence report from the Standing Group in 1951 completely neglected the Baltic Approaches and the need to control all of Denmark if one wanted control of the Approaches. This in spite of quite precise comments from the Danish C-in-C in the preparation phase. But two years later, Denmark got more attention in the annual intelligence report, SG 161.

The 1954 war plan had much focus on ground forces and it appeared that the NATO planners did not really understand the problems of the Danish narrows. The planners assumed that Sweden would also be attacked when Denmark and Norway were attacked. Most forces were to be concentrated in Schleswig-Holstein, but the four to five divisions required only existed on paper. The naval defence focused on the Danish narrows and actions south east of Zealand with eight destroyers and 40 MTBs which were in real life not available – and the three planned submarines to operate in the narrows must have been a misunderstanding of littoral warfare. But the mine fields could be laid. In the air, it was the same story: a large number of planes was required for supporting the army and navy and intercept enemy planes, but few were available.

The NATO directives, then, only partly understood the issues of littoral warfare. In particular, the staff of the Standing Group had more of a "Blue Ocean" perspective, mostly neglecting the Baltic Sea and its approaches and showing no interest in understanding the problems of littoral warfare. Their focus was on Norway and Sweden (as a stepping stone to Norway). SHAPE's tactical staff grasped the littoral issues better, stressing the need for recce in the Baltic, minefields in the choke points and at the beaches, and the need for reinforcement forces.

The British Chiefs of Staff did not trust the plans of AFNORTH to be effective. The defence forces of Schleswig-Holstein were inadequate and the Soviet forces would soon conquer Jutland and the forces withdrawn to Southern Norway. Unless Sweden intervened, the Zealand islands would also soon be taken by the Soviets. But the only viable solution would be to re-arm Germany.

Like the Danes, the British thought that some NATO planners did not understand the importance of the Baltic Approaches and the need to use choke points to block Soviet submarines from getting out into the Atlantic. NATO had expressed the need for attacking at source in the Baltic, but not much was planned. The British took a quite radical approach and suggested an intensive bombing campaign to obliterate Soviet bases and airfields in the Baltic Area. They wanted to hit medium and light bombers on airfields, submarines and surface vessels in their bases, communication lines such as the Kiel Canal (bombs); the Danish Belts and the Sound (mine fields); the Trave-Elbe Canal and the Baltic-White Sea Canal (bombs); and they wanted to hit oil production. About 75 nuclear bombs would be necessary. The Brits did not have the resources for this and the plan was shelved. But a few years after something like this was planned by SACEUR under NATO's New Approach, which we shall return to later.

AFNORTH had a strong interest in getting support from Aircraft Carriers, but most of them were under the command of SACLANT from its initiation in 1952. SACEUR Eisenhower and the British navy backed AFNORTH strongly with a concept of Carrier Strike Groups involving four carriers with 350 airplanes. An agreement was reached with SACLANT that carrier strike groups would be sent to Northern Norway to bomb Soviet bases in Northern Russia, but SACLANT was also willing to let carrier strike groups operate in the North Sea to bomb Soviet bases in the Baltic. However, the range of aircraft carrier based aircraft was limited to reach East Germany only, and then the carriers were at risk for Soviet counter air attacks. But they could also support the Danish navy in the narrows from a more safe distance in Skagerrak. Their size did not permit them to enter the littoral seas of Kattegat and the Baltics.

Exercise MAINBRACE in September 1952 was designed to test Eisenhower's ideas about Carrier Strike Forces. The evaluations differed. SACLANT and SACEUR were quite satisfied, stressing the adverse weather as a main cause for problems; Carriers would be important in the future. The British Chiefs of Staff were quite critical, stressing that the cancelling of four out of five aircraft sorties hardly was a success. And bomber attacks on the carriers had been successful. An American magazine pointed out that the costs of bringing the Strike Carriers to work were far too high.

The Danes were quite satisfied with the amphibious landing in Northern Jutland and the naval exercises in the Baltic Approaches, but the original plans which would have tested littoral warfare more in depth were not implemented due to political protests. The Danes furthermore were not so sure that carrier operations to support naval and army operations were to be trusted – would they be available?

Chapter 4
NATO in control: Annual Review and intelligence reporting

As military planning took form, the NATO leaders realised that they needed quite comprehensive insight in how to finance the proposed actions and guarantee delivery of military equipment and supplies. Furthermore, intelligence about the Soviet Union and its military forces had to be reported systematically. For the first purpose, the Annual Review was established and followed by a series of Combat Effectiveness Reports, and for the second, the SG 161 reports (see chapter 3) were updated. Both were reported annually to the Standing Group, and we shall take a look of some of the early reports from the 1950s in this chapter to understand how NATO step by step built up instruments of information as well as control.

Towards the Annual Review

What were the realistic politico-economic capabilities of the countries seen in the light of the military plans? In September 1951, the NATO Council decided to set up a Temporary Council Committee – the TCC – to examine that.[1] The task of the TCC was to systematise information from the member countries regarding civilian as well as military affairs, including information about difficulties due to public finance instability, production problems, manpower deficiencies or lack of raw materials, as well as information on factors limiting the present defence build-up. Also included was information on the size of the forces available to NATO, their state of training and their equipment, and, finally, a forecast of the equipment which would be available in 1952 and the additional trained manpower which could be expected by the end of 1952.

In three months, the committee prepared a draft report which was sent to the member countries for comments. In essence, the account used the military targets set out by previous strategy decisions like the DC 13 (see chapter 3) and subsequent force requirements from the Military Committee to fulfil the strategy. Table 4.1 gives us an idea of what was required by the day of mobilisation:

---

[1] SHAPE. *SHAPE History Volume I*, 225–26. Versailles: SHAPE, 1953.

Table 4.1: NATO Force build-up 1952–54. Source: TCC Report December 1951 Part 7, p. 2.

	1952	1953	1954
Army divisions M-day	25	36 2/3	41 2/3
Aircraft M-day	4230	7005	9965
Destroyer escort & larger M-day	354	367	402

These measures were put within the macro economic capabilities as measured by the information gathered in questionnaires and supplemented by hearings in each country. On this basis, the Committee made an evaluation of the capability of each country and recommended a future frame in 1952, 1953 and 1954 for the economic contribution to military spending.

In most cases, the Committee found a gap between what was desirable in terms of military targets and what was planned by each country to be spent. Thus for Denmark:

Table 4.2: Military spending Denmark, million USD. Source: TCC Report December 1951, pp. 99–91.

	1951/52	1953/53	1953/54	Total
NATO requirements	205	282	339	826
Country planned Program	94	108	119	321
Recommended Program	123	152	173	448
Gap	82	130	166	378
Planned programme % GDP	2.8	3.2	3.5	
Suggested programme % GDP	3.7	4.5	5.1	

The table shows significant differences between the nationally planned program and the ideal level of expenditure as desired by NATO according to the strategic goals. The NATO-recommended program did not even fill the gap in costs. The costs in per cent of GNP are illustrative in that, historically, the Danish expenditures for the defence have neither before nor after 1954 exceeded 3.2 percent of GNP.

In other words, there were considerable differences between what NATO desired and what the member countries – in this case Denmark – were politically prepared to pay. Nonetheless, the NATO members approved the report at the Lisbon meeting in February 1952. They also approved that the activities of the Committee be reinforced and resumed in an "Annual Review" procedure.

The Annual Review Committee was set up to supervise and co-ordinate all work within this domain. One of the Annual Review's goals was to produce a transparent presentation of the defence effort country by country. Over the years, the Annual Review process was streamlined to enhance its impact in the member states.

In general, the documents of to the Annual Review constituted: a preface and directives for preparing the memorandum; three sections on the various forces (army, navy and air force); an economic and financial section; and annexes instructing how to answer the questionnaire. The process as a whole and the documents written demanded an impressive series of work. There were questionnaires, replies, SHAPE comments and documents going through the hierarchy of the Standing Group and the Military Committee with comments along the way from individual countries and answers to comments. Step by step one got incremental corrections to the papers and then the final recommendations.

We shall discuss the Annual Review of 1952 and 1957 in more detail below.

Annual Review 1952

The Lisbon meeting decided to appoint a Secretary General, Lord Ismay, who set up his staff in Paris in the ensuing months. A primary task became the Annual Review which was directed by a Review Committee chaired by the Deputy Secretary General with members from all countries. The tasks were to revise the reporting system used by the TCC for measuring military requirements and costs and then issue a questionnaire in order to amend military force goals for 1953, 1954 and 1955. In addition they had to evaluate infrastructure and equipment requirements; to develop strategic guidance with respect to prioritising the build-up process; to mitigate requirements and capabilities, the military risk considered; to draft proposals for revision of countries' defence efforts and thereafter re-examine the means of reconciliation followed by discussions with representatives of each country; and, finally, after negotiating a draft with the member countries, to prepare a report to the Council with recommendations for action.[2]

Quite a comprehensive task! An agreement was made between the civilian administration and the staff of the Standing Group how to integrate the work on military and economic/political factors so that the respective types of expertise were used productively. Four technical teams were set up to draft the questionnaires and go through the answers when they came in and formulate questions to clarify the answers.

---

2 SHAPE. *SHAPE History Volume II*, 193–94. Versailles: SHAPE, 1959.

We shall take a look at how this process turned out in Denmark in 1952.[3] It took the staff of the Committee four days to analyse the answers to the questionnaires, and this led to 87 questions to the Danish delegation coming to Paris. The delegation wrote answers; most of the "technical" questions were solved, and more complicated answers typically relating to infrastructure and economic capabilities were then discussed in a formal meeting with the Committee. Remaining questions were apparently typical for most member states and referred to the standards of readiness: how quickly and with what forces could the member state meet an attack or call up forces in times of a crisis?

Denmark's main problem was the relatively few professional soldiers in a system that relied on conscription; and the question logically following from NATO was how to ensure that the previously conscripted personnel sustained their military capacities? NATO's idea appeared to be annual exercises of up to four weeks – a heavy requisition on the Danish male work force, and possibly as a consequence a setback for the Danish production economy. An alternative would be to extend conscription time to 18 months, a solution which soon became reality in Denmark.

Another important theme for questioning was the lack of qualified personnel for air control and warning; this was not a contentious issue but Denmark had severe problems in recruiting personnel for those roles.

Some issues concerned the infrastructure development. Given the fact that SACEUR's investment program was not ready, Denmark had conveyed its own program for investment which included two stationary coastal forts. The military rationale of building these forts, however, had been questioned several times by the supreme commander who preferred solving the blockage of the Baltic Approaches by minefields laid partly by aircraft and partly by naval mine layers (see chapter 6). The Danes responded that Denmark had no capacity to expand forces to such tactics and given the availability of suitable 150 mm guns (from the German occupation), the building of the two forts had been an economically sound solution. There were additional, but minor questions, and agreement was reached that until NATO's program was ready, Denmark would not finalise investment plans for those tasks.

A final theme which apparently was shared with other countries concerned supplies which were in store for 30-days use. NATO recommended more supplies, but Denmark saw it as a zero-sum game, so immediate resources for forces proper would then have to be reduced, and the Danes were not willing to do so.

---

3 Notat vedr. "Annual Review" HEM Forsvarsministeriet 11. kontor 8-11-52 831/52.

The report was supposed to be ready by early December, but the process drew out, so a first report was written by December 18, 1952. It concluded that progress in military spending after the Lisbon conference had not been as good as hoped for but, still, expansions of military capability were made. Regarding force goals, the report for Denmark stated that for the army, Lisbon goals were met in terms of number of divisions, but they were all under the standard required. For the navy, Lisbon goals were not reached in Coastal Escorts, Submarines and MTBs. For the air force, Lisbon goals were 131 but the actual level was 73, leaving a deficit of 58 aircraft (44 per cent, with the NATO total about a 10 per cent deficit).[4]

The Final Report from April 1953 concluded that "there has been substantial but still insufficient progress in the building up of collective forces for NATO defence".[5] Regarding Denmark, the key comments were as follows. For the army, the main problem was lack of quality because of the brief time of conscript time, 12 months. Denmark was going to prolong it to 18 months, fully implemented by 1954; a request to prolong recall services of the reserve was hardly feasible. Stores were below the desirable level. For the navy and the air force the main theme was shortage of skilled personnel for the many complicated services on board and in aircraft workshops. The issue of the two coastal forts raised in November was omitted in the final report.

The NATO International Staff made some recommendations. The first was an appeal for more resources to military spending, but the Staff realised that there was a political barrier towards that. The second was a corollary: to extend conscription time to 18 months as soon as possible. The third was an enlargement of the air force. And finally the International Staff felt that the increases suggested should be seen as fair and reasonable.

In other words, the NATO International Staff had difficulties in accepting the slow pace of increase in Danish military spending and the limitations on the use of military conscripts. They even noted that Denmark lacked a "military tradition", and this "hampered the growth of the military forces".[6] But of course they also knew that the main obstacles were found in the Danish Parliament.

In April 1953, SACEUR summarised his understanding of the status of the defence of AFNORTH:[7]

---

4 C-M(52) 130 Part III.
5 C-M(53) 55 Introduction, p. 6.
6 C-M(53) 35 p. 30.
7 Letter HEM C-in-C to minister 21-5-53 FST C 3823-4480/53.

We can not yet defend this area efficiently against a real Russian attack. Denmark and Norway can not with own means shoulder sufficient forces for such a defence. They need help from outside, and we must consider this in our planning. But a careful evaluation of the situation shows that these two nations can set up more military forces which can expand the capabilities to defend our vital northern flank.

For the three forces there were the following deficiencies:
- The army lacked units of supply and support forces to become fully efficient when fighting. There was a critical lack of ammunition for the artillery, but also lack of ammunition beyond a few days for all entities – one had to expect the army to cease fighting when those weapons could not shoot any more.
- The navy lacked sufficient vessels to defend the LOCs at sea.
- The possibilities to operate with the air force and get reliable information about an air attack were extremely limited. The lack concerned radar material, but also radar crews. There was a lack of airplanes, particularly night fighters, and the air force was the weakest link in the defence and required high priority to obtain a better balance. The lack of warning radars meant that airplanes would be destroyed on the ground and the enemy could only be met in daytime to a very limited extent.

The supreme commander also found lack of progress regarding logistics, and the existing system was inflexible. The intelligence system lacked resources to warn against surprise attacks and to guarantee mobilisation and readiness in time. Finally, there was a need to inform the populations better about NATO and its purposes.

In the ensuing years, the military expenses were increased – to a record high of 3.2 per cent of the GDP in 1954. The 18-month issue was solved, and the issue of more aircraft was raised, but not solved (see chapter 5).

Alternative understandings of 'controlling' ministers

In April, 1953, the NATO council was to approve the second Annual Review. Preparing the meeting, the permanent representatives (diplomats) met with the Chairman (Lord Ismay) to go though the final drafts of the documents to be finally decided upon by the ministers who were the formal members of the Council. Lord Ismay has been characterised as follows: "(Ismay) ran NATO in the best tradition of the British civil service which he admired: he functioned as a quiet behind-the-scenes conciliator and coordinator".[8] The following incidence indicates otherwise.

---

8 Jordan, Robert S., and Parley W. Newman. "The Secretary-General of NATO and Multinational Political Leadership." *International Journal (Toronto)* 30, no. 4: 736.

The incidence regards the final resolution of the Council meeting.[9] The discussion became rather terse. The text below is verbatim, but emphasis has been added a few places, and some sentences have been omitted or shortened:

Chairman: "We come to a bracket where our draftsmen are silent. I have a form of words which has been given for that. If I could read it very slowly". (Reads a complex text loud) "It is rather important – apparently this came out of the first draft and it was decided to leave it blank . . . but I should have thought it was wiser not to leave a complete blank for Ministers. Let's give them something to bite on."

US representative: "The language of the Resolution is subject to discussion and change obviously."

Chairman: "But give them something to discuss. If you leave it blank they might do anything. . . . May I have views . . . Is it agreed that we should give them some form of words? . . . Would anyone prefer to leave it blank? Denmark."

Danish representative: "In our opinion, this is a question which the Ministers are going to discuss as the principal item of the meeting. I therefore think it would be most appropriate to leave it open or put it in brackets to show that we have not gone in advance of our Ministers."

Chairman: "Do you suggest putting a footnote to say 'subject to discussion that the Ministers have on the whole paper'? They **are** going to discuss the whole paper. . . . It is only a base of discussion, and it is much easier to discuss a form of words than it is a blank. Well, there seems to be general agreement on that then. We read on." (Reads complex paragraphs) "I will assume approval unless anybody stops me."

(reads on, several paragraphs) "I am sorry. Denmark."

(Danish representative presents an alternative text) "We also thought that the same applies to this as to the other. It should not be fixed before the Ministers have had their discussion on Soviet peace moves. But perhaps we could put a footnote on this as you suggested on the other thing."

Chairman. "But Denmark, the whole thing is a draft. It is **headed** "draft". I will underline draft four times if you like. It is **all** a draft. This is for the Ministers to decide on."

Danish representative: "But if you do not call their attention to specific places, they may overlook them."

Chairman. "Oh well, you would like an asterisk against the existing paragraph to say, 'This is, of course, subject to the decisions reached as a result of the Ministers' talk about Soviet intentions'?"

Danish representative: "Yes."

---

9 MC-CS-008 19-4-53. MC and Permanent Council Joint meeting 20-4-53.

US representative (intervenes): "Might it not be better to simply have the asterisk and this language at the foot of the page as suggested by the Danish delegation, if they insist on leaving this in?"

Chairman: "Do you want to press your alternative?"

Danish representative: "No, if only there is some reservation that this is going to be subject to the discussion of the Ministers then I am satisfied."

Chairman: "What would the Council feel?"
 (some discussion leading to a suggestion that an asterisk be put to the particular points needing the Minister's attention)

Danish representative: "Thank you very much. I think that was a very good idea."

Chairman: "Any objection to that?"

Denmark: "No, I think that was a very good idea."

Chairman: "That meets your point then? That was the two points with asterisks. Now we continue." (reads on)

So back to the characterization of "Conciliator and coordinator"! Lord Ismay obviously wanted the ministers to decide according to his ideas of a suitable resolution, while the Danish representative had a more classical understanding of the neutral role of a civil servant. Risso's comment ". . . while he kept within the limits of his official role during most formal meetings . . . he was proactive during the weekly sessions with the Permanent Representatives"[10] seems more appropriate. And one cannot deny that there was a slightly humorous tone in the chairman's comments.

Combat effectiveness

As a follow-up to the Annual Review, SACEUR decided to use the information and add some features based on other observations to create an overview, the Combat Effectiveness Report, which gave a uniform basis of assessment, equally applied to all nations. The first report (from November 1953, SHAPE 1002/53) only dealt with army and air forces, the subsequent annual reports also included the navies.

In the report, SACEUR particularly called attention to the problems of mobilisation: many units were not to be considered ready because the personnel was

---

10 Risso, Linda. "'I Am the Servant of the Council': Lord Ismay and the Making of the NATO International Staff." *Contemporary European History* 28 (2019): 349.

called up – they needed training up to 30 days or even more before they would be ready to face the enemy.

The themes for evaluation were levels of manning and equipment, percentage of regular personnel, strength of leadership, morale, mobilisation factors, training and a fully practised command system and cooperation among forces. Evaluations and on-site visits by the supreme commander's subordinate C-in-Cs also played a role.

From 1953, only Denmark was militarily present in the Baltic Approaches (apart from a British surveillance unit). The combat effectiveness evaluation for the army comprised three divisions and two smaller entities. In 1952, SHAPE had given them a status of being ready 30 days after mobilisation; the Danish government claimed them to be ready after 15 days, and SHAPE now evaluated that they would need more than 30 days to reach the "proper state of battle efficiency". The actual content of the divisions was very low, only manned between 15 and 25 per cent; several divisions had never been completely assembled or mobilised, and reservists had not been called up for training. However, exercises in 1953 had shown high morale.

The Danish Air Force had 164 aircraft, of which 136 were evaluated to be effective. There was a serious shortage of aircrew and technical trained personnel. The radar surveillance system had shortage of personnel.

The Danish forces, then, were not high on the scale of combat effectiveness; there were particularly low standards in the army. But this was a recurrent pattern for many of the small countries in NATO in 1953.

The Combat Effectiveness Report of 1953 was a first stab at the issue, and quite incomplete. In the following years, the report was expanded, as we shall see below for the year 1957.

Annual review 1957

For starters, we may quote the SHAPE history of 1957:

> In a report at the highest NATO level following the conclusion of the 1956 Annual Review, NATO authorities found grave inadequacies in existing NATO forces. . . . The ground, sea and air forces in early 1957 were inadequate to enable the Commanders to defend NATO's area. This was particularly true in the Central Region of Allied Command Europe where, owing to withdrawal of French forces, there had been a marked decrease during 1956 in the number of army M-day units available to fight in case of invasion. There were serious shortages in naval forces, and there were considerable deficiencies in the air forces. Although the German authorities had said they would provide a significant contribution to the NATO forces by 1957, the full number of NATO forces from Germany was not expected to be ready

until 1959 or even later. Some progress towards establishing an integrated atomic capability for Allied Command Europe had been made.[11]

The problems were not solved in 1957. On the contrary, Great Britain and Belgium reduced their force goals. Britain faced a general economic crisis, and as part of an across-the-board reduction of military spending, they reduced ground forces in Europe by 35 per cent and air forces about 50 per cent by March 1958.[12] SACEUR nonetheless initiated the Annual Review process with estimates of military forces as if no warning had been received. The British did not take this lightly and found the estimates "not useful". As to the Belgians, the government reduced conscript time from 18 to 15 months, thus reducing the quality of the forces.[13] Both reductions were unwelcome because the Germans announced that some of their forces would not be ready in 1958 as expected, but in 1959.

These reductions and late developments had consequences for the defence of Schleswig-Holstein where the Germans were supposed to take over in 1957, but an agreement was reached to let the Danish and British troops stay until April 1958[14] (see chapter 6).

Table 4.3: NATO Force build-up 1956–57. Source: C-M 57 143 part 1, p. 4.

	Actual 1956	estimate 1957
Army divisions M-day	32	37
Other combat teams	15	27
Aircraft M-day	6,534	6,351
Major vessels M-day	609	626

If one compares with the force build-up from the 1952 Review (see above), it can be seen that the army figures and particularly the aircraft figures (lacking 3,000!) are lower than the 1954 projected figures from 1952. However, some of the discrepancy is due to different definitions of force measures. Nonetheless, the table reflects cut-backs made by most of the NATO countries in the years between.

---

11 SHAPE. *History 1957*, 37. Mons: SHAPE, 1967a.
12 Ibid., 48–49.
13 Ibid., 59.
14 Ibid., 64.

Denmark

In 1957, there once again was an analysis of the "gap" between SACEUR-desired military build-up and the actual national military budgets. The Danish army operated with regimental units whose strengths were below the desirable. The Navy fell one major and seven minor units short on M-day. The air force, however, was in accordance with plans. The level of military expenditure as percentage of GDP was 3.4 per cent in 1956.[15]

The Annual Review process in Denmark ran as scheduled, but the Danish politicians in a ministerial Defence Committee were in a process of curbing or reducing military spending (see chapter 5). In a first meeting with the NATO examining committee on 11 June 1957, the Danish permanent secretary announced possible reductions due to the new three-party cabinet with minority parties in favour of reductions.[16] However, he felt that discussions of such reductions at this time would "not be profitable". Instead, he invited comments on what seemed politically feasible, including the expected HONEST JOHN and NIKE batteries and ways to renew the ships of the navy.

Five months later, the discussions with the examining committee from NATO continued in a somewhat unpleasant atmosphere.[17] The Danes repeated the possibility of a reduction of force goals in relation to SACEUR's numbers. The chairman of the NATO committee retorted that this was the first time any member country indicated that SHAPE's force goals could not be fulfilled (given the problems with military cuts in Belgium, Britain and the Netherlands in 1956–57, the veracity of this statement may be questioned, PB) and claimed that the goals of MC-70-to-come had to be understood as minimum. The Danes informed him that since the reductions were still in a process of being negotiated, the figures for the 1957 Review would hardly be affected. The chairman stated that if they were this was a case for discussions with NATO authorities. He added that as far as he could see, the planned savings in the Danish State budget were all put into the military accounts. He felt it absolutely necessary to increase, not decrease, military spending. Since nothing had happened since the previous year, the Review statements from last year had to be repeated.

Indeed, after stating that "The sums now available are insufficient to cover the operating costs, replacement and modernisation", and noting "with great concern" the possibility of reductions, the final recommendations were not to reduce military spending and to discuss any changes with NATO authorities.[18]

---

15 The figure is not comparable with the figure reported in 1952.
16 Manuscript HEM in Forsvarsministeriet 11. kontor 11-6-57.
17 Foreløbige kommentarer vedrørende eksaminationen af Danmark i Annual Review-komiteen den 7 november 1957. HEM. Forsvarsministeriet 11. kontor 12-11-57.
18 C-M(57) 143 Part I p. 14–15.

As reported in chapter 5, the political discussions of military spending were not concluded until 1960, and therefore the Danish Annual Review became a statement of the status quo rather than future expectations.

The Annual Review[19] summarised the Danish force goals and the recommendations from the NATO.

- The army Country Plans for the end of 1959 had slightly less forces than recommended by NATO, but the NATO recommendations for the end of 1961 were higher and mirrored NATO's desire for Denmark to have more combat ready forces available at D-day; given the political negotiations at that time this was not likely to happen.
- The navy force numbers indicated a deficit of destroyers and FPBs ready for D-day.
- The air force numbers from Annual Review indicated that NATO recommended Strike Fighter Bombers while Denmark had Attack Fighter Bombers prioritised; furthermore Denmark had too few recce planes.

West Germany

As for Denmark, there was a discussion of the SACEUR-desired military build-up. The army met the NATO goals with five divisions and two Regimental groups. The navy was three major and 10 minor vessels over the planned level. The air force fell 10 airplanes short of plans, but progress for 1958 looked good. The level of military expenditure as a percentage of GDP was 4.4 per cent for Germany in 1956.

Unlike the Danish negotiations, the talks in Germany were polite and to the technical points.[20] A major theme in the discussions was availability of depots. In Germany, all war depots were built west of the river Weser and north of the River Schlei in order to not make them easy targets for attacking Soviets. Germany was dependent on depots to be built abroad, but until now no such plans had been finished. Regarding training, a major problem was capacities to speak English, particularly for signal personnel; many Germans did not speak English, and there was a lack of teachers. The Bundesmarine had a comprehensive building program for ships, and some plans turned out to be questionable because of new military demands or new knowledge undermining received views. Furthermore, not all money had been approved by the parliament. Overall, Germany

---

19 Annual Review 1958 C-M(58)141 PART II ANNEX.
20 Protokoll der Sitzung des Annual Review Visiting Teams mit Vertretern des Führungsstabes der Bundesmarine am 10.6.1958. Streng geheim. Anlage zu Fü M II – Az 03-06-00 – Tgb.Nr. 90. BM 1/1639 ARQ.

lacked means for two mine layers, ten FPBs, 14 aircraft, 12 small submarines, ten patrol craft and probably 18 amphibious craft.

In general, the review found the German endeavours laudable and recognised the main problems for progress: lack of junior officers, technicians and rank and file personnel and lack of suitable accommodation and training areas. Plans to expand the conscripted personnel were frowned upon because the service time foreseen for conscripts would be too short. The standard of the forces was, as expected, well beyond desirable, and war stocks were far too low. Government spending had been lower than promised, but now seemed to move in the right direction.

The Annual Review[21] summarised the West German force goals and the recommendations from the NATO Annual Review Committee:

- The army plans exceeded the NATO numbers for 1959, and one could expect Germany to fulfil the goals for 1961.
- The navy faced strong demands for the year 1963, but it had initiated a large building program.
- The air force plans were higher for Attack bombers in 1959, and a little less in interceptor fighters, and non-existent in all weather fighters. The demands for 1963 were quite high.

Combat effectiveness 1957

SACEUR's 1957 Combat Effectiveness Report was much more comprehensive than the first (1953) report. Now the combat units were graded on a scale from A to D, A signifying full preparedness for battle, and D indicating that the unit was not operational. Denmark and Germany, protectors of the Baltic Approaches, did not fare well in those terms.

Denmark

The combat effectiveness of the Danish army forces was rather low. One brigade group got a B, most of the rest a C and one a D. Retraining was not satisfactory, so several units were not considered capable of entering battle without further training. Some units had a very low manning level, and only few of the reserves had been recalled.

---

21 Annual Review 1958 C-M(58)141 PART II ANNEX.

Furthermore, there were serious shortages in the operational reserves of some ammunition and equipment items; Combat and Service Support units available for earmarked forces were not sufficient; Recall training of Post M-Day units was far below SHAPE requirements; there continued to be a shortage of regular personnel and skilled technicians; and finally, due to the introduction of a personnel replacement system, the army forces were in a reorganisation period and this adversely affected the combat effectiveness. When the system was fully implemented and the brigade groups were composed of sub-units of the same echelon, the combat effectiveness of the units was expected to increase.

The Danish navy was *en route* to a rather bad standing because many ships were about to be obsolete, and the existing units could not be improved. A new building programme therefore was desirable. The largest units shared a lack of adequate firing control, no ahead throwing ASW, no electronic Friend-Foe system and a lack of petty officers; furthermore, there were too many conscripts and too few regulars. Therefore, most units got a grade B or C, but the (new) FPBs and (new) coastal mine sweepers got an A.

Training was improving, but most armament and equipment was obsolete, and the logistics and supplies were too concentrated and vulnerable, but building two new naval stations in Korsør and Frederikshavn would improve this.

The air force of Denmark fared better. While in 1956, none had reached that level, most units now got a B and one (recce) a D (due to obsolete METEOR aircraft, otherwise it would have got an A!). All squadrons lacked technicians and some crew; the F-84 aircrews were not combat ready, whereas the Hawker Hunter aircraft were not combat ready.

The air control systems were well manned, but the equipment inadequate; overall assessed to B; the communication system, however, was inadequate. There were shortages in technicians and regular personnel. Pilots were well trained. Ninety per cent of combat aircraft was on hand. Equipment and supplies were satisfactory except for drop tanks and 30 mm ammunition. The concentration of aircraft on three airfields made them vulnerable.

West Germany

The Bundesarmee was in a process of being created and therefore got a D; it was not ready for battle at all. Particular points made were: a shortage of specialists and junior officers; lack of training areas, inadequate logistics and no war supplies. Shortage of accommodation prevented satisfactory deployment of forces.

The air force was non-existent in 1957.

The Bundesmarine had just started with FPBs and coastal mine sweepers, which were graded B, their tenders A. Training systems were being built up, foreign country schools had been used. English communication was under-developed. Logistics was under construction, for now war supplies were lagging behind. All these problems were to be expected in a new force with obsolescent ships.

The enemy: Intelligence reporting to the standing group

How was the military strength of the enemy assessed by NATO? The various types of information from the SG 176 and SG 161 (see chapter 3) were brought together and from 1954 reported systematically to the Standing Group in an annual SG 161.[22] We shall not go into all the reports, but having taken a look at the Annual Review 1957, we shall take the report from the same year, the SG 161/10: "The Soviet Bloc Strength and Capabilities 1957–1961" in two parts of 39 and 208 pages, respectively, the first part being a general overview, the second a report on the strategic and tactical themes, including high-class, detailed information about weapon platforms, weapons and communication systems. It was a comprehensive document, reporting on a host of political, economic and military issues, but we shall limit our interest to the tactical discussions related to the Baltic Approaches, found in the second part.

The report explained the basic Soviet ways of thinking within the three forces. The army doctrine emphasised mobility, manoeuvre, surprise, coordination and concentration of combat power. All Soviet commanders had to be able to regroup rapidly, and in principle only offensive battle was considered acceptable – retreat was solely a means of preparing to resume the offensive. Command powers were decentralised, whenever possible, giving local commanders possibilities for adapting to the situation. The forces, then, were mobile and trained in night operations, river crossing and infiltrations. They could conduct airborne and amphibious operations and cooperate with aircraft. They stressed continuous artillery and air support of infantry and armour, and they preferred a superiority of three to one in the main effort point. Thus they would shatter an attacking enemy and create conditions for passing to the offensive.

As to equipment, a large-scale modernisation had taken place regarding tanks, armoured personnel carriers, amphibious vehicles and infantry weapons in general. The Soviets now had modern artillery, heavy mortars and multiple rocket launchers. Tanks had increased firing power, mobility and armour protection. Their anti-tank tanks had a fixed gun which was heavier than a normal tank gun.

---

22 SHAPE. *SHAPE History – The New Approach 1953–1956*, 389. Mons: SHAPE, 1976.

Regarding the navy tactics, there was strong emphasis on air cooperation in reconnaissance, ASW, fighter and strike missions in close cooperation with surface vessels, including FPBs. Whenever possible, units operated at high speed, also when firing guns and torpedoes. Torpedoes were fired in formation, but also in sector attacks. Smoke screens were frequently laid, while formations of large ships often did not seem to pay attention to ASW or anti-aircraft defence in depth (in other words, stressing attack, no matter what, PB). FPBs operated in groups, boats 200 feet apart, and fired torpedoes 2,000 yards at a speed of 35 knots, often in cooperation with aircraft and destroyers. Submarines were supported by reconnaissance aircraft in search and attack operations. Long-range operations were centralised tactically by use of VHF radios.

The naval air force had fighters, light bombers and medium bombers. They were used for attacking enemy naval forces, reconnaissance, aerial mining, defence of own bases and supporting seaward flanks of army forces. The Soviets were developing air-to-surface guided missiles with a range of about 55 miles. ASW capability was limited, but improving.

The air force was large and found use over a broad range of activities. Its tactical branches were located at the periphery of the Soviet union, coincident with the army units. The main aircraft were fighters and light bombers. Long-range bombers were organised by themselves, predominantly in the Western USSR, with targets far away in Great Britain and the USA. As we saw above, the Navy had its own land-based air force (no carriers).

Many airfields had fighter planes ready for immediate response: two to six immediately with pilots sitting in the cockpit, another group ready close to the runway and more aircraft ready within a short time. Interception tactics were carried out in sections of two or groups of six. Large formations of 20 to 50 fighters had been seen. A number of tactical manoeuvres for fighters, escorts and fighter-ground attacks were described as well as tactics for light bombers and bombers and reconnaissance activities, but we shall not go into those details. The report also discussed the development of various types of aircraft and missiles until 1961.

The various forms of attacks – labelled campaigns – on NATO were described within sub-chapters on the three forces, respectively, rather than a description by areas to be attacked. We shall restrict the discussion to the Baltic Approaches.

Air campaigns were mainly aimed at the USA, Britain and the bases for NATO nuclear weapons – which are out of scope of this analysis. But the air force had many roles supporting army and naval campaigns. Thus airborne and amphibious attacks were expected in the Baltic Approaches. Paratrooper operations were under technical development. For now, one could only expect small-scale airborne raids for sabotage etc. and small operations for specific targets. Larger drops would normally be made close to forward troops so that linking could be established within a few days. No heavy equipment could be expected to be dropped. Similarly, the amphibious capabilities were limited to short-haul operations. The Soviets had an unknown number of obsolete landing ships and landing craft, but they could move forces by merchant vessels and fishing craft to enemy harbours.

The main campaigns against Scandinavia and the Baltic Approaches were listed under army campaigns. In 1956–57, there was a strong pressure from SACEUR to include Denmark and the Baltic Approaches (see chapter 9) in AFCENT, and this is probably why they were treated as part of the section on the army campaign against Western Europe, and Norway was therefore reported on separately. The operations to gain Soviet control of the Baltic Approaches would include two steps in rapid succession:

> First, an attack against Denmark to make possible the passage of Soviet vessels and to secure the flank of their forces in Western Continental Europe. The attack would be launched against Jutland in conjunction with seaborne and airborne attacks on the Danish islands.
>
> Second, an assault against southern Norway, either directly from Denmark or through Southern Sweden, to secure complete freedom of passage to and from the Baltic. If Sweden's neutrality were respected, the force landed on southern Norway would be limited to four divisions for logistical reasons.
>
> Sweden might also be attacked directly as part of the campaign against Norway; in the previous (1956) report, SG 161-9, the Norwegians had protested against the negligence of such a possibility, and the Standing Group clearly had concurred and included such an attack in the 1957 report; their wording made it clear, however, that the Standing Group considered such an attack unlikely.[23]

There was not much changed in comparison with the pictures painted in AFNORTH's first war plan, as told before (see chapter 3). The attacks were illustrated with maps identical to those used in 1953.

Soviet logistics as perceived by Danish Intelligence

SG 161 raised the question of keeping Soviet divisions ready for battle with equipment, food etc. The Danish Intelligence did a study of the possibilities by Baltic LOCs, and included the possibility that Sweden was attacked.[24] Six areas in the Baltic were considered "loading areas" for stores for the army.

The capacity for each loading area per 24 hours was indicated in "long tons", and from each area, a circle measuring a distance of 400 nautical miles was drawn into the map to indicate how far away the Soviets could keep one division battle ready with four merchant ships. There would be about 64

---

23 The issue is discussed in depth by Espenes from a Swedish perspective Espenes, Øistein. "'Den dolda alliansen' og svensk Natodebatt." *Kungl Krigsvetenskapsakademiens Handlingar och Tidskrift* 2015, no. 1 (2015): 140–48.

24 Note Forsvarets Efterretningssektion: Sea Communications. HEM January 1955 X3/55.

such ships available (over 1,000 tons) in the Baltic. A campaign against Denmark would require up to eight divisions, Southern Norway five to six divisions and Northern Norway one to three divisions. Some of these could be used for a later attack on Southern Sweden. An attack on Northern Sweden through Finland would require five to eight divisions.

So if all attacks were initiated, there would not be enough capacity by merchant ships. But a large fleet of fishing boats (as Admiral Heye had pointed out in 1949, see chapter 2) and barges could take up the slack; 23 fishing boats or 12 barges could supply one division, but this would require a continuous stream of such vessels from loading areas to the receiving port and back.

Figure 4.1: 400 miles limit to keep one division with stores by four merchant ships. Source: Rigsarkivet.

The report stressed that in any campaign against Scandinavia the main purpose of a Soviet attack would be to obtain control of the northern seaboard of Norway, hence priority would be given to operations against northern Norway. We shall not go into those operations, since our focus is on the Baltic Approaches, but we must take note that one of the ways to attack Norway would be to land Soviet forces in Southern Sweden after Denmark was conquered and then move north towards Norway.

The main threat against NATO from the Soviet navy was attacks by submarines in the Atlantic and North Sea, first of all from those based in the Northern USSR, hence the strong interest in conquering Northern Norway. Submarines were expected either to have left the Baltic before war broke out or to wait for Soviet forces to gain control of the Baltic approaches before they moved into the North Sea.

As to the Baltic Approaches, the use of the Soviet Baltic Fleet – with the Danish straits dominated by NATO – was also discussed; the main Soviet roles were then to protect own shipping and harbours in the Baltic, to support raids on NATO areas and support army forces by artillery from the sea and protect LOCs along the coast. Finally, the navy could lay minefields to prevent NATO ships from going eastwards in the Baltic and to block NATO harbours. The Navy's aircraft could play a strong role in such tasks.

The Baltic Fleet was essentially expected to be consigned to operations within the Baltic, as it was estimated that they would not attempt to break out at an early stage in the war. In planning Baltic Fleet operations the Soviets had to consider the status of Sweden; hence Baltic Fleet requirements had to take into account operations against the Swedes as well as tasks in connection with operations against the NATO powers alone.

One of the principal tasks of the Soviet Baltic Fleet would be to support ground campaigns. Here the Soviet Baltic cruiser destroyer force would be most useful. Large ship amphibious operations were not considered likely in the early stages of the war because of the allied air threat. However, light, high-speed craft would probably be employed to put ashore harassment or raiding groups. Particular significance was seen in the large number of FPBs. Naval Forces would be used to assist in seizing islands in the vicinity of the Baltic exits.

Large areas of the Baltic are suitable for mining. Soviet mine laying was expected in an attempt to deny Allied access to the Baltic, especially by aircraft and fast surface units and perhaps by submarines. In addition aircraft of the Baltic Fleet would be used in missions directed against the ports of NATO countries. Protective minefields would probably be laid off Soviet controlled ports.

Raiding groups could be landed by sea or by air to facilitate Soviet troop movements and to sabotage communications and installations.

The navy's air force would be used to keep control of the air space over the Baltic, defending bases and covering warships and merchant shipping. Air reconnaissance would be an important role. Light bombers could strike, supported by fighters, and would probably also conduct ground attacks when necessary. Their main role, however, would be torpedo and bombing attacks in daylight on NATO naval forces and merchant shipping. By night, they would conduct mine-laying sorties against allied ports in the Baltic and in Northwest Europe.

Summing up: NATO's instruments of information and control

After a first examination by an ad-hoc committee, the TCC, an annual procedure was initiated to produce an Annual Review of the resources and readiness of each NATO-country. The Review was written in consultation with the national authorities. The first report, however, was hardly a pleasure for the Danish military to read, particularly because, contrary to military advice, the politicians refused to accept the stationing of foreign forces in Denmark.

It concluded that efficient defence of AFNORTH was not possible (yet) without help from the outside. Denmark and Norway should expand their military capabilities. Denmark's army lacked supplies, particularly ammunition, and had too few support forces to become fully efficient. The air force could not get reliable information about an air attack because of lack of radar material and trained personnel. It had not enough airplanes, in particular lacked night fighters, and as a result they would be destroyed on the ground. The navy lacked sufficient vessels to defend the LOCs at sea. The logistics was problematic, and the existing system was inflexible. The intelligence system lacked resources.

NATO also introduced reports of combat effectiveness. Denmark did not score high, with combat effectiveness particularly low in the army. But this was a recurrent pattern for many of the small countries in NATO in 1953.

The 1957 Annual Review did not paint a better picture of the NATO forces; several countries cut back their contributions, and West Germany did not deliver promised forces in time. Denmark was in the middle of an intense negotiation process among the political parties; the Social Democratic government wanted to cut back on forces, and the bourgeois opposition was dead against this. Therefore, it was exceedingly difficult for the military planners to give NATO any trustworthy numbers. West Germany, on the other hand, by and large fulfilled the goals previously set by NATO, except for the Air Force which took more time than planned to start up.

The 1957 Combat Effectiveness Report was much more comprehensive than the 1953 report. Units were graded on a scale from A (full preparedness for battle) to D (the unit was not operational). Most of Denmark's army got a C; the navy B and C (but the new FPBs and mine sweepers got an A); and the air force mostly B. The army had serious lack of ammunition and equipment items; combat and service support units were not sufficient; Recall training was far below requirements; regular personnel and skilled technicians were too few. Most of the navy's ships were close to being obsolete; modern electronic systems were lacking, there were too many conscripts and a lack of technicians and petty officers. In the air force there was lack of modern electronic systems. The pilots were well trained but technicians lacked relevant knowledge. Aircraft was too densely located on only three airfields. Germany's army was only just being started; the navy had FPBs and mine sweepers which operated quite well, but the air force was non-existent.

The intelligence in SG 161 had increased vastly, now bringing quite detailed information on the various doctrines, instruments and tactics of the Soviet forces. Maybe somewhat surprising for a Western observer, the army stressed mobility and decentralisation of powers, but also put weight on the offensive, in operations combined with the air force and navy. Large-scale modernisation had taken place, enhancing mobility and use of tanks. The report told about a number of naval tactical doctrines with torpedoes and use of the the naval air force for attacking enemy naval forces, reconnaissance, aerial mining and defence of own bases. Air-to-surface missiles were under development. The air force was well developed and aircraft was on immediate alert with pilots in the cockpit. As for navy, tactical manoeuvres were described.

The threat against AFNORTH was not much different from the pattern described in the previous chapter. SACEUR planners still saw attacks against Northern Norway as the most dangerous. The Baltic Approaches would probably not be attacked in the first days of a confrontation – the Soviet Baltic Fleet was seen mainly as an instrument for the army, securing Soviet army LOCs and securing the flank of the army rather than attacking NATO vessels. The navy could also lay minefields and attack NATO convoys.

Chapter 5
Denmark almost alone

In the aftermath of World War II it took five years to reorganise the Danish defence into three forces – army, navy and air force, the air force being a new creation. The national economy was in a bad shape, so money was scarce. Technically, WWII had meant a revolution in weaponry, communication and control systems, so there was much to learn about and invest in.

We shall not go into detail with the long journey towards rearmament and reorganisation; the details are told elsewhere.[1] Denmark's defence capabilities were almost annihilated during the German occupation, so in 1949, when Denmark joined NATO, the forces were poorly equipped, lacking in armoured vehicles, modern vessels and jet aircraft. The army was mainly infantry, the navy obsolete torpedo boats and a few WWII German FPBs, and the air force piston engine SPITFIREs plus a few METEOR Jets.

By joining NATO, Denmark gave up 85 years of neutrality, and politicians as well as the military leadership had to learn how to think anew. Danish forces were the only ones to guard the Baltic Approaches in 1949. In this chapter we first go though the (poor) quality of the Danish defence and list the plans for the three forces to reach higher quality, and the next section deals with the changes of the role of the air force in 1955, involving attacks at source on the bases and airfields in the Baltic. The next section analyses the navy's attempts to create cooperation with the air force. The sixth section deals with the military cooperation between Denmark and Norway. Then follows reports from a comprehensive exercise in 1957. The subsequent section analyses the relations between Danish defence and AF-NORTH, and the final section discusses how, for five years, the politicians were unable to reach a compromise on defence spending.

Denmark's weak defence in 1949–50

As a neutral state, the role of the defence forces had been to observe the military moves of other countries and react to attempts to breach the conditions of neutrality. As a member of NATO, any military undertaking to cross the Danish bor-

---

[1] Schrøder, Hans A. *Historien om Flyvevåbnet*. Komiteen til udgivelse af "Historien om Flyvevåbnet," 1990; Bogason, Peter. *Søværnet under den kolde krig – politik, strategi og taktik*. København: Snorres Forlag, 2015; Clemmesen, Michael H. "Udviklingen i Danmarks forsvarsdoktrin fra 1945 til 1969." *Militært Tidsskrift* (1987), 7–81.

ders on land or at sea by non-member states was to be regarded as a possible aggression and hence one had to be ready to respond with armed resolve. As a neutral state, all types of military moves had been thinkable towards any type of enemy. As a member of NATO, the enemy was known – the Soviet Union – and the use of military means had to be thought out as a reaction to what the enemy was perceived to have in mind.

We start out in October 1950, when the defence was reorganised with three forces – army, navy and air – and a C-in-C who had a small staff and an intelligence section. In addition, he had as a deliberative special body the Joint Chiefs of Staff – the three chiefs of the forces plus the chief of staff for the C-in-C. They met once a week to discuss issues and set priorities.

The newly appointed C-in-C, Admiral Qvistgaard, turned in his first "annual statement" of the Danish defence to the minister of defence in December 1950,[2] and his report was quite alarming. He introduced his 25-page letter by saying:

> It is imperative for me as early as possible to call Your Excellency's attention to the absolutely catastrophic lack of capability of this country to defend itself. . . . This is a particularly sinister background for today's tense foreign policy situation . . . at risk for triggering the third world war.

The strength of the mobilised Danish defence was as follows:
- Army. The field troops (divided between Jutland and Zealand): 17 infantry battalions; eight artillery batteries (64 guns); two light anti-aircraft batteries and one heavy; a few pioneer and signal groups.
- Local defence: nine light infantry battalions, 64 patrol companies plus the home guard.
- Navy (some additional units in reserve): two coastal destroyers; four large patrol craft; five MTBs, two submarines, three mine layers, 14 mine sweepers, two escort frigates. All six forts manned. All naval districts operational with small craft for local purposes. All naval lookouts (102 in all) manned.
- Air force (a few units in reserve): one squadron Meteors; one squadron Spitfires, one photo group and one SAR group. Three airfields with local defence forces.

The C-in-C summarised the following features:

Army. In general too few men to fulfil the tasks. In particular, there were no tanks; a lack of anti-tank weapons; no heavy and middle heavy artillery and very few light artillery; extremely weak anti-aircraft weaponry; a severe lack of signal

---

[2] Letter HEM C-in-C to minister 5-12-50 0.252.

units and consequently a poor ability to fight in coordination; an unfortunate mix of Danish, Swedish, British and American weapons and material; lack of reserve ammunition.

Navy. Shortage of coastal destroyers to attack an invasion fleet; new patrol crafts too weakly armed; too weak anti-aircraft guns on many ships and the forts; crews not sufficiently trained; not enough mine sweeping gear to maintain swept routes. There were 1,000 mines in stock, only one third of what was needed to block the straits and invasion beaches efficiently and protect a number of harbours, including Copenhagen. Finally, repair facilities were sparse.

Air Force. The only up-to-date fighters were 16 Gloster METEOR; 24 SPITFIREs were close to obsolete. No radar of any use, therefore interception of enemy aircraft was extremely difficult. The army and navy could not count on support. Reconnaissance flights possible to a limited extent. No flying at night.

In sum, the C-in-C estimated that the Danish defence (before mobilization) would not be able to resist a coup-like attack of trained troops, and Copenhagen had no anti-aircraft defence worth speaking of. After mobilization, there were insufficient signal systems to support the command headquarters and hence poor conditions for directing the fighting units which were anyway poorly armed and insufficiently trained.

Shortly after, the Danish Intelligence Section issued a note about such coup-like attacks.[3] They would not be carried out by landing craft on open beaches, the Russians had none of those in the Baltic area; but they had a large number of smaller vessels which could enter Danish harbours at night. Seven Polish and East German harbours were named as possible departing points for ships which could reach Danish harbours overnight. If such operations were carried out, the Russians did not have to cross the Kiel Canal and attack through Schleswig-Holstein to conquer the territories adjacent to the Danish straits and establish land-based control of those thoroughfares to the North Sea.

Coup worries aside, the general Soviet operation possibilities against Denmark had been assessed by the Danish Intelligence Office at the time of the C-in-C's note.[4] If they decided to attack the West, the Soviets would move quickly through West Germany towards the English Channel, and they would have to conquer Denmark to eliminate the threat of airplanes operating from Danish airfields against their flank; airborne Soviet supporting forces could be expected to land in Northern Jutland. At the same time, the Soviets would open the Baltic Approaches for their submarines after landing forces in Danish harbours at the Bal-

---

3 HEM note Russisk Østersø strategi 19-3-51, Forsvarsstaben 1160/51.
4 Sovjets operative muligheder mod det danske område. HEM 20-12-50 Forsvarsstaben 1072/50.

tic Sea. For the attack against the West there were 28 Soviet divisions in East Germany and Poland, and 8 divisions could easily be added unnoticed; three more division could be used for seaborne landings in Denmark. If the Soviets attacked, an attempt to cut off their provisions from the east would have little effect because the West would not be able to resist the attacks and hence little ammunition and petrol would be used by the Soviets for their operations.

One year later, in October 1951, the C-in-C called the minister's attention[5] to the developing NATO forward strategy which – until Europe was in a better military situation – might push Russia to act soon and start an attack while the military balance "quite definitely" was in Russia's favour. It would be in the nation's interest to build up sufficient forces to counter such an attack and make help possible before the country became lost. The C-in-C quoted some passages in a letter from SHAPE:

> Unless the D-day forces are operationally and logistically in all aspects and maintained, in peace time, in a permanent state of readiness for battle, they will not be fit for combat on D-day and may thereby jeopardize the plans for the defence of Western Europe. . . . Thus SHAPE requires an accelerated buildup of forces . . .

Two years later, the annual report from the C-in-C indicated an improvement mainly because of American support of military material, but the situation still was undesirable.[6] The army needed ammunition, anti-tank weapons and tanks. The navy needed larger artillery-armed ships and bases outside Copenhagen. The air force needed material for its systems of air control, ammunition for F-84 fighter-bombers and training ranges. The military defence as such needed experienced personnel and equipment, it needed a general system of supply and had insufficient reserves of petrol, oil and most other materials.

The C-in-C noted that AFNORTH was militarily weak, but it seemed that NATO was beginning to realise this (understood: and hopefully would take action, PB). Three courses of action would be necessary. First, strengthening the defence of Schleswig-Holstein by NATO-forces; second, stationing of NATO aircraft in Jutland already in peace time; and third, a strengthening of the Danish navy and the possibilities for getting NATO-support in a crisis.

But there were not enough budgetary resources from the political arena for the necessary build-up, and the C-in-C soon had to take the blame from NATO-generals. One military suggestion for a solution was to take in forces from other countries, particularly American aircraft and ground forces in Schleswig-Holstein.

---

5 Letter HEM c.401/0 4511 22-10-52.
6 Letter HEM to the minister "Tilstanden inden for værnene primo 1953", FCH G 81/0 2000 11-5-53.

However, these solutions were met with fierce resistance from some of the political parties. We shall deal with these discussions in chapter 6.

Danish defence principles in the early 1950s

Denmark received extensive military equipment for all three forces as aid from 1950 to 1955, mainly from the USA. Without that help the Danish defence had been rendered without any significant strength. Still, there was a lack of effectiveness, seen with military eyes. This becomes apparent from the annual report the Danish C-in-C sent to the minister in December 1954. It contained an overview of the nation's defence plan,[7] which we shall use below.

The plan was the Danish contribution to fulfil AFNORTH's mission in the south: "... To defend the land area ... to close the Baltic exits and control the adjacent sea area of strategic importance."

However, this broadly formulated mission was too ambitious, given the weak forces at hand. Consequently, the overall goals were formulated less demanding: "To hold *selected areas* in the theatre and, for as long and as effectively *as possible*, to deny the enemy the exits from the Baltic. All means available will be utilized to *disrupt* the Soviet advance, *delay* and *destroy* Soviet forces and equipment as far to the north and south *as possible*" (Italics added, PB).

The general tasks were implemented by the sub-commands of AFNORTH (see chapter 3).

The Danish Army

The task of the Danish army was to control the territory: first, to counter any attempt by the enemy to land troops by amphibious or paratrooper operations, which required mobile forces; and second, to maintain national security by safeguarding military key points and important infrastructure.

The size of the army we saw above. The country was divided in two commands – one for the east: Zealand and surrounding islands plus Bornholm, and one for the west: Jutland and the island Fyn with roughly 50 percent in each command. Thus the strait of Storebælt divided the country in army terms; there was no bridge or tunnel crossing until a long time after the Cold War.

---

7 Kortfattet redegørelse for nuværende planer for forsvaret af Danmark. HEM bilag til FCH skrivelse C.K.10/0.5154 8-12-54.

The traditional army setup was based on regional groups spread over the country, each mobilising troops and then organising the defence of their area. This was the general doctrine all over Europe which therefore – allied troops in Germany not counted – in "daily order" had very few fully trained army soldiers ready for combat. By 1951, SACEUR formulated a NATO doctrine as a "shield" with larger forces permanently under arms. The desired size for each country was determined by the NATO Council meeting in Lisbon in February 1952 (see chapter 4). Denmark now had to organise the army into mobile groups which could operate individually but together formed up to four divisions, each with a commanding general coordinating the activities. To obtain the required number of soldiers, conscription time was increased to 18 months (later 16 months).

In Jutland's Western Command, the mobilised defence force would have to distribute groups to guard airfields and other key points from airborne attacks. The rest would move south across the border to Schleswig-Holstein to join the allied forces already there: a mix of Danish, Norwegian and British troops (see chapter 6 on Schleswig-Holstein). The river of Eider formed the defence line, if NATO had to give up the Kiel Canal.

In the Eastern Command, the forces were to prepare for an invasion on the south-eastern coast of Zealand or Falster, and possibly airborne attack forces. At a certain alert, forces would leave their barracks and move towards planned camp areas relatively close to the eastern and south-eastern coasts, ready to move towards the areas (beaches) under attack.

Until 1958, Denmark had a (reduced) brigade in Schleswig-Holstein together with a Norwegian brigade which was withdrawn in 1953. The Danes learned much from exercises together with the British who, of course, had extensive experiences from the war.

The main heavy weapons of the army were American and British tanks such as SHERMAN, CHAFFEE, ACHILLES, CENTURION and WALKER BULLDOG. Among guns we find 105 mm, 155 mm and 203 mm howitzers, a 155 mm gun and A-A guns. Late in the 1950s the army got HONEST JOHN missiles.

In 1954, the threat pattern from the perspective of the army was as follows:
- In the east, an amphibious attack against Zealand, starting from Baltic harbours. The Soviet goal was to take Copenhagen, open the Baltic exits and create a base for a possible attack on Sweden. Bornholm would be attacked by amphibious forces to destroy the early warning capabilities from this island.
- In the west, a ground force attack through Schleswig-Holstein to take Jutland and Fyn. There were three defence lines in the west: in Schleswig-Holstein the brigade would prepare defence along the Kiel Canal, destroying crossings and keeping the enemy at bay in order to secure mobilization of forces in Jutland; the Jutland corps would prepare defence along a line of small rivers

across Southern Jutland, with one regiment kept in Northern Jutland to defend airfield Karup and the Limfjord area; the final defence line would be the Limfjord with Frederikshavn as main base and harbour for evacuations to Southern Norway or Sweden.

We can clearly see the expectations of the army from a letter, sent by the Eastern Command in 1957 to the Danish C-in-C, protesting against the assessment of the threat pattern in SACEUR's Minimum Force Study, MC-70.[8] The study stated that WAPA attacks against Denmark could be met by SACEUR's counter nuclear offensive; that the Danish air defence would weaken an assault (resulting in "small, uncoordinated attacks, developing after the landing"), and that German and Danish reconnaissance by air and sea would reveal the threat early, resulting in NATO attacks either in a harbour or at sea, degrading the attack so that "it could be met by Danish ground forces with limited air support".

The Danish army command found that this was close to wishful thinking, exaggerating the capabilities of Danish defence. First, due to political restrictions, a NATO attack on forces approaching Denmark could not be carried out until the WAPA forces were recognised as openly aggressive, i.e. long after they left the harbour, and certainly not early in the build-up in the Baltic harbour. Second, the eventuality of limited war (i.e. not massive retaliation) was increasing because nuclear war simply would destroy both parties. In the case of limited war, the Soviets could probably hide the preparations for paratrooper attacks on D-day. On that day, the NATO air forces would have their hands full from the counter-nuclear offensive; hence few, if any, aircraft would be available to support the Danish army. Consequently, the prediction of the army was that the defence of eastern Denmark would mainly rest with the army on the ground, and before that the navy in national territorial waters and the air force in the air space, but therefore close to the beaches and harbours to be attacked by the Soviets. In that perspective it was crucial for the army that surviving NATO air forces be used as tactical support in the decisive fight about the land territory.

Consequently, a battle with amphibious forces before and after landing had to the utmost extent take place with support from tactical aircraft, not just SACEUR's "limited air support". The army therefore recommended that the Danish C-in-C took issue with the supreme commander's formulations and, furthermore, took the initiative to improve the possibilities for using aircraft as tactical support for the army and the navy in the defence of the Danish coasts.

---

8 Bemærkninger til Allied Command Europe Minimum Force Study 1958–63. YHM. 4-12-57. O.110/13958. Østre Landsdelskommando: KC. Klassificeret kopibog (afklassificeret) (1950–1979) 10.

The Danish Navy

The first comprehensive war plan for the navy was written in 1951.[9] The navy had four instruments: minefields mainly in a defensive capacity; torpedoes carried by submarines and FPBs and some of the larger ships; coastal forts to support minefields and block narrow straits – two new forts with 150 mm guns were under preparation; and a few larger ships with 102 mm guns – the hope was that soon one could get destroyers with 127 mm guns.

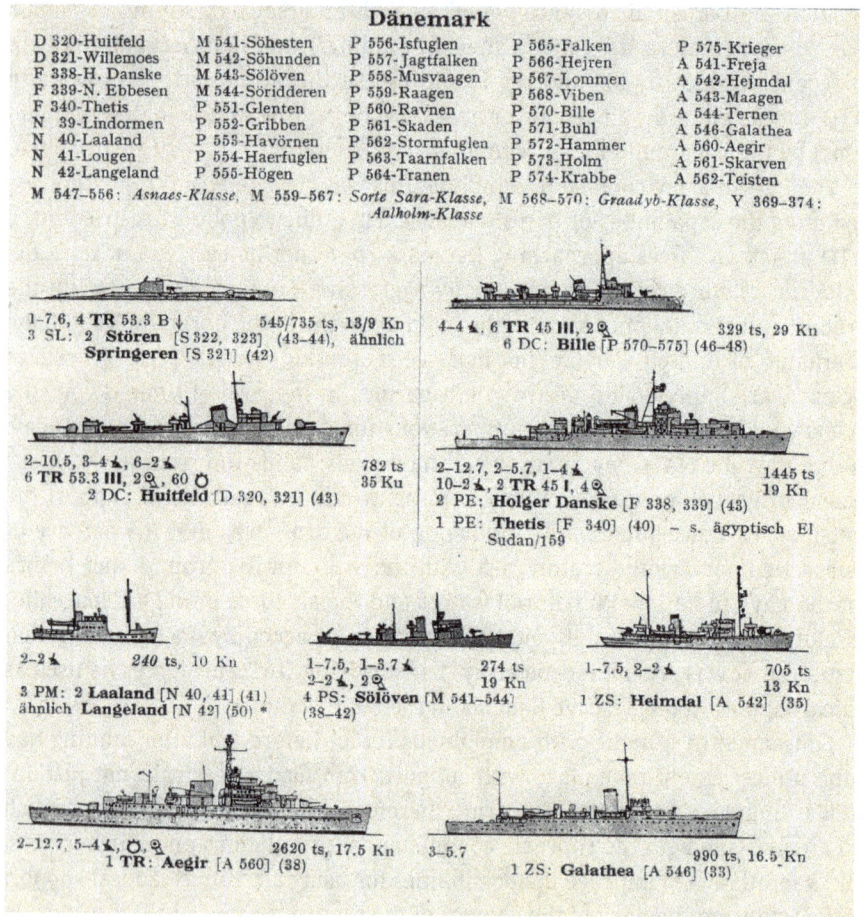

Figure 5.1: The Danish navy 1952. FPBs are not included. Source: *Weyers Flottentaschenbuch* 1953.

---

9 Marinestaben: KC. Hemmelig kopibog (afklassificeret) (1946–1975). U 252, 16. marts 1951.

The navy had lost nearly all ships during the German occupation. After the war, two small (800-ton) coastal destroyers and six medium-size (350-ton) torpedo boats were built, and 18 ex-German FPBs bought from the Americans. Two frigates and one corvette were bought (for training purposes and service at the Faroe Islands and Greenland), and three submarines were rented from the Royal Navy. Ten mine sweepers were on loan from the Royal Navy and 25 ex-German mine sweepers borrowed from the Americans, some of them later bought and changed into patrol vessels. The navy had four small mine layers, but many other vessels were able to lay mines. In the 1953 the navy got three ex-British HUNT II class escort destroyers and two American-built mine layers, and the navy started building four Danish-designed submarines.

The tasks in case of an attack from the east were: to prevent amphibious landings; to block the narrows for Soviet ships; to protect one's own LOCs at sea; to participate in air defence around the capital; to cover the flank of the army in South Jutland; and to attack enemy LOCs in the Baltic.

There were three straits: Øresund, Storebælt and Lillebælt. The two first ones were international passage waters which Denmark according to a treaty of 1858 was committed to keep open for passage for commercial traffic at any time. Warships were also permitted to pass but submarines must pass surfaced. Accordingly, blocking the passage was not permitted in peace time.

The Danes, then, prepared for war by planning to mine the waters reserved for international passage, following the mission for NATO to prevent passage by Soviet vessels of any kind. In 1950, the planned mine fields were as indicated on the map below.

Initially, minefields were to be established in southern Øresund and in the south eastern bays of Zealand; in the southern waters of Storebælt and in Lillebælt, and in the approaches to Copenhagen harbour and the main harbours to the south. Later, a minefield had to be laid in Kattegat and Skagerrak, in cooperation with Norway and England. Two ex-American amphibious ships were converted into Danish mine layers, and almost all other ships had mine laying capacity.

The main tasks were preventing an invasion on Zealand and maintaining lines of communication (ferries). Therefore the main forces were formed in Øresund and Storebælt and the southern Approaches. In the early 1950s two new 150 mm batteries were built on Eastern Zealand and Southern Langeland to protect the mine laying process and the completed mine fields. Cooperation with the air force was a must, and plans included allied forces to operate in Danish waters.

Lacking large ships to carry big guns, the main offensive weapon for the navy became the torpedo. For the 18 ex-German FPBs the navy developed offensive tactics in the Baltic together with the two coastal destroyers completed just after the

Figure 5.2: Danish planned mine fields 1950. Stars: Controlled fields; bubbles: not controlled fields, X-marks: Coastal mining.

war. The tactics for submarines (three ex-British) were completely revised and changed into surveillance tasks and attacks on invasion vessels in the waters east and south of the island of Bornholm.

Three British HUNT II destroyers escort were rented in 1953. They yielded a guarantee for naval operations in all forms of weather; in addition, their artillery was welcome for protecting the minefields and for supporting the army's flank in Southern Jutland. Four new corvettes were built in Italy in 1955–56 to strengthen anti-submarine warfare and anti–aircraft gunnery when protecting mine layers.

A number of old mine sweepers and the six in reality obsolete torpedo boats were used as patrol craft and (fast) mine layers.

After 30 days a convoy system had to be in place between England and Norway, with some of the ships to continue to Danish harbours: starting at Skagen about 140 merchant ships per month would continue to five large harbours.

The plan was minimal, and the army was very dissatisfied with the support for its flank in South Jutland. But the Danish navy had no more resources, and the British (using Kiel and Flensburg as bases) were unwilling to set aside ships for this purpose.

The 1954 threat pattern was the following. Enemy navy forces would probably focus on keeping control of sea areas important to his other targets, giving support to amphibious operations and cutting off allied sea lines of communication. NAVNORTH had to oppose seaborne invasion with all available forces, and for as long and effectively as possible deny the enemy the exits from the Baltic. Furthermore, the navy had to support the flank of the army and when possible attack enemy forces in the Baltic. Finally there was the task to support convoys between Denmark and Norway.

In general, most navy activity would take place during dark hours due to the risk for air attacks. Forces available were at mobilisation during the day (+3 days in parathesis):[10] 1–2 coastal destroyers, 1–2 frigates, 7–8 (10–11) MTBs, 5 (11) mine sweepers, 2–3 mine layers, 2 submarines. Four patrol craft manned by M+3 needed training before they became operational. Forts were ready after three days. British and Norwegian FPBs could possibly be available soon after mobilisation. A British mine layer was reserved for minefields in Northern Kattegat.

Minefields were planned for as above with Fehmarn Belt added. MTBs and submarines would establish support together with coastal forts. More minefields were planned at large harbours (as above) and invasion mines expanded along the coasts between Copenhagen and Gedser.

Radar stations, loop stations (detecting submarines) and coastal lookouts would establish surveillance of all naval traffic. If possible, air reconnaissance was desirable. After minefields were completed, actions against bases and support ships for amphibious attacks had priority: destroyers and patrol boats would operate from the Storebælt area, MTBs from Grønsund and submarines around Bornholm. Attempts by enemy naval crafts to break through the Baltic Approaches would also be compromised where possible.

Mine sweeping of harbours and lines of communication would be carried out. Two frigates would be reserved for convoys between Norway and Denmark. About 90 civilian auxiliary ships were planned for guarding approaches and patrolling local waters – from fishing boats to tankers and tugs, and coasters for diverse transport and supply services.

The Dreams of the Danish Navy: Naval Plan 1953

Based on the Lisbon goals and MC 14/1 (see chapter 1), the Danish Navy set up a plan to fulfil its objectives. Part of it was public and used to argue for more money for the navy; part of it was secret and only known to a few.[11] The secret part contained the tactical plans for war.

There was a serious lack of ships to fulfil the plan, as indicated by Table 5.1.

---

10 It should be noted that 1954 was at an absolutely low point for the navy. One year later it had added 3 frigates, 6 MTBs, 2 corvettes, 3 mine sweepers and 2 mine layers.
11 Marinestaben: KC. Hemmelig kopibog (afklassificeret) (1946–1975). U. 688 12. februar 1953.

Table 5.1: Ships required for Naval Plan 1953. Source: Naval Plan 1953.

	Plan	Deficit
Coastal destroyers	7	2
Frigates	5	3
Patrol craft	6	1
Submarines	9	1
MTB/MGB	24	
Mine layers	9	3
Mine sweepers	54	8
Gun boats 500 tonnes	12	12
Small patrol craft	12	6
Depot vessels	2	
Other	3	

The most serious deficits were, first, the lack of coastal destroyers which were supposed to act as Flotilla Leaders for groups of MTBs and would be guarantees for navy presence even in rough weather. Second, as a new feature, the navy found a demand for large gunboats to serve as watch ships and defenders at the minefields. Third, there was a deficit of escorts for convoys and small patrol craft for maintaining various LOCs.

The plan presupposed a tight coordination with the air force for air recce and fighter support. During daytime, most ships would be withdrawn to Copenhagen, Aarhus Bay, Lillebælt and Korsør to get adequate air defence.

The secret tactical setup was based on four groups:
- In the south-east Baltic seven submarines for recce and attack
- In Øresund a main force of two destroyers and 16 MTB/MGB
- In Storebælt another main force of four destroyers
- In Kattegat two to three frigates and patrol craft.

Mine layers, mine sweepers and patrol craft and gunboats would be spread as necessary in the situation. The plan presupposed that about 25 per cent of all ships would be under repair, replenishment etc., and therefore not available for operations.

The plan was quite offensive in character because the passive mine laying capacity was large and hence destroyers and MTBs were available for offensive mining at the coast of the enemy and for attacking enemy ships.

The plan did not specify the need for auxiliary craft. In a later document, the demand was tallied to 25 watch ships, 25 auxiliary mine sweepers, six auxiliary mine layers (ferries) and at least 40 transport ships and tenders[12]

The plan never came to fulfilment. The ministry in principle agreed with the principles of the plan and noted that the NATO-Lisbon goals were high, but desirable.[13] But, as we shall see later, the politicians cut back on defence spending from 1954 onwards, and the plan was put aside.

---

12 Marinestaben: A. Sagsarkiv (afklassificeret) (1950–1961) 2: 1953–1955. U. 823 29. september 1953.
13 Kortfattet redegørelse for Søværnskommandoens flådeplan 1953. Forsvarsministeriet 1. kontor 1-12-53 113.22-8.

The Danish Air Force

From the start of Danish military aviation around 1910, the navy and the army had separate air forces and had to start over from scratch after the German occupation, but from 1947 they were under a common leadership controlling e.g. planning and acquisitions. They were merged into one Danish Air Force in October 1950.

By 1952, the development plan[14] mustered six squadrons (25 aircraft each) of fighter bombers, one squadron of fighters, one of all-weather fighters plus some transport and reconnaissance aircraft: all in all, about 200 fighters or fighter-bombers. In its plans for 1956, the Air Force wanted three squadrons of fighters, four squadrons of fighter-bombers and two of all-weather fighters. This was an expansion of 25 all-weather aircraft, and in addition some reconnaissance and SAR aircraft.

A particular issue was recruiting and training pilots. Given the change to jet planes, one had to start all over, but there were few pilots from the old squadrons anyway. For each airplane 1½ pilot was needed in order to secure full operation capability at any time; about 300 pilots when all airplanes were phased in. The C-in-C, however, thought that full reserve capacity would be difficult to obtain, but enough could be mustered for daily operations.[15]

The growth in aircraft over a few years was considerable and rapid, given it was peace time. The Air Force received its first F-84 fighter-bombers in 1952, which were in active service until 1961. All in all, the air force got 238 F-84s over the years, and tragically many were lost in the early years. From 1950 to 1955, 79 aircraft (not all F-84, though) were lost and 62 persons killed.

In 1956, the METEOR fighters were replaced by 30 HAWKER HUNTER fighters. In 1958, F-86D fighter-bombers were introduced to replace some F-84s; others were replaced by the SUPER SABRE fighter-bomber in 1959. The RF-84F THUNDERFLASH served as reconnaissance aircraft from 1956.

The air force also had CATALINAs and other aircraft for rescuing and transport tasks.

The 1954 threat for the air force was as follows. Soviet ground and sea attacks would be supported by comprehensive air operations to destroy allied aircraft, prevent mobilisation and destroy lines of communication. Key points (headquarters, infrastructure) might be attacked. AIRNORTH were to impose the greatest delay and attrition possible on the enemy's attacking forces and – if forced to withdraw – make a maximum air contribution towards holding a defensible position.

---

14 Letter C-in-C to ministry of defence, HEM 20-2-53, C G 36/0 712.
15 C-in-C HEM letter to minister 12-10-51 C.40/0 4335.

The numerical superiority of the Russians might be about 5:1, and the Russians would try to get air superiority over Denmark. MIG-15s as fighter-bombers were expected to give intensive support for enemy ground and naval operations and for attacks against airfields and harbours.

The primary tasks[16] of the flying forces of the air force in the early 1950s were to protect Danish territory: the capital of Copenhagen and support military operations on the Zealand islands. In addition, they were to cooperate with the army and navy in solving tasks. Airplanes were to have forward stations on Zealand, but also be prepared to relocate to Norwegian airfields.

Two of the four Danish fighter-bomber squadrons were below the desired fighting efficiency. The control- and surveillance system also had serious defects. The four main radar stations were obsolete or incomplete. Air recce capacity was very low.

The main task would be to fight enemy aircraft attacking the airfields, particularly Karup (with four squadrons of fighter-bombers) and Ålborg (with two interceptor squadrons), and key points in the Danish defence. Other airfields had to be prepared for allied reinforcements and for their own interceptor-aircraft operations. The secondary task would be to attack targets whose destruction would impede enemy operations at the maximum.

Heavy anti-aircraft artillery would be concentrated at Copenhagen and Frederikshavn, light artillery would be distributed to airfields and the bridges across the Limfiord at Ålborg. Mobile artillery from the army would supplement these.

Counter-offensive attacks in the 1950s

In the early 1950s, the role of the air force was to defend Danish territory. But with NATO's New Approach from 1954 (see chapter 7), the perspective of air defence took a dramatic turn towards forward defence by bombing the Soviet bases in the Baltic area, partly with nuclear warheads, and thus destroy the logistics of the Soviet forces moving westwards and defeat aircraft on the ground rather than in the air.

In 1955,[17] the air force took note that a centralisation of command of all NATO's air forces would be necessary to obtain the new goal of a large-scale offensive against Soviet forces. Danish forces would get a task to support this offensive. The threats against Denmark would come from the areas south and south-east of the country. First, it would be necessary to expand the recce capacity of the Danish Air force sig-

---

16 Flyverkommandoen: Direktiv til flyverkommandoen vedrørende flyvevåbnets opgaver i tilfælde af et østmagtangreb på Danmark. Brev til forsvarschefen. HEM. Udkast. 1-6-51.
17 Flyverkommandoen: CINCNORTH's bemærkninger til SHAPE's 1957 Capabilities Plan. YHM. C. nr. 56, 30-3-55.

nificantly in order to get information about targets profitable for a nuclear warhead attack. Second, it would be necessary to spread the existing airplanes to more airfields. Third, the plan presupposed faster and around-the-clock vigilance reporting to a broader range of regions. Finally, anti-aircraft missiles were warranted. All in all, the costs of the air defence were to rise significantly.

These changes were analysed in more detail in the years to come, and soon the vocabulary of a defence planning group had included the new concepts of counter air offensive and interdiction. In 1957, the C-in-C of the Danish Air Force gave the air force three offensive tasks:[18]

- in case of enemy attack to immediately initiate an air counter offensive against enemy installations and airfields in the Baltic area in order to reduce those parts of the enemy war potential that represented a nuclear threat or an air threat against their territory.
- as the war escalated – in coordination with the other two military forces – to perform offensive operations against enemy naval bases, communication lines and harbours and against enemy army forces in Northern Germany which were deemed threatening to their territory.
- to perform air recce to support all military forces.

It is clear, then, that the tasks of the Air Force now included counter-offensive actions, attacks on enemy infrastructure and military key points. Attacking air bases and particularly those with nuclear bombers had first priority, then came other military bases in the Baltic – specified as the coast from Lübeck to Riga – and army forces close to the Danish border. Beyond the obvious roles of defending Danish territory and maintaining an air warning and control system, other important tasks included reconnaissance of "nuclear targets" (presumably targets for nuclear NATO warheads, PB) before and after attacks by AFNORTH airplanes; daily recce of certain bases, harbours, communication centres and "nuclear targets", recce of exits from the Baltic and recce to aid army and naval forces.

In another document from the same month, the Danish Air Force warned against consequences of future "mass, low flying bombing" Soviet attacks in day time.[19] First, facing high performance day fighters escorting the bombers, the composition of the Danish force (all weather fighters and fighter-bombers, PB) would not permit it to participate effectively in a day air battle. Second, the expected NIKE air missiles (see chapter 6) would not be effective against low flying bombers. There-

---

18 Flyverkommandoens synspunkter vedrørende målsætning og opgaver for det danske flyvevåben. YHM bilag til FLK skr. 12081/1081/C314 23-12-57.
19 Comments by Royal Danish Air Force on minimum force study Allied Command Europe (SHAPE/154/57, volumes I and II). YHM. 110.13/C16-11-57.

fore, until a low level missile was available, the best defence would be based on interceptor fighters. Consequently, an additional fighter squadron was desirable, and when a low level missile was operational, eight units of those was warranted, primarily to be located south of Copenhagen. Furthermore, a doubling of recce planes was supported.

SACEUR also had proposed the introduction of surface-to-surface missiles, and – noting that no decision had been made regarding this by the Danish government – the Danish air force supported this, expecting that such missiles would be used primarily against heavily defended targets in Eastern Europe and thus reduce the risk for fighter-bombers in counter-air-attacks – and at the same time, the Danes called for a revision of the interplay of Danish fighter-bombers and the supreme commander's strike forces "to maintain an adequate separation between manned aircraft and nuclear explosions".

These comments reveal that the Danes were well aware of the nuclear scope and some details of the operational pattern. But there are no Danish declassified documents describing how such operations could be executed with Danish airplanes, so let us instead take a look at what the Norwegian air force planned to do in the 1950s.[20]

The operations were planned in advance, and if war broke out recce aircraft initially flew to the target area(s) to create a situation image of what the bombers might expect. Later, after the attack, those planes had to return to generate a photo basis for assessing the effects. The operation took place as follows: the recce planes took off from their home base with drop tanks to increase their action range, went to march altitude (high up to save fuel) and flew east – if necessary crossing Swedish territory using a special method of identification so that Swedish fighters would not attack.[21] Before they could be spotted by Soviet radar, they descended to a low altitude, and increased speed to 420–480 knots until an initial point where course and time to target was adjusted. The relevant cameras were selected, and just before the target they were started. After the photos were taken, they could get rid of the drop tanks and go back at a higher speed.

The Norwegian fighter bombers were ready for action when the necessary information from the recce planes had been digested. They were slated to participate in the so-called SNOWCAT operations (Support of Nuclear Operations with

---

20 Korstad, Dag Inge. "Luftforsvaret i kald krig." In *Alt henger sammen med alt!* eds Karl Erik Haug, Ole Jørgen Maaø, and Steinar Sanderød, 107–24. Oslo: Forsvarets Høgskole/Luftkrigsskolen, 2020; Sandnes, Hans Ole. *The 1970–1974 Combat Aircraft Analysis*, 23–25. Trondheim: Tapir Academic Press, 2010.
21 Dalsjö, Robert. *Sweden's Squandered Life-Line to the West*. Parallel History Project on Cooperative Security. http://www.php.isn.ethz.ch/, 2007.

Conventional Attacks) in the first wave of war to smash enemy radar installations and airfields before larger strategic bombers were set in. After take-off they climbed to high altitude and proceeded to the range limit of the Soviet radar system. Then they descended to low altitude, below radar coverage, down to about 50 feet with an airspeed of 450–480 knots, and with no other navigational help other than a stopwatch and eyeballing. The flight course followed a zigzag pattern with course alteration every six to eight minutes, indicated with turning points on the pilot's map. This was because it was supposed that the Soviet radar took two to three minutes to spot a hit and needed three more hits to create a prediction of the course and speed of the plane. Continuous changing course would create difficulties for the radar operator. In some cases the plane had to pass the target and attack from behind, hoping to evade the defence system. A few seconds before letting the bomb go the pilot made a pull-up to 600 feet and headed towards the target in a 35–40 degree angle. The pilot only had a few seconds to find the target and let go of his weapon. Afterwards he returned to very low altitude to disappear on the radar, helped by the terrain. Later he would return to high altitude to save fuel for the home trip.

The targets were planned in advance, and they were allocated to each pilot in a paper containing long descriptions with maps, indicating flight course and target areas. In the 1950s those maps were without the detail the task really demanded. Flying a plane under those circumstances was challenging. Early in the 1960s target folders were introduced – a folder with the necessary maps positioned so that the pilot, as he advanced, could change to new maps with the necessary detail – for navigation, low level flight and target map. The folder was fastened on his thigh.

Some of the fighter bombers could carry nuclear warheads. They were mostly sent off in a group whose other planes were without nuclear weapons to reduce the risk that the nuclear carrying plane would be shot down. But other operations could be carried out by one plane only, and those pilots were instructed not to share any knowledge about the operation with other pilots. They were updated on their target once or twice a year by the military intelligence section.

Being part of the first wave was risky business, planned to hit important military targets, but also to create havoc in the Soviet warning systems because of the large number of aircraft approaching the area. Some pilots called these operations one-way missions, and in 1959 CINCNORTH Murray characterised them as suicide operations in a conversation with the Norwegian minister of defence.

And Denmark? The Danish air force had a large proportion of its aircraft as fighter bombers to be used mainly against surface targets; there were relatively few fighters to attack incoming enemy aircraft. So we may assume that there was advanced planning of counter attacks against targets along the Baltic coast. Indeed, this is what SACEUR told Danish politicians in the fall of 1955 at a meeting in Paris:[22] at the order of the supreme commander, Denmark was to allocate a maximum of sorties for direct and indirect support of his nuclear counter-offensive. Supporting aircraft would have to operate in ways that copied those of the nuclear-armed aircraft and thus help blocking or saturating the enemy's air defence system. They might imitate normal fighter movements, simulate dog fights, attack ground-to-air defence, escort other fighters and patrol over bases to protect nuclear-carrying aircraft on the ground.

There is a hint of the possible targets in one source (see chapter 7): in a large exercise in the fall of 1957, the Danish air force was sent out to attack Wismar, Warnemünde, Rostock, Stralsund, Swinoujscie and the naval aircraft stations in Peenemünde, Kolobrzeg og Gdynia. Of course, these targets were transformed into exercise targets in Denmark.

Cooperation between the Danish navy and air force

The creation of the separate Danish Air Force in 1950 meant that the army and the navy lost the capacity to command delivery of air support; instead support became an issue of negotiating the priorities of the Danish air force activities in any given moment.

By 1954, the new offensive NATO actions for the air force in the Baltic were being planned (see above), giving fewer possibilities for national support in the first phase of a war. In 1955, the navy formulated its needs for air support, spurred by a request from AFNORTH,[23] and one year later the Danish C-in-C summarised the solicited support to the Ministry of Defence.[24]

The C-in-C stressed that naval activities in a severe crisis or after the outbreak of war would emphasise mine laying in the southern waters together with recce activities to spot amphibious and invasion craft. When minefields were ready, offensive activities in the Baltic would be in focus. Most of the activities would take place in the dark hours and in periods with poor visibility.

In its 1955 letter, the navy wanted:
- Recce activities in the Baltic: photos of harbours and land installations. Visual observation of harbours, land installations and sea areas, preferably by a naval

---

22 Minutes of meeting HEM, in Rigsarkivet; Forsvarsministeriet, Forsvarsudvalget: Materiale (1950–1960): 6. More of this later in the chapter.
23 The demands of the navy are found in Marinestaben HEM U. 45 30-4-55.
24 C-in-C letter HEM M.71/0 2514 6-6-56.

officer in two-seater planes or by pilots with special training. In addition, radar observation of the sea.
- Attacks against surface craft at sea, single as well as convoys, and against transport ships and their escorting navy units, and particularly mine sweepers. If the enemy was forced to concentrate their forces they might become a profitable target for nuclear weapons. Such attacks also required special training of pilots.
- Attacks against targets in harbours and on land. Targets in the Eastern Baltic had first priority, then enemy targets in Danish harbours, on Danish territory or in the process of landing.
- Fighter support for naval operations in daylight – during one's own mine laying, during attacks on enemy surface ships, in convoys and during evacuation of own military personnel.
- Mine laying from the air when areas were no longer subject to NATO operations in the Baltic.
- The C-in-C confirmed those needs and added
- The need for detecting enemy submarines from the air. However, demand would be strongest in the Northern waters, and SACLANT was expected to take care of such activities.
- Mine sweeping by helicopters.

The Danish air force planned neither ASW capacities nor capabilities for mine laying and mine sweeping. Furthermore, while recognising the needs, the air force could not at this time perform radar based recce of the sea. The air force could support attack activities by the navy. It could also attack sea and land targets, but not in the scope desired.

The air force developed a general system of air control, the COMBAT AIR PATROL, which had a number of aircraft permanently airborne during periods of crisis or war. Each patrol – until 1974 typically HAWKER HUNTERS – had a geographical area as its responsibility and would attack enemy aircraft in that area. The COMBAT AIR PATROL CONTROL would decide the priorities in attacks, which therefore could include support to naval attacks, when requested. The navy was formally included in the patrol control from late in the 1950s, which became quite important for offensive activities in the Baltic.[25]

---

25 Bork, Jørgen F. *Åbent hav. Mit liv i Søværnet 1945–1990*, 83. København: Gyldendal, 2010.

Cooperation with the Norwegian and British navies

Until the creation of SHAPE, there was no command system in NATO beyond the national defence systems. But for Denmark and Norway, there was an obvious demand for coordination of certain activities, and – at least seen from Denmark – a need for a sort of "forward defence" of Norway in the Baltic Approaches. In 1949–50, the Danish Navy had a series of discussions with the Norwegian Navy,[26] and cooperation continued in 1950. They never reached a formalised plan, but AFNORTH did.

The Baltic Approaches were perceived as a passageway:[27] Norway could be reached by passing through the Danish Straits and/or Danish territory. Therefore, the defence of Norway had to begin in Danish waters and even south of Denmark, and the main idea was to deploy Norwegian forces to the south. Danish support to Norway – apart from auxiliary craft and transport – was not foreseen before defence of Denmark had been given up. According to the NATO Short Term Plan, the primary task was to muster maximal resistance against invasion and to maintain certain vital areas. The following tasks had first priority:

- Defence against invasion should be initiated as far out in the Baltic as possible, but the capabilities to do so were dependent on other activities
- Minefields in the narrows were expected to be efficient as long as the coastal area was not occupied by the enemy; Norway could support if a secondary line of mine fields was deemed necessary north of the straits, in Kattegat;
- Submarine patrols in the Baltic between the island of Bornholm and Zealand; Norwegian submarines could assist there and, in case of partial withdrawal, in Kattegat;
- Surface entities (destroyers and MTBs) for raids into the Baltic; Norwegian destroyers and a flotilla of MTBs could strengthen the activities considerably;
- Coastal batteries for support for ships and defence of minefields and harbours;
- Mine sweepers for clearing own lines of communication; no Norwegian participation was foreseen here;
- Escorts for convoys and ferries; Norwegian ships could participate in such activities in Kattegat.

Norwegian capabilities for deploying ships to Denmark were quite limited. But in the 1950s, Norwegian MTBs of the ELCO and D-classes regularly participated in NATO ex-

---

26 Marinestaben: V. Atlantpagten (1949–1951) 1: Atlantpagten 1949 – Atlantpagten 1951. Unless otherwise noted, the presentation below is based on documents found there.
27 HEM Maj 1950 PM vedr. gensidig dansk-norsk bistandsydelse til søs inden for "short term plan".

ercises in the Baltic, and MTBs and destroyers from the Danish navy regularly had exercises in the Norwegian fiords.

As the Soviet forces in Murmansk were strengthened in accordance with Soviet strategy development towards the Atlantic, Norway's defence interests gradually became more oriented towards west and North. From the mid-fifties, Norway's primary defence forces were located in Northern Norway, and hence, Norwegian capability for activities in Danish waters became even more limited.

There were also some possibilities for British help. The fast mine layer APOLLO was until 1962 dedicated ("if available") to mine laying in Kattegat with mine supplies stored in North Jutland.

Danish, Norwegian and British FPBs started common exercises in 1950 (as we saw above, this was also part of the MAINBRACE exercise), and in December 1952 the commanders had a conference on their future cooperation within NATO.[28] They discussed the following scenario:

The Soviets had landed parachute forces in Jutland and the landing of amphibious forces on Zealand and Bornholm was in progress. The Soviets now wanted to pass the narrows with surface craft. The task of the navy was to close the straits with mines, to initiate counter attacks on amphibious forces and protect the flank of the army in Jutland. There would be no warning; immediate action was necessary.

This being the situation, a southern front would be divided into two parts by the Fehmarn Belt. Given that most other Danish ships would be involved in mine laying, the jobs for the MTBs would be the following:
– protecting mine laying;
– anti-invasion activities;
– offensive activities including mine laying; and
– defending activities of the army against amphibious forces

When war broke out, Danish MTBs would be active in the south-eastern sector, but the Danish army would need support from Norwegian and English FPBs in the western part of the Baltic. The commanders would in the east select Masnedø or Stubbekøbing as a forward base for the Danish MTBs and in the west Sønderborg for the Norwegian and British forces. The Danes wanted to avoid Korsør –a normal choice of base – because the MTBs then had to be guided through minefields, and one also expected air attacks on Korsør which was a communication port east-West (ferry boats) and in addition had many military posts. Furthermore, one might expect heavy naval traffic because Korsør was a main post for loading mines. Problems

---

28 Marinestaben: A. Sagsarkiv (afklassificeret) (1950–1961) 1: 1950–52. Minutes sent 18-5-53, NATO No 498, J.NATO D-1.

of logistics were to be solved by MOBA, the navy's mobile base, with oil, generators, repair shops and systems of pressured air for the torpedoes. Repair facilities would be available in various Danish base harbours.

The question now was when Norwegian and British FPBs could be available. The British could be there within four days, if they came from combat ready forces, but five weeks, if they were in the reserve fleet; only six larger and six smaller were under command and the Royal Navy expected to cut them back to eight due to lack of personnel. Norway need 48 hours, possibly only 24, for combat ready forces (six in all), and for reserve boats it would take one month. Denmark had eight to ten MTBs under command.

The conclusions of this scenario was that in order to fulfil the intentions AFNORTH must earmark Norwegian and British FPBs for Danish defence. Denmark furthermore had to take care of the problems related to logistical support, and one had to analyse possibilities for waiting positions and forward bases for FPBs. A formal plan was never written, but the situation was trained in exercises.

Exercise brown jug 1957

What did the Danish military do regarding nuclear weapons? None was available, but we have several indications that the use of such weapons was foreseen and exercised in the 1950s. In 1957, "special strikes" were a feature of the national autumn exercise of the armed forces.

The Danish defence executed exercise BROWN JUG in the fall of 1957 with other NATO forces, focusing on the capability to withstand amphibious attacks on Zealand and surrounding islands.[29] For each 24 hours, the planned movements of Orange forces are first summarized, then we take FOD's intentions and plans, and finally we summarise what actually to place. The analysis is based on the reports of the navy. Army and air force reports have not been found in the archives apart from an army report on interrogation.

The strategic starting point was a slow deterioration of the relations between East and West. Therefore, the Atlantic strike fleet carried out exercises south of Iceland, certain HQs were manned with operation room and communication systems running, some elements of the NCS (Naval Control of Shipping) were in force and some large harbours had been evacuated. At 0100 hours on 19 September, Orange forces initiated an intensive offensive with airplanes, submarines and mines, and NATO responded with full alert.

---

29 The following text is condensed from Bogason Bogason, op. cit., pp. 147–53.

Figure 5.3: Danish navy in Danish waters on Day D-1.[30] S: Submarine. D: Coastal destroyer.
F: Frigate. PC: Patrol craft. N: Mine layer. MTB: MTB. MOBA: Mobile MTB base.

The day before (D-1) camouflaged fishing boats had landed sabotage groups in a bay north of Copenhagen, and other groups had been parachuted to Mid-Zealand.

On D-1 the Danish navy had the following forces ready, five of which with recalled crews:
- Two submarines in Helsingør,
- Two coastal destroyers at anchor off Copenhagen;
- Two frigates on patrol east of Møn
- Six MTBs in waiting positions off Bagenkop, off Hesnæs and of Klintholm; their mobile base was established in the Grønsund area,
- Two large patrol craft in Korsør,
- One large mine sweeper in Storebælt
- One mine sweeper in Ebeltoft Vig;
- Four mine layers at anchor south of Copenhagen and one in Korsør, all ready for mining
- Six patrol craft at various places in Danish waters

---

30 Bogason, op. cit., p. 148.

18 September, D-1 before attacks

Orange plans were as follows: FPBs were to do surveillance in Danish waters, avoiding offensive action. Escort destroyers and light frigates were to enter the sea south of Trelleborg and then withdraw.

FOD's plan comprised mine laying in Øresund and Storebælt with all mine-carrying units. The six MTBs were to mine enemy waters at Wismar and Warnemünde; afterwards they were to secure the defensive mine fields in Danish waters. Submarines were to patrol at Bornholm and, if possible, to attack; en route to the patrol area they were to lay mines in the enemy's supposed build-up area.

Actually, Danish territory was overflown several times by Orange aircraft without any offensive actions. Danish intelligence had reports about concentrations of Orange forces in Swinoujscie, Kolobrzeg, Gdansk and Klapeida. A request for air surveillance towards east was first denied, but then granted at dawn and American radar planes were asked to patrol further east and north in the Baltic. Norwegian FTPs started towards Danish waters late in the day. NCS control was executed from 10.30, and the four largest Danish harbours were evacuated. During the day the presence of sabotage groups was recognised. Early in the night three enemy FPBs were spotted, but a report never reached FOD. The frigates on patrol met two escort destroyers and exchanged fire. Three other orange FPBs were found by coastal radar, and a Danish patrol boat was sent to investigate. They were found and FOD (erroneously) supposed that they had laid mines and therefore ordered the ferry connection from Korsør to Nyborg stopped. When the army demanded transport eastwards, another ferry connection was established, and mine sweepers were sent to the original route to sweep it.

19 September, D-day

General Alert at 00.20. The submarines headed south, laid mines at Rügen and continued to patrol waters north of Bornholm. In Danish waters, mine laying was initiated with coastal destroyers and four mine layers in Øresund between Stevns and (Swedish) Falsterbo. The frigates covered mine layers south of the fields but were reported as orange forces to FOD. In Storebælt mines were laid by the large patrol boats and one mine layer, but due to enemy attacks the mine fields were laid further to the north than planned. The MTBs laid their mines as planned in enemy waters but some had engine trouble. The British APOLLO fast mine layer was ordered to leave the North Sea to lay mines as planned in Kattegat, but did not answer. After the first mines had been laid, the coastal destroyers were sent north around Zealand to bunker oil and take more mines on board, initially to Kalundborg, but the destination was changed to Korsør – the naval district, however, forgot to reroute the oil delivery. The four mine layers called at Køge to take new mines on board; they were attacked in the harbour by orange aircraft. In Storebælt the mine laying vessels went back to Korsør to take mines on board and bunker oil.

During the day NATO planes attacked Wismar, Warnemünde, Rostock, Stralsund, Swinoujscie and the naval aircraft stations in Peenemünde, Kolobrzeg og Gdynia. Orange aircraft dropped nuclear bombs over Copenhagen and Aarhus late in the day, but the naval infrastructure was unharmed in both cities.

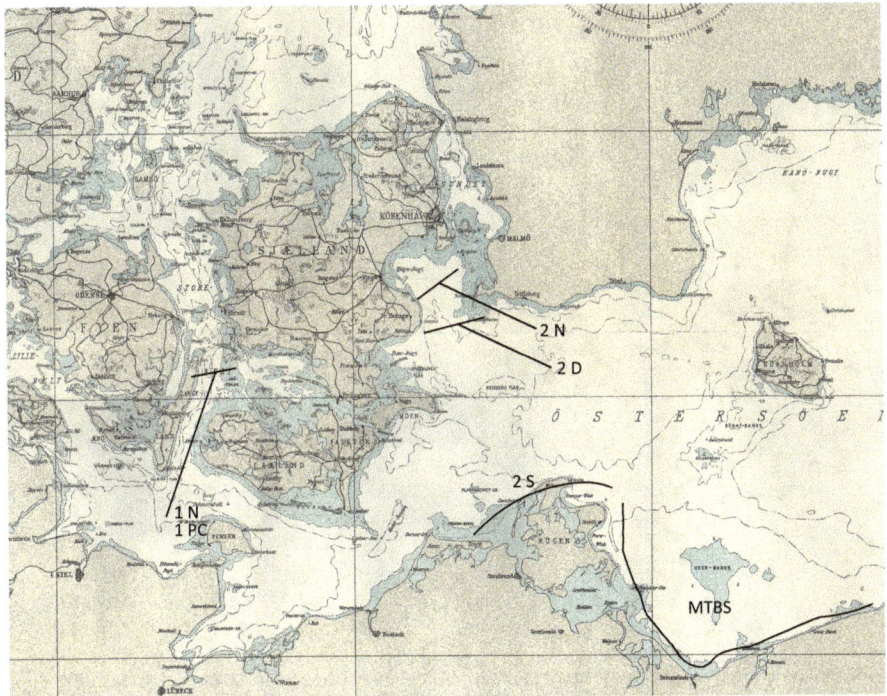

Figure 5.4: Danish mine laying night to D-day.[31]

At 18.00 several orange cruisers and ten destroyers had been sighted at Gotland heading south. Several smaller orange craft were gathered in the Baltic harbours, and there were amphibious craft in Swinoujscie, Kolberg and Usika. Actual landing was not expected yet, but attempts to stop mine laying, commando raids and attempts to land saboteurs were expected.

---

31 Ibid., 149.

20 September, D+1

Orange plans were the following: two destroyers and two frigates were to enter Øresund from the south and obstruct NATO mine laying. They also were to cover three MTBs slated to raid Køge Harbour, and late at night they were to lay mines SE of Møn and at the entrance to Grønsund.

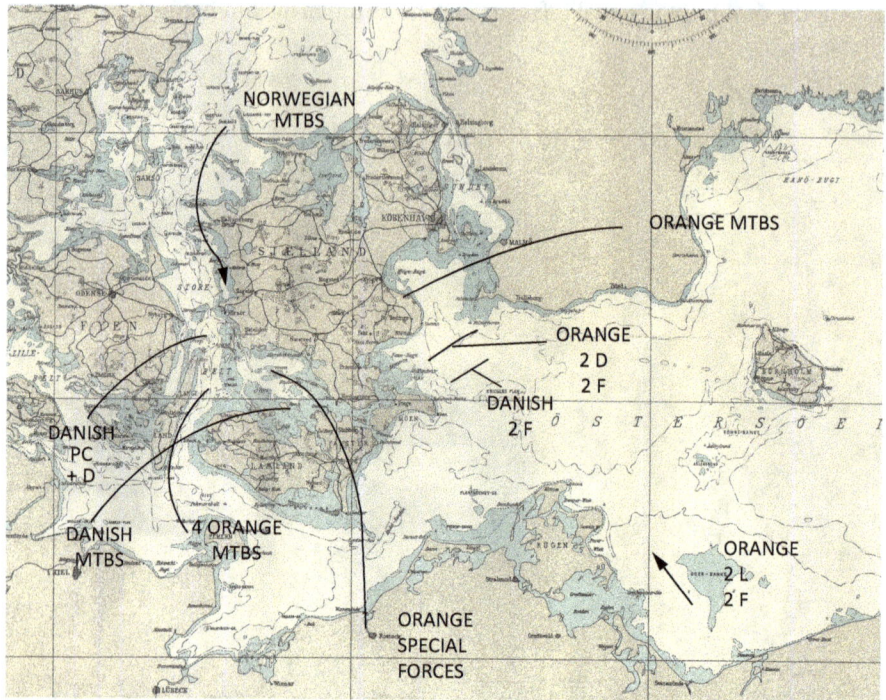

Figure 5.5: Orange attacks in the straits and Danish defence. Invasion force moving west along the Polish coast.[32] L: Landing craft.

The three MTBs were to land 110 special forces in Køge to destroy the harbour infrastructure and take the local mining officer of the Danish Navy prisoner. Furthermore, a MTB was to deliver some frogmen to a fishing boat at Falsterbo; the frogmen then were to attack ships in the Copenhagen harbour. Four MTBs were to obstruct mine laying in Storebælt and attempt to sink civilian ferries. By midnight two amphibious ships were to leave Polish harbour and have a rendezvous

---

[32] Ibid., 150.

with two destroyers as escorts for westbound sailing in daylight in the Baltic. Some of the previously landed saboteurs were to attack the bridge between Zealand and Falster, and others were to sabotage the mine depot Enø.

FOD as yet had no report from APOLLO, the Norwegian MTBs had arrived in Korsør, RAF was to mine Fehmarn Belt from the air. The Danish MTBs were under camouflage in the waters between Falster and Zealand; the mine laying vessels were to take mines on board, the frigates were at anchor at the Copenhagen approach, and the submarines were on patrol at Bornholm.

Night came. In Storebælt the fort of Langeland reported orange MTBs heading north; they were shot at, but disappeared northbound where they attacked mine laying patrol boats and later launched torpedoes against one coastal destroyer. When the mines were in place, the coastal destroyers covered for the other mine laying vessels and attacked their own MTBs which did not respond. This created some confusion, but the Danish force once more took mines on board and headed south, but at dawn they were attacked by aircraft. Therefore, all mines were dropped in condition "safe", and the ships returned to Korsør. The two coastal destroyers were sent to Øresund.

Figure 5.6: Special forces raiding Danish harbour Køge from MTBs. Source: Forsvarsgalleriet.

In Øresund the frigates were patrolling at Falsterbo and got radar contact with Orange frigates. The Danes withdrew to the west and then met two Orange destroyers which they tried to entice away from the mine layers; they did not succeed, and one group of mine layers did not observe the enemy before it was too late, and some were sunk. In the end the mine layers went to Køge once more where they were fired upon by mistake with handguns when they entered the harbour. The frigates went to the Copenhagen approaches and anchored.

In Køge the orange raid started at 23.00 with a group landing south of the harbour by RIBs; the group took the home guard at the harbour with surprise and then signalled to the three MTBs which entered the harbour but received a surprise counter attack by the home guard armed with handguns. The raid force, however, landed and won control over the harbour. They did not succeed in catching the mine officer. On Øresund the fishing boat failed to get into contact with the MTB and had to return without frogmen. The Orange MTBs were supposed to lay mines after the Køge raid; they were attacked by Danish MTBs, withdrew but later returned to lay mines at Grønsund. Orange destroyers and frigates also laid mines at Klintholm and Møn.

Sabotages: the bridge connecting Zealand and Falster was sabotaged from a canoe: While a group attacked the home guard protecting the bridge, another group used a fishing boat to approach the bridge; they launched a canoe and used a crossbow to shoot a rope across a section of the bridge. Then the canoe group climbed to the deck of the bridge with a bomb. The group was caught afterwards because their fishing boat went aground and was reported by another fishing boat. Another group was put ashore by the Stevns Fort; their RIB was found by a patrol, but the group remained undetected. A third orange group sabotaged the HQ of the FOD and destroyed all communication lines.

The day brought fine flying conditions, and almost everyone experienced an air attack: forts and radar stations; the MTBs (camouflaged) in the area of South Zealand; Korsør was laid waste for 12 hours.

The APOLLO created great confusion because several signals were either not received or misread. The APOLLO ended in Frederikshavn, bunkered and took mines on board and was ordered to lay a minefield in the northern part of Storebælt, but it had already gone to the Northern Sound to lay mines there. Since there was plenty of time, both minefields were established.

The Orange group of cruisers and destroyers south of Gotland were approved by SACEUR for a nuclear strike. A request for a normal air attack on the frigates south of Trelleborg was denied because "they were not a threat to AFNORTH". The harbours in Wismar, Warnemünde, Rostock, Stralsund, Swinoujscie, Stettin and Kolobrzeg were destroyed. The intelligence section reported a group of six frigates, eight MTB and ten amphibious craft in Greifswald; the amphibious ships were bombed and later in the day the amphibious group at sea, now reported heading north towards Øresund, was also bombed by F-84 fighter bombers. The MTBs waiting south of Zealand were not brought into action against them.

At 18.00 FOD regarded a landing operation to be in progress in spite of several special strikes and the destroyed harbours in the Eastern Baltic.

21 September, D+2

This was the first day of Orange forces going ashore. The amphibious force was strengthened by a cruiser and set course for Stevns to land forces one kilometre west of Rødvig. Supporting frigates bombed the coast, and three MTBs were to enter Rødvig Harbour and occupy it so that the amphibious craft could use the harbour for landing heavy equipment after the troops had been landed on the beach. A group would be set ashore at the Stevns Fort to meet with the previously landed group, destroy the radar system and later the guns. Paratroopers were to land at Fakse, Karise and Vallø. Air support would be available at dawn. Several groups of MTBs were on patrol to the west to protect from Danish MTBs, if any.

FOD had planned all available ships to be used against amphibious craft and to make the enemy concentrate their forces so that a strike with two nuclear warheads – being prepared at Karup Airfield – would pay off. The Danes made a co-ordinated attack with frigates and coastal destroyers from the east, and MTBs from the west; the Orange forces only observed the MTBs and consequently the larger group initially got a free run from the east. The MTBs fired torpedoes against the Orange cruiser and returned to their mobile base for new torpedoes to make another attack, but this time they were attacked by orange MTBs. Nonetheless, a torpedo attack against the amphibious force was carried through.

The sabotage operations at the Stevns Fort did not succeed, and the group was taken aboard a fishing boat at Højrup Kirke. Then the landing at Rødvig started; the MTBs landed forces in the harbour, and the amphibious vessels landed infantry shortly after. The support group anchored SE of Stevns and started a bombardment. The MTBs covered this force and attacked two Danish frigates. Two nuclear strikes came too late to hit the landing forces which had landed 25 minutes earlier and therefore now were supposedly spread inland. Instead, the amphibious force and the support vessels were attacked five miles out, as their own forces had been ordered to vacate the target area.

FOD had reports about landings at Rødvig as well as Højrup (the departing point for the saboteurs) and for several hours he thought that two landings were taking place and reported so to the army command. The roads slated for getting the army to the Stevns area were ruined by air bombardments and also threatened by

Figure 5.7: Orange Forces landing on South-East coast of Zealand.[33]

the air support of the enemy. Therefore, Orange forces quickly occupied Stevns in a bridge head until the main road from Vordingborg to Copenhagen. Late in the day the army could move forward. In the light of the enemy moving forward FOD ordered MOBA to withdraw to Korsør, and all harbours south of Helsingør were evacuated so that Zealand henceforward got supplies from the western harbours and the Isefjord.

---

33 Ibid., 152.

Figure 5.8: Red forces landing on beach at Rødvig. Source: Forsvarsgalleriet.

When the day was over the navy was done mining Storebælt and also mined the Northern part of Øresund. VINDHUNDEN was ordered to anchor at Samsø with mines on board to prepare for offensive mine laying. BESKYTTEREN, LANGELAND and HOLM were sent to lay mines in Lillebælt.

22 September, D+3
Orange forces planned to land second wave of infantry at 0200 hours near Rødvig, covered by destroyers and a cruiser which also had a role to bombard the radar system at Møn and then return to Bornholm which in the meantime had been occupied by Orange forces.

The Danish army now succeeded in blocking the advance of Orange forces. The navy had some minor fights with MTBs in Storebælt and a larger, coordinated attack on the amphibious convoy of the orange forces en route to Rødvig. Mining was completed in inner Danish Waters, and the APOLLO – finally – laid mines in the Northern Kattegat.

23 September, D+4
Orange forces had several cruisers in the Baltic which wanted to break through the Baltic Approaches to the Atlantic. They chose to enter Storebælt early in the day after orange MTBs had sailed through a couple of times to attack enemy vessels and then support passage of the cruisers. Land stations would be bombed beforehand, and the force would have air cover *en route*; the efficiency, however, would be reduced as the distance to their own air fields was increased. A cruiser and a destroyer would pass north of Anholt and continue towards the Swedish coast while two frigates would pass west of Læsø to look out for air attacks from airfields in Jutland.

One example of the attacks was operation MIXED GRILL at the island of Sejrø, involving a cooperation between aircraft, MTBs and coastal destroyers. The cruiser group sailed with two frigates in the front, then the cruiser and a destroyer in formation one with MTBs covering both sides. The coastal destroyers initiated a bogus attack from Kalundborg Fjord; the cruiser opened fire and the covering MTBs attacked the coastal destroyers and fired their torpedoes. This created room for the Danish MTBs which attacked from several angles (sectors) when the Orange group reached Sejrø. Three minutes before the MTBs fired their torpedoes, the aircraft attacked and the torpedoes were fired at two to two and a half miles distance. Thus the Orange group had been attacked with maximum conventional forces.

Evaluation
Below we quote some of the critiques formulated on the basis of a comprehensive reporting from participants.

Command. Different types of operation had different locus of command which created confusion – some ships were directly under FOD; the mine layers were under the marine district of the area and the MTBs were under FOD, but via the mobile base MOBA. Accordingly, the mine layers did not know the whereabouts of the covering force, and it was reported as an enemy; a patrol unit moving from Storebælt to Øresund was not reported to the Langeland Fort and consequently came under friendly fire; a mine layer at Kelsnor was not aware of the identity of Danish MTBs acting as covering force for him. It was recommended to let FOD have command over all ships, but maintaining MOBA as coordinator of the MTBs.

Mine laying. Only two thirds of the planned mines were laid on time, and it took three nights. The MTBs and submarines laid all the designated mines correctly.

The efficiency of the forts against MTBs was questionable. The forts received massive air attacks because the attacker saw them as very dangerous for his operations. It was recommended to establish comprehensive camouflage of the forts.

Five of six of the recalled crews had fairly high efficiency. The sixth was for a coastal destroyer, and it turned out that only a handful actually had previous experience from such a vessel; first at the end of the exercise one could see acceptable efficiency.

Losses were heavy in the start of the exercise, but all vessels were relived by the next day. But it was obvious for the participants that the navy had a serious shortage of large ships, given the number of tasks to be fulfilled.

There had been quite a few problems in getting the operation rooms of the command centres operational because of a lack of qualified personnel, but also for concrete communication and for leadership. This could be improved by moving more command roles to FOD. The efficiency of the coastal radar stations was low because of lack of qualified personnel for plotting as well as communication. The reporting system was too complicated but again, if FOD took over, improvement was expected. Generally, NATO communication was too complicated. The IFF system was not sufficiently developed. The radar station system of the navy was of poor quality in the Baltic and Kattegat.

The air force. The navy longed for its past own air force to give the desired cover and execute the desired surveillance. During action pilots often mistook friend and foe. Air warning was run by the air force and often ships got notified of a danger after the attack was over – the signal was sent quickly, but on the receiving side it took time because all signals were treated the same way; taken down, written by hand on a form and sent on with an orderly.

The navy called for a procedure for sudden needs so that airplanes in the area could come to assistance; this might have saved the mine layers in Storebælt in the morning of D+2 when they because of unfortunate conditions were still at sea at dawn and were annihilated by Orange aircraft. Cooperation in general went well, but always on the conditions defined by the air force, also time wise. Unfortunately, a few demands had been denied. Air reconnaissance was below standard.

Air protection. The SUND class mine sweepers had insufficient A/A guns. In general, it would help the crews if the Marine commands had personnel to man the A/A guns on the ships when they were in a harbour. In general, the air protection at the approaches to Copenhagen was insufficient. Furthermore, camouflage of the ships in harbour was an item for future discussions.

The procedures for special strikes were slowing the operations down – at the landing on D+2 the forces had landed and spread themselves before an attack could be initiated. Furthermore, special strikes were to be followed up by conventional strikes.

The submarines had operated under very unrealistic conditions – the commanders thought that their main role was to attack, not to observe and report – reporting required the submarines to surface and hence risk detection.

Integrating Danish Defence into NATO

In war, CINCNORTH would take command over forces within his area, and his four subcommands would take operational responsibility. The Danish defence law of 1950, however, put the Danish C-in-C in supreme command; therefore, the law was changed in March 1952 to reflect the NATO organisation. The C-in-C remained as chief of the Joint Chiefs of Staff and as chief advisor to the Minister of Defence, he became the military representative for the minister of defence in a number of international bodies, including NATO's Military Committee.

But when in a crisis would AFNORTH take over? If war broke out, forces had to be assigned to AFNORTH, and there were different rules in NATO-countries about this assignment. The Danish and Norwegian Constitutions limited the possibilities to conditions of war. The only forces assigned beforehand to AFNORTH were the brigades stationed in Schleswig-Holstein because they were not on national territory and hence subject to another rule regime. All other Danish forces would become assigned as soon as the Danish parliament decided that the country was at war, but this was not likely to happen until NATO had reached the state of General Alert. If Denmark was attacked by surprise, the cabinet could assign the forces to NATO.

All defence actions therefore were to be implemented by AFNORTH in war time. The war plan for 1954 was presented above. CINCNORTH had different organisation principles for the three forces.[34]

- The army command was placed with the two national commanders, but an allied army corps was under consideration for use in Jutland, and it would require its own command under AFNORTH. Furthermore, CINCNORTH considered setting up an integrating commander for all army forces in AFNORTH.
- The naval command COMNAVNORTH would be based on using the commanding officer in each national navy as Flag Officer, and possibly adding a flag officer for the Skagerrak and Kattegat area.
- The air command COMAIRNORTH would be divided into three sectors with 15 per cent of the aircraft in Northern Norway, 35 per cent in Southern Norway and 50 per cent in Denmark; the command system would run through each nation's national commands. However, a special contingent of light bombers was under consideration for use anywhere in the region; therefore, it would be commanded directly by COMAIRNORTH.

---

[34] Ekstraktafskrift af AFNE's skrivelse af 11/3 1952 . . . HEM Forsvarsministeriet 11. kontor 451/52 9-6-52.

The Danish C-in-C, however, strongly advised against having any division of the army command structure in Jutland; all forces fighting there had to be under the same command.[35] Likewise, he did not appreciate a new integrating army command in Oslo; it would be a bureaucratic waste. The idea of a new Flag Officer for Skagerrak and Kattegat was acceptable. However, the devil is in the detail, and a Danish approval was based on the fact that in reality all AFNORTH forces in Denmark were already commanded by Danish officers in peacetime; in war they were just allocated to NATO.

The year after, in 1953, it turned out that the new CINCNORTH, General Mansergh, did not agree to this construction; he wanted the roles split between war and peace, and therefore the suggested system did not get implemented. It took several years to solve the disagreements, but in 1956 the Danes acquiesced and split the command system between three operational chiefs in war.[36] Each force kept its national chief whose responsibility in war was reduced to organisation, administration and supplies.

The formalisation of the command principles were, first, delayed until the Danish parliament reached an agreement to redefine the law on Danish defence in 1960; then delayed until the organisation of BALTAP was in place; then again delayed because a working group to finalise the principles took time in getting an agreement;[37] and not really solved until 1967 when a special Danish command was set up under a NATO umbrella. COMBALTAP – who was always a Danish officer (see chapter 9) – became C-in-C for the operative forces of the defence. This construction meant that this C-in-C would take over the command of all Danish forces when the alert level was raised; when General Alert was reached, he would seamlessly change hat to being COMBALTAP; at the same time, the Danish operational commands would change into their NATO war status. This solution was in accordance with a tradition within NATO; for example, General Norstad was SACEUR and Commander in Chief, U.S. European Command at the same time. Before that, he was Commander-in-Chief of the US Air Forces in Europe and (NATO) Commander-in-Chief of Allied Air Forces, Central Europe.

---

35 Notat om nordregionens kommandoorganisation under krig. HEM Forsvarsministeriets 11. kontor 9-6-52 451/52.
36 Notat om ansvarsfordelingen . . . HEM Forsvarsministeriet 11. kontor 27-7-56 26-15-56.
37 Notat vedrørende afgivelse af regeringserklæring . . . HEM Forsvarsministeriets 11. kontor 11-11-64 26-25-1/64.

Squeezing the Danish military budget 1955–60

A Social Democratic cabinet came into power in 1953, and this meant trouble for the defence budget.[38] While in opposition in 1950–53, the Social Democratic party had been part of a pro-defence coalition which supported the growth of the defence budget to 3.4 per cent of GDP. But after the election of 1953, the new cabinet became dependent on the support of the anti-military Radical Left (which in spite of its name was not a revolutionary party). In 1955, a special Committee for Defence chaired by the minister was given the role to prepare for a new defence. The "special" thing was that in order to avoid the Communist Party partaking, the committee was not parliamentary, but ministerial.

It took five years of strong disagreement among the political parties before a compromise between profoundly divergent attitudes could be reached in the parliament. The details of the alternatives discussed are found elsewhere.[39]

What did the politicians making decisions in the parliament know about the organisation and weaponry of the military? Since the members of the committee got briefings from four sources – the ministry, the Danish Joints chiefs of Staff, SHAPE and AFNORTH – the preparatory work in 1955 is a good indicator of how their information base was created.[40]

Of course, this information was based on military assessments and data, but the minister was boss. In a preparatory meeting with the Danish Joint Chiefs of Staff he called for temperance in the presentations they were supposed to give the committee the next day. In particular, he noted that the air force had prepared comments on the need for stationing foreign air forces in Denmark (a politically hot potato, see chapter 6), which he found challenging. He also noted that the navy had strong wording in expressing its needs: the draft warned that unless new ships were built in the near future, the navy would become obsolete; in addition, the bases needed upgrading. He emphasised this again in his conclusion. The minister commented that if those formulations were very significant for the chiefs, so be it, and he would exert no pressure. However, both chiefs agreed to change their wording; the air force took out the possibility of stationing foreign aircraft on Danish territory, and the navy softened the gloomy perspectives for the future.

Consequently, the presentations by the Danish military top were not very challenging. But the politicians also visited SHAPE in Paris and AFNORTH in Oslo

---

38 Ibid., 103–10.
39 Clemmesen, op. cit.
40 This section is based on minutes and papers, most graded COSMIC and HEM, in Forsvarsministeriet, Forsvarsudvalget: Materiale (1950–1960): 6. The sequence of the papers is not followed. We only digest operational and tactical issues, not the details of economy, personnel and weapon types.

and learned about the perspectives of those two NATO commands: the role of the Baltic Approaches as a choke point; the potential for blocking Soviets LOCs in the Baltic; the importance of preventing the Soviets from landing forces in Denmark; and the importance of Bornholm as an early warning post. NATO could win a war with nuclear weapons because Russia could not attack all the bases for NATO's air forces at the same time, and NATO's radar system would warn early enough to start an air counter offensive. SACEUR outlined the principles of the counter offensive we have seen above. NATO commanders anxiously awaited the West German rearmament.

As to air attacks, Denmark was a weak link, and SHAPE would be happy to discuss possibilities to strengthen the air defence.

So SHAPE was quite friendly. But the AFNORTH staff followed up with a comprehensive criticism of the Danish defence. A Soviet attack could start immediately on D-day – it was crucial that the Danish defence was fully prepared for fighting, creating a protecting shield for the total mobilisation of the defence which would then form a sort of second wave or echelon. However,

- the Danish army had too little D-day strength (entities had to be reinforced from 30 to 75 per cent) and had to reorganise its D-day structure favouring Zealand. Artillery, tanks and supporting entities were not strong enough; bare infantry could not do the job. Stocks were insufficient.
- the navy had obsolete ships and none Danish-built were planned except three submarines; the crews did not have enough professional hands and such were non-existent for the reserve entities, and stocks were insufficient.
- the air force had an insufficient control- and warning system and lacked trained staff. There were not enough airplanes and pilots ready for action. Stocks were insufficient.
- Furthermore, the service time for conscripts was too short and ideally would be increased to 18 months. In addition, the percentage of permanent technical staff had to be increased significantly.

All in all, the members of the committee were briefed quite well, seen from a military angle. Step by step, they were informed that the military top, particularly in NATO, did not perceive the Danish defence forces to be adequate. And it appears that what the minister asked his Chiefs of Staff to remove from their papers in the introductory meeting in may 1955, NATO officials took up by removing the gloves and rendering an intense critique of the status of the Danish defence. The members could not possibly be in doubt what the military top thought.

That, however, appears not to have had much influence on the ideas of the majority of the committee. We shall proceed to the outcomes of the political processes in the committee.

In the Annual Review process of 1953, the Danish C-in-C had estimated a growth of the military budget to 1190 million. DKK. In 1954 the new government cut it to 940 million after a budgetary compromise with the support party, but with an increase to 978 million in 1955.

Consequently, there was a stop for most planned military investments. In January 1956, the Joint Chiefs of Staff had worked out the Long Time Plan for the Danish defence. The planned budget was 1280 million, based on the 1957 Capabilities plan (see chapter 7). The negotiations among the three forces had been tough, and the air force in particular was very discontent with a reduction of two squadrons, compared with the NATO plan. The minister answered with a demand that a budget of 900 million be set up.

The chiefs of the three forces also disagreed among themselves. In June 1958, the minister asked the chiefs to set up a defence system which first of all took care of peace time operations, and among those surveillance and alert warnings. The defence proper was to create the basis for NATO to assist Denmark, i.e. the defence had to be very strong in the short time horizon, but no one would expect the forces to withstand for very long.

Such principles, of course, would favour the navy and the air force who had the strongest roles in surveillance and warning activities. Furthermore, both forces were relatively expensive because they had a high percentage of permanent personnel while the organisation of the army was based on conscripts to be mobilised in a few days. The chief of the army could not accept the proposal coming out of the negotiations and suggested that, instead, one should take point of departure from the physical territory with local defence forces and the Home Guard as pillars and a mobile field army as "the fist" for real battle. Once those activities were in the budget, the navy could get resources for a coastal anti-invasion defence, and the air force could solve limited air defence tasks, expecting support from other NATO-partners in a short while.

The supreme commander followed the budgetary fights at an annoyed distance, but he used the Annual Review to express a critique:

> The limits imposed . . . on defence expenditures during these last few years have led, as a result of rising costs and increased requirements to a deterioration of the effectiveness of the Danish forces. . . . The standard of Danish forces is thus considerably below military requirements and the matter is one of grave concern to the NATO military authorities.[41]

---

41 Annual Review 1958, Country Report on Denmark, p. 1.

The Danish C-in-C attempted to reach a compromise with SACEUR in Paris, and he did succeed (see table 5.2) – only to learn that the Danish government could not accept it.

Table 5.2: Alternative forces. Source: C-in-C documents.

	Government	NATO	Compromise
Army	2+1 infant/armour 1 HONEST JOHN 1 NIKE 1 small reserve unit 10 local def. units –	3 Armour-infant.grp 2 HONEST JOHN 2 NIKE (same) (same) –	2 Armour-infant.grp 2 HONEST JOHN 1 NIKE 1 larger reserve unit 15 local def. units 15 local batteries
Navy	8 small destroyers 4 small mine layers 9 patrol craft 12 MTB	14 small destroyers 7 small mine layers 11 patrol craft 12 MTB	11 small destroyers 6 small mine layers 10 patrol craft 17 MTB
Air Force	36 fighter bombers 32 AWF fighters 18 recce	75 fighter bombers 48 AWF fighters 18 recce	68 fighter bombers 48 AWF fighters 18 recce

After this attempt the process went back to square one, and when the parliament reconvened in October 1959 the politicians took over. The bourgeois opposition re-entered negotiations because the Social Democrats wanted a broad compromise. Therefore, intense negotiations took place until mid-January 1960 when a compromise was reached at 1054 million DKK. The army got about the same as the C-in-C had negotiated in Paris, but the navy had a cut corresponding to three small destroyers and some patrol craft. The Air Force got 20 fighter bombers and two recce airplanes less.

The C-in-C complained in a secret note[42] that the relative success for the army came about because the army chief knew that some of the Social Democrats would favour the army, and he persuaded one of them to call him as a witness several times to the parliamentary committee. The C-in-C himself was only called in once, the air force once and the navy not at all, so the army chief had the possibility to exert "undue" influence. He also discussed issues privately with the Social Democrats without informing his C-in-C.

---

42 The C-in-C personally became quite upset and made a HEM note about the process which was not accessible for the public until a few years ago. Forsvarschefers arkiv: Journalsager (1950–1962) 2: 090 Paris forslag 1959–1960 m.m. Notits om Parisforslaget.

This, then, was the military force Denmark was willing to pay for when the final discussions of the future BALTAP command took place in 1961.

Summing up: A weak defence of the Baltic Approaches

When Denmark entered NATO in 1949, its defence was in shambles, and while a rearmament took place in the 1950s, the forces never reached a level that satisfied the NATO commands.

The new C-in-C wrote shortly after he took over in 1950 that there was "an absolutely catastrophic lack of capability of this country to defend itself". The army had too few men to fulfil the tasks; no tanks; a lack of anti-tank weapons; next to no artillery; extremely weak anti-aircraft weaponry; a severe lack of signal units; and little reserve ammunition. The navy lacked coastal destroyers; gunnery in general was weak; crews were not sufficiently trained; there was not enough mine sweeping gear to maintain swept routes; there was only one third of the mines needed; and repair facilities were sparse. For the air force, the only up-to-date fighters were 16 GLOSTER METEOR; no radar of any use, and the army and navy could not count on support. There was no flying at night. In short, the Danish defence (before mobilisation) would not be able to resist a coup-like attack of trained troops.

One year later, not much had changed. Military hardware, particularly for the air force, helped out, but in 1954 the Danes still were not be able to fulfil NATO's goals. In particular, the defence of Jutland was weak because of very few army forces in Schleswig-Holstein and a mobilisation system that was based on local battalions which had to move south towards the border. Most airfields were in Jutland and needed ground defence forces. The navy's capacity for laying mines depended until 1955 on the use of small destroyers and patrol craft; two new forts and two more mine layers did, however, increase the capacity to lay and defend the minefields. The air force got modern fighter-bombers, but the number was too small and the defence therefore depended on foreign reinforcement (see chapter 6). All three forces demanded more resources but the budget did not permit expansion.

As AFNORTH took shape, most sub-commands became identical with the national commanders in Norway and Denmark – but the air command had both countries under its turf. The Danish C-in-C advised against splitting army commands in a territory (Jutland) and thought that a special army staff in Oslo would be a bureaucratic waste. But the integration between forces needed in littoral warfare in the Baltic Approaches did not come about within AFNORTH in the 1950s. On the contrary, coordination had to be made *ad hoc*.

Denmark and Norway initiated ways to cooperate with their navies in the Baltic Approaches and together with Britain started exercises with FPBs in Danish waters.

Furthermore, Britain was asked to support laying minefields in Kattegat, north of the narrows of the Baltic Approaches. Thus the creation of AFNORTH helped supporting international cooperation to handle the obvious lack of Danish forces.

From 1954 the role of the air force changed dramatically, from defending Danish territory to being part of SACEUR's counter-offensive nuclear bombing in the Baltic in order to reduce those parts of the enemy war potential that represented a nuclear threat or an air threat against their territory. The Danes were to support such actions. In addition, to (non-nuclear) bomb enemy naval bases, communication lines and harbours. The air recce tasks also grew before and after such operations and as early warning. Thus the air force became part of a sort of AFNORTH mission command system when war was about to start – but strictly within the air forces. This, in turn, made other mission commands – integrating air force actions with army and/or navy – difficult in the introductory days of a war.

The operation area being littoral waters with short distances from a large number of enemy airfields, the navy knew that unless NATO had some degree of air superiority it would be difficult for naval units to operate in daytime. Until 1950, the navy had its own air force, but the new system of defence took it away to favour a stand-alone air force. Realising the need to integrate several forces in the littoral warfare, the navy therefore tried to create closer cooperation with the air force to get as much support as possible, but the result was meagre.

From 1955, the government wanted to reduce the Danish military budget because a coalition partner demanded it. A committee worked for four years to get a solution, but in vain. The Danish chiefs of staff tried to paint the bleak picture of the Danish defence, but it was NATO officials that made quite clear that the Danish army had too little D-day strength, that artillery, tanks and supporting entities were not strong enough. The navy had obsolete ships and new ones were hardly planned; the crews did not have enough professional hands and stocks were insufficient. The air force had an insufficient control- and warning system and lacked trained staff. It also lacked airplanes and pilots ready for action. Stocks were insufficient. Finally, the service time for conscripts was too short.

A political compromise was reached in the parliament in 1960, much to the chagrin of the C-in-C whose attempts to reach a compromise with SHAPE in Paris fell on barren ground in Denmark. The final result gave the army a better deal at the expense of the navy and air force.

The Danish defence was weak, but of course, this was why Denmark joined NATO. Kesselring has a rather brief characterisation: "Until 1960, NATO was not capable of closing the Baltic exits by conventional means. Hence, the only way of defending them would have been to drop nuclear bombs, entirely in line with NATO's doctrine of 'massive retaliation'."[43]

The descriptions in this chapter and in the chapter on NATO strategy qualify that sweeping statement to a considerable degree. Kesselring ignores a number of facts that made the dropping of nuclear bombs unlikely: there was a Danish ban on such weapons, and procedures for using the existing platforms for nuclear weapons in the area had not been exercised, and hence a "go" from the Americans was not possible. Furthermore, Kesselring makes a (incomplete) count of Danish versus Soviet warships the proof of the pudding,[44] sidestepping the fact that the Danish main defence would be minefields, blocking the Danish straits. Finally, he ignores the plans from that time for NATO reinforcement of the air force, slated to several Danish airfields, to which we shall return below.

---

[43] Kesselring, Agilof. "The Nordic Balance and the Realities of Defence in the Baltic Region, 1948–1961." In *Periphery or Contact Zone? The NATO Flanks 1961 to 2013*, edited by Bernd Lemke, 30. Freiburg: Rombach Verlag KG, 2015.
[44] Ibid., 35–36.

Chapter 6
NATO Policy and Danish military issues in the 1950s

Strengthening the military defence of the Baltic Approaches in the 1950s was not an easy task. This chapter illustrates the problems by analysing a number of issues, all involving the Danish military. Some of them created fierce public and political debates.

The first issue originated from the Russian occupation of the island of Bornholm 1945–46 and the interpretation of an agreement of what forces might come to the island. The second theme is the territorial defence of Northern Germany, or more precisely Schleswig-Holstein, which became part of AFNORTH while the rest of West Germany was under AFCENT. A third issue was the location of depots in Denmark for military supplies for NATO forces in combat; many Danes were fiercely against any type of West German troops to enter Danish soil. Another problem was resources for more naval offensive operations in the Baltic which required more units than the Danish navy had.

The Danish navy had not only ships, but also forts and coastal batteries. The Danes planned two new forts, but the Americans did not want stationary forts, they recommended mobile batteries. The Danes would not accept this.

In the early 1950s, SACEUR put strong pressure on Denmark and Norway to accept the stationing of American warplanes in peace time. This, however, saw strong political resistance on the political left side. In addition, the Danish government dragged its feet in allocating Danish air forces to SACEUR.

Soviet uses of the Bornholm agreement

The location of Bornholm is quite special (see figure 6.1 below). Geographically, it is close – 35 kilometres – to Sweden, and when Denmark ceded the southern part of the Scandinavian peninsula to the Swedish king after a war was lost in 1658, Bornholm was also slated to become Swedish. But a resistance group overwhelmed the Swedish occupation force on the island in December 1659 and the Danish king was allowed to keep the island, a monetary compensation to the Swedish king pending.

In May 1945, the German occupation forces in Denmark surrendered to the British. The island of Bornholm, however, was to be occupied by Soviet troops in accordance with the Yalta Conference. When the Germans on the island refused to surrender to any one but the British, the Soviets bombed two cities from the air, and then the Germans surrendered. The Soviet troops occupied the island until 5 April 1946, when Danish forces took over. They did so subject to the conditions of an agreement between Denmark and the Soviet Union, stating that "Denmark will without any participation of foreign forces immediately be able to occupy the island of Bornholm and there fully execute the administration."

The history and wording of the declaration is discussed in detail elsewhere,[1] and we shall not go into the semantics of it. But in the decades to follow, the Soviet Union used the declaration to assail Danish security policy several times.

When Denmark became member of NATO, Bornholm became an important intelligence and early warning outpost. In October 1951, the Danish C-in-C issued a note on the strategic importance of the island.[2] The distance to Poland and East Germany (Rügen) is only 90 kilometres. First of all the island was a warning outpost, making possible visual and electronic observation from the island, supported by observations from navy units at sea. One could monitor air traffic along the Baltic coast south of the island and over the territories of Pomerania and West Prussia; naval traffic in the Baltic and along the coast to the south; Russian and Polish naval exercises (the Danish navy could observe the eastern Baltic to Memel); radio traffic in a large part of the Baltic and submarine activities around Bornholm. The Danish air force's radar control would be extended 150 kilometres to the east and the navy could use the island as a forward base for MTBs and submarines. For the Russians, the island was a military problem in the above terms, but the island was not necessary for them to hold for attacking forces moving west, if only the electronic installations on the island had been silenced.

The C-in-C stressed that the island could not expect any help from other NATO forces in case of an attack, but the defence on the ground would have relatively good conditions, given the fact that landing forces from the sea was only possible in a few places. The largest harbour, Rønne, should have a harbour battery (this was never built, PB). The limited air force support was problematic, however.

The Soviet Union exploited the 1946 declaration several times. Specifically, the Soviets asserted that non-Danish NATO troops, including warships, could not visit the island, and even NATO-exercises in the adjacent waters were frowned upon. In 1952 the Soviet daily *Pravda* complained that in the exercise MAINBRACE (see chapter 3), NATO planned to include Bornholm and thus the Danish govern-

---

[1] Jensen, Bent. *Bornholmske Samlinger III række 9. Bind*, 271. Rønne: Bornholms historiske samfund, 1996.
[2] Bornholms strategiske betydning og nødvendige styrker til øens forsvar, HEM C. 422/0 4626 30-10-51.

ment was in breach of the Bornholm agreement of 1946. This created some worries among the NATO top decision-makers.[3] The British government expressed "some concern", indicating that the exercises in the Baltic should be cancelled. The Americans, in contrast, were dead against any changes, but accepted the view that one should avoid "provocations". CINCNORTH then decided that NATO aircraft would not fly there, and foreign men-of-war would not come closer to Bornholm than 25 nautical miles (47 kilometres) west of the island. The Danish minister of defence therefore countered the Soviets by declaring that Danish participation in NATO exercises was business as usual and, anyway, NATO exercises were aimed at defence, not attack. As to Bornholm, the governing of it was not influenced by the exercise in any way. Regarding the military side, "only Danish army and air forces were involved on Bornholm, while the naval exercises included a few British and Norwegian ships, and they would not dock in Bornholm".[4] This declaration was meant as a rejection of the Soviet understanding of the agreement, but one could say that by explicitly stating that no foreign ships would dock in Bornholm, the Danish government *de facto* accepted it.

The Danish military top was not pleased with the restrictions. They wanted the MAINBRACE exercise to encompass more activities in the south and south-east, the area where most Danish military activities would take place in the event of war.[5] As a consequence of the restrictions, a planned minefield laid east of Bornholm by the British mine layer APOLLO was instead planned to be laid by the Danish LINDORMEN, and a planned landing of NATO troops on Bornholm had to be changed to Danish troops carried by the Danish frigate HOLGER DANSKE.[6]

So there is no doubt that, formally, the Danish government did not accept the Soviet interpretation, but in actual fact, it observed it fairly closely. On 18 March 1953, CINCNORTH expressed his dissatisfaction with the Danish limit on exercises 25 miles east of Bornholm[7] and recommended the Danish government to allow air and naval exercises, including submarines, east of the island. His rationales were that, first, one should not implicitly acknowledge the Soviet claims about foreign forces in the area. Second, the area to the east would be the operating field of NATO forces in case of

---

3 Dansk Institut for Internationale Studier. *Danmark under den kolde krig. Den sikkerhedspolitiske situation 1945–1991. Bind 1: 1945–1962*, 236–39. København: Dansk Institut for Internationale Studier, 2005a.
4 Udenrigsministeriet. *Dansk Sikkerhedspolitik 1948–1966*, 160. København: Udenrigsministeriet, 1968a.
5 FSS 23-4-52 1.
6 FSS 19-8-52 4.
7 HEM Beretning vedrørende øvelser i Østersøen. 14-9-53 Forsvarsministeriet 11. kontor 35-41/53. Written by the Ministry of Foreign Affairs.

Figure 6.1: The proposal from the Danish C-in-C for extending exercise areas to the east of Bornholm.

war and, therefore, they should have access to train operations there. The Danish C-in-C concurred and suggested that NATO forces could operate until 115 kilometers (17 degrees East) east of Bornholm (see figure above).

The C-in-C added that under all conditions – including exercises – Danish military units needed permission to go as far as the nautical territorial borders of East Germany and Poland.

An inter-ministerial committee of the Foreign and Defence Departments analysed the problems, and the Foreign Ministry maintained that no general permission could be granted for non-Danish entities; every case had to take the political circumstances in that particular situation into consideration. One had to avoid "incidents" provoked by the Soviets. Therefore, the committee suggested that the proposal by the C-in-C be approved under the condition that exercises be limited to what would technically be the absolute minimum, and that no ship larger than destroyers were involved. Exercises had to demonstrably be of a defensive character, and only Danish and Norwegian vessels be allowed to call at harbours on Bornholm. The participation of allied aircraft had to be limited, and no planes would be allowed to land on Bornholm. As an exception to the general rules one would allow Danish-Norwegian-British FPB exercises including calls at harbours in those waters provided that no other type of vessel participated.

The creation of the BALTAP command also spurred Soviet diplomatic interference with reference to the Bornholm agreement (see chapter 9). In December 1961, the Soviets noted that the Danish government "supported a German attempt to conquer territory in the area . . . (and) that including Bornholm under the BALTAP command was contrary to the spirit and letter in the Danish Government's assurances of 8 March 1946 . . .".[8]

The Soviet government might have had to take the necessary steps to secure the safety of its own country and its allies. The Danish government rejected the interpretation and specifically noted that the BALTAP command was a NATO command – a defence activity – and not a Danish-German setup; hence Denmark did not specifically support Germany. And regarding Bornholm, there were no changes: "there are only Danish forces present on Bornholm under Danish command".

In general, NATO ships were allowed to visit the island when they were not part of exercises, but military NATO activity on land was banned. According to Bent Jensen,[9] not even an American military orchestra was allowed to play at an agricultural fair on the island in 1982. It is true, but the tone of that assessment is moot. In fact, several top generals visited the island in the 1950s, but normally in civilian clothes, and in the 1960s and 1970s whole groups of officers visited.[10] One example was in August 1974, when COMBALTAP Helms inspected the Bornholm detail accompanied by a group of six NATO officers, all in uniform. His deputy chief of staff informed him that this was against government policy, so the guests should be in civilian clothes, but lacking a document substantiating this, Helms

---

8 Ibid., 112.
9 Jensen, op. cit., p. 312.
10 Geckler, Niels, and Morten Friis Jørgensen. *Bornholm i krig og fred*, 205–11. Rønne: Hakon Holm Publishing, 2021.

challenged his deputy and chose to let the officers do the inspection over two days.[11]

In 1983, the Danish foreign minister initiated a formal change of policy by allowing a deputy American secretary of state to visit Bornholm with a staff of uniformed officers; shortly after the naval exercise area was expanded to 18 degrees East, NATO vessels were allowed to participate, and single aircraft was allowed to land.[12]

We shall return to the Bornholm agreement when relevant in the chapters to follow.

The territorial defence of Schleswig-Holstein 1949–62

After WWII, North-Western Germany was occupied by British troops. Soon a civilian British administration was set up, and the role of the military reduced correspondingly to preserving inner security. This meant maintaining law and order in case of civilian unrest, but only if prompted by a demand from the civil administration for military support. From 1947, a Danish, a Belgian and a Norwegian brigade, each comprising 4,000 men, took part in these tasks, and the British also had some forces there.

When the Federal Republic of Germany was founded in 1949, the role became to protect the area from a military attack by the Soviet Union, which was close by, occupying Eastern Germany. The Danish and Norwegian brigades were relocated to Schleswig-Holstein in order to defend that area together with the remaining British forces, all in all about 6,000 men.[13] As the war organisation of NATO unfolded in 1951–52, this force was placed under AFNORTH, operationally under COMLANDENMARK who commanded army forces on Danish territory.[14]

The quality of the overall NATO defence of the Cimbric Peninsula at that time – and actually until the German Bundeswehr was created and took over the defence of the area – was questionable indeed. The main defence line of North-

---

11 Helms, Adam. "Min tid som Commander Allied Forces Baltic Approaches 1970–75. Anden del 1973–75." *Tidsskrift for Søvæsen* 176, no. 2 (2005b): 73–103.
12 Geckler, and Jørgensen, op. cit., p. 213.
13 Vegger, A. C. B. *Slesvig-Holsten fra 1945 til 1962*, 29. Viborg: Det kongelige Garnisonsbibliotek, 1985.
14 For a comprehensive analysis of the dislocation of the Danish army in this period of time, see Clemmesen Clemmesen, Michael H. "Udviklingen i Danmarks forsvarsdoktrin fra 1945 til 1969." *Militært Tidsskrift* (1987), 7–81.

Western Europe at that time was at the Rhine-Ijssel, meaning that NATO would let the attacker go forward to that line, but no further.

During the first years of NATO, Denmark and Norway repeatedly called for what later became a NATO strategy, namely a "forward" defence line starting east of Lübeck and extending south along the Trave Canal to the river Elbe.[15] This would give the Denmark a considerable buffer against attackers heading for the Danish border behind which the Danish territorial defence proper was organised. The Danes asked for British support to such a defence and together with the Norwegians they estimated that a Danish-Norwegian division of about 10,000 men might be possible to set up. But the British Chiefs of Staff declined because, in their opinion, this force would not suffice. The British saw a need for two Danish-Norwegian divisions and a total force of about five divisions plus three in reserve – as well as air supremacy. This could not be done by NATO without rearmament of West Germany, so until 1958 the Schleswig-Holstein area remained a weak spot in military terms.

In the summer of 1952, the Danish C-in-C wrote a memo on the defence of the area.[16] First, he called to attention that although the Kiel Canal was quite a "natural" defence line, the value of it would have to be assessed in the light of the strength of the force allocated to its defence. Since the Russians had specialised in crossing such natural hindrances, small NATO defence forces might easily be run over. Second, no less than one division could do the job. A lesser force might be cut off, it might not get to the fighting positions in time and the groups might be annihilated group by group. Third, a correct dislocation of the forces would secure that the planned destructions of the Canal were implemented, but continued fighting could not be expected. After one day, they would have to withdraw north. After that, the main role for Danish forces would be to protect vital military points in Jutland.

NATO wanted Denmark to keep the brigade south of the border in order to at least temporarily stop the enemy by demolishing the Kiel Canal together with a British armoured regiment.[17] Thus a strengthened Danish Brigade would be an important first defence of Denmark, allowing time for a proper mobilisation. Furthermore, SACEUR might agree to allocate more forces if the Danes stayed; if not, NATO would maintain the forces in AFCENT. Furthermore, all ideas about getting

---

15 Rasmussen, Peter Hertel. *Den danske Tysklandsbrigade 1947–1958*, 283. Odense: Syddansk Universitetsforlag, 2019.
16 South Jutland Covering Force, HEM C.J.23/0. 2584 3-7-52.
17 Meeting with CINCNORTH in Copenhagen 20-1-53. Minutes HEM Forsvarsministeriet 1. kontor 21-1-53 98/1230-199.

air forces to airfields in the area (see below) would wither away if there were no ground defence.

So in winter 1952–53, the Danish bourgeois government proposed a policy change permitting the Danish brigade to be strengthened to 4,000 men, but failed to get parliamentary support; the opposition demanded a stronger NATO-representation in the area. But the supreme commander would not allocate forces from AFCENT; the British would not allocate more forces than the regiment already present in the area; and in spite of a first positive stance from their Foreign Minister,[18] the French also had declined.

The Danish government now approached the French and British governments which confirmed an intention to participate in discussions of increasing the NATO forces, and at the same time the American government indicated that a solution might be found. But the American solution soon materialised as an allocation of a fighter wing to the Schleswig Land Airfield – if and only if there was a sufficient number of ground forces to secure the area. The other NATO countries wanted the Danish government to assure that about 5,000 Danish soldiers would be stationed south of the Danish border if other NATO forces were to be expanded.

However, the main Danish opposition party demanded that NATO's big powers guarantee a substantial force to help cover the deficit; the party would not support an increase of the Danish forces. Consequently, the Danish government was in a sort of stalemate or maybe rather a catch-22. Both NATO and the Danish opposition required the other party to move (increase forces) before they would approve. Therefore, the Danish bourgeois government's wish for a stronger Danish force did not materialise. The Norwegians withdrew their brigade in the spring of 1953 to build up their defence of northern Norway – in accordance with the overall NATO strategy – and the Danish brigade, already reduced to about 1,400 men, was not strengthened to fill the void south of the Danish border.

In 1954 the issue was discussed with deputy SACEUR Montgomery in a rather hostile negotiation setting about pushing the border between AFCENT and AFNORTH to the Danish-German border and thus leave the defence of the area south of the border to AFCENT (we shall return to this in chapter 9). The Danish Joint chiefs of Staff disagreed, seeing the problem for the territorial defence as follows:[19] if forced to withdraw, land forces under the command of AFCENT – as suggested by Montgomery – would naturally move to the west to keep contact with other AFCENT forces. This would leave Schleswig-Holstein open for the Russians, and the next natural defence line would be Limfjorden – a natural water

---

18 Signal HEM 10-2-53 from Forsvarsministeriet to Danish SHAPE representation 981.230-199.
19 Memo for General Collins, C-in-C 13-5-54.

barrier in the north of Jutland, but 250 kilometres away from Kiel. In other words, most of Jutland would be laid bare for the attackers, leaving all but one airfield to the enemy. Therefore the main defence line had to be in the south with NATO forces.

Montgomery's plan did not materialise, but nor did the NATO reinforcement to the area. The minuscule remaining forces in Schleswig-Holstein prepared on their own a defence line at the Kiel Canal and the river Eider. A number of bridges were to be destroyed, and minefields prepared in conjunction with flooding of low-land areas.[20] But there was not enough strength to build up a force to counter the aggressor. The most likely action after destroying the infrastructure therefore would be a withdrawal across the Danish border, unless an early Danish mobilisation of the army's two divisions (later merged into one) in Jutland would make it possible to move those forces into Schleswig-Holstein and establish a defence line – until 1953 at the Kiel Canal, after 1953 at an east-West line, Schleswig-Husum. One of the divisions was supposed to move into Schleswig, if necessary, to support the existing defence. If the plan failed, an alternative defence line (far south of the Limfjord) would be about 25 kilometres north of the border in a line from Tønder to Aabenraa, divided between two divisions. The defence positions followed various waterways when possible and involved a series of destructions of the infrastructure.[21]

There was a lack of air support in the area. The Danish air force had a total of about 200 fighter and light bomber planes and could not be expected to assist south of the border. This was one of the reasons for the American offer of stationing aircraft in Denmark (see below).

The New York Times speaks out
The weak defence of Schleswig-Holstein was no secret to the general public. Thus *The New York Times* on 26 February, 1955 stated:

> Schleswig-Holstein, the anchor point of free Europe's northern flank, should, as a flank, be strong at its junction with the centre. Instead, it is one of the weakest spots in the Allies' defences. . . . as the situation stands, armoured divisions from East Germany could move through Schleswig-Holstein into Denmark in a few hours . . .
>
> (West German forces) will not be ready for at least two years, In the meantime the only troops in Schleswig-Holstein are an under strength British armoured regiment and a reinforced Danish battalion. The Allies are not prepared to station any more forces there because of supply-line difficulties.

---

20 Ibid., 303–4.
21 Ibid., 361; Steinkopff, Klaus Christoph. *Die geostrategische Bedeutung der Cimbrischen Halbinsel in der westlichen Verteidigungsplanung*, 85–87. Kiel, 2003.

> Of course, the Soviets knew this. Their passivity is an indication that other matters than the local military defence played a role in military decision-making and international politics.

The Bundeswehr took over the defence of Schleswig-Holstein April 1, 1958, with its headquarters called LANDSCHLESWIG, linked to LANDENMARK and hence to CINCNORTH. The Germans originally planned two divisions, but in the end only one armoured division was set up. It was to have a particular military strength by having its "own" allocated air support, an additional armoured vehicle group and access to tactical nuclear weapons.[22] More specifically, the air component was planned to be two squadrons of bomber fighters by 1959, two squadrons of day fighters by 1960 and two reconnaissance squadrons by 1961.[23]

The Germans perceived the Kiel Canal as the main defence line. It would not be difficult for the Soviets to cross the canal, but in terms of defence infrastructure, the bridges over the canal formed 90 per cent of all road connections and about 60 per cent of all railroad connections. So as long as it was under NATO control, it was decisive in all NATO force movements and supply delivery in all aspects.

A special corps headquarters based on the German sixth division and one Danish brigade was formed and had its first exercise in HOLD FAST (1960); we shall give some detail from the exercise below.

The background for the exercise was a deteriorating political climate during the summer.[24] In early August the NATO Council published a report expressing serious concerns over the situation. At the end of August SACEUR initiated a state of military vigilance, and Denmark and Norway followed suit.

In the first week of September, comprehensive WAPA exercises took place in East Germany. On 10 September, the Danish government prepared for assigning forces to NATO and receiving nuclear warheads immediately upon request. The parliament authorised the cabinet to raise the alert levels and to lay out sea mines. The navy called up reserves for mine layers and the army initiated exercises. On 18 September CINCNORTH declared simple alert, Denmark followed and the navy started laying mines at the coasts and in controlled blockades at Copen-

---

22 Thoss, Bruno. *NATO-strategie und nationale Verteidigungsplanung. Planung und Aufbau der Bundeswehr unter den Bedingungen atomaren Vergeltungsstrategie 1952–1960*, 267. München: R. Oldenbourg Verlag, 2006.
23 SHAPE. *SHAPE History 1958*, 33. Mons: SHAPE, 1967b.
24 Unless otherwise noted, the ensuing paragraphs follow a series of HEM notes by Forsvarsministeriet 1. kontor 1959–60, j. nr. 171.11–13.

hagen and Southern Zealand. The day after the Danish army crossed the border to Schleswig-Holstein, and the navy increased mine laying.

On the night between 19 and 20 September enemy special forces were landed at various locations in Denmark and Germany. The next morning Danish forces were assigned to CINCNORTH, and the country started to mobilise.

Now the German sixth division was south of the Kiel Canal, the Danish 3. division north of the canal and orange forces moved across the border towards Lübeck, supported by aircraft, paratroopers at Rendsborg and Aabenraa, and an amphibious for landed at Eckernförde. The plan for blue forces was to retreat slowly towards the Danish border.

We shall not detail the quite comprehensive ensuing exercise movements. The evaluations of the participants follow.

The joint HQ with staff and signal battalion had to be operating in peacetime at a 60 per cent level in order to function adequately from the day of alert, it wa to be fully mobile, and officers working there had to be able to speak English. The joint command took over the operations at reinforced alert. This was too late; it had to take place at simple alert. For the Jutland area, in the future one was only to have one joint command, not two.

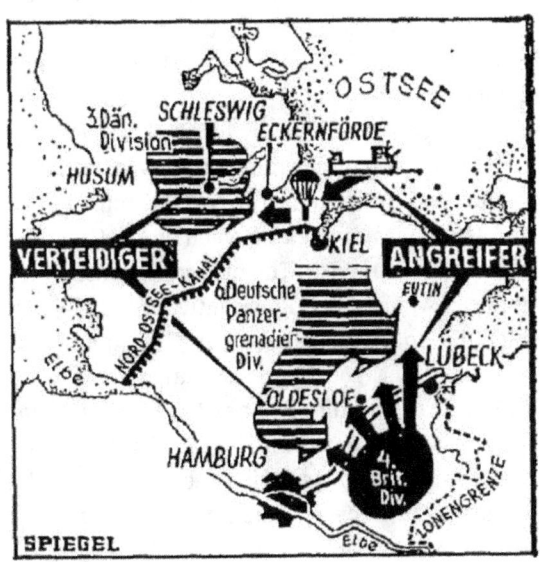

Figure 6.2: Map of HOLD FAST area. German sixth Division south east of the Kiel Canal, the Danish third division to the north west. Based on drawing in *Der Spiegel* 1960 no 41.

Fighting units were to be brought together more often in minor exercises. They were to be under NATO HQ command no later than simple alert.

In general, reservists were usable at the level of the company, but had problems in the larger formations. In particular, the signal sections had problems in cooperating across nations. Called-up reservists needed some time for re-training; after three days things went much better.

Forces were not strong enough south and east of the Kiel Canal, and cooperation with the German local defence (home guard) was difficult. The regular forces should number three, not one, armoured infantry divisions, and in addition an armoured reserve and a strong artillery unit.

Sixteen nuclear warheads were available, four by plane. Seven were used, five of those by artillery or missile. Those who called for the warheads found that it took too much time from identifying targets to getting the warhead delivered by aircraft. One should not forget that use of warheads required governmental approval in each case. But the participants in the exercise recommended that, first, nuclear warheads should be available when SACEUR called for their use (R-hour), and if the enemy used atom weapons, response should come automatically.

Logistics required a major comprehensive analysis of its organisation.

From COMLANDSCHLESWIG-HOLSTEIN[25] it was pointed out that it was necessary for all forces in the area to be under tactical command of the joint HQ. If not, serious problems would arise in times of crisis, e.g. if the sixth division had to retire and cross the Kiel Canal; the bridges would create bottlenecks and there was a risk of clashes between civilian fugitives and military forces. Therefore, the German home guard (Territorialheer) had to be under the joint HQ – as the Danish home guard was in Denmark – and this HQ had to be the NATO command.

Regarding aircraft, Schleswig-Holstein was divided between 2. ATAF (air defence) and COMTAFDEN (air recce and close support). The officer responsible for "air" war in tactical issues was under 2. ATAF which apparently regarded COMTAFDEN as a northern add-on which did not have their interest; their focus was on Central Europe. Consequently, COMTAFDEN got little information about what happened in the air. Therefore, in the future all air "business" was to be under COMTAFDEN. That command, however, had too few recce aircraft. Therefore, the joint HQ did not get any ordered recce from aircraft during the exercise. In the future, a fixed number of recce flights were to be allocated; this so much more

---

25 COMLANDSCHLESWIG-HOLSTEIN. Erfahrungsbericht NATO–übung HOLD FAST. Streng geheim. 19-12-60. j.nr 039/1700.1/60. BH 1/3.

because the fighting would be determined by nuclear warheads which required good recce support.

The Danish COMLANDENMARK planned to use one third of the special corps south of the Kiel Canal, the rest north of the canal; this did not please the German military top which saw this disposition rather as a defence of Denmark, not Germany.[26] As to the outcomes of the exercise, the movement of the unified corps towards the south had been so slow that a first defence line could only be established between the Elbe and the Schlei, way north of the planned defence line, and in effect forcing NATO to give up the southern part of the area. In addition, the use of nuclear tactical weapons by aircraft had been delayed because one had to request them from SACLANT's carrier group; AFNORTH had none available. In short, the German judgment was that whether one could talk of "defence" or "delay" was to be decided by the enemy rather than by COMLANDENMARK. The German troops were basically on their own south of the Schlei.[27] This conflict of interest strengthened the German pressure for getting Schleswig-Holstein as part of AFCENT rather than AFNORTH.

From the summer of 1962, the BALTAP command solved some of the problems of military focus in war in the sense that the territorial defence of Denmark was divided into two commands. The staff of the western army component, COMLANDJUT, which included Schleswig-Holstein, was located in Rendsburg, south of the Danish border, with alternating Danish-German top command. The Danish dominance in military thinking was over. Nonetheless, the defence under COMLANDJUT remained weak.[28] The cooperation between Danish and German troops was less successful than desired, and the ability of the Danish forces to move south quickly was constrained, leaving the forward defence of the Elbe-Trave line open (in 1975, COMBALTAP Helms analysed the relocation time and found that it would take about 90 hours for the Danish division to take up battle positions in Schleswig[29]). Furthermore, neither country allocated the resources desired by NATO to their army components.

---

26 Vegger, op. cit., pp. 61–62.
27 Thoss, op. cit., pp. 271–72.
28 Ibid., 275.
29 Helms, op. cit.

Logistics: NATO storage in Denmark

Shortly after SACEUR was installed in 1951, his staff began analysing the logistics of the member countries. The supreme commander had no say over the stores of the individual countries, but it was obvious that something had to be done to secure deliveries in case of war. Denmark was a case in point: it could not provide more than a small proportion of the equipment necessary. If NATO forces could hold Schleswig-Holstein, supplies would pass through Germany. But if not, stocks had to be sailed from Norway or Great Britain. The issue was raised of whether an advanced NATO base in Denmark was needed.[30]

The discussions of the scope and location of NATO's depots are linked to other themes in this chapter, particularly the permanent stationing of NATO forces and the various forms of cooperation between forces in times of crisis and war.

SACEUR saw it as his responsibility

> to ensure that complete logistic support including initial equipment, replacement equipment, supplies, maintenance parts, facilities and installations, and all essential services, procedures and techniques be provided for three purposes. First, so that forces could be trained; secondly, so that combat operations could be sustained until full NATO reserves could be mobilised; and lastly, so that the transition from peace to war could be achieved in such a way that logistics kept pace with the expansion of forces.[31]

These goals for supplies presupposed, however, that there was an infrastructure available to store supplies, communicate about their use and move them as needed during times of crisis or war. The existing systems were insufficient and only geared towards supplying own forces, and since one could expect other forces to become involved during crises and war, the systems had to be expanded. An annual program with "slices" of investments paid by NATO was initiated.

Getting depots and infrastructure in place turned out to be difficult. For one, the disagreements regarding stationing foreign aircraft in Denmark (see below) made firm decisions impossible regarding depots servicing airfields. More progress was made on the communication infrastructure, e.g. a 140 mile-long petrol pipeline linking airfields in Jutland to stocks.

But as time progressed and West Germany came closer to a membership of NATO, the demand for a more forward strategy also came up, and therefore SACEUR in 1955 decided that all supplies for Denmark should be located in Den-

---

30 SHAPE. *SHAPE History Volume I*, 260–61. Versailles: SHAPE, 1953.
31 Ibid., 262.

mark.³² The revised plan was discussed with the Danes in October 1955.³³ It presupposed that German forces would keep the enemy at bay in Schleswig-Holstein and that their communication lines went through Jutland with Frederikshavn (in northernmost Jutland) as main harbour. Danish army supplies were to be stored on Zealand (60 days) and in mid-Jutland and north Jutland (90 days plus 30 days for Zealand); navy stores were to be decentralised from Copenhagen, favouring Korsør (at Storebælt) and Frederikshavn plus some minor harbours at the Baltic (these should be open for the future West German navy): air force stores at the airfields plus large stores in north Jutland. The Danes agreed to the principles but wanted a more precise calculations of the costs – there was not room for increased costs in the military budget.

The procedures for getting access to various forms of supplies were not determined, and it took two years to reach a common understanding and create a quite complicated usable system,³⁴ where one set of rules determined SACEUR's powers vis-a-vis national authorities, the processes to follow and the information to be given to the supreme commander about resources available. Another set delineated SACEUR's use of such stores made available and particularly principles for storing and using the stocks of one nation in another nation's territory.³⁵

These clauses created major problems in the relations between Denmark, West Germany and the supreme commander. Given that the German forces were planned to operate in Schleswig-Holstein with stores in Jutland, and given that the German navy in all probability would have to get access to replenishment in Danish harbours, there was from a military point of view no doubt that storing capacity must be built. But seen from the political side, the perspective differed radically.

Informal discussions between Danish and German military about stores for German forces started in Winter 1957–58.³⁶ The Germans wanted storage room for 20,000 tons of ammunition, 1,600 tons of equipment and 10,000 m³ of fuel. The Danish representative suggested that security etc. be taken care of by the Danes with a few German advisers on site, but the Germans would have the right to inspect the contents at their discretion. Formal negotiations about the issue took place in late January 1959, and a draft agreement written but kept secret for other political parties. However, the minority partner in the cabinet, the Radical Left,

---

32 SHAPE. *SHAPE History – The New Approach 1953–1956*, 400. Mons: SHAPE, 1976.
33 Minutes 18-10-55 HEM in Forsvarsministeriet 11. kontor.
34 SHAPE, *SHAPE History – The New Approach 1953–1956*, 396–403.
35 Changes are summarized in note HEM 17-10-57 "Aftale med AFNORTH . . . " Forsvarsministeriet 11. kontor 663/07.
36 Note HEM Oplægning af forsyninger til tyske styrker 11-5-58 662/58.

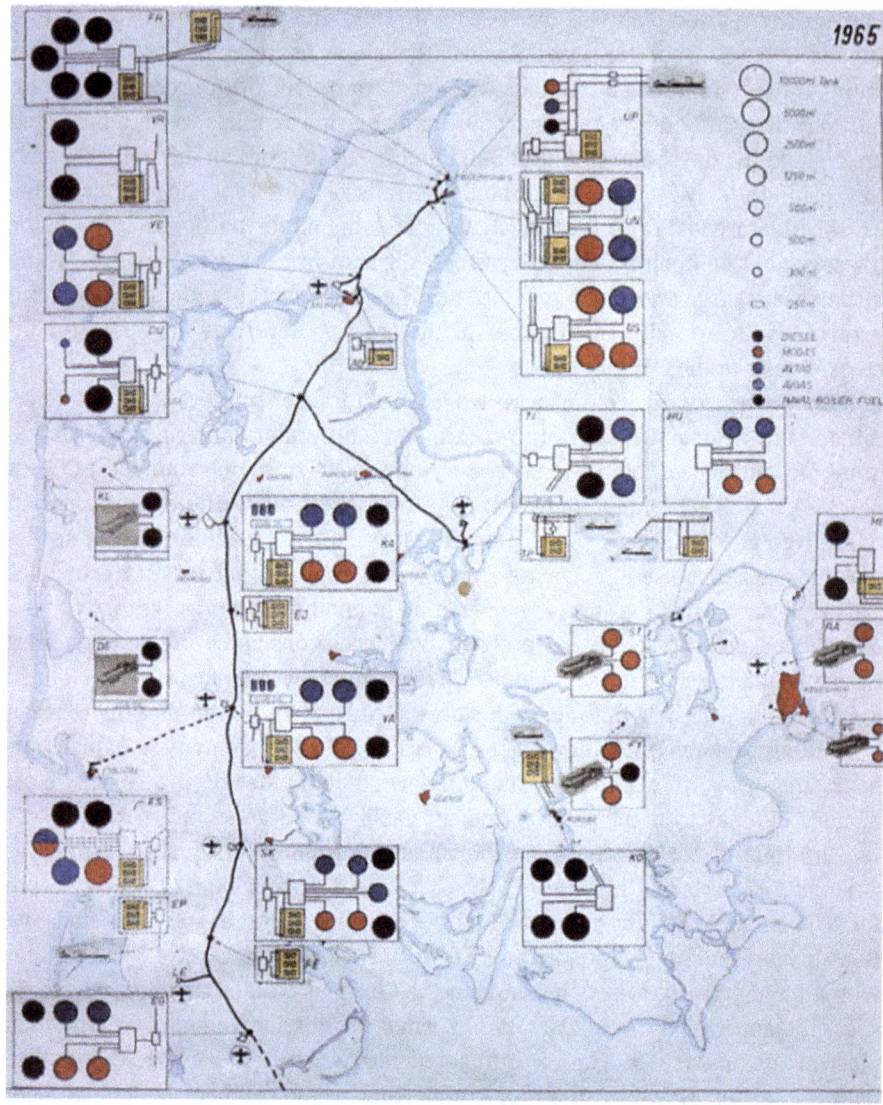

Figure 6.3: The NEPS pipeline for Danish airfields was initiated in 1955. The colours indicate various types of POL. Later it was expanded to the German airfields.[37]

---

37 Kulturministeriet. *Kold krig. 33 fortællinger om den kolde krigs bygninger og anlæg i Danmark, Færøerne og Grønland,* 72. København: Kulturministeriet, 2013.

had reservations, and the negotiations were halted after the German newspaper *Frankfurter Allgemeine* revealed them, a very unwelcome situation for the Danes. The Danish minister feared political unrest in the population and particularly within the coalition cabinet.[38] The Germans suggested that the negotiations be changed to concern NATO depots rather than German depots. The minister agreed but wanted the negotiations about the future Danish defence (see chapter 5) to be completed before the depot issues could be solved.

When the negotiations started over,[39] The German demands had grown substantially: two depots containing 5,000 tons ammunition each; three depots for 10,000, 25,000 and 25,000 tons equipment, respectively. Existing structures had been found usable. Furthermore, access to 40,000 m^3 petrol by pipeline to the Danish border from Skrydstrup airfield, which would be a NATO investment. The Ministry of Defence noted several problems in establishing such NATO-depots: existing depots could not be transferred to another nation according to existing rules, and new depots required financing by NATO; this would undoubtedly trigger new demands from other NATO countries. A possible solution could be to grant SACEUR access to the existing depots and then let the supreme commander grant access to the Germans; such a solution was recommended by AFNORTH and was likely to withstand a judicial review.

This solution passed the scrutiny of the minority party. The party had fierce discussions internally about the issue and ended up demanding a contractual guarantee that the depots were not for nuclear warheads and that maintenance and security were to be carried out by Danish personnel – to be reimbursed by SACEUR who apparently established a clearing office for this purpose, thus permitting the Germans to pay their share without involving the Danish treasury.[40]

Offensive operations in the Baltic?

The military possibilities for Danish forces were, by and large, confined to defending Danish soil and waters. And according to the nature of NATO, one could only react to an attack by the Russians, not vice versa. But the Danish top military re-

---

[38] Minutes HEM Forsvarsministeriet 1. kontor 15-4-59 See also Villaume 1991 Villaume, Poul. "Mulig fjende – nødvendig allieret?" In *Danmark, Norden og NATO 1948–1962*, Carsten Due Nielsen, Johan peder Noack, and Nikolaj Petersen, 167–68. København: Jurist- og Økonomforbundets Forlag, 1991.
[39] HEM Notat om oplægning af allierede militære forsyninger i Danmark 2-5-59 662/59.
[40] Notits om AFNORTHs bestræbelser i sagen om tyske depoter i Danmark. HEM Forsvarsministeriets 11. kontor 29-4-59 668/59.

alised that attacking the Russians – once they had initiated a conflict – deep into the Baltic Sea could give a handsome payoff. As soon as war had broken out, offensive operations by air and sea in the Baltic were warranted, targeting lines of communication, harbours and bases.

Admiral Heye had pointed this out in his notes to the Danish navy in 1949 (see chapter 2), calling for operations by rather small craft, submarines and air forces. The idea was to sink ships transporting goods and mine the harbours and narrow straits.

However, Heye also produced another paper[41] whose contents, in his own wording, would "paralyse Soviet initiative, as it will burden the Soviets with uncertainty concerning the plans of the West.... (and) give the West a firm basis for its political negotiations with the East..." The paper built up a NATO standing naval force as "armed force in being" consisting of battleships, aircraft carriers, cruisers, destroyer flotillas, small fighting craft and a big landing craft pool, supported by fighters and bombers, and having army landing troops stationed in the vicinity. The ships were to be stationed in Norwegian, Danish and West German ports and have very frequent operations in the Baltic, showing force and making exercises that left no doubt of their potential. This force would constitute a permanent threat, be directed by SACEUR and create an uncertainty as to what could be expected, when and where. This threat would bind large numbers of Soviet troops in the area and weaken any idea about attacking West Europe.

Given Heye's general propensity to recommend small craft and submarines for operations in the Baltic, this large scale project seems a little surprising. The paper was sent by the C-in-C's intelligence deputy chief to the Danish representative at SHAPE asking him to explore the possibilities to implement it, apparently to no avail. But it became of use for the Danish C-in-C who in the summer of 1951 prepared a note on offensive operations in the Baltic, presented in September to the Danish military top.[42] Operations would be of help locking Russian ships in the harbours and create doubt among the Russian military leadership regarding the feasibility of naval operations which would be hampered by the need for extended mine sweeping. Thus offensive operations would help:
- the defence of the Baltic Approaches which the Russians would desire for free passage towards the North Sea and the Atlantic as well as getting access to bases and airfields in the area. In addition, the area would be useful as a base for Allied offensive operations into the Baltic;

---

41 Forsvarets Efterretningstjeneste: V. Diverse sager (afklass.) (1940–1966) 4: Diverse 1942–1966, Heye.
42 Memorandum vedrørende betydningen af offensive operationer i Østersøen. Forsvarschefen 21-9-51, C.422/0. 3787.

- hinder the Russians in using Bornholm as a forward base or oblige them to use more forces for an attack because "lively NATO activity" would create doubt as to what forces NATO would use;
- support one's own forces in Northern Germany and Jutland by hampering the transport of Russian supplies for their forces (land transport through Poland was cumbersome) and
- indicate to Sweden that it might make sense to join the NATO forces. Sweden would be hesitant to take action in the Baltic alone, but if NATO showed force there, participation might be more attractive for the Swedes.

Possible operations were: air-bombing harbours, airfields and (future) missile batteries close to Denmark; mining harbour entrances from the air; direct attacks from aircraft, light warships, submarines on transport ships and other elements in the lines of communication.

The island of Bornholm was mentioned as important in surveillance before war and as a station for naval and air operations. If taken by the Russians, it could serve same purposes for them. But the island was not important in Soviet operations aiming at taking Zealand. Strong naval presence by NATO in the Baltic might force the Russians to allocate much stronger forces to take the island, if they so desired.

Strong NATO naval and air presence in the Baltic would also in war interfere with Russian LOCs securing supplies to land forces advancing in Northern Germany.

The memorandum therefore – clearly inspired by Heye's paper quoted above – called for more demonstration of NATO naval power in peacetime. The Danish navy alone could not do much, but frequent visits by a combined NATO naval task force using aircraft carriers, cruisers and destroyers plus marine infantry in the area would indicate to the Russians that NATO was prepared for counter-attacks. Such temporary presence would presumably also impress the Swedes and the populations of Russian-dominated areas in the Baltic.

The memorandum was addressed to Danish military leaders and the minister, but the reaction from the political side is not reflected in the archives. However, only one year later the theme was indirectly discussed during the preparation of the NATO exercise MAINBRACE. The decisions in the wake of the exercise did not leave any room for the wishes by the Danish C-in-C for any NATO task force to demonstrate force in the Baltic.

But the idea of a NATO naval task force became reality 16 years later with the STANAVFORLANT – albeit at a much more modest level.

Stationary forts or mobile batteries?

This case concerns the financing of Danish coastal forts and it was, unlike many of the other cases in this chapter, never discussed in public. But it is an important example of the consequences of being in disagreement with the NATO top brass.

In 1947–48, a second Danish naval commission was to recommend on the implementation of the ideas of a former commission on building new coastal batteries.[43] They analysed the costs and benefits of mobile 150 mm batteries – instead of the traditional fixed property ones. Each gun weighed about 14 tons and it took between two and three hours to prepare it for action. The maximum speed was 40 kilometres per hour, and transport required good quality roads. Radar and a communication system for fire directing was imperative. For air defence, each battery of four guns needed six 40 mm and three 20 mm guns. Furthermore, the battery needed an infantry company for ground defence. All in all, one battery would need about 450 men and cost an investment of about five million kroner – half the planned costs of the preferred solution, a stationary battery on Stevns; or a little less than the planned costs of one 250-ton submarine.

The commission ended up with a proposal building new forts at strategic points. After Denmark joined NATO, a governmental commission analysed the Danish defence and recommended that new forts be built at the southern entrances to the Danish straits.[44] One year later, the navy included two forts in its investment plans, one at Stevns and one on the southern part of Langeland.

The ensuing years would show that the distinction between fixed and mobile batteries formed a watershed between military experts; a severe disagreement between NATO and the Danish C-in-C nearly stalled the construction of the two new forts in 1952.

The Danes wanted to get NATO money to reduce the costs for the Danish treasury. The Military Assistance Advisory Group (MAAG), which oversaw the American weapon help to Denmark, however, was very critical towards the Danish plans.[45] They saw fixed forts as easy to pass, isolate or attack from land. The Danish Joint Chiefs of Staff responded that the decision was based on the facts that the guns were available and could be installed relatively quickly and then were ready for action. Mobile batteries, on the other hand, were not available, would

---

[43] Bogason, Peter. *Søværnet under den kolde krig – politik, strategi og taktik*, 33–36. København: Snorres Forlag, 2015.
[44] Ibid., 55.
[45] Larsen, Margit Bech. "Vejen til Danmarks sidste kystforter: Stevnsfort og Langelandsfort 1945–1954." *Fra Krig og Fred* 2014/1 (2014): 181–234.

not be available in a foreseeable future and would require special training which the Danish forces could not set up within the present organisation.

The critique was not welcome in Denmark and it only confirmed the Danish perception that the Americans and SACEUR's staff were uninformed about the military geography of Denmark and the Baltic approaches. The Danes held the formulation that "Denmark is the key to the Baltic" dear and saw the forts as key assets in guarding the minefields that were planned to keep the Russians in the Baltic and prevent them from entering the North Sea to fight the NATO transport system from the USA to Europe.

The Danes made a strong case for having NATO finance the two forts as part of the Infrastructure Programme.[46] At first, AFNORTH rejected the suggestion because the forts were not "infrastructure" – as for instance the base harbours being planned. The Danes retorted that the forts were built only because of NATO – if Denmark were alone, one would never dare to do so against the Russians: first, the forts only merited existence due to the fact that Denmark had to block the narrows for NATO to prevent the Russians from reaching the Atlantic with their submarines; second, the blocking served the purpose of permitting NATO to bring in reinforcements to Denmark and Norway. In short, without NATO, no forts. AFNORTH accepted this line of thought and supported the claim vis-a-vis SACEUR. The supreme commander, on the other hand, did not give in. The official answer was that the forts did not fit into the categories of the Infrastructure program. But in addition, SACEUR added that "the whole history of warfare in modern times points to the fatal fallacy of reliance on such works".

The supreme commander's decision settled the discussion. CINCNORTH bit the bullet and told the Danish Joint Chiefs of Staff that he was worried about the possibilities of defending the forts from air attacks and that he would prefer ships and/or mobile batteries to protect the minefields. Denmark thus had to finance the forts out of their own pocket.

US aircraft stationed in Denmark?

In the early 1950s there was a comprehensive political and military discussion about stationing American and British aircraft in Denmark. There was a long debate – most of the military details unknown to the general public, but nonetheless much discussed by the media at that time – among Danish and foreign politicians, and the Soviet Union repeatedly expressed concern. This national and interna-

---

46 Ibid., 222–27.

tional political debate is laid bare in painstaking detail by Villaume[47] and shall not be repeated here beyond some quite decisive facts; the final decision was for the politicians to make, and they did not follow the advice of their military top and NATO. The Danish official analysis of the Cold War also analyses the debate with an emphasis on international politics and foreign policy.[48] In this section we focus on the military analyses of the issue, based on documents which have recently been made accessible; they were not so when Villaume made his groundbreaking work.

In January 1949, Norway was verbally attacked by the Soviets because of the possible, but not yet decided, association with NATO. The Norwegians reacted with a declaration that "The Norwegian Government will not join in any agreement with other states involving obligations to open bases for the military forces of foreign powers on Norwegian territory as long as Norway is not attacked or exposed to threats of attack", followed by an assertion in the parliament in March that it would not "grant bases for foreign military forces on Norwegian territory as long as Norway is not attacked or subjected to threats of attack".[49]

In Denmark, the situation was somewhat different; there was no Russian pressure. But when the country joined NATO in 1949, several politicians, both from the right and the left, had declared that this would not imply that foreign troops would be based in Denmark. This was repeated as late as in February 1951 with a reference to the Norwegian policy.[50]

In 1950, both Norway and Denmark had stressed (in October and December 1950, respectively) that granting military facilities to foreign forces in peacetime was out of the question. What constituted "war time" was not specified, however, and the Danish Ministry of Defence was aware that action in war time would presuppose some preparations in peacetime, e.g. communication lines, bases and other forms of infrastructure and various kinds of storage.

But discussions regarding the use of Danish facilities by British, American and Norwegian forces in war time had taken place already from early 1951.[51] The negotiations were based on some observations on the Regional Short term Plans

---

47 Villaume, Poul. *Allieret med forbehold*. København: Eirene, 1995; Villaume, Poul. "Amerikanske flybaser på dansk jord i fredstid? En studie i Danmarks base- og stationeringspolitik i NATO 1951–1957." *Historisk Tidsskrift* 15, no. 2 (1987): 238–98.
48 Dansk Institut for Internationale Studier, op. cit.
49 SHAPE. *SHAPE History Volume II*, 157. Versailles: SHAPE, 1959.
50 Villaume, "Amerikanske flybaser på dansk jord i fredstid? En studie i Danmarks base- og stationeringspolitik i NATO 1951–1957," 241.
51 Notat vedrørende militære baser og rettigheder indrnfor den nordeuropæiske region. YHM 4-5-51 Forsvarsministeriets 11. kontor 82-51/2.

of NATO made by the Standing Group in SG 26 in October 1950, that "the implementation (of defence plans) depends in certain instances upon the forces of certain member nations being granted military facilities in the territories of other member nations".

For the USA, there was a particular interest to make an agreement with Denmark regarding Greenland in those respects, and an agreement was made on 17 April, 1951. That agreement is not within the scope of this book.

The issues to be negotiated by Denmark, USA, Great Britain and Norway concerned a long list of rights to inspect, establish, occupy, operate, prepare, expand, protect, maintain, store and support air and naval bases and other military facilities which were significant for the execution of NATO plans. The policy stance of the Ministry of Defence was that these issues were to be negotiated individually with the three countries, and the ministry expected the USA and Great Britain to take the initiative. Norway was to be dealt with informally.

But over the summer of 1951 no initiative was taken. In October, a first indication that NATO would actively take an initiative towards stationing aircraft in Denmark came when CINCNORTH told the participants in a C-in-C meeting that this type of defence aid would be ready in the fall of 1952.[52] A few days later, the American general Taylor asked the Danish C-in-C whether the stationing of six to seven rescue aircraft, most of them helicopters, in Denmark would be possible. The C-in-C made it clear that in spite of the fact that such aircraft were unarmed, this required a political policy decision, and in his opinion, Danish politicians were not ready for deciding at this point of time, and if so, the decision might be negative. He would, however, mention it to the minister. To his minister he noted that General Taylor's request could be regarded as a first step towards stationing fighters and light bombers in Denmark. So on 30 October, the minister decided that no Danish initiative was to be taken, but he would allow the Danish C-in-C to investigate the issues informally.

In November 1951, the Air Deputy of AFNORTH wrote a memo[53] stressing that according to plans, the number of aircraft demanded by 1953 in the region was 934, the number delivered by the Danish air force was 154 and the Norwegian number was 226, all in all 380 units. That left AFNORTH with a gap of 554 aircraft which might be filled by foreign assistance. Some had suggested a rotation of aircraft between Denmark and Norway to avoid accusations that they were permanently stationed. But such a solution appeared to be out of step with reality: it

---

52 Letter HEM from C-in-C to minister of defence 30-10-51 C. 6/0. 4621.
53 Translation into Danish of COMAIRNORTH note 24-11-51, Forsvarsministeriet 11. kontor 82–7/51.

required a double set of airfields, two systems of supply and a costly and risky move of a large number of personnel and aircraft in a precarious situation of imminent attack.

The Danish Ministry of Defence analysed the problems:[54] Given that an expansion of aircraft had already been touched upon in the Emergency Plan, it was time to prepare the politicians for a broader policy stance towards stationing of foreign forces in a not too distant future; particularly naval and air forces, whereas army stationing was unlikely until NATO entirely lost confidence in Danish defence (sic!). The immediate positive consequences – improving the readiness of forces – were seen as crystal-clear by the office writing the memo, but, obviously, problems in national and international politics could arise. Nationally, the majority of the population was expected to welcome a strengthening of the defence, but a negative minority was to be kept in mind. Internationally, the NATO countries would hardly understand a negative policy stance. Regarding the Soviet Union, the possible reactions should be analysed more closely.

In early 1952, the issue of stationing aircraft came up again from documents by the TCC. The Danish C-in-C apparently had foreseen this, so he wrote a letter on the matter to his minister,[55] stressing that air power was an absolute precondition for operations by the army as well as the navy, and aircraft for that purpose had to be at hand. Since Denmark did not have the required number of aircraft, foreign aid was necessary in the shape of aircraft stationed in Denmark already in peacetime, accompanied by ground personnel servicing the units. It would take some time for them to learn the specifics of the Danish territory and adjacent waters. A possible, but less desirable alternative could be a rotation of aircraft among several NATO-countries. The C-in-C called attention to a comparable need for stationing naval forces which had to be present all the time since they could not be moved as fast as aircraft (as we saw above regarding offensives in the Baltic). Consequently, the C-in-C recommended that the politicians approve the principles of stationing air and naval forces in Denmark in peacetime, and persuade the population to understand that this was to be seen as a guarantee by NATO for Danish security, not as yet another occupation.

Denmark was an ideal location for fighter bombers which could easily reach a large number of enemy airfields and ports in the Baltic from Denmark and initiate a bombing campaign during the first days of a confrontation, destroying aircraft, ships, infrastructure and lines of communication.

---

54 Notat vedr. stationering af en "Air Rescue Flight" i Danmark, Forsvarsministeriet 11. kontor 11-12-51 82-77/51.
55 Letter HEM from C-in-C to minister of defence 1-2-52 C. 6/0. 111.

Such use was planned in the Strategic Guidance Directive no. 1, stating that "for the northern flank, the (first) object will be to hold base areas in Denmark and Norway for offensive and counterattack operations".[56] This concerned naval bases as well, but in this chapter we shall stick to the airfields. SHAPE set the goals for aircraft in AFNORTH to 865 by 1952–53. But Denmark and Norway did not have, nor did they plan to have, such an air force. They did not have the financial strength to do so.

Hence, the TCC in February 1952 recommended that foreign forces should constitute 40 per cent of the available aircraft: in Norway, one USAF group; in Denmark, two USAF groups, and two RAF wings.[57] At this time the defence of AFNORTH relied heavily on land and naval forces which would not be mobilised until an emergency state – and this would take some time. Therefore, the ability to react immediately and the efficiency of the air defence system and the defence and support of the air forces were crucial. Lack of air power would critically affect the ability to ensure the security of AFNORTH in war.

If one took just the numbers into consideration, the demand for external aircraft became rather obvious. But different actors discussed below used different sources for their claims and hence figures do not always square exactly.

The 1953 Lisbon goals were for Denmark 175 fighters or fighter-bombers and 20 night fighters, and for Norway 150 fighter-bombers. If one took all possibilities of assistance into account, only 80 per cent of that number could be attained.[58] If the planned foreign wings did not materialise, a military disaster would be imminent in case of a Russian attack – in terms of civilian losses, in terms of material destruction and in terms of missing support for army and navy.

The Russians used the TCC plans to protest against any idea of stationing foreign forces in Norway, and in the end the Norwegians did not deviate from the promises. But for quite some time, Norwegian politicians in the cabinet hoped for another solution, accommodating NATO which had suggested the stationing of a wing (75 aircraft) of American fighters in peacetime. But realizing the problems on the political side, NATO aired the solution mentioned above with only 25 aircraft present at any time in Norway while the rest of the planes were stationed on the other side of Skagerrak, in Northern Jutland, to be transferred to Norway when necessary.

The Danes, however, were not keen on this idea[59] because they already faced an offer from NATO of permanently stationing two wings – each comprising 75

---

56 SHAPE, *SHAPE History volume I*, 341.
57 SHAPE, *SHAPE History volume II*, 161.
58 Minutes from meeting "Forsvarsmøde" 24-10-52, Forsvarsministeriet 11. kontor 86-778/53.
59 Minutes of meeting with CINCNORTH 26-4-52, Forsvarsministeriet 11. kontor 12-5-52 101-3/52.

American fighter and light bomber planes – at two airfields in Jutland. One wing more might be difficult to house in terms of airfield space, but the wish increased the NATO-political pressure. The Danish politicians now realised that they might have to reverse their previous standpoints of no-stationing, but they were not happy to do so.

In other words, NATO had spotted the difference between Denmark and Norway in terms of having a binding policy (Norway) and a less binding series of political stances earlier on the theme (Denmark) and now put pressure on Denmark to help makie an all-encompassing plan for stationing foreign aircraft in AFNORTH's southern part.

What was at stake? In a series of meetings in the spring of 1952, the military magnitude of implementing such a program became clear, as did the problems of Danish politicians to accept the plans.[60]

For NATO and the USA, implementing the program was a comprehensive task. New aircraft had to be ordered and produced; pilots and service staff had to be trained; air control systems to be developed; service systems to be set up etc. The number of pilots and support staff for an American wing of 75 aircraft would be about 3,000 people. Preparing a wing for stationing would take about one year. Therefore, commitment from the host-countries-to-be was essential in a rather early phase. As a minimum, a declaration that the country was prepared to receive visiting air forces now and in the future was warranted. This was a solution circumventing the realities, but soon it turned out that the support staff had to remain in Denmark, once they were deployed. Such an influx of Americans in an airfield in the Danish countryside could not remain unnoticed by the local population – after all, one could not lock them up in the barracks – and a negative reaction was what the politicians feared.

But this was what the NATO chiefs pressed for. On the Danish side, the military top agreed in principle, but the politicians pressed for less binding decisions. For instance, they wanted to accept airfields to be built, but without an binding agreement on stationing. They also might accept to receive visiting forces and gradually expand the purposes by having exercises with them. The purpose of such a strategy would be to gradually let the population get used to seeing foreign troops in Denmark. On another count, the politicians felt that one should be careful not to anger the Russians who might initiate repercussions, for instance in Finland.

---

60 Minutes of meeting with CINCNORTH in Danish Ministry of Defence 17-3-52 82-77/52; minutes of meeting 26-4-52, Forsvarsministeriet 11. kontor 12-5-52 101-3/52.

However, for a while the Danish politicians believed that the mood of the population might swing to a more positive stance towards stationing foreign aircraft and they told SACEUR so. But the cabinet turned down the idea of having aircraft slated for Norway stationed in Denmark because a new airfield in the countryside would mean loss of farm land which was important for the Danish export economy.[61] They suggested that an airfield be built in Schleswig-Holstein for the "Norwegian" wing, but the chief of air forces from AFNORTH did not second such a plan.

In late August 1952, the Ministry of Defence summed up the situation, apparently fearing a reversal of policy:[62] Denmark was ready to start work reinforcing the two airfields (Tirstrup near Aarhus and Vandel in South Jutland); a team of American experts was ready to discuss the technical details of an agreement between Denmark and the USA regarding stationing American personnel; Danish political declarations of commitment were persuasive and SACEUR had approved the work on the airfields as a common NATO project (i.e. financed 96 per cent by NATO). Therefore, a reversal of the Danish policy would create very negative reactions in NATO; one might fear that NATO would more or less be inclined to give up Denmark in the defence plans. The note then discussed in some detail a proposal of having the Americans pay for two wings completely manned by Danish personnel, but the conclusion was that Denmark would risk losing credibility in NATO because until now the Danish policy stance had been that it could not increase its military personnel, so a sudden recruitment of 6,000 would indeed undermine Danish credibility in NATO. The Ministry recommended that the matter be presented to the Danish Military Top.

The C-in-C responded with a note[63] analysing the demand for personnel if the wings with 75 F84 fighter-bombers in 1953 and 75 F86 fighters in 1954 were to be manned by Danish personnel. The count came to 2,679 men, of which there were about 300 officers (of which 33 pilots), 192 other pilots, 390 non-commissioned officers, 1,400 privates and 380 civilians. In addition, there were military personnel for ground defence. Given the fact that the present plans for accommodating eight squadrons in the Danish air force were already difficult to fulfil because of a lack of officers and enlisted men, such an expansion was hardly possible. Furthermore, pilots could not be trained to the task within the time horizon. Consequently, although an expansion of the Danish Air Force would be welcome in the Danish population, the C-in-C could not recommend it and strongly advised that the ideas of

---

61 Minutes of meeting between NATO SACEUR Ridgeway and Danish ministers 3-7-52, Forsvarsministeriet 11. kontor jour. 19-10/52.
62 Note 28-8-52 from Forsvarsministeriet 11. kontor, j.nr. 82-77/51.
63 Forsvarschefen 6-9-52 PM HEM vedr. mulighederne for udbygning af flyvevåbnet, Forsvarsministeriet 11. kontor. 82-77/51.

stationing foreign aircraft be implemented. If that were not the case, Denmark would face a serious loss of prestige among NATO partners, and one should take note that the American personnel for the first wing was already in training. One alternative might be to prepare airfields and supplies for receiving aircraft if war broke out, but the process was technically difficult and risky and could not be recommended. Strategically, this might lead NATO to give up strengthening the air forces and move the defence line (which prevented the Russians from leaving the Baltic) from the Danish straits to the Kattegat and Skagerrak waters, with bases in Southern Norway, i.e. in effect giving up the defence of the Danish isles and Southern Jutland.

The C-in-C had based his numerical analysis on a PM from the Danish air force,[64] but he did not follow the conclusion of that PM. The C-in-C of the air force had recommended an expansion of six wings in the Danish Air Force in order to create a better balance for Denmark in NATO issues, and alternatively a reduced Danish expansion and a smaller American permanently stationed force.

The Committee of Foreign Affairs discussed the issue on September 10, 1952.[65] The minister of foreign affairs stressed that the airplanes were solely for tactical use in Denmark and vicinity, and the majority of the parties supported the stationing but did not approve it formally. One party – the Radical Left which one year later became decisive in Danish defence policy – declined support, referring to Norway and a previous statement on non-stationing by the Danish Foreign Secretary in March 1949 when he negotiated Denmark's membership of NATO.[66] The Social Democrats reminded the cabinet that it was unfortunate if the Norwegians maintained their "no".

At this time, there were four types of stationing in play: the two original "Danish" wing, one "Norwegian" wing and now the British would like to add 64 light bombers in Schleswig, but with a possibility of redeployment to the Danish Karup airfield. In the fall months of 1952, quite comprehensive negotiations about the stationing of two American wings on Airfields Tirstrup and Vandel were carried out as technical issues, and tentative agreements reached.[67]

---

64 PM HEM Mulighederne for ved udbygning af flyvevåbnet at gøre en stationering af allierede flyverstyrker i Danmark i fredstid unødvendig. Danish Air Force 3-9-52. Flyverstaben, NATO-kontoret: KC. Klassificeret kopibog (afklassificeret) (1950–1965) 2.
65 Minutes in Rigsarkivet.
66 Lauridsen, John T., Rasmus Mariager, Thorsten Borring Olesen, and Poul Villaume. *Den kolde krig og Danmark*, 119. København: Gads Forlag, 2011.
67 Notat af 5-1-53 vedrørende fredstidsstationering af NATO–flyverstyrker i Danmark. Forsvarsministeriet 11. kontor 82-77/51.

While these technical issues were discussed, the political aspects came under public scrutiny. Of course, one should not be blind to the possibility of a number of other uses of the American aircraft, particularly outside Denmark. One use – bypassing national borders – would be as SNOWCAT (see chapter 5) escort for long-range strategic bombers coming from airfields far away; and this became part of the Danish public debate in the fall of 1952.[68] The discussion became international when Denmark became involved in an unfortunate diplomatic exchange of views with the Soviet Union in October 1952 about stationing foreign aircraft,[69] referring to the Bornholm agreement (see earlier). They claimed that handing over "war bases" to foreign armed forces would equal threatening the Soviet Union.[70] Specifically, the Danish government "deviated from its position of not accepting foreign troops on Danish territory, a position stated in 1946" regarding Bornholm.[71] The minister of foreign affairs denied any analogy.

As the clock ticked, CINCNORTH was pressed by SACEUR to have decisions made; air forces were in high demand and poor supply, and he needed more forces for AFCENT. So if the Danes could not make a decision, the supreme commander would reallocate the "Norwegian" wing to AFCENT. On 3 of December, 1952, the regional commander therefore had a meeting with the Danish minister of foreign affairs, presenting three alternative ways of distributing the 289 American and British aircraft among Danish and Schleswig airfields.[72] In two alternatives, a new "main" airfield (fully equipped) had to be built at Karup; in one, the demand was reduced to an "alternative" (less facilities) airfield. Unfortunately, the Americans, CINCNORTH and the Danes each preferred their own alternative, the Danes leaning towards the cheaper alternative airfield in Karup. The regional commander hoped that the Danes would switch to a "main" airfield but would accept any of the alternatives, if it meant that AFNORTH could keep the third American wing.

Although there were strategic and political grounds to do so, the British Chiefs of Staff in January 1953 decided that due to costs of building infrastructure and inconvenient logistics and training conditions, the plan of bombers had to be

---

68 Villaume, "Amerikanske flybaser på dansk jord i fredstid? En studie i Danmarks base– og stationeringspolitik i NATO 1951–1957."
69 See detailed analysis in DIIS report Dansk Institut for Internationale Studier, op. cit., pp. 271–75.
70 Udenrigsministeriet, *Dansk Sikkerhedspolitik 1948–1966*, 92.
71 Udenrigsministeriet. *Dansk Sikkerhedspolitik 1948–1966. Bilag*, 289. København: Udenrigsministeriet, 1968b.
72 Letter SECRET from CINCNORTH to Minister of Foreign affairs n.d., but written 5-12-52, Forsvarsministeriet 11. kontor 82-77/51.

abandoned.⁷³ Consequently, the Danish Ministry of Defence concluded that the "Norwegian" wing now could be based in Schleswig with a redeployment airfield in Torp, Norway.⁷⁴ Nonetheless, CINCNORTH would like an "alternative" airfield built in Karup to increase Danish capacities for receiving supporting aircraft. He asked for a swift decision on approval of the alternative airfield in Karup (which the Danes supposed would be built for NATO money), and the stationing of two American wings in Denmark. The problems with the British had to be decided on when one knew whether their alternative was viable.

Early January in 1953, the status therefore was that the Danish Ministry of Defence was ready to negotiate an agreement about the two remaining wings with the Americans.⁷⁵ There was in principle still a possibility of a British wing (formally cancelled mid-February⁷⁶) and an American wing, but the main points of the discussions concerned American stationing in the Tirstrup and Vandel airfields. However, the ministry called attention to the fact that, for a long time, the cabinet had postponed a political decision about the main issue: stationing foreign aircraft in peacetime. Going on with the negotiations without political clearance might lead to a *de facto* positive decision because of the quite large investments approved along the road.

The Russian contentions about Danish aggression were repeated in January 1953.⁷⁷ Due to the death of Stalin the Danes did not answer directly, but a speech by the minister, Ole Bjørn Kraft, in April, was held as an informal answer. The minister referred directly to the Soviet note and stressed that Denmark had no aggressive intentions at all. And in particular, the agreement had no validity whatsoever beyond Bornholm. Denmark had created a Danish administration, and "furthermore, we have maintained this position and therefore *de facto* behaved as if a commitment for the future was in existence." Denmark "never has considered, or even planned to, stationing foreign troops on Bornholm". Denmark would "always take the special conditions of Bornholm into consideration, given its geographical position".⁷⁸ This wording could be understood as accepting the So-

---

73 C.O.S. (53)54 28th January, 1953 Allocation of fighter bomber aircraft to SACEUR – possibility of stationing in or near Denmark.
74 Notat HEM af 5-1-53 vedrørende fredstidsstationering af NATO–flyverstyrker i Danmark. Forsvarsministeriet 11. kontor 82-77/51.
75 PM HEM om fremskridt i forhandlingerne om fredstidsstationering Forsvarsministeriet 11. kontor 21-11-52 82-77/51.
76 Notits HEM om fredstidsstationering Forsvarsministeriet 11. kontor 17-2-53 82-77/51.
77 See detailed analysis in DIIS report Dansk Institut for Internationale Studier, op. cit., pp. 279–84.
78 Udenrigsministeriet, *Dansk Sikkerhedspolitik 1948–1966. Bilag*, 300.

viet demands, at least regarding Bornholm – despite the fact that the whole speech concerned a denial of the Soviet interpretation.

During the discussions, the bourgeois government had all the time kept contact with the Social Democratic opposition as part of the ongoing compromises regarding the development of Danish defence. The Social Democrats had been relatively positive in the Committee on Foreign Policy in September 1952, but later in the fall of 1952 when the public debate took form, the Minister of Foreign Affairs told his colleagues that he felt some wavering among Social Democrats – apparently after the Swedish Social Democrats had expressed concern because they saw the stationing as a threat to Sweden's position.[79] A couple of months later, the Danish party would not support the proposal and asked for a quid-pro-quo. They demanded a stronger NATO allocation of ground forces to Schleswig-Holstein to balance a stronger Danish risk (by accepting the aircraft), but this was not possible (see the section earlier on Schleswig-Holstein).

When the government initiated concrete discussions with the Americans about an agreement in January 1953, the ministers realised that the Social Democrats were about to block the case. They did briefly after by formulating five requirements for their support to the government – such as that the aircraft could not be stationed outside Danish territory unless approved by the Danes, and furthermore that contingent had to be under Danish supreme command.[80] These were unacceptable to the Americans. None of the representatives had discretion to change their policy stances and therefore the discussions stopped by the end of January.[81]

In February, the polling firm Gallup conducted a poll on the stationing issue with the result that 20 per cent of the population supported stationing, but 57 per cent were against. Gallup chose not to publish this result, but a number of leading politicians were probably informed about this outcome.[82] By March, SACEUR and CINCNORTH agreed to postpone the issue until after the Danish elections.[83]

The "borderless" use of aircraft, and probably the possibility of use in Northern Germany and Southern Norway, easily explains the American rejection of the attempt to limit their operations to Danish territory. The clause of only using the airfields for tactical use – on which the parties agreed – was formulated to prevent the use for fighters allocated to escort bombers passing over Danish territory.

---

79 Foreløbigt referat af forsvarsmøde 24-11-52, Forsvarsministeriet 11. kontor 26-11-52.
80 Dansk Institut for Internationale Studier, op. cit., pp. 277–78.
81 Notat HEM om udviklingen i fredstidsstationeringen . . . Forsvarsministeriet 11. kontor 29-9-53 82-77/51.
82 Lauridsen, Mariager, Olesen, and Villaume, op. cit., p. 120.
83 SHAPE, *SHAPE History volume II*, 175.

At the annual meeting of the Social Democrats in June 1953, the chairman followed these sentiments and declared that due to the popular resistance and because of Norway's no to a stationing, the policy of the Social Democrats would also be a "no". Consequently, as the Social Democrats won the election in the fall, the Danish government, now Social Democratic, rejected the offer of stationing aircraft "under the present conditions" in the opening statement by the prime minister on October 6.

One consequence, however, of the yearlong discussions was that two Danish airfields – Tirstrup and Vandel – were reinforced but their status changed from "main" to "alternate", meaning that there were few facilities for ground staff. So in times of crisis each of them could take in a wing of American or British aircraft, but makeshift facilities then were to be set up. On the other hand, the supplies stored there were more comprehensive than on other alternate airfields. The work on runways etc. had started in 1952, and according to the Danish Ministry of Foreign Affairs, the decision by NATO to allocate the funds were not dependent on permanent stationing of foreign aircraft.[84] Therefore, the Danes now at least could say that they had prepared for the worst case, and nothing prevented NATO from using those airfields in exercises – or stationing aircraft there in times of severe crisis.

One might also say that because of the condition of Danish approval of use outside Denmark mentioned above, the Americans probably would not sustain the offer,[85] but those negotiations were not taken up again. As to Schleswig-Holstein, the aircraft wing south of the border also withered away as the Danish Brigade was not reinforced.

The decision on the alternate status of the two airfields was accepted by the bourgeois opposition in the Foreign Policy Commission half a year later, on the 8 April 1954. They did not do this gladly and criticised the government, but they did not want to renew a public discussion.

Behind closed doors they had protested and agreed to keep most of the contents of a meeting in the Foreign Policy Committee on December 2, 1953 secret from the press which normally would get a briefing about the themes of the discussions.[86] The new Social Democratic cabinet had held an arms length distance to the Danish C-in-C and did not inform the opposition about this. The point was that the new Minister of Defence had held a meeting in Copenhagen with SACEUR

---

[84] Notat HEM om udviklingen i fredstidsstationeringen . . . Forsvarsministeriet 11. kontor 29-9-53 82-77/51.
[85] Villaume, "Amerikanske flybaser på dansk jord i fredstid? En studie i Danmarks base- og stationeringspolitik i NATO 1951–1957," 290.
[86] In general, the minutes of the Committee are kept secret for 30 years.

on the 18 November 1953[87] – quite exceptionally without the participation of the C-in-C who therefore was not really in a position to give the comment expected by the former minister at the meeting in the Committee.

But the reaction – a very critical one – of the C-in-C came on December 8, i.e. six days after the political Committee meeting. The minutes from the cabinet meeting with the supreme commander were the point of departure for his letter. The minister was quoted for saying that a stationing of foreign aircraft in peace time "not in a decisive way will change the possibilities for defending Denmark and Norway" and furthermore that "an addition of 150 aircraft in Denmark at this time would not mean increased military security for Denmark if the Soviet Union would start a war today." Admitting that the addition would not mean a total turnaround, the C-in-C wanted to call to the minister's attention that an increase from 190 to 340 aircraft was nearly a doubling of the air forces in Denmark. Furthermore, the C-in-C would refer to the statement by SACEUR that "The Danish decision results in a definite and substantial change in the military strength that I may count on in the Northern area . . . In my judgment there is in fact no alternative solution of a degree of military effectiveness which I consider satisfactory."

The C-in-C continued that it was not realistic to think that Allied aircraft could come to assist immediately if hostilities broke out, and especially not now when technical ground facilities in Denmark were taken out of the plans. He quoted SACEUR: "Allied Command Europe will not be able at present to earmark a specific unit or units for post D-day deployment to Denmark." Furthermore, there was hardly any hope for fulfilment of what the minister had hoped for, namely that aircraft carriers would be close to Denmark in the first critical days of a war, nor was there any guarantee that they could come later. That would among other things depend on the presence of necessary land-based aircraft to secure air power of the area. Furthermore, even though there might be air forces present in Northern Germany, there were no indications that such would be used in Danish air space; they were reserved for land military operations in Northern Germany.

The lack of the 150 aircraft would mean a fatal reduction of air power for NATO in the area. Consequently, naval and army operations would lack the necessary support from the air. The C-in-C of course acknowledged that the final evaluation of the international was the privilege of the political institutions, but he had to point to the military fact that the lack of the 150 aircraft, present and ready in Denmark, meant severely reduced abilities to resist an attack.

---

87 C-in-C letter HEM 8-12-53 to Minister, C. 582/0 5144.

There is no answer from the minister in the archive, and the opposition was not informed in any detail about the critical stance of the C-in-C.

During the annual NATO-meetings in Paris one week later, several solutions were discussed; we shall lay the details aside. But an American proposal was found to be negotiable, and one week later the Americans came to Copenhagen to do so. They suggested to strengthen the Danish air force by getting more American-built aircraft than already planned, and a corresponding pilot training as an extension of the existing military aid programme.[88] But as we saw earlier, a large increase of Danish aircraft had been analysed in 1952 with a quite negative conclusion. The minister consequently answered that since such an increase would incur running costs for maintenance and personnel in the future; it would require a change in the Danish defence plans and a re-allocation of the military budget. This would be very difficult. Therefore, the minister could not recommend the American offer. This was grudgingly accepted by the Foreign Policy Committee on April 8, 1954; the bourgeois opposition maintained, however, that a solution might be to accept foreign stationing of aircraft, to be gradually reduced until full force was reached by 1962. The minister then quoted the British minister of defence, Lord Alexander, a "considerable military authority", for maintaining – when challenged – that such stationing was of minor importance.

All in all, the two American wings originally suggested were allocated to AFCENT and thus lost for AFNORTH. Only the already planned deliveries of the American aircraft were carried out. From 1958, 59 F-86D SABRE and 72 F-100D/F SUPER SABRE were delivered to the Danish air force, but they only replaced the existing fleet of F-84G THUNDERJETs which were all gone by 1961.[89]

What had the Danish minister of defence hoped for? In a private conversation in October 1953, the recently appointed minister had indicated to the Danish Chief of the Navy that if the ongoing EDC-negotiations about the future German involvement in the defence of West Europe went well, the Germans would take over the defence of Schleswig-Holstein, and the Americans would station aircraft there. The chief of the navy had answered that there was not enough airfield

---

[88] PM: Møde hos forsvarsministeren den 21-12-53 kl. 15 vedrørende amerikansk End-Item-Aid. Forsvarsministeriet 11. kontor 82-77/51.

[89] Thus Villlaume's claim – that the 162 fighter- and fighter-bombers delivered 1956–61 roughly corresponded to the two USAF wings and that Denmark consequently got what it needed, but under Danish command in Villaume, "Amerikanske flybaser på dansk jord i fredstid? En studie i Danmarks base- og stationeringspolitik i NATO 1951–1957," 278 – is quite misleading. In 1956, 30 British HAWKER HUNTERs *replaced* the Danish METEOR squadron, and from 1958 132 American fighter-bombers step by step *replaced* the old THUNDERJETs.

space for that in the area.⁹⁰ But nonetheless, the minister appeared to hope for such a solution which would reduce the need for more aircraft in Denmark. The Danish joint chiefs of staff did not share his opinion. They thought that air forces south of the border would be allocated to the defence of that area only, and consequently there would still be a serious deficit of aircraft for defending Denmark. The EDC treaty was voted down on August 30, 1954, in the French Parliament, thrashing the hopes of the Danish minister.

Integrated air defence in Europe

From the start, air defence in NATO was basically a national task, and the nations developed air defence systems on the basis of individual doctrines and national concepts of operations. The systems were not necessarily compatible and hence not guaranteed to reinforce one another.⁹¹

Given the comprehensive threat from WAPA aircraft, SACEUR soon initiated analyses to make the NATO efforts at air defence more encompassing and coordinated. Therefore, the Standing Group in 1954 asked the supreme commander to carry out a study of what was needed for integration. The large scope of the study is indicated by these themes to be taken into consideration ("but by no means limited to . . . "): control and reporting systems including radars; types and location of aircraft; anti-aircraft artillery and missiles; passive defence such as black-outs, balloons; counter-measures and offensive air action etc.; logistics support and infrastructure; manpower and training; command, control and coordination structure.⁹²

The analysis set up some requirements with a time horizon for 1957, but the subsequent questioning of national representatives revealed serious deficiencies:⁹³

> Only about 55 per cent of the aircraft required were expected to be available by 1957, and a large proportion of these could be expected to be ineffective because of the shortage of trained technicians and pilots. Reserves of operational aircraft were virtually non-existent, and this situation was not expected to improve . . . Of 2,350 medium anti-aircraft batteries required, only 675 batteries had been formed . . . and only 390 batteries would have sufficient modern equipment by 1 January 1975. . . . No guided missiles were expected to be available for air defence before 1957.

---

90 Reported in the minutes of the Danish Joint Chiefs of Staff October 16, 1953.
91 SHAPE, *SHAPE History – The New Approach 1953–1956*, 205.
92 Ibid., 215–16.
93 Ibid., 219.

Furthermore, the existing radar did not afford continuous coverage. There was insufficient radar coverage in Norway and Denmark and very little likelihood of continuous plotting above 30,000 feet. In Holland and Belgium the radars were obsolete. ... So few operators and men were available in SHAPE that only one group was capable of manning radar on a 24 hour basis. Radars only operated four hours a day in the North.

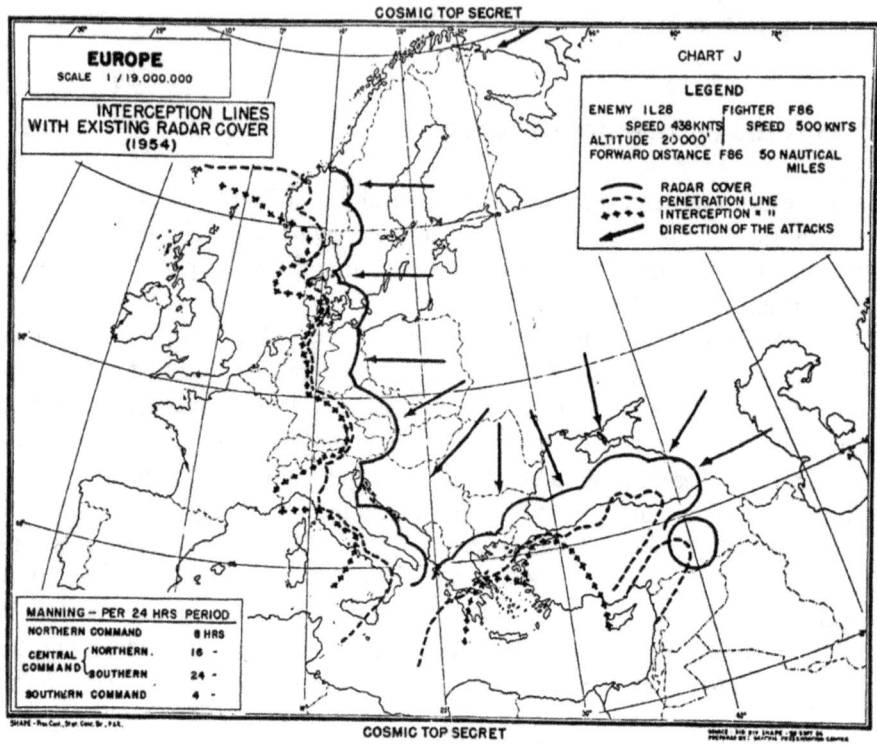

Figure 6.4: Radar coverage 1954 is the full line to the east; interception is the strong-dotted line showing that fighters cannot protect most of Norway, Denmark, Northern Germany and most of Italy from incoming Soviet aircraft. Source: SHAPE 626/54.

It was obvious to SACEUR that some of these deficiencies were due to the fact that air defence had been national. He therefore wanted more NATO insight and control and suggested that the supreme commander be given a stronger role in air defence in the future.

This led to the formulation of MC 54, a document that gave the supreme commander a coordinating role, recommending air defence steps to be taken within Europe which was divided into four air defence zones. But he did not get any powers to directly control air defence; this would be a future task. For now, the

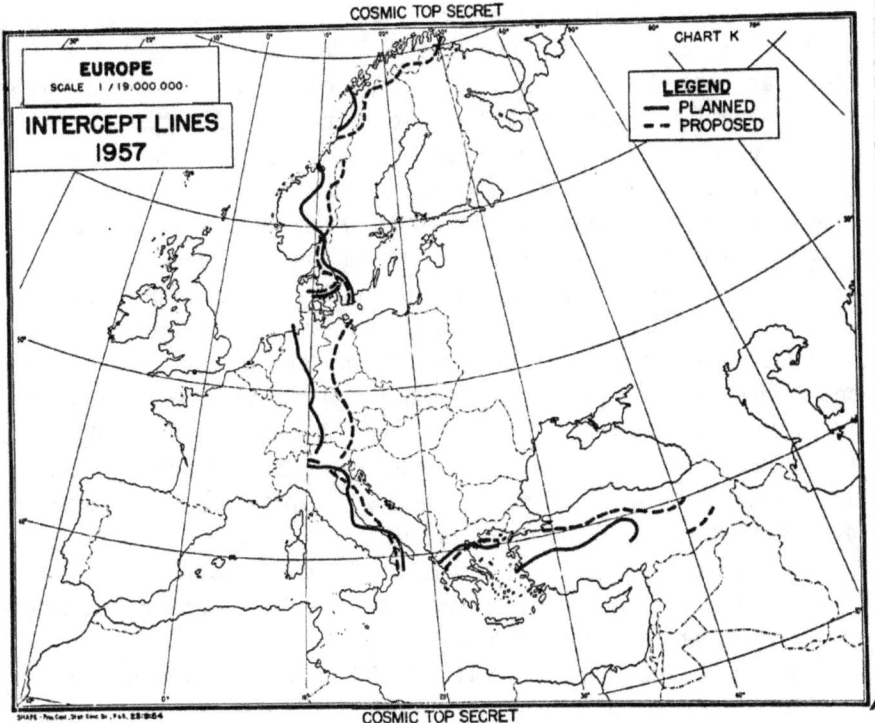

Figure 6.5: Hoped-for interception lines 1957 with new radar and command system. Source: SHAPE 626/54.

role was to make the regions organise for future commands and induce the countries involved to invest in the endeavours.

As time went by, SACEUR improved his organisation for the task; however, it soon became evident that coordination was worth its while but in the end it would be necessary – for the air defence system to work – to create an integrated command system.

In December 1957, the supreme commander pointed out[94] that while some progress had been made, especially in planning, it had become more and more obvious that real improvement in air defence now depended on shaping a gradual evolution from present national air defence organisations into an integrated Allied Air defence system. Three factors weighed in. First, the need for air defence would be at an absolute maximum during the first few hours of a war, necessitating now a change of operational control from national to allied, but this would almost cer-

---

94 SHAPE. *History 1957*, 246–47. Mons: SHAPE, 1967a.

tainly result in chaos. Therefore, the war system had to be in place and operational already in peacetime. Second, important future weapons would be surface-to-air missiles, and those had to be directed at an international, not a national scale; enemy missiles did not respect national borders and had to be intercepted at the earliest time possible. Third, the emerging build-up of German forces under NATO (not national) command necessitated a non-national system of air defence.

So it was necessary to build an integrated system of air defence. In order to respect national interests, the following principles had to be followed:

National air defence units were to be assigned to SACEUR in peace and war; air Defence units would not be used for other tasks without national approval; national forces would in general be deployed in national territories; the composition of Allied staffs was to be broadly in proportion to the forces contributed to each Allied Command; centres and stations would be manned primarily by the nation in whose territory they were located; logistics and administration would remain a national responsibility; and finally SHAPE-prepared air defence plans would be coordinated with individual nations.

The supreme commander also pointed out that the proposal was for integration of the command and control system, not the integration of the national fighting units which were operated by the system.

One of the four zones was AFNORTH which had the air forces under national command when in action. The air space was divided between Norway and Denmark, and in the south (Schleswig-Holstein) between Denmark and the 2. ATAF (the Northern air command of AFCENT, directing British, Dutch and later German war planes). Normally, these commands would run their business without operational contact with the neighbouring command. This could create problematic situations. First, an enemy could exploit the chances offered by flying on the border line between two commands – which NATO command was then to react, and how would they coordinate their actions? Second, if and when enemy aircraft crossed borders, how to coordinate actions between two NATO commands. In the late 1950s, more problems were created by the introduction of surface-to-air missiles: how to coordinate the target determination as well as the division of labour between interceptor aircraft and missiles. This was especially obvious on the border between AFNORTH and AFCENT.

The state of the art of Danish air defence 1959

The Danish Air Force analysed the problems of integrating the Danish air defence system in 1959.[95] It illustrates some of the problems perceived by SACEUR.

---

95 Note Forsvarsministeriet 1. kontor HEM Ledelse af luftværnsraketenheder og bemandede luftjagere i forsvaret af Danmark 16-2-59 125.2.2.

The present Danish warning- and control systems for airplanes and the system for the planned NIKE missiles were not compatible and, therefore, only some degree of coordination could be attained. Furthermore, there was a significant difference in the response time for missiles and manned aircraft. Missiles could be fired rapidly after identification of enemy aircraft. Manned aircraft depended on the reaction time of the pilot and the manoeuvrability of the airplane.

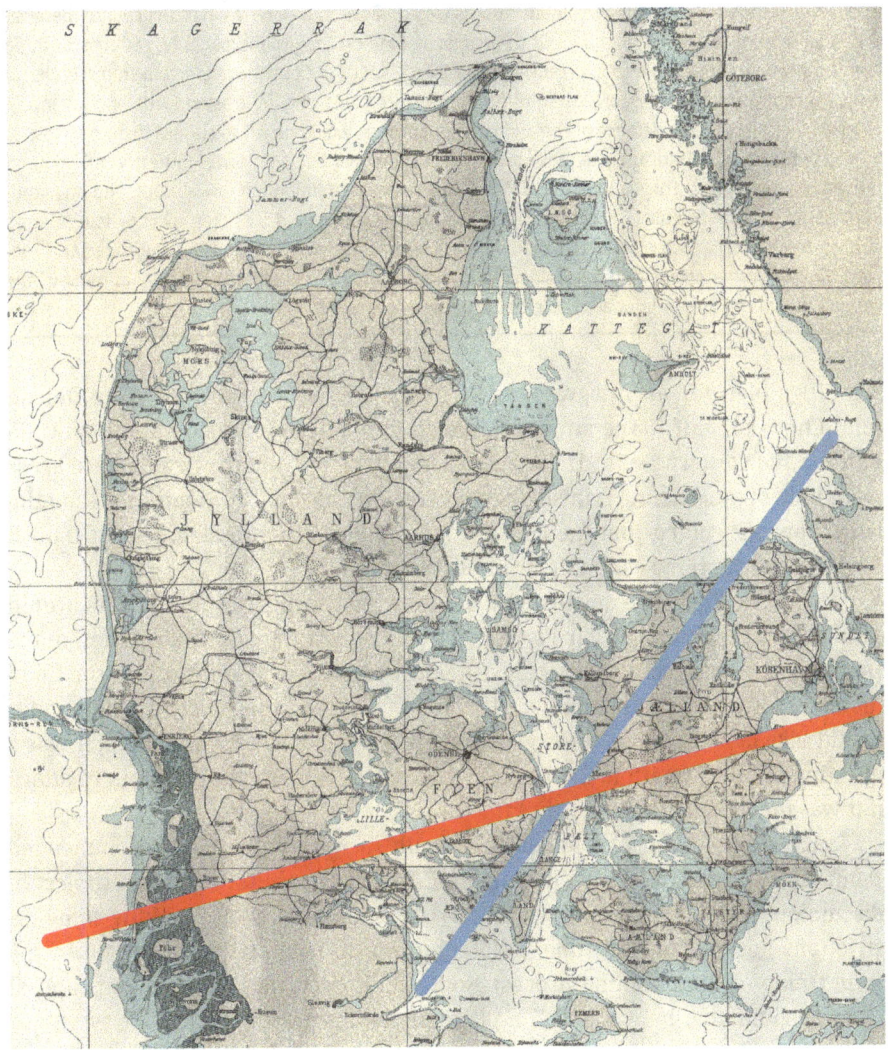

Figure 6.6: Lines of fighter interception in high altitude (blue line, aircraft from Karup) and low altitude (red line, aircraft from Aalborg) in 1959.

Air fighters took a relatively long time to be ready for action: the preparation phase on the airfield, the start procedure and relatively low airspeed. These factors required a relatively long distance, a sort of no man's land between the enemy- and one's own airfield. This, however, was not possible for Denmark; the distance was quite short. The Danish fighter airfields were in Northern Jutland, and the response factors determined that middle and high altitude attacks from Poland or East Germany could only be intercepted north of a line between Flensborg and Halmstad (in Sweden), meaning that most of Zealand and Fyn were not defendable. Low altitude attacks were difficult to counter all over the country because the radar systems were not adequate. If the response time on the ground could be reduced to three minutes it would be possible to intercept at a line a little south of Copenhagen, drawn from Tønder to Køge. In conclusion, the present system of fighter defence could only be trusted to defend Jutland. It followed logically that the defence of Zealand and Copenhagen would be left to surface-to-air missiles.

Consequently, the Danish air defence system in 1959 would be as follows. Fighters would defend Jutland in all altitudes. They would also defend the area east of Jutland in low altitude and any landing operation from the air – it was assumed that these tasks would be taken over by low altitude surface-to-air missiles later. Missiles would defend Copenhagen and Øresund in all altitudes and Zealand, Fyn, the other straits and the Baltic Sea in high altitudes. Low altitude defence in most of the country would require additional missile batteries and new radars.

SACEUR's plan for an integrated air defence was well received by the Danish Joint Chiefs of Staff.[96] The air force pointed to the need for cooperation with AFCENT in the western Baltic. If the operational systems from the two defence areas were linked, the existing Danish system of command could still find use. The ministry, however, noted that the constitution did not permit assignment of Danish forces to the supreme commander in peace time.

Denmark therefore suggested a solution that in peacetime SACEUR would send orders to the Danish Air Force Command with a copy for information to the Danish C-in-C who could then block the order (and it was crucial that the Command be aware of this possibility). If war was obvious, the supreme commander would take over anyway. In the grey zone when war might be imminent, it was a question of interpretation; the Danish rules prescribed any military unit to attack if it was under direct military threat.

SACEUR, however, was not satisfied with such a solution and recommended Denmark to formally approve his plan MC 54/1 in the Military Council, subject to discussion later during implementation; the plan had a clause making some restrictions possible at that time.[97] No compromise could be reached within the time frame of the planning process, so SACEUR decided, backed by a proposal from Belgium, that he would go on planning the integrated air defence system as

---

96 Note HEM Notat om integrering af luftforsvaret i Europa. Forsvarsministeriet 11. kontor 5-5-58.
97 Minutes HEM from meeting 2-12-58 Udenrigsministeriet 105.I.1.0.1.

set out in the proposal, hoping that the problems of political (in Denmark: constitutional) character would be solved over time.[98]

The technical improvements of Danish air defence due to the investments in the integrated air defence system were tangible. The fighter command centres were merged into one in Karup, capable of tracking 290 objects and handling 50 fighter engagements over Denmark at the same time; an alternate command, capable of tracking 164 and engaging 36 objects, was established in Vedbæk. Both centres would integrate the use of fighter planes and missiles. The radar systems were modernised, they became better protected against jamming and data transmissions were made semi automatic. The system was linked to NATO's early warning radar systems; one of those located on Bornholm, another on the Faroe Islands.[99]

The problems were not solved to the supreme commander's satisfaction because the Danish constitution was firm on the ban against foreign control of Danish forces in peacetime. MC 54/1 was replaced by MC 54/2 which Denmark did in principle approve by letter on 15 February 1962, subject to negotiations about the constitutional clause.[100] But the release to NATO command was made easier by an organisational change in 1965, to which we shall return later.

Summing up: Trouble spots in military policy in the 1950s

The Soviet Union occupied the island of Bornholm in May 1945. They left in April 1946 under an agreement with Denmark that Denmark would "fully execute the administration" of the island, meaning without help from other (military) forces. This declaration caused much political trouble in the years to come because the Soviets used it to demand that no military forces came near the island. Denmark protested against that interpretation, but in actual fact the Danes observed it rather closely until the 1980s, much to the chagrin of NATO commanders. The situation became quite threatening in December 1961 when the BALTAP command was decided upon and the soviets claimed that Denmark "supported a German attempt to conquer territory in the area". The Danes denied this and the Soviets kept their distance.

The defence of Schleswig-Holstein – so to say the entrance to Denmark/Jutland – was weak throughout the period until BALTAP was created in 1962. Two

---

98 SHAPE, *SHAPE History 1958*, 202–3.
99 Note HEM Forsvarsministeriet 1. kontor 19-1-61 and note 7-12-60 on SACEUR's long term requirements, both 125.0-4. Also note HEM 16-11-61, 11. kontor on SACEUR's langtidsplan for luftforsvaret af Europa.
100 NATO MCM-22-62 21-2-62.

Danish and Norwegian brigades had the task until 1953 when the Norwegians withdrew for other NATO tasks. The Danes remained with a reduced brigade which could in no way defend the area. The issue was addressed several times, but the Danish Social Democrats were opposed to strengthening the brigade without NATO assurance about more forces, and NATO did not want to assure anything without a stronger Danish commitment. Therefore, the defence until 1958 was reduced to the demolishing of the Kiel Canal bridges and then withdrawal to the Danish forces on the other side of the border. When the Germans took over in 1958, a much stronger force was set up, combined with the Danish forces in Jutland.

Storage of military resources became a NATO issue when Germany was re-armed: for army forces withdrawing northwards through Jutland or being cut off from supplies from the rest of Germany; and for the German navy using Danish harbours or bases for its ships, as well as for reinforcements using Danish airfields. SACEUR wanted NATO to have supplies for 90 days, initially split between Denmark and Britain, later mainly in Denmark. Storing supplies for German forces, however, turned out to be a hot potato in Danish politics, and a formal solution took time to reach – one solution was to name the phenomenon "NATO" supplies, another to grant the supreme commander, rather than the Germans, the authority to distribute the contents. Symbols matter in politics!

The defence of the Baltic Approaches was basically very passive in character, but there was a Danish wish for a more offensive strategy. In 1951, the Danish C-in-C sketched out a plan for a large-scale naval force into the Baltic. He suggested that NATO set up a standing naval force as an "armed force in being" consisting of battleships, aircraft carriers, cruisers, destroyer flotillas, small fighting craft and a large landing craft pool, supported by fighters and bombers, and having army landing troops stationed in the vicinity. The ships were to be stationed in Norwegian, Danish and West German ports and have very frequent operations in the Baltic, showing force and making exercises: air-bombing harbours, airfields and (future) missile batteries close to Denmark; mining harbour entrances from the air; direct attacks from aircraft, light warships, submarines on transport ships and other elements in the lines of communication. In spite of its character of a mission command, integrated with army and air forces, such a plan was in stark contrast to the conditions of littoral warfare in the Baltic – waters were shallow and distances to land-based aircraft short, making operations with aircraft carriers and battleships very risky. The plan never materialised, but 16 years later, a much smaller force, the STANAVFORLANT, was set up to indicate NATO's resolve, when necessary. It had mission characters, but only involving the navies. It was only to operate in the Baltic if NATO had air superiority.

Denmark had a tradition of using coastal batteries, and after WWII several commissions reviewed the pros and cons of various types. The German occupiers had left a large number of such fortifications in 1945, and the Danes decided to keep a few and to build two new forts on the southern part of Langeland and on Stevns, for general defence and for guarding the minefields planned for war time. Mobile batteries were considered, but deemed too costly and difficult to manage in a time of crisis: the guns were heavy, many Danish roads could not support them and the setup of AA-guns and fire direction system required much space and personnel. The Americans and SACEUR, however, disagreed strongly and blocked NATO financial support for the construction of the fixed batteries. Denmark therefore had to finance the forts without support, and the Danish military top felt that this confirmed that the supreme commander's staff did not understand the military geography of the Baltic Approaches.

Over a period of two and a half years a policy for stationing foreign, mainly American, aircraft in Denmark was discussed among politicians and military chiefs. The result – a Danish no to such stationing in peacetime – is well known and most of the political processes researched, but the details of the military side's arguments and the attempts to make them heard by the cabinet have not been known. They are now declassified. In 1950–51, ways of rotating aircraft and naval vessels in wartime among Danish, British and Norwegian bases were discussed in a mood of "need-to-do-it", based on military advice, but formal agreements never materialised, and the Danish government did not press the issues. In early 1952 AFNORTH started a process of negotiating the stationing of American aircraft in peacetime in Norway and Denmark, based on the obvious deficit of national military airplanes to fulfil NATO's war plans. Norway and Denmark did not have the means to do so. They could muster up to 380 aircraft where SHAPE demanded more than 800. The discussions about foreign stationing concerned between 225 and 300 aircraft, mainly American, but British also were on the palette at certain times. Even so, only about 80 per cent of SHAPE's demands could be fulfilled. The negotiations were complex in terms of solutions to what "permanent" would mean and included permanent processes of rotation of wings among the countries. The costs were larger, the more permanent the aircraft were stationed, but so were the resources the receiving countries had to deliver. But NATO would bear the brunt of the costs. An American group of 75 aircraft required personnel in the vicinity of 3,000.

The Danish C-in-C several times pressed the government to accept the stationing, and for a while he seemed to succeed. He analysed the costs of expanding the Danish air force and found it impossible (contrariwise to the chief of the Danish air force, though) due to costs and a likely lack of qualified personnel. SACEUR was involved several times, noting that unless Denmark acquiesced, the aircraft would go to AFCENT. In a series of last minute meetings in December 1952 and January 1953, a solution was analysed, but now the Social Democratic party began to cast doubt on the project and set up a series of demands that they probably knew the Americans could not accept. In the light of an upcoming election the theme petered out. After the elections the political powers changed into the hands of the Social Democrats. But the new cabinet was dependent on a minority party that was dead against foreign forces, and the Danish public sentiment also appeared quite negative – imagining the effect of 3,000 Americans residing in and around a rural Danish village.

The final outcome of the yearlong discussions was that two Danish airfields – Tirstrup and Vandel – were reinforced but with few facilities for ground staff. So in times of crisis each of them could take in a wing of American or British aircraft. The cabinet had held the Danish C-in-C on arms length and did not let him participate in a series of meetings with SACEUR. The C-in-C reacted with a lengthy note, from which we shall quote: "The Danish decision results in a definite and substantial change in the military strength that I may count on in the Northern area ... In my judgment there is in fact no alternative solution of a degree of military effectiveness which I consider satisfactory."

He quoted the supreme commander: "Allied Command Europe will not be able at present to earmark a specific unit or units for post D-day deployment to Denmark."

The note was not made known to the political opposition. The airplanes were lost for AFNORTH and allocated to AFCENT.

The air defence in Europe was a national task in the early 1950s, and hence the systems of direction and control differed among countries. This created weaknesses in the defence of any area close to a national border. From 1954, SACEUR initiated a large-scale project to coordinate and integrate the air defence in Europe. First a comprehensive analysis of all aspects of the air defence – from types of aircraft over guns and missiles to logistics, personnel and direction and communication systems. The analysis showed large–scale deficiencies in numbers of aircraft, missiles, control systems and communication. SACEUR therefore planned a system of direction and coordination within four zones of Europe. For the Baltic Approaches, particularly coordination between the Danish Air Command and the 2. ATAF in Northern Germany would be important. Regarding missiles, they would be very important for the defence of Zealand and Copenhagen because of the short warning time; Jutland could be defended by air fighters.

One might conclude, then, that AFNORTH and NATO did much to integrate the air forces and the air defence of the Baltic Approaches with the rest of Europe, but apart from a few mission command exercises with naval units not much happened to integrate the defence. Denmark was quite stubborn politically by preventing the stationing of reinforcement forces in peacetime.

Chapter 7
NATO's New Approach and The Danish "No" to nuclear weapon: A Janus Head?

In the 1950s, the governments of both Great Britain and the United States relied increasingly on nuclear weapons in their national security policies. This was followed by a shift away from large-scale conventional forces. In Britain the policy was named the British Global Strategy and in the USA the New Look security policy. Since USA and Britain were leading players in NATO, it comes as no surprise that they put pressure on the NATO organisation to apply these principles to NATO's strategy. Growing acceptance of the New Look policy in NATO was marked by the approval of two new strategy documents in 1954, MC 14/1 and MC 48, which relied heavily on the use of nuclear weapons.

During the first years of NATO, the decision about using nuclear weapons rested with the governments that actually had such weapons in stock. We shall ignore Great Britain and France which never offered these weapons for use by other countries, and focus on the American weapons. They remained under the control of the President, but over time the possibility of use by other forces than those American came on the agenda of NATO. The discussion below concerns the political and military discussions of the use of nuclear weapons. We shall also ignore the international politics dimension set by the relations to the Soviet Union which several times made clear its dissatisfaction with Danish policy. That theme has been analysed by several authors.[1]

First we shall briefly take a look at the concepts of nuclear warfare, particularly at the level of operation: transporting and firing the weapons for tactical use. The second and third sections of the chapter deal with the objectives of the New Approach and the comprehensive military campaigns that were to fulfil those objectives. Then follows the reactions by the Danish defence system – what to do under this new nuclear umbrella, and how to prepare for using such weapons. The politicians, however, soon grasped what the consequences of a nuclear attack could be, namely devastation of large areas, and the political parties to the left decided that they would not permit the use of such weapons on Danish territory. But in many ways it was a discussion with a Janus Head, and the "no" was

---

[1] Agger, Jonathan Søborg, and Lasse Wolsgård. "Den størst mulige fleksibilitet: Dansk atomvåbenpolitik 1956–60." *Historisk Tidsskrift* 101, no. 1 (2001): 76–110; Dansk Institut for Internationale Studier, *Danmark under den kolde krig. Den sikkerhedspolitiske situation 1945–1991. Bind 1: 1945–1962.*

never without some form of "maybe". Consequently, the Danish military prepared for the use of nuclear weapons for about a decade, and the possibility of using them was part of many exercises.

Nuclear tactical warfare – A primer

Our main theme is the defence of the Baltic approaches within AFNORTH. As we shall see below, the Danish and Norwegian governments did not permit the storage of nuclear weapons in their territories in peacetime, and neither country was party to bilateral nuclear agreements with the US – a prerequisite for having access to using such weapons in war. But Schleswig-Holstein was part of West Germany, and most of the waters were international, not national, and the USA operated naval and maritime air nuclear forces in the area.[2] Hence, it was possible to operate with nuclear weapons in certain areas of AFNORTH, and certainly within the Baltic Approaches.

There are few sources from the 1950s about the uses of tactical nuclear warheads. So we must go to the early 1960s. What were the consequences of a nuclear exchange of warheads by then? One scenario stems from an command post exercise in Eastern Germany with 1,200 NATO warheads and 1,000 Soviet warheads being employed.[3] The consequences were devastating; we shall not go into any detail except that in their first "strategic" nuclear strike, Warsaw Pact forces would attack a total of 1,200 stationary NATO targets (422 in West Germany) within 30 minutes with approximately 400 nuclear attacks on mobile targets such as troop concentrations or nuclear weapons.

Regarding the use of NATO nuclear war heads, the question arises whether the governments in the area of the Baltic Approaches would have a say. Until 1962 there was no guarantee that this would be the case, but the so-called Athens Declaration by the British and American governments in April 1962 laid down the following elements of a deliberation with the NATO council (i.e. not the individual country):[4]

---

2 Gregory, Shaun R. *Nuclear Command and Control in NATO*, 54. Hounds, Basinstoke, Hampshire: Macmillan Press Ltd, 1996.
3 Schulte, Paul. "Tactical Nuclear Weapons in NATO and Beyond: A Historical and Thematic Examination." In *Tactical Nuclear Weapons and NATO*, eds Tom Nichols, Douglas Stuart, and Jeffrey McCausland, 32–33. US Army College: The Strategic Studies Institute, 2012.
4 Conclusion to Athens meeting NATO SECRET C-M(62)48 17-4-62.

- In the case of an unmistakable Soviet attack with nuclear weapons, NATO would respond in a scale appropriate to circumstances, and there would be limited possibilities for consultation;
- In the case of a full-scale Soviet attack with conventional forces, NATO would answer with nuclear weapons if appropriate; in this case there would probably be time for consultations;
- In the case of a Soviet attack not of the type above, and if forces could not be held back with conventional weapons, a decision to use nuclear weapons would be subject to prior consultation in the NATO council.

What, then, would happen in a situation of crisis? On the military side, the process was quite comprehensive. First, no nuclear weapons could be used without the approval of the President of the USA in tandem with one more person in the National Command Authority. This right, however, could be delegated – presumably during periods of crisis – to groups of persons at a lower level, and it would normally be subject to consultations with relevant parties, e.g. national governments. In practical terms, this was an opportunity to veto the nuclear weapon.

The procedure for nuclear weapons in "Aggression less that general war", i.e. local fights, was quite extensive.[5] The objectives were to halt and contain the aggression and to restore the integrity of NATO territory and to preserve the general war capability of nuclear strike forces. In contrast to the general war plan, the aggression less than war plan had no previously determined targets; they would depend on the developing situation. Therefore the procedure would be one of "selective release" which involved an exchange of messages between SACEUR and a subordinate commander about the circumstances as they arose. The message transmitting the supreme commander's approval would contain all the necessary information and authority to enable US weapons custodians to unlock and transfer weapons to the appropriate NATO commanders, and for them to employ the necessary procedures (see below).

The authorising procedure was elaborate. First, a request from a subordinate to the supreme commander had to be made; to speed the process up it would go directly to SACEUR with a copy to the commander in charge of firing. The format was standardised: it had to specify the type and number of weapons required together with a statement of the restraints or limitations to be placed on the use of the weapons. The names of commanders in charge locally had to be specified. And the question of why use nuclear weapons had to be answered in a concise way: a description of the situation, a specification of the actual threat, a statement

---

[5] Statement by deputy SACEUR PO/65/616 COSMIC 27-11-65 to Special Committee.

of why conventional weapons were not adequate and a discussion of the consequences of a disapproval.

Upon receipt of this message, the supreme commander would analyse the situation and deliberate with subordinate commanders, where relevant. If he considered the request should be approved, he would inform the NATO Council and request political authority; at the same time he would ask the US European Command for approval from the American authorities. If permission was granted, an execution message would contain code words that were transmitted to custodial and command and control centres, releasing for action.

Quick Reaction Alert (QRA)

SACEUR had a number of aircraft ready for immediate reaction with nuclear weaponry to attack the most urgent and time-sensitive targets. What happened if they were to be put in use? A British former pilot has told some of the story from around 1960.[6]

In 2. ATAF which commanded the air forces in Northern Germany, the British used the two-man crewed Canberra B(I)8 aircraft for a nuclear strike role based on low altitude bombing with the US-provided Mk7 1650 lb weapon. Four squadrons were allocated to the supreme commander as part of Britain's light bomber force.

The QRA aircraft would provide immediate response to SACEUR's call for strikes, and would be able to do that either individually or as the vanguard of a fully generated force if there had been enough time (from a period of alert state development) to the weapon loading and crew preparation to make the whole squadron available for selective release against targets on the supreme commander's strike program. Due to the Canberra's relatively low range of action the targets were almost all confined to tactical airfields in one or other of the Warsaw Pact satellite countries.

The primary QRA target was exhaustively studied by crews in regular sessions in the Operations Wing vault, and the day before a QRA watch started was a mandatory study day. Other sessions were programmed in with all the other routine training requirements. The crew's knowledge was regularly checked by visits of the so-called Weapons Standardisation Team; this was "a regular challenge to the memory glands".

The squadron operations were totally focused on low-level operation in 250 feet. The attack was a trifle mechanical, and involved pre-computing release parameters prior to take-off, which were set by the navigator on the release computer at the rear of the aircraft before he climbed aboard. In-flight adjustments were possible. There were two methods of releasing the bomb: the standard forward toss and the reversionary over-the-shoulder attacks. The approach speed was 434 knots. Just before release the plane had to increase altitude to 4,000 feet, which was triggered by pressing the bomb release button and waiting until the computer-driven timer ran down and gave the cue. After release there was a mildly aerobatic escape recovery from 4,000 plus feet back to the 250 feet approach height. Proficiency in this manoeuvre was of fundamental importance, both for consistent weapon accuracy and for one's own survival.

---

6 Wilkinson, P.J. "Offensive Operations – Strike." In *Royal Air Force in Germany*, Royal Air Force Historical Society, 71–85. Brighton: Royal Air Force Historical Society, 1998.

What happened in the battlefield on the ground? First, one should realise that the storage and delivery systems for weapons to be used and the entity actually launching the weapon were separate organisations. Weapons were stored at particularly secure places and heavily guarded. Guns, missiles and aircraft able to fire the weapons were somewhere in the theatre field. Delivery to the field could be made by truck, helicopter or by plane. Special units – always under US command to maintain the presidential influence on use – were at hand to bring the war heads to those who should fire them, and they followed special procedures to recognise one another. In peacetime, the weapons were stored at particular US facilities; the smallest would house about 25, the largest several hundreds. But during crisis periods, at a certain NATO alert level, some weapons would be deployed to places of operation – one, to make them available quickly, and two, to reduce the risk of the enemy bombing the larger arsenals and destroying large quantities in one blow.[7]

Second, it took time to make the nuclear warhead ready for firing.[8] If we take the 203 mm army howitzer as an example, one complication was that the warhead required careful assembly of about one hour right before firing in order to guarantee accurate detonation. Computation of firing data also took about an hour in the pre-computer era. In order to cause the projectile to detonate in the air over a target, careful use of data was necessary. To insure accuracy, two white phosphorous "spotting" rounds were fired to check data and make corrections. Although these were not fired over the actual target, it is safe to say that the Soviet side would see such firing as a warning of imminent nuclear attack.

MC 48 and the "New Approach"

After Eisenhower became president of the USA, he increasingly stressed the possibilities of using nuclear weapons and wanted such options as an integrated element of NATO's strategy. Shortly after General Gruenther took over as SACEUR in July 1953, he initiated a process of changing the strategic concepts for the defence of Western Europe in that direction. MC 14, which since 1952 had served as strategic guidance, was built upon a massive army and air defence system in Central Europe. It was clear, however, that the Soviets had more ground forces and more aircraft than the West, and the Annual Reviews (see chapter 4) revealed

---

7 Gregory, op. cit., pp. 95–96.
8 Burns, William F. "Tactical Nuclear Weapons and NATO: An Introductory Reminiscence." In *Tactical Nuclear Weapons and NATO*, eds Tom Nichols, Douglas Stuart, and Jeffrey McCausland, xiv. US Army College: The Strategic Studies Institute, 2012.

that it would be difficult to make the European members of NATO fulfil their quotas of military investment based on the Lisbon goals. Furthermore, the development of nuclear weapons continued with high speed, and it seemed obvious to the military top that nuclear weapons would be used in some capacity if war broke out.

At the CPX-4-exercise in April 1954,[9] SACEUR Gruenther gave an overall presentation of different aspects of the use of nuclear weapons. He offered as his opinion that if NATO states approved the plans under preparation, they would also make assurance that nuclear warheads would be used from the start of a war and not just as counter strike. As we shall see below, he did not succeed on that particular point.

The essence of what became known as *The New Approach* was presented in SACEUR's *1957 Capability Plan* and later formulated coherently as MC 70, valid for the period 1958–1963. The first formal step was taken in November 1954 when the NATO council approved the document MC 48, covering all NATO commanders, which explicitly integrated nuclear weapons in the policy of the alliance.[10] The formulation "in the event of aggression, NATO forces would be able to initiate immediate defensive and retaliatory operations including the use of atomic weapons" initiated the massive retaliation or massive response epoch of NATO. This was to be done by two separate types of force.[11] The Sword was the American air force and its strategic bombers were to wipe out Soviet infrastructure and major military targets during the first days or weeks of a general war. The Shield was all other forces in Western Europe which were to meet surviving enemy forces in a forward strategy towards the East – as time went by, increasingly with tactical nuclear warheads. But it also served a deterrent purpose by being so strong that in and by itself it would keep the Soviets from initiating a surprise attack.

If the Soviet Union initiated aggression, the response would be immediate with strategic (the Sword) as well as tactical (the Shield) nuclear weapons against the Soviet Union and its infrastructure, including airfields for its bombers. A war started in Europe would immediately escalate to a comprehensive all-out war, directed by the Americans who even had the option to attack the Soviets in a preemptive strike, if there were sufficient indices of them initiating an attack.

However, a decision to respond rested with the governments of NATO, not the military commanders, and many of the European politicians – not the British, though – had some reservations about an immediate retaliation with nuclear weap-

---

9 PM HEM Forsvarschefens notater om CPX-4, C.H.81/0.2001 12-5-54.
10 Pedlow, Gregory W, op. cit., pp. xvii–xviii.
11 Ibid., xix.

ons. Therefore, the concept step by step was modified over the ensuing three years and was reflected in the documents MC 14/2 and MC 48/2 from May 1957. Thus, MC 14/2 called for conventional forces to be able to deal with such lesser contingencies "without necessarily having recourse to nuclear weapons", and MC 48/2 called for NATO to be able to deal with "a limited military situation in the NATO area which an aggressor might create in the belief that gains could be achieved without provoking NATO to general war". To deal with such an eventuality, NATO forces had to be capable of acting "promptly to restore and maintain the security of the NATO area without necessarily having recourse to nuclear weapons".

Still, the paper stated that "in no case is there a NATO concept of limited war with the Soviets". Not all members of the NATO councils were happy with the formulations; in particular the Dutch delegation expressed reservations and therefore all NATO commanders got the directives, but also a printout of the political discussions preceding the formal decision.[12]

So, what were the commanders to do? MC 14/2 was an incoherent and self-contradictory document, formulating a non-nuclear way of acting while stressing that limited war was not a NATO instrument. A political compromise? Since this book has the military responses and actions as its primary focus, we shall not go into the intricacies of these political debates. The reader will find them elsewhere; for an overview regarding the above, see Heuser.[13] Suffice to say here that from the outset, there was political doubt about massive retaliation, and step by step it was softened until the formal change into "flexible response" in 1967, to which we shall return later.

The analysis – objectives and campaigns

The analysis forming the basis for The New Approach was comprehensive, with themes like the need for forces for the New Approach, Soviet capabilities, consequences of new weapons for operations, efficiency of conventional forces, structure and limitations of NATO logistics, the promises in integration, mobilisation of reserves and much more.[14]

1957 became a focus year in the ensuing years for all SACEUR's sub-commands because it was the planning horizon for The New Approach, and the supreme com-

---

12 Ibid., xx.
13 Heuser, Beatrice. "The Development of NATO's Nuclear Strategy." *Contemporary European History* 4, no. 1 (1995): 41–47.
14 SHAPE, *SHAPE History – The New Approach 1953–1956*, 31–32.

mander initiated a "Capability Study 1957" to be carried out by all sub-commands and later put together to a whole by SACEUR.

The supreme commander's planning group came up with a series of objectives for the New Approach, to be achieved by a series of campaigns[15] which we shall go through:

Objectives

The first category of objectives were the basic ones for survival:
(1) protecting shipping and lines of communication against Soviet attack so as to keep losses under a critical level;
(2) countering the Soviet nuclear and/or air attack sufficiently so that Allied will and ability to continue the fight would not be destroyed;
(3) keeping the Soviet ground attack from penetrating very far beyond the general area astride the Rhine/Ijsel; and
(4) preventing any Soviet advance in the south from severing the Mediterranean Command.

The second category of objectives were to delay Soviet progress and attack Soviet LOCs and concentration areas and to prevent the build up of enemy forces coming in from support areas.

The last category of objectives was made up of those further objectives which had to be achieved insofar as circumstances would permit – we only quote those relevant for the Baltic Approaches:
a. Hold in Western Germany as far to the east as possible.
b. Maintain a continuous front through Schleswig-Holstein and Northeast Germany.
. . .
g. Conduct limited offensive naval operations, primarily submarine and reconnaissance, in the Baltic.
h. Limit losses of Allied forces and territories from Soviet air attack.
i. Limit losses to, or interference with, Allied naval forces and shipping.

In effect, the defence in Europe moved towards the east from the Rhine to the river Weser and even nearly to the border to East Germany in the North; if

---

15 Ibid., 35–37.

successful, this "forward strategy" would save large areas in West Germany from becoming battlefields.

Campaigns

The New Approach had nine campaigns, of which we only shall discuss those five most relevant for AFNORTH and the defence of the Baltic Approaches. Behind the campaigns lay the premise that NATO's forces in much larger numbers than before were action-ready from day one of a war; that they were trained for nuclear warfare tactics; and that NATO would use nuclear weapons from day one, based on authority delegated from the member nations to SACEUR. Finally, there was also the premise that West Germany would be re-armed as part of the EDC and deliver a substantial number of army divisions for the defence.[16]

Below we introduce the essence of the relevant five campaigns, followed by some details giving the reader an idea of how comprehensive the nuclear potential was, together with some details of the military actions involved:[17]

– Interdiction of the Soviet Build-up of Support and Sea Lines of Communications. To limit Soviet capability rapidly to replace losses, conduct amphibious operations and/or build up forces, a preplanned air interdiction campaign would be undertaken in the Eastern European area. Air and submarine action would also be conducted against Soviet sea LOCs in the Baltic, to be accomplished by naval and air forces.

Most of the attacks were counter-air operations, with comprehensive attacks (e.g. QRA) carried out against the enemy's assets behind the front line, preventing the provisioning of resources to entities that were active in the front line. In the Baltic, the campaign would be carried out by airplanes and, as we saw in chapter 5, the Danish Air Force might take part, but not by carrying nuclear weapons.

– Arrest of the Soviet Land Advance in Western Europe. An active defence would be conducted, thereby channelling the Soviet forces and inducing sizeable concentrations. These concentrations would then be attacked with air, ground and missile delivered nuclear weapons. A maximum Allied effort with all forms of atomic support was to be made to hold on to the Rhine. This campaign included

---

16 France turned down the EDC plans in August 1954, but this led to the integration of West Germany in NATO in 1955, so the German participation was ensured nonetheless.
17 Italics added by PB. Detailed assessments and military force figures (including nuclear weapons) are quoted from the original Capabilities 1957 document SHAPE 330–54.

the defence of Schleswig-Holstein, blocking Soviet forces from entering Danish territory (Jutland).

The fundamental principle in positioning ground forces was to use them to create large and concentrated targets of the enemy for NATO nuclear weapons.[18] Minimum NATO covering forces, probably one battalion every 12,000 to 13,000 yards, would man the initial obstacle for the enemy. In Schleswig-Holstein, that defence line would be along the Trave-Elbe Canal up to the Baltic Sea. If the enemy penetrated the covering forces and crossed the river or canal, they would have to "mass" troops prior to an attack on AFCENT's main positions.

No Danish forces were planned to participate in this campaign after the Germans' rearmament – designated to take place in the last year of the Capabilities plan, 1957. The plan was a sort of guarantee that the Danes did not have to plan for a battle in Southern Jutland. See below for the Danish territory defence.

– **Combating of Soviet Attacks on Allied Shipping, Convoys and Naval Forces.** Maximum local protective measures for Allied shipping, convoys and naval forces were to be instituted to cope with the Soviet submarine, air and mining threat on D-Day and immediately thereafter. Progressively, mining reconnaissance, anti-submarine warfare, and other appropriate operations in the Danish Straits area were to be undertaken to impose effective closure of these exits. Firm control over land areas contiguous to both Straits would be maintained, and any Soviet-acquired bases in the North Sea were to be subjected to nuclear attack.

The campaign in the Baltic would involve (air) attacks on enemy naval bases, interdiction of enemy LOCs and ships, establishing naval control of the Baltic exits and countering any enemy amphibious attacks. But importantly, the task also was to control allied shipping, organise escort activities and maintain shipping centres for receiving goods (Naval Control of Shipping, NCS). In that respect, the New Approach did not change the traditional understanding of littoral warfare, but NCS had not been spelled out in detail in NATO documents before.

The New Approach document acknowledged some of the demands to littoral warfare in that it took note that the Danish narrows were shallow and bordered by very low lands and islands on which defences such as batteries would be relatively easy to locate and exposed to destruction by atomic attack – a rather frank critique of the Danish decision to build fixed forts two places. The document, however, interfered with the Danish understanding of how to wage littoral war there by suggesting that the narrows could be closed, at least temporarily, by ae-

---

18 Ibid., 57.

rial mining – a tactic which had been opposed several times by the Danish Joint Chiefs of Staff, (see chapter 5). As long as the Allies held the adjacent land masses, they were capable of denying the straits to the enemy by operating mine layers, controlled minefields, detection devices, air, surface and submarine patrols. To a certain degree they could then be kept open for Allied use.

The figures for naval forces in the document combined the Danish and Norwegian navies and were valid for the mobilisation day (with M+30 in parenthesis); the numbers for the tasks above in the Baltic Straits would probably be about half:

Destroyers 2 (4);
Destroyers Escort: 6 (11);
Patrol craft: 10 (31);
Mine sweepers: 18 (46);
MTB: 18 (28);
Mine layers: 8 (23);
Submarines: 6 (10).

In addition, the document set up expected West German (EDC) ships from 1957 with 18 Destroyers Escort, 60 MTBs, 60 mine sweepers and 24 maritime aircraft. This was the first time German forces were explicitly used in NATO planning documents.

The existing naval forces were insufficient to prevent enemy seaborne assaults or infiltrations of Zealand. However, submarine operations in the Baltic could cause some damage to enemy amphibious invasion forces, and counter attacks on Soviet naval bases, allied mining and limited submarine operations in the Baltic would reduce the risk involved, as would land forces available to oppose these operations. Soviet difficulties in supporting forces that had been landed by sea after SACLANT forces were in the area (see below) further reduced the risk to the Allies.

Regarding nuclear weapons, estimates of the Soviet naval base complex in the Baltic indicated that approximately 18 A-weapons and 5 H-weapons could be profitably employed on these objectives.

– **Arrest of the Soviet Land Advance in Denmark.** With a view to arresting the Soviet advance south of the narrows area, operations were planned at the base of the Cimbric Peninsula and coordinated with action planned against the threat from Northern Germany, in order to channel the Soviet attack and force it to mass. The enemy would then be attacked with air, ground and missile delivered atomic weapons – thus preventing the enemy from entering Jutland. The main risk for Jutland would therefore be landing troops from the air. The same risk plus risk for amphibious landing would threaten Zealand.

The forces available for the defence of the Baltic Straits – in essence, Danish territory – were
- Army: three divisions infantry supported by some tank forces.
- Air Force: 150 fighter-bombers and 25 interception fighters plus a small number of recce and transport planes. Some conventional air support might be provided to this area from the SACLANT Carrier Task Force, when this would not detract from their principal tasks in an atomic delivery role, and from naval operations in the eastern Atlantic area (see campaign for north Norway below).
- Navy: see above.

As to nuclear weapons, some were to be used in the Schleswig-Holstein Campaign. At the time of formulation of this plan, the Danish government had not taken any decision on the use of nuclear weapons. For the defence of Denmark proper, NATO estimated that 40 to 60 nuclear weapons might be used in support of the forces in this area. Although there might be some requirement for the use of nuclear weapons against Soviet amphibious efforts towards Denmark or against lodgements resulting from airborne operations, no weapons were allocated in the plan (but reserves were available). This was because in the overall plan enemy airfields and naval bases which could be used for such purposes would have been destroyed by campaign number one and three (presented above).

– Combating the Soviet Land Advance in Norway. As nuclear capabilities of SACLANT carrier forces became available after completion of their initial pre-planned counter-air and naval missions, these would be concentrated on interdiction and close support in Norway, Sweden and/or Denmark, depending on criticality of the situation.

This last campaign was for Northern Norway, so we only take note of the possibility that aircraft carriers could later deliver air support to the Danish narrows (from the North Sea), probably including beaches where Soviet troops would go ashore. But such NATO attacks might include the use of nuclear warheads, and that would change the game parameters of littoral warfare in the Baltic Approaches.

The New Approach: Danish general strategy

In November 1954, the Danish ministry of defence wrote a paper summing up the strategic consequences of the New Approach for Danish defence, based on a draft version of the 1957 Capability study which was summarised above.[19] The note had a quite critical stance, but it was heavily biased towards the ground forces and had little to say about the naval and air defence forces.

The note repeated two requisites for the New Approach – that immediate use of nuclear warheads was authorised and that West Germany is rearmed. Then six points for adaptation of strategy and tactics in the New Approach were commented on:

1. NATO-forces had to be technically able to use nuclear warheads. Ministerial comment: this was hardly relevant for Denmark.
2. In case of war NATO forces had to be authorised to use nuclear weapons from the very start. Ministerial comment: it was politically unlikely that such an authority be granted in advance.
3. An effective alert system had to be created to make NATO able to react as soon as there was substantiated information about a Russian attack.
4. Top priority had to be given to improve intelligence systems and radar systems and create broader coverage of the planned radar system. Ministerial comment: no. 3 and 4 were technical in character and would increase military costs and demand for personnel.
5. Standing forces and their training in nuclear warfare had to have high priority together with the integration of German forces in the NATO defence. Less priority should be given to non-standing (mobilised) forces. Ministerial comment: this would create greater dependence on our standing forces (which are small and exist in order to wait for and defend mobilisation processes).
6. The tactics and organisation of NATO forces had to be adapted to the demands of nuclear warfare. Passive defence elements also had to be adapted, particularly if there was a need to spread aircraft to a large number of airfields. Ministerial comment: this could become quite costly if airfields were to be equipped with sub-terrain hangers etc., and less costly if they just reinforced alternate reserve airfields.

Finally, the ministry took note that the Danish Joint Chiefs of Staff wanted SACEUR to reserve nuclear warheads for use in Denmark (see below). The NATO draft version had no such provisions. The ministry acknowledged this as a Danish

---

19 Notat. De militære NATO-myndigheders bedømmelse af NATO's forsvarsmuligheder i de kommende år. YHM Forsvarsministeriets 11. kontor 12-11-54 711/54.

military request but stressed that one had to keep the probable Danish political problems with such warheads in mind.

In short, the paper was very hesitant towards NATO's intentions. It was written as a basis for instructing the Danish member of the Military Council advising the Standing Group. In so far as the reservations to the use of nuclear weapons were spelled out in the final plan, the member was authorised to accept it.

In an addendum, the tactical consequences for Danish defence were drawn up.[20] Since a major part of the defence was fought out in Schleswig-Holstein by non-Danish forces with comprehensive use of nuclear weapons, the Danish ground defence of Jutland would be reduced to fighting airborne troops or groups coming by amphibious means to target airfields and military key points and infrastructure. Therefore, the main theatre for the Danish territorial defence would be Zealand against paratroopers and amphibious landings. But the area had no nuclear warheads reserved by SACEUR. An early attack would be difficult to resist because the Danish defence still depended on mobilissing reserves. But one could expect SACEUR to bomb the Baltic bases and harbours required to build up the Soviet forces for the attacks.

The Soviet forces might use nuclear weapons against certain troops, airfields and the major harbour cities, but since those facilities would be important for their own use after they were conquered, the Soviets might refrain from such use. Note was taken that after two weeks, aircraft carriers might become available.

The note discussed the tactical profile of the Danish defence. In order to prevent the Soviets from taking Zealand and gain control of the Baltic straits and landing forces by various means, the defence had to
- blocks the narrows for passage;
- stop any Soviet attempt to access Jutland and the Danish islands; and
- attack enemy Baltic bases used for aircraft and amphibious craft, if possible by nuclear weapons because the enemy was particularly vulnerable in those positions.

Reconnaissance by aircraft and the navy was indispensable to create information about the intentions of the enemy, but Danish resources were not sufficient for recce in the Baltic. There was also a need for aircraft to support nuclear attacks on targets in the Baltic. One could hope for assistance when the planned German Naval Air Force became available.

---

20 Bilag II. Notat om den militære omvurderings betydning for forsvaret af Danmark. YHM Forsvarsministeriets 11. kontor 12-11-54 711/54.

Other weak points in the Danish defence were the poor ability to withstand a surprise attack at the Elbe/Trave defence line; and lack of ground forces at D-day on Zealand.

The note concluded that in so far as the defence in Schleswig-Holstein was successful, the main problem for Danish defence was having weak ground forces on Zealand. This could be remedied before 1957 (the target year of the Capability Plan).

SACEUR's Atomic Strike Plans (ASP) by 1956

In 1956, the ASP was based on a situation where war was imminent, and SACEUR had been authorised to use special weapons by the announcement of a General Alert.[21]

The supreme commander had a theatre-wide system of plans, the Scheduled Program, which contained targets selected for immediate and automatic attack as soon as practicable. The program included those counter-air targets which posed the major atomic threat facing SACEUR.

In addition, an Interdiction Program would include targets which the supreme commander deemed important at the theatre level on movement of surface forces and supplies. Regional commanders could recommend such targets. Peacetime planning could not be expected to cover new threats and emergencies. Therefore, regional commanders were expected to submit new plans to meet such threats.

In 1956, strikes could only be performed by US forces, normally by aircraft. The process was guided by SACEUR SOP 1-56 which allowed commanders at the Flag Officer level to make a request which had to be approved by the senior command level having the authority to release. The strike force then had to coordinate its intentions, and after the attack the results had to be made known to concerned commanders.

The SOP 1-56 had been criticised by a number of commanders who wanted a more decentralised system of authority.[22] Getting an authorisation took time which was proved in an exercise: due to overload in communications, the time for transmissions between local commanders and SHAPE averaged four hours and 10 minutes. One message took 18 hours and 18 minutes to transmit. Shifts of priority were cumbersome and some times impossible: in one instance during the exercise, four enemy divisions were concentrated in one area; the US seventh army fired two of its remaining three weapons on the target but needed eight to 10 more to complete its task. A local request to SHAPE to have 12 CODE BLACK ground-delivered weapons changed to CODE GREEN was denied, and the weapons were never used.

SACEUR Gruenther's response to these problems was to formally establish a number of Joint Centres of Command at all joint levels of command, down to and including field army/tactical air force/naval-task-group or equivalent level.[23]

---

21 The procedures below are described in an undated YHM note for the Danish Joint Chiefs of Staff 7a-1. Forsvarsstaben: KC. YHM-skrivelser (afklass.) (1956–1969) 1: 1954–1969 m.m. See also SHAPE report SHAPE, *SHAPE History – The New Approach 1953–1956*, 126–27.
22 SHAPE, *SHAPE History – The New Approach 1953–1956*, 118.
23 Ibid., 252.

The New Approach: Control of warheads

The New Approach campaigns were highly dependent on nuclear weapons. But only the Americans and the British had nuclear warheads. Both countries could perform the roles for delivering strategic bombing of Soviet targets. The British would use their capacities in coordination with British land forces. So in practice only the American forces were likely to carry out nuclear tactical military tasks linked to other NATO countries, but American law prevented any handling of those by personnel of foreign countries.

The New Approach, however, required that nuclear weapons were available for SACEUR from day one of a war, as it appears in the first draft:[24] "The ability of NATO to survive depends on SACEUR's ability to launch immediately a devastating counter air action using atomic and thermonuclear weapons. . . . SACEUR must have authority to initiate immediate counter air action using atomic and thermonuclear weapons."

Furthermore, when NATO's forces had adapted their tactics to the use of nuclear weapons, the conventional strength would be reduced to such a level that there was no other option than to use nuclear weapons from day one: "Therefore, in the event of war involving NATO, the commitment to action of forces by NATO countries under Article 5 of the North Atlantic Treaty should encompass full authority for the employment of atomic and thermonuclear weapons in their defence of these forces. This authority should be written into the terms of the General Alerts."[25]

In other words, the New Approach, if implemented, would assure a general nuclear war in case the Soviet Union initiated an attack that triggered the musketeer oath (article 5) of the NATO countries.

The purpose was to deter the Soviets from doing so. But it was not implemented as planned. SACEUR did not get the desired authority to control nuclear weapons from day one of a war and hence initiate nuclear war. The NATO Council approved the document in December 1954 as a foundation for planning and preparation, but it emphasised that the right to initiate military responses had to remain with the national governments.[26]

The American forces remained under national control. But in the years to follow, new programs of cooperation between USA and individual European countries step by step changed the pattern. The process to get support from nuclear weapons became simplified, giving nations authority to stock and transport war-

---

24 NATO SG 241 12-8-54, p. 6.
25 NATO SG 241 12-8-54, p. 11.
26 Ibid., 82.

heads (but not fire them). More precisely, a stockpile of nuclear weapons was created, and under specified alert conditions, SACEUR was given authorisation to release nuclear weapons to those NATO countries that were included in the atomic strike plan.[27] Denmark was not one of those.

We shall return to the significance of the stockpile concept below.

Danish first reactions to nuclear warheads

In May 1954, the Danish ministry of defence discussed the issue of nuclear weapons in a note.[28] The New Approach was still under preparation, but one could see from other NATO documents that decisions to use nuclear weapons could not be made by field commanders, but who then could do so was not articulated. The Danish C-in-C declared that while strategic nuclear weapons would not be used on Danish soil, and while the government could expect to be asked about such use if it became pertinent, one could expect tactical nuclear weapons to be used immediately from the start of a war. There was no procedure for hearing the Danish government about this, and the C-in-C recommended that such procedures be initiated by SHAPE and AFNORTH. The note concluded that Denmark only could hope to be asked in cases of using nuclear weapons on Danish territory or against foreign territory from bases in Denmark.

In other words: Denmark had no formal influence on the use of nuclear weapons anywhere. In 1954, the Danish military forces had no technical capacity to use nuclear weapons, but nonetheless AFNORTH initiated exercises involving the use of them on Danish territory.

The military chiefs

The Danish Joint Chiefs of Staff discussed the New Approach in a series of meetings in October 1954, based on a framework set out by the C-in-C.[29] The chiefs took note that nuclear tactical weapons would favour NATO's side. But because of NATO's weak conventional forces NATO would have to use nuclear weapons even though the enemy refrained from doing so. Consequently, SACEUR had to have

---

27 Twigge, Stephen, and Len Scott. *Planning Armageddon. Britain, the United States and the Command of Western Nuclear Forces 1945–1964*, 152–58. Amsterdam: Harwood Academic Publishers, 2000.
28 Notits om anvendelsen af atomvåben, Forsvarsministeriet 11. kontor 13-5-54 HEM 26-22/54, 21-16/55.
29 Draft note from the C-in-C of 14-10-54, C. J. 157/0 4138 in the archive of Forsvarsministeriet 11. kontor.

authority to use such weapons forthwith and without having to wait for further permission (as we shall see, he did not obtain that, PB). SACEUR did not reserve any nuclear warheads for the defence of Zealand, but the Chiefs thought that Denmark should ask for such artillery with stores on Zealand, and if this for Danish political reasons were impossible, they should be stored in Southern Norway. Beyond the transfer of authority to the supreme commander regarding nuclear warheads, the Chiefs foresaw that Denmark would have to reorganise its defence in ways that were as yet not clear; the army had to have larger standing forces; the navy had to be modernised; the aircraft of the air force had to be spread in a wider area; stores had to be increased and be prepared for supporting forces retreating from Schleswig-Holstein; and the radar recce systems had to be completed (to cover all Denmark) and manned around the clock.

What did the military chiefs know about nuclear warfare, and how did they react to the New Approach?

In the army, a few senior officers had followed American courses on the issue, and they did not hesitate to inform participants in the staff courses for Danish army personnel.[30] Some even informed the general public (see box). In 1954, the Army staff wrote a memo on organisation, emphasising the importance of larger standing forces because recently mobilised troops could not be expected to withstand the chocks caused by nuclear weapons. The standing forces were to be put together as mobile entities having all types of weapons and function permanently at a high level of readiness. Size mattered because the enemy would have to concentrate their forces to fight a strong enemy; by doing so they would invite a nuclear counterattack.

A public lecture on Nuclear Warfare
Major General Kragh, chief of the Army staff, delivered a lengthy lecture on nuclear warfare for several publics,[31] stressing first the decisive role of strategic nuclear bombing if war broke out, and second that the threat factor was crucial in making the enemy abstain from attacking. Nuclear weapons were not enough in themselves; the threat had to be kept viable by well trained standing military forces, ready to counter any attack. The role for future German troops in Schleswig-Holstein would be to stop the Soviet army, while the Danish army had to protect vital military points in Jutland and prepare for countering an invasion on Zealand from sea or air. If the invading enemy succeeded in creating a bridge head and attack, the Danish army had to use tactics forcing the enemy to concentrate their forces (in order to gain sufficient potency) and thus create suitable targets for nuclear weapons.

---

30 Clemmesen, Michael H. "Den massive gengældelses lille ekko. De taktiske atomvåbens rolle i dansk forsvarsplanlægning i 1950erne." In *Danmark, Norden og NATO 1948–1962*, eds Carsten Due Nielsen, Johan Peder Noack, and Nikolaj Petersen, 129–30. København: Jurist- og Økonomforbundets Forlag, 1990.
31 Dansk forsvar i atomalderen, archived by Forsvarsministeriet 11. kontor 772/55, approved by the minister 23-2-55.

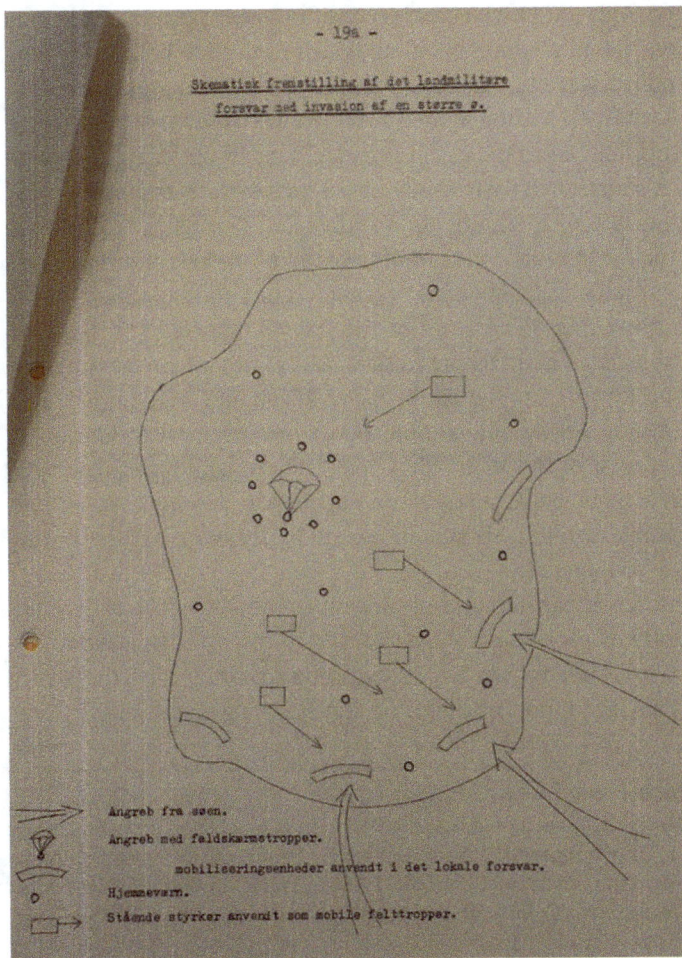

Figure 7.1: A figure from General Kragh's lecture illustrates attack (landed on south-east beaches and from the air) and defence (squares: standing forces, bent boxes: local mobilised forces; circles: Home Guard) on Zealand. Source: Rigsarkivet.

The Danish navy did not really change any tactical principles because of the nuclear threat. The crews were trained to make the use of systems to spray away the waste, and future ships would be designed differently. The navy would prepare for more mobile stores and maintenance systems. But the chief of the navy was quite dissatisfied with SACEUR's document on the New Approach.[32] He took issue with the nuclear-weapon-based approach which neglected that, e.g. in Denmark, many focal points were too small for such weapons and would be dealt with by conventional forces. Furthermore, the supreme commander neglected that modern defence would be a task for all three military forces in an integrated approach, whereas his approach was mainly based on separate actions by army and air forces. In the case of the Baltic approaches and Denmark, SACEUR neglected the role of the navy which was not only based on vessels. The navy also ran radar systems, mine fields, submarine detection loops and maintained various bases and transport lines. The chief of the navy supported the supreme commander's offensive ideas of attacking Russian LOCs with air forces, but only east of Bornholm and Rügen. A minefield between Rügen and Zeeland (i.e. west of Bornholm) was a new SACEUR invention, never discussed with the Danish navy which held that west of Bornholm ship operations should have priority to counter amphibious actions, but if the area was opened to mining from aircraft this would be impossible. Mine fields should be laid by ships so that their accurate positions were determined.

The Danish air force apparently did not formulate a policy at that time but took a stance indirectly by recommending aircraft to be dispersed on several airfields and noting the roles inherent in SACEUR's planned counter-offensive which the Danish air force would support by diverting and escorting operations.

Use of NATO tactical nuclear weapons on Danish territory?
In the fall of 1954, COMAIRNORTH requested that the Danish navy designated promising target areas to bomb attacking Soviet troops with nuclear warheads.[33] This brought new features to the traditional Danish understanding of littoral warfare. The navy interpreted the request as regarding amphibious forces in the process of landing on Danish beaches or harbours. Furthermore, it was presumed that a certain size of the target was desirable. At sea, concentration (creating target for nuclear warheads) would be forced by passage of narrow straits, and in other areas the navy could induce a concentration of ships by laying minefields in which the enemy would then create relatively narrow access channels by mine sweeping. Furthermore, land batteries could force a concentration on the outside of the range of the guns of the battery. Finally, landing troops at beaches in minor bays and inlets and in harbours would create a concentration.

The result is shown at the map below, with the best areas marked in red.

The navy emphasised that this designation was premature and further investigation was desirable. Furthermore, it was pointed out that the issue of civilian losses needed an in-depth analysis.

---

32 Letter from Naval Staff to C-in-C on "Capabilities Plans 1957", NATO nr. 985, NATO E-6.
33 "Potential Atomic Targets" Note SVK NATO-arkiv.L-5, 23-11-54.

Figure 7.2: Map over possible nuclear target areas in Denmark 1955. Source: Rigsarkivet.

The politicians: A policy of not rocking the boat

The Danish minister of defence was invited to participate in exercise SKY BLAESER (mainly using aircraft) in Oslo in February 1955. He declined because he did not want publicity about his participation in such an exercise, but commented on the issue:[34]

> The use of nuclear weapons in exercises seems to me a logical consequence of last years (1954, PB) decision in the NATO council to include such use in military planning, and I have no issue with that. . . . The use of new weapons in exercises with troops might create psychological reactions in the population. . . . Therefore, I want to stress that one must be very careful with the type of information that is disseminated to the press regarding the use of atomic weapons. . . . My C-in-C will participate in the exercise and keep me informed about the outcomes.

Consequently, the Danish Government in 1955 did not formulate any reservations regarding the use of nuclear weapons on Danish territory.

The technical development of weapons went fast, and in late 1956 Denmark was offered HONEST JOHN missiles with nuclear capacity. The issue was discussed with CINCNORTH Sugden at a meeting in the Danish ministry of defence on 28 December 1956.[35] The proposal was to integrate six HONEST JOHN batteries, four on Zealand (mainly to attack amphibious crafts and ships in an invasion fleet), two in Southern Jutland or Schleswig-Holstein (for use against ground troops), with delivery probably in 1957. The six batteries were not to replace conventional artillery which still would find many uses.

Why the atomic warheads? General Sugden stressed that in military terms the Danish army did not have the desired strength. Therefore, stronger firing power must compensate for numerical inferiority. The nuclear warhead of one HONEST JOHN missile had the power of ten conventional artillery batteries, firing for half an hour. Normally, one would expect aircraft to deliver atomic warheads, but first the air force had other tasks and the land commander would have greater trust in his own weapons; second, weather conditions might prohibit air attacks; and third, approval of air attacks was a fairly slow procedure involving military top decision-makers – this would not be the case on the ground.[36] Finally there was the moral question: why put own forces in a questionable position, preventing them to retaliate nuclear use by the enemy?

---

34 Letter (Danish draft) to General Mansergh of 27-1-55, HEM, Forsvarsministeriet 11. kontor 35–54/55.
35 Minutes by Forsvarsministeriet 11. kontor, YHM 14-1-57, 91–26/57.
36 The veracity of the last statement may be questioned, given the discussions in SHAPE, PB.

A particular issue, however, was the division of responsibilities between Denmark and AFNORTH in wartime – this question had been discussed several times and still was not solved (see chapter 3).

Defence minister Poul Hansen found the theme "rather scary". While he understood the military reasons, the political problems were twofold: first, the stationing of foreign forces in peacetime, although the number of foreign experts apparently would be fairly low; second, the issue of stockpiling nuclear warheads on Danish territory which probably would be met with opposition in the population. That said, the minister encouraged AFNORTH to make its recommendation to SHAPE, and then – taking the reaction of the Danish population into consideration – the Danish government could formulate its policy on the issue.

The minister perceived this meeting as purely informational involving no decision. General Sugden concurred.

Nuclear warheads: A formalized "no"

In the spring of 1957, Denmark was offered 48 launchers of NIKE anti-aircraft defence missiles which also had capacity for nuclear warheads, and according to the minister of defence he had to accept the offer immediately, or the missiles would go to other countries.[37] At the same time, a number of HONEST JOHNs – as we saw above, discussed informally in December – were now formally offered. The NIKE offer was accepted in principle by the Danish cabinet on 23 April, and the Committee for Foreign Affairs was told on 26 April that the government would also approve the HONEST JOHN offer in principle, but neither offer would be formally approved until after the next election to the parliament, when all technical aspects of the offer had been analysed.

We cannot know what the political decision on nuclear warheads would have been if the Social Democratic government had continued unchanged – apart from the fact that with the bourgeois parties a majority was secured. But in May 1957, a general election led to the creation of a tripartite majority cabinet with a Social Democratic prime minister. The other two coalition parties both were rather anti-defence oriented, and in a declaration of 29 May 1957, the prime minister stated that during the negotiations regarding HONEST JOHN nuclear warheads had not been offered by the Americans, and the government was not inclined to accept, if so offered.

---

37 Dansk Institut for Internationale Studier, *Danmark under den kolde krig. Den sikkerhedspolitiske situation 1945–1991. Bind 1: 1945–1962*, 295.

As the minutes quoted above indicate something else, the question for an analyst is what is meant by "offered". There is no doubt that the original discussion had nuclear warheads as the main theme because the HONEST JOHN missile had little military meaning if used with conventional warheads. But the minister indeed declared that the meeting was purely informational – no formal offer had been made.

Denmark's "no" was officially formulated in the winter of 1957–58. At the NATO Council meeting of 17–19 December 1957, Denmark (together with Norway) expressed reluctance towards storing nuclear warheads in Europe and having mid-range missiles (IRBM) stationed in the country. The final communique from the meeting indirectly stated that not all NATO countries had to have such stocks and missiles on their territory because decisions had to be made "in agreement with the states directly involved".[38] On 21 January 1958, the Danish prime minister declared in the Danish parliament that "under present conditions, the Danish government will not accept to receive nuclear ammunition". This debate concerned the construction of new NATO depots and the statement meant that no nuclear ammunition could be stored on Danish territory.

The Danish C-in-C handled the issue in his own professional way,[39] noting in a letter to the minister that he expected a discussion of the supreme commander's forward strategy in a future meeting in NATO's Military Committee, and therefore, being a member of said committee, he found it his duty to call the minister's attention to the fact that in spite of the government's rejection of a possible offer to receive nuclear warheads SACEUR's forward strategy was actually precisely built on the premise that such weapons were available because without them the defending troops could not fight effectively. Two weeks later, in another letter, he underscored that the minimum forces required by NATO only made sense if there was imminent and direct access to depots of nuclear warheads for tactical use. If not, the defending conventional forces could not stop an attack by forces which would be expected to have tactical nuclear weapons.

The government maintained its negative stance.

---

38 New York Times 20th December 1957. The Americans were quite surprised by the statements. The political process at the NATO Council Paris meeting was dramatic behind the scenes, see Villaume Villaume, *Allieret med forbehold*, 550–56.

39 Clemmesen, Michael H., "Den massive gengældelses lille ekko. De taktiske atomvåbens rolle i dansk forsvarsplanlægning i 1950erne," 137.

New SACEUR and the stockpiling of nuclear weapons

General Norstad had relieved General Gruenther in November 1956, and he soon acknowledged the authority of his political masters in the NATO Council.[40] In a speech in November 1957 he pointed out that no nation had ever precisely codified the borders between political and military authority in times before hostilities. So politicians and military leaders had to keep a dialogue open about eventualities and the perspectives as perceived from each sphere. However, this would be difficult in times when instant reaction was desirable.

Soon after, a process of revising the massive retaliation started – but for reasons that varied among the member states of NATO.[41] In strategic terms, the essence of the desired changes was to allow for less than massive retaliation – but opposed by Britain and the staff of SHAPE.[42] Thus the general rule of massive retaliation was kept in place – exempting only specified situations such as local attacks performed with conventional weapons and no use of nuclear weapons.

These revisions were decided as a Political Directive (C-M(56)138) by the NATO Council on 13 December 1956. The changes, indicating a certain flexibility in NATO responses, called for renewed planning. This triggered the ensuing military planning process towards MC 70 which we shall deal with below.

As we saw above, the supreme commander did not in the New Approach get a general authority to the use of nuclear weapons. But the stockpile concept became an instrument for giving him quite a strong role in the forward defence of NATO.[43] Until now, the American forces were the only ones allowed to fire nuclear weapons. But by using the existing system for storing, transporting and releasing American nuclear warheads, one could create additional custodian groups of American personnel and let the tasks of security (defence against attacks by enemy troops, saboteurs or para-military entities) be taken care of by the hosting nation which also could fire the weapons – given that the American president had released them.

Therefore, SACEUR set up a plan for stockpiling such weapons and for the transport of them to the delivery forces. In the supreme commander's plan for 1958, the following conditions for the use of stockpiled atomic weapons were found in Annex C:[44] SACEUR had the command over such weapons, but the increasing number made delegation to lower levels of command necessary to promote the efficiency of the weapons and their means of transportation. The supreme com-

---

40 SHAPE, *SHAPE History 1958*, 10.
41 Duffield, op. cit., chap. 4.
42 SHAPE, *History 1957*, chap. II.
43 SHAPE, *SHAPE History 1958*, 62–69.
44 SACEUR's forsvarsplan for 1958, Forsvarsministeriet 11. kontor, 18-11-57, YHM 314/57.

mander would notify his regional commanders of the number of special weapons they could expect to have under their command; SACEUR would keep a number of weapons as reserve for unforeseen use (this was what the Danish Chiefs of Staff, quoted above, hoped for to be used on Zealand, PB). Joint Command Centres with the chiefs for all three forces would be established to perform execution of special weapons within their area of responsibility. Use of special weapons near centres of population were to be avoided, if possible. The goal for the use of special weapons was to deny the enemy use of special weapons, reduce enemy air threat, help stopping enemy advance and support allied forces in Europe. The priorities for use of special weapons were:

a) fast reduction of the enemy capacity to perform nuclear warfare by immediate and automatic attacks against a large number of predestined targets;
b) attacks on non-planned, but now rewarding targets;
c) attacks on Russian radar systems and Air Control Systems;
d) attacks on bridges, railroad centres and harbours. Some automatically, some after order.

In case good results might be reached by conventional weapons, special weapons were not to be used. AFNORTH would automatically have eight aircraft from Third US Air Force at disposition for nuclear bombing.

The American public knew
The New York Times 14 March 1955 edition had an article describing such bombing for Danish defence:
   This exercise (supporting AFNORTH, PB) was based on the availability of the Forty-ninth US Air Division, stationed in Britain, to go to the aid of the Northern Command on a 'call and deliver' basis. . . . Its F-84F Thunderstreak fighter-bomber is armed with 'baby' atomic bombs . . .
   Denmark, essential to Atlantic Alliance because she controls the approaches to the Baltic, is particularly vulnerable to attack from Soviet airfields in Northeastern Germany, from which jet planes can reach Danish targets in thirteen minutes. . . . Tacticians hold that the speed with which the Allies could drop atomic bombs on those airfields is crucial to the defence of Denmark. That mission might also be expected to fall to the Forty-ninth Air Division.

MC 70 – facing the economic facts

By 1955, a perceived improvement of the Cold War climate contributed to a decline in immediate military preparedness in the West, so the interest to increase military spending waned. The original attraction of MC 48 for European politicians was a promise of reduced expenditures on conventional forces. But nonetheless, NATO commanders continued to call for sizeable forces because they wanted large conventional forces which would force Russia to mobilise large-scale for a planned invasion; the mobilisation could hardly happen unnoticed and hence NATO would get a warning and lead time for implementing own plans.

As we saw above, the previous documents MC 14 and MC 48 were amended in 1957. The new documents (MC14/2 and MC48/2) were intended to develop a politically meaningful defence concept, and in order to establish future force goals the document MC 70 was written, integrating the various concepts and commands.

New features in MC 70

MC 70 became the main document for the military commanders to follow, comprising the Minimum Force Requirements of SACEUR, SACLANT and CINCHAN. It was prepared through 1957 in a quite lengthy process under close and apparently somewhat grumpy attention by the Standing Group due to protraction of several understudies.[45] Beyond desired numbers for military forces in 1963, it addressed in essence the need to initiate a planning process to modernise NATO forces, since it was unlikely that NATO's members could increase resources for the military expenses.

Given the political demand for NATO-actions short of general war with its use of nuclear warheads, MC 70 listed a number of other possible Soviet aggressions to be met by NATO:
- Gradual political and economic penetration of countries with Soviet armed forces present in a more or less threatening way behind the scenes;
- Encouraging limited wars outside the Soviet block and supporting one or more of the parties involved;
- Using armed forces for limited operations in areas bordering to the Soviet block; and
- In times of perceived weaknesses in NATO forces: initiating limited operations like infiltrations, hostile attacks or local operations within NATO territory with open or covert Russian support.

MC 70, then, opened the possibility to counter aggression without using nuclear weapons, but at the same time stressed that in no case was there a NATO concept of limited war with the Soviets (MC 70, p. 26).

---

45 The review below is based on YHM Notat om Styrkemål, Forsvarsministeriet 11. kontor 31-3-58 111.2-2. The MC 70 draft version is dated 29-1-58.

So what was the gist of the nuclear policy of MC 70? The formulations in reality made anything possible. The military side (the Military Committee) of NATO appeared to maintain the permanent threat of nuclear weapons; the politicians, however, kept the upper hand by not allowing the military commanders to use such weapons without the consent of the political bodies, nationally as well as in NATO.

MC 70 elucidated that, technically, weapons had developed so that in the future, missiles and submarines would challenge NATO's defence capacities. Satellites would yield communication and steering systems guiding these weapons, some of which would be programmed to hit key points in the West. NATO had to answer by installing new intelligence and warning systems; developing missile systems; making ground forces more mobile; and making aircraft less dependable upon stationary airfields. All forces had to be highly prepared for action:

- Army forces had to be organised in relatively small entities, be mobile and flexible and integrate all types of weapons, including nuclear warheads, in their operations, based on modern communication systems.
- Naval forces had to participate in deterrence (aircraft carriers), develop anti-submarine weapons and establish systems of information, warning and control, also against aircraft.
- Air forces were particularly important in the first phase of a war for deterrence and retaliation. Missiles were expected to replace some aircraft later. Air defence would rely more on missiles fired from the ground.

Consequences for the Baltic approaches

As can be inferred from the above, the situation in the area of the Baltic approaches did not match certain parts of MC 70 well. Aircraft carriers were out of bounds due to shallow waters and had to stay in the North Sea (but might assist from there or approach later), large submarines were unlikely to operate here and large army movements were unlikely outside Schleswig-Holstein which from 1958 was the responsibility of the Bundeswehr. Nuclear weapons were a Fata Morgana, at least for now. At the same time, the area of the Baltic Approaches was a possible candidate for some of the new operations mentioned: limited attack (Bornholm); gradual penetration (the political left wing was relatively strong in Denmark); and more or less subtle international pressure (the declaration of Bornholm) were phenomena the Danish politicians and military chiefs had to take into account.

On the military technical side, the defence was not strong if one took a look at Denmark alone (West Germany is discussed in chapter 8). MC 70 had the following force requirements, compared with requirements in the previous plan:

Table 7.1: Army.

	MC 70	Previous Plan
Brigade Groups	3	3
HONEST JOHN Groups	1	1
LITTLE JOHN Groups	2	0
NIKE Groups	3	0
1st Reserve Brigades	4	4
Local defence Brigades	5	5

LITTLE JOHN was never implemented. NIKE groups were moved to the air force 4 years later.

Table 7.2: Navy D-day.

	MC 70	Previous Plan
Mine-laying destroyers	2	0
Escorts	7	5
Patrol Craft	not included (11)	9
Submarines	4	2
Mine sweepers	not included (15)	12
Mine layers	5	6
MTBs	16	12

In order to muster the above number of ships on D-day, approximately 20 per cent more ships would have to be "in stock".

Mine-laying destroyers were soon abandoned and replaced by two large fast frigates (larger than WWII destroyers).

Table 7.3: Air Force.

	MC 70	Previous Plan
Fighter-bomber squadrons	3 (1 "Strike")	5
Day fighters squadrons	0	1
All-weather fighter squadrons	3	2
Reconnaissance squadron	1	½
Aircraft total	141	178
Ground-to-ground missile grp.	1	0

One fighter-bomber squadron was planned to carry nuclear warheads – contrary to the Danish policy. The ground missiles were never implemented.

These technical measures do not reveal that Denmark as a special bonus for NATO's vigilance step-by-step built up a sophisticated reconnaissance and warning system based on radar and other forms of electronic systems and thus played an important role in the general NATO information system.

Strong criticism

MC 70, a very comprehensive document of 111 pages, was ready as a draft on 29 January 1958, and one month later a staff document from the Danish Ministry of Defence launched a strong critique of the force requirements expressed in that version.[46] First, it was noted that the plan required a Danish increase in defence spending of 40 per cent, politically impossible to reach; the government wanted to reduce spending. Second, a surface-to-surface middle range missile was included to be operated by the air force – probably the MATADOR cruise missile with a range of 800 kilometres; this would also be politically difficult. Third, the NATO-political precondition was fast access to nuclear warheads – equally questionable for Denmark.

Specific topics were criticised in the document: first, the plan apparently required a 10–15 per cent increase of military spending in all countries (more for Denmark), and this was not likely to get Danish approval. The draft was based on previous decisions in NATO (which were unalterable), and only preconditions, required forces and head counts were revisions; as such they might be undercut. An evaluation, however, would require military expertise, i.e. from the C-in-C (understood: we in the ministry don't want that, PB). This being so, the only way for the ministry to question the draft on its own would be to raise a discussion of the particular circumstances for Denmark, different from the other countries, regarding warning time, threats and possibilities for defence. This, however, would call for cooperation by the Joint Chiefs of Staff, and that was seen as just as improbable (!).

Consequently, the ideas of the ministerial staff presented above were "condemned to die" (sic!) beforehand. The ministry had no power. A radical alternative would be to declare that Denmark trusted NATO's general nuclear umbrella to keep the Soviets at bay and in the future only would prepare for local attacks from the Soviets. Such a declaration, however, would not be "pleasant" to present

---

46 Kommentarer til MC 70 YHM, Forsvarsministeriet 11. kontor 10-2-58.

in the Council, and probably there would also be national political problems in doing so. What remained, then, was to declare that the resources required were not available in the Kingdom of Denmark. This would be equally unpleasant to express.

Therefore, in the belief that Denmark was not alone in lacking resources, the document recommended that the Ministry chose to let the ensuing processes in Annual Review reveal that the MC 70 was built on sand, as country after country had to testify their problems. The tactics for the upcoming meeting would therefore be that the Council "took note" (but did not approve) of the study as a basis for military planning, to be pursued by activities of the Annual Review over the Summer. Judging from preparatory meetings, such a solution appeared to be feasible. At a later stage, NATO authorities would then have to review the goals and requirements of MC 70.

This ministerial document – clearly written for insiders – is interesting as an example of bureaucratic politics: what to do when squeezed between strongly diverging interests: military and party political. The ministry of course had to follow its political masters in the cabinet, but did not wish to show weaknesses in the NATO community, to say nothing of the military leadership.

The tactics turned out to work well for the ministry. A subsequent note[47] tells us that the Council took note that MC 70 was for planning purposes requiring further study for the 1962–63 figures and that the figures for 1958 were advisory. In the SHAPE history (which is SHAPE's own accord), we indirectly see the problems of such evasive political decision-making seen from the military side: the decision by the NATO Council was characterised as "a rather nebulous seal", and added that "no single nation had definitely stated that it would raise any particular size or type of force by any particular date."[48]

Consequently, SACEUR got no binding promises from the politicians. MC 70 was never approved as a document that formally directed the force requirements for NATO. It was too expensive.[49] But it remained as an indication of the supreme commander's desires.

Denmark was a case in point; the Danish military budget was far below the level desired by MC 70. SACEUR tried to reason with the Danes about the rationale for NATO:[50] the threat pattern was the same, and the need for NATO to defend

---

47 Tillæg til kommentarer til MC 70 YHM, Forsvarsministeriet 11. kontor 28-3-58.
48 Ibid., 21.
49 David, Francois. "The Doctrine of Massive Retaliation and the Impossible Nuclear Defense of the Atlantic Alliance." In *The Routledge Handbook of Transatlantic Secutiry*, eds Basil Germond and Soutou Hanhimäki, Georges-Henru, 41. Milton Park: Routledge, 2010.
50 SHAPE, *SHAPE History 1958*, 35.

Denmark and the Baltic approaches was also unchanged, so no reduction in military spending could be justified. Any successful defence against enemy attack would require that the military commanders had access to forces of the general type and magnitude indicated in MC 70. Should Denmark reduce her effort, other nations might feel justified in doing the same thing. The supreme commander knew that a reorganisation of the Danish forces was being discussed, but savings from a reorganisation could not possibly create the means for front-line forces required by MC 70.

The "reorganisation" of the Danish defence and hence the NATO contribution was not solved until 1960 when a long overdue compromise about defence policy was reached in the Danish parliament (see chapter 5). But in Denmark, the "no" to nuclear warheads was repeated in a debate in the parliament on 2 March 1960: "... there is no reason for the government to change its policy on this matter".

The ministry seized the opportunity to do an internal review of the NATO policy on "this matter". Regarding the use of special weapons in Denmark, the NATO rules in April 1960 were as follows:[51]

- Any use of special weapons would require the approval of SACEUR, even though the use might be part of an approved plan. If possible, the approval of the respective national government was required, too.
- Concerning Denmark, the latest draft for turning over powers to AFNORTH stated that as soon as the Danish government had declared that the country was in a state of war, CINCNORTH would take over command of Danish assigned forces. Thus the regional commander could carry out military actions that were part of an approved plan.
- Regarding the use of nuclear weapons against centres of population or industrial areas, the approval had to be given by the Danish Government beforehand. If there was disagreement, the decision by the Government was binding for NATO.

These rules were presented to the minister, who resolved that this matter – which pertained to the rules of turning military command over to CINCNORTH, a theme which had been unsolved for at least eight years – had to remain undecided until after the next general elections.

One must take note of this formulation – "against centres of population or industrial areas". In July 1959, the Danish representative in the Military Committee was instructed[52] that regarding the SACEUR Emergency Defence Plan, it was

---

51 Note Forsvarsministeriet 11. kontor 11-4-60 and 29-4-60 YHM 314/60, 91-26/60.
52 YHEM notits til den permanente danske repræsentant i militærkomiteen 22 juli 1959.

obvious that the Norwegian government had made any use of nuclear weapons impossible without a governmental permission on Norwegian territory. But the Danish government declaration (then still a draft version) said that permission was to be asked for in cases of serious political or economic consequences for Denmark, for instance the use of nuclear warheads against population centres or industrial areas. In other words, since the contrast to Norway was mentioned, one may conclude that nuclear weapons might be used without governmental approval in thinly populated Danish areas. We shall return to this below.

The military make-do

In 1957, the army strongly supported the acquisition of missiles – to be operated by the army.[53] As to the HONEST JOHN armed with a nuclear warhead, it was short range (up to 25 kilometres) but it would reduce the need for fighter-bomber nuclear support – experience from exercises revealed it could take a long time to get approval. Regarding NIKE, it would be a welcomed strengthening of the defence of Copenhagen. The army realised that budgets were tight, and since both types of missiles meant less dependence on fighters (NIKE) and fighter-bombers (HONEST JOHN) from the air force, money might be taken from that branch of the Danish defence, if no increase of the defence budget was possible.

In a note to the parliamentary Defence Committee in March 1958, the Joint chiefs of Staff remarked that keeping the policy of "no" to nuclear warheads raised doubts regarding the value of having NIKE and HONEST JOHN missiles; without nuclear warheads their effect did not justify the costs of introduction and maintenance.[54] One year later, the Defence Committee received more detailed information:[55] the NIKE missile could only be used against targets above 6,000 feet and it was constructed for nuclear warheads which could destroy a whole formation of aircraft, while with conventional warhead only one plane could be destroyed. At a price of 500,000 Dkr. this was uneconomical. In comparison, an anti-aircraft shell for a 90 mm gun cost 400 Dkr.

For HONEST JOHN a similar rule of thumb was that with a nuclear warhead one could destroy most military equipment within 500 meters with a 15 KT load; with a 100 KT load the range would be increased to roughly one kilometer. A con-

---

53 Two letters HEM from the Army Command to the C-inC: EK/II 3747 2-4-57 and BHI/II 4391 24-4-54.
54 Clemmesen, Michael H., "Den massive gengældelses lille ekko. De taktiske atomvåbens rolle i dansk forsvarsplanlægning i 1950erne," 138.
55 YHM Bilag til svar på spørgsmål nr. 11, Forsvarsstabens skr. G.1216/0.1842 15-4-59.

ventional load for the missile would hardly be efficient within more than 150 meters, whereas a conventional gun would work within about 90 meters. Furthermore, a gun would hit its target within 30–40 meters while the missile only had a precision of 25 per cent to hit within 250 meters. At a cost of 77,000 Dkr. compared with the cost of a shell at no more than 400 Dkr, the missile was highly uneconomical without a nuclear warhead.

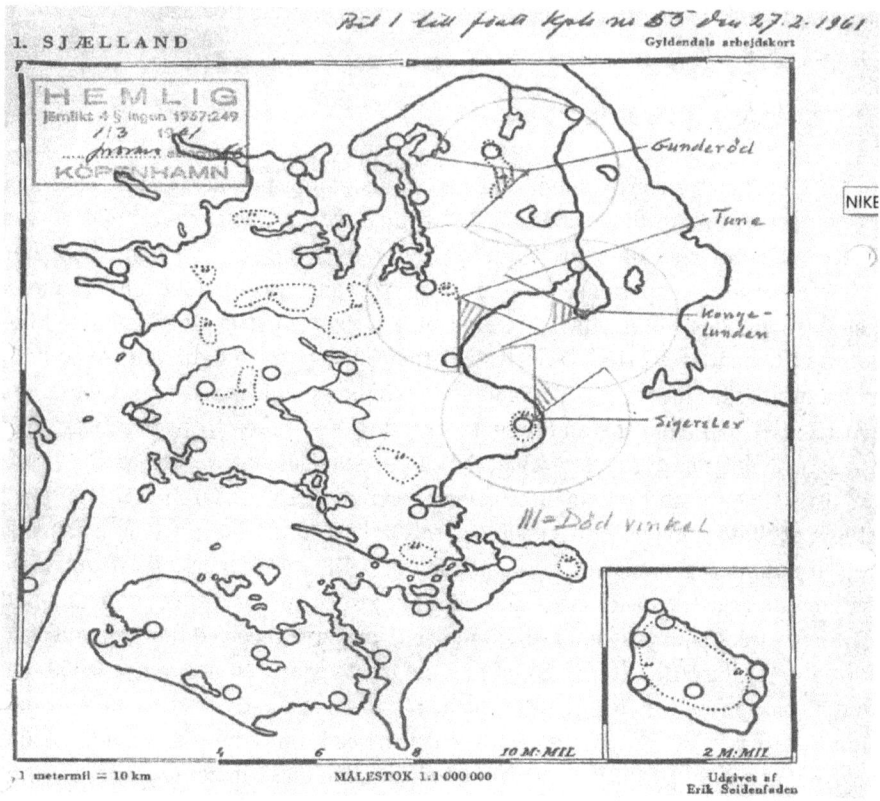

Figure 7.3: NIKE-batteries (Gunderød, Tune and Sigerslev) surrounding Copenhagen.[56] One notes the "blind angles" of the batteries, probably due to local obstacles.

Nonetheless, the HONEST JOHN missiles were delivered to Denmark in 1959, as were F-100 fighter-bombers, capable of carrying nuclear warheads. Stores suited for nuclear warheads were built for the aircraft at the Karup airfield, and like-

---

56 Görtz, *Skandinavisk försvarsutredning 1948–1949 – uppstarten och dess inverkan under kalla kriget*, 120.

wise stores were built for four NIKE batteries on Zealand.[57] The American policy for nuclear ammunition required American personnel to safeguard and handle said ammunition, and hence buildings for housing such personnel were to be constructed together with the magazines. But as long as the Danish "no" to nuclear war heads was valid, such buildings might stand empty; this could cause (Soviet) observers to consider the buildings a provocation because they indicated that sooner or later the "no" would become a "yes". Therefore, none were built, and the problem was circumvented by a declaration by the Danish government to CINCNORTH that in case Denmark would accept nuclear warheads, such personnel could be housed in existing buildings.[58]

The depots for nuclear warheads for HONEST JOHN missiles were never built because of difficulties in getting suitable areas for them, and since the missiles were put into reserve from 1965, the plans became less relevant, given the priorities for other buildings in the NATO-committee for infrastructure. However, the Danish Army Command maintained that there was a need for the depots as long as there existed a possibility that nuclear war heads could be fired by Danish weapons (i.e. the policy of the Danish government might change, PB) and missiles were part of the Danish defence system – for psychological reasons (meaning the prevention of war) and for reasons of morale in the army which would be proud of having such an advanced system of weapons.[59]

The ministry of defence then briefly analysed what the preconditions were for receiving special ammunition in critical situations.[60] The ministry "had no knowledge of any allocation by SACEUR to Danish forces" and it did not know whether the supreme commander in his reserves had any kept for Danish forces in case Denmark declared a change in its policy on receiving special ammunition. Magazines fulfilling the demands for special ammunition were available for the air force at Karup airfield and for NIKE missiles. But the ministry noted that American special ammunition was to be controlled and maintained by American personnel – for a HONEST JOHN battery 25, for an air squadron 60 and for a NIKE battery 75 people – and it would normally take six months to obtain the ammunition and the personnel and prepare them for action. In a case of emergency this time span could be reduced if air transport were available.

---

57 The contention by Agger et al. that the ministry planned magazines for nuclear war heads at six airfields for strategic air forces is not substantiated by the archives consulted for this book. Agger, and Wolsgård, op. cit., p. 94.
58 Note Forsvarsministeriet 11. kontor HEM 22-2-60 91-26/60.
59 Comment added 17-8-64 to note by Forsvarsministeriet 11. kontor 27-2-64 9-20/64.
60 Note by Forsvarsministeriet 11. kontor 9-9-64 HEM 31–26/64.

The note offered no conclusions, but it is not difficult to guess that Denmark could not expect any quick allocation of special ammunition in times of crisis. However, there were in principle possibilities south of the border, where the Germans were planning magazines for nuclear warheads in Schleswig-Holstein, and in the years 1959–60 the army command investigated some possibilities for bilateral agreement about such stores. But in the Summer of 1960 the German Foreign Minister declared that Denmark could not expect Germany to take on the burden of establishing nuclear storage for Danish units on German territory in order to make it possible for the Danish government to maintain its negative – "but politically welcome" – policy towards nuclear war heads and nonetheless obtain a certain improvement of military preparedness.[61] One year later, the Danish ministry noted that an enhancement of the German nuclear stockpile was being negotiated, and they expected one relatively small magazine to be built close to the Danish border.[62]

This note, of course, is open for interpretation as the reader wishes. The magazine has been referred to by several authors as accessible for the Danes in the case of war.[63] The HONEST JOHN missiles were fully retired from active service by 1967, but the principled capacity to fire nuclear warheads was maintained by the army because of new 155 Howitzer self-propelled guns,[64] which were expanded to eight batteries. The question of actually preparing and training for use of these guns with nuclear warheads was not taken up by the ministry.

NATO planning in spite of the "no"

Both Denmark and Norway had declared that they would not receive nuclear warheads in peace time. Nonetheless, NATO continued planning for the use of those weapons. The text below concerns SHAPE's concerns regarding force goals of Spring 1959:[65]

AFNORTH. Specifically, in the North there was great concern for Northern Norway, where the basic force requirements were not going to be met. The nuclear strength capability in the North would be only about 15% of the MC 70 requirements, which meant that its strike forces would not be able to perform counter nuclear tasks in general war. The forces could provide limited nuclear support to surface forces and a significant degree of non-nuclear support. Reconnaissance would be critical.

SHAPE's judgement was that since next to no Danish information was available beyond 1959, an evaluation in terms of progress toward 1963 objectives was not very meaningful. In 1959, a beginning would have been made towards nuclear striking capability from new F-100s for one Danish

---

61 Notits HEM Forsvarsministeriet 11. kontor 3-11-59, continued 2-6-60 and 10-10-60.
62 Note Forsvarsministeriet 11. kontor HEM 18-8-61 91–26/61.
63 Clemmesen, Michael H., "Den massive gengældelses lille ekko. De taktiske atomvåbens rolle i dansk forsvarsplanlægning i 1950erne," 139.
64 Fortsættelse af notat dateret 3 MAJ 1965-1. Kt.242.13-1. HEM. Forsvarsminiseriet 1. kontor 9-3-67.
65 SHAPE, *SHAPE History 1958*, 23–24.

Fighter-Bomber squadron. However, the neutralisation of enemy airfields and missile sites continued to depend on forces outside the area. The air defence capability would improve with surface to air missile in both Norway and Denmark. The mission of defending the Baltic Straits could be fulfilled in spite of shortfalls, and it was conceivable that passage through the narrows could still be denied to the enemy. Interdiction of sea lines of communications in the Baltic probably could not be accomplished. This would mean that the sea and land defences of the Baltic Straits would have to withstand a heavier enemy threat than anticipated, but the impact of landings might be nullified by nuclear attacks.

A "no" turned into a "maybe"?

The Danish ban had certain limitations, being issued "under the present conditions" in 1957. One question therefore was whether the conditions were to change some time in the future, and then what? If war was declared, or actually in process? What if German troops, armed with nuclear weapons, withdrew from Germany to Danish territory? What about American air forces brought in as reinforcement to Danish airfields? And what about Danish use of tactical nuclear weapons on enemy territory?[66]

The command post exercise IRON OUT in late March 1958 indicates an answer because the issue of NATO nuclear bombing of their own (Danish) territory was played out.[67] As we saw above, NATO had in 1955 asked what Danish areas might be suitable for nuclear bombing of WAPA forces after they had landed. In IRON OUT, the situation came up that enemy forces had been landed successfully on the Rødvig beach on the southern edge of the Stevns peninsula on the eastern side of Zealand, and the NATO command expected reinforcements including heavy tanks to be landed by using the Rødvig harbour so that the bridge head could be solidified and expanded and the forces move westwards. At this moment, the enemy forces were stuck. Therefore, permission to strike with a 50 kiloton nuclear bomb from a low-altitude bomber was requested. The civilian population of the area was about 1,300, but 400 had been evacuated. The enemy had ordered those remaining to stay in the house, preferably in the basement. If the reinforcements succeeded, the enemy would attack, and the Danish forces would not be able to resist successfully. If a nuclear attack was carried though now, the reinforcements would be eliminated, and the Danes would succeed finishing mobilisation. Since the enemy probably could not muster new reinforcements within eight to ten days, the Danes would

---

66 Questions formulated by Nikolaj Petersen in newspaper Jyllandsposten 18-1-2005.
67 Papers HEM in the archive of 11. kontor March 1958, no journal number. Defence Staff journal H.8100/C.898, 25-2-58 (regarding a draft version of the exercise plan).

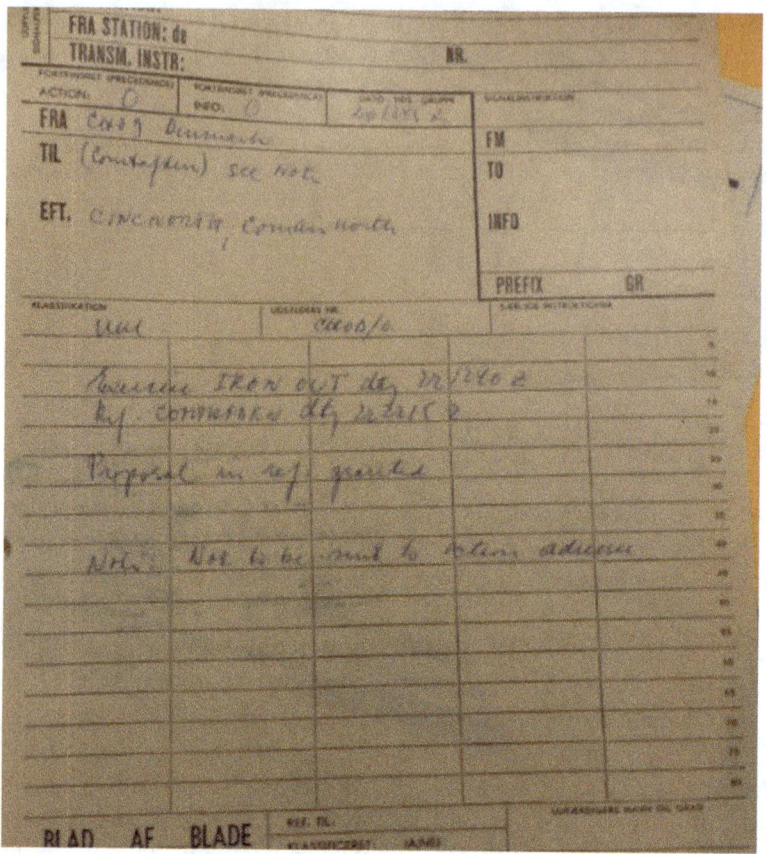

Figure 7.4: This is the handwritten draft for an IRON OUT exercise order granting permission to drop a 50 kiloton nuclear bomb a little north of Rødvig, Denmark. Source: Rigsarkivet.

be able to stop the aggression. Civilian casualties were expected to be heavy, 80 to 90 per cent, but the military gains were so large that a strike was recommended.

Given that the country had reached a "state of war", and therefore the "present circumstances" (of peace) used by the government declaration of 1958 of no-use were not the case, permission to strike was granted. The papers do not state whether the government was involved. Two explanations are possible. Firstly, the comments from the C-in-C staff on the drafts for the exercise were that the government had to be involved if "larger population segments or vital industries" were at risk. But the area at Rødvig was rural and densely populated. Secondly, if the government were incapable of making a decision, CINCNORTH and the Danish C-in-C could make decisions under the general clause that Denmark was under attack (demanded in the constitution), and enemy attacks had to be resisted (at any cost).

In any case, the strike was granted in the exercise IRON OUT. Of course, this was only an exercise, but exercises are made to test possible actions when they are in demand, so one may at least conclude that the use of nuclear weapons was not to be ruled out in Denmark in 1958.

Orders for nuclear warfare in the Danish army
In 1957, the Danish army had standing orders for nuclear warfare.[68] The Danish forces had to be vigilant regarding the enemy's possibilities for to make nuclear warfare: indicators of enemy use of nuclear warheads could be unusual recce flights, sudden withdrawal of forces, preparation of armoured units for attack behind the front, mounting of missiles and presence of specialist groups etc.

The Danish army also had to assess the enemy's vulnerability towards NATO nuclear attacks, and therefore the army had to watch for promising targets for such attacks. Consequently, immediate reporting was necessary for such information including assessment of the state of the enemy after a NATO attack.

There were standardised forms for requiring a nuclear attack. Any massing of enemy troops and establishment of missile platforms would be possible targets for NATO nuclear attacks. Examples of worthy targets were two 75 mm artillery units, a battalion of armoured vehicles and a reserve group of 5,000 men in preparation and large supply units.

All information about one's own commands, support firing plans for nuclear attacks, marked maps, photos etc. relating to NATO use of nuclear warheads was to be kept at the staff level.

After 1958, things changed step by step. In 1960, Danish F-100 SUPER SABRE pilots were trained in delivering such weapons, but in the years after such training was absent.[69] Furthermore, the Danes had HONEST JOHN missiles which did not make sense in use without nuclear war heads, and Denmark had some artillery also capable of using nuclear war ammunition.

In September 1961 the Danish chiefs of staff discussed SACEUR's plan for the Berlin crisis.[70] The chiefs agreed that at a certain level of NATO alert, nuclear warheads should be prepared for use. The chief of the army wanted training in preparing nuclear warheads by the Americans; the chief of the air force mentioned that such a team of Americans just had visited a Danish airfield – he did not say directly that they had trained Danish personnel. The C-in-C had brought the theme of levels of alert and nuclear warheads up in a letter to the minister on

---

68 Østre Landsdelskommando: Blivende bestemmelser for EK(ELK) under feltforhold. Tillæg A. Atomkrigsførelse. FTR. 0.122.94-375. 13-9-57.
69 Newspaper Berlingske Tidende 21-11-2004.
70 FSS meeting 19-9-61 issue 1.

30 August; he would not, however, bring this theme up again in the present situation because the minority party in the cabinet might react very negatively.

Hopes for nuclear warheads were wishful thinking. During a seminar conducted by CINCNORTH three months after, in December 1961, the participants were told[71] that it was unlikely that nuclear warheads could be delivered to firing platforms within AFNORTH because there were no depots fulfilling the American requirements for storage of nuclear warheads, and even if there were depots there was no American personnel cleared for handling them in the region. The closest depots to AFNORTH, capable of storing nuclear warheads, were in the northern half of AFCENT, and there were only three. If non-American forces were to become involved in handling nuclear warheads, a rigorous and thorough training process was required beforehand, followed by a formal American approval. This took time; for example a German armoured division had taken one year to reach a satisfactory level.

All in all, we can conclude that the use of nuclear tactical weapons under conditions of war was possible in Denmark and desired by the military top at a certain level of NATO alert, but given the American strict procedures demanding approval of personnel involved and training completed, it is not likely that Danish military personnel would be directly involved after the early 1960s. But in Denmark and in areas close to Denmark, the use by other nationalities was certainly possible in a war situation if nuclear warheads could be brought forward to forces trained to such use. Alternatively, nuclear weapons could be fired by aircraft or long range missiles, e.g. from Northern Germany. But still, nuclear weapons could not be used without unanimous authorisation from the NATO Council; the politicians' ultimate powers were upheld.[72]

Summing up: More becomes less

The introduction of tactical nuclear warheads changed the military perspective radically. It opened the possibility of more constrained use of nuclear weapons. But precisely such limited use was difficult to put into the strategy of NATO. On the contrary, NATO's military chiefs wanted an all-out response to any attack by the Soviets – not because they wanted the war, but because they wanted the Soviets to abstain from attacking in fear of the risk of total destruction by retaliation.

---

71 Minutes YHM from a briefing 14-12-61 at COMLANDENMARK, Forsvarsministeriet 1. kontor 644-3.
72 Afgørelse om atomvåbens anvendelse. Definition af den politiske myndighed. HEM. Forsvarsministeriets 11. kontor 22-11-61. 905-1/61.

The tactics of using smaller nuclear warheads – mainly American – was developed in the mid-1950s. Basically, the military tactics were to induce the enemy to concentrate their forces, making them a nuclear "valuable" target. In principle they could only be released by order of the President; American law prohibited non-Americans to be active in the processes. Weapons were stored at particularly secure places and heavily guarded. Guns, missiles and aircraft able to fire the weapons were somewhere in the theatre field. Special units – always under US command to maintain the presidential influence on use – were at hand to bring the war heads to the platforms destined to fire them, and they followed special procedures to recognise one another. Once brought into the theatre, the firing procedure could take several hours.

SACEUR initiated an elaborate analysis of the prerequisites of conducting a nuclear war – the *New Approach* with massive retaliation to any attack. In 1954 he released a draft of the *1957 Capabilities Plan* of NATO in Europe. The basic idea was an all-out nuclear response to any Soviet attack, with comprehensive attacks with tactical weapons in various theatres, but also with elaborate use of counter-offensive tactical attacks on Soviet bases and airfields to cut off provisions for the army fighting in Europe. The NATO Council, however, could not reach an agreement on letting the supreme commander have the powers to release these weapons, they wanted political influence. Step by step, exemptions to the massive retaliation were introduced – but nonetheless, the massive retaliation concept remained in the documents.

The Capability Plan had many objectives and sketched out nine campaigns to fulfil them. Five of those were relevant for the Baltic Approaches. Each campaign had a series of goals and listed the activities and the forces necessary to perform those roles:
- A preplanned air interdiction campaign would be undertaken in the Eastern European area by naval and air force elements pre-designated and trained for the purpose.
- In Central Europe, an active defence would be conducted, channelling the Soviet forces and inducing sizeable concentrations to be attacked with air, ground and missile delivered nuclear weapons. This campaign included the defence of the Baltic Approaches with Schleswig-Holstein, blocking Soviet forces from entering Danish territory (Jutland).
- In the Baltic and North Sea, maximum local protective measures for Allied shipping, convoys and naval forces were to be instituted. Various (mine) operations in the Danish Straits area were to be undertaken to impose effective closure of these exits.

- Operations were planned in Schleswig-Holstein and coordinated with action planned against the threat in Northern Germany, in order to channel the Soviet attack and force it to mass, to be attacked with atomic weapons.
- If SACLANT carrier forces became available after completion of their initial missions, these would be concentrated on interdiction and close support in Norway, Sweden and/or Denmark, depending on criticality of the situation.

The majority of these campaigns did not relate to littoral warfare; they were massive attacks to prevent Soviet forces from moving and from getting the necessary equipment and stores and thus prevent them from waging war, also in the approaches. The third campaign concerned mine laying in the approaches and the protection of such choke points from the contiguous land areas, but SACEUR undercut the Danish tactics of littoral warfare by indicating that mines could be laid by airplanes (making controlled minefields impossible). The fifth campaign opened the possibility for aircraft carrier support from the North Sea; carriers were not to enter Kattegat or the narrows, but carrier airplanes could easily support warship operations there. A new feature for littoral warfare – potentially changing the mission planning – was that the carrier airplanes could bomb Soviet amphibious forces landing on the Danish (or German) beaches with nuclear weapons. The Danish navy had informed AFNORTH about where such attacks were feasible.

The consequences of the New Approach for the Danish strategy and tactics for the Baltic Approaches were tangible, but also problematic from the military perspective because of the Danish political ambiguity towards use of nuclear weapons. They were not seen as relevant for Denmark, and it was politically unlikely that an authority to use such weapons (by SACEUR) be granted in advance. The Danish Ministry of Defence summarised a number of issues: the principles of the New Approach made intelligence systems imperative; an effective alert system had to be created to make NATO able to react quickly: and top priority had to be given to improve intelligence systems and radar systems and create broader coverage of the planned radar system. This would increase military costs and demand for personnel. Standing forces had to have high priority; this would create problems with the Danish conscripted defence. In general, the tactics were not new: the defence had to block the narrows for passage; stop any Soviet attempt to access Jutland and the Danish islands; and attack enemy Baltic bases used for aircraft and amphibious craft. A weak point in the Danish defence was the ability to withstand a surprise attack at the Elbe/Trave defence line; in so far as the defence in Schleswig-Holstein was successful, the main problem for Danish defence was having weak ground forces on Zealand.

The Danish military top wanted access to nuclear warheads, and the C-in-C recommended NATO to set up procedures. The army included nuclear tactics (creating enemy mass) in the staff courses; the navy did not do much except preparing to protect its personnel. The air force appears to have had some training of pilots. SACEUR started to involve nuclear warheads in exercises, and AFNORTH asked the Danes to point out what coastal areas would be suitable for nuclear (NATO) attacks on landing forces.

The Danish government did not want nuclear warheads. In 1956–57 Denmark was offered HONEST JOHN and NIKE missiles which, however, were not of much use without such warheads; the government accepted them nonetheless without warheads. The cabinet was dependent on minority anti-military parties and could not get political acceptance of storing warheads in Denmark. The Danish C-in-C informed the minister that defence of Denmark would be impossible if the enemy had nuclear weapons and Denmark none. The cabinet did not give in, and the government made this a formal policy "under the present circumstances" in 1957–58 – i.e. in peacetime, but the formulations did not prevent use in wartime.

SACEUR realised in 1957 that the economic means for fulfilling the New Approach were not to be granted by the member countries. NATO's forces had therefore to be modernised to use less personnel. More options for non-nuclear responses were included so that all-out war became less likely. In tactics, army forces had to be organised in relatively small units, be mobile and flexible and integrate all types of weapons, including nuclear warheads, in their operations, based on modern communication systems. Naval forces had to participate in deterrence (aircraft carriers), develop anti-submarine weapons and establish systems of information, warning and control, also against aircraft. Air forces were particularly important in the first phase of a war for deterrence and retaliation. Missiles were expected to replace some aircraft later. Air defence would rely more on missiles.

These ideas, however, did not reduce military costs and rather quite the opposite. Danish costs would rise with 40 per cent, NATO's in general 20 percent. Many countries protested, and the document was only therefore accepted by the NATO Council as a starting point for planning, but not as an operational plan.

The Danish military for some years exercised the use of nuclear warheads, but the investments necessary to build the infrastructure for depots etc. were not budgeted. Quite a large contingent of Americans would have to be housed at the depots, and the government did not want such visible signs of preparations for nuclear weapons. So an active decision to go ahead was never taken; only a few depots were built and the infrastructure to follow suit was so to say blowing in the wind.

To conclude, the use of nuclear tactical weapons was a Janus head. Under conditions of war it was possible in Denmark in the 1950s, but given the American strict procedures it is not likely that Danish military personnel would be directly involved after the start of the 1960s. But in Denmark and in areas close to Denmark, the use by other nationalities was certainly possible in a war situation if nuclear warheads could be brought forward to forces trained to such use. Alternatively, nuclear weapons could be fired by aircraft (e.g. from aircraft carriers) or long range missiles, e.g. from Northern Germany.

Chapter 8
West Germany's rearmament

The rearmament of West Germany is a sizeable theme and there is a comprehensive, mainly German, literature detailing its various aspects; see e.g. Thoss[1] for an analysis emphasising the political reactions to NATO's nuclear retaliation policies. One should realise, however, that for many years following the surrender in 1945, Germans were participants in military activities; thus a large contingent of German mine sweepers with German crews cleared mine fields under British and American command. We shall deal with that below.

Politically, rearmament was contested, especially because the three allied Western powers did not agree on much; every goal reached was a compromise. For several years, the process was one of creating a European Defence Community (EDC) with troops in about 20 divisions from Benelux, France, Italy and Germany, governed by a supra-national system of committees, not unlike the solution in the European Coal and Steel Community. In 1954, the EDC was abandoned because the French Parliament did not approve it. Germany then became member of the Brussels treaty and after that NATO, and since NATO became the military system that governed the rearmament, we shall limit the analysis to what was relevant within NATO and forego a discussion of the various models that were discussed in preparing the EDC.

In Germany, a considerable German movement was created against rearmament with the slogan "Ohne mich" (Without me), supported by the SPD and some of the labour unions. The bourgeois parties CDU and CSU under the leadership of chancellor Konrad Adenauer, however, maintained that rearmament was necessary in order to get a say in the military defence of one's own country. Without its own military, West Germany would be reduced to a battlefield at the mercy of Soviet and American decisions. With a military reinstalled, West Germany could be a partner in decisions that would push the battlefield as far to the east – the forward strategy – as possible and hence spare West German civilian lives. The bourgeois parties also got their way in the difficult theme of providing German troops with nuclear warheads.

In this book we shall not follow the political discussions in their own right. We focus on the military side and mainly deal with NATO and the Baltic Ap-

---

[1] Thoss, Bruno. *NATO-strategie und nationale Verteidigungsplanung. Planung und Aufbau der Bundeswehr unter den Bedingungen atomaren Vergeltungsstrategie 1952–1960*. München: R. Oldenbourg Verlag, 2006.

proaches, and therefore we delimit the discussion to the geographical area which to some degree is part of the Approaches (the Western Baltic and its coastline). For practical purposes, we mainly discuss rearmament of forces in Schleswig-Holstein which was included in the AFNORTH command. Of course, this cannot be done without some information on the Bundesrepublik's military *in toto*; this will be dealt with at a principled level.

Furthermore, the main emphasis of the analysis is on the new *Bundesmarine* and its naval air force,[2] but we do not totally neglect the *Bundesheer* which had to be ready to meet amphibious forces and land forces crossing the border to East Germany, and the *Bundesluftwaffe* which had certain roles in bombing, particularly with nuclear warheads.

Initial conceptions of German rearmament

Out of fear for a re-creation of the spirit of the Nazi armed forces, the Allies made sure in 1945 that it was forbidden to work for the re-creation of German military forces. But the Korean war changed their minds, realising that without a contribution from the newly created West German Bundesrepublik to the military forces, the West would come into a serious deficit vis-a-vis the Soviet Union. So in the fall of 1950, former German officers began to work for such cause, invited by the German Bundeskansler, Konrad Adenauer.

The first secret discussions took place in early October 1950 in a seminar at the former monastery Himmerod, and the resulting report, the Himmerod Memorandum (*Himmeroder Denkschrift*), became the starting point for Adenauer's negotiations with the three West Allies for the rearmament of West Germany. The memorandum launched the idea of creating a contingent for the defence of Western Europe – not as an independent German force, but rather within the framework of an International Fighting Force. Late October, 1950, an office for rearmament, the Blank Agency (*Amt Blank)*, was set up by Adenauer in the Chancellor's office to serve as administration for that purpose. Soon thereafter, the West Allies agreed to discuss the issue, and the Germans became involved in the process of creating the European Defence Community, the EDC.

The Himmerod group thought that the navies and air forces of the West were relatively strong, so their main focus became the threat from the east on the

---

2 An overview is found in Monte, Peter. "Die Rolle der Marine der Bundesrepublik Deutschland." In *Deutsche Marinen im Wandel. Vom Symbol nationaler Einheit zum Instrument internationaler Sicherheit*, Werner Rahn. München: R. Oldenbourg Verlag, 2005.

ground,[3] and the principal discussions concerned the territorial defence and the creation of German army forces of 250,000 men. The air force of 821 airplanes plus transport planes was mainly linked to the operations of the army, but it also had a strong fighter component to attack incoming Soviet bombers.

For most of the participants, the perceived main naval threat was the Soviet submarines, estimated to be 200 in the Atlantic and North Sea (to be dealt with by the Americans and the British) and 100 in the Baltic. The Baltic approaches – Denmark and Schleswig-Holstein – were seen partly as a cork in the bottle for the passage of Soviet submarines, partly as a theatre for counter-attacks once the Soviet attacks were stopped. This called for a West German naval presence in the Baltic with MTBs, submarines and amphibious vessels. They were to be supported by British and American ships – not smaller than destroyers – and by air forces.

Comprehensive planning of the Bundeswehr-to-be took place in the 1950s, but we shall not go into the details of various first plans except for the *Bundesmarine* which is dealt with below. Suffice it to say that expectations in numbers were high, especially for the army, but the results somewhat lower, as the ministry took the stance that it would prefer quality to quantity, meaning that the forces to work within NATO had to be of high military standard. This took time because of problems in recruiting officers and non-commissioned officers as well as getting suitable barracks and training areas in the right places. For the air force numerous problems came up regarding training, creating workshops and even getting planes. For the navy, the problems were in the abstract the same – getting new vessels, establishing training facilities and repair yards, as well as recruiting personnel.

In 1956–57, the first armed forces were formed, so let us see what the expectations for future military forces were at that time. Below, we use the figures from the Annual Review 1957, projecting forces for 1961.[4]

Army: Bundesheer

In 1957, the size of the army planned for 1961 is indicated in table 8.1.

Each infantry division (as in the exercise at Hameln, see box) was organised into three combat commands, each consisting of three motorised infantry battal-

---

[3] Sander-Nagashima, Johannes Berthold. *Die Bundesmarine 1950 bis 1972*, 34–40. München: Oldenbourg Wissenschaftsverlag, 2006.
[4] Greiner, Christian. "Die militärische Eingliederung der Bundesrepublik Deutschland in die WEU und die NATO." In *Die NATO-Option*, Hans Ehlert, Christian Greiner, Georg Meyer, and Bruno Thoss, 831–41. München: R. Oldenbourg Verlag, 1993.

Table 8.1: Army divisions.

Infantry divisions	4
Armoured divisions	6
Airborne divisions	1
Mountain divisions	1
Honest John groups	3

ions and an armour battalion; it would have combat support from light and medium artillery batteries. In addition, they would have antiaircraft, engineer and reconnaissance battalions, a communication battalion, and diverse support units. The armoured divisions were organised in the same way, but with more armoured vehicles. The airborne and mountain divisions had another organisation better suited to their special purposes.

In Schleswig-Holstein, the original plans were to house two infantry divisions, but as things turned out, only one – very large – infantry/armour division was located there, as the basic concept was changed in 1959 (see below). It was the sixth Panzergrenadier Division which was merged by divisions from the previous organisation.

This new division had up to 30,000 men in two infantry brigades (16 and 17) and one armoured brigade (18); it was the largest division in NATO. It had 5,800 wheeled vehicles and 1,200 track vehicles.[5] It had (after 1965) 252 Leopard tanks and more than 220 armoured personnel carriers. It had 21 helicopters and 24 transport helicopters plus 14 special helicopters for fighting tanks.

After 1981, the sixth division was supported locally by the fifty-first home defence brigade with 4,500 men organised in two infantry-, two tank- and two artillery battalions.

In war, the sixth division was until 1962 commanded by COMLANDSCHLESWIG, followed by COMLANDJUT. The division had as its main task the forward defence at the border to East Germany, especially east of the freeway between Hamburg and Lübeck, and was to prevent enemy sea and air landing of troops in Schleswig-Holstein. The task was to prevent WAPA forces from getting across to the North Sea and thus cut off the AFNORTH from AFCENT and in addition cut off the sea lines of communication from the west to Germany.

The MC 70 specified that West German troops would get nuclear warheads. The issue was strongly contested in the German public, but in the end West Germany accepted the proposal from NATO.

---

5 https://de.wikipedia.org/wiki/6._Panzergrenadierdivision_(Bundeswehr).

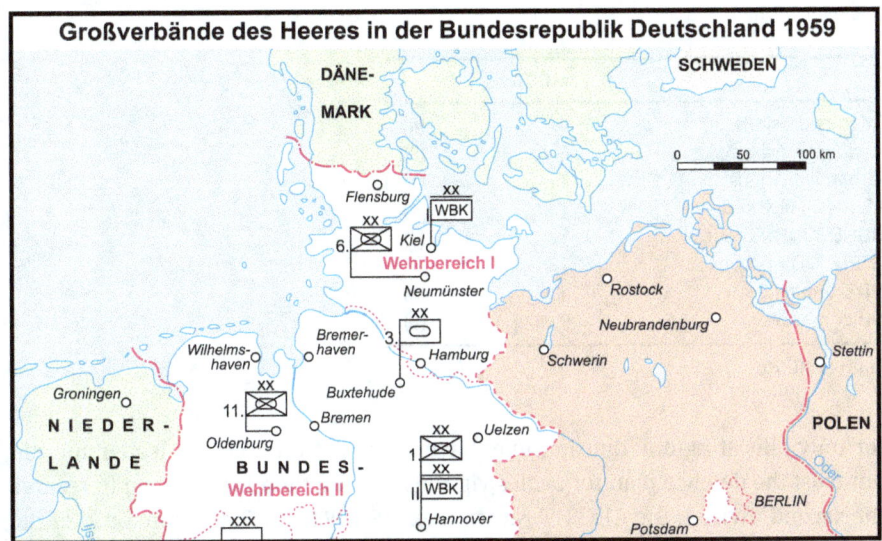

Figure 8.1: Location of army divisions in Northern Germany 1959.[6] Copyright ZMSBW.

As a consequence, the planned army was restructured, to some degree inspired by the American ideas for the "Pentomic"[7] division, working on the basis of a high degree of decentralisation and hence flexibility. The mountain- and airborne divisions were sustained. The remaining ten divisions were organised into three brigades which were organised so that they could each independently provide for themselves in five days of combat.[8] Four "panzergrenadier" divisions with 216 tanks had one armoured brigade and two infantry brigades. Six armoured divisions with 270 tanks had two armoured brigades and one infantry brigade. All brigades had artillery and rocket launchers capable of both traditional and nuclear warheads. Conscription time was increased from 12 to 18 months.

The table below shows the MC 70 target figures for 1963 with the 1959 figures in brackets.

The reorganisation was one rationale for only allocating one "panzergrenadier" division to Schleswig-Holstein from 1959. Such a division was stronger than the two infantry divisions originally planned for the area.[9] But another reason

---

6 Hammerich, Helmut R., Dieter H. Kollmer, Martin Rink, and Rudolf J. Schlaffer. *Das Heer 1950 Bis 1970. Konzeption, Organisation, Aufstellung*, 262. München: R. Oldenbourg Verlag, 2006.
7 See https://en.wikipedia.org/wiki/Pentomic for details of Pentomic organisation.
8 Ibid., 187.
9 Ibid., 453.

Table 8.2: Army.

	MC 70	
Infantry divisions	4	(4)
Armoured divisions	6	(3)
Airborne divisions	1	(1/3)
Mountain divisions	1	(1)
HONEST JOHN Groups	12	(4)
LITTLE JOHN Groups	12	
NIKE Groups	3	(1)
Other missiles	9	(3)

Source: MC 70.

for only allocating one division may have been that the German leadership did not trust the defence plan for Schleswig-Holstein and therefore wanted to reserve the second division for AFCENT rather than AFNORTH.[10] The planned use of the sixth Panzergrenadier division in Schleswig-Holstein is found in chapter 6.

Air force: Luftwaffe

Ten years after WWII there were no previous pilots from the Wehrmacht with intimate knowledge of the technical development of aircraft, so the Germans had to cooperate closely with the Americans to organise the new Luftwaffe, get new planes, set up technical support and train pilots and ground staff.

The West Germans planned the new air force based on the following perception of a Soviet attack:[11] initially a large number of aircraft would attack NATO's nuclear weapon depots and firing stands, and in the process they would attack the West German air defence, primarily with light bombers and fighter-bombers. The large bombers would pass Germany for more remote targets, possibly in Britain. After that, the Soviet air force would be used for air support to the ground troops.

The Germans planned an Interception Defence Force to support army operations, and a interceptor force to attack enemy bombers in up to 25,000 meters altitude, and a missile system on the ground.

---

[10] Ibid., 126.
[11] Lemke, Bernd, Dieter Krüger, Heinz Rebhan, and Wolfgang Schmidt. *Die Luftwaffe 1950 bis 1970. Konzeption, Aufbau, Integration*, 153–54. München: R. Oldenbourg Verlag, 2006.

In 1957, the tactical air force and its wings were organised in two geographical divisions north and south, following the allied organisation of the second and fourth Allied Tactical Air Force (ATAF) under British and American command, respectively. Thus the organisation of the air force was tuned to the military tasks of AFCENT: preventing various attacks against the central territory of West Germany. But making the new air force operational took its time. The first fighter-bomber wing was ready for action by Summer 1958, but the staffs of the two divisions were not ready for directing combat until early 1961.

For starters, 450 F-84 F fighter-bombers, 108 RF-84 recce and 20 Douglas C-47 were rented in the USA and 75 F-86 Sabre 5 fighters in Canada. Some 225 F-86 Sabre 6 fighters were bought from Canada, 90 F 86 K all-weather fighters from Italy and 157 transport Noratlas from France.[12] Sixteen airfields were destined for these forces. In addition, 300 training airplanes of various sorts were used at four training airfields.

The tasks for the aircraft were the traditional ones. The main role for the fighters was air defence by attacking all sorts of enemy aircraft. The fighter-bombers had three main roles: counter air (destroying enemy airfields and infrastructure in enemy territory); interdiction (closing off battle areas for enemy ground forces); and close air support (attacking enemy ground forces for the army's operations). These three tasks were distributed among the wings which specialised their operations accordingly.

Regarding the Baltic Approaches, Schleswig-Holstein got wings from the air force in three locations: fighters (54) in Leck, fighter-bombers (75) in Husum and transport (18) in Hohn. In addition, a G-91 wing was planned to be forward-located to Hohn in times of crisis. Furthermore, the navy got its own air force (see next section below).

The split into two commands meant that the northern division, 2. ATAF, had the role of operational control of aircraft in Schleswig-Holstein, and remained in that role even after the BALTAP command was established; COMAIRBALTAP only had operational command of air forces north of the Danish-German border.[13] COMAIRBALTAP did, however, have tactical command of the air forces within BALTAP.[14]

MC 70 planned the following strength of the German air force by 1963 as indicated in table 8.3.

Compared with the original composition of the air force, MC 70 put less emphasis on fighter-bombers (the same for Danish forces) and more on all-weather fighters. Thus the ability to meet enemy bombers in the initial phases of a conflict

---

12 Ibid., 569.
13 Steinkopff, Klaus Christoph. *Die geostrategische Bedeutung der Cimbrischen Halbinsel in der westlichen Verteidigungsplanung*, 98. Kiel, 2003.
14 Ibid., 92–93.

Table 8.3: Air Force.

Fighter-bomber squadrons	8/200
Day fighters squadrons	8/160
All-weather fighter squadrons	16/256
Reconnaissance squadrons	11/206
Transport	8/125
Aircraft total	1047
Air def. Missiles groups	28

Source: MC 70 Annex Tables.

was strengthened. But the air force planned to get F-104 STARFIGHTERs which were fighters, but also usable as fighter-bombers with nuclear warheads. This aircraft was expensive, but fast and efficient.

The maps below indicate the number of infrastructure centres and airfields within the range of STARFIGHTERs. The maps were used in 1959 for a top-military discussion of the tricky question of whether Germany should make use of nuclear warheads. The author of the paper using the maps discussed the possibilities for the air force and argued that there were many more targets that the German air force could destroy over a number of days, meaning that the attacking Soviet forces had solid support possibilities and hence could sustain their attacks. Consequently, there would be no way to escape the issue at hand: the Germans had to resort to the use of nuclear warheads from the very beginning of a war.[15]

Missiles were being developed to take over the general air defence. Two types of missiles stood out: NIKE missiles for aircraft in higher altitude, and HAWK missiles for low altitude aircraft. The missile air defence was organised in two belts through West Germany; to the east a belt of HAWK missiles, to the west a belt of NIKE missiles. Regarding Schleswig-Holstein, the HAWK-belt crossed the area at Husum. The NIKE missiles were farther away, in Ostfriesland, but close enough to yield efficient cover for the northern territory.

A comprehensive radar warning system was constructed with 11 radar installations in the whole of West Germany. One of these radar systems was located in Brekendorf close to Kiel.

In addition to this general air defence system there was local air defence of various military key points.

---

15 Lemke, Krüger, Rebhan, and Schmidt, op. cit., pp. 205–14.

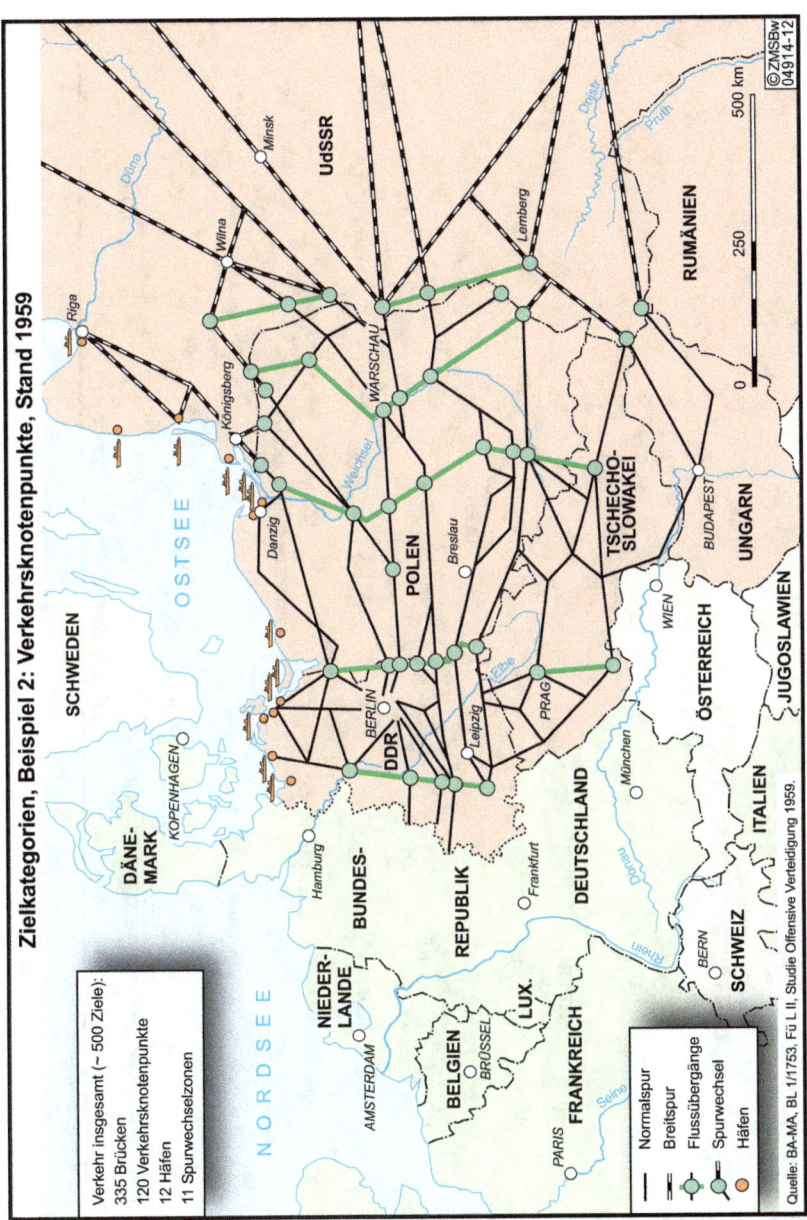

Figure 8.2: Infrastructure targets in Eastern Europe.[16] Copyright ZMSBW.

---

16 Ibid., 211.

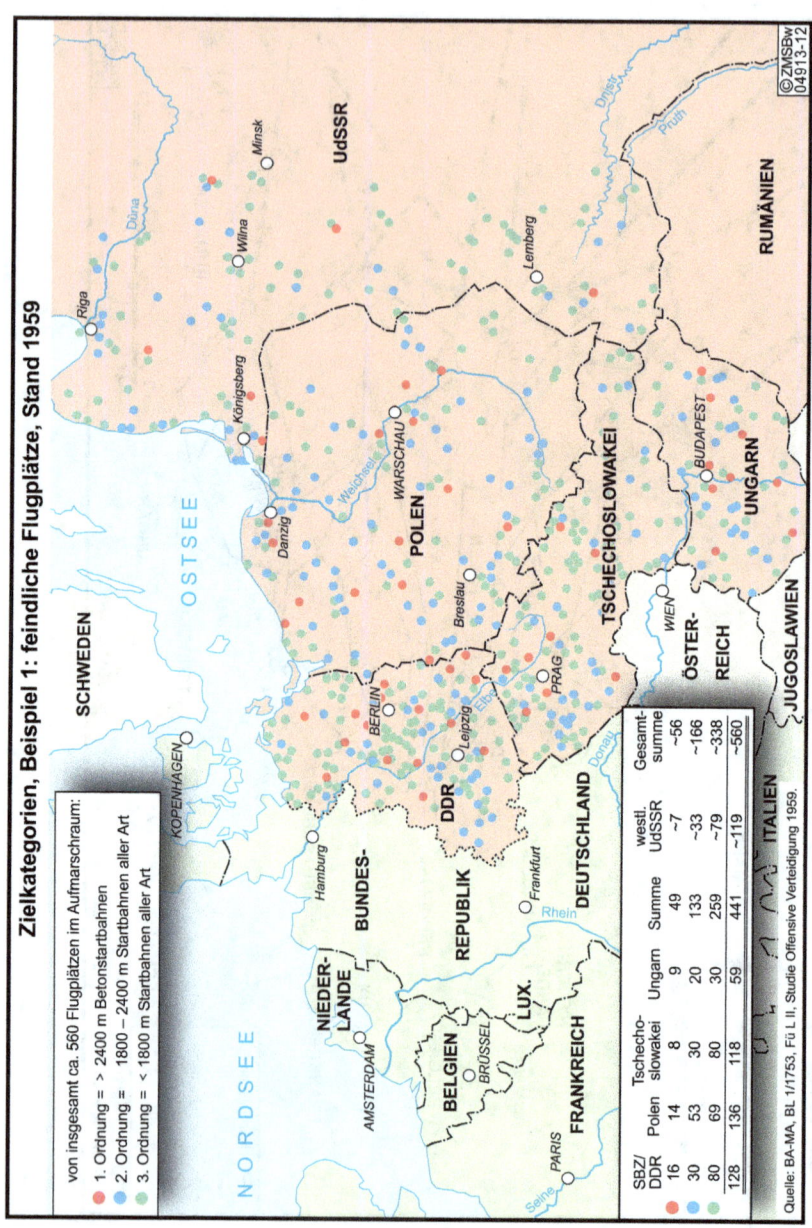

Figure 8.3: Airfield targets in Eastern Europe.[17] Copyright ZMSBW.

---

17 Ibid., 210.

Navy: Bundesmarine

Since the main tasks of defending the Baltic Approaches lay with the West German navy (including its air force), we shall go more in detail with the conceptualisation of the Bundesmarine.

Nearly from day one of the German surrender in 1945, some Germans were still engaged in military affairs.[18] A large number of mine sweepers swept mines: the *German Minesweeping Administration* (GMSA) worked under British command, but had a German sub-commander. It was dissolved on 1 January 1948, but 12 mine sweepers with 600 men in civilian clothes continued sweeping mines from Cuxhaven under British command. The unit was closed down in 1951, but some continued under the new German sea police, others under the American *Labor Service Unit B*, sweeping mines, stationed in Cuxhaven. The British created the *British Baltic Fishery Protection Service*, using ex-German MTBs under British colours, formally for fishery inspection, but really working as a clandestine network of gathering intelligence and transporting agents to and from the Baltic states.

Klose and the *British Baltic Fishery Protection Service*
As we saw in chapter 6, the Danish government was quite concerned about NATO warships entering the waters around Bornholm. After the exercise MAINBRACE (see chapter 3), a note was written, preventing British FPBs to call at harbours at Bornholm during exercises. Be that as it may, any call of foreign warships had to be approved by the Ministry of Foreign Affairs.

In the Fall of 1953 the Ministry of Foreign Affairs received a note from the Ministry of Defence, asking if there were any objections against a British MTB 5208 – functioning as fishery inspection vessel – calling at the harbour of Rønne at Bornholm now and then to get supplies. As a matter of fact, this had been the case in all of 1952 and 1953 until now as a mutual, non-formal agreement. Diplomats are by nature prudent, so the ministry issued a note of October 1, 1953:

> The Ministry of Defence today informed the Ministry of Foreign Affairs that according to the Danish C-in-C of the Navy, this non-formal agreement has functioned in an exemplary way. The vessel has called about once a month . . . calling Rønne has been regarded as a normal instance and has not been mentioned in the local press. We recommend to approve this but to bring this matter into formalization ASAP.[19]

---

18 Pfeifer, Douglas. "Forerunners to the West German Bundesmarine: The Klose Fast Patrol Group, the Naval Historical Team Bremerhaven, and the U.S. Navy's Labor Service Unit (B)." *International Journal of Naval History* 1, no. 1 (2002).
19 Hornemann, Jacob. *Bornholm mellem Øst og Vest. En udenrigspolitisk dokumentation*. Rønne: Bornholms Tidendes Forlag, 2006.

This was a carefully formulated rebuke to the navy, but the permission was granted. MTB 5208 was one of the vessels of the *British Baltic Fishery Protection Service*, a former German MTB 208, commanded by Hans-Helmut Klose.[20] Formally, it protected West German fishery in the Baltic against Russian interference. In reality, the main tasks were to land and take back agents behind the Iron Curtain, and to eavesdrop on Soviet communication. But the Danish Foreign Ministry knew nothing about this, so the recommendation to grant the permission above was based on the premise that there were no foreign policy issues involved. The ministry noted, however, that the minister should check possible national policy problems – this was a warning to the minister that the communist party representation in the Danish parliament might raise objections.

In other words, Denmark supported a comprehensive system of espionage – apparently without any minister knowing about this – by letting Klose get supplies in Rønne and permit him to visit other harbours, among those Christiansø which is the easternmost (small) Danish island (see photo below). Most of the time MTB 5208 sailed along the coasts of the Baltic using powerful electronic listening devices and observing what went on close to Soviet territory. Thus Klose and his crew created invaluable information about Soviet Radar installations, gun batteries, searchlights, airfields and exercise areas along the Baltic coast.

Figure 8.4: Wild Swan at Christiansø in 1954. Note the British jack. Source: www.s-boot.net.

At this time, the Danish navy had no ships suited to such tasks, but from 1956 new corvettes could do the job, and they did take up the task of gathering information for NATO about the Soviet bloc and its activities in the Baltic.

---

20 Hess, Sigurd. "Die Schnellbootgruppe Klose." In *Die deutschen Schnellboote im Einsatz*, edited by Hans Frank. Hamburg: E S Mittler Verlag, 2007.

Hans-Helmut Klose did the groundbreaking work for such activities. He joined the new Bundesmarine in 1956 as group leader of MTBs. He rose later to vice admiral and C-in-C of the navy.

The Himmerod group was mainly occupied with the defence by army forces, but the navy also was discussed. The tasks in the North Sea and the Baltic were, according to the Himmerod Group:

- Protection against Soviet attacks at sea and prevention of landing troops
- Preventing submarines from breaking out;
- Blocking Soviet LOCs at sea (the Baltic would be an important supply channel for Soviet land forces);
- Protecting own LOCs against submarines and air forces and keeping them free from mines;
- Protecting own land forces against bombardment from the sea and against the landing of troops.

Knowing, however, that the US and Britain had not reserved forces for the Baltic, that Sweden was neutral and that Denmark did not have forces worth mentioning, a strong West German component was needed. The Himmerod Group recommended a navy as indicated in the table below, which includes figures from two other analyses in the 1950s which we shall return to below:

Table 8.4: Navy targets.

	Himmerod	SACEUR	1956	MC 70–1963
Destroyers/ large torpedo boats	12	18	12	10*
Escorts/ frigates	12	–	6	6
Patrol Craft large/ small	24/35	10	0/10	36
Submarines	24	12	12	30**
ASW	12	–	–	–
Mine sweepers large/ small	24/35	30	6/48	6
Mine layers	2	–	4	4***
MTBs	36	40	40	50
Amphibious craft	12	yes	36	
Aircraft fighter-bombers/ ASW	84/30	58/0	72	

*originally 12 destroyers. **originally 8 350-t subs plus 100-t subs. ***all later taken out. Source:[21] MC 70.

---

21 Sander-Nagashima, op. cit., pp. 38–39, 144–45; Frorath, Gerd, Dieter Matthei, and Hans W Worringer. *Die Crew X/62 im Spiegel der Zeit*, 16–17. http://www.crewx62.de/Texte/DokuCrewX62+Schlussversion+HP.pdf, n.d.

These recommendations became the starting point for negotiations in the years to come. For the naval members of the section there were two main themes to negotiate: getting larger units – destroyers – and getting a navy as active as possible, i.e. with as few ships as possible decommissioned in a reserve.

This was exactly what the French were opposed to in the negotiations of the EDC. They did not want German destroyers and preferred most units in the reserve, and consequently the future German navy was reduced to a sort of coastal defence and mine sweeping force. This was initially supported by SHAPE, but during Winter 1951–52, the Germans got an opportunity to present the German ideas, as seen by the ex-naval officers, for SHAPE,[22] and got an audience that had a broader understanding for their demand for destroyers and only a small reserve, but still they got no destroyers and submarines.

The Danish Joint Chiefs of Staff then were heard for opinions in March 1952.[23] But they did not quite agree about the need for German rearmament. The chief of the Navy, as we saw in chapter 2, had been in close contact with Admiral Heye and supported a West German build-up of a navy in the Baltic, with destroyers and submarines also. He did not trust the other NATO countries to allocate forces for the area, and, even so, it would take them several days to get there while the Germans were present and ready for action any time. The army and air force supported his views, but the C-in-C had more doubts. He feared that while the other countries in the EDC-to-come would see to it that proper oversight was established over German army and air force, such control mechanisms would be more difficult regarding the navy. Only the Danish navy was close by, and remembering the failure of the control mechanisms from the Versailles peace treaty, the C-in-C had his doubts about the prospects for success. So why not entice the British to allocate some naval forces to the Baltic? He had suggested a rather large NATO force in the Baltic the year before (see chapter 5). However, he acquiesced to his subordinate chiefs and ended up supporting the German ideas.

In a meeting with the chairman of NATO's Standing Group, General Ely, in late July 1953, the Danish Joint Chiefs of Staff reconfirmed the desirability of West German forces – army forces in Schleswig-Holstein were crucial for the defence of the area, and a West German navy in the Baltic Sea was necessary because one could not rely on naval assistance in time from other NATO countries.[24]

---

22 Sander-Nagashima, op. cit., p. 45.
23 FSS 7-3-52 and 19-3-52.
24 Minutes of meeting 31-7-53, SGM-1666-53 dated 6-11-53.

In the WEU-negotiations the French had tried to curtail the Germans. In NATO, the French had less influence and West Germany used the change of setting to get destroyers and submarines included in the proposals for a navy by asking SACEUR for an advisory opinion. This was contrary to normal procedures, but underscoring that the statement was tentative and informal, the supreme commander defined the future roles for the navy:
- to prevent enemy ships from leaving the Baltic
- to block Soviet LOCs
- to participate in the defence of West German and Danish coasts and
- to maintain own LOCs.

This could be done by a navy of 18 small destroyers, 12 coastal submarines, 10 escort crafts, 40 FPBs, 30 mine sweepers and a number of auxiliary craft.[25]

The West Germans now took the lead and defined the roles for their future navy, adding two tasks to the above:[26]
- Limited participation in operations in the North Sea; and
- Suitable representation of the country at sea and performing naval education
- Given the geographical conditions, the tasks of the new navy were split into two areas:[27]
- In the Baltic the task was to prevent attacks on the German coast by using fast units to carry out repeated surprise attacks on the enemy. Thus NATO could take advantage of the geography and quickly set up new task forces; in particular, MTBs, fighter-bombers, submarines and mine vessels would be useful for such tasks, but further to the east in the Baltic one would need destroyers.
- In the North Sea the navy would have to protect NATO LOCs, and in Skagerrak they were to block the connections between the Baltic and the Atlantic, if the defence of the Baltic Approaches was run over. This required ships with great endurance and ability to operate in all kinds of weather – this required destroyers and frigates, ASW airplanes, submarines and fighter-bombers.

The resulting plan for the navy is shown in Table 8.4 above, under "1956". The table also indicates what the MC 70 planned, a somewhat reduced strength of the German navy by 1963. The numbers were the desired size of the navy; in actual fact,

---

25 SHAPE. *SHAPE History – The New Approach 1953–1956*, 366–69. Mons: SHAPE, 1976.
26 Sander-Nagashima, op. cit., p. 49.
27 Jeschonnek, Gert. *Bundesmarine 1955 bis heute*, 142–43. Koblenz/Bonn: Wehr und Wissen, 1975.

the numbers of destroyers and submarines became smaller. Since our focus is on NATO and the Baltic Approaches, the main theme in the remainder of the book will be the tasks in the Baltic with an outlook to the North Sea when necessary.

The navy had eight stations (see map); the main stations were in Flensburg and Kiel (the Western Baltic), and Cuxhaven and Wilhelmshaven (the North Sea). The Kiel Canal connected the two seas. The naval air force was located in Jagel in Schleswig and Nordholz close to Cuxhaven.

As we saw above, the navy had to serve two separate geographical areas. The NATO command For the North Sea NORSEACENT in Cuxhaven was under AFCENT, and the actual commander over the Baltic forces in peacetime, the FOG (Flag Officer Germany), was a sub-command. But the tasks in the North Sea and in the Baltic were quite different; consequently in wartime the German Baltic navy under the FOG came under the NAVNORTH command together with the Danish navy under the FOD (Flag Officer Denmark). This of course was a too complicated system which was solved by the creation of BALTAP in 1962 (see chapter 9).

The locations of the navy stations were problematic because of their proximity to East Germany and the short distance for attacking land forces. One could not be sure of keeping them under NATO control after a surprise attack (later on, in the 1960s, the risk for the German bases would include attacks from a large distance with missiles). Therefore, much emphasis was put on ways to handle supplies to the navy.[28] A large fleet of supply ships was planned to avoid that the ships would have to return to a German base – exactly as admiral Heye had advised in 1949. Two types of depot ships were planned. Mother ships would carry supplies for 10 days and would deliver supplies directly to the fighting units. Special transport supply ships (tankers, munition ships etc.) would bring supplies stored in German or foreign country depots (Denmark and the Netherlands, possibly Norway) to the mother ships. The mother ships would deliver supplies at sea. Consequently, one could imagine that the whole German Baltic navy went to sea at a certain alert level and positioned itself in Danish or Norwegian waters together with depot ships. However, the issue of depots in Denmark was not easily solved (see chapter 6). In 1963, the navy had 13 mother ships and 15 other supply ships built or planned, a quite sizeable support fleet, but in 1958, 47 ships had been planned for.[29]

---

28 Minutes of German naval logistics conference held on Friday, 12th Sept. 1958 in Aircent main briefing room. BM 1/720.
29 Protokoll der Sitzung des Annual Review Visiting Teams mit Vertretern des Führungsstabes der Bundesmarine am 10.6.1958. Streng geheim. Anlage zu Fü M II – Az 03-06 – 00 – Tgb.Nr. 90. BM 1/1639.

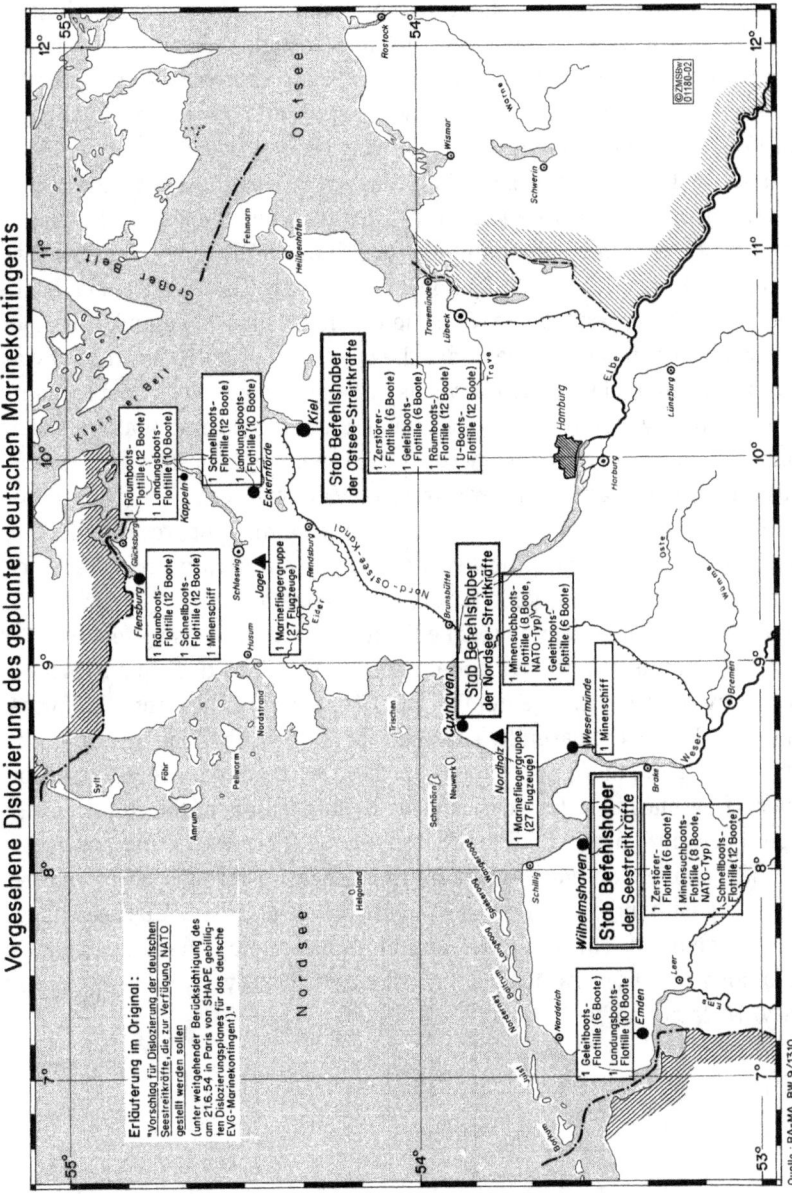

Figure 8.5: Map of planned navy stations 1956.[30] Copyright ZMSBW.

---

30 Greiner, op. cit., p. 843.

The *Bundesmarine* started out with mine sweepers and FPBs from the organisations maintained by the British and the Americans, and personnel from those organisations became a resource in forming the first crews. A comprehensive program for building new destroyers, submarines, mine sweepers and MTBs was initiated.

Until 1963, the organisation had the following general features:[31] in the Ministry of Defence in Bonn, the Inspector of the Navy, a vice admiral, resided with his staff, far away from the naval stations at the North Sea and the Baltic. Three operational staffs took care of commanding the operations of the navy, logistics (harbours, support ships etc.) and education, respectively. The Commander of the Navy had two subsidiaries: Command of the North Sea and Command of the Baltic. These two commands would be under the command of NATO in times of war, and hence the Commander of the Navy was an administrative position, responsible for the day-to-day quality of the operational units. The operational units were organised in flotillas or squadrons according to their type: destroyers, submarines, FPBs (fast patrol boats), mine sweepers, navy aircrafts etc. During operations they were assigned to the North Sea or the Baltic commands, residing in Cuxhaven and Kiel, respectively. After 1963, education and a number of technical services were merged into one Central Services Command.

Altogether, the young navy had gone through a comprehensive "exercise" of training a large number of officers and crew in a very short time span. This only was possible by re-hiring a large number of officers and ratings from the former Kriegsmarine. These were carefully screened for Nazi sympathies. Education became important. First, there was a focus on the non-commissioned officers from the former Kriegsmarine to let them run the daily business of the ships and use their experiences in a new school for NCOs. Second, there was a focus on future admiral staff members among the officers to let them go through a two year advanced training without, however, them having privileges in the final selection of officers for promotion. Third, a fairly large number of ships were dedicated to training, among those several former British escort destroyers of the HUNT and BLACK SWAN classes and a three-mast sailship.[32]

---

31 Jeschonnek, op. cit., pp. 29–36.
32 Wagner, Gerhard. "Die ersten Jahre der Bundesmarine." In *Seemacht un Geschichte*, Deutsches Marine Institut, 229–38. Bonn: MOV-Verlag, 1975.

Admiral Ruge's forward defence in the Baltic Approaches

What were the expectations for the Bundesmarine-in-being? Early work in the 1950s on tactical principles made itself felt later. The C-in-C (Inspector) of the West German navy, Admiral Ruge, had participated in the work of the Himmerod Group and in May 1958 he wrote a note on sea strategy for the Bundesmarine, with strong roots in the Himmerod Denkschrift.[33] In a sense, he continued the thoughts we have seen above (by the British Chiefs of Staff, chapter 3, and the Danish Navy C-in-C, chapter 6) about offensive operations in the Baltic: thoughts which the French had opposed strongly in the WEU-negotiations. But now we had NATO.

Ruge stressed the need for forward defence to keep the Cimbric Peninsula in the hands of NATO and prevent the Soviets from attacking the north flank of the AFCENT forces (and thus protect the Soviet north flank). The Baltic Approaches and the Baltic were key to staying in power, or losing it, with severe consequences for the war in Central Europe. Therefore, the initial NATO counter strikes against Soviet Baltic bases were important, and instead of just defending the AFNORTH area, NATO was to counterattack along the Baltic Coast into enemy territory and establish military power by using amphibious forces to land army contingents in key points and thus cut off the Soviets LOCs for the army units moving westwards. SACLANT air carrier strike forces could be important helpers, navigating in the North Sea to launch air attacks against the Baltic. Air supremacy was a must, but uncertain; all actions in daytime were dependent on it. Since the German bases were so close to East Germany, most of the navy would have to initially use bases in Denmark and even South Norway and have a large number of depot ships so that the fighting units could find safe haven against air raids during daytime and have stations for supplies. Consequently, close cooperation with the Danes was a must in the preparations for war, and obviously a joint NATO integrated command was necessary in wartime (and therefore, the border of AFCENT was to be moved to Skagerrak). For forward defence activities destroyers, FPBs and small submarines were essential, but the two first types were dependent on the local situation in the airspace. The navy also had to employ a relatively large number of amphibious craft, and the navy air arm would support actions at sea and at enemy ports. In addition, it could do important recce.

This theoretical analysis left the German navy, and hence AFNORTH, in a rather weak condition. The area needed a NATO force booster. Admiral Ruge decided to address the issue during a visit in January 1959 to the American Admiral Burke, Chief of US Naval Operations. Burke had some months before indicated

---

33 Sander-Nagashima, op. cit., pp. 73–80.

that such a note would be most welcome.[34] However, Ruge never got to present the paper because it was met with some resistance from the German military top.

Initially, Ruge's staff wrote a 40-page note addressing the issue which was christened "A Study of an Offensive Strategy in the Baltic".[35] The title says much: Ruge did not just want to react to a Soviet attack, waiting in the AFNORTH waters; he wanted to move the front into enemy areas, and this required more NATO forces than the present plan (MC 70) mandated.

The note followed much of the argumentation from May 1958, but it was adapted to an American perspective. Ruge more or less made the Baltic Approaches the cornerstone of winning (or preventing) a war in Europe. First, he stressed that the Baltic Approaches were exits for Soviet submarines to the Atlantic, threatening American as well as European interests. Second, the Soviet navy had to be countered: it was so large that it totally dominated the Baltic; it could protect their LOCs (in general, but also to Soviet forces attacking Western Europe), it could probably conquer the Baltic Approaches and then Southern Norway, followed by attacks in the North Sea area and subsequently with submarines in the Atlantic; and it could – after taking the Approaches – use all the shipping resources of the Baltic for the whole navy and particularly for replenishing and repairing the submarines. Third, the Baltics had previously not played a special role in NATO's defence plans – plans were, as far as the German Navy knew, to mine the Exits in the north and in the south by British air planes and mine layers (as we have seen, this was blatantly untrue, PB), but now the new German navy had the role of defending the Baltic Approaches together with the Danish navy. In addition, the German navy was to carry out offensive operations, particularly against Soviet LOCs; this, however, would be difficult because the tasks of defending own territory so close to the enemy took nearly all resources. Furthermore, the Danish forces were weak and Denmark did not show much interest in expanding them.

The tactical problems for the Germans were the following: first, the Soviets had air supremacy over most of the Baltic so there was a need to counterbalance the Soviets; second, the whole land-based logistical system of the navy was threatened because of the short distance to the Eastern bloc and the defending ground forces of NATO were weak; third, German military resources were limited and weak because a military tradition had been lost; fourth, Denmark was militarily weak – in spite of an obvious military need for reinforcements Denmark had refused such in peacetime – and in spite of this gap did not want West Germany to

---

[34] Aktennotitz Geheim by Capt. Wegener: Vorwärtsstrategie in Ostsee und Schwarzem Meer. 3-11-58. BM 3174a.
[35] NATO top secret. Sent to the Inspector of the Bundeswehr 13-1-59, Tgb.Nr.3/59. BM 3174a Ostsee-strategie.

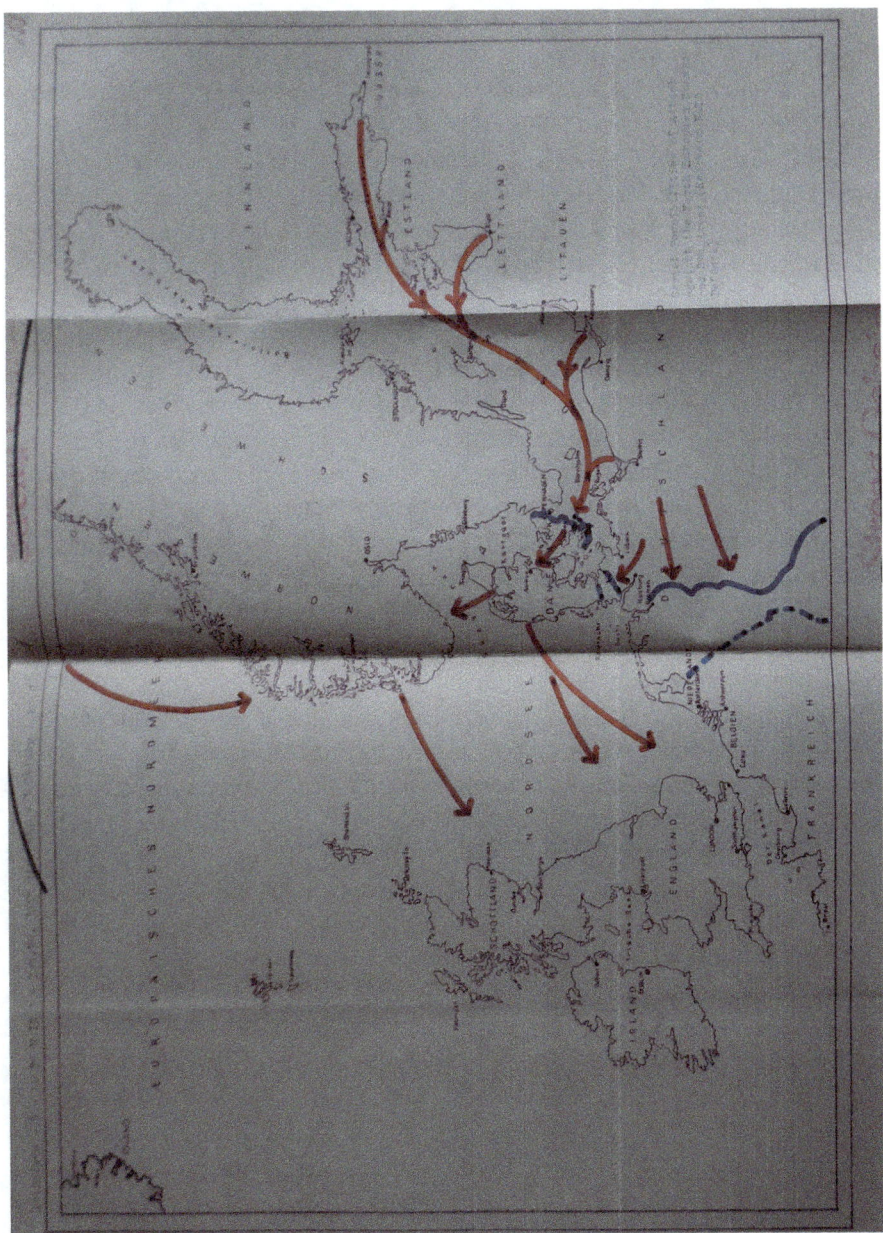

Figure 8.6: A map from Ruge's note indicating the risks of Soviet aggression if the Baltic Approaches were not held by NATO (Blue lines: Defence lines). Source: Bundeswehr Archiv.

take a lead in the defence of the Baltic Approaches; therefore, Germany wanted the AFCENT border moved north.

In the light of the above, Ruge stated that it had been quite a mistake of the Western Allies not to fill the military void in the Baltic created by the disarmament of Germany after the war. They ought to have build up a carrier or strike force based in North Sea and Baltic ports, somewhat like the American sixth fleet in the Mediterranean. And if the French and the Dutch realised the importance of the Baltic Approaches for their own security, they would probably also have seen an interest in participating.

At this time (1959) NATO was discussing a more forward defence line, a concept that was at the heart of the Germans. And if one wanted offensive operations in the Baltic, holding the defence line was paramount. Given that NATO altogether had a very strong naval potential, NATO was to allocate more of that potential – together with ground forces – to initiate an offensive along the Baltic coast, for starters in Mecklenburg and possibly Rügen (both in East Germany), and at the same time reinforce NATO forces on Bornholm. Thus NATO could outflank the Soviets in Central Europe, endanger a Soviet attack against the Baltic Exits, hold the NATO bases and create a favourable starting point for attacks against Soviet LOCs, and finally take the initiative from the Soviets. Ultimately, NATO naval dominance could be attained in the Baltic up to the Finnish Gulf.

How to do it? The US Navy would have to take the lead to provide for a carrier strike force and a strong amphibious strike force, operating from the northern ports of Britain, Ireland and Central and Southern Norway. In a conventional war their tasks would be to eliminate the Soviet air supremacy in the Baltic, and the amphibious units would land forces on Danish isles early on in a period of tension. Other NATO navies might station submarines, FPBs and aircraft for use in the Baltic. They were to develop rather small submarines, about 350 tons, for that purpose; they were to be stationed in mid- and northern Baltic. Additional aircraft would open new possibilities for the use of destroyers.

The Baltic would furthermore be suited for submarines (1,000 tons) carrying missiles, but such had to be developed. Mining could be done by airplanes, possibly departing from aircraft carriers. Both tasks were to be of interest for the American navy.

Ruge also pointed to some restrictions for the German navy, with roots in the WEU negotiations, which ought to be abandoned if the Germans were to become efficient.

Ruge's note did not square well with the ideas of his former colleague in the American-financed Naval Historical Team, admiral Heye, who helped the Danish navy formulating its tactics for littoral warfare (although he did not coin that phrase) in 1949.

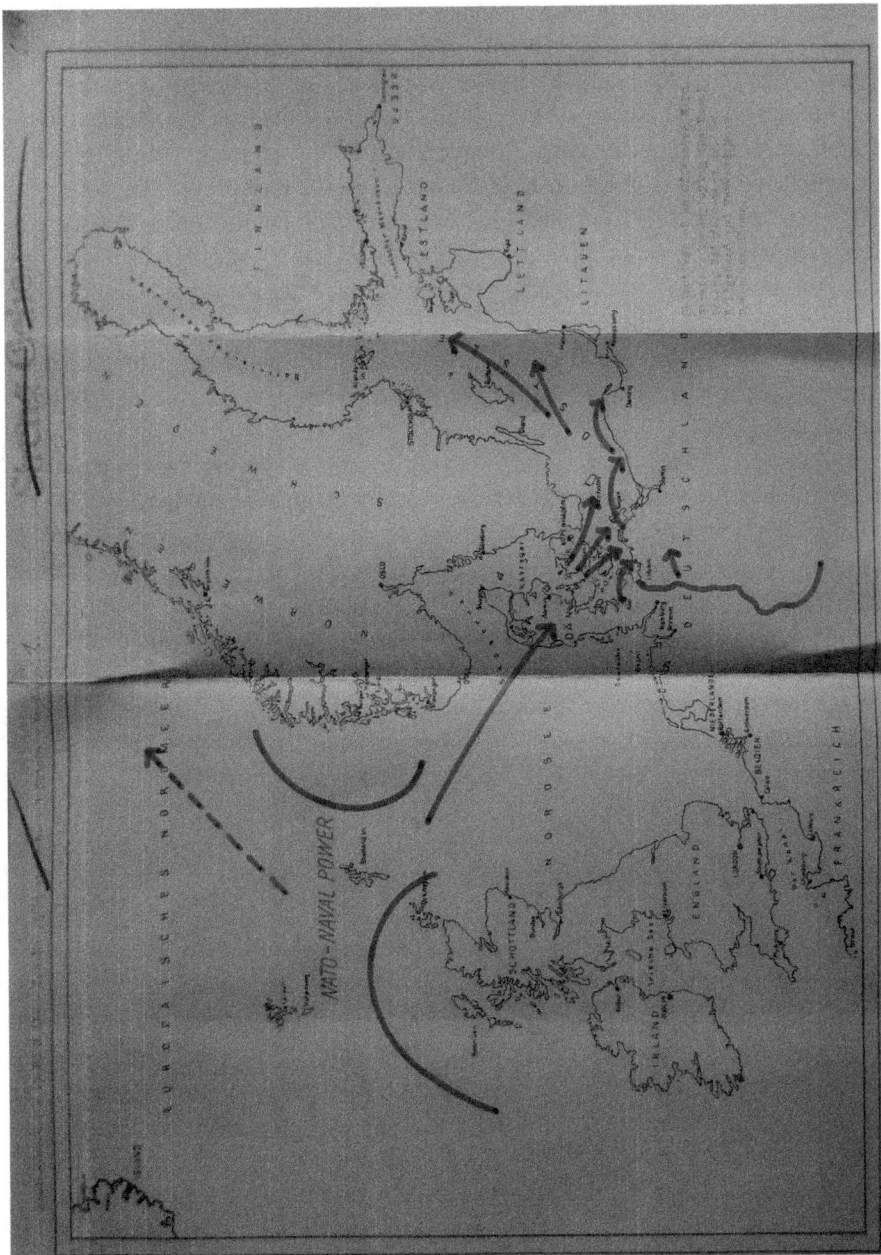

Figure 8.7: Map from Ruge's note indicating the possibilities for forward offensive counterattacks in the Baltic. Source: Bundeswehr Archiv.

The note did not please the top commander of the German forces, Inspector General Heusinger. First, and on the political side, the comments about Denmark were hardly tolerable, and for now it was not politically desirable to air the problems of the border between AFNORTH and AFCENT.[36] Second, the French and the Dutch were mentioned separately while the British were assumed to be part of the great sea powers; the British would easily get the impression that their presence was only tolerated, not desired. Third, one might get the impression that the Germans wanted a major offensive in the Baltic; offensive-strategy, forward strategy, counterattack and other phrases were used indiscriminately, and foreign readers might get confused; this had to be toned down. Fourth, the future Luftwaffe did not get the role it probably deserved – it was destined to get a most important role in the Baltic together with the navy air arm which could not operate alone.

Therefore, Heusinger deemed the study not suitable for eyes outside the German military top, at least not in writing. As a consequence, the permissible contents of the note were only used as a basis for an oral discussion between (then) Captain Wegener and top officers of the US Navy in Washington as a friendly "navy-to-navy" exchange of opinions.[37] The ideas of the note were well received by the Americans and appeared to get the desired impact; they would support a removal of the WEU restrictions. Wegener hoped that a condensed version could be written and brought to Admiral Burke later, but even if that happened the ideas of Ruge never got accepted. On the contrary, analyses of naval tactics in the subsequent years undermined his ideas about an offensive navy.

Navy tactics: Conceptual analyses

The leadership of the new Bundesmarine initiated a series of analyses to create starting points for discussions among high-ranking officers about the various types of weapon platforms being planned and their tactical use. The Ministry of Defence wrote papers of a similar kind. Below we shall see some of the analyses and their conclusions; they have differing points of departure regarding the enemy – in particular, they differ regarding air powers. Unfortunately from an analytical point of view, the question of air power has great significance for the conclusions that can be drawn. Most of the studies are taken from Sander-

---

[36] Letter Streng Geheim 12-1-59 from Capt Smidt (Bonn) to Capt. Wegener (Washington DC). Az. 31-02-01 Tgb.Nr. 3 II/59. BM 3174a.
[37] Letter Geheim from Wegener (German Embassy) to Captain Schmidt (Bonn) 12-2-59. Az.31-02 Tgb Nr. 2 III/59 geh. BM 3174a.

Nagashima[38] who goes through them in great detail, for a fascinating study of detail the reader is referred to in the book.

Destroyers, frigates and FPBs

The new German navy planned for destroyers, but obviously such vessels were better suited for "blue ocean" tasks than for littoral warfare operations in the narrows of the Baltic Approaches, and everywhere in the Baltic the enemy's aircraft were close by. In 1955, plans for destroyers were discussed among various decision-makers, and Admiral Wagner wrote a paper to explain why he thought that destroyers were necessary in the Baltic.[39] First, there was a need for ships able to counter the larger ships of the Russian navy; destroyers would have mid-size guns, anti-aircraft gunnery, torpedoes and ASW weapons. Thus destroyers could serve many purposes in supporting MTBs and mine layers, and they could attack amphibious craft. Second, the critique that destroyers were lame ducks vis-a-vis aircraft was unfair. The Baltic destroyers would be relatively small and well armed and thus more safe; and if the enemy was able to maintain air superiority, one could withdraw to the Western Baltic and ultimately to the North Sea (one reads the doubt about the Baltic between the lines, PB). Third, a destroyer as weapon platform was too small for attacks by nuclear warheads. Fourth, if built in the right way, a destroyer would form a good platform for weapons of the future like missiles. Finally, there was a demand for a weapon platform that would operate under all weather conditions and in that respect they were irreplaceable by smaller (and cheaper) ships.

Those were the arguments for destroyers, but they had to be relatively small.[40] In the Baltic, they would be a guarantee for all-weather operations and security for smaller units. Their main role became – together with the MTBs and the naval air force (see below) – to prevent amphibious landings by the enemy.

The naval C-in-C, Ruge, recommended to rent American destroyers for starters, and to build new destroyers on German shipyards.[41] The roles of destroyers would be numerous: offensive and defensive mine laying, protection of one's own mine operations, attacking Soviet amphibious actions, supporting and protecting offensive FPB operations, attacking enemy LOCs, protecting one's own

---

38 Ibid.
39 Ibid., 63–67.
40 Ibid., 129–31.
41 Inspekteur der Marine: Probleme der Seekriegsführung, NATO-Kommandostruktur. Geheim.8-4-58. Az 31-03-01-02. Tgb.Nr.N 322/58. BW 2/2569.

Figure 8.8: The German navy rented six American FLETCHER destroyers as a starter for destroyers as the backbone of the navy operations. This is D179, renamed Z5. 2050 tons, 35 knots, 4 127 mm, 6 76 mm, torpedoes, depth charges. Source: Forsvarsgalleriet.

LOCs, protecting one's own mine sweepers, protect one's own amphibious actions and support with artillery, supporting one's own army flank with artillery and protecting it against Soviet naval shooting, and attacking enemy amphibious actions in the back of the NATO front. Destroyers were useful because of their size which permitted them to operate in all kinds of weather with a relatively strong weaponry and high speed. The only danger in the West Baltic would be enemy aircraft, so one had to rely on the efficiency of SACEUR's counter air offensive against Baltic enemy air fields.

Six Fletcher-class destroyers (2000 tons) were rented from the Americans for six years in the period 1958–60, all stationed in the West Baltic. The Germans knew that the destroyers were somewhat outdated, but one had to start somewhere. From 1958 to 1964, four new destroyers (2800 tons) and six frigates (2100 tons) were built and stationed by the North Sea. They could, however, easily be moved to the Baltic through the Kiel Canal.

In the years 1957–61 40 new MTBs were built and stationed in the West Baltic. As we shall see, these investments in destroyers and frigates came under fierce critique later in the 1960s, and the tactical plans for their use were radically changed.

Destroyers, frigates and FPBs — **253**

Figure 8.9: The navy built four new HAMBURG-Class destroyers, here D181 HAMBURG. 2850 tons, 35 knots, 4 100 mm, 8 40 mm, torpedoes, depth charges. Source: Forsvarsgalleriet.

Figure 8.10: A ZOBEL class FPB NERZ. 160 tons, 42 knots, 2 40 mm, 4 torpedo launchers. Source: Forsvarsgalleriet.

Submarines

Submarines were initially planned and built as quite small units because larger ones were deemed unsuitable for the Baltic, and the WEU accord limited the size of them. In 1958, the C-in-C of the navy set up these tasks for submarines to be built over the following years, following NATO plans:[42] attacking enemy war ships, attacking enemy LOCs, laying mines outside enemy harbours, recce, fighting other submarines, securing the flank of one's own forces, landing commando forces and rescuing one's own air crews.

The risk of being detected was smaller than the risk for surface vessels, and the smaller the submarine, the lower the risk. The presence of NATO submarines in the Baltic would commit a considerable number of enemy ASW units and aircraft for chasing them and thus drain Soviet war resources. The main domain for operations was initially thought to be the waters between Gotland and the approach to the Gulf of Finland, some 600 miles away from the home base; later a more thorough analysis pointed to more operation areas in the Baltic.[43] The main interest was attacking LOCs in waters that made ships tend to "bundle" because of navigational issues or because of a need to follow a particular route. The West Baltic was not suited for submarine operations because of low depth. In the Middle Baltic there were a few areas for mid-size submarines, and more for mini submarines. But the area around Rügen would probably see much naval traffic and therefore was assumed to be an excellent "hunting ground". The same was the case in the Gulf of Gdansk. Finally, the area east and north-East of Gotland would form an excellent operation field. The map below illustrates where and how many submarines the navy would like to place in the Baltic. A main problem, however, was getting the submarines to the operation areas and back. The waters south of the Danish Islands were shallow and passage therefore dangerous in war times. Submarines from Germany would have to go north around Zealand, have safe passage south through Øresund and then go east along the Swedish coast. This was a bit cumbersome, so the German navy hoped for a solution with a number of German submarines exercising in the Middle Baltic; a depot ship then should have more or less permanent access to a harbour on Bornholm. In any case, submarines should be in their operation area before a war broke out.

---

42 Inspekteur der Marine: Probleme der Seekriegsführung, NATO-Kommandostruktur. Geheim.8-4-58. Az 31-03-01-02. Tgb.Nr.N 322/58. BW 2/2569.
43 Fü M II Einsatz von Ubooten in der Ostsee. Geheim. Az. 31-05-14-03. Tgb.Nr. 851/58 geh. 4-8-58. BM 10/22.

In 1960–61, the submarines of the future – small and middle sized – were analysed in depth.[44] The point of departure was German WWII experiences with submarines close to the coast. In the Baltic, the tasks would include intelligence gathering and attacking targets like large warships, troop transports and supply ships. In addition, tasks would include mine laying and special tasks. At that time, German submarines were limited by the WEU to 350 tons. Analysing the Soviet navy brought the conclusion that since the Soviets did not emphasise ASW in the Baltic, they had no capacity for systematic submarine hunting, and because of different layers of salt water it was difficult anyway to detect submarines by sonar. The Soviets had few experiences with submarine hunting from WWII, and they would probably seek to deny them access to their likely routes and watch their own transport routes closely.

In 1961, two types of submarines were analysed: small units of 100 tons for the waters north of Rügen and larger submarines of 350 tons for various areas further to the east, mainly close to larger harbours. A war game analysed the possibility to deploy a number of 350-tons submarines to the southern part of Kattegat. They could then pass the Øresund to the Baltic and do surveillance and attack with torpedoes; after that possibly mine laying, landing special forces etc; the boats then had to get supplies from Danish and Norwegian bases. Snorkeling was a must during operations close to Swedish territorial waters.

The conclusion regarding the small submarines was that their weaponry and crew (six men) were too small, given the size of the investment. Therefore, the larger boats were recommended, and preferably they would be 500 rather than 350 tons (this was allowed a few years later).

The rule of thumb for submarine actions was that one third would be in the operation area, one third *en route* from or to the area, and one third on its base for repairs and supplies. Consequently, if one wanted 15 submarines in action, a total of 45 was needed.

---

44 Ibid., 132–56.

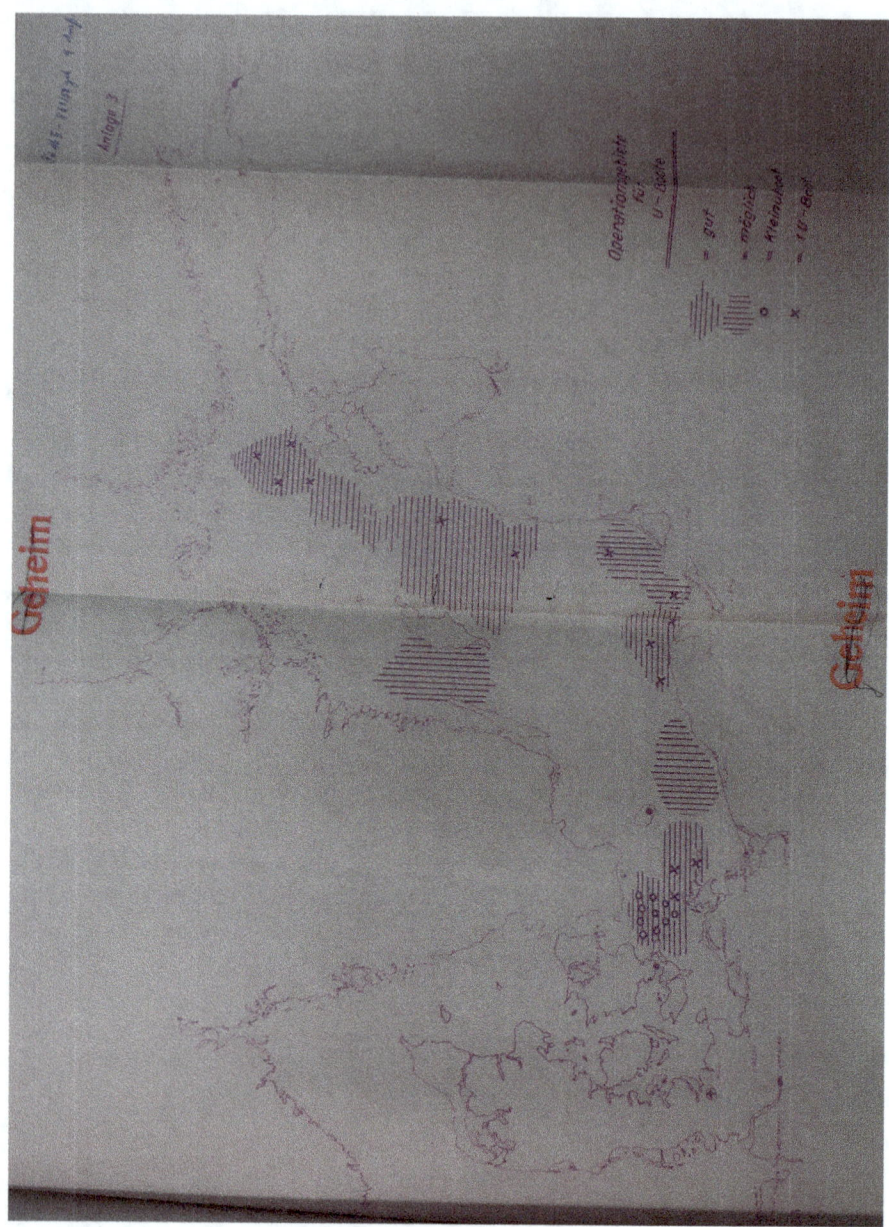

Figure 8.11: Map (1958) of possible operation areas for submarines in the Baltic; mini submarines were planned for waters west of Bornholm; larger submarines would operate east of Bornholm. Source: Bundeswehr Archiv.

Figure 8.12: Type 205 Submarine S 180 U1. 350 tons, 17 knots, torpedoes. Source: Bundeswehr Archiv.

Mine laying

In 1960 a war game analysis of feasible uses of sea mines was carried out.[45] The starting point was a strong enemy with ships as well as naval aircraft, and if one was to keep the enemy at bay, the Bundesmarine had to have a high level of activity together with the allies. The question now was what the aims of the enemy were – did they want immediate access to the Atlantic for their submarines, or would they hold them back, waiting for the army to conquer the territories surrounding the Baltic Approaches and in the meantime just attack the ships of the West with naval aircraft? The analysis emphasised the first possibility.

In that case, an offensive war with mines could be implemented by using MTBs, fast mine sweepers, submarines and (non-German) aircraft for laying mines in Polish and East German waters and harbours. Furthermore, one might lay a mine field south of Bornholm but only if the enemy was not too aggressive. Such an operation required eight destroyers, two mine layers, 22 MTB and air

---

45 Ibid., 159–74.

support. In order to guarantee safe passage for one's own forces, no mines were to be laid north of Bornholm; if the enemy entered the area, one could lay a temporary minefield with MTBs so that one's own units could later operate in the Baltic east of Bornholm. In general, the risk of offensive mining was high because of the enemy's radar coverage and their large number of aircraft and FPB etc.

A defensive mine war should deny the enemy access to NATO waters, but still make it possible for one's own units to manoeuvre. The analysts did not expect to be in a position to defend those minefields, so they had to be set up with different types of mines, making them difficult to sweep. Some fields were to be laid by the Danes in Danish waters threatened by invasion – the Danish straits and the bays at Zealand. West Germany had to lay mines in the Gedser Passage, Fehmarn Belt and Fehmarn Sound; this could be a task for the two ferries servicing Gedser and Grossenbrode. In addition one would have to lay mines blocking the harbours in the area. It would not be necessary to lay mines in the Western Baltic immediately.

The analysis however, led to the conclusion that the Warsaw Treaty probably would prioritise the occupation of Lolland, Falster, Zealand and Fehmarn so much that they would succeed in doing so, and consequently, a comprehensive mine war would be out of the question if NATO did not get sufficient lead time: planned minefields south of Bornholm would be impossible to establish, and the question was whether the enemy's aircraft would prevent NATO ships in attacking the amphibious forces. In that case NATO would have to resort to nuclear weapons against the troops during the landing process.

Altogether, the analysis had quite negative conclusions: offensive mining would only be possible under very favourable circumstances; defensive mining in the Baltic was only possible if the enemy was quite passive, but mining close to one's own coast would probably be possible if the relevant mine layers were accessible and ready immediately for taking mines on board.

The analysis had two other conclusions which were of interest for the Danish navy. First, destroyers were seen as very vulnerable and the risk of using them in most of the 24 hours was very high. Second, it was risky to use large mine layers because they, too, were vulnerable. One should resort to smaller mine layers. The Danes had come to opposite conclusions (see chapter 13).

In spite of the negative conclusions of the war game above, the Germans prepared for mine laying[46] using LSTs (Tank Landing Ships) and FPBs. For the Baltic Approaches, the following minefields were considered necessary.

---

46 Führungsakademie Bw/Abt. Marine TgbNr 231/61. Vorschläge für eine Minenkriegsplanung der Bundesmarine. Kurzstudie. Entwurf. Geheim. 26-20-61. BM 1/88a.

Table 8.5: German mines to be laid.

Area	Number of mines	Mine layers
Fehmarn Belt (sequence 1)	1400	3 LST (or ferries)
Fehmarn/ Lillebælt (sequence 2)	1400	3 LST (or ferries)
Fehmarn Sound East	120	1 FPB division (3)
Gedser Passage	1200	4 FPB groups (40)
Tactic Fields Rügen-Bornholm	900	3 FPB groups (30)
Sum	5020	

In addition, 650 mines were to be laid at various harbours, and about 2,500 mines were to be laid in Skagerrak and at inlets and harbours in the North Sea. This, however, was only the immediate need. Over time, and if offensive mining was desirable (with destroyers, FPBs and submarines), about 20,000 mines should be available.

The navy did not have the desired mine layers planned for in the analysis – the LST were large amphibious craft to be taken over from the USA and modified – and it was not possible to lay all these minefields at the same time. This document planned to use three large amphibious craft or ferries, but a rather large number of FPBs had to be included. There would be no more than two or three large mine layers available, and the FPBs had many other tasks to fulfil. Therefore, the tactical situation would determine when and how the fields were to be laid.

Mine sweeping

In 1960–61, the Germans analysed the missions for their own mine sweepers.[47] There were two main tasks: in the west to secure LOCs from England and the USA; in the east to secure freedom of operation for own forces.

The main problem in mine sweeping was a technical one: there was a lack of technology to sweep mines using pressure ignition. One solution could be using *Sperrbrechers*, ships constructed or modified to be difficult to sink. Typically one took an old freighter and built a large number of water tight cells into it or filled it with empty oil barrels so that it would not sink because of a couple of mines exploding. Such vessels would be sent through a minefield as a sacrificial lamb, leaving a mine-free (exploded) passage. Other types of mines could be dealt with by normal sweeping procedures.

---

47 Ibid., 169–74.

Figure 8.13: Mine sweeper M1072 LINDAU of the LINDAU Class. 370 tons, 16 knots, 1 40 mm. Source: Forsvarsgalleriet.

In the west, mine sweeping would be necessary at the harbours and in the routes of the LOCs. Mines would probably come from aircraft, so it would be necessary to keep the routes secret and do mine sweeping continuously, especially at night and under poor visibility.

One's own forces in the Baltic also had to be protected by own mine sweepers; mines could be laid by aircraft as well as ships and submarines. The question was where? For one, NATO harbours in the Western Baltic, but also other areas. But at the same time the units of the Warsaw Pact would secure their own manoeuvres, and if they wanted to land troops on eastern Zealand and Falster, they might mine the waters south of Gedser and at Fehmarn to prevent NATO from coming to the rescue from the West. Consequently, one had to establish mine lookouts and continuously mine sweep important transport channels and harbours. This, however, presupposed that some mine sweepers were located in Danish harbours and therefore came under Danish command.

In the long run, it might be necessary to sweep mines further to the east in the Baltic, but this was not analysed.

Amphibious forces

One main tactical rationale for having amphibious forces was to disturb the WAPA's right (northern) flank by landing forces on the East German and Polish coasts and thus attacking WAPA transportation channels and disturbing their military activities in various ways. In turn, this would reduce the enemy pressure on CINCENT's forces and the AFNORTH forces in Schleswig-Holstein. The second main reason was to use them for moving one's own army forces in various ways.

A number of war games tested the concepts in 1960.[48] They mirrored in more detail the operations the navy wanted to carry out, if necessary:
- The landing of supplies and reinforcements to forces that had previously been set ashore;
- Evacuation of units from an area under enemy pressure;
- Landing of reinforcements to army forces that had been surrounded by enemy forces;
- Landing special forces in the eastern part of the Western Baltic to raid enemy control centres;
- Carrying out navy seal operations to demolish a bridge;
- Evacuating of field hospital units, wounded soldiers etc.;
- Strengthening a bridge head south of the Flenburg Inlet;
- Evacuating the same bridge head after enemy pressure;
- Landing a force on Zealand to attack an enemy group that was in the process of landing;
- Landing a force on the western side of Fyn to attack an enemy force that had conquered the bridge to Jutland.

The exercises showed that support was necessary from sea and air. From destroyers one would get artillery support, but then the first landing groups had to bring along artillery spotters to create direction for the artillery. They also could direct support from the air, but the naval air arm needed pilots with special training for ground support; their support could be quite decisive for the success of the operation.

Furthermore, helicopters were indispensable for connecting small groups and fast movement of forces. With six helicopters NATO forces could quickly land a small company behind the back of the enemy. Furthermore, staffs and various forms of supplies could quickly be brought to where they were needed.

---

48 Kdo der amphibischen Stritkräfte an der Kommando der Flotte Tgb.Nr 435/60. Geheim. 1-11-60. BM 1/1102.

Figure 8.14: EIDECHSE amphibious craft. 743 tons, 13 knots, 2 40 mm. 10 tanks.
Source: Forsvarsgalleriet.

The report pointed out that the possibilities by using amphibious forces hardly were perceived by the army until exercises had proved their utility; this was especially the case in Schleswig-Holstein and Jutland because of the many inlets and beach-like coasts. This had to be built into the operational thinking of the Army staffs.

The staff of the amphibious forces foresaw several problems.[49] Cooperation with army staffs and air forces was necessary, and operating across the boundaries of AFNORTH and AFCENT added to the problems of coordination and they would have to involve SACEUR to make things operational. The staff concluded that the unit could handle an army brigade, but due to the slim staff organisation one could only handle operations in one place at a time; if demand should come up from another area, it could not be fulfilled. All in all, landing troops was a complicated business requiring repeated training and the setting up of a staff across the forces to make various groups cooperate properly.

In 1964, it was estimated[50] that 17½ WAPA divisions were linked to the northern flank, partly to be able to counter such amphibious attacks, and therefore not

---

49 Ibid., 156–59.
50 Notes on Die Rolle der Seestreitkräfte bei der Verteidigung der zentraleuropäischen Nordflanke. Geheim. 28-1-64. Fü M II 1 – Az 31-02-02. TgbNr N-251/64. BM 1/65.

able to attack in the CINCENT area as long as NATO kept a pressure on that flank by numerous limited amphibious attacks or raids with special forces. The Soviets, however, had set up a relatively large number of coastal radars to warn against such attacks. Furthermore, they now had missile destroyers of the first generation (three KRUPNY/KILDIN) in the Baltic. In addition there was a large number of missile fast patrol boats. Therefore, comprehensive NATO attacks on the coast and coastal sea traffic e.g. by using amphibious forces were becoming difficult.

CINCENT, however, wanted the navy to maintain the amphibious force – it should be used to disorganise the back country of the Soviets. Operations could have a spreading effect, blocking Soviet movements westwards. Consequently, it was a way of easing the NATO forward defence strategy; the area was a sort of springboard for attacks. After a number of landed transport corridors had been destroyed by NATO's counterattacks, the coastal routes would become even more important for the Soviets.

Originally, the number of amphibious units in the future navy was set to 36, organised in four groups with one large docking ship (LSD), three LST for tanks, three mid-sized craft (LSM) and two gunboats for artillery support. This never materialised; military spending cuts made the leadership prioritise the "normal" navy. By the mid-1960s, six LSM were available, new prototypes planned, but not implemented.[51] Some 22 smaller multi-purpose landing craft (LCU) had been built, able to carry 140 tons; they corresponded to the change in tasks from large attack operations to smaller logistical operations supporting one's own forces.[52]

Naval air arm

During the years of preparing the Bundesmarine, air support by a dedicated naval air force had been on the table most of the time. This separation of aircraft into two forces, one of the Luftwaffe proper and one of the navy, was not supported by the Luftwaffe. Based on the so-called Dahms-analysis, its leadership pointed out that during times of conflict, having two systems of air command over the Baltic Approaches was not wise.[53, 54] In and by itself, the navy contingent of 58 aircraft was in no way enough to get a controlling power in the air over the Baltic; in addition, the proposed aircraft, the Sea Hawk (which was constructed

---

51 Ibid., 257.
52 https://de.wikipedia.org/wiki/Amphibische_Gruppe 19-4-22.
53 The author of the paper disregarded that there was a third system of command, the AF-NORTH COMTAFDEN in Karup.
54 Ibid., 109–17.

for British aircraft carriers), was technically at a lower level than the fighters of the enemy they were supposed to meet in action. Therefore, close coordination with the Luftwaffe (with its proper fighters) would be necessary, but in effect creating double channels of command – two air forces flying next to one another instead of with another. If one accepted the fact that the naval air force faced special tasks not mastered by the Luftwaffe, there was a need for a coordinator located at the control centre of the Luftwaffe to prepare for the particular naval tasks. Furthermore, some pilots of the Luftwaffe were to be trained for those tasks. This suggestion from the Luftwaffe was turned down by the navy, and the question of controlling air defence over the Baltic sea was left unanswered. But there was agreement that many tasks of the two air forces could be solved in common: basic training of most personnel groups, maintenance, airfields, communication, logistics etc.

Behind the operational disagreement were different perceptions of war in the Baltic Approaches. Luftwaffe saw the area as an entity over which you flew your aircraft, carrying out your air force war tasks. The navy perceived the naval aircraft as a direct and permanent part of naval action only, requiring a deep understanding of the many facets of the war at sea. The roles of the naval air arm and the air force were in the opinion of the navy as follows:[55]

- Naval air arm: tactical recce; fighting sea targets in tactical cooperation with warships; protecting warships; sub chasing; mine sweeping and mine laying; and SAR.
- Naval air arm cooperating with the air force: fighting warships in general; common action to support own landing operations and to fight enemy landings; and protecting warships.
- Air force operations: interdiction – strikes – against targets that were important for the war at sea; recce for those purposes; and interception within the frames of the general air defence.

Within NATO this was the normal division of labour. The Luftwaffe agreed to this in so far as a separation was a fact.

The success of cooperation between ships and aircraft was analysed.[56] The issue was how to attack a fleet of amphibious craft situated between Rügen and Southern Sweden, for FPBs (30 knots) two hours from Gedser, three hours from Fehmarn. But the aircraft of the enemy were only between three and eight minutes away. If the Germans had F-104 aircraft ready, the flight time would be

---

55 FüM II: Marineflieger. Geheim. 25-9-58. Az 31-05-10-20. Tgb.Nr. 1048/58. BM 10/21.
56 Ibid., 117–23.

Figure 8.15: SEA HAWK fighter-bomber in its absolutely final position.

about 11 minutes from Germany, and they had to use *Tiefflug* (30 meters above the sea) in order not to be detected and attacked by enemy aircraft before they reached their targets. The FPBs would be detected at least 15 minutes before they reached their firing distance and risked enemy air attack. These differences in reaction time for aircraft made it very difficult to create fighter air security for the FPBs. Hence, the conclusion of the analysis was that clear sky day operations by surface craft were next to impossible due to the air dominance by the enemy. On the other hand, if flight operations took departure from Værløse airfield outside Copenhagen and the FPBs operated from Grønsund between Zealand and Falster, chances for success were somewhat better because the radar coverage of the enemy was poorer in those areas.

The overall conclusion for all surface craft was that if the enemy had air power, operations with surface vessels were extremely dangerous. Still, operations during the night and in foul weather were possible.

The navy initially had Gannet aircraft for recce and submarine chasing, and Sea Hawk fighter-bombers, but planned to get F-104 in the early 1960s, and their number would be increased from 58 to 72. The question then came up whether one should rather buy a number of the Fiat G 91 planes which had been developed as NATO aircrafts.[57] The plane was slower than the F-104, but it was more versatile and it could operate from very simple airfields where the F-104 required quite long and undamaged concrete runways – and the airfields of the navy were close to the border of Eastern Germany, so they were at risk. In addition, the Fiat plane only cost half of the F-104, so one could get twice as many planes. But the decision-makers stayed with the F-104. They saw it as very potent – it would be possible to carry nuclear warheads – and as a replacement for surface ships when they could not operate (as we shall see below).

Helicopters were in the first years of the Bundesmarine mainly used for rescue and transport purposes, and helicopters were also used for landing purposes within the amphibious section of the navy. From 1963, a squadron with Sikorsky H-34G helicopters was organised for testing ASW and mine laying roles; SACEUR's force goals for 1971 indicated that the navy should plan for helicopters for both roles. The navy planned 2 x 18 mid-sized helicopters (able to land on a ship) for those roles by then, noting that efficient instruments for those roles still were under development, possibly requiring the navy to take over systems from other navies.[58] The number later was reduced to 18 plus four in reserve.

More offensive roles with frigates and destroyers were discussed briefly in various papers, but the navy lacked in ships able to take helicopters on board; tests were made with the frigates of the KÖLN class and the HAMBURG class destroyers,[59] but a permanent solution was not reached until the frigate class 122 became operational many years later.

The emerging threat: Ship-to-ship missiles

In 1958, the first Russian destroyer armed with surface missiles was sighted in the Baltic; one year later FPBs with such weapons were also seen; by 1961, six destroyers (Kildin- and Krupny-class) and six FPBs (Komar- and Osa-class) were identified. This caused some alarm in NATO, and the German Ministry of Defence started analysing the phenomenon in order to decide how to counter these missiles.[60] The navy's staff wrote a comprehensive analysis assessing the magnitude of ships carrying such missiles and how to respond by the navy.

---

57 Ibid., 123–29.
58 Anlage zu 3-530/65, Kdo Flotte A3/Az 9 0-15-20. BM 1/1600.
59 Ibid., 376.
60 Letters and note: Sowjetiskë Überwasserschiffe mit FK-Waffen. April–May 1961. Geheim. BM 1/87b. The contents of this section is based on that note unless otherwise stated.

The Krupny destroyer was supposed to carry up to 18 missiles, probably radio-guided with a range of over 100 miles (requiring a forward target spotter for direction at long distances); for now probably not terribly precise, but progress was expected over the next years. The primary target for the missiles would be other ships; nuclear warheads might be used for large targets. The Krupny had only small-gauged anti-aircraft guns and therefore would probably operate where their own air dominance was established.

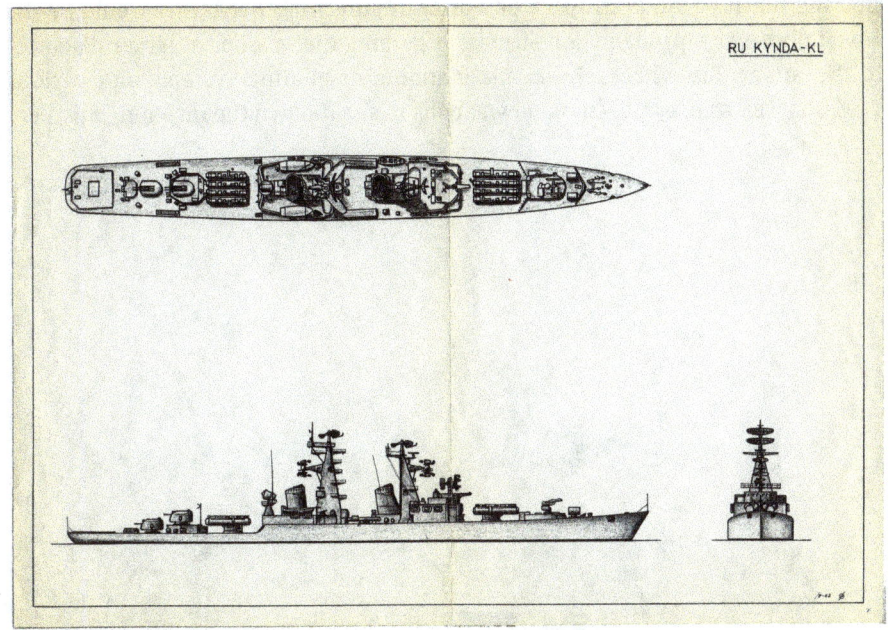

Figure 8.16: Soviet missile destroyer/cruiser of the KYNDA-class from 1962. 4,400 tons, 141 meters, 34 knots. 2 x 4 sea missile launchers, 1 x 2 air missile launchers, 2 x 76 mm guns, torpedoes. Source: Forsvarsgalleriet.

The OSA-class had four surface missiles available, probably non-guided with their own target homing instrument in the terminal phase and a range of 20 to 30 miles.

The missile destroyers would revolutionise naval warfare in the Baltic; even if they were dependent on fair weather-and radar conditions, they could fire their weapons before any NATO destroyers of 1960 could open gun fire. They could reach targets in Kattegat or in the Kiel Bay from the Mid-Baltic. The missile FPBs likewise had to be perceived as major threats against nearly all types of vessels; however, they were more dependent on fair weather. Both types, however, were vulnerable to air attacks, and the German Navy Air Arm could become efficient against them. Furthermore, various ways of jamming the radio direction system and/or radars might help NATO units. The efficient response to the Russian missiles would be to develop NATO missile destroyers and FPBs. In the meantime, it was important with recce giving information about the missiles: their velocity, range, control system, homing system, size of warhead etc.

For now, it was necessary with new weapons for the naval fighter-bombers, for instance the Bullpup missile which had a range of 10 miles and thus was outside the reach of the destroyer's anti-aircraft guns. Another target would be the Soviet observer – probably a helicopter – guiding the missiles at larger distances to the target. Elsewhere, there was jamming of guiding systems and various ECMs, as well as use of decoys and weapons to shoot down the incoming missile.

Figure 8.17: OSA-class FPB firing a missile. Source: Forsvarsgalleriet.

The above analysis was written as a response to a brief note of 10 April 1961 to the minister from "Abteilung T" in the Ministry, headed by Dr. Karl Fischer, who caused considerable anger ("a very one-sided and insufficient answer") in the staff of the navy by suggesting that the right answer to missile destroyers would be hydrofoils which due to their speed could reach the enemy fast, and due to their relatively small size would be very economic to build and use, and in addition that they could avoid sea mines and were easy to hide away.

The German navy soon decided to recommend buying American-built missile destroyers and to build missile-FPBs. We shall return to those later. Fischer did not give up his ideas about hydrofoils (and giving the Luftwaffe a stronger role). In the spring of 1963, two German shipyards were asked to analyse the possibilities for a Hydrofoil, but the projects were soon abandoned, probably because Fischer lost the infight with the navy after Minister Strauss had to leave office and was replaced by von Hassel.[61, 62]

In 1969, however, the Americans took the ideas about a hydrofoil up in NATO, and Boeing was asked to develop an already existing prototype into an operational, 265 tons version with four EXOCET missiles and a 76 mm gun. The project was named "Type 162" in Germany and there were thoughts to let this type replace the ZOBEL class, but the development of type 143 ALBATROS took priority, and Type 162 was abandoned.[63]

Nuclear weapon platforms under German control

The depictions in the various NATO strategic papers of a future nuclear general war between the West and the East in the 1950s were very gloomy. In the first period of up to 30 days, both parties would maximise their use of nuclear warheads against the enemy and thus seek to get the military overhand. Bombs would annihilate military key points, infrastructure, industrial production and whole cities. NATO expected to win this battle in the sense that NATO in the ensuing period of time would be able to reorganise, resupply and take back lost territory (if any) and force the enemy to negotiate peace.

The published NATO strategic papers never came beyond this very general description of a nuclear war. There was no analysis of the second phase. NATO papers instead concentrated their efforts on describing how to organise the military for the first phase of destruction – in the hope that the organisation would deter the enemy from initiating the general war. Furthermore, more emphasis was put on developing the infrastructure in Europe to secure both basic civilian and military supplies in a future conflict.

---

61 Ibid., 248–51.
62 Sander-Nagashima does not mention these two nor later projects.
63 Tactical demands are found in BM 1/26109. A drawing and details are found on https://www.freundeskreis-schnellboote-korvetten.de/Bootstypen/Schnellboote/, one has to select "162" on the left side.

NATO's New Approach laid out the defence of Middle Europe on German soil by the use of nuclear warheads and the stronghold of NATO at the Rhine.[64] The Germans were supposed to bring more troops to the defence once they became members of NATO. But after the Germans did so, it dawned upon the top politicians and military as well as SACEUR that the German troops would not increase the NATO troops as much as foreseen and thus improve the chances of a forward strategy. What happened was that the other NATO members, against the recommendation of the supreme commander, reduced their military budgets, withdrawing from German territory and cutting back on military units at home. At the same time, however, the New Approach in the MC 70 version demanded that tactical nuclear warheads be introduced in the defence of West Europe, operated by European NATO forces and thus taken out of the centralised American control system. As we saw in chapter 7, this happened, but SACEUR's hope to get the overall authority failed; the political bodies of NATO and the individual countries kept control over the nuclear weapon triggers.

The initial West German military top was not prepared to plan the use of nuclear weapons. Until membership of NATO, they were not even informed about NATO plans for nuclear warfare. The army had planned for traditional but very mobile divisions with infantry at the fore and a strong armoured force behind to give strength and depth to a counter attack. Furthermore, various ideas about having local reserve light infantry divisions for "testing" the seriousness of an attacker and possibly keeping the clash at the local, non-nuclear level were discussed. In the navy, not many thoughts had been given to nuclear warheads because they were not yet developed to efficient use at sea. Only the air force saw the possibilities and even necessities of nuclear warheads, given the ultra short time for reaction in an age of jet planes.

Submarines after a nuclear exchange?
In 1962, a naval analysis put special emphasis on the perspectives for using submarines in the Baltic after a nuclear exchange.[65] The point of departure was that an all-out nuclear war was being fought. Most military forces were stationary, locked to a particular territorial position. Only ships organised by a navy with depot ships (the Germans planned a large fleet of those) could get beyond the territorial lockdown. That said, the modern naval wonder, the aircraft carrier, was vulnerable because of its size, and only the modern submarine was able to hide away and escape the nuclear battle. It would not need replenishment until after several weeks. Therefore, the German navy should focus on submarines for use after the first nuclear exchanges.

---

64 Unless referenced otherwise, the following is based on Thoss, op. cit.
65 Kommando der Amphibischen Streitkräfte: Der Einsatz von U-Booten in der Ostsee unter dem Aspekt des nuklearen Krieges. Geheim. 25-6-62. BM 10/33.

A comprehensive nuclear war would probably have the effect that most military activities in the Baltic would come to a standstill; for NATO until reinforcement came from other NATO countries, particularly Great Britain and the USA. On the Soviet side, amphibious forces could be expected to try landing on the Zealand isles, particularly if they had been loaded on ships earlier on and dispersed so that the nuclear battle would not affect them. The best operation area for submarines, however, was east of Bornholm, and the submarines had to be there before the war started, and somewhere in that area there had to be resources available for a first replenishing; an analysis of this issues had been initiated. The best solution would be that Sweden joined NATO when war had broken out.

The role of the German submarines would be to attack what was left of the Soviet military resources after the nuclear strikes – partly surviving naval ships, partly resources that could be transported by other vessels – to prevent the Soviets from re-building their military powers. The submarines had to exercise in peacetime and to be in place east of Bornholm before war broke out. In a period of tension they would perform recce. If non-nuclear war started, they should continue the recce tasks and attack all larger naval vessels and ships for transport. During nuclear exchange they should report results. After nuclear war they were to continue the attacks, particularly on LOCs.

If the submarines were on site in time with well trained crews, with correct types of weapons and own LOCs in place for continued action, then they would become a worthwhile contingent to NATO's deterrence system. The German navy would need 40 modern submarines of about 400 tons for this purpose.

The leadership of the navy perceived the paper as a recommendation for more attack-submarines. They welcomed such an analysis, but did not share the perspective.[66] First, apart from the replenishment issue, there would be little variance in operating submarines with or without nuclear exchange. If harbours were destroyed, loading and unloading for sea transport would have to take place so that submarines could easily attack, but maybe most would take place by small boats, not worth a torpedo. Second, the possibilities for communication from submarines would be limited, and aircraft could much more efficiently do recce over a large area. Third, the possibilities for submarines to wield sea power alone was doubtful, given their special operation forms; they had to operate as part of a more balanced navy. Fourth, while the German navy would have submarines in the Eastern Baltic, the main tasks for the German navy were in the Baltic Approaches, and submarines were not suited for the Danish Narrows. Operations in the Baltic were possible as long as the Danish Narrows were controlled by NATO; replenishment solely from depot ships was dubious, as was support in Swedish harbours. In sum, the issues of risky access to the Eastern Baltic, passing the relatively shallow waters north or south of Bornholm, and replenishment problems in general made a comprehensive use of such submarines doubtful. The number of 40 submarines was too high. The author of the above note also had thoughts about using American Polaris submarines, but such were absolutely outside the aspirations of the German navy's top.

---

66 FÜ M II: Betr. Studie Einsatz von Ubooten. 30-11-62. Geheim. 10-71-04. Tgb. Nr. 4459/62. BM 10/33.

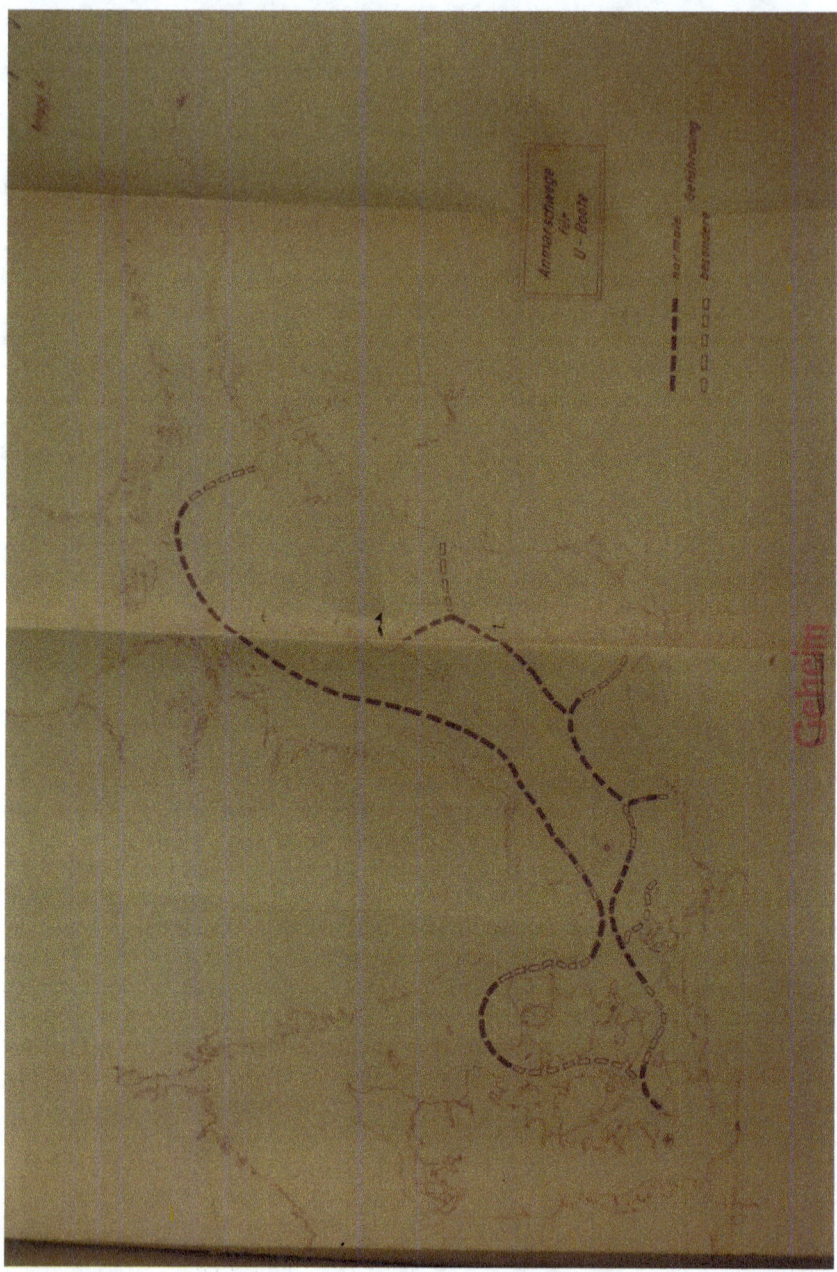

Figure 8.18: Submarine routes (map from 1958) from German waters to the operation fields in the Baltic. Source: Bundeswehr Archiv.

The German military top was not alone in this empty space of nuclear information. Very few non-American officers in NATO had specific knowledge about the technology as well as the planned use of such weapons, to say nothing of their effect. Consequently, one might say that the quite comprehensive discussions about the future use of nuclear weapons were held in an atmosphere of veiled circumstances; one is tempted to use the parable of the three blind men discussing the physical appearance of the elephant.

A command-post exercise, LION NOIR, in 1957 revealed the devastating consequences of nuclear warfare in Germany. One thing was commanding and controlling the military forces, but it was soon shown that the military commanders were unable to control the civilian sector – how to get prioritised military access through the infrastructure, controlling behaviour in residential as well as industrial areas, and coordination with civilian authorities. Far worse, a large number of cities were simply destroyed by nuclear warheads. In conclusion, the German military top said in SHAPE headquarters: "We must pray that nuclear weapons are only used on German soil if all other means to reach the tactical purpose are deemed insufficient."[67]

But within NATO commands, the issue was not the principles, but the practical allocation of nuclear weapon platforms – guns, missiles and aircraft for one's own use. So the German military decision-makers could only prepare the troops for behaviour on the nuclear battlefield: protection against nuclear waste, physical protection of material and personnel while waiting for an attack and securing supplies after an attack. And following the development of NATO they had to work for getting the most advanced weapon platforms integrated in the German military forces, primarily the army and the air force. So by 1963 the army had 12 HONEST JOHN missile battalions with 72 launchers and four SERGEANT guided missile battalions with 18 launchers. In addition the army had 203 mm howitzers capable of delivering nuclear warheads. Apart from the SERGEANT missile, these platforms were allocated and controlled army division by army division. The air force over time got five F 104 G STARFIGHTER squadrons with 36 aircraft each, and 153 Nike-Hercules air defence launchers and four Pershing medium-range ballistic missile launchers.[68] The platforms were run by the Germans, but the nuclear warheads were under American control until released. So there was no way a German commander could start his own nuclear war.

Not that they wanted to: there is no doubt that the main problem for the Germans was the costs to the German civilian population in the case of a nuclear

---

67 Thoss, op. cit., p. 348.
68 Hammerich, Helmut. "Fighting for the Heart of Germany: German I Corps and NATO's Plans for the Defence of the North German Plain in the 1960s." In *Blueprints for Battle: Planning for War in Central Europe.*, eds Jan Hoffenaar, Dieter Krüger, and David T Zabecki, 158. Lelxington, KY: University Press of Kentucky, 2012.

war. Hence the pressure for developing NATO's forward defence tactics, beginning at the border between East and West Germany, where possible. But it was not until 1958 that the traditional stand of NATO – the Rhine-Ijsel line – was officially moved by AFCENT to the east, to the Ems-Neckar line, and defence would start at the Weser–Lech line, and in April 1962, SACEUR Norstad ordered a mobile defence line to start at the border.[69]

Exercises

Participation in NATO exercises was of course important for the young German navy, but in 1959, the reports from an exercise[70] made the navy staff in Bonn conclude that while participation in NATO exercises allowed many lessons to be learned, the general training level of the crews was low, so more rigorous national training and less participation in NATO exercises was the logical step to take. The destroyers had problems with communication because the crews were not sufficiently trained to fast (blink) signals and lacked knowledge of the English language. Their radars (from 1943) were out of date and did not catch airplanes in low altitudes. Merchant ship officers needed training in convoy sailing. MTBs were more suited to operate in the Baltic than in the North Sea.

In 1960, the navy fared better. The NATO exercise TIGER GRIS took place in the south of the North Sea from 25 September to 1 October 1960. Four FPB divisions (two Danish, eight boats; two German, 14 boats) were available for attacking convoys. Destroyers and aircraft also participated, but we shall only deal with the FPBs in detail.[71]

26–9. A convoy of five merchant ships, escorted by two (German ex-Fletcher class) destroyers were eight hours away to the north west. Another group of three frigates and five destroyers escort were coming from the west. The FPB commander evaluated that an operation against the merchant ships would demand that the FPBs were at sea for about 16 hours. He decided therefore to attack the warships in the upcoming night with two divisions. But due to bad weather he sent a "weather boat" out to check the conditions, and that boat reported back that the sea was too rough. The operation was cancelled.

---

69 Ibid., 161.
70 Fü M II: Stellungnahme zur Auswertung des Kommandos der Flotte zum TB (man) des BSW über die NATO-Übung WOLF JAUNE vom 21.5-29.5.59. NATO Secret 31-10-59. BM 1/1107.
71 The text is based on a) Abschlussbemerkungen des Kommando der Flotte zu NATO-Manöver Tiger Gris vom 25.9 bis 1.10 1960. Geheim. Az. 34-71-15. Tgb.Nr. 191/61A3a. 28-2-61, and b) War diaries by Commanders Matzen and Wülfing. BM 1/1258.

27–9. A group of supply ships was headed towards Borkum, at a speed of nine knots. The commander of the FPBs decided to use all divisions and first attack the escorts of the convoy, and then sink the amphibious vessels. The FPBs left Cuxhaven at 16.30 and at 20.00 they were at the starting point for the operation. They moved west, at a speed of 24 knots. At 21.08 one of the Danish FPBs spotted six objects on the radar, at a distance of 12 miles, and a speed of 10 knots; the FPB maintained contact at that distance. The commander ordered a sector attack at 22.30, meaning that the FPBs approached the convoy from different angles but so that they could fire their torpedoes at the same time from the same distance. See the map below for the navigation patterns of the FPBs to get to a sector and then attack on time.

After the sector attack the FPBs were ordered to attack a group of amphibious ships approaching Borkum, and then go back to base.

28–9. Around 20.00 orders were given to prepare to go to sea and attack a convoy at Ostende sailing north east, at a speed of eight knots. It was so far away that the trip back to base would have to be done in daylight; the conditions in the air were unknown. It was decided to postpone the attack to the day after.

29–9. All FPBs had to be ready for leaving harbour at 16.00. Air recce had found a convoy of four vessels and four frigates sailing course north east not far from Yarmouth on the British east coast, at a speed of 15 knots. The commander thought that the assessed speed was far too high; it should rather be eight to nine knots. He decided to attack with two divisions and left harbour about 1700. See map below.

En route west the commander received various information about the convoy, some contradicting one another. He was ordered to proceed with high speed towards five merchant vessels and two destroyers off Yarmouth. The two divisions split, and the commander ordered the other division to approach the convoy from north east; the commander then approached from north west, the divisions thus attacking like a tong. The destroyers escorting the convoy all were to the east of it, leaving the west side unprotected. The commander evaluated that ten torpedoes had hit their target. The divisions returned to base and the exercise was over.

The evaluation of the exercise was that the FPB divisions worked well together across nations; they took turns in commanding all four divisions, and previous training together paid off: in the coordinated attacks no mistakes were made. The Danish Mobile Base (MOBA) delivered good service, including radar signals from its land base. On September 28 the weather was rough (wind north east 6, sea state 4) and the FPBs were at the border of their capabilities; they could not operate fully in certain directions. The escorts of the convoy attacked did not spot the attackers, partly because they did not believe FPBs were able to operate in a sea beyond state 4 and therefore had not posted sufficient outlooks. The Gannet aircraft from the new air arm was another story with many communication problems and misunderstandings, often due to the technical side with

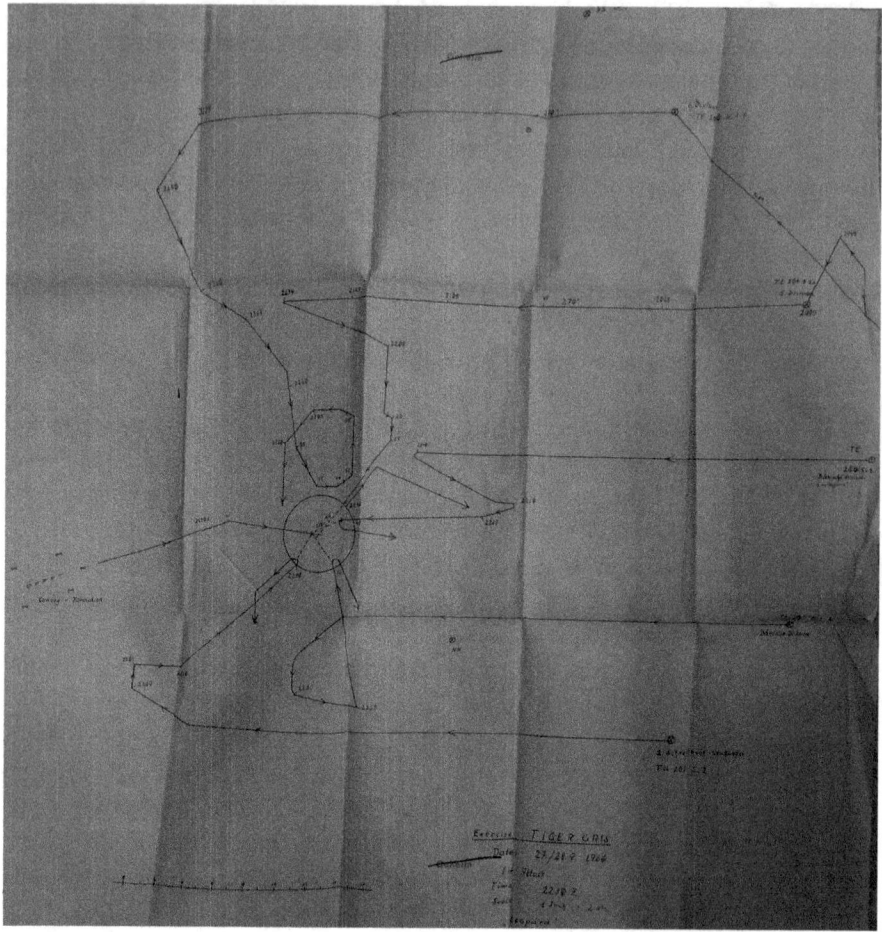

Figure 8.19: The map shows the convoy approaching from the west; the FPBs coming from the east, dispersing in order to come from different angles (sectors) to the convoy so that they all can fire torpedoes at time 22.30 at a distance of 5,000 yards (indicated by the circle). One sees how some of the boats have to do a full circle in order not to come too early. The convoy changed course shortly before planned firing of torpedoes, and therefore the division furthest to the west did not reach a firing position (the circle) in time. Source: Bundeswehr Archiv.

insufficient or outright missing receivers (incorrect wave bands), but also delays in reports, missing reports on take-offs and wrong or missing code words. Radars were outdated and therefore air control from some destroyers was not possible. Cooperation with British recce airplanes was not possible due to misinformation about communication channels. Overall, a proper overview for the command centre was not possible to create.

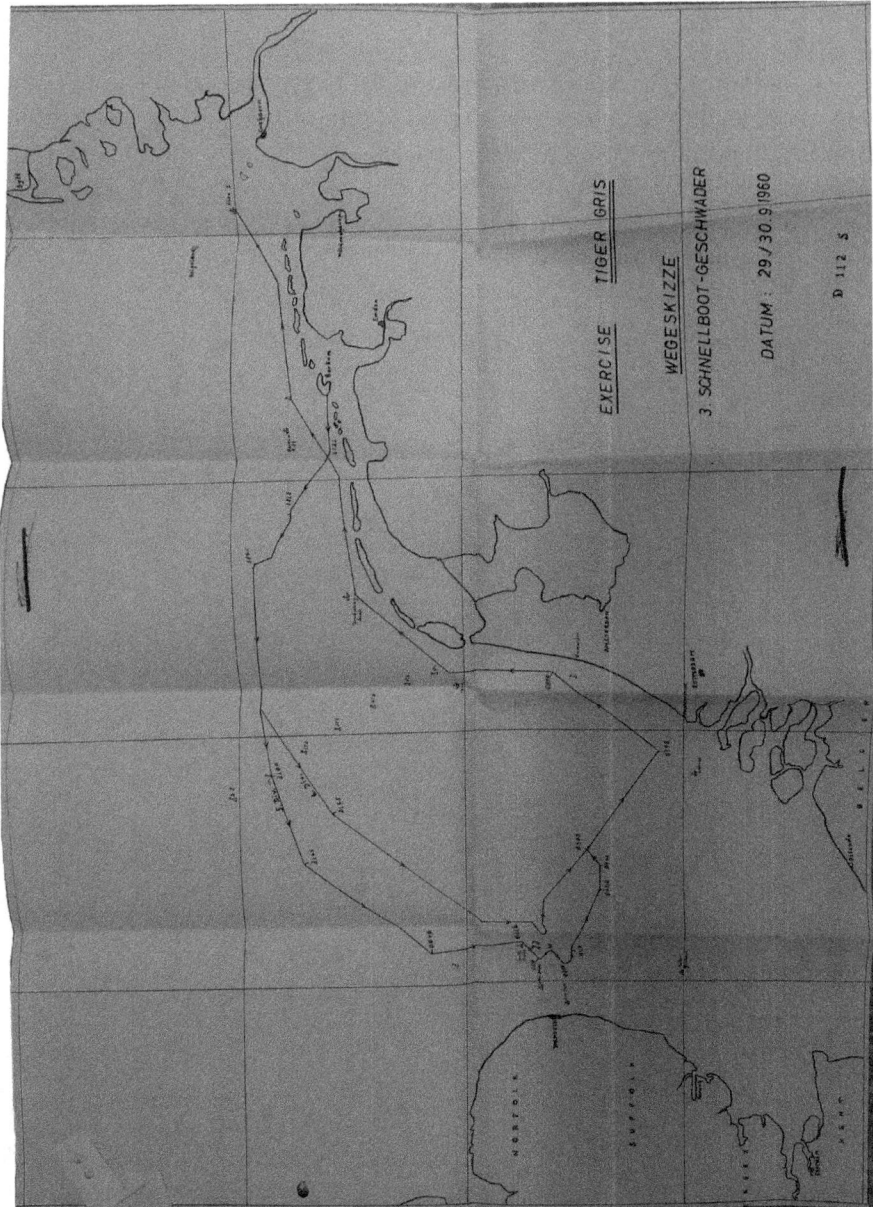

Figure 8.20: This map shows the two FPB divisions going west from Borkum, splitting into two formations, attacking the convoy off Yarmouth from two sides with torpedoes and then joining for the home trip.

Summing up

The discussion of German rearmament started in 1950, based on a treatise, the *Himmerod Denkschrift*, written by a group of former German top-officers. NATO members quickly realised that West Germany was needed for a future defence against the Soviets, and after various negotiations West Germany became a member of NATO and started rearming in 1956. Around 1962, the defence of Schleswig-Holstein was as depicted below.

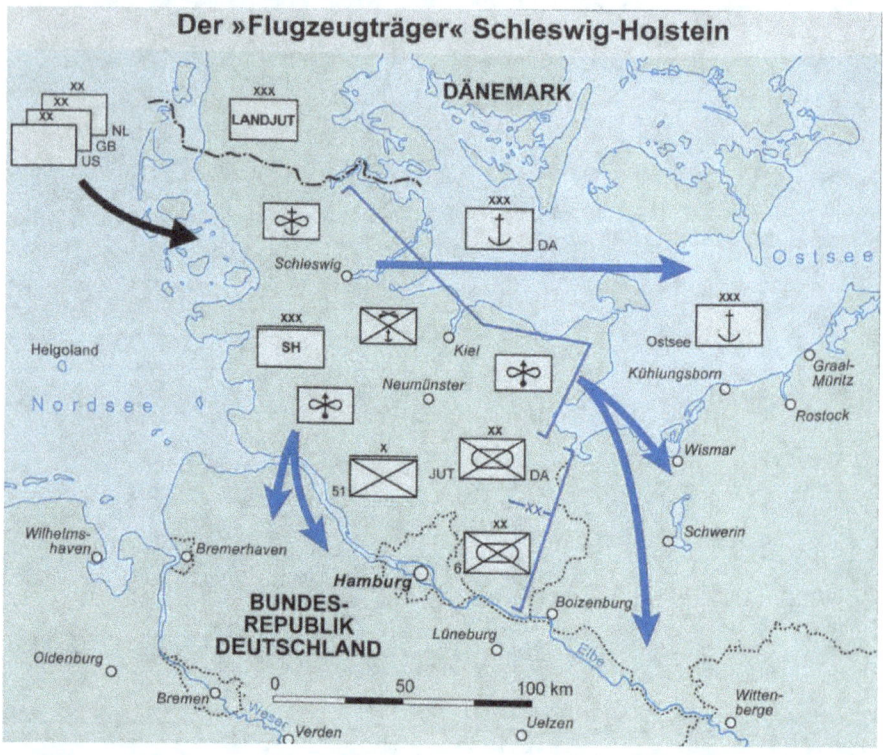

Figure 8.21: Schleswig-Holstein as a "Aircraft Carrier" with Danish forces north of the border and at the eastern border with the German army (in two corps), Danish and German navies at sea and three airfields for the Luftwaffe and the Naval air arm. Reinforcements coming in from the west.[72]

---

[72] Kollmer, Dieter. "Schleswig-Holstein: 'Flugzeug Träger' Im Kalten Krieg." *Militärgeschichte*, no. 3 (2016).

For the army, only forces (one large armoured division) located in Schleswig-Holstein were under AFNORTH and relevant for the Baltic Approaches; the bulk of the army forces was located south of that area, under command of AFCENT. The air force had some squadrons in the area, but mostly to the south, and all forces were directed by the 2. ATAF, under command of AFCENT. The operations of the navy in war were completely within AFNORTH's jurisdiction. Consequently, we have analysed the navy in more detail than the other two forces.

The tactics of the army were to counter a Soviet attack by denying the enemy access to waters, forests and other natural hindrances and thus channel the advancing troops into tracks suitable for nuclear attacks, particularly at the rivers and the Kiel Canal. German troops had access to nuclear warheads. Danish forces were supposed to join the West Germans, moving south through Jutland to the battle area.

The air force planned a fighter-bomber force to support army operations, and a interceptor force to attack enemy bombers in up to 25,000 meters' altitude, and a missile system on the ground. The air force was not operational until 1961 and planned heavy reliance on F-104 STARFIGHTERs.

In 1958 and again in 1959, the C-in-C of the navy, Vice Admiral Ruge, had defined the main tasks for the new navy as part of the NATO concept of forward defence using submarines, aircraft, destroyers and FPBs for offensive mining in the Baltic and attacks against the LOCs of the enemy. A main role also was to prevent amphibious landings and prepare counter attacks with own amphibious craft. These tasks were to be solved with sufficient air support from fighters, but the navy did not prepare integrated staffs with the air force and army to facilitate such complex operations of littoral warfare; the navy wanted its own air force for support.

The tactical analyses which we saw above did not support such an aggressive naval policy. The use of submarines (east of Bornholm) and minefields (creating choke points) was possible, but that was not sufficient to keep the enemy at bay. But the forward tactics with surface vessels was "Blue Ocean" tactics rather than littoral warfare tactics. Because of the short distances to airfields on land the Germans would face severe resistance from Soviet air force – the German air forces would not be in a position to yield sufficient air fighter support, and the split between the naval air force and Luftwaffe was not conducive to creating a workable tactics.

The problems were indirectly recognised by the Navy because the four new destroyers were stationed by the North Sea rather than in the Western Baltic. As the 1960s progressed, the overall concepts were changed to reflect the problems with air support. Furthermore, the introduction of Soviet surface missiles in the

Baltic created solid doubts about the possibilities for German destroyers to operate. We shall return to the challenges to the German tactics in a later chapter.

The West German military top was not prepared for planning the use of nuclear weapons. A command-post exercise LION NOIR in 1957 revealed the devastating consequences of nuclear warfare in Germany. But the Germans had to follow the American lead, so by 1963 the army had secured HONEST JOHN and SARGEANT missiles and 203 mm howitzers capable of delivering nuclear warheads; the air force was getting aircraft capable of carrying nuclear warheads. A general assessment was that the WAPA forces had so many options regarding an attack through Schleswig-Holstein that they were unlikely to resort to nuclear weapons unless NATO forces – under strong pressure to withdraw – used them.

Chapter 9
The Creation of Baltap

The issue of rearming West Germany created new considerations about the organisation of NATO forces and particularly the problems related to the defence of the Baltic and the Baltic approaches. It took many years to reach a decision that accommodated all interests by creating the BALTAP organisation, integrating the command of all NATO forces in Denmark, Schleswig-Holstein, the Danish Straits and the Baltic into one chief, responsible to CINCNORTH, with four subcommands: two army (one East Denmark, one the "Cimbric peninsula"), one air and one navy.

The main stumbling stone for the Integrated NATO Command was a strong averseness among Danish politicians to see German soldiers on Danish soil after five years of German occupation during WWII. They claimed that an integrated command – necessitating German soldiers on Danish territory – would not be acceptable for the Danish population. The Danes were not alone in Europe in having this animosity and fear of German re-militarisation. Another obstacle for agreement on this issue was a West German wish for a NATO integration of all German forces within the territory of West Germany, including Schleswig-Holstein. This would mean a change of the border between AFNORTH and AFCENT, possibly integrating Denmark in AFCENT and pushing the border to the sea of Skagerrak. This was unacceptable for Denmark as well as Norway. In the end, the conundrum led to a compromise between various demands, but the Danes blocked for a decision until 1961, and BALTAP first became fully organised from July 1962.

The political side of the negotiations is fairly well described in the literature.[1] The main primary source for the Danish discussions has been a White Paper from the Ministry of Foreign Affairs, describing Danish Security Policy from 1948 to 1966, published with a comprehensive addendum with source material.[2] But as we shall see below, the White Paper is deficient in several aspects, first of all by omitting a number of discussions and negotiations involving the Danish Joint

---

[1] Nielsen, Jens Perch. *Socialdemokratiet og enhedskommandoen 1961*. Århus: Institut for Statskundskab, 1987; Thoss, Bruno. *NATO-strategie und nationale Verteidigungsplanung. Planung und Aufbau der Bundeswehr unter den Bedingungen atomaren Vergeltungsstrategie 1952–1960*. München: R. Oldenbourg Verlag, 2006; Dansk Institut for Internationale Studier. *Danmark under den kolde krig. Den sikkerhedspolitiske situation 1945–1991. Bind 1: 1945–1962*. København: Dansk Institut for Internationale Studier, 2005a; Villaume, Poul. *Allieret med forbehold*. København: Eirene, 1995.
[2] Udenrigsministeriet. *Dansk Sikkerhedspolitik 1948–1966*. København: Udenrigsministeriet, 1968a; Udenrigsministeriet. *Dansk Sikkerhedspolitik 1948–1966. Bilag*. København: Udenrigsministeriet, 1968b.

Chiefs of Staff, secondly by mentioning but then omitting any detail of the substance of two years of negotiation of the very topic in 1954 and 1955. One can say that the White Paper is the story as perceived by the diplomats of a Ministry of Foreign Affairs with less regard for the military points of view. Of course, some files may have been kept classified by then. In any case, those military angles have more weight below.

The military side of the discussions is to some extent described in the literature,[3] but recent declassification of Danish military archives has added significant information about military perspectives on the creation of BALTAP, and the German Bundeswehr Archiv has the papers of the Holtenau planning group of 1957–58 which are not found in Danish archives. The decision on organisation was to be taken by SACEUR, to be approved by the Military Council and finally the NATO Council. In most situations, the supreme commander did not operate in an empty space; he had to consult with his two sub-commands, CINCENT and CINCNORTH, and in addition the military top of West Germany and Denmark.

The discussion in this chapter deals mainly with the military conceptions, but it also dwells on those political considerations and actions that had a significant impact on the process, some of which have not before been made public. As we shall see, it took 10 years to solve the problems of the NATO-organisation of the area. Montgomery started the disputes, and his wishes never came true, even though the West Germans for a number of years supported the claim. The long story is unwrapped below; for a short version, see Henriksen.[4]

Overview of discussions 1954–1961

1952: Montgomery raises the question of best location of border – no success

1954: May: Discussions of border with Montgomery; November: Denmark blocks change of border AFCENT-AFNORTH; December: CINCNORTH opens negotiations for Naval NATO Command

1955: Summer: Danish-German private talks about future naval cooperation

1956: West Germany declares interest in fully integrated NATO Command; January: SACEUR proposes COMNAVBALT under AFNORTH; March: SACEUR meeting with Germans; Denmark dragging its feet; June: Denmark impedes SACEUR's proposal in NATO's Standing Group; September–October: Discussions of Denmark-SACEUR; "infight" AFCENT vs. AFNORTH; December: Denmark postpones discussions until after election. SACEUR blocks discussions of AFCENT-AFNORTH and continues working on a compromise

1957: SACEUR proposes planning group in Holtenau which commences work in October

---

3 Thoss, op. cit.; SHAPE. *SHAPE History – The New Approach 1953–1956*. Mons: SHAPE, 1976; SHAPE. *History 1957*. Mons: SHAPE, 1967a; SHAPE. *SHAPE History 1958*. Mons: SHAPE, 1967b.
4 Henriksen, Jesper Thestrup. "Der Weg zum Einheitskommando." In *Grenzen überwinden – Schleswig-Holstein, Dänemark und die DDR*, eds Aaron Jessen, Elmar Moldenmauer, and Karsten Biermann, 49–70. Husum: Husum Druck- und Verlagsgesellschaft, 2016.

1958: Spring: reports from Holtenau group, proposal for COMNAVBALTAP, Spring–Summer: Admiral Ruge and CINCENT suggest moving border AFCENT-AFNORTH; September: Denmark approves COMNAVBALTAP (in principle) under AFNORTH; October: German Minister of Defence supports moving border; November: SACEUR intervenes to maintain border, Germans accept

1959: January: CINCNORTH reinvigorates discussions about integrated BALTAP command: Spring: Denmark postpones negotiations; September: Denmark formally approves COMNAVBALTAP; November: SACEUR agrees with Germany to establish integrated BALTAP and stops COMNAV-BALTAP; December: Denmark postpones negotiations until after election late 1960

1960: Spring: Danish Joint Chiefs of Staff hesitant towards integrated BALTAP; June–September: SACEUR presses for solution, meeting in Denmark; November: new Danish cabinet; December: West Germany recommends integrated BALTAP, SACEUR presses for decision

1961: January: Newspaper publishes SACEUR's ideas, Danish minister seems positive, meeting with German Minister, Joint Chiefs of Staff meets SACEUR; Spring: Several counter-proposals from Danish minister and Joint Chiefs of Staff; June: SACEUR threatens with changing borders North-South if no solution; August–September: Danish Cabinet close to compromise; meetings with SACEUR; Danish acceptance of principles in SACEUR's proposal; November: Compromise reached in Oslo; December: BALTAP approved by the Danish parliament

First step: Discussions of the border

The borders between AFCENT and AFNORTH were created at a time when Danish, Norwegian and British troops were stationed in Schleswig-Holstein. Therefore, the area – from 1949 a Bundesland, a state within the German Federation – was made part of AFNORTH with a special command named COMLANDSCHLES-WIG-HOLSTEIN, while the rest of West Germany came under AFCENT. The Norwegian troops were withdrawn in 1953; the Danes were foreseen to be withdrawn later, and so were most of the British as soon as Germany was rearmed and took over the defence. With the foreign troops gone (1958), the new Bundeswehr was divided between two NATO commands, and hence the border became a problem for military planners.

The border was politically desirable – the consistency of the Nordic tradition of cooperation was accentuated by this solution from 1951. However, the practical, military soundness of the border between AFCENT and AFNORTH was contested. A Danish colonel, Erik Kragh, Danish representative in the negotiations about the war organisation of NATO in Paris in 1951, was instructed to support Norwegian points of view and did so. Personally, he disagreed. In a book he noted that "From a military and strategic angle it had been a logical solution to let Denmark be a part of AFCENT and let Norway be part of SACLANT. The defence problems of the two countries are radically different; for Norway the main tasks are in the Northern part of the country, for Denmark the main task lies in the western part of the Baltic."[5]

Apparently such a view was out of bounds at that time, but Deputy SACEUR Montgomery raised doubt about the border at a meeting with CINCNORTH in September 1952; however he did not get any one to support him. Two years later, the border was openly disputed by Montgomery.[6] At that time, negotiations about the European Defence Community (EDC)[7] were about to be finalised, and the rearmament of Germany and the allocation of German troops was a crucial theme. In early April, Montgomery opened a discussion about such a change of the border with the Norwegian minister of defence, and the day after, CINCNORTH Mansergh sent a letter to the Danish minister of defence, informing him about the discussion and notifying that if such a change took place, the Danish forces in Schleswig-Holstein had to be moved to Jutland.[8] Montgomery was expected to discuss this with the Danes in May. Mansergh called attention to the fact that such a change would mean that he would losee command of the area south of the border and that this would create problems in commanding land-, air- and naval forces in the Baltic area.

This would have consequences for the defence of Jutland. The Danish ministry of defence took Montgomery's suggestion under analysis,[9] pointing to the risk that under AFCENT command, retiring NATO (German) forces would probably go west rather than North and hence leave the entrance to Jutland open for the enemy. Coordination between Danish and German forces would be very difficult.

What was the rationale of Montgomery – why this change of border? The New Approach and its re-orientation of the NATO defence strategy was under way, heavily dependent on the use of atomic weapons and therefore making possible a reduction of ground forces (see chapter 7). In the process of working out a draft for the SHAPE Capability Plan 1957, Montgomery wanted the defence line in Northern Germany to move forward from the river Weser towards the east, using the Elbe as the main defence line, and planned four future German divisions to defend Schleswig-Holstein from there. This, however, required that Schleswig-

---

5 Vegger, A. C. B. *Slesvig-Holsten fra 1945 til 1962*, 31. Viborg: Det kongelige Garnisonsbibliotek, 1985.
6 Also mentioned by Henriksen, Jesper Thestrup. "Side om side i det kommende Europa." *Sønderjyske Årbøger*, 2016 2016, 100.
7 We shall not deal with the details of the negotiations 1952–54 about the EDC which failed recognition in 1954 when the French Parliament would not approve the treaty. See e.g Fursdon Fursdon, Edward. *The European Defence Community: A History*. London: Palgrave Macmillan, 1980.
8 Letter 6-4-54 AFNORTH 361/54, Forsvarsministeriet 11. kontor 26-25/54. See also SHAPE's report SHAPE, *SHAPE History – The New Approach 1953–1956*, 53.
9 Notits om ECD-styrkers anvendelse. Forsvarsministeriet 11. kontor YHM april 54 26-25/54.

Holstein came under the command of AFCENT, and the border be moved to the Danish-German border. This was from his point of view militarily sound, and in addition he thought that future German troops could not be expected to fight for Denmark, maybe even under a Danish general.

Montgomery met with the Danish minister of Defence in Copenhagen in May 1954. Montgomery strongly emphasised that if a future defence force in Schleswig-Holstein had to retire, he did not want them to go towards Hamburg; on the contrary, they were to go north towards Jutland, and logistically the supplies were therefore to come from north, not west. Thus the forces would protect Denmark, not Hamburg. Nonetheless, the Danes informed him that changing the border was not the policy of the Danish government, and on the military side, the Danish Joint Chiefs of Staff were also against such a change.

Montgomery's ire
The discussions in Copenhagen did not go well because before Montgomery arrived, the Danish C-in-C and his Joint Chiefs of Staff had a written a memo to General Collins – the Chief of the NATO's Standing Group – about the matter. The memo was based on a previous (1952) force size of two divisions in the area and it found Montgomery's proposal "absolutely unacceptable" because the Baltic, the Danish narrows and the territory around those waters constituted an area of operation that could not be divided.[10] Moving the border between AFCENT and AFNORTH might make it impossible to defend Schleswig-Holstein and hence Denmark (see chapter 6 for details).

Montgomery saw this action as a circumvention of his office, a stab in the back. He became furious and told the Danish Minister of Defence so, much to the dismay of the minister. In two hectic meetings on the 24 and 26 May between the Danish C-in-C and the minister, the C-in-C was ordered to heal the wounds. The minister would not accept a bad standing with Montgomery because it was a question of protocol. Still, he maintained the Danish policy of no change of the border:[11] the Danes saw the proposed change as a serious weakening of the defence of Danish territory, fearing that AFCENT – in spite of Montgomery's assurances – would focus on the defence of Hamburg in the west and leave the path to Denmark in the north open if the troops would have to retreat from the first line of defence.

The C-in-C had to write a new letter[12] to General Collins, acknowledging that Montgomery had in fact set off four future divisions for the defence of the area. The C-in-C also had to call back the last paragraph of the first letter because it made the whole letter a plea to the Standing Group – which could only be addressed as part of a governmental, not a military process.

Still, putting Schleswig-Holstein under command of AFCENT ran counter to the Danish wishes for AFNORTH, and the minister stressed this at a meeting with SACEUR in June 1954.[13]

---

10 Memo for General Collins, C-in-C 13-5-54. Also quoted in HEM Notat vedrørende Nordregionens sydgrænse, Forsvarsministeriet 11. kontor 16-4-56, 26-25/56.
11 Minutes of the meetings in Forsvarsministeriet 11. kontor j.nr. 313/54 29 + 31-5-54 HEM.
12 Dated 24-5-54, HEM FCP 60.
13 Udenrigsministeriet, *Dansk Sikkerhedspolitik 1948–1966*, 82.

In the final draft capability plan, Montgomery's ideas were not followed because the planners in the New Approach Group stated that holding the Elbe forward defence line would be beyond the NATO capabilities in 1957. The eastern defence line therefore was kept at the Weser.[14] Montgomery nonetheless kept his view of the border, and since CINCNORTH and CINCENT could not agree, he "felt that SACEUR would have to settle the matter".

Later that year, SACEUR made a formal proposal to do so in the final plan, but this time he overestimated his powers, so in November 1954, the Danish representative in the Military Committee of NATO blocked this idea which was to be implemented by MC 48, and the supreme commander was told that while the Committee approved the overall strategy (including the massive use of nuclear weapons), he was to re-examine the idea of reorganising the North-Cent border in the light of the task of defending the Danish Straits as well as Jutland under the command of AFNORTH, and in addition, one had to discuss the problems of withdrawing ground forces from Germany to Denmark.[15]

But in June 1955, SACEUR's planning process had retained AFCENT to defend Schleswig-Holstein, and this created some concern in the Danish Ministry of Defence.[16] It appears that the supreme commander, as requested by the Standing Group, had done an analysis of the logistics of an AFCENT army corps dislocated in Schleswig-Holstein, and it was recommended that the supplies for the corps were to be located in Jutland, i.e. under the turf of AFNORTH, and consequently, the corps – named "the hinge" – was to retire towards Jutland, if necessary, and then the command was to be turned over from AFCENT to AFNORTH. The Danish C-in-C found such a shift of command troublesome. But the basic tenet was that the corps must not retire; the area was to he held at all costs.

The ministry summed up the costs and benefits of a change of border:

Costs:
- The physical border between Demark and Germany had no military defence value in terms of natural holding points. From the Kiel Canal, the next nature-given defence line to the North would be the Limfjord, and one would then have to give up four airfields in Jutland. Of course, one would try to establish a defence line more to the south, but it would be difficult.
- COMLANDENMARK would lose control over military access to Denmark and would have to rely on reconnaissance information from AFCENT.

---

14 SHAPE, *SHAPE History – The New Approach 1953–1956*, 66.
15 Ibid., 80.
16 There is a series of letters and memos on the matter in Forsvarsministeriet 11. kontor in 1955, 1956 and 1957, more or less identical, j. no. 26–25.

- It would be more difficult to plan integrated operations across the border because of differing commands and likewise it would be more difficult to have naval forces support the flanks of forces in Schleswig-Holstein.
- Competing demands for naval assistance from North and south would be difficult to prioritise.

Benefits:
- Forces in Schleswig-Holstein would probably get better air support because AFCENT had larger air forces.
- There would be fewer German officers in allied staffs located in Denmark (this was a political, not a military problem).

It is not difficult to see that there were more costs than benefits, and Denmark could not support a change. SACEUR's suggestions, however, however, did not come to a test in the Standing Group. One can say that they withered away because he had to push his implementation year for the Capability plan forward from 1957 to 1959, and in the meantime the Baltic Approaches became the object of another and major reorganisation, as we shall see below.

Second step: Naval integration?

AFNORTH would be responsible for defending NATO's left (northern) flank of the fight resulting from a Soviet attack on West Germany, and hence it had to be in control of the offensive naval forces in the Baltic and the Danish narrows. The regional commander was not inclined to give up his command over West Germany north of the river Elbe and, by implication, the Baltic. In 1952, when SHAPE was preparing a policy for the future West German naval forces, CINCNORTH had indicated that such forces together with the Danish navy had to be under one flag officer under his command; this was supported by the Danish Joint Chiefs of Staff in a statement from March 1952;[17] they also indicated that a future "Flag Officer Baltic" should be a Danish officer with an integrated Danish-German staff.

The Danish Joint Chiefs of Staff discussed the issue of Baltic command again one and a half years later.[18] The chief of the navy now had reconsidered the command question, and, realising that neither the Danes nor the Germans would be pleased by having a Flag Officer from the other nation in command, he recom-

---

17 FSS 19-3-52.
18 FSS 17-11-53.

mended that one should aim towards getting a Baltic Naval Command under a British Flag Officer.

The question of a Baltic naval command, then, had been in the minds of top officers for several years; it had been suggested by Admiral Heye when he consulted with the Danish Navy in the years 1949–52.[19] Probably as a reaction to the Danish blocking of SACEUR's proposal in the Military Committee, CINCNORTH in December 1954 suggested that a new naval command, COMNAVBALT, be established to control the important defence tasks expected in the Baltic. It would integrate Danish and West German naval forces – each under their own national command – under AFNORTH. The upcoming seventh slice of the NATO Common Infrastructure Programme could finance the proposed headquarters with an international staff, headed by an international flag officer, probably British.[20] This new headquarter was meant to command offensive operations by Danish and West German naval forces – including naval air forces – in the Baltic, possibly in cooperation with other NATO navies. Danish administration, local defence and supplies would remain under Danish control. The new command under AFNORTH would become operational when war broke out with headquarters near Aarhus in Denmark. In peacetime, the German navy would be under command from Kiel.

As preparation for the meeting, the Danish C-in-C listed a number of concerns to his Ministry of Defence:[21]

– First, he questioned the soundness of having different command posts in peace and war; alone the change from one command post to another was problematic.
– Second, it had to be ruled out that the flag officer was German. The post should preferably be Danish, since a Dane would have the necessary knowledge of the conditions in the quite tricky Danish and Baltic waters. A British admiral might be acceptable as a compromise, but one then had to foresee that all naval flag officers in AFNORTH might be British. This would be less fortunate seen from the perspective of the Danish population (a fact the politicians would have to take into consideration, PB). On the other hand, British leadership might be more acceptable for the Germans who respected the Royal Navy and its indisputable experience from war. However, one had to foresee a future demand for leadership from the Germans; in that case, alternations between Denmark and Germany would be preferable.
– The geographical position of the future command should be in Denmark, organised as such – under AFNORTH – in peace as well as war.

---

19 Die Rolle der westlichen Seemacht in einem Krieg gegen Russland. Forsvarets Efterretningstjeneste HEM K4A Tyskland, 3506/55.
20 FSS 4-2-55 4f.
21 PM vedrørende den fremtidige kommandoorganisation i Østersøen, C.K.10/0789 13-2-55.

In conclusion, the C-in-C recommended that the policy of the Danish government should favour a permanent NAVBALT under AFNORTH, located in Denmark with a Danish chief.

A meeting in February 1955 between CINCNORTH – General Mansergh – and the Danish Minister of Defence did not create any agreement.[22] It turned out that the Danish C-in-C and the chief of the navy did not agree regarding the nationality of the future chief of NAVBALTAP, because the navy preferred an Englishman. Nor did they agree regarding the location of the headquarters; the navy preferred Kiel in peacetime and Aarhus during war.

The minister was not helpful. He declared from the start that he could not decide anything without backing from the cabinet. The issue was politically sensitive in that the proposed headquarters, located in Aarhus, would include German officers. The Danish population was not ready for this only ten years after the occupation; NATO should consider a location in Kiel, at least in peacetime. Furthermore, the disagreement between his top military advisors did not make his position any easier.

CINCNORTH recognised the problems for the minister and intended to bring the proposal to SACEUR as his own, with no recommendations from Denmark. The supreme commander wanted swift action, given the upcoming West German rearmament. Mansergh added that in his opinion, the Germans would not accept a permanent Danish chief – just as the Danish would not accept a German – and hence he recommended a British.

After the meeting, the Danish minister consulted with the prime minister and the minister for foreign affairs; no one wanted German officers in Denmark and they recommended Kiel as the location for the command in peacetime.[23]

In the light of the less than enthusiastic Danish policy stance and having to deal with practical decisions regarding the new German Bundeswehr, SACEUR put work on the NAVBALT command on hold in June 1955.[24]

Representatives from the Danish navy and the West German Ministry of Defence-to-be discussed the possibilities for a COMNAVBALT at a "private" meeting in a manor house in Holstein in the late summer of 1955.[25] The main theme was the size and composition of the new German navy.

---

22 Minutes are from Forsvarsministeriet 11. kontor 17-2-55.
23 PM Forsvarsministeriet 11. kontor 16-3-55.
24 Note from Forsvarsministeriet 11. kontor 4-7-55.
25 Thostrup, S. S. "Chief of Staff from 9th January 1962 to 31st March 1965." In *Safeguarding Security in the Baltic Approaches 1962–2002*, Ove Høegh-Guldberg Hoff, 11. Viborg: Public Information Office Joint Headquiarters NORTHEAST, 2002.

But the Germans wanted more than suggested by AFNORTH. In early 1956, the German Ministry of Defence decided that, first of all, West Germany would be interested in an integrated NATO command in the Baltic Area – i.e. one comprising all three types of military forces – and that the allocation to AFNORTH or AFCENT was only of secondary importance. The Germans saw an obvious need for integrating all military forces in the defence system for the Baltic area, for instance when defending the coast of Northern Germany against amphibious attack.[26, 27] This strategic conception was voiced six years earlier in the note on the Baltic by Hellmuth Heye, as we saw in chapter 2.

NATO, however, was not yet ready to go so far. On 21 January 1956, SACEUR – General Gruenther – forwarded a suggestion to the Danish Ministry of Defence that a naval command, COMNAVBALT, be established for the Baltic, the Danish straits and Kattegat, under AFNORTH,[28] much along the lines of the previous proposal from 1954, but for starters in the Kiel area. In peacetime, German forces were answerable to AFCENT, but Danish and other forces were linked to AFNORTH.

According to the Danish White Paper on Security Policy from 1968, there were "no significant discussions" between NATO and Danish authorities after the proposal was sent; instead NATO suggested that the proposal be analysed by a planning group.[29] This statement is quite far from what actually took place. In fact, comprehensive and close but fruitless (regarding a COMNAVBALT) contacts were pursued, involving the Danish political and military top as well as SACEUR and the Standing Group – which blocked SACEUR's plans by a Danish veto. The process is detailed below.

- The Danish C-in-C and the chief of the navy came to an agreement that the headquarters should be located in Denmark in peace as well as war, and that the chief preferably should be Danish, and under no circumstances German.
- The Danish C-in-C wrote a note to the Minister of Defence in March, emphasising the military benefits from a close cooperation with future West German military forces.[30] Realising that there would be much animosity against

---

26 Thoss, op. cit., p. 262.
27 Jens Perch Nielsen notes that the idea of an integrated command probably was born in AFNORTH Nielsen, op. cit., p. 119, but the initiative taken by AFNORTH in 1954 was, as we saw above, only a command integrating Danish and German naval forces. The Germans wanted an all-forces integrated command in the Baltic area from the very start of the rearmament i 1956. Nielsen's presentation is based on an interview with the Danish General Vegger who thought that American and British officers originally brought the concept forward as an experience from WWII (Personal communication from Nielsen 10-8-21).
28 Note from Forsvarsministeriet 11. kontor 18-5-56.
29 Udenrigsministeriet, *Dansk Sikkerhedspolitik 1948–1966*, 100.
30 C-in-C letter HEM 6-3-56, B 4282/O.1032.

such cooperation in the general public, and realising that certain parts of the press already voiced opposition, the C-in-C stressed the need for Danes to understand the tangible military necessities in the light of a substantial increase in defence strength when the Germans joined the NATO.
- Regarding the defence at sea, a future German navy would increase the ability to resist amphibious enemy forces and strengthen the sea power controlling the Danish narrows. This, however, presupposed a NATO command coordinating the actions of the two navies. The C-in-C reminded the minister that SACEUR's proposal for the COMNAVBALT organisation fulfilled this purpose. The Danish Joint Chiefs of Staff agreed with the supreme commander that the command should be permanently located in Jutland, not in Northern Germany, but given the lack of suitable headquarters, the command could initially be placed in Germany. Furthermore, the C-in-C called attention to the future need for supplies for German forces, to be located in Jutland in order to make them less vulnerable to enemy attacks.
- Regarding the defence on land, the Danish defence of Jutland required close coordination with German forces, and the need for common planning already in peacetime was obvious. In addition, a supply line for German forces was inevitable if one wanted to secure a defensive retreat from Northern Germany to South Jutland. Lack of such supplies would mean that the Germans retreated towards west (Hamburg) and left Jutland more open for enemy attacks.
- Regarding the air defence, a need for cooperation was unclear at this point of time because the air defence of Western Europe was under reorganisation, but one could foresee a need for cooperation sooner or later.
- Finally, the C-in-C reminded the minister that Denmark's standing within NATO was rather low, given that the Danes had declined the offer of stationing American aircraft in Jutland in 1953. If Denmark once again resisted cooperation within a new NATO with West Germany as a partner, it would have serious consequences for the willingness of NATO partners to help Denmark in the future. The C-in-C asked for a political backing and a policy baseline for future cooperation with German military forces.

Apparently this note had no immediate consequences; the Danish minister of defence did not respond to SACEUR's proposal for COMNAVBALT. But the supreme commander had a meeting regarding the proposal with the German Ministry of Defence on 8 March 1956. The Danish Joint Chiefs of Staff got a condensed report of what had happened from the Danish ambassador in Bonn.[31] First, as we saw

---

31 Note from Forsvarsministeriet 11. kontor 9-4-56.

above, the Germans wanted the future NATO command in the Baltic area to be an integrated command for all three military branches. Second, the chief of the planned COMNAVBALT should be British for a start, but later Germany should take over the role as chief because of the size of its new navy. The chief of staff, then, could be Danish and chief of operations German, or vice versa. Third, the Germans suggested that the location of the command be in Kiel-Holtenau, to be moved to Mid-Jutland when buildings etc. were ready.

In April, several NATO top brass informally complained that Denmark was dragging its feet; indeed, SACEUR's vice naval deputy was "chocked".[32] The Danish Joint Chiefs of Staff tried to persuade the minister to make a decision on 30 May.[33] The C-in-C stressed that the proposal for COMNAVBALT was militarily sound, that the headquarters should be located in mid-Jutland and that the chief should be British or American. The minister understood these partly military, partly practical, arguments, but he foresaw a number of political difficulties. Therefore, a new meeting was held one week later, now also including the prime minister (who also held the office of Foreign Affairs), and the permanent secretaries of the three ministries.[34] The military rationales for the new NATO command were spelled out in detail: the operations of the Danish and German navies in the Baltic area had to be planned beforehand and coordinated during action to create maximum efficiency towards a strong enemy and had to be exercised. For instance, submarine activities had to be carefully planned to avoid collisions and misinterpretations. Minefields had to be planned and coordinated to make navigation safe. German ships covering Danish mine layers had to exercise cooperation, particularly during night time. The German navy would need to withdraw to the Danish straits during daytime. All this required one centre of command with a common set of directives and communication, thoroughly exercised during peacetime. The nationality of the COMBALTAP was under discussion in a small committee.

The prime minister accepted the military justification, but he disagreed regarding the time schedule. Why such haste? He needed time to discuss the plans with the opposition, and the matter had to be discussed by the parliamentary Committee for Foreign Affairs. He doubted that the parliament would support the plan, and personally, he was quite sceptical towards the plan. No decision could be taken that day, and the plan was to be kept top secret.

The minister, then, saw a conceivably quite strong opposition among the political parties in the Danish parliament to the proposal. Politicians did not want

---

32 FSS 6-4-56 4/3; note HEM from Colonel Grüner, NMR, to C-in-C 5-4-56, C-in-C archive 220.02.
33 Minutes from Forsvarsministeriet 11. kontor 7-6-56.
34 Minutes from Forsvarsministeriet 11. kontor 9-6-56.

German officers in Denmark, and to make things worse, some feared that a location in Kiel would create the reaction that the Danish navy was run by the Germans.

SACEUR repeatedly asked for a response, but the Danish minister stalled the process until late June, and at that time he replied (through his representative in SHAPE) that he needed to consult with opposition parties in parliament, and this could not take place until August.[35] Neglecting this response, the supreme commander on July 24, 1956, sent the proposal to NATO's Standing Group. He notified the Danish representative in Paris that the matter probably would take some time in the Group which might perceive it as a hot potato. The Dane responded that some Danish political parties likewise might treat the matter as a hot potato and hence avoid a decision.[36] Whatever the case, Denmark, probably as a tough answer to SACEUR, blocked a decision in the Standing Group.

SACEUR followed up by meeting on 18 September with some members of the Danish cabinet and the Joint Chiefs of Staff.[37] He pushed for a Danish decision, noting that there had been no problems whatsoever in integrating German officers in other staffs in Europe. The Minister of Defence responded that the matter was very sensitive in Denmark; personally he accepted the military rationales, but politically it would be difficult. The planned meeting in August with the opposition had been cancelled due to the Suez crisis, but a new one was planned.

On 10 October, SACEUR's naval deputy, admiral Sala, met with the Danish Minister of Defence and the Danish Joint Chiefs of Staff.[38] He informed them that the COMNAVBALT was to be located in mid-Jutland, close to the commands of the army and the air force. Indeed, the supreme commander was informed that there were particular Danish political problems linked to the proposal, and SACEUR therefore would propose a small planning group of eight officers headed by a British admiral and located in Kiel-Holtenau, to carry out analyses of the future military tasks in the Baltic. The expected time frame would be six months. As the Bundesmarine would become operational from early 1957, one had to solve the problems related to Danish-German naval cooperation. The admiral also had to oversee the training of the Bundesmarine, and he would bring seven more officers for this task, and therefore the group was placed under AFCENT.

The minister once again informed the participants of his personal acceptance of the COMNAVBALT, but he had to quote a recent Gallup poll, indicating than

---

35 FSS 30-6-56 3c.
36 Forsvarsministeriet 11. kontor "Ekstraktudskrift fra Kontorchef Svend Hansens møde med General Gruenter 10 juli 1956".
37 Minutes by Forsvarsministeriet 11. kontor 25-9-56.
38 Minutes by Forsvarsministeriet 11. kontor 25-10-56.

only one out of four Danes was positive to the command. However, the minister found the idea of a study and planning group interesting and he would expect the cabinet to follow suit, provided that it was clear that this did not in any way constitute an acceptance of COMNAVBALT.

Late 1956 the Danish government notified SACEUR that no Danish formal policy position was possible until after parliamentary elections expected to take place in the fall of 1957[39] (actually, the election took place in May 1957, PB). This happened after a series of meetings in parliamentary committees and informal groupings in October and November 1956. The Danish Prime Minister was in favour of the command, but the opposition was rather lukewarm, and the idea of having German officers on Danish soil in particular appeared to be unacceptable, particularly to the leadership of the party Venstre.[40] Given this fact of Danish politics, the supreme commander – now General Norstad[41] – ordered his C-in-Cs in the centre and north not to discuss the problems of military commands in the Baltic with national authorities, fully aware that the C-in-Cs actually did work on comprehensive analyses of this particular problematic from their respective perspectives.[42] CINCNORTH wanted an integrated command under his control. CINCENT wanted – in accordance with what he perceived as the wishes of West Germany[43] – a change of the borders between AFCENT and AFsNORTH and intended to create a command – initially under SACEUR[44] – that integrated all three branches of the Danish and German forces.

What were the German ambitions for the Baltic Command?

Commodore Gerlach, recently named C-in-C of the German navy in the Baltic (BSO), wrote a letter in July 1957[45] to one of his younger colleagues about the aspirations for the German Bundeswehr in the longer run. His colleague had expressed a fear that German interests were not met in the negotiations and wanted a German leadership. Gerlach perceived the issues differently and explained the German tactics:

---

39 SHAPE, *History 1957*, 154.
40 Notes HEM in Danish C-in-C archive, group 220.02, dated 3-10-56, 4-10-56 and 2-11-56.
41 Some sources, e.g. Pedlow and Thoss Pedlow, Gregory W. "The Politics of NATO Command, 1950–1962." In *U:S: Miliitary Forces in Europe. The Early Years*, eds Simon W. Duke and Wolfgang Krieger, 15–42. Boulder, CO: Westview Press, 1993; Thoss, op. cit, mention Norstad as SACEUR and initiator to COMNAVBALT in the Summer of 1956, but he did not take command until 20 November 1956, and as we have seen, the idea originated in AFNORTH late 1954.
42 SHAPE, *History 1957*, 154–59.
43 PM page 3, YHM attachment to letter from C-in-C C.635/O.1249 15 March 1960.
44 He was in agreement with the German Minister of Defence on this point Nielsen, op. cit., p. 52.
45 Letter Secret 12-7-57 to Fregattenkapitän Waldemar Holst in the NATO Defence College. BM 1/1097.

First, an integrated, joint command would unquestionably be a military necessity in the Baltics. The Soviets would attack with all three forces, so NATO had to coordinate its responses accordingly. The joint command should be under AFCENT, and in order to create military coherence, AFNORTH should be reduced to Northern Norway in close cooperation with SACLANT, and AFCENT expanded correspondingly. British participation in the command would be essential because the air defence of the Baltics would be dependent on aircraft support from air carriers from the great sea powers. Since the main battles would be three-force, but carried and supported by the navies, the integrated command had to be headed by an admiral.

Second, such a goal could not be reached right away. The resistance in the Danish population had to be reduced step by step. The present idea (July 1957, PB) about a naval Planning Group was a first, but of course not sufficient, step, and the German navy top and the Bundeswehr Top were satisfied. Unofficially the group would work together with the Danish and German naval top, thus preparing the ground for a future joint command. In Gerlach's opinion, the Planning Group could not but conclude that an integrated planning process together with army and air force was a must, and thus carry the issues towards the integrated command desired by Germany. And a task for the German members of the group would precisely be to nudge the work in that direction.

Third, Germany should be happy with an British admiral as leader of the group, even though it had been tempting to push for a German leadership. It was a German interest to maintain the interest of the Royal Navy in the Baltics, and the Royal Navy would be a good partner in re-building the German navy, not least in logistical issues. In addition, this cooperation would reduce the antipathies from WWII which were so to say in the bones of many British naval officers. Over time, the cooperation would create an understanding that the Germans had wholehearted and honest wishes for a common future. Finally, this British admiral would be gone in three years or so, and a Danish or German admiral could then take over.

As we shall see, Gerlach was right about the integrated necessity (thus following the ideas of littoral warfare), but not about the strength of the AFCENT and the superiority of the navies, and the process too, six years, not three.

The outcome of the Danish elections in May 1957 was a three-party coalition cabinet lead by the Social Democrats, but the two associated parties were rather anti-defence. This meant that the expenses for the Danish military forces were frozen and under pressure for reductions during the following three years, and all discussions of NATO were difficult and often inconclusive.[46]

A further complication was found in the organisation of the West German navy. For NATO-political reasons, the whole Bundeswehr was from the outset controlled by AFCENT[47] which made sure that the Bundeswehr in its totality became an asset for, rather than a threat against, Western Europe; one must remember that WWII only was 11 years away. In peacetime, the West German navy both in the North Sea and the Baltic were under the naval command of AFCENT,

---

46 Kaarsted, Tage. *De danske ministerier 1953–1972*, 139–41, 158–61. København: PFA Pension, 1992.
47 Sander-Nagashima, Johannes Berthold. *Die Bundesmarine 1950 bis 1972*, 5. München: Oldenbourg Wissenschaftsverlag, 2006.

the COMNAVCENT, which oversaw the training and daily actions of the navy. But the Bundesmarine would be placed under two separate commands in wartime. One command (COMNORSEACENT) was for forces in the North Sea, located in Cuxhaven and linked to AFCENT, one (COMNAVGERBALT) for the Baltic, located in Kiel and linked to AFNORTH.[48] Whereas the navy in peace time was under one German navy C-in-C, the split in case of war and hence NATO-command was less fortunate.

SACEUR could neither get German nor Danish support to let the Holtenau planning group work under CINCENT,[49] so the proposal was changed into an international group to work under the joint responsibility of CINCENT and CINCNORTH with two tasks:
a) Study the organisation and command problems and the naval strategy in the Baltic area and make appropriate recommendations; and
b) Formulate war plans for all Allied Baltic Naval Forces and undertake NATO exercise planning in this area.

More specifically, the group should plan the future organisation of the NATO command; assess the need for and the use of aircraft in the Baltic; plan communication systems, minefields and mine sweeping tasks; assess logistics; and make strategic studies of the Baltic Approaches.[50]

This indicated that SACEUR put the ideas of an integrated command aside for a while and focused his interest on the naval command. Denmark approved the group in June 1957, having earlier noted specifically that this decision did not prejudice the formation of a COMNAVBALT in any way.[51]

The group was approved by the Military Council, taking note of the Danish special condition, and started its work by mid-October 1957, directed by a British admiral. CINCENT and CINCNORTH 8 October 1957 agreed that Denmark, Schleswig-Holstein and the Western Baltic were to be regarded as one tactical area, preferably under a single tactical commander, and that the borders between north and centre were to be unaltered.[52] The West German navy, however, was kept under the split command of CINCENT and AFNORTH in wartime, but under AFCENT in peacetime.

---

48 Ibid., 68.
49 SHAPE, *History 1957*, 154–59.
50 Draft Terms of Reference 17-5-57, Forsvarsministeriet 11. kontor 14-6-57.
51 Telegram to SACEUR 23-5-57, Forsvarsministeriet 11. kontor.
52 PM page 2, YHM attachment to letter from CINC C.635/O.1249 15-3-60.

Third step: Integrated naval command

The first report of the Holtenau Planning Group[53] was ready on 14 February, 1958.[54]

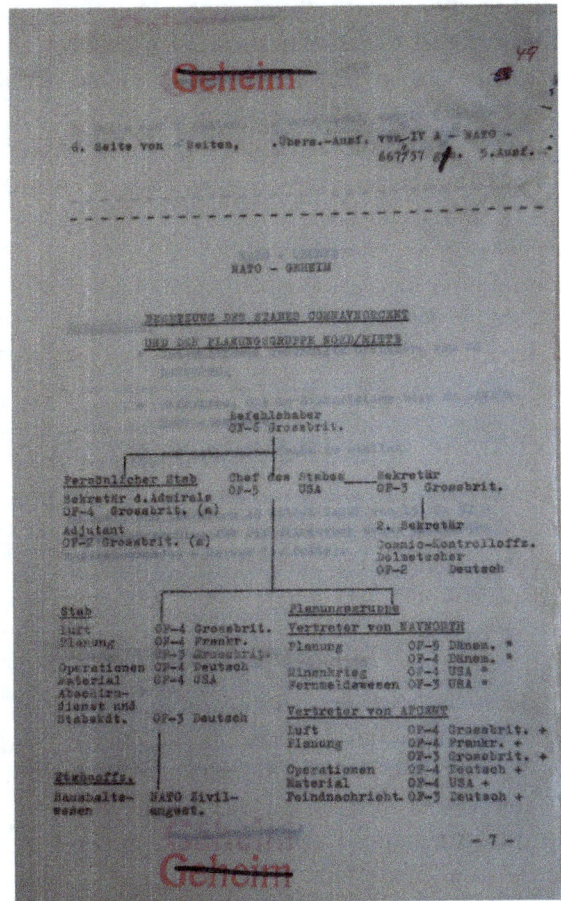

Figure 9.1: The organisation of COMNAVNORCENT with the Planning Group. The Germans had resisted a British Flag Lieutenant to the Admiral. The British argued that they had special competent officers for such a task. The Germans pointed out that Germans needed to learn the ropes of staff work. As a compromise, the Admiral got two secretaries. Source: Bundeswehr Archiv.

---

53 The reports have not been found in Danish archives, but most of the papers are in the German Militärarchiv in Freiburg. Some of the contents are discussed in other Danish papers. We combine the two sources in this chapter.
54 Tasks of Baltic Naval Force. NATO Secret. BM 1/1000c.

All reports were to be discussed at quarterly meetings within a group which at the first meeting consisted of representatives from COMNAVNORCENT, COMNAVCENT, CINCNORTH, COMNAVNORTH and SACEUR. The number of participants could be quite large; 15–19 officers were there to comment and participate in subgroups, solving disagreements and clarifying texts at the meeting.

Initially, the Planning Group wrote up a document describing the foreseen process of hostilities initiated by the Warsaw Treaty forces.[55] First, air raids would take place against naval bases, air bases, radar and coastal defence stations, ships at sea, and mine depots and loading harbours. One would expect mines to be laid and various attacks by special forces. Second, balanced naval forces would be set in against NATO ships as far towards north and west as possible; main targets would be mine layers and their escorts and other NATO-units in the straits of Fehmarn and Øresund. As soon as possible, amphibious attacks would be initiated against the Zealand islands and Schleswig-Holstein. At the same time, ground forces and airborne troops were expected to try to conquer Jutland.

The Planning Group first suggested that the area should comprise Skagerrak, Kattegat, the Danish Straits and the Baltic. The report contained some fairly general principles for planning and preparing for war, and how to execute these principles by various instruments: submarines, minefields, air operations, electronic warfare, convoying, clandestine operations etc. In addition, to establish defence against amphibious activities, attack enemy ships and submarines, defend harbours and own LOCs, attack enemy LOCs and neutralise their bases.

The future organisation and location of a HQ was dealt with in more detail, analysing available buildings and possible future locations. A main theme was the necessity to coordinate navy, army and air forces in the relatively small area. Therefore, distances to other HQs (army and air force) was to be small. A particular Danish political hot potato was the stationing of German officers in Denmark in peacetime, which meant that the command should be located in Kiel – but in wartime preferably close to Karup (but not closer than 20 kilometres due to the risk of nuclear bombing of Karup).

---

55 Note YHM from Danish Foreign Ministry j. no. 105.I.19.c dated 29-9-58 and 13-10-58.

Planning issues

Over the ensuing eight months, more themes were analysed by the group, and existing themes were re-formulated. As time went by, plans for various actions were written, discussed and approved. The main thrusts of those issues follow below.

The overall organisation

There was considerable disagreement among the parties regarding the overall principles of the command. The first report concluded that one was to avoid sub-dividing the area into a German and Danish area, and avoid a large general HQ for the two navies. Instead one was to rely on already existing groups of the two navies which were to operate all over the area as task forces.

The Germans, however, saw this as a two-pronged British, non-expressed assault against West Germany.[56] First, an attempt to keep the Germans away from power (a large area command would probably get a German C-in-C because of the size of the German navy) and, supported by the Danes, secure their own power as C-in-C of the Baltic naval command. Second, to ensure that no nationally homogeneous German Navy would (re)appear. According to the Germans, the British wanted to keep the command because of, first, a real interest to keep Schleswig-Holstein and Jutland from Soviet hands – as a base for Soviet missiles this would threaten the British isles; second, to get a new power base now that they were losing power in the Mediterranean to the Americans; third, a historic naval interest in the Baltic; and fourth, a suspicion that the Germans were planning to re-create a strong fleet of submarines for the high seas.

The planning group only suggested two task forces: one of mine layers under Danish command, and one strike force under German command. This did not please the Danes who had to make it very clear that such a division of labour would in no time reduce the Danish navy to a second class navy with severe problems in recruiting qualified personnel, and they maintained that both nations needed a balanced navy.[57] The suggestion was removed (see below).

---

56 Bericht und Stellungnahme des B.S.O. NATO Secret, Anlage zu BSO Tgb.Nr 86 sach 58, no date, signed by Gerlach. BM 1/1000e.
57 Petersen, Jørgen. *Mit liv i Søværnet 1934–80*, 85. Odense: Odense Universitetsforlag, 1985.

Geography

The first meeting of the Coordination Group led to a reduction in the suggested delineation of the command to Denmark, Schleswig-Holstein, Kattegat, the Danish Straits and the Baltic until 16 degrees east (50 kilometres east of Bornholm), thus leaving the Skagerrak to the naval command of AFNORTH.[58] This was a first step in the process of not accepting the German wishes to extend AFCENT first to Skagerrak and later even farther to the North.

The expected "line to be held" by NATO forces against Soviet attacks would be in the area east of the Danish island Falster, and past Bornholm. Given that the Danish and German forces would fight in this common area, given the need for coordination, and given the Danish critique of the mine task force, the ideas of a small HQ and task forces were given up and instead a common HQ was suggested to be established with a Danish and German flag officer as sub-commanders, each with their national forces.

In this organisation, the Danish forces were primarily to defend the Danish straits and Kattegat, the Germans the Kieler Bay and the Straits of Fehmarn and Gedser. The area further to the east, however, was to be a shared war theatre, and action taken – possibly joined under one commander – as required in any situation, particularly against amphibious assaults and surface forces attacking or threatening NATO territory. Furthermore, submarines were to be under one commander only (initially Danish since the Germans had none), to avoid any confusion regarding the whereabouts of them. Likewise, naval aircraft had to be under one commander, for now COMNAVBALTAP.

Surveillance

A basic activity of the whole NATO system was a continuous, ongoing surveillance of the Soviet military activities. The NATO alarm system was based on early warning, whenever possible. The planning group analysed three issues in surveillance: short range, long range and a particular electronic detection loop in the Strait of Fehmarn.

The long range system concerned activities east of Bornholm. Apparently it was dependent on the surveys carried out by the USAF ADVON (Advanced Operational Node) forces[59] which were to survey two areas in the Baltic by radar on

---

58 Naval Command Structure in the Baltic Approach Area. NATO Secret. North/Centre Planning Group. PG/P(58)4, 12-3-58. BM 1/1000e.
59 New page 2 to Annex B to pg/P(58)10 of 22-8-58. NATO Secret. BM 1/1000d.

General Alert, continuing for 72 hours and then upon request. One area was south east of Bornholm (until Gdynia) every four hours, the other north east of Bornholm every 24 hours. Since identification of radar echoes from the Americans was difficult to interpret, intelligence from those sorties had to be followed up by own recce units – airplanes or vessels – for positive identification. COMTAFDEN was slated to do recce on the Baltic ports, so intelligence from those flights would also come to use.

The Short Range system[60] was aimed at detection and identification of all surface and sub-surface activities in the Baltic Approaches, beginning around Bornholm. The system was based on coastal radar stations, nine patrol craft, visual look-out stations, underwater detection devices, local command and control systems and local inshore patrol craft as available. The primary instruments for detection, then, were radars, sonars and other electronic systems, stationary or on ships. Shipborne systems were particularly important at night and during reduced visibility. A system of communication was to be set up to make sure that relevant information reached the right commander(s).

The Planning Group also analysed the possibilities for establishing an underwater detection system to survey for submerged submarines – passing in order to reach the Kiel Bay (to lay mines or attack otherwise) or Storebælt (to pass and continue towards the North Sea and the Atlantic.[61] Denmark had three such loops – in Storebælt, Lillebælt and in Øresund north of Helsingør. Therefore, a new loop would be particularly important for the defence of the Western Baltic, serving as a warning post that an attack or a mine laying scheme in the Kiel area might be imminent. Alternatively, the personnel at the loop in Storebælt would be warned that a passage might be on the way. The loop would be laid down in the Strait of Fehmarn between Ohlensburg-Huk and the Danish town Rødby. The strait had an average depth of 24 meters which a submarine could easily pass submerged.

Mine laying

The most important military instrument in the Baltic Approaches probably was mine laying. Three general plans were written: mining the straits, mining the beaches for landing and tactical mining in enemy waters. Mines in one's own

---

60 Short Range Surveillance System. NATO Secret. Annex A to PG/P(58)10 of 22-8-58. 15-10-58. BM 1/1000d.
61 North/Centre Planning Group Holtenau: Underwater Detection Station in the Fehmarn Belt. NATO Secret. Memorandum PG/T(58)1. 3-10-58. BM 1/1000d.

waters were to be laid before D-day. All types of mines were to be laid: acoustic, magnetic and contact; the ship counters should mostly be set to one so that they exploded by first contact. In general, they would be laid at night because of the air threat, and there was a risk of enemy attacks by FPBs and destroyers; therefore, surface units like destroyers, destroyers escort and FPBs would be allocated to protect the mine layers which were only armed with small-calibre guns.

Previously the Danes had prepared for mining the two Belts and Øresund. Now the Germans were involved, and this meant that the Strait of Fehmarn could be mined, blocking access to the two Danish Belts, and the Danes now could concentrate the initial mining procedures to the southern part of Øresund. Plan "C" dealt with this.[62] The purpose was to prevent amphibious forces from passing the straits and approach their targets, and to prevent any enemy from entering to attack allied LOCs and military units. Four Danish mine layers were allocated for Øresund, and two German and one UK mine layers plus 24 mine sweepers were allocated for the Strait of Fehmarn. Other units equipped with mine laying capability could be allocated in both areas, if possible. The minefields would be laid at night, consisting of a mix of magnetic, acoustic and contact mines with safe channels for their own forces' passage. Exact navigation was to be ensured by Decca (started on demand) or radar.

Plan "I" concerned the mining of invasion beaches.[63] There were three directions amphibious attacks might take: transit the Strait of Fehmarn to land somewhere on the Jutland peninsula or the main Danish islands; transit southern Øresund to land in Faxe Bay or Køge Bay; or land on the southeastern coasts of Lolland, Falster or Møn. The second and third possibilities were considered most likely, but landing on the peninsula might also happen to support Soviet forces there. The mining of Øresund and the Strait of Fehmarn (according to Plan C) formed an obstacle for the two first types of attacks; Plan I was meant to block the third one and add mines at the relevant beaches if the minefields of Plan C were surpassed. The main tasks were allocated to the Danish navy with two mine layers plus various auxiliary craft for priority one: the beaches of Falster, Lolland and Møn (53 miles). Priority two was the beaches of Køge and Faxe Bays (56 miles), also with two mine layers. Priority three was certain areas west of the Strait of Fehmarn (75 miles); no mine layers were assigned beforehand.

---

62 Mining Plan for Southern Sound and Fehmarn Belt. NATO Secret. Annex C to PG/P(58)10 of 22-8-58. 15-10-58. BM 1/1000d.
63 Mining Plan for the Invasion Beaches. NATO Secret. Annex I to PG/P(58)10 of 22-8-58. 15-10-58. BM 1/1000d.

Plan "J" dealt with tactical mining against "worthwhile targets" in the area south east of Denmark.[64] Tactical mining was a dangerous endeavour and only to be used when there was a great opportunity for success and if no other methods were possible or desirable at that time. Tactical mine laying was to be performed by FPBs which were reassigned from other tasks to one of the task force commanders. Tactical mining by aircraft also was a possibility.

Combined surface action

This plan[65] would be dormant until activated by COMNAVBALTAP. It combined the forces from Denmark and Germany and was to be initiated only if the enemy was perceived to become a "major threat", e.g. when a seaborne invasion was being initiated. Most other plans for NAVBALTAP would have to cede. The forces available would be eight destroyers, six destroyers escort, 48 FPBs and 15 patrol craft. Furthermore, there would be eight midget submarines, 18 attack aircraft plus up to 18 recce airplanes, as well as shore-based supporting forces. In addition, there would be non-naval aircraft if required and possible. The mission for this maximum NATO force was to attack the enemy continuously until they were destroyed or turned back. Pre-planning such an operation would not be possible; the operational commander would be given maximum freedom of action. A loose and open enemy formation would be attacked by light, fast surface forces. Concentrated forces might be attacked by an atomic strike in accordance with the ASP. If an invasion force got close to its destination, it had to be attacked again and again to stop the invasion. Large enemy transport vessels and heavy naval units would be priority targets.

Submarines

The Baltic was foreseen to become a major LOC for the Soviets in the east-west direction with a large number of ports, airfields and radar stations. It might become the only way to transport goods after an initial atomic exchange, which had destroyed transport channels on land. If the enemy had air supremacy, submarines would be the only NATO instrument to attack the sea transports.[66] Eight small (up to 150 tons) and 12 coastal submarines (up to 600 tons) were allocated to

---

64 Tactical Mining Plan. NATO Secret. Annex J to PG/P(58)10 22-8-58. 15-10-58. BM 1/1000d.
65 Combined Surface Force Action Against Major Enemy Forces Threatening The Area. NATO Secret. Annex F to PG/P(58)10 of 22-8-58. 15-10-58. BM 1/1000d.
66 Submarine Striking Plan. NATO Secret. Annex H to PG/P(58)10 of 22-8-58. 15-10-58. BM 1/1000d.

this plan under one commander. Submarine operations in the Baltic were difficult due to shallowness, restricted size of the theatre and the expected naval superiority of the Soviets, working with a large number of radar stations. But the presence of NATO submarines would force them to operate in convoys, to form hunter groups and keep mine sweepers active around ports in fear of mines being laid by submarines.

When the submarines were in their operation area, they had to proceed submerged during the whole patrol, and this required advanced gear for the navigation, surveillance of the enemy, observation and communication. Preferred targets would be larger vessels for all kinds of transport and large naval units. The small submarines would preferably be used for torpedo attacks. The medium submarines would operate with torpedoes and mines in the south eastern part of the Baltic. They would operate widely separated in order to create a feeling of insecurity for enemy forces. The enemy then had to provide escorts for protection.

Nuclear weapons

The effects of nuclear weapons were discussed in fairly general terms.[67] SACEUR's plans for use of nuclear warheads would be found in ASP 1 from 31 December 1957. Factors reducing the likelihood would be fog, rain, low clouds, darkness and heavy ice. As prevailing winds were from the west, nuclear bursts might affect Sweden with serious political consequences. Since the wind would also carry nuclear waste to the Soviet Union, the Soviets might think twice before they used an atomic bomb as water or ground burst. This would not stop NATO use, and not stop air bursts from the Soviets. Both NATO and the Soviets would find ports and bases "attractive" for nuclear bombing, but if the Soviets wanted to use some as bases later, they might not use them. For NATO, attractive targets would be concentrated forces like amphibious landing parties.

A follow-up note added some guidelines.[68] The NATO commanders should prepare for countering a nuclear attack by taking measures to reduce the effects from blast, thermal and radioactive waste on their equipment and personnel. They should be prepared to request atomic strikes against favourable targets as the tactical situation developed by land- or ship-based or by air delivery, but only

---

67 Strategic Survey. Chapter V – The Effect of Strategic Factors on the Use of Forces/Weapons. Section 7 – Nuclear Weapons. NATO Secret. PG/P(58)1. 17-4-58. BM 1/1000c.
68 Atomic Warfare Plan. NATO Secret. Annex K to PG/P(58)10 of 22-8-58. 15-10-58. BM 1/1000d.

if conventional weapons could not be used. The Karup command centre was delegated releasing authority if Code GREEN was declared. One had to ensure that their own forces could be moved away from a desired ground zero at short notice.

Command over naval aircraft – AFNORTH or AFCENT?

The issue of commanding the future German Naval Air Arm turned out to become a major stumbling stone for COMNAVBALTAP – but not regarding the desirability of those airplanes. The future Danish and German Task Force commanders would be able to call on support from the German Fleet Air Arm, commanded by the German Navy. The Danes would have to request support through COMNAVBALTAP. The Planning Group perceived the upcoming German naval aircraft as a force under the command of the German Navy, also when in action, but the actual control of airborne aircraft had to be with the command having air command of the Baltic.[69] In the spring of 1958, this was COMTAFDEN, under AFNORTH, located in Karup. To coordinate air control and tasks for the aircraft, a system of liaison officers had to be set up between sea commanders and air control. The planning group suggested accordingly.

But the Germans took this opportunity to beg to differ, with severe consequences for the organisation, with the reasoning as follows. The special roles of the Naval Air Arm made the aircraft vulnerable to the enemy fighters, and they were not themselves able to participate in the creation of air supremacy. On the contrary, they needed support from fighters.[70] The whole area of the future NAVBALTAP was small and only one air command could control it. So there would be no particular naval air command centre. Given the present command system, the naval aircraft would then have to be controlled by COMTAFDEN; this was recommended, as we saw above, by the Planning Group. But the perception of the Germans was that COMTAFDEN only had fighters to protect the Danish islands, not the Baltic. The upcoming Luftwaffe, by comparison, would have much larger capability to operate over the Baltic, but then the Naval Air Arm had to be controlled by the 2. ATAF. If so, the future NAVBALTAP should be under AFCENT, not AFNORTH, to create cohesion.

---

69 North/Centre Planning Group: Command and Control of the Naval Air Arm in the Baltic. NATO Secret. Draft 29-3-58, final PG/P(58)7, 17-4-58. BM 1/1000e.
70 Befehlshaber der Seestreitkräfte der Ostsee: Vorschläge Planning-Group: Führung der deutschen Marine-Fliegerverbande im Einsatz. NATO Secret. 2-4-58.Tbg.Nr. 155/58. BM 1/1000e.

The German naval commander for the Baltic asked the German Ministry of Defence to instruct the German representative in the Planning Group that the Germans would not be in a position to support any suggestion for the time being (in April 1958), until the roles of the 2. ATAF – planned to control the Luftwaffe – were cleared. He added that this might the opportunity to change course (towards AFCENT, not AFNORTH). The Germans did so on the second coordination meeting May 6,[71] but of course the Planning Group had to go on working with a command system under COMTAFDEN until instructed otherwise, and the group made some amendments clarifying the powers of COMTAFDEN over all aircraft in the Baltic, also regarding air surveillance and the need for all other air commands to coordinate accordingly. Liaison officers connecting all commands were essential.

Over the summer of 1958, these disagreements about the borders between AFCENT and AFNORTH came up in the public. They had been aired in Germany and within NATO while the Danes were busy getting their way with the (primarily) political suggestions. The disagreements were between the two C-in-Cs, but also between Denmark and West Germany.

A first military opinion came when two military commanders voiced ideas about the future organisation of NATO in the Baltic area (we saw Admiral Gerlach's opinion above). CINCENT wanted an integrated command of all forces in the area and link them to the supreme commander. SACEUR Norstad, however, retorted that such a proposal would be unacceptable to the Danish as well as the Norwegian government.[72] CINCENT did not budge. CINCNORTH then intervened with the comment that although he could understand that over time the "forward defence battle" – moving the NATO defence line from the Rhine to the border of the Iron Curtain – in Northern and Central Germany would have to take place as an integrated project, now (1958) was not yet the time for such a solution because the forward strategy of NATO was far from operational. The proposed change of organisation was politically impossible and since there already was a command centre for ground as well as air forces existing in Jutland, it would be easy to add a naval command centre.[73]

The second military intervention came from the West German admiral Ruge who in August 1958 stated that the entire German navy needed a common command; that the Germans needed a fair share of the command posts; and that British influence over Baltic affairs had gone far enough by now. Hence, all German

---

71 Headquarters NAVNORCENT: Minutes of the second quarterly coordination meeting of the North/Centre Planning Group. NATO Secret. No. 2030/PG, 21-5-58. BM 1/1000d.
72 SHAPE, *SHAPE History 1958*, 113.
73 Ibid., 114–15.

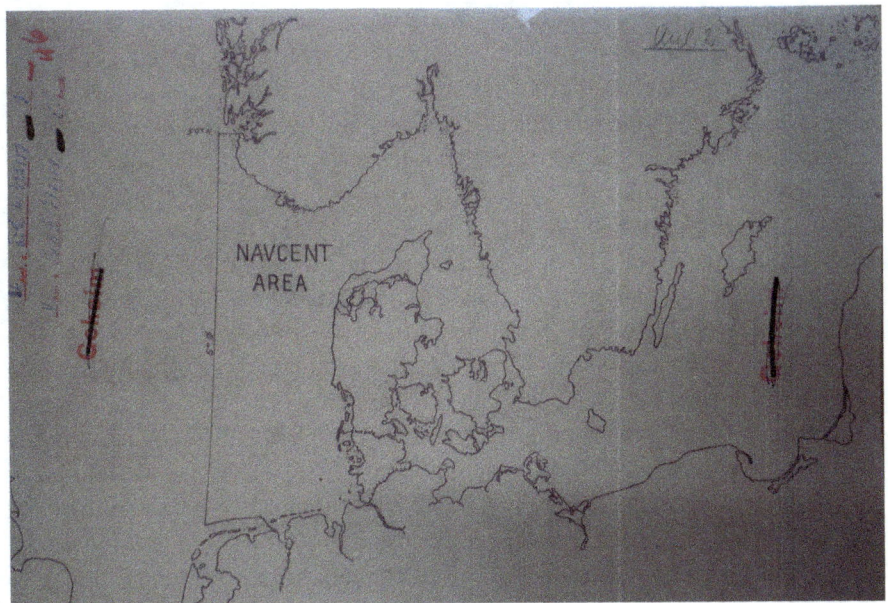

Figure 9.2: Admiral Ruge's suggestion for incorporating all waters until Norway in AFCENT. This also took some SACLANT domain. Source: Bundeswehr Archiv.

forces should be under AFCENT.[74] He had made that point internally[75] in April, suggesting that at the very least the border between AFCENT and AFNORTH should be moved to the Danish-German border, and the German navy command be integrated; Denmark should take of the Danish Narrows; and Germany should defend the Baltic outside the Danish sovereignty. But the most preferable solution from a military perspective would be to move the border to Skagerrak and include Denmark in AFCENT.

He was not alone in this line of thinking. The German Minister of Defence supported this and at a meeting with the NATO Standing Group in Kiel in the Summer of 1958 he suggested that if the Danes and Norwegians would not accept a division between the two countries, the border of AFCENT could first be moved to Skagerrak and later to Bodø (about half way to Norway's Northern tip). Consequently, in the longer run AFNORTH was to be closed down and Northern Norway turned over to SACLANT.[76] The Germans had a number of military reasons

---

74 Thoss, op. cit., p. 267.
75 Inspekteur der Marine: Probleme der Seekriegsführung, NATO-Kommandostruktur. Geheim.8-4-58. Az 31-03-01-02. Tgb.Nr.N 322/58. BW 2/2569.
76 PM page 3, YHM attachment to letter from C-in-C C.635/O.1249 15 March 1960.

for demanding a change of border:[77] coherence of European ground defence; air support to the navies in the Baltic; logistics of supplies; coherence of Luftwaffe and naval air arm etc.; we have gone through those in detail above. These issues pointed to an integrated solution of the command system, combining all three forces into one command that comprised the eastern North Sea, Skagerrak, the Baltic Approaches, Schleswig-Holstein and the Western Baltic, in a separate, integrated command under AFCENT. For now (fall of 1958), the creation of a naval command would suffice, but the integrated command was the ultimate goal.

Meanwhile, the Planning Group went on preparing the basis for organising the defence activities in a new COMNAVBALTAP. On 2 September, 1958, the Danish Ministry of Defence approved the proposed, but temporary, organisation in a letter to the supreme commander[78] – even the terms of reference for the future C-in-C were ready[79] – to be located with a small staff of 22 officers (total number of personnel 65) from Denmark, Germany, France, Norway, England and USA in Kiel-Holtenau under the command of the British admiral running the planning group. In May, the Germans had been opposed to a British admiral, but would accept a proposal of a Canadian admiral. Canada, however, was not ready to name one, and then the Germans accepted the Brit. The Command was answerable to CINCNORTH. But the case was stranded in NATO's Standing Group because some countries aired reservations.

In September 1958 the new plans for the future air defence of Germany were ready, making 2. ATAF responsible for air defence in the area south of the Danish/German border, continuing along a line through the centre of the Strait of Fehmarn to Bornholm and to the centre of the Baltic. Since the German Air Arm would be stationed in Schleswig-Holstein, the 2. ATAF would have command over their air operations as long as they were within that area, but a liaison had to be established to COMTAFDEN regarding coordination. At the coordination meeting on 30 September, 1958,[80] the Germans stressed that until the command system was finalised, the matter should be postponed. This blocked for further negotiations, and the command system for aircraft differed from the naval system. Until 1961 this solution with 2. ATAF was in force, then a new AIRBALTAP command took over.[81]

---

77 Note: Besprechung mit Vertretern der Standing Group in Kiel am 18-7-58. NATO Secret. Fü M II Az.:10-70-03, Hardthöhe 21-7-58. BM 1/730.
78 Mentioned in note Forsvarsministeriet 11. kontor 11-9-59.
79 Copy in Forsvarsministeriet 11. kontor 28-8-58.
80 Headquarters NAVNORCENT: Minutes of the third quarterly coordination meeting of the North/Centre Planning Group held at Holtenau 30.9 – 1-10.58. NATO Secret. BM 1/1000d.
81 Lemke, Bernd, Dieter Krüger, Heinz Rebhan, and Wolfgang Schmidt. *Die Luftwaffe 1950 bis 1970. Konzeption, Aufbau, Integration*, 519–20. München: R. Oldenbourg Verlag, 2006.

Still, the two tasks of air offensive and air defence remained split between AIRBALTAP (offensive operations until the Elbe river) and 2. ATAF (air defence for the whole of Schleswig-Holstein.[82] The 2. ATAF controlled the two missile defence systems (HAWK and NIKE) in Northern Germany, and those tasks had to remain under the same command in order to secure coordination, also with NATO interception aircraft. Offensive actions would often be linked to the Naval Air Arm and hence remain under the control of AFNORTH. In 1978, a compromise between these interests was reached by the creation of an Air Space Control Authority to coordinate the two commands.

SACEUR intervenes

In October, after the problems with NATO's Standing Group and the problems with delineating the borders for air control, SACEUR stopped the work on a COMNAVBALTAP.[83] He upheld the status quo by having the Holtenau planning group to continue its work and decided that in the event of war, the present command of the West German Navy in the Baltic would be placed under the planning group in Holtenau under CINCNORTH.[84] The supreme commander was fully aware that in actual fact this decision meant that a sort of COMNAVBALTAP was created – the only thing missing was the name. He was quite content with this outcome.[85] In the light of the strong resistance from Denmark and Norway, SACEUR told the Danish C-in-C that he did not intend to accommodate the German pressure for changing the borders between north and centre.

The Planning Group continued working, now with an aim to prepare for exercises and ultimately war, under the command of CINCNORTH.[86] Over the next months, they wrote the operation orders for NAVNORCENT.

In November 1958, the Germans agreed to give up the idea of changing the border. There was a quite heated discussion in the Danish public and subsequently in the Danish parliament about the matter,[87] and it was evident that if

---

82 Fü M VI 1: Sprechzettel. Luftverteidigungsgrenzen zwischen AFCENT und AFNORTH. 18-1-79. App 4477. BM 1/25112.
83 By letter 18 October 1958, Forsvarsministeriet 11. kontor 11-9-59.
84 SHAPE, *SHAPE History 1958*, 119.
85 Note by the Danish CINC regarding a conversation with SACEUR 14 Nov. 1958, YHM attachment to G 38/MC. 5948, 19 Nov. 1958.
86 Minutes of the third coordination meeting between GFOD and BSO helt at HQ NAVNORCENT, Kiel-Holtenau, 8 & 9 December, 1958. NATO Secret, 17-12-58. BM 1/1000e.
87 Udenrigsministeriet, *Dansk Sikkerhedspolitik 1948–1966*, 102.

the Germans kept the idea, the Danish government would have to stop negotiating the integrated NATO command. Indeed, the Germans now again supported the wish for an expanded and integrated command, COMBALTAP, for the Baltic area. In January 1959, CINCNORTH seized the opportunity to boost the matter and suggested that SACEUR created an integrated command for the Baltic Approaches, Denmark and Schleswig-Holstein.[88, 89] But now the Danish government stalled the discussions because at the same time negotiations regarding establishing German supply depots in Denmark were initiated; this created heated discussions in the Danish public but was solved in the fall when the theme was changed into "NATO" rather than "German" supplies.[90]

In September 1959, the Danish government finally and formally accepted the naval reorganisation and the Danish C-in-C could notify the supreme commander that Denmark would accept a joint naval command under a British admiral until May 1961, and after that, a Danish flag officer would be appointed chief. The subsequent leadership would then alternate between Danish and German admirals.[91] This concession, however, came too late to get the desired effect because SACEUR was in the process of negotiating with the Germans and on November 18[92] they reached an agreement to set up the naval command soon, and after 1961 it would be permanently run by a German admiral. However, this was but one element in a bigger reorganisation of NATO commands. The agreement with the Germans read that an integrated BALTAP command be established with a Danish three-star officer permanently as chief. Four subcommands would be formed: one for Jutland and Schleswig-Holstein (alternating chiefs Germany-Denmark), one for Zealand (Danish chief), one for air forces (Danish, or possibly alternating chiefs) and one for naval affairs (German chief). It had been indicated informally that SACEUR would be willing to accept alternating chiefs for both naval and air affairs.

As a consequence of the German deal, the supreme commander did not establish the proposed COMNAVBALTAP which Denmark had accepted. He wanted to change the command system overall, not piecemeal. But the overall plan, agreed with the Germans, was not made public and the Danish government – which would oppose several of the planned steps – was not formally informed.[93] The Danish C-in-C, however, was informed. He told SACEUR at a conference in December 1959 that

---

88 Thoss, op. cit., p. 268.
89 Also noted in PM page 4, YHM attachment to letter from CINC C.635/O.1249 15 March 1960.
90 Nielsen, op. cit., pp. 49–51.
91 PM page 5, YHM attachment to letter from CINC C.635/O.1249 15 March 1960.
92 Note YHM from Danish Foreign Ministry j. no. 105.I.19.c, 9 January 1960.
93 PM page 6, YHM attachment to letter from CINC C.635/O.1249 15 March 1960.

the Danish government was not prepared to agree at this point of time and that the matter should be kept from the Danish public until after the upcoming election in 1960[94] (which was held 15 November, PB).

SACEUR now started a process of influencing the main actors. The Danish C-in-C met with him again on 5 April 1960 and told him that although the Danish government was prepared to accept a naval command, the integrated BALTAP command – which the Danish minister still perceived as "under discussion among the military experts" – would have to be postponed until the Danish public was better prepared to accept it,[95] The C-in-C recommended (contrary to the supreme commander's ideas) to start out with the naval command, then step by step create commands for air and ground forces and thus approach an integrated BALTAP command.

However, the devil is in the detail, and now the main obstacle for an integrated command was the Danish Joint Chiefs of Staff dragging its feet. Their point of view was that while they could understand a political reason for it, an integrated BALTAP command was not really necessary from a military standpoint.[96] Integration between the two navies and between the Danish and the German armies clearly was desirable, but only at that level, so no chief beyond CINCNORTH was necessary. Regarding the Danish Air Force it was dependent on coordination with as well as assistance from German air forces. A war would in the first days be fought by aircraft (counter-air offensive), implying no need for an integrated NATO command, only coordination with other air commands. But acceptance of an integrated command of some sort in the Baltic area was inevitable, and an integrated command might also be useful later in a war when operations by army and navy were under development. The Danes could see that CINCNORTH, located in Oslo, Norway, was a bit far from the action. So why not just send a Task Commander to Karup, Denmark, where the "Baltic" sub-commands would be located, to deal with the problems in that area?

The Danish Chiefs of Staff thus neglected the need for general coordination in littoral warfare by a command spanning all forces, but accepted some need after the initial attacks by suggesting a mission command to be established when necessary by sending a Task Commander to Karup. An observer cannot but comment that this solution appears to serve one's own interests of the Danish military top rather than the NATO organisation.

So SACEUR Norstad did not buy the suggestion. He wanted to meet with Danish politicians and the Joint Chiefs of Staff in May, but fell ill and the meeting first took

---

94 Note YHM from Danish Foreign Ministry j. no. 105.I.19.c, 9 January 1960.
95 Letter YHM from CINC to Ministry of Defence, FCP 36, 9 April 1960.
96 FSS 21-3-60 2.

place August 12, 1960.[97] He detailed his proposal (as agreed with the Germans the previous fall) of one BALTAP integrated command under AFNORTH, not AFCENT, and directed by a Danish officer, with four sub-commands, now with alternating Danish or German chiefs. At the same time, AFNORTH was to be reorganised.

The supreme commander saw the proposal as a bonus for the Danes. The top commander would be Danish. The defence of Denmark would be facilitated by this integrated command. The alternative might be that the Germans organised the defence of Schleswig-Holstein themselves, without NATO interference. The Danish minister answered that politically, an integrated command was not feasible because of a negative mood in the Danish public, and furthermore, he needed his military experts to comment. But he invited the supreme commander to go ahead with COMNAVBALTAP. SACEUR, however, preferred BALTAP as a unified command; the naval command would be established as planned under BALTAP, once there was agreement. But the prime minister wanted to postpone a decision until after the next general election, supposedly in May 1961. SACEUR expressed his disappointment because he needed to act soon.

The general election, however, took place November 15, 1960. It meant a farewell to the three-party cabinet and a new one based on two parties was formed. Late November 1960, after the election, the Danish Joint Chiefs of Staff met again to discuss the problems of the NATO-organization. CINCNORTH now had intervened by proposing to make a shortcut and integrate all three forces in one staff under a new deputy CINCNORTH (who could be a Dane).[98] The Danish chief of the air force voiced deep scepticism towards the idea of an integrated BALTIC command because he saw it violating modern principles of air warfare. Apparently he saw the proposal as a way of "convoluting" the Danish air force solely for operations in Denmark, linked to army and navy operations, preventing it from participating in more comprehensive counter-air operations in Southern Norway or Northern Germany.[99] The chiefs concluded that they needed more detailed information about the proposal.

Fourth step: Public discussions and a political solution

In December 1960 at the NATO meeting of Defence ministers, the German minister Strauss once again recommended an integrated Baltic Command. A few days later, on December 23, 1960, SACEUR wrote to the Danish Minister of Defence a

---

97 Minutes Forsvarsministeriet 11. kontor 15-8-60.
98 FSS 29-11-60 2.
99 Note Forsvarsministeriet 11. kontor 17-11-61.

letter asking for the policy stance of the newly formed Danish Government regarding the COMBALTAP organisation. The minister answered on January 14, 1961 that he needed the advice of his military chiefs before he could answer. He recommended a meeting between the supreme commander and the Danish Joint Chiefs of Staff.

On January 20, 1961, the Danish daily Politiken published the contents of SACEUR's proposal, apparently quite unexpectedly, and subsequently the Minister of Defence indicated a positive stance towards it.[100]

The Danish Joint Chiefs of Staff met three days later and now sought for quick action because shortly before CINCENT had once again suggested that Schleswig-Holstein became part of AFCENT. They decided that in the light of the risk that all German air forces be allocated to AFCENT unless Denmark gave in to the pressure for an integrated BALTAP command, one had to accept the proposal. One might even hope for an even larger allocation of German air forces to the Schleswig-Holstein area for use in the Baltic approaches and tactical air support to army and navy activities. If not, Denmark would be without German help in the case of a limited attack on isolated parts of Danish territory. In sum, an integration with German forces would reduce such risks.

The Danish Minister of Defence visited Germany in late January and had a private meeting with the German minister, Strauss, in the afternoon of January 26, in the home of the Danish ambassador.[101] Poul Hansen told about the political situation: one party in the parliament was against NATO; the coalition partner in the cabinet was very reluctant towards military expenses; most Danes were negative towards Germany and the politicians feared their reaction if cooperation was initiated. These political problems had repercussions for the defence policy of the government, particularly the ideas about COMNAVBALTAP and the question of nuclear weapons in the hands of Germany. The minister wanted to emphasise that, personally, he was not against a rearmament of Germany and saw NATO as the right platform for this. His prime minister was of the same opinion.

Minister Strauss had been approached unofficially by the supreme commander before the meeting[102] and was advised to stress the importance of clarifying and deciding the BALTAP issue quickly. The minister was to be very distinct and to the point, but "not too rough", and point to the risk of moving the border between AFCENT and AFNORTH (but he was to refrain from actually proposing

---

[100] FSS 23-1-61 1.
[101] Minutes YHM by Forsvarsministeriet 11. kontor 30-1-61.
[102] Note from General Butler Geheim 21-1-61 to the German Minister of Defence. NMR-Az 03-26-20. Tgb. Nr. 268/61. BW 2/2569.

this!). In the conversation with the Danish minister, Strauss pointed to the paradoxical situation that, on the one hand, NATO wanted Germany to build up the military and complained that not enough was done to comply with MC 70; on the other hand, many Europeans were scared because of the German rearmament. Strauss wanted to call attention to the fact that Germany only had supplies for one week's fighting, and it had no real military leadership outside NATO. Hence the fear of German rearmament had a weak foundation.

The Danish minister agreed and concluded that integrating Germany in NATO was the right policy to pursue. Strauss then discussed the Baltic problems. He considered a change of border between AFCENT and AFNORTH impossible; the defence of Jutland would be difficult, and Germany needed access to the Baltic Sea. The organisation, however, had to be ameliorated. He supported the proposal by SACEUR for an integrated BALTAP command with four sub-commands. Strauss suggested – in accordance with his earlier agreement with the supreme commander – that for the first three to five years, the top and three sub-commands should have a Danish commander, the NAVBALTAP a German. Chiefs of staff were to be the same nationality, but chiefs of operation the other nationality.

Poul Hansen said that he knew of the proposal, but before the government could make a decision, he needed his military top to comment. For now, the nationality of the commanders was to be kept open; he was not quite sure that a German should be the first to head the NAVBALTAP. In any case, he would postpone any decision until he had advice from his advisors.

This rejection is at odds with the autobiography of vice admiral Ruge who wrote that an agreement was reached between the two ministers in January, 1961, to name Rear Admiral Wagner as chief of the Holtenau Planning Group by June 1961.[103] Wagner did become chief of NAVNORCENT in 1961 and did head the Holtenau planning group which in war would act as a NAVBALTAP (see above about SACEUR Norstad's "coup"), but that was before NAVBALTAP was formally created. It seems, then, that Poul Hansen, by stressing a postponement, did not see this decision as one creating a NAVBALTAP before the fact. But the supreme commander probably did, as we saw above.

While their minister was in Bonn, the Danish Joint Chiefs of Staff were invited to a meeting with SACEUR about the proposal in Paris on 27 January.[104] SACEUR stressed that if the Danes did not accept, Schleswig-Holstein would go to AFCENT. It was agreed that the chief would permanently be a Dane, that the chief

---

[103] Ruge, Friedrich. *In vier Marinen. Lebenserinnerungen als Beitrag zur Zeitgeschichte*, 354–55. München: Bernard & Graefe Verlag, 1979.
[104] Note Forsvarsministeriet 11. kontor 31-1-61.

of the air forces likewise would be Danish, and that the chiefs of the two other sub-commands could interchange between Danes and Germans. The supreme commander wanted at least the army and navy commands to start out at the same time (at that time, the dislocations of the German air force were not known, PB).

Although a number of questions still had to be answered, the C-in-C nonetheless recommended the establishment of the BALTAP command, noting especially that the future command did not change anything regarding Danish parliamentary control of nuclear weapons.[105]

---

3 weeks of squeezing the lemon

In early Spring 1961, the supreme commander lost patience: a telegram from the Danish representative at SHAPER on 14 March requested a prompt Danish reaction to his proposal because the German minister of defence was slated to visit SACEUR the following day. This set off a series of quick Danish negotiations. The minister was on an excursion of the north of Copenhagen with the Scandinavian ministers of defence and since the ministry regarded the telegram important, a senior naval officer participating in the outing was contacted by phone. He then discussed the matter with the minister and obtained an instruction for the contents of a response telegram. It was sent the same day to the supreme commander, indicating a positive stance in principle, but the government "would like to address some details, wishing a more marked NATO influence e.g. by having American, British and Norwegian officers in the staffs".[106] This may have been formulated on the basis of demands from the minor cabinet partner[107] in order to weaken the German element in the new organization and thereby make it more acceptable to the general public. "NATO" would sound better than "German".

SACEUR responded on 20 March, expressing concern over the answer, and once again pleaded for an answer as soon as possible to his original proposal. The Danish Minister of Defence then asked an *ad hoc* committee from his ministry and the Ministry of Foreign Affairs to create a counter-proposal to the supreme commander's.[108] The group considered a number of possibilities to be negotiated with SACEUR. First, they proposed that an American, Canadian, British or Norwegian deputy be added to COMBALTAP. This did not satisfy the minister. Then they added similar deputies for staffs with alternating Danish/German chiefs, and in addition recommended the inclusion of NATO-officers as ordinary members of the staffs in general. These three points for negotiation were approved by the minister, but he added a fairly tough introduction to the proposal, in effect indicating that unless this was accepted by SACEUR, the Danish government would stop the negotiations. The Danish C-in-C commented that he did not agree to the wording and did not have support to this from his chiefs. Therefore, the final wording was toned down, asking for a negotiation of these wishes.[109]

But in addition, outside the formal statements, the minister notified the supreme commander that there was a precarious political situation in Denmark due to problems in the labour market

---

105 C-in-C note to the ministry C.635/0.994 HEM 25-2-61.
106 Note Forsvarsministeriet 11. kontor 14-3-61.
107 See the discussion in Nielsen, op. cit., pp. 74–75.
108 Note Forsvarsministeriet 11. kontor 25-3-61. The process appears rather hectic.
109 The final statement is found in Foreign Office report Udenrigsministeriet, *Dansk Sikkerhedspolitik 1948–1966. Bilag*, 315.

(wild cat strikes), and this demanded the time and resources of the government which therefore could not negotiate the details right now.

The three ideas of the note were negotiated with the supreme commander by a Danish Foreign Office chief who recommended the change from a Danish-German venture into a true NATO-institution. SACEUR agreed that this was NATO-matter, however, he turned the wishes for deputies down, but accepted the idea of more NATO-officers in the staffs. In the days to follow, the Danish government and the supreme commander exchanged views regarding the contents of a public statement by the supreme commander, which on April 6 got the following wording (formulated by the Danes): "SACEUR's proposal has been studied by the Danish government which has put forward some ideas for change. The government will return to the matter when Danish political difficulties regarding the labour market have been solved".[110]

CINCNORTH happened to have a meeting with SACEUR in Paris after the Danish delegation had left. He reported to the Danish C-in-C that the supreme commander was quite upset, thinking that the Danish government wanted to protract the process; he believed that the labour market situation was but a bad excuse.[111] If the Danish government stood by its proposal, he would – if asked – recommend to the NATO council that the border between AFCENT and AFNORTH be moved. But this was not made public.

By April 1960, SACEUR still had nothing but a very principled acceptance of COMBALTAP and a promise to get deeper into the organisational features at a later date, at the discretion of the Danes. This prolongation had its roots in the Joint Chiefs of Staff.

The Danish Joint Chiefs of Staff were involved in the wording of the Government's answer to the supreme commander. But before this incident, the group had its own problems with COMBALTAP. They accepted the integration, but not the details of the proposed organisation.[112] SACEUR's proposal had four sub-commanders, of which two were army commanders in east and West Denmark (plus Northern Germany). The Danes asked for a reduction of the number of sub-commanders to three: army, navy and air force. The army sub-commander would then have five sub-sub commanders, of which only Schleswig-Holstein and South Jutland could have a German chief; the rest would command different parts of Denmark, separated by the straits, and hence all with Danish chiefs. The chief for the army forces was permanently to be a Dane with a German deputy; chiefs for the two other subcommands could alternate between Denmark and Germany.

According to Danish files, the supreme commander as well as CINCNORTH had informally accepted this idea.[113] But other archived actions show otherwise. SACEUR Norstad went to Copenhagen in early June and presented his own pro-

---

110 Note Forsvarsministeriet 11. kontor 6-4-61.
111 Note Forsvarsministeriet 11. kontor 5-4-61.
112 FSS 31-1-61 1.
113 Note Forsvarsministeriet 11. kontor 6-4-61, attached letter 10-5-61.

posal once more, now to the public; and he had a conversation of warning with the Danish minister Poul Hansen. He had trouble with the coalition partner and wrote about it to his Norwegian colleague, Gudmund Harlem, in a letter on 9 June, 1961:[114]

> ... it is very difficult to get our cabinet partner to accept this proposal, even in a moderate form, which gives the integrated command a stronger NATO-imprint.... I would be interested in all arguments recommending the proposal that may impress that party. Therefore, I am interested in a Norwegian indication that such a command is desirable and that Norway would be concerned if it does not happen.... General Norstad has indicated to me that in the case of no acceptance, he will recommend that the German forces in Schleswig-Holstein be transferred to AFCENT. This will mean a serious weakening of the defence of Jutland and ... it cannot be in Norwegian interest.

The Danish and Norwegian Ministers of Defence had a meeting with the supreme commander in Paris on 21 June:[115] Norstad once again pressed for a cabinet decision and went as far as saying that a negative decision would be better than no decision. Poul Hansen said that the matter was under discussion in a cabinet committee, and he hoped for a decision by August. But the formal decision had to be made by the Danish parliament which would not meet until October. He asked for a declaration of support from Norway – as we saw above, he had prepared this in a letter on June 9 – and the Norwegian minister offered to ask for an evaluation by his military top, to be sent to the Danish government.

SACEUR once again made it clear in a conversation with the Danish minister that if his proposal was rejected, the consequence would be that all West Germany would come under AFCENT; the border would be moved to the Danish-German border.[116] Denmark would lose influence on NATO commands, whereas the Germans would gain influence.

It appears to be the first time that SACEUR officially declared he would act with such grave consequences. But he was under pressure from AFCENT to do so,[117] and the consequences had been clear for most participants for at least six months. Now the Danes had reached the limits of his patience.

The Danish minister continued to have problems with his coalition partner in the cabinet which had demanded that three questions be clarified before they could take a decision:[118] first, if Denmark agreed to BALTAP, and Germany subsequently got ac-

---

114 Forsvarsministeriet, Minister Poul Hansen: Sagsakter (1956–1962) V008: 1959 Juli 1–1961 September 30.
115 Note Forsvarsministeriet 11. kontor 23-6-61.
116 Note Forsvarsministeriet 26-6-61, probably to the cabinet committee on defence.
117 Note Forsvarsministeriet 11. kontor 12-6-61.
118 Note Forsvarsministeriet 11. kontor 13-5-61.

cess to nuclear weapons, was Denmark still free to decide whether or not they would use such weapons? Second: if West Germany were involved in an "isolated" war, would Denmark have the right to opt out? And third, would membership of the BALTAP mean that they were more easily involved in a war? The short answer to the first question was that the autonomy of the Danish government to decide this for Danish forces was unaltered. One should, however, take note that Danish officers holding NATO command posts did so as NATO officers and might be involved in taking decisions about the use of nuclear weapons allocated to NATO forces. The answer to question number two and three was that the NATO treaty saw an attack on one member country as an attack on all member countries. Still, the Danish constitution prescribed that it was up to the Danish government to decide acts of war and hence to allocate forces to NATO. That said, one should note that the build-up of the NATO organisation was to ensure defence measures according to formulated NATO plans. Of course, an overall strategic evaluation of the particular situation was required case by case. But anyway, the NATO system was made to persuade a would-be attacker not to attack.

On 31 August, 1961, the government published a note which formally had some further demands (see box), but in reality this was an approval and invitation to final discussions.

Fifth step: Final negotiations

The day before the government declaration, on 30 August in the afternoon, SACEUR had sent a signal requesting the Danish C-in-C to approve the contents of a message informing the Standing Group about his proposal.[119] Given the non-decision mode of the Cabinet on that day, Qvistgaard naturally could not approve anything. He had informed the minister about the signal, and the minister had instructed him to "pacify" General Norstad with a message that the cabinet still was considering various questions, but the main party, the Social Democrats, had approved the principles two days previous and hence a majority in the parliament was at hand. But it was not possible yet to know a date. The minister awaited a meeting the day after with the supreme commander's Chief of Staff, General Moore, to discuss certain details. After that meeting, the supreme commander could expect a written response.

Moore was called out of the meeting because of a telephone call, asking him to report to SHAPE what "the lay of the land" was because SACEUR wanted to send his message immediately to the Standing Group in order to avoid a reminder from them. The message had one change from the original proposal, namely that the first

---

[119] The following paragraphs are reported in FSS 1-9-61 3.

COMBALTAP was to be Danish. The Danish C-in-C commented that this change was completely unacceptable, and if SACEUR maintained it, he would throw the baby out with the bathing water. The C-in-C, the minister, the parliament and the Danish public would revolt against it. The C-in-C then introduced the organisation suggested by the Danish Joint Chiefs of Staff in May to Moore, who once again telephoned with SHAPE and asked for a reaction by the supreme commander, who according to Moore was sole decision-maker, consulting with no one. The response came a little later, in effect asserting that SACEUR's original proposal now had been approved by the Germans, and any change had to be negotiated with them. If the Danish proposal to establish three instead of four sub-commanders were accepted, one must expect the price to the Germans to be an alternating COMNAVBALTAP since COMAIRBALTAP was to be permanently Danish. This suggested in the opinion of the C-in-C that the Germans did not expect to allocate but a few aircraft to BALTAP.

September 1, the day after the above declaration by the Cabinet, the Danish Joint Chiefs of Staff had a meeting with General Moore about the supreme commander's proposal. Before the general arrived, the members had a rather candid exchange of views, mainly reflecting the interests of each of the three branches of the military in avoiding a German chief. Furthermore, the chief of the army wanted his five sub-sub commanders to be sub-commanders under COMBALTAP. The Danish C-in-C told him that he wholeheartedly disagreed with him, and then General Moore entered the room to discuss the situation with them.

General Moore reported that SACEUR wanted a decision now; the Germans agreed with his proposal, and he did not want to spend more time for re-negotiating changes with them. Anyway, he believed that the Germans would not accept the Danish proposal, and if they did they would demand alternating chiefs of the army part, which the Danes in return could not accept. The Danish proposal was discussed in some detail, Moore trying to substantiate the positive elements of the supreme commander's proposal. The Danish chief of the air force once again reiterated his "gut feeling" that with SACEUR's two army sub-commanders, COMBALTAP would have to come from the army and in addition a large proportion of his staff would have to be army. Moore rejoined that, on the contrary, it was only a question of the right man to the right job. The Danish C-in-C concluded that it seemed as if they would have to go on based on the proposal by the supreme commander, but in that case they still had to wait for an approval by the minister – there was a meeting with him and General Moore later that day.

It turned out that the minister did not really care about the proposal by his C-in-C,[120] with the idea of only three sub-commanders not important for the politi-

---

[120] Minutes Forsvarsministeriet 4-9-61.

cians. General Moore then stated that the Germans probably would demand alternation between Denmark and Germany for the COMLANDBALTAP, if created – and if one followed the supreme commander's proposal, Denmark would get four out of five high command posts. The minister retorted that the Danish proposal would be withdrawn, if SACEUR supported such a German demand. He then turned down the supreme commander's request for a detailed message to the Standing Group but allowed a message that a positive decision was under way. It would be okay to start preparing the organisation, but absolutely nothing could be told in public.

Yet another meeting regarding the proposals was held in Paris on 8 September. The reason for the minister's caution vis-a-vis General Moore was that he had not yet – despite the cabinet declaration – obtained final approval to go on by the minority party in the cabinet. On a cabinet meeting on September 5, he had reported that the meeting in Paris would take place, and he would like to call attention to the fact that there was a majority in the parliament supporting the Integrated command.[121] In the weeks to follow, the minority party grudgingly accepted the fact and a majority supported the Integrated Command.

So when asked about the desired pace of the negotiations-to-come, the minister had answered: "Not too fast".[122] The Paris meeting accordingly was a discussion of the two alternatives with no conclusions drawn.[123] But the Germans indicated that if the Danish proposal was implemented, Germany would demand alternation for the army chief. This was in contradiction to the Danish government declaration of August 31 and therefore impossible for Denmark to accept.

On September 29, the Danish minister therefore gave in and informed SACEUR that given the German demands for top posts in the Danish proposal, he would accept the supreme commander's proposal as a basis for final negotiations towards a BALTAP-organisation – to be done under the auspices of AFNORTH,[124] as recommended by SACEUR himself.

But on 11 October, the Germans accepted the Danish proposal as the basis for negotiations.[125] They wanted however, as predicted, the COMLANDENMARK to alternate between the two countries. This would mean that Danish forces on the islands would come under German command, and therefore the idea was incompatible with the declaration of the Danish government on August 31. Consequently, the negotiations became based on the supreme commander's proposal,

---

121 Kaarsted, op. cit., p. 219.
122 Letter 5-9-61 from the permanent secretary of the Ministry of Defence to the chief of section 11 who should participate in the upcoming negotiaions.
123 Forsvarsministeriet 11. kontor notes 11-9-61 and 3-10-61.
124 Danish text of telegram Forsvarsministeriet 11. kontor 29-9-61.
125 Note Forsvarsministeriet 11. kontor 11-10-61.

and given the minority party's hesitant accept, the final negotiations, to take place in Oslo, could be put in the calendar.

The Oslo meetings went smoothly,[126] and the parties agreed on the following structure:

The top officer COMBALTAP was to be Danish together with his chief of staff, but a German deputy was put into the system to accommodate German demands. Three of the sub-commanders were to be Danish "initially", but only the COM-LANDZEALAND would be permanently Danish, with the three others to have alternating German and Danish chiefs, and their chiefs of staff preferably coming from the other country; if not, the senior member of the staff was to be from the other country.[127] The headquarter for BALTAP was planned to be located in Jutland.

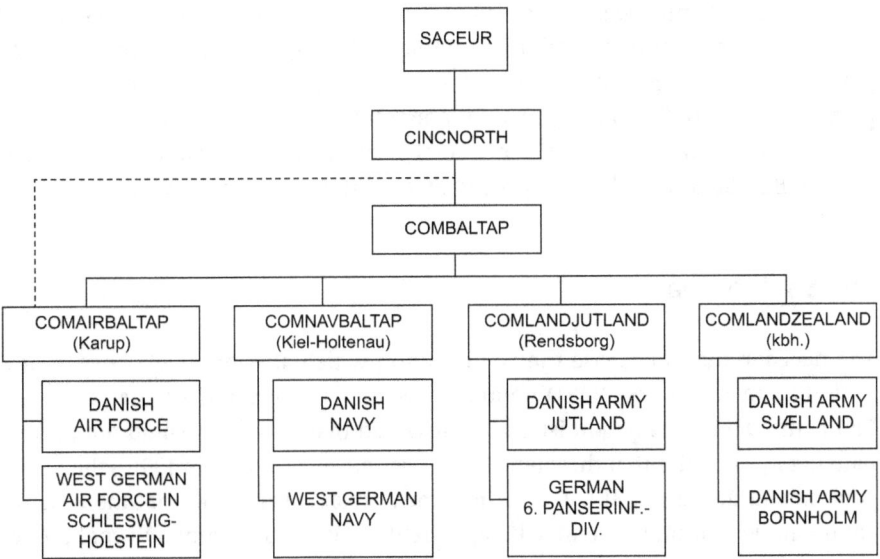

Figure 9.3: BALTAP organisation 1962.[128]

---

126 Petersen, op. cit., pp. 101–3.
127 This veracity of this distribution has now and then been discussed, particularly whether the air command should be permanently Danish, as reported by Forsvarskommandoen. See *Ved forenede kræfter. Forsvarets øverste militære ledelse. Forsvarschefsembedet og forsvarets udvikling 1950–2000*, 107. Vedbæk: Forsvarskommandoen, 2000. I have used the Danish translation of the report to SACEUR, Forsvarsministeriet 11. kontor 24-11-61.
128 Thostrup, S. "Enhedkommandoen." *Tidsskrift for Søvæsen* 135 (1963): 224.

The Germans had pressed for high ranks – three stars – in several positions. The Danes were reluctant to accept this because they knew that the Danish politicians did not want more high ranking officers than absolutely necessary.[129] The Danish system of pay was linked to a system of permanent positions. Once you were a general major, you stayed general major and got your pension accordingly. The many NATO positions required more high-rank officers, and the Danish politicians tried to circumvent the consequences by promoting officers *ad hoc*, meaning that when they returned to Denmark they got their former rank back, and, unless they later got a permanent promotion, a lower pension. Officers from other countries did not know nor recognise such a system, and Danish *ad hoc* ranking officers were regarded with a little disrespect because they would have to accept a demotion upon returning.[130]

The compromise was presented in the Danish parliament on December 7 with protesters chanting outside the building. Three days before, the minority party had a meeting in its national executive board, and the proposal was approved by a mere 34 votes against 31, apparently to avoid a cabinet crisis.[131] In the final vote in the parliament, one member of the minority cabinet party voted against. But the proposal was approved by a comfortable majority.

The Soviets react

The decision did not please the Soviet Union which already in 1957 had sent a note that an Integrated NATO Command would complicate the situation in the Baltic; the Danish Prime Minister had answered that Denmark would not participate in any activities that threatened other countries.[132] Now – in 1961 – the Soviet government on August 31 had informed the Danish government that the BALTAP command would make Denmark dependent on West Germany and make Denmark part of the "aggressive and revanchist plans" of that state.[133] The Soviet Union warned the Danes that an Integrated Command would deteriorate the situation in the Baltic and North European area. On October 7, the Danish government responded that it did not share the perceptions of the Soviet Government regarding West Germany's intentions, and the Danes hoped that the Soviet Union

---

129 FSS 27-11-61 1.
130 Petersen, op. cit., p. 120.
131 Kaarsted, op. cit., p. 220.
132 Udenrigsministeriet, *Dansk Sikkerhedspolitik 1948–1966*, 101.
133 Ibid., 107.

would agree that any government had the right to protect the security of its land and population.

Five days later after the final vote in the Danish parliament, on December 12, the Soviet Union again protested against the establishment of the BALTAP command by sending the Danish government a note, declaring that the relations between the Soviet Union and Denmark deteriorated because of the decision and made Denmark's neutral position difficult.[134] In particular, making Bornholm part of the Command was against the agreement of 1946 (see chapter 6). The Soviet government "would have to make the necessary steps to reciprocate and sustain the security of own country and its allies".

The Soviet declaration could not but be understood as a threat, and the note was discussed in the Committee for Foreign Affairs of the parliament on December 14.[135] The Danish prime minister noted that the wording was unclear, and that it also could be understood as a message that the Soviet Union would do what was necessary within its own area. The Swedish ambassador in Moscow had been handed a copy of the declaration and had asked about the meaning, but the answer was inconclusive. The draft of a response was discussed. The prime minister found it essential to refute the Soviet interpretation of the Bornholm agreement. Apparently several of the members had not understood the agreement of 1946 properly, so they were informed about the Danish understanding and the earlier Soviet reference to it in 1953. The prime minister wanted to make the response brief: Denmark had the right to determine how its interests were to be pursued; NATO was defensive in character and Germany's participation did nothing to change that; the BALTAP Command was part of NATO with a Danish C-in-C and hence not dominated by West Germany. Finally, the Danish government did not share the Soviet interpretation of the Bornholm agreement, and it still was so that only Danish forces were on the island under Danish command.

The Danish Joint Chiefs of Staff discussed the Soviet note on December 13. They saw no reason to military alert, but asked for an overview of capacities on the island of Bornholm. Russian forces in the Baltic area had been increased from about 330,000 to 400,000, and information was being gathered regarding Polish forces. The air warning radar was on 24 hours a day, and surface radar during dark hours; a mobile radar could be alerted in one hour. The communication system for surveillance was being tested. The chief for the air force doubted that an airborne attack was imminent, and the chief for the navy did not want to send a corvette for investigation unless is was deemed absolutely necessary. The army

---

134 Ibid., 111–12.
135 Minutes of the Committee in RA.

had no action planned. All in all, there was agreement that any step in the direction of alert would be noted and would possibly be subject to misinterpretation or even provocation.

The Danish C-in-C contacted SACEUR whose opinion was that the Soviets would stay put, but he asked his staff to prepare a mobile force for Bornholm, if conditions changed. Likewise, the American Secretary of State indicated to the Danish Minister of Foreign Affairs that there was no reason to worry, and if necessary, Bornholm would see American intervention.[136]

The perception of these military actors was proved right. The Soviet Union did not go further.

Summing up: Eight years of bureaucratic and symbolic politics

The need for integration in the NATO command system for littoral warfare in the Baltic Approaches was formulated already when the Danes worked on their future strategy about 1950. Their German helper, former Admiral Heye, pointed to the possibility of putting the Danish navy and a future German navy under the same command. But it took about ten years to work out a solution, mostly because the Danes would not accept the Germans as partners worthy of influence.

A recurring theme was the border between AFNORTH and AFCENT. Respecting the wishes of Denmark and Norway to keep cooperation in the defence of Scandinavia, the border had been drawn so that Schleswig-Holstein was the southern "barrier" against Soviet attacking forces, and the two countries each had a brigade there, Norway until 1953 and Denmark until 1958 when the German army took over. The Germans, however, were not content with having their country divided between two NATO commands, and much of NATO-military thought that the border should be in Skagerrak – making Denmark as a whole part of AFCENT. This, however, was politically impossible with fierce opposition from Denmark and Norway, and several NATO top people had to give up trying to change the border.

The military issue was that the defence of the Baltic Approaches had to be coordinated; if Denmark was included in AFCENT, the command would be integrated by the organisation. If not, coordination issues would come up in the southern part for the army forces and for air traffic, and for the navies and armies to get air support. A side theme was where retreating army forces would be headed; the Danes feared that troops under AFCENT-command would go west to-

---

136 Dansk Institut for Internationale Studier, op. cit., p. 362.

wards Hamburg instead of going north and protect Jutland from advancing Soviet forces.

The political issues were the wish to work together with Norway, but also the remaining animosity towards Germans, and particularly soldiers, because Germany had occupied Denmark during WWII. In addition, the Danish cabinet from 1953 and many years after was dependent on minority parties that were not amicable towards any military spending and therefore blocked for decisions on several military themes.

Politicians and military top shared a consternation for Danish forces coming under German command.

The integration issue was first played out regarding the two navies from Denmark and Germany. Obviously they had to work closely together; they were dependent on one another in issues like minefields, operating submarines and any forward defence operation in the middle or eastern Baltic. In addition, the German navy was dependent on using Danish waters for stores, replenishment and hiding units during day time. And on the flip side, the Danes would benefit from the upcoming large German units with artillery to support various operations.

The Danish navy was aware of these needs from day one of discussions on Germany's rearmament and worked out a solution with a common command under Danish leadership. So when AFNORTH brought up the issue in 1954, the Danes were well prepared. But they disagreed militarily or the organisation, and the politicians did not want any Germans on Danish soil. The project stalled until in 1956, Germany came up with a suggestion of an integrated command – army, navy and air force – for the Baltic Approaches. But NATO was not prepared to go so far and instead set up a proposal for an integrated, but only naval, command. The Danish military pushed for such a solution, but the Danish minister did not want any decision at this point of time; he saw no need to rush the issue. Denmark blocked SACEUR's attempt to make the Standing Group decide the issue. Several people in the NATO top resented this passivity, and the supreme commander then suggested that a working group be set up to analyse the issues at hand.

The Holtenau working group drew up the expected scenarios for warfare in the Baltic Approaches and the challenges for the two navies, but – realizing the need for coordinating across force types in littoral warfare – also to some degree for army and air force. They suggested that the two navies remained under national flag officer command, but also under NATO supreme command with a relatively small staff, first in Kiel and later in Jutland (Karup). But now bureaucratic infights broke loose. The Germans wanted the AFCENT border moved north to the Danish border. Some military wanted a comprehensive, integrated command instead of the one-force suggestion. Furthermore, there was the question of what country should have the top post of the command. These disagreements made SACEUR stall the project, but continue the analyses of the military issues. Meanwhile, new suggestions for the organisation came up; the Germans now wanted an integrated command, the BALTAP, but the chances for a compromise about this seemed bleak.

Now it was up to the politicians to make progress. The Danish and German ministers of defence met privately and exchanged points of view, also about the top posts. SACEUR pressed for a solution and threatened to let AFCENT get Schleswig-Holstein, if no decision was made. To make bad things worse, the Danish Chiefs of Staff got into an internal disagreement, made a compromise and tried to make the supreme commander change his proposal. SACEUR did not want to follow them. At the same time, the Danish minister did his utmost to stall any decision because of political disagreements with the supporting parties in the parliament. The issue was so important for the minor party that there was a threat to leave the cabinet, but in the end a compromise was reached.

After the Danish elections one of the anti-NATO parties left the government, but the cabinet still was dependent on one anti-militaristic party. In December 1960, Germany raised the issue of an integrated BALTAP command, and the supreme commander now had to deal with the dodging Danes. The Danish and German ministers had a private meeting, and the Dane indicated his personal agreement with the proposal, but still needed advice from the Danish C-in-C and he foresaw serious problems of acceptance in the parliament. The Danish military top agreed to accept the proposal because the alternative might create a military disaster at the Danish border. Still, there were certain details in the composition of the staffs blocked for formal acceptance. SACEUR lost his patience and pressed hard for a decision. The Danish minister found a rather lame excuse of political problems because of a labour strike, but behind the scenes he was working for acceptance from the minority party in the cabinet. The Danish military top once more tried to change the suggested organisation, but now the supreme commander put his foot down. The political stalemate continued over the summer, but finally a principled accept came by the end of August. The details of the organisation then were put in place, first by quite complicated negotiations in the fall, and finally by the military top in a meeting in Oslo. The Danish parliament accepted the deal.

The Soviet Union had followed the complicated processes of deciding BALTAP. The deed done, a protest came in, referring to the Bornholm agreement of 1946 once more – stating that the Soviet government "would have to make the necessary steps to reciprocate and sustain the security of [one's] own country and its allies". This threat created some concern in Denmark, but agreement was soon reached to ignore the threat because any step in the direction of an alert would be noted and possibly subject to misinterpretation or even provocation. SACEUR agreed but asked his staff to investigate the possibilities for a mobile NATO force, if things got serious. But nothing happened.

Chapter 10
The Warsaw Pact and its Tactics – as seen by NATO

This chapter deals with various aspects of the Warsaw Pact military organisation and its tactics as perceived by the West until the early 1960s. We shall not deal with this theme in depth, as other books have done so.[1] Therefore, we draw on those sources to create a first overview. Then we dig into the NATO-military analyses of various Warsaw Pact (WAPA) activities and its exercises and consolidate that information into a pattern of threat, as perceived by NATO.

Organising the Warsaw Pact

As a response to the inclusion of West Germany in NATO, the WAPA was created in 1955, and from then on the Soviets included military forces from all of Eastern Europe in their defence planning. The other countries had no say in the overall planning which was based on a system of various War Theatres which had a system of "Fronts", i.e. planning units. In Western Europe, there were four[2]"
- The first, the West Front (Middle Germany and westwards) involving forces from East Germany and Russia;
- The second, the Coastal Front (Northern Germany and northwards) involving forces from East Germany, Poland and Russia; and
- The third, the South West Front (Southern Germany and southwards) involving forces from Czechoslovakia and Russia.
- A special Naval War Theatre of the Baltic Sea involving the navies of East Germany, Poland and Russia, together they formed a Unified Baltic Navy.

In this book, the Coastal Front and the Baltic Sea form the main military-geographical area of interest. They correspond roughly to NATO's AFNORTH and later, in the southern part, the BALTAP command.

---

1 Wenzke, Rüdiger, ed. *Die Streitkräfte der DDR und Polens in der Operationsplanung des Warschauer Paktes*. Berlin: Militärgeschictliches Forschungsamt, 2010; Minow, Fritz. *Die NVA und Volksmarine in den Vereinten Streitkräften. Geheimnisse der Warschauer Vertragsorganisation.* Friedland: Steffen Verlag, 2011; Nielsen, Harald. *Die DDR und die Kernwaffen – Die nukleare Rolle der National Volksarmee im Warschauer Pakt*. Baden-Baden: Nomos Verlagsgesellschaft, 1998.
2 Nielsen, op. cit., pp. 26, 49.

The command of the Coastal Front was integrated, so all forces in the area were coordinated, no matter whether they were army, air force or some special group[3] – thus corresponding to the principles of BALTAP. It is noteworthy that the coastal front command was Polish, but the command was under orders by the Soviet General Staff which was sure to apply the Soviet military principles to the lower levels and interact with them in the planning stages. Command-in-action, however, was decentralised and thus belonged – except for missile- and artillery batteries, reserves and special forces – to the forces in the area. These battle forces, of course, had to be guided by plans for action, but the precise movements were to be decided on the battle ground. The plans for action directed a first and second echelon, the actions of particular army groups (often behind the enemy), the use of aircraft and naval resources, and dislocation of missile- and artillery batteries. In addition there were the use of reserves, when applicable. Still, the Soviet military organisation in the battlefield strived towards high mobility and ability to regroup when necessary.

USA had a monopoly on operational nuclear warheads until 1953, and therefore Stalin discouraged any public discussions about atomic warfare; this did not mean, however, that the Russians did not secretly prepare the use of atomic weapons.[4] Until 1956, the Soviet system of defence was publicly based on conventional weapons – a comprehensive use of motorised and mechanised divisions and a large air force to aggressively break through the enemy's defence. From 1956, the Soviet Union had intercontinental bombers available for strategic nuclear bombs, and in the early 1960s more tactical nuclear warheads were ready for use by missiles in Europe, and war plans were based on an aggressive use of atomic weapons in Europe, if necessary.

The Coastal Front had four German and two Polish divisions, but it would not go into action until the Polish forces were ready at the border to the west, and this would take two days, so the front would not be operational until two days after the Central Front.[5] There were aircraft and naval units at disposal. The plans allocated the WAPA forces to stop the NATO forces and then attack into NATO territory; in the Coastal Front the role for the East Germans was in the first two days to keep the NATO forces at bay and prevent NATO landings on the coast; when the Polish forces had arrived, the Germans were to support them in the at-

---

3 Ibid., 34–47.
4 Diedrich, Torsten. "Zur Rolle der Nationalen Volksarmee der DDR." In *Die Streitkräfte der DDR und Polens in der Operationsplanung des Warschauer Paktes*, edited by Rüdiger Wenke, 15–17. Potsdam: Militärgeschichtliches Forschungsamr, 2011.
5 Nielsen, op. cit., pp. 48–52.

tacks against the NATO forces and break through to NATO territory.[6] At this point, under strong pressure to withdraw, the Soviet assumption was that NATO would initiate the use of nuclear warheads, and since WAPA had no tactics of flexible response, the counter nuclear attack would be massive and make the way for the Coastal Front forces to move north across Schleswig-Holstein into Jutland and annihilate the NATO defence. Even if NATO did not use nuclear warheads, the plan implied that the WAPA forces were so strong that NATO could not resist them, apparently without using nuclear warheads.

Cooperation with the naval forces from the Baltic Sea Front was required.[7] The East German navy had to protect transport in the coastal waters and prevent NATO forces from landing on the coast and attack the flank of the Coastal Front forces. The navy also had to take part in the expected attacks on the NATO coasts when the NATO attack had been stopped and the WAPA counter attack initiated. The navy had to sweep mines, attack NATO naval forces and sail landing craft to the enemy coasts. One group was destined to land on the island of Fehmarn, others in the Kiel Inlet, and yet others on the coast of the Danish island Lolland in order to set up a coastal battery. In addition, the navy should land special forces to attack the Danish fort on Langeland. Later in the 1960s larger operations by the United Baltic Navy were planned, including the landing of a Polish division on Zealand while the East Germans landed on the islands of Falster and Lolland.

NATO's perceptions at the command level

Earlier (Chapter 4) we followed the threat pattern as perceived by NATO intelligence in the annual SG 161 reports. They were fairly general in their approach and therefore did not help in preparing for an attack in any detail. The intelligence gathered by the Danish Intelligence Office was intended to fill out the gaps, and in addition the small-scale types of information from exercises etc. could send warning signals of changes in WAPA tactics and maybe even strategic elements.

If we take a look at the tactics analysed in SG 161, we may take the tenth report from 1957 as an example. In Part 2, the Soviet naval tactical doctrine is presented on page 32–33:

---

6 Ibid., 60–61.
7 Diedrich, op. cit., pp. 25–28.

- There was close air cooperation; all types of surface vessels including FPBs worked with use of aircraft on reconnaissance, ASW, fighter and strike missions.
- Surface action forces operated at speeds up to 30 knots; destroyers attacked with torpedoes at better than 25 knots and gunnery firing up to 24 knots.
- As to gunnery, cruisers practised firings at 8–12 miles, destroyers at 3–7 miles. They operated at night and carried out shore bombardments.
- Torpedoes were used in coordinated attacks using both formation and sector methods.
- Smoke screens were used for concealment and deception.
- Reconnaissance was very important in all operations, using aircraft, submarine and shore radar stations.
- Escort screens were used as bent lines and circular screens, with units about 2,000 meters apart; formations did not appear to pay attention to ASW or AA defence in depth.
- FPBs were attacking in line of bearing formation about 65 meters apart from an angle of 45 degrees on the bow. Firing range was about 2,000 meters at a speed of about 35 knots, often in cooperation with bomber and fighter aircraft. At night this was in cooperation with aircraft, destroyers or other FPBs which illuminate the target.
- Submarines carried out coordinated tactical training, supported by reconnaissance aircraft; long range operations are controlled by radio. Most surface guns had been removed but for limited AA purposes.

The above information was of course useful, but quite limited in scope. The intelligence gathered by the Danish Intelligence Office gave much more information about how military action might take place. So let us turn to Denmark.

Danish Intelligence sources

As perceived by NATO, the WAPA strategy was more or less determined beforehand as a principle (world dominance), but more precisely how to accomplish that in specific war theatres was the object of intense intelligence gathering by various intelligence offices of NATO. Important sources are found in the archives of the Danish Intelligence Office which gathered and analysed military information which it used for creating and disseminating images of what the East could do and how they were going to do it.

The Danish Intelligence Office was set up in 1950 by merging the previous intelligence services of the army and the navy into one, covering all forces and organised in the C-in-C's staff. The bureau had a broad range of interests, but one of the main tasks was to monitor all shipping in the Baltic Sea and the Baltic Approaches closely, creating a day-to-day map of what ships – both military and merchant – were where. This monitoring can be seen as a follow-up of Klose's activities in the Baltic in the early 1950 (see chapter 8), and it was important NATO-wide. A system of surveillance was set up, using radio and radar as well as eyeballing. Information about ships was relayed to a number of plotting stations. Over the years, the system created a map of "electronic fingerprints" for all WAPA ships so that one could monitor them no matter where they were stationed.

In the archives there is a large number of reports. First, on the military systems: order of battle, technical details including electronic information and evaluations of the armies, navies and air forces. In addition there were reports on exercises, and updating of various forms of information. Furthermore, the economies of the countries were monitored and reports written on themes like population, commerce, industrial production, agriculture, fishery, natural resources etc. Estimates on future development potentials were made.

Researching all this would lead to a book in itself, so we only scratch the surface of those archives, focusing on military information and exercises.

Routine reports

Several report types were recurring by week, month or year, and thus information was built up step by step. Various aspects of the orders of battle of the military in WAPA countries were analysed, often in English so that NATO authorities could make use of them, and all passages and manoeuvres by WAPA units in the Baltic approaches were monitored and reported. Examples follow below.

The Polish forces

A 10-page note from 1957 briefly analysed the Polish armed forces for a SHAPE intelligence conference in the summer of 1957.[8] The note goes through the order of battle for all three forces, discussing recent cut-backs, particularly in the army. In that vein, the note suggested that in the light of the Hungarian revolt in 1956, the removal of a number of Soviet-trusted top officers and the deep-grained hate of the Russians in the Polish population, the Soviets would not trust the Polish armed forces to be supportive of an attack against the West. On the contrary, in

---

8 Note NATO SECRET An estimate of the Polish armed forces. Forsvarsstaben, efterretningsafdelingen Z. no 313/57, X3 749/57 n.d. (June 1957).

order to protect Soviet military key points and LOCs, they might have to neutralise and disarm the Polish forces by a massive influx of Soviet security forces. This would take three to four armies with air support eight to ten days. A follow-up to guard the country would take up to 20 divisions.

The reductions had been made due to severe shortages of labour in the general economy and amounted to about 190,000 men, leaving the army with 160,000, the navy with 8,000 and the air force with 22,000 men. The note detailed the types of divisions in the army, the composition of the navy and the air force and gave some information about the HQs and the location of (radar) warning systems. In addition, there were short presentations of the exercise patterns and the logistics, including the dependence on Soviet deliveries, particularly oil and petrol.

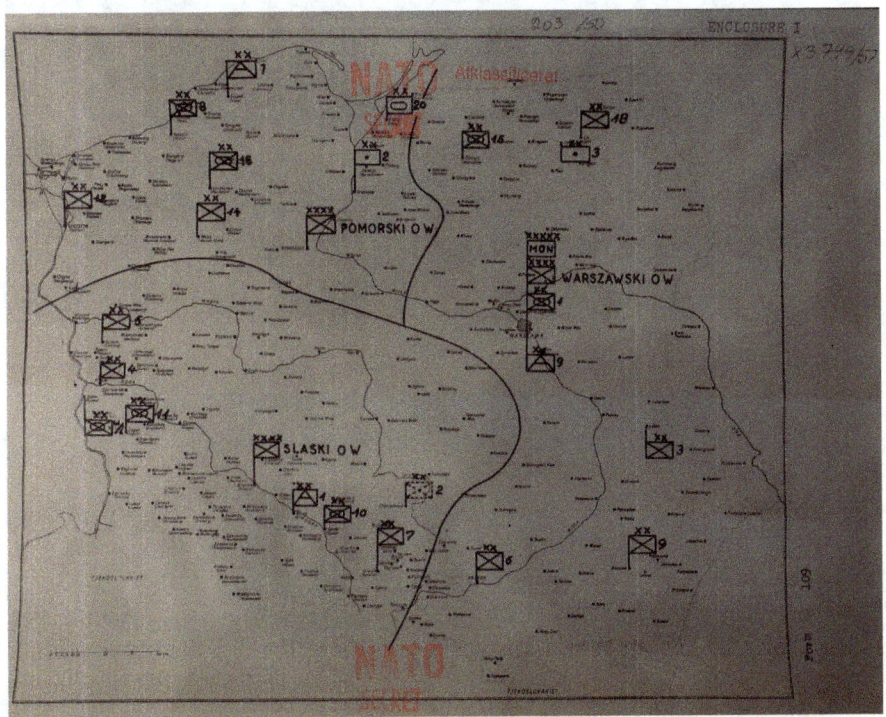

Figure 10.1: A map of the location and strength of various Polish army divisions in 1956. Source: Rigsarkivet.

Figure 10.2: A map of the location and strength of the branches of the Polish Air Force 1956. FGT: Fighters; GR-ATT: Fighter-bombers; LT-BMB: Light bombers. Source: Rigsarkivet.

The Soviet navy

The intelligence office regularly reported the order of battle for the Soviet navy, and annual summaries were made. A 1957 short (five pages) summary was written in 1958, probably for AFNORTH.[9]

The 1957 report summarised which ships had passed the Baltic Approaches, most of them being transferred to the Northern Fleet. It also indicated the details of the order of battle, noting a reduction in mine sweepers and patrol craft due to an ageing fleet, a stagnation in the building of cruisers, and new classes in the destroyer and FPB segments. Missiles had not yet been sighted on surface ships, but some submarines were believed to have them, and aircraft had been observed with air-to-ground missiles. The coastal defence was becoming more mo-

---

9 Note: A survey of the Soviet navy 1957, NATO SECRET, The Defence Staff, Z 7/58, X3 149/58, n.d.

bile, and the fighting control systems modernised. All vessels now had improved ECM equipment.

Spying in 1956: Russian cruiser and destroyers

In August 1956 a Russian squadron consisting of the cruiser (Sverdlov class) ORDZHONIKIDZE and two destroyers of the Skory-class visited Copenhagen. The Danish Intelligence office did not miss the opportunity to gather information about their construction and reported a host of details to NATO.[10] The intelligence was based on on-the-spot observations, from high-definition photographs taken during the visit, and from conversations with Soviet naval personnel.

The report had eight subjects: radar equipment; ABCD-service; construction and armour; engine rooms; armament; torpedo; depth charge and mine installations; and degaussing (magnetism reduction). We shall not go through all these details in the 15-page report, one example may suffice: torpedoes on the destroyers. They were installed in quintuple launchers which had an overall length of 8.65 meters and were fired with gun powder or compressed air. Training (turning) was controlled from a cabin on the launcher. Adjustment of the torpedo run (depth and angle) could be made from the outside of the tube or by control system from the bridge. The torpedo director (on the bridge) was a tall column with one binocular for main sight and another for regulating the angle. The column had a few handles (one for adjusting speed at 34, 39 and 51 knots) and presumably got various information (deflection, range etc.) from a computer which was installed on the forepart of the bridge (see the drawing below).

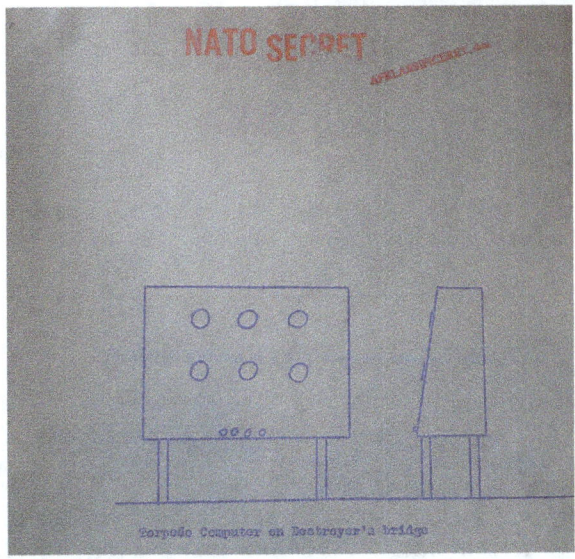

Figure 10.3: The drawing shows the torpedo computer on the bridge. The various scales indicate: torpedo speed (0–45 knots); range (0–12 km); torpedo angle (0–45 degrees); training (45–135 degrees) course of ship; "tubes ready" and firing switches; sundry control lights. More details were in the report. Source: Rigsarkivet.

---

10 Note Visit of Soviet Squadron to Copenhagen, HEM, Z 306/45, n.d.

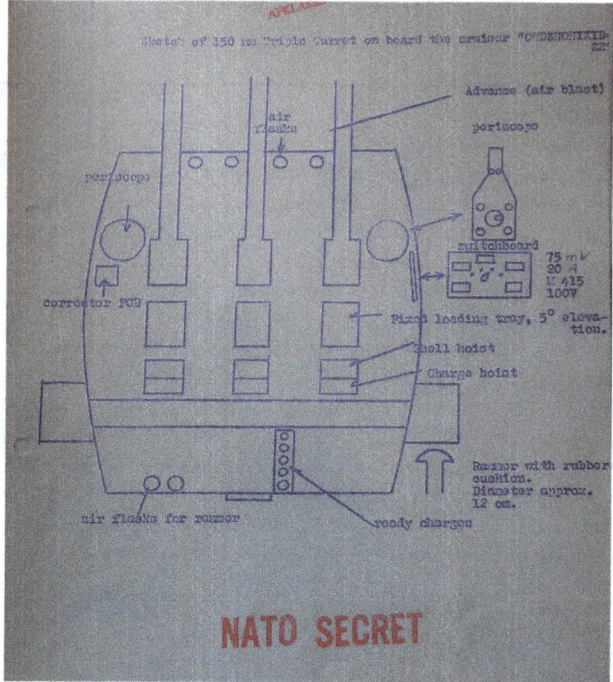

Figure 10.4: The drawing shows the infrastructure of the 150 mm turret on the cruiser. More details were in the report. Rigsarkivet.

There also was considerable interest in the 150 mm main armament of the cruiser; two pages were devoted to a detailed insight in the operation of the turret, getting ammo to the guns, direction system, armour etc.

Special reports

Until about 1960, the Soviet navy had mostly had the role of a "Fortress fleet", meaning that it was supposed to defend the Soviet territory, prevent the enemy from entering the Baltic and support the army, and thus was a fleet in being rather than an attack force. A naval exercise in August 1955 illustrated such a role. It was reported[11] that a cruiser and four destroyers were anchored for a week. When they entered, six mine sweepers performed a number of sweeps. Later, various attacks were initiated by MTBs and submarines. The role of the destroyers were to fend off

---

11 Danish Defence Staff: Russian Naval Activity in the Waters off Rügen Medio August 1955. HEM Z 144/55 n.d.

the MTBs, and ASW vessels were called in to perform a protection against submarines. The main force later left in a formation with the four destroyers screening in a rectangle of two miles with the cruiser in the centre.

A report from 1958 also indicated a certain degree of passivity. It went through the activities in two Soviet naval districts in the middle Baltic;[12] we shall quote from the Swinoujscie district. It had three destroyers, four ASW, six to eight mine sweepers and 24–30 MTBs plus various auxiliaries. There were 90 fighter aircraft at three airfields, at least two mobile coastal batteries and a battalion of marines. But "No remarkable activity has been observed" for years. The ships were usually in harbour, and within the previous year only two exercises of any importance had been set up, both of them ASW. MTBs performed navigation and formation exercises frequently, but real attack exercises with torpedoes had never been observed, nor had mine sweeping exercises. The Danish Intelligence office concluded that the districts were made for defensive purposes, responsible for free access to harbours.

Two exercises in the late 1950s indicated a change of role. They involved "break-through" of (the Irben) strait and landing forces by amphibious craft and aircraft, including helicopters (see report on more details below) and thus indicated preparations for a more offensive role against the Baltic Approaches and the Western Baltic. At the same time, the submarine segment was being reinforced with larger submarines, probably for a more offensive role on the oceans.

A seven-page note on the modernisation of the navy was written in 1960.[13] It reported on destroyers (KILDIN and KRUPNYI) and FPBs with surface-to-surface missiles. As to submarines, there were indications of atomic powered units being built, and the Z-class was developed into missile submarines. New mine sweepers were being built, and the amphibious segment was extended, as were tenders.

On the weapon side, new anti-aircraft guns and control systems were being developed. ASW was becoming more effective with rocket launchers and modernised sonar and control systems. Radar systems originally were of a western type, but now Soviet systems were developing rapidly in general, with systems for air warning, gunnery, height finding and navigation. Other electronic systems for IFF ad ECM were under development, as were UHF-band radios and infrared communication systems.

Exercises, which earlier on were mainly carried out with a few ships, were now much more complex and comparable with large NATO exercises. It seemed

---

12 The Soviet, Polish and East German Navies during the first Quarter of 1958. HEM. Defence Staff Z 174/58 n.d.
13 Note: Trends and technical developments in the Soviet navy. NATO SECRET. The Defence Staff, n.d. E1115/60, 00127.

that the Soviet Union was preparing for a larger role on the oceans, mainly with submarines, also atomic driven, and destroyers with missiles.

Special themes

Now and then the intelligence bureau wrote reports on specific themes like the quality of runways in airfields, Russian development of frigates, or the WAPA use of electronic navigation systems under passage of Danish territory.

Passive ECM

One example is a report on the passive use of ECM on WAPA ships.[14] Many of those navigated in Danish waters as part of the intelligence gathering by the WAPA states. The report went through the various systems in use: radio bearing and communication, and radar interception (specifying the various band systems frequencies etc). The report identified the various ships used for intelligence and identified the visible systems on their superstructure (see photo).

Russian ASW tactics

Another example is the way the Russians traced and attacked submarines.[15] This brief report noted that the Russians had improved their search instruments (magnetic systems, systematic hydrographical measures); they increasingly used aircraft and helicopters; and their attack weapons had improved. They had set up a research institute to improve ASW.

A common search tactics was as follows. Up to four destroyers or frigates moved forward in abreast formation with a distance of 1.6 times effective sonar coverage, up to about 6,000 meters with a speed up to 20 knots. When contact was made, data from contacts were used to determine the course and speed of the submarine, and the division commander determined which ships were to attack in which sequence. After the attack the ships were to re-try getting contact, and, if so, a new attack would be initiated. The figure below from the report illustrates the attack sequence.

If the distance was very short, the submarine had to be attacked immediately by all means in order to make it dive and thus prevent it from firing its torpedoes (it was apparently assumed that torpedoes could only be fired based on periscope vision).

---

14 Note Østmagternes skibsbaserede passive ECM. HEM. FST-E 702/62. n.d.
15 Note Sovjetisk A/U-krigsførelse. HEM. 23-3-61. E490/61. 2.4.b.13 Rusland.

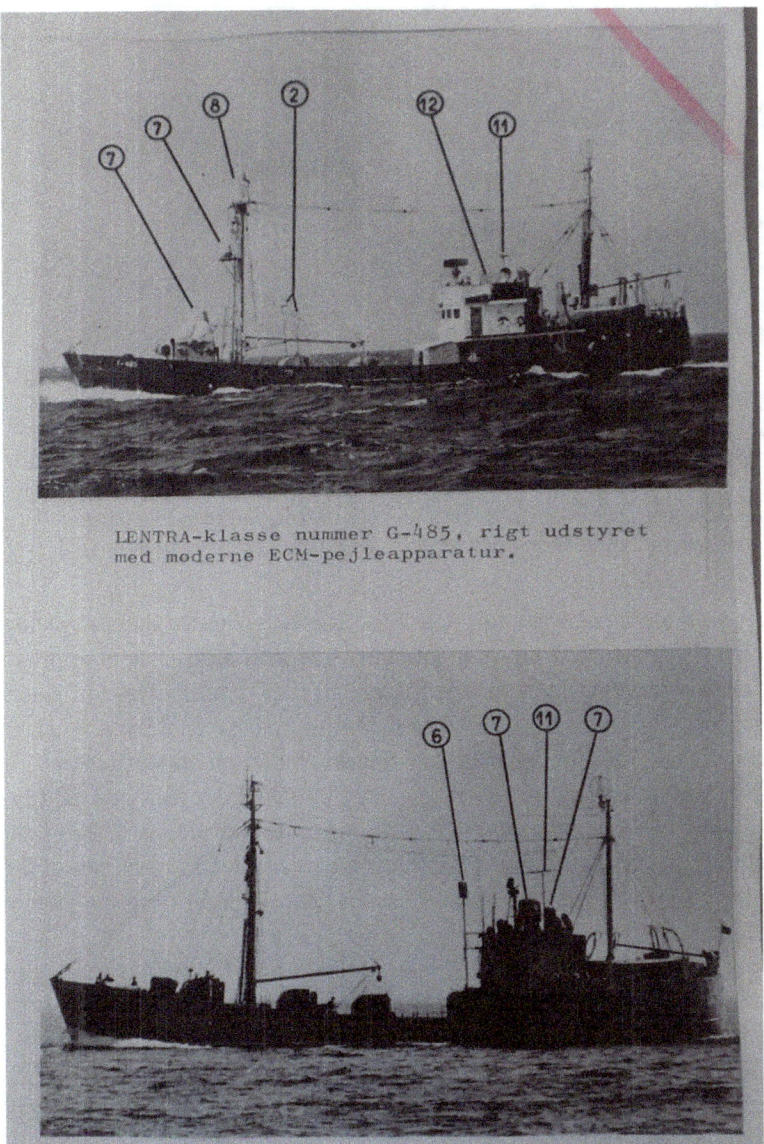

LENTRA-klasse nummer G-485, rigt udstyret med moderne ECM-pejleapparatur.

Figure 10.5: Examples of (fishing) vessels carrying systems of ECM. Each antenna is identified by a number. Thus no. 4 is BRICK SQUARE, covering the frequencies X, S and L, approx. 750–10.000 Mc/S. Source: Rigsarkivet.

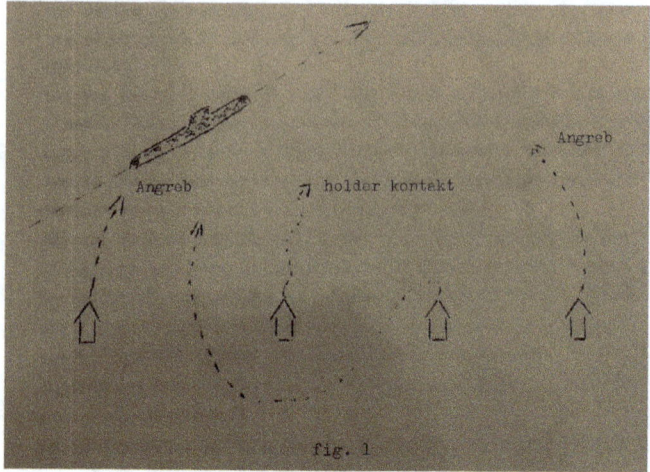

Figure 10.6: An illustration of how the submarine (upper left side) is attacked by four frigates (Danish "angreb" = attack; Danish "holder kontakt" = keeps contact). Source: Rigsarkivet.

Attack tactics with airplanes were also described. Normally, two to three airplanes cooperated by dropping sonar buoys in straight lines with a distance of approximately one mile between each buoy. The buoys had radio transmitters to the airplanes. When contact was made, an airplane would approach one of the submarine hunters in the area and ask it to follow to the relevant buoy and initiate a search. At the same time, MAD searching (measuring changes in the earth's magnetic field because of the body of the submarine) was initiated by the airplanes. They might drop more buoys in the direction the submarine was assumed to proceed. If the submarine had been observed by eyeballing, the planes might drop buoys in a circle around it.

The report finally described the war organisation of the ASW system and showed how the submarine detection and blocking system is set up around the naval bases (see figure below).

The report concluded that the Soviet ASW-system was not as good as NATO's, but it was improving. A number of tables finally listed the weapons, the search systems and the ships able to perform ASW roles.

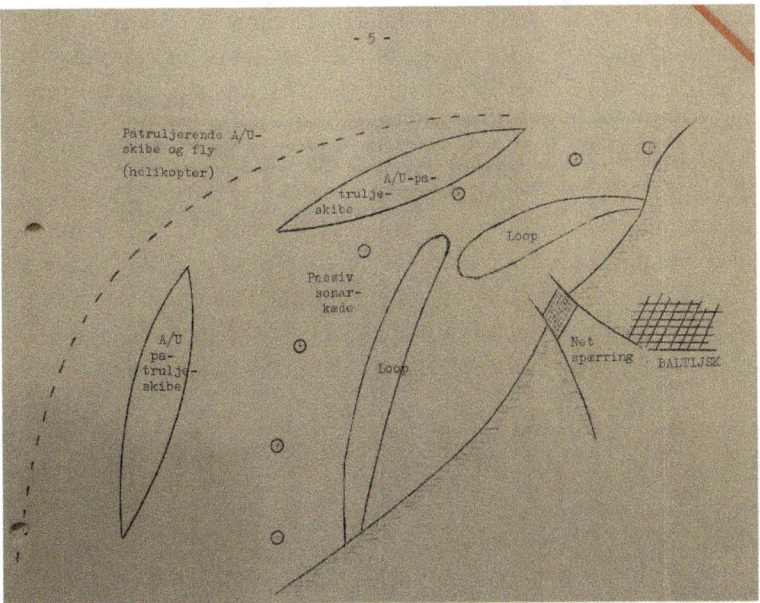

Figure 10.7: The figure indicates the protection system against submarines at the naval base Baltysk. There is a net barrier at the harbour, two listening loops outside, a number of minefields and ships on patrol. Source: Rigsarkivet.

Exercises

The Danish Intelligence Service followed movements of the WAPA closely, in particular naval and air exercises – no wonder, given the expected nature of military activities against most of Denmark. But some army exercises were also monitored. We shall go through several reports on such exercises below.

Integrated exercise

An exercise involving all three Soviet forces, including landing of amphibious forces and paratroopers, took place on 5–14 September, 1957, in the eastern part of the Gulf of Riga and the passages from the Baltic into the bay, more precisely on the south-Eastern part of the island Saaremaa near the Keskrana Beach and in the inlet, Irbe Strait.[16] A large number of details from the Danish report are omit-

---

16 Russisk flåde-flyøvelse i Østersøen i tiden 5–14 september 1957. Forsvarsstaben HEM 501/58 1-11-57.

ted below, e.g. details on the radio communication system and its stations; the radio reporting variables and code systems including hours for shifting codes; systems and procedures of enemy reporting; weather reports; and the use of radar. All those analyses were, of course, immensely important for the intelligence group, but we shall stick to the contents of the exercise.

The map below shows the wider exercise area with two forces, BLACK and WHITE, WHITE holding the northern area, and BLACK having the southern area.

The Danish intelligence office found that these exercise locations were used because there was a close geographical resemblance between that area and the area of Øresund and Køge Bay south of Copenhagen, believed to be one of the areas the Soviets would select for landing amphibious forces.

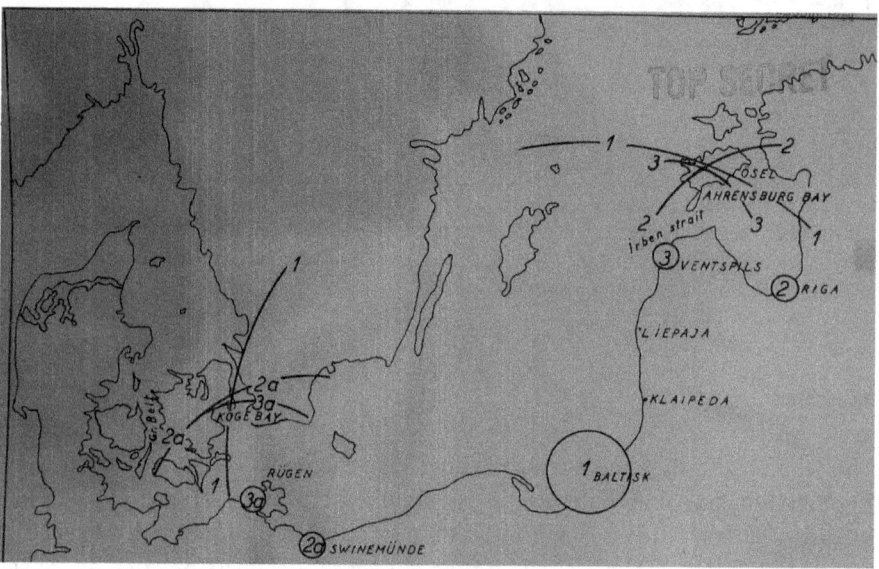

Figure 10.8: The map shows how the two areas compare in general and their distances from Soviet strongholds in the Baltic. The Soviets then were able to exercise the convoying of the amphibious force and also how to attack such a force. The Danish Intelligence used the names from WWII. Saaremaa was Ösel, Irben Strait is Irbe Strait and Ahrensburg Bay is the bay at Kuressaare. Source: Rigsarkivet.

Both naval forces were quite large, WHITE using a Tallin based squadron of two or three cruisers and 12 destroyers, BLACK using a squadron based in Baltijsk with three cruisers and 18 destroyers. Both also had FPBs, mine sweepers and submarines, and from the air force fighters, light and medium bombers. There were army groups involved on both sides; BLACK had an airborne division with transport planes and helicopters.

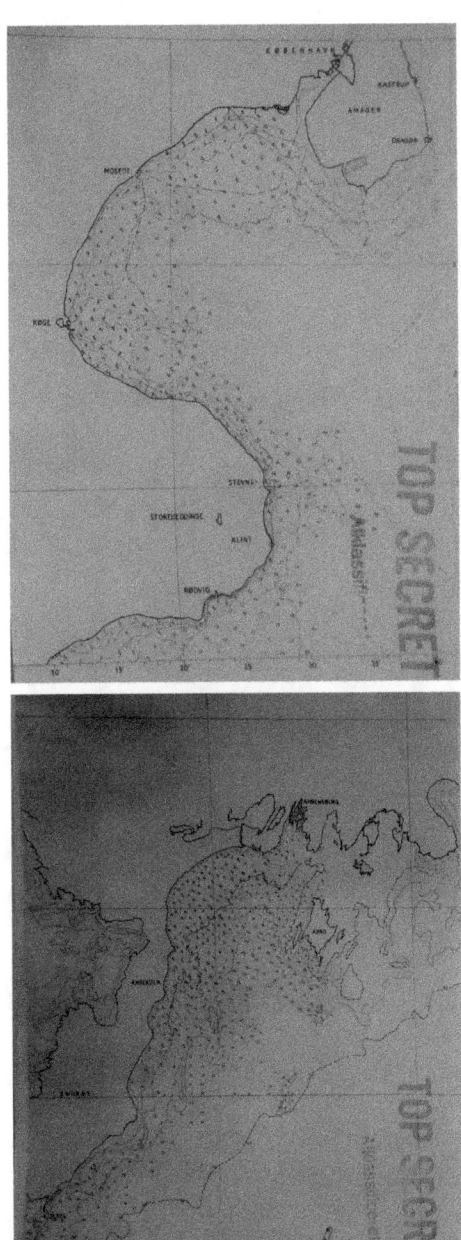

Figure 10.9: The maps show the general similarity of the two areas (White = land) Irbe first, Køge second. Source: Rigsarkivet.

Figure 10.10: This photo (from 2021, not 1957) illustrates the beach area of Køge, similar to Keskrana, with sand beaches and relatively shallow waters. Source: private photo.

In the first phase of the exercise, WHITE was the aggressor carrying out strategic bombing in BLACK hinterland, and the Tallinn squadron operating in the southern Baltic. BLACK carried out light bombing on WHITE ports and installations. But after a few days, the air situation changed to the disfavour of WHITE, and BLACK now took the lead.

These circumstances are easily translated to the real world as it was perceived by Soviets: WHITE (NATO) attacked, but BLACK (WAPA) stopped the aggression and now was able to initiate a large-scale counter attack against enemy territory.

On 8 September BLACK naval forces left their base areas and pressed the WHITE forces northwards, ending in a naval battle off the Saaremaa with WHITE losing at least one cruiser and withdrawing to the Tallin area. BLACK mine sweepers cleared the Irbe Strait, covered by destroyers and naval air forces. During the exercise both parties used jamming of radar and VHF-bands.

Phase three started: BLACK forces landed at the Keskrana area with two types of amphibious craft under cover of smoke. Paratroopers were flown in with transport planes, and troops were landed with helicopters. The manoeuvres were covered by ships and fighters and light bombers which also produced the smoke concealing the landing forces. All in all, two divisions were landed; the defending force was one division. The whole island was conquered the following day.

BLACK now controlled the island and the strait, and submarines were sent through the strait and into the Gulf of Riga.

The Danish Intelligence Unit translated the exercise into the real world as follows: NATO attacked WAPA, allowing WAPA to start its large-scale attacks westwards. The WAPA now had air supremacy and forced the NATO navy to withdraw northwards. The WAPA has conquered the island of Zealand, rendering control over the Baltic approaches and making way for its submarines to come out into the North Sea and from there to the Atlantic.

Coastal exercise

On July 19–21, 1958, a coastal defence exercise was held in the area of Swinoujscie.[17] Soviet, Polish and East German navy units participated together with aircraft from the Air Force of the Soviet Baltic Navy. This was the first time the Danes detected active cooperation within a tactical framework among WAPA forces at sea. The Soviet dominance was obvious, and no common communication system was observed beyond common time settings. Communication was probaby established by exchanging signal teams. The participants were:

Soviet: one destroyer (SKORY-class), four frigates (RIGA-class), five ASW (KRONSTADT-class), ten mine sweepers (T-301 class), one command ship, 22 MTBs (P-6 class), one amphibious craft and one surveillance ship, two coastal batteries at Swinoujscie, three fighter air regiments (MIG-17 FRESCO), several bomber divisions (IL-28 BEAGLE) and one reconnaissance unit (BE-6 MADGE).

Polish: two destroyers (one SKORY-class), two submarines (M-class), 11 minesweepers (T-43 & TR-classes), four ASW (KRONSTADT-class), six amphibious craft.

East German: one frigate (RIGA-class), six mine sweepers (KRAKE-class), four patrol craft (KS-class), one cable ship, one command ship.

The attacking force was: bombers and recce aircraft and two operation groups: group west all participants from East Germany; group east two Soviet destroyers and the Soviet and Polish amphibious crafts.

The defending force was: one destroyer, four frigates, ASWs, mine sweepers, MTBs, submarines and air fighters from Peenemünde.

---

17 Rapport verdørende sovjetisk kystforsvarsøvelse i Swinemündebugten i juli måned 1958. Forsvarsstaben YHM 18-11-58 1080/58.

The exercise started out on July 19 with Soviet bombers attacking the naval base in Swinoujscie and probably laid mines in the approaches to the harbour. The defending force then swept the mines, covered by air force fighters, two frigates at sea and a number of MTBs. The defenders sent out ASWs near the coast, large mine sweepers south of Bornholm and submarines east of Bornholm. The attackers' aircraft initiated a jamming of enemy radar station by dropping chaff (in 1958 called "window").

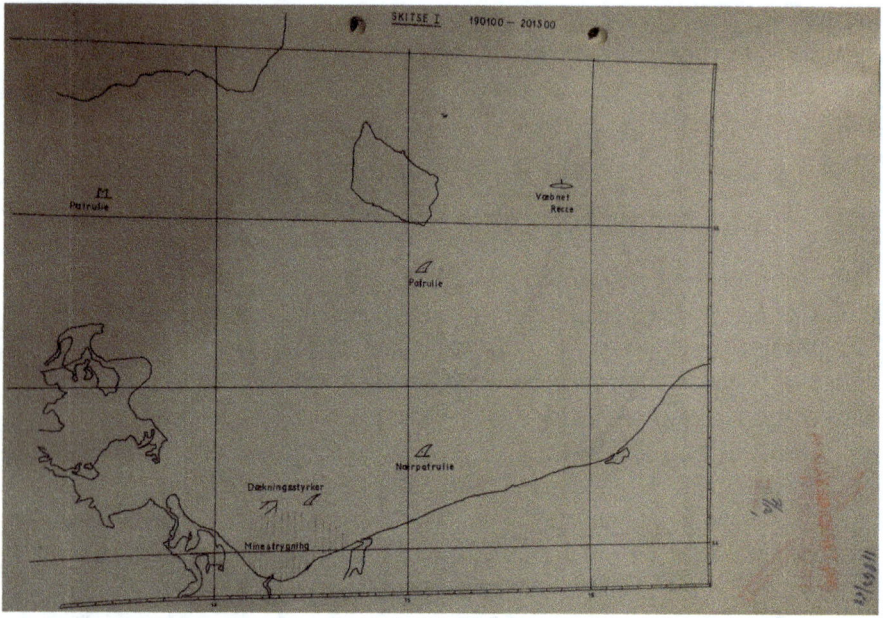

Figure 10.11: Coastal exercise day one indicating a situation with the mined area at Swinoujscie and various patrols around Bornholm. Source: Rigsarkivet.

On day two and three two different forces attacked: the East German group came from the west, the Polish and Soviet group from the east. The East German force was attacked by up to four defending frigates and half a division of MTBs at 0300 on July 21 and was presumed to suffer losses. The force coming from the east was two destroyers, presumably acting as a larger force, and was at 0700 attacked by aircraft and probably at the same time submarines. The group continued and was joined by six Polish amphibious craft. They were attacked again at 1015 by three half divisions of MTB under the cover of artificial fog. The movements are indicated on the map below.

The exercise was completed by 1300 hours, and the participants went first to Swinoujscie for a final parade; later they returned to their own bases.

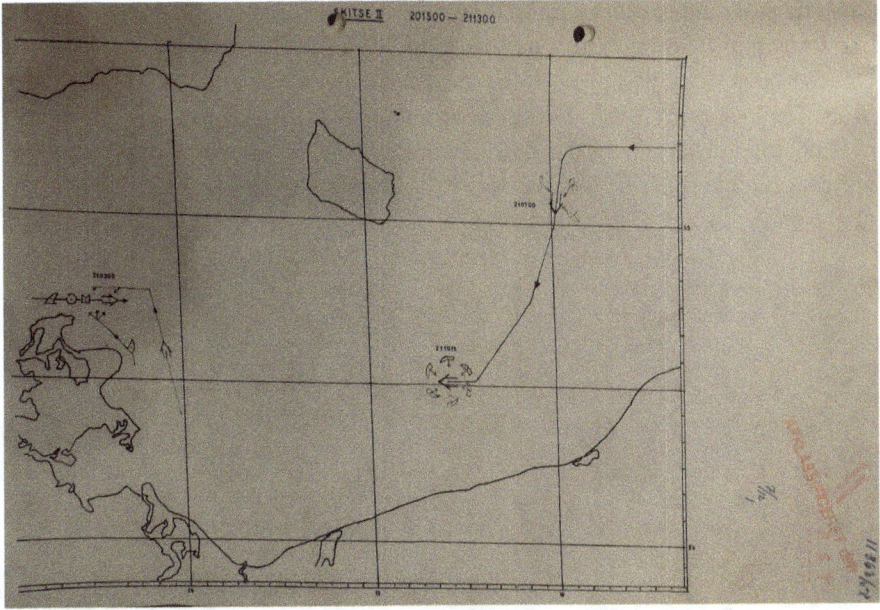

Figure 10.12: Two attacking groups, one operating outside Rügen, one from the eastern Baltic. Source: Rigsarkivet.

The Danish Intelligence noted that the Soviets strongly emphasised the use of aircraft in naval warfare and trained in cooperation between the forces during attack as well as defence; they appeared to maintain their military pressure until the enemy was done with. The Soviets also used MTBs in relatively large numbers, attacking using artificial fog in a syncronised, concentrical (sector) action (see the eastern group attack on the map above). At night the MTBs only used one radar per half division, so they had to use passive ECM in their operations, probably supported by the frigates which used their navigational radars intensively. The MTBs apparently were directed by a mission commander located on the coast, directing their attacks. In sum, the Soviet dominated coastal defence appeared very efficient, at the level of what NATO could marshal.

Army exercise

On 18–20 October, 1960, the East German army had an exercise in the area north of Dresden.[18] The exercise followed the well-known pattern of a West (NATO) part attacking the east, a counter attack then started and the enemy driven back into its own territory by use of overwhelming force.

The West party was parts of the fourth and eleventh motorised infantry divisions. The East party was the seventh armoured division, some paratroopers and possibly units from the Border patrol police. The air force planned to participate, but cancelled because of bad weather. The area of the exercise is shown on the map below.

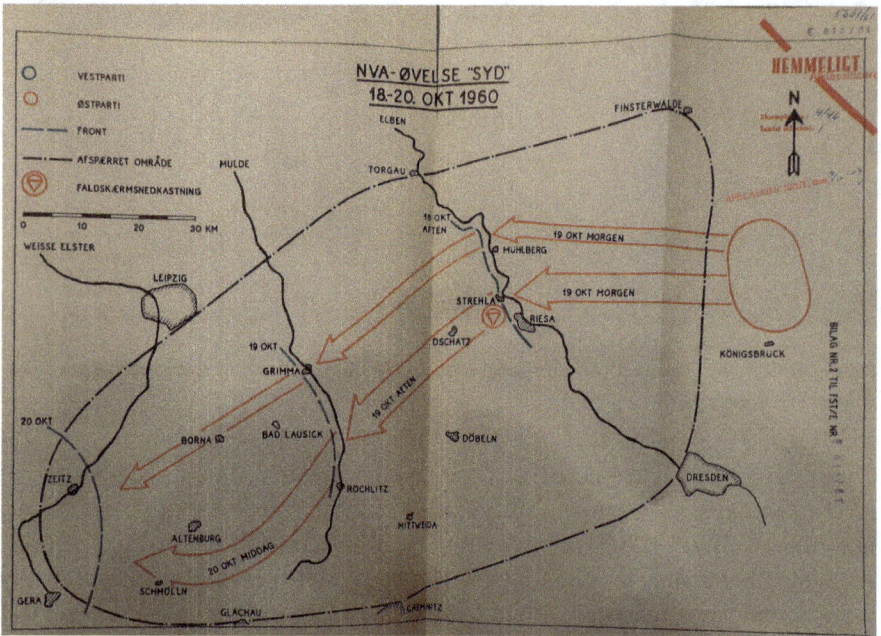

Figure 10.13: Map of the area. The West forces started out in the westernmost part, attacking to the east until the River Elbe. Here the counter attack stopped them and they were forced to withdraw. Source: Rigsarkivet.

---

18 Forsvarsstaben: Efterårsøvelser ved østtyske nationale styrker 1960. HEM. E 616/61 18-4-61.

The West attackers were gathered in the area at Gera and Zeitz on 13–15 October; on the night between October 17 and 18 the East party was alarmed and moved by train and its own vehicles to the area north of Königsberg.

On the morning of October 18 the West attackers quickly moved to the north east and reached the Elbe in the evening. They brought along material for mobile bridges, but on the morning of October 19 they were stopped by a counter attack from the east defenders, apparently by paratroopers in the area of Strehla. The seventh armoured division soon followed after passing the Elbe by normal bridges. The plan had been to use amphibious material for the passage (paratroopers having secured the area for passage), but the bad weather prevented such action. The West attackers were pressed back the following day to their starting point, and the exercise then was called off.

Typical features (compared with other army exercises) were the use of transport by railroad, even at short distances; use of groups of border police units as a first counter attack to create time for alarming the designated army units; use of armoured units in areas normally not considered "armour-friendly"; and night passages of river. The use of paratroopers as support for the counter attack was new: prior exercises had used paratroopers to create havoc behind the front.

Air forces were not in use, so there was no fight about air supremacy. In another exercise the week before, about 50 aircraft had participated from four airfields, doing recce in the morning and attacking ground targets in the afternoon from 2,000 feet altitude. Paratroopers had been flown in.

In its conclusions about the exercise, the Danish Intelligence doubted that these East German units would be allowed to operate separately in a real situation; they supposed that the East Germans would be brought into this type of action only if they were together with a Soviet division, possibly to cover its flank.

Air defence exercises

Twelve exercises in September and October 1959 formed the basis for a comprehensive report on air defence in East Germany.[19] Eight of the exercises were done together with the army and there was no opposing party involved; those exercises therefore were training in cooperation rather than exercising war-like conditions.

Activities trained were: recce and the interception by fighters of recce aircraft; use of chaff to block radar systems: supporting army units crossing a river, including visual and photo recce support to artillery; interception of incoming

---

19 Forsvarsstaben: Efterårsøvelserne 1959 ved 24. luftarme i Østtyskland. HEM 20-10-60. 317/40.

bombers; bombing army units and airfields; escorting bombers *en route* to their targets and defending them against intercepting fighters; relocation to other (war) airfields and training landing outside the concrete runways.

The Danish Intelligence drew out a number of conclusions regarding the tactics of the East German Air Force:

Fighters operated in groups of two or four, now and then six. Ground based actions were supported by fighter groups of four. Recce was performed in low altitude grouped two by two, often covered by a group of four in higher altitude. After interception of bombers, they were often attacked by two fighters for the first bomber, another pair for the second and so forth.

Bombers were mostly escorted by fighters, often 1:1. Bombing took place from 500 meters altitude in groups of three to five, or some times two. In larger exercises groups of 15–20 bombers were often seen, but now and then up to 50 units – this was a bit unusual, but was maybe to boost the morale of own troops or due to lack of fighters for escort. There was no sign of use of nuclear warheads.

The tactical systems of control looked much like what was done by NATO. Liason officers from the Air Force advised army officers on the use of aircraft, but apparently did not perform visual observation of targets to be relayed to the aircraft; they probably used maps for target reconnaissance. The targets appeared to be decided by the army officers who then gave the orders to the air force liasons for execution. Communication was carried out by VHF or the like. Each fighter wing had about four fighters with photo systems to carry out smaller tasks like photoing army groups, post-strike recce and the like; they appeared to be able to deliver reports, possibly with pictures, within one hour.

Relocations of aircraft wings were done in three phases. First a column of vehicles left with ground equipment, petrol lorries, radar equipment, food etc. Then a group of transport aircraft with key personnel and the most important ground equipment left and finally the flying echelon left. There was no fixed pattern, however; some times much was moved by air, while some times it was nearly only by ground transportation.

Helicopters had for the first time been used by East Germany for artillery observation and landing of small groups e.g. by rivers. A new helicopter regiment had been set up.

Summing up: information from exercises

Intelligence offices work with marginal bits of data which they put together in the light of previous experiences. So gradually they construct images of how the enemy's military forces operate; their weapons, their communication, their sensors etc.

The information stored by those offices is enormous. We have only seen a few examples above, and this is not the place to create an overview. Taken together with many other reports we can see that together they gave NATO a fairly good impression of what to expect if war broke out – and therefore also how to counter the tactical steps taken by the WAPA forces.

Chapter 11
The 1961 Berlin crisis

The First Berlin crisis was in 1948–49 when access to the city was blocked by the Soviets and all traffic and supplies to the city were handled by airplanes. The second Berlin crisis was a series of incidents in the years 1958–62.[1] In November 1958 the Soviets demanded that Berlin be demilitarised by the four previously allied powers within half a year. East Germany would take over and thus control access to the city. A series of meetings was held, but no agreement reached, and the Soviets backed down from their deadline.

This chapter deals with the second Berlin crisis as it was revived in the summer of 1961. This meant that a defence plan, Live Oak from 1958, was an instrument of possible use, but it was not a NATO issue. As the Berlin wall was raised, it became obvious that NATO might be involved anyway, so a process of creating a NATO plan – the BERCON – was initiated.

The Baltic Approaches were at a distance from Berlin, but any aggression around Berlin could easily spill into the Baltic, so especially for the navy and the air force, the crisis would cause concern. Denmark and Germany both analysed their military capabilities; Denmark not to the satisfaction of SACEUR, with Germany faring better.

The Warsaw Pact did a command post exercise in the fall of 1962; it did fulfil the premises and Paris was reached in 10 days, but the exercise unveiled a host of problems, particularly in the communication among the national forces, casting doubt on the realism of the quick defeat of NATO.

Live Oak 1958–59

Seen from the West, the military problem was that Berlin was not part of NATO. The three Western powers therefore initiated a planning group, *Live Oak*, under General Norstad (in his capacity of C-in-C of American forces, not his SACEUR

---

[1] For various mainly political angles on the second Berlin crisis, see Gearson & Schake Gearson, John, and Kori Schake, eds. *The Berlin Wall Crisis*. London: Palgrave Macmillan, 2002. The military side is discussed by Thoss, Bruno. *NATO-strategie und nationale Verteidigungsplanung. Planung und Aufbau der Bundeswehr unter den Bedingungen atomaren Vergeltungsstrategie 1952–1960*, 291–329. München: R. Oldenbourg Verlag, 2006. Live Oak is discussed by Nes, Harald van. "Crisis Management During the Cold War Illustrated by 'Live Oak'." In *Periphery or Contact Zone? The NATO Flanks 1961 to 2013*, edited by Bernd Lemke, 185–96. Freiburg: Rombach Verlag KG, 2015.

command) to prepare for military action in case the access to Berlin was once again blocked by the Soviets or East Germany. *Live Oak* plans included various responses to blocked access routes from West Germany (Helmstedt) to Berlin. The planned actions were strictly conventional in terms of weapons, and the first planned light responses were first of all seen as a "probe" to test a Soviet response. They ranged from sending a few infantry platoons to demand access to the freeways, over the use of a battalion to the initiation of secured air corridors.[2] These measures would come about step by step. But a full military solution by conventional forces would demand 40 divisions plus air support, and forces of such magnitude were not available.[3]

The staff of *Live Oak* therefore pointed to a general NATO response under SACEUR. General Norstad, however, in his double capacities of being the supreme commander and commander of *Live Oak*, disagreed quite strongly with any thoughts of nuclear response. He called for planning stronger demonstration by a battalion-sized or even stronger force.[4] Furthermore, he pointed to non-military intervention such as trade blockages (which the staff had considered out of their hands).

As time went by, no confrontations came about; the Berlin issue was discussed in various political settings, but petered out until the summer of 1961.

Berlin crisis summer 1961

The Kennedy administration took over in the USA in January 1961, and soon it became obvious to NATO and the world that the new president was no fan of nuclear weapons.

In the Spring of 1961, the American top military expressed dissatisfaction with the Live Oak plans.[5] In May, the Secretary of Defence had called the existing Live Oak military contingency plans deficient, stating that the designated forces could be stopped even by the East Germans acting alone. Therefore the Americans had to have at least the level of forces required to defeat any such Satellite force, without resorting to a nuclear response. The British and the French, how-

---

2 Maloney, S. M. "Berlin Contingency Planning: Prelude to Flexible Response." *Journal of Strategic Studies* 25, no. 1 (2002): 104–5.
3 COS (59)154, 29-6-59 Berlin Contingency Planning. More elaborate military measures.Top Secret.
4 Letter Norstad to Cooper LO-TS-59-1005, 26-6-59, archived by COS (59)155, 29-6-59.
5 Pedlow, Gregory W. "NATO and the Berlin Crisis of 1961: Facing the Soviets While Maintaining Unity." Supreme Headquarters Allied Powers Europe, 2002.

ever, were hesitant towards larger scale operations, and SACEUR Norstad noted that such greater forces would be taken from the NATO forces in West Germany, weakening the general NATO defence.

In June 1961, phase two of the second Berlin crisis was initiated with the Soviets threatening to sign a peace accord with East Germany and hence make the agreement of access to Berlin for the West null and void – and the West answering that the agreement would stand anyway. The Americans announced an increase of military spending, and it was clear to many observers that there was a need for a general strengthening of NATO. The American President issued a direct appeal to the NATO allies on 20 July 1961 to undertake an immediate military build-up to meet the Soviet challenge over Berlin. On August 8, the American Foreign Secretary addressed the NATO Council on this issue and the need for a military build-up. The day after, the Live Oak staff moved into the SHAPE HQ, and got a German liaison officer, but the Germans could not participate in Live Oak operations. In principle, Live Oak remained a separate organization.

In the night between August 12 and 13, the East Germans started building a wall in Berlin. In and by itself, the building of the Berlin wall did not interfere with the status or rights of the Western Allies in Berlin, and hence there was no basis for countering the closure of the border, nor any basis for military action. But the wall was a sign of Soviet resolve and hence NATO had to analyse its possibilities if some sort of conflict should arise – and to show resolve as well.

US Secretary of State Rusk addressed the NATO council with a speech indicating a number of possible steps towards Soviet interference with Berlin access, indicating that the USA was prepared to go quite far in a response, but it also showed fairly low-level possibilities.

SACEUR was relatively quick in his response. Since he had already been working on these problems, he could present his amended plans[6] to the NATO Council by 21 August, recommending a strengthening of equipment and personnel levels in existing combat units; the addition of new combat units; the addition of fresh combat and service support units; and an improvement in the status of the reserves. These four principles were followed by very specific suggestions to be implemented by each NATO member country. The council members agreed to respond by 4 September.

It took a little more time, and two countries did not respond at all. All in all, some progress was seen, thus the number of army divisions was increased from 21 to 24 and they now had a higher combat potential. But still, NATO's capabilities

---

6 SHAPE 167 61 Plan of action NATO Europe.

by 1962 were not as desired by the supreme commander. In Northern Europe, the answers from Denmark and Norway did not reach the desired force level.

The details of these SHAPE plans for Denmark and Germany and the Danish and German responses are dealt with below.

Denmark

On 21 July, when the Berlin crisis was building up, the Danish Ministry of Foreign Affairs initiated an internal review of the state of preparedness of the Danish defence, including the question of mine laying in Danish waters, in cooperation with the Ministry of Defence.[7] But there was no information on plans for mines in either ministry. One may speculate that the issue of mines came up because the Chief of the US Navy had assured President Kennedy on a meeting three days before that the navy would be able to harass Soviet shipping in the Baltic and handed him a note on this and various other issues. The note stated regarding blockade (not harassment):

> Danish straits: Straits can be closed by mining and naval forces in the North Sea Approaches to the Baltic.[8]

Whether this was to be done by the American or Danish navy was not stated, but the Americans may have asked the Danish Foreign Office about Danish mine plans, and this question then was passed to the Ministry of Defence. As we shall see, SACEUR was very interested in the issue.

The Ministry of Defence issued an analysis of possible initiatives to strengthen the military forces within a short time horizon.[9] There were few beyond speeding up the implementation of matters already decided and speeding up the training of recruits in boot camps. Politically, one could call attention to the decision to recall 10,000 men for exercises in the fall – as a foreign policy indicator for the level of preparedness.

In a note, the Ministry summarised the preparedness, detailing what forces were available:[10]

- The army had a standing force of 13,800 plus 6,300 in boot camp plus 7,000 other personnel. They were formed in eight infantry battalions, two tank bat-

---

7   Notits HEM Forsvarsministeriet 11. Kontor 26-7-61.
8   JCSM-486-61, Berlin 18-7-61, Annex B to Appendix B, p. 16.
9   Notat HEM om hvilke foranstaltninger, der eventuelt vil kunne træffes til forstærkning af forsvaret. Forsvarsministeriet 11. kontor 27-7-61.
10 Notat HEM vedrørende beredskabssituationen. Forsvarsministeriet 28-7-61 j.nr. 120.2-1.

talions and four artillery battalions (of which one was a HONEST JOHN group), organized in two one-third brigades.
- The navy had available for their regular purposes (numbers decommissioned or unavailable in brackets): frigates 1 (2); corvettes 2 (2); large patrol boats 2; MTBs 9 (7); submarines 3 (1); mine layers 2 (2); mine sweepers 5 (7); depot ships: 1 (1). Three Coastal forts, 11 radar stations and 41 lookouts were alerted. The force could be increased if ships laid up came under command and if ships reserved for training were made war operational.
- The air force had six operational airfields and five radar stations with the following state of readiness (number/actually ready)

Table 11.1: State of readiness.

	Aircraft	pilots
fighter-bombers	52/22	65/16
All weather fighters	49/17	62/53
Day fighters	25/12	19
Recce aircraft	7/1	11/8

4 NIKE missile AA batteries

The number of pilots ready for fighter-bombers would increase as soon as final training for new aircraft was implemented – the air force was in the process of changing from F84 to F100 aircraft.

It was pointed out that a decision on the BALTAP command (see chapter 6) was desirable. Furthermore, a governmental statement authorising NATO-command of Danish forces still had not been worked out (lacking since 1952!). In a series of meetings in late July in the Foreign Policy Committee, the bourgeois opposition asked if any Danish military steps were to be taken; the ministers answered that such steps had been discussed with the Joint chiefs of Staff, but none decided.

In the days after the Wall was built, the Ministry of Defence daily reported on possible military issues in the area, but there were none. The Soviet and East German armies put several battalions on alert, but this appeared to be in order to support the police forces against the population, not against NATO.

The Minister of Defence had a meeting with the Danish Joint chiefs of Staff on August 14 regarding the preparedness of the defence. The decisions were made public in order to demonstrate the Danish solidarity with the people in Berlin.[11] The air force was ready for action any time; there was a lack of technicians,

---

11 Notat HEM om Berlin-situationen. Forsvarsministeriet 11. kontor 15-8-61 905-1/61.

but if needed, some could be recalled. The army could in a short time mobilise two brigade groups. The navy's situation was like that in the air force. In order to concentrate forces available in Denmark it was decided to cancel an exercise for a tank battalion in Germany, cancel a navy show-the-flag trip to the Mediterranean and cancel a missile exercise for the air force in North Africa. The squadrons of the air force were temporarily expanded from 12 to 16 aircraft. Finally, the investments for later years were taken up for consideration to expedite them.

From an observer's standpoint, the statements from the Joint chiefs of Staff regarding preparedness do not square well with the numbers in the tables above (from July 28); in particular, the number of pilots for fighter-bombers seem to be below what one might hope for, and the number of ships out of service is relatively high. The supreme commander's reactions are detailed below.

A budgetary increase of about eight per cent was decided. A few measures were prepared to be implemented on short notice: call-up of reserves for the army; keep conscripts on a number of ships in the navy; call-up of technicians for the air force. These actions were not implemented, but by the end of September two mine layers took war mines on board and kept them there for at least one month, staying at sea, ready to block Danish straits.[12]

SACEUR's above-mentioned suggestions for a Danish strengthening of the military capability were these:[13]

a. Raise army manning levels of M-Day units to at least 90% and insure readiness of the remaining mobilization increment.
b. Raise combat-ready crew level in the air force (now at 33%) to 100% and aircraft combat-ready rate (now 55%) to at least 70%.
c. Activate the Unified Command in the Baltic (BALTAP).
d. Phase forward to Category A readiness two frigates, four patrol craft, three submarines, and two mine layers (with mines aboard).
e. Procure and store in Denmark additional mines required to meet plans.
f. Man Control and Reporting units for 24 hour operation.
g. Procure 13 additional F-I00 aircraft.
h. Increase balanced logistic support for all services in phase with force improvement.

Finally, SHAPE noted that the effectiveness of the Danish army and air force would be greatly enhanced by the achievement of a nuclear capability.

---

12 Note Forsvarsministeriet 1. kontor 31-10-61, 120-1-10.
13 SHAPE 167 61 Plan of action NATO_Europe.

The Danish ministry of defence asked the C-in-C for comments.[14] They came one week later:
- Suggestions a, b, d and g created an increased demand for personnel and would mean recall of reserves and postponement of planned dismissals of conscripts. In the army, an extension to 22 months conscription was necessary to fulfil the supreme commander's demands fully. However, the army had limited space in existing barracks, so one had to recourse to 18 months service which would probably be manageable. The air force could not increase the number of pilots in the short run, and there was already now a serious shortage of technical personnel. The navy would be able to add decommissioned ships to the active navy, but other activities would then stop, and conscription time increased. All in all, a budgetary increase of about 12 per cent was required. Furthermore,
- The BALTAP command was a cabinet issue, not a military one, to be decided upon fairly soon (see chapter 9 about the statement of the cabinet on 31 August).
- The supply of mines was sufficient to existing plans, and Control and Reporting units were already alerted.
- More supplies and logistic support would demand a considerably higher financial contribution, about a 13 per cent increase of the budget.
- The issue of nuclear warheads might be solved if the Danish government would permit warheads to be imported at red alert.

Based on these facts, the response of the government to SACEUR – or rather the NATO Council – was that

> The Danish military authorities are instructed, to the extent possible, to make preparations to the effect that such measures – which will imply an increase of military personnel including calling up again of disbanded personnel and postponement of disbandment of personnel on active service – can be taken within a very short time.[15]

For certain investments the cabinet would reserve 75 mio DKR (about seven per cent of the normal budget).

This was close to a polite "sorry, but no". Sufficient resources were not available, and therefore only marginal changes in the Danish defence could be ex-

---

14 Notat HEM om beredskabsforanstaltninger i forbindelse med Berlin-situationen. Forsvarsministeriet 11. kontor 21-8-61 905-1/61.
15 Note SECRET "Danish Delegation to NATO" 4 September 1961 to the NATO Council.

pected.[16] It was also implied that the Danish government was aware of the problems raised and would keep them in mind. The government did not comment on SACEUR's observation regarding nuclear warheads (which could be read as a polite insult, PB).

This answer to the supreme commander did not please him, and he responded that both Denmark's (and Norway's) actions within AFNORTH were appreciated, but did not reach the desired goal. SACEUR formulated his reactions by September 15,[17] reiterating what was desired, as we saw above.

In Denmark, the minister once again asked the Danish Joint Chiefs of Staff for comments. As we saw above, they had already analysed the consequences but not expressed a policy stance. Now they stated that militarily it would be desirable to follow the wishes of the supreme commander except for the proposed enlargement (8,000 conscripts) of the army.

The cabinet, however, declined the proposal, referring to the formulations in the law of defence which stated that the proposals of extending conscription and recalling certain reserves could only be implemented in times of war or severe crisis. The cabinet did not consider the present situation a severe crisis.

Ready for war mining in the Baltic Approaches

> Bjarne Romme tells: I sailed with VINDHUNDEN from September 1960 to October 1961 as a radio operator. During the Berlin crisis VINDHUNDEN and BESKYTTEREN (sister ship) went to Køge and took war mines on board. BESKYTTEREN was sent to Storebælt and VINDHUNDEN to the southern part of Øresund. We sailed with low speed from Kastrup to the Swedish 3-mile border and back for 14 days. During the whole period of time we had a sort of Action Stations; everybody was on two-shift watch.
>
> After two weeks we were allowed to approach the harbour of Copenhagen, access to the quay was blocked for the general public. We took stores on board, and after six hours we returned to sea. We were on patrol, ready for mine laying, for four weeks. Then the crisis was over. To the best of my recollection we had war mines on board for three or four months. We were not allowed to go to the naval base with those on board.[18]

---

16 FTR Beredskabsforanstaltninger i forbindelse med Berlin-krisen. Forsvarsministeriet 3-10-61 905-1/61.
17 SHAPE 168/61 15-9-61 SECRET.
18 Bogason, Peter. *Søværnet under den kolde krig – politik, strategi og taktik*, 145–46. København: Snorres Forlag, 2015.

Figure 11.1: Danish Mine Layer VINDHUNDEN, an ex American LSM. 750 tons, length 62m, 12 knots, 4 double 40 mm AA, 6 20 mm AA, 150 mines. Source: Forsvarsgalleriet.

In response to SACEUR's renewed demands, the Danish delegation now gave a detailed note[19] explaining a number of problems: the consequences of the lack of technical personnel in both navy and air force made it impossible to buy more aircraft, impossible to take over two Fletcher class destroyers and very difficult to keep more ships in the active category. Furthermore, the combat ready rate of pilots would be 100 per cent from January 1. Third, more mine layers would be in the active category and put in operation with mines on board. Finally, the army was to now had more ammunition supplies and exercises were to be made on the desired brigade level.

The final conclusion was about the same as before. Militarily, Denmark was not in a position to do what the supreme commander demanded. Politically, only marginal resources were given to improve the defence. By January 1962, the status of the army was the same; the navy had one more frigate, one more mine layer, one more mine sweeper and one more depot ship ready for action. The air

---

[19] SECRET Danish Reply to Remarks made by SACEUR in Doc.SHAPE 188/61, 29-9-61 Paris.

force had 19 more aircraft and 28 more pilots ready, particularly for the fighter-bombers whose pilots had gone through a change for a new type of aircraft.[20]

West Germany

SACEUR's suggestions were as follows:[21]
   The Federal Republic already had proposed to:
a. Bring the eight divisions not committed to full strength by early 1962
b. Provide two brigades to a ninth division by early 1962
c. Accelerate the delivery of military equipment and supplies
d. Provide two more divisions of two brigades each during 1962

SACEUR recommended the following additional measures for implementation by January 1962:
e. Provide temporary or permanent sites for programmed infrastructure projects and accelerate construction.
f. Complete training and assign eight additional Air Force squadrons.
g. Phase forward to "Category IIA", seven destroyers, ten FPB and three mine layers.
h. Activate the Unified Command in the Baltic (BALTAP).
i. Increase balanced logistic support for all Services in phase with force improvements

SACEUR's suggestions meant that existing army forces would be strengthened and one more division created in 1961, increasing the personnel from 101,000 to 150,000, and adding three more divisions in 1962, bringing the total number up to 230,000. The navy was only required to prepare better for mine warfare. The air force was asked to add about 50 per cent (8) squadrons in 1961 and 50 per cent (13) of the new total in 1962. The Germans were also asked to help establishing the new BALTAP command.

The Germans nearly fulfilled the suggestions for 1961, but could not add more than two new divisional HQ and four brigades in 1962. The capacity of mine layers would remain lower than desired. Regarding the air force, there would be a deficit of around 200 planes (25 per cent) by the end of 1962 due to lack of technical staff, infrastructure and training of pilots.

---

20 Note Forsvarsministeriet 1. kontor 22-1-62 120-1-10.
21 SHAPE 167 61 Plan of action NATO Europe.

All in all, West Germany was doing what was possible within the constraints coming from technical labour and pilot shortage; there also was lack of airfields and other infrastructure.

As to the Baltic Approaches, the army division in Schleswig-Holstein was strengthened, and the state of the navy was nearly as SACEUR had suggested. The air force had problems in getting combat ready pilots. Regarding BALTAP, West Germany was ready to negotiate the final points.

NATO and Live Oak

The four countries involved in Live Oak from August 1961 were aware that future action could not be implemented without coordinating with NATO, and they initiated a series of policy discussions which they wanted to end with an involvement of NATO to such a degree that NATO would have to take over the lead of Live Oak.

We shall not go into detail with the quite intensive political discussions in September–October 1961 which ended with a decision by the NATO Council on 25 October 1961.[22] Some NATO commanders hoped for Denmark (and Turkey) to block their straits for Warsaw Pact ships and thus press the Soviets to give up blocking access roads to Berlin, but the Danes turned it down,[23] probably referring to international law. The main theme in the NATO council was the recourse to use of nuclear weapons, and having secured that such a decision was to be taken only by the political authorities, not military, a NATO agreement on an instruction to SACEUR was reached. The goal for NATO would be to maintain presence and security of the three Western garrisons in West Berlin; to maintain the freedom and viability of West Berlin; and to maintain freedom of access to West Berlin.

The task now was for the supreme commander to plan for NATO's military steps if these goals were jeopardised and no political or other intervention could remedy the disagreements between the Soviets and the Western powers.

Based on the North Atlantic Council's instructions, SHAPE went on to prepare the Berlin Contingency (BERCON) plans that included operations from one to four army divisions on East German territory, air operations within the air corridors but also over portions of East Germany; maritime operations against Soviet bloc shipping; and even nuclear demonstrations to show how serious the West was about reopening access to Berlin. At the same time, SACLANT's planners prepared

---

22 Pedlow, op. cit.
23 Henriksen, Jesper Thestrup. "Der Weg zum Einheitskommando." In *Grenzen überwinden – Schleswig-Holstein, Dänemark und die DDR*, eds Aaron Jessen, Elmar Moldenmauer, and Karsten Biermann, 63–64. Husum: Husum Druck- und Verlagsgesellschaft, 2016.

Maritime Contingency (MARCON) plans for use against Soviet bloc shipping all around the world. These plans were ready early 1962 and finally approved by NATO Council in October.

In May 1962, the first BERCON draft was ready.[24] It presupposed that NATO's governments had declared reinforced alert (a rather high level, PB). The Berlin corridors were close to the Baltic Approaches, so of course, any military action there might infer spill-over to the North. But only the SACEUR naval actions were directly relevant for the defence of the Baltic Approaches: naval forces could be used for surveillance of Soviet bloc warships and merchant shipping, hindrance of Soviet bloc ship activity, board and search measures, seizure of Soviet bloc merchant ships, and blocking Soviet ships from specific areas. SACLANT had MARCON plans ready with the same range of naval actions; he saw a possibility to establish the relevant measures at sea 100–150 miles from the Baltic Approaches. There were several possibilities for action; which ones to be used would be signalled when relevant. All these measures had to be approved by the NATO Council before they could be executed.

The Danish C-in-C foresaw the possibility that blocking by mines and impounding Soviet freighters could take place in Danish waters. The Danish Ministry of Foreign Affairs pointed out that the Soviets would likely see any hindrance of passage in the Danish narrows as *casus belli* and consequently they were high-risk measures. The Ministry wanted this caveat included somehow in the text.[25]

The total Berlin Contingency Plan, however, contained more than the above.[26] The Americans had named it the Poodle Blanket,[27] but it falls outside the scope of this book. It was a step-by-step process involving, first, small-scale military confrontations which might not even lead to use of weapons. Then there were exerting pressures of other kinds – but those were probably to be used during the whole process. BERCON, then, would scale the military intervention up and finally an all-out war might change the regional conflict into a total NATO-WAPA war.

---

24 Note YHM Militære planer til imødegåelse af sovjetrussiske krænkelser i og omkring Berllin. Forsvarsministeriet 11. kontor 11-5-62 905-1/62.
25 In YHM Notat om militære planer til imødegåelse af krænkelser i omkring Berlin, Forsvarsministeriet 11. kontor 18-9-62 905-1/62. The note claims that the passage is now part of the introduction to the final document. Upon inspection of document SHAPE 70-A/62 of 10-9-61, this author is unable to trace that change.
26 YHM Notat om Berlinplanlægningen i relation til NATO. Forsvarsministeriet 11. kontor 14-11-62. 905-1/62.
27 Maloney, op. cit., p. 115.

BERCON DELTA: Problems of legality

The actions in the naval part of the BERCON plan were likely to be carried out by the Danish and German navies on the high seas (the Baltic, Kattegat, Skagerrak and the North Sea) in coordination with SACLANT's MARCON. But after a legal scrutiny by the legal adviser to NATO,[28] it dawned upon the actors that any other intervention than surveillance on the high sea was likely to be in breach of international law.

BERCON DELTA comprised activities like shadowing Soviet bloc merchant ships and as a step up also shadowing warships in designated areas. Further steps up would be to hinder and annoy ships, to board merchant ships, to seize merchant ships and to establish blockade or enforce diversion and exclusion of Soviet bloc ships from specific areas.

For territorial waters there were also sincere doubts about the legality of some interventions. The Danish navy would have the role of acting in its territorial waters, particularly the straits: Storebælt and Øresund. They were in principle open to "innocent passage" which was defined as follows in the Geneva convention:[29]

> Passage is innocent so long as it is not prejudicial to the peace, good order or security of the coastal State. Such passage shall take place in conformity with these articles and with other rules of international law.

The question, then, for Danish authorities having the role of "coastal state" was whether one could deny passage to East bloc ships if access to Berlin was blocked by the Soviets or by East Germany? The above paragraph opened the possibility to stop and search ships that were in disregard of laws of the coastal state or threatened its security, but not on the basis of motives of any other character.

The convention also stated that innocent passage was allowed for passage of warships if the strait connected two international waters – which is the case for the Danish straits. Interestingly enough, this rule was supported by the NATO countries four years before 1962 at a conference on the issue, but not approved by the WAPA countries. In that light, it would be difficult for Denmark to deny innocent passage for East bloc warships in the Danish narrows.

The legal adviser to NATO concluded that in actions other than surveillance, the coastal states would have to determine for their territorial waters what rules

---

28 NATO Archives: Note by the legal adviser, Annex I to Cj(63)43, 18-2-63.
29 NATO Archives: Danish Delegation to NATO: Comments on the note of the Legal Adviser, file no 105 I. 1a. 20-11-62.

would apply to hindrance, board and search, seizure of Soviet bloc ships and blocking access to specific areas. In most cases, it would be difficult to subsume under international law. And all four measures would be breach of international law in international waters.

One more question, however, was whether blocking access to Berlin could be regarded as action that merited reprisal. But international law forbade armed reprisal unless the security of the state was threatened directly by attack or other warlike means in which case self-defence was permitted. Unarmed reprisals then were possible, but probably unlikely to be accepted by the Eastern powers. Legal scholars disagreed on several aspects, and therefore the legal adviser concluded that it was up to each state to determine what to do regarding unarmed reprisal.

Finally, if the event could be classified as armed attack or an imminent threat of armed attack, the rules of self-defence applied, and MARCON and BERCON actions could be implemented, but only regarding the Soviet Union and East Germany as long as no other WAPA country participated. In other words, if the Berlin crisis developed into an armed incident or immediate threat against NATO, actions could be initiated as part of self-defence.

West German considerations

The problems discussed above related much to the problems of international waters. But in national waters the issue was different. The Germans would take upon them to harass WAPA vessels in the Kiel Canal and in German harbours. This was discussed with the German Ministry of Transport in December 1970.[30] Until now (1970) no plans had been issued because the harbours and the Ministry for Transport had protested against taking such roles; particularly, the officers of the harbours pointed to their duty to perform their services as good as possible, and not consciously treat any customer sloppily. But at a meeting on 8 December the following priorities had been set up to hinder WAPA vessels from coming forward: not yielding or postponing pilot services; holding back the vessels in harbours in the canal; and holding back the vessels in the entrance harbours to the canal. These measures should be selective, i.e. used against single, selected WAPA vessels.

---

30 Fü S III 2 and Fü S III. Maritime Gegenmassnahmen der Viermächte. LO TgbNr L 1724/70 Geheim. 10-12-70 App 9218. BW 71/6.

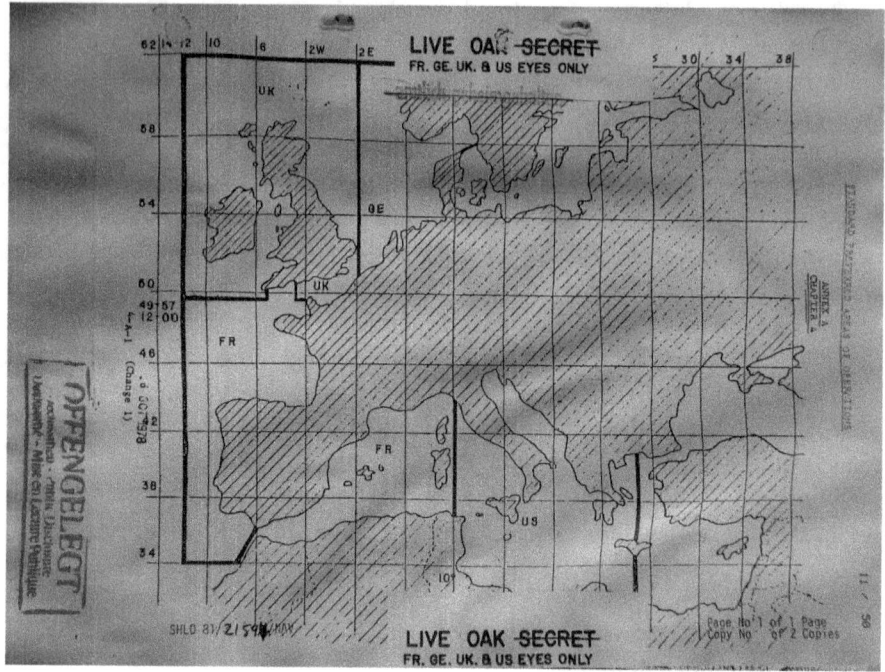

Figure 11.2: Map of division of labour between Germany, Great Britain, France and the USA in Live Oak Maritime Countermeasures in European Waters. Source: Bundeswehr Archiv Freiburg.

The Ministry for Transport pointed out that this only could be implemented if one was sure that the large competitors (Rotterdam, Antwerpen) did the same; if not, the competition among the large harbours would leave the Germans behind.

The Ministry of Defence concluded that the implementation appeared to come closer, but one could not be sure that all problems perceived by the Ministry of Transport had been solved.

Regarding maritime countermeasures at sea, the top commanders of the navy had sealed orders of what to do when necessary in the Baltic and the North Sea.[31] Most of the initial measures we saw above were, however, at odds with international law, so what remained as legal actions were at various degrees of reconnaissance and surveillance of WAPA ships, and shadowing WAPA vessels – merchant or naval – in such ways that they were not harassed. Furthermore, naval exercises could be held to indicate dissatisfaction with the actions of the

---

31 German Delegation LIVE OAK TgbNr 576/80 Secret. German National Plans for Maritime Countermeasures. 15-10-80. BW 71/10.

adversary. The German naval leadership shared this perception of legal possibilities on the high sea.[32]

AFNORTH implementation of BERCON

The regional NATO Commands were to implement the general plan. Three years later (!) AFNORTH was ready with the measures for navy and aircraft actions as well as some precautions by army forces:[33]

COMBALTAP:
- Increase the readiness of forces to meet and halt enemy incursion at the Elbe/Trave Canal
- Be prepared to deploy German forces in Schleswig-Holstein to their battle positions based on the Elbe-Trave Canal
- Be prepared to reinforce Bornholm with one Danish reinforced battalion from Zealand

COMNAVBALTAP:
- Deploy naval units to their war stations
- Be prepared to execute the signalled parts of BERCON DELTA
- Be prepared to conduct naval air operations in support of naval operations.

COMAIRBALTAP:
- Provide early warning information (according to the Joint Emergency Defence Plan Northern Europe)
- Be prepared to conduct air defence of your area
- Increase the readiness of air forces and be prepared to execute regional air tasks on order, to include reconnaissance missions and surveillance of East Bloc shipping
- Coordinating and organising training and equipping earmarked air forces to facilitate the effective wartime employment
- Participate with other commanders in the preparation of co-ordinated joint tactical operations plans pursuant of this plan.

---

32 Comments by the Federal Ministry of Defence 20-10-81. Secret. Annex A to GLNO, Az: 02-20-20-10, TgbNr: 458/82, dated 24-9-82. BW 71/12.
33 YHM Notat om AFNORTHs Berlin Contingency Support Plan. Forsvarsministeriet 11. kontor 19-1-66 905-1/66.

For the army and the air force, these preparations were mainly types of vigilance; but the air force had to be active in recce. The COMNAVBALTAP preparations were those closest to real action. But CINCNORTH commented (to SACEUR) that his naval units did not have the desired strength, and therefore he could not recommend using the whole range of possible naval interventions. He would be able to perform the first two – to shadow designated Soviet bloc merchant ships and as a step up also shadow warships in designated areas. But regarding the remaining four actions he could hardly hinder and annoy ships, board merchant ships, seize merchant ships and establish blockade or enforce diversion and exclusion of Soviet bloc ships from specific areas. Most of it would require more naval forces. CINCNORTH saw the plan as risky because he did not have sufficient forces to handle neither small incidents nor larger attacks in Northern Norway, Schleswig-Holstein or Bornholm.

The Danish C-in-C endorsed CINCNORTH's comments and added, first, that the opinion of the Danish government was that almost any intervention towards Soviet ships would be considered *casus belli* by the Soviets, and second, that transferring an army battalion to Bornholm required approval from the Danish government.

An American desk analysis of some BERCON measures concluded that purely conventional operations would most likely fail, and thus nuclear weapons would have to be used in conjunction with ground operations.[34]

The BERCON plans were never used for real in the Baltic Approaches.

And the Warsaw pact?

NATO, then, planned a number of answers to imagined steps by the Warsaw pact. What did the war planners in the East prepare for? We have no knowledge of any specific plans, but in the early fall of 1961, Exercise Buria was carried through to test what might be done, if a confrontation became a reality.

Buria took place between September 29 and October 10, 1961, shortly after the building of the Berlin wall.[35] The exercise rehearsed the actions of the Unified Armed Forces (the Warsaw pact) in the Western European theatre of war in the event of an all-out nuclear war. It was a command post exercise with a number

---

34 Ibid., 124–25.
35 Uhl, Matthias. "Storming on to Paris. The 1961 Buria Exercise and the Planned Solution of the Berlin Crisis." In *War Plans and Alliances in the Cold War. Threat Perceptions in the East and West.*, Vojtech Mastny, Sven G. Holtsmark, and Andreas (eds) Wenger, 46–71. London: Routledge, 2006.

of field tactical components added, among these the crossing of rivers and landing operations.

In the exercise, the East Germans closed all checkpoints and prohibited Allied aircraft from using the air corridors to West Berlin. Attempts by the Western Allies to re-open access to West Berlin using military force locally escalated into the use of nuclear missiles as of midday on October 6. Ten days later the Warsaw pact entered Paris.

We shall restrict our narrative to the Baltic Approaches. On day two of the attack the fiftieth Polish Army received orders to occupy Schleswig-Holstein and to push through the Jutland Peninsula into Denmark. At the same time, two Polish divisions undertook air and marine landings on the Danish island of Falster. Airborne troops also occupied the strategically important bridge at Nykøbing and thus safeguarded the advance toward the island of Zealand. On the fifth day, the forces of the Coastal and Western Fronts occupied the northern part of the Jutland Peninsula and Zealand, and thus the Baltic Approaches were lost for NATO.

So the job was well done. The East, however, learned some lessons which were quite severe:[36]

- problems of mobilisation, transportation and logistical support of the advance of such large numbers of troops were still completely unresolved,
- considerable weaknesses and flaws in the combat training and control of the forces involved were revealed,
- communications between neighbouring fronts and armies could be established only with very great difficulty, and they were repeatedly interrupted. Thus, no coordinated combat command was possible; the national commanders hardly knew what was going on in the adjacent front sections,
- language problems were the main reason for these communication problems, in addition to faulty communication technology. Only very few East German commanders were able to hold conversations with Soviet or Polish general staffs without interpreters.

The troops deployed in the exercise therefore hardly corresponded to the Soviet idea of unified forces.

Seen from the perspective of the Berlin crisis, the reaction of the Warsaw pact to a military aggression from NATO in the transport corridors was obvious: it would end with an all-out war. Fortunately it was only an exercise, but the problems summarised above may have been instrumental for Khrushchev and the Soviet Union not carrying through the separate signing of a peace treaty with East Germany.

---

36 Ibid., 58.

Summing up: Close to a stalemate

The Berlin crisis of the Summer 1961 followed a verbal attack from the Soviet leadership regarding a separate peace treaty with East Germany. This was probably to test the new presidency of the USA. The American response was firm, and NATO countries were called upon to prepare for action, if necessary. Denmark and Germany both analysed their forces. Denmark did not show the capabilities desired by SACEUR and got a list of ways to better the military preparation. But Denmark did not have the financial means to follow this up. Germany, on the other hand, nearly performed as desired according to the plans. The Berlin wall was built mid-August 1961 to stop the exodus from the East to the West. But, by itself, this was not a NATO issue.

NATO developed a plan, BERCON, to counter future Berlin aggressions. It was quite comprehensive, particularly regarding the air forces, but since the Baltic Approaches could have been affected by what happened on the plains of Northern Germany, there was a naval component as part of it, affecting the Danish as well as the German navy. It mainly contained measures of harassing merchant ships, from hindrance of passage to seizing them. But international law turned out to be a strong barrier against most of the interventions, particularly for the Danes for whom it was difficult to declare that actions around Berlin threatened Danish authority.

Both the Americans and the Warsaw Pact tested their plans in a simulation and a command post exercise, respectively. None of them bore promise. The West plan concluded that aggression only could be held at bay by nuclear warheads, and this might end in an all-out nuclear exchange. The WAPA exercise succeeded on the formal level, but in reality it cast serious doubt about the capacity of the various military leaderships to cooperate because of language difficulties.

So one may say that the two parties kept one another in a deadlock. Neither dared take a step that would initiate an armed confrontation.

Chapter 12
Making BALTAP operational: Organising for WAPA threats

Unlike AFNORTH in 1951–52, BALTAP did not start in an empty strategic space. Various NATO commanders had been working on emergency and contingency plans since 1950, and the Germans in particular had spent much time on producing military concepts and plans for the new Bundeswehr. From a NATO-perspective, the working group in Holtenau had started naval planning already in 1957.

The NATO strategy at the time of BALTAP's initiation was heavily dependent on nuclear weapons. SACEUR Norstad presented the general picture at a meeting with the German Bundespräsident on July 12, 1962.[1] NATO's aim was to let the traditional war be history. The US Strategic Air Command and the British Bomber Command were key. If the Soviet Union wanted to provoke a general war, those two commands would initiate a series of attacks to destroy everything vital in the USSR. The Soviets knew this because the USA had made public technical information about the atomic weapons intended to be used and their power, if exploded. NATO's response to nearly any attack would be of a magnitude close to general war. Therefore, the former demands for a large number of army divisions in Europe were now reduced; about 30 divisions would suffice today, if they were located at the right spots; they could easily meet an enemy trying out NATO's resolve, and the nuclear forces were ready to attack if it turned out that the Soviets really wanted to wage war. The issue, then, was how to balance nuclear capacity with conventional strength, and this was what NATO's planning was about.

In this chapter, we shall go through the threats from the Warsaw Pact, as perceived by various branches of NATO: the Standing Group and the Danish Intelligence Office, and – although our main interest is NATO perceptions – we season those views with a Polish plan for attacking the Baltic Approaches. Then follows a discussion of NATO's state of preparedness as reported in the Annual Review and the Combat Effectiveness Reports. A possible partner, Sweden, had reorganised its defence in 1958, and the Germans analysed it in depth. We finish the chapter by discussing how the BALTAP command was set up and the perceptions of strategy there, and a brief analysis of the changed roles of the Swedish defence in the Baltic.

---

1 BW 2/53917 Norstad 1960–62, minutes 115–77.A/62.

https://doi.org/10.1515/9783111235752-012

The threat picture: SG 161, Danish intelligence and a Polish plan

What were the risks for a Soviet attack in the first years of BALTAP? We have in previous chapters used the SG 161 reports for the outlook of NATO. We have also seen reports from the Danish Intelligence Office. Finally, a Polish exercise plan from 1970 indicates what might have been the case, it the WAPA attacked.

SG 161/15

In 1962, the SG 161/15 report updated the risks of a Soviet-led attack. This 1962 issue was shorter in the military sections than the 1957 version due to strict editing in a format giving the main issues only a brief description, and due to the fact that the sections on campaigns were abbreviated: from 50 pages to 12. On the other hand, more details about different weapons and their platforms were given under a general description of the army, navy and air force, respectively. Special attention was given to various missiles. Thus the report was more like a catalogue of the capabilities of the forces while their use in campaigns was more up to the reader to deduce.

As before, the Standing Group's main interest regarding Scandinavia was not the Baltic Approaches, but Norway. Campaigns to seize Norway could be launched directly from northwestern USSR, through Finland, and from west central Europe through Denmark and the Baltic Approaches. However, a campaign against southern Norway probably would not be initiated until Soviet forces controlled Denmark. Soviet forces would probably prefer to start with a campaign in Northern Norway.

The Standing Group stated that the USSR would seek to seize the Baltic Sea exits immediately. But then the special NATO interest in Norway came back in the report: how the Soviets might take Norway through Denmark. The campaign in Norway would probably be continued until the forces advancing over land from the north had merged with those coming from the south.

The Soviet leaders might estimate that they could gain their main objectives in this campaign without violating Swedish neutrality. However, they could, if necessary, gain control of the eastern Baltic exits by occupying the part of Sweden adjacent to the Strait of Øresund. If Sweden were forced by Soviet pressure to allow passage of Soviet troops, this would facilitate attacks on Norway. If the Soviets moved against Sweden, as many as six additional divisions could be employed across Finland and four across the Baltic Sea.

Regarding the navy, the Soviets had recently added new classes of missile-firing FPBs to the surface fleet; they were particularly suitable for operations in the Baltic. Amphibious forces were being modernised. Polish and East German naval forces could augment the Soviet Baltic Fleet.

Naval and naval air units would be used in defence of Soviet and satellite shipping, sea lanes and coastal targets, against Allied surface and submarine forces, in the support of amphibious landings, and for flank support of ground forces. These forces could break out into the open sea, if the straits came under Soviet control, but there is some ambiguity in the report, especially the second part which lets the Soviet Baltic navy concentrate on protecting one's own forces and laying mines to bother NATO pushing forward – rather than attacking the Baltic Approaches. But on the other hand, a section on attacks against Western Europe opens the possibility of a rapid take-over of the Baltic exits and Denmark.

All options were thus open.

A Danish report

In May 1965, the Danish Intelligence Bureau presented a highly classified analysis of the threat against Denmark[2] at a conference held by AFNORTH in Oslo, and the report formed the basis for subsequent updates of the threat picture, published in Danish until 1988. This was the first comprehensive analysis, combining existing knowledge of all WAPA forces. The study was made under the assumptions that conventional war would be most likely, possibly with the use of tactical nuclear weapons, and that Sweden maintained its neutrality. The Soviet Union's goals would be: annihilation of NATO's nuclear forces and neutralisation of NATO's vital industrial production areas by using strategic missiles, bombers and naval vessels; defeat of NATO's conventional forces by WAPA conventional forces on land, at sea and in the air; and a cut-off of Western Europe from the USA by use of WAPA naval forces from Northern Russia and possibly the Baltic Sea.

The military strength of the WAPA ground forces was considerable, but of course, not all forces were expected to be used against Denmark. The armies of Russia, Poland and East Germany altogether had 29 motorised infantry divisions, 20 armoured divisions and six airborne divisions in the area of the Baltic and Central Europe. Of these, up to three Soviet divisions might be initially used to secure the Northern flank in the Cimbric Peninsula. Alternatively, five Polish divisions could be used for attacking Schleswig-Holstein and afterwards Jutland; a few East German divisions might be used to follow up. Some Soviet units from the Baltic Area might be used against Denmark, but three regiments from the marines were

---

2 Forsvarets Efterretningstjeneste: Truslen mod Danmark. YHM.

probably the first wave to be landed by amphibious vessels on Zealand, possibly together with two Polish marine regiments. Alternatively, a reduced Soviet division might be landed, later to be reinforced by a division transported by ordinary merchant ships. Two to three airborne Soviet regiments could be used against Zealand and Jutland, depending on the availability of transport airplanes.

The size of the combined navies also was considerable. Three cruisers and 21 destroyers (three with sea missiles) were organised in two brigades and constituted the main force, supported by 49 FPBs with sea missiles and 146 MTBs. Seventy submarines were mostly somewhat old and were not considered fit to operate West of Bornholm (shallow waters) except for recce, landing special forces and the like. A total of 129 ASW vessels were considered to be less efficient than their Western counterparts, but still they could be serious adversaries in the Baltic Sea. Some 282 mine sweepers were thought to be no more efficient than during WWII.

The Baltic fleet had 96 landing craft available which were considered seaworthy. However, there had been no landing exercises since 1957, so several months of training would be necessary to put those forces up to date. The existing force would be able to transport a reduced motorised division of 5,000 men with 112 tanks and 194 armoured personnel carriers, 120 other vehicles and 36 guns.

The combined air forces also had large numbers: 600 fighter-bombers, 290 bombers, 1,565 fighters and 315 recce, but only 140 fighter-bombers and 60 recce airplanes, all Polish, were considered likely to be used against the Baltic Approaches, depending on the nature of the attack operations on the ground.

However, there were also about 940 transport airplanes which could bring in paratroopers; 380 helicopters which could transport any type of force, but within short distances. Again, most military units were supposed to be occupied with other tasks, and a maximum of three Soviet regiments, one Polish and one East German battalion were foreseen to be available, possibly in South Jutland.

The Soviet Union finally had a large number of strategic missiles, but given the fact that the Danish analysis did not presume any use of strategic weapons, they were not discussed in any detail.

The analysis informed the reader about what beaches on the Zealand islands were considered favourable for the landing of enemy amphibious forces. See the map.

The capacities of the most likely beaches were: on Møn, Falster and Lolland the "fighting element" of one regiment, on Stevns of two regiments and on West Zealand a motorised infantry division (but the navigation to this area was complicated). Furthermore, the Zealand islands fwere well suited for dropping paratroopers. The report had the beaches around Stevns as the most likely ones to be attacked due to capacity and location – the attacking forces could cross the island, split the defence forces into two and take over important harbours in the southern

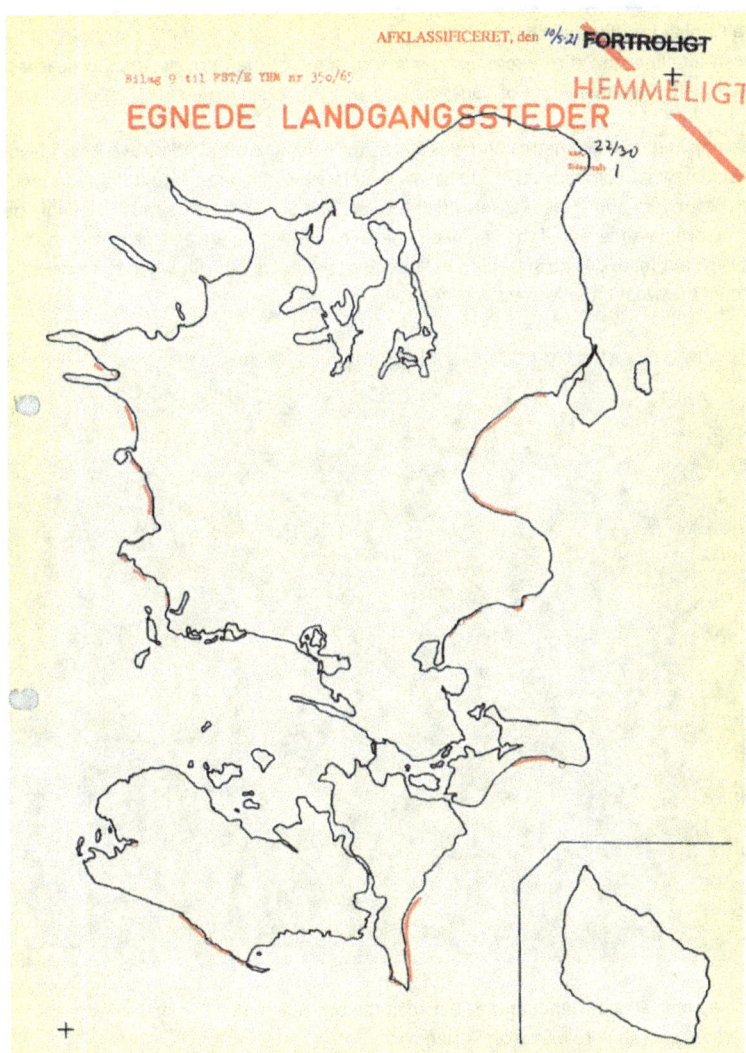

Figure 12.1: This map from the Danish Intelligence report indicates the possible landing beaches with red. This information remained classified until May 2021.

part. But the report foresaw landing on several beaches in order to spread the forces and reduce the risk of nuclear counterattack.

Description of a Danish landing beach

In 1966 the Danish Intelligence Office wrote an overview of some of the possible landing beaches. Below is the description of an area South of Køge:[3]

> The beach comprised five kilometres and was suited for landing craft all the way. Access from the sea was somewhat complicated, and shallow waters NE of the area would limit manoeuvrability for destroyers and larger vessels off the coast. The Stevns fortress must probably be neutralized before passage, and if the planned mine fields in the area were actually laid, considerable losses would follow. Mine sweeping in Køge Bugt would be difficult while mine fields at Falsterbo could be swept if the fortress was neutralized.

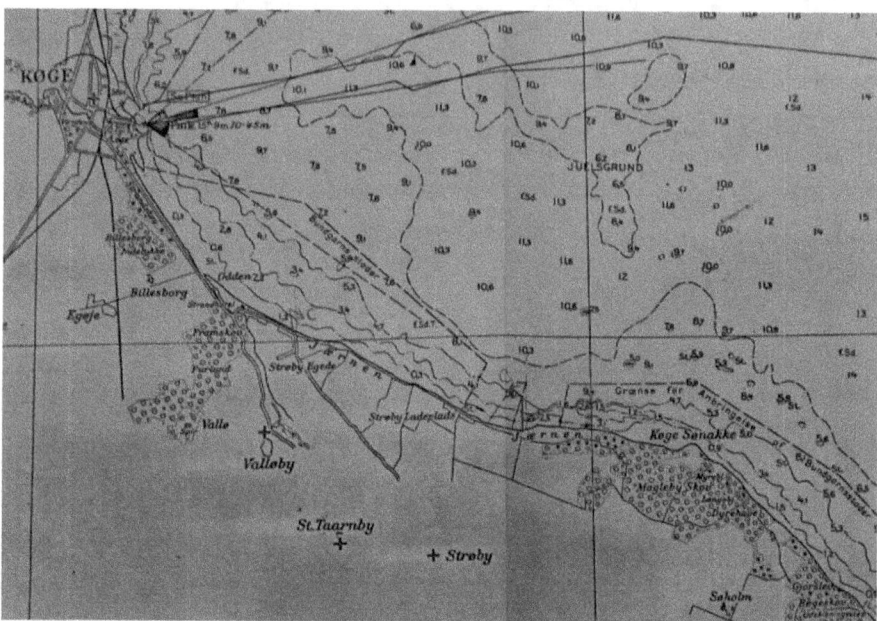

Figure 12.2: The map indicates the landing area between the two red marks. The shallow water is the Juelsgrund north east of the area. Source: Rigsarkivet.

Soviet doctrine demanded two kilometres between landing parties, permitting two landing points on this beach, each for one battalion transported in four to eight relatively large landing craft in order to reduce the size of the landing area. If the whole beach were taken in use, about 25 amphibious craft could land there simultaneously. But this would eliminate the demand for distance between landing parties and increase vulnerability. The maximum landing would therefore be one regiment.

---

3 Bedømmelse af visse sjællandske kyststrækninger. HEM. 359/67. 6-4-67. Forsvarets Efterretningstjeneste: KC. Kopibog med bilag (afklass.) (1947–1967) 24.

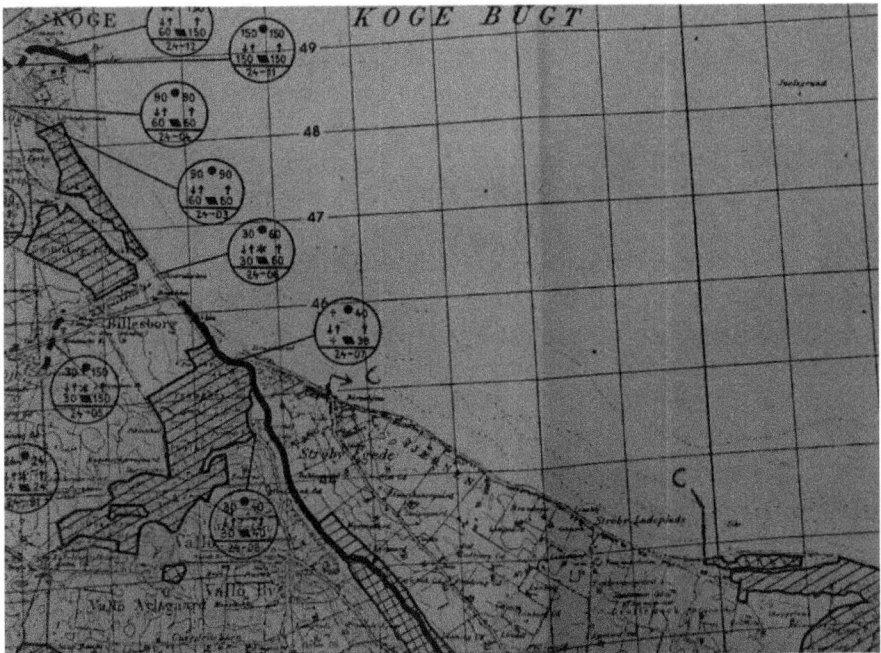

Figure 12.3: The map indicates problem areas when continuing from the beach inland towards Køge: A stream (full black line) cannot be crossed by tanks, and the road bridges have weight limits (e.g. 30 tons for tanks and 40 tons for wheel vehicles) for passage. The semi-crossed areas are areas difficult to pass, those crossed are impassable, and the dotted black line indicates a creek difficult to pass. Source: Rigsarkivet.

The rest of the Danish report discussed the ways an amphibious attack might be played out, starting from the harbours close to the island Rügen in East Germany; they had considerable capacity for goods and there were many inlets close by enabling landing craft to lay up, presumably hidden for recce airplanes. But there were also many other possibilities along the Baltic coast. Airborne operations could be initiated from airfields on the Baltic coast.

The report had two scenarios for attacks. The first was based on "maximum surprise" on day one of hostilities, meaning that airborne forces could land no later than 30 minutes after radar detection, and amphibious forces had to be ready to land within six to eight hours after leaving their own harbour. Denmark had one mobile brigade ready on very short notice to defend Zealand; therefore a sizeable enemy force would be necessary: one motorised reduced infantry brigade to be landed on South East or East Zealand and to be followed by two marine battalions with helicopters; up to two airborne regiments, one for securing the bridge head, one for the airfield of Værløse and to cut off Danish forces in North Zealand from moving south. Over the following days, more forces would land. The operations depended on Soviet air supremacy and direct support from air, ships and missiles.

The second scenario played out an attack later than (in central Europe) D-day plus two; then Denmark would have mobilised its war forces, now having three brigades on Zealand. In that case, the enemy had to land one motorised infantry division reinforced by two marine battalions and a reduced airborne division (role as above). No later than two days after, another motorised division would have to land to participate in defeating the defending forces; possibly more forces would also have to be brought in.

In all cases key NATO military points would be sought neutralised, and the laying of NATO minefields would be opposed. Small reconnaissance groups would probably be landed from submarines, and air supremacy attempted. Mine sweeping would be necessary before landing craft were set in; gun support would come from larger units, and tactical air support from the air force. When a bridge head was established, the enemy navies would have to support LOCs.

The report also dealt with an attack on Jutland, but with little detail; the operation would start in Schleswig-Holstein to safeguard the Northern flank of the forces in Central Europe, and then develop – according to the degree of success to the south – with several divisions.

The main points of the Danish report dealt with enemy army forces, their possible landing spots, their equipment and the means and capacities for transporting them by air or by sea. So it was a study of overall military capacities of the WAPA and the possible sub-allocations to an attack force on Denmark, including the need for landing craft and transport airplanes. Aspects of the transports themselves like naval escorts, air support, bombardment, mine clearing etc. were not covered, which came up in subsequent editions. It was indicated that air support was to be delivered by the Polish air force with up to 200 airplanes.

In another report we find a discussion of the possible support from the Polish and East German navies.[4] First, they would be used for denying NATO forces access to attacking the Baltic bases. Thus the Soviet Baltic flank was secured. The navies were capable of mining own approaches and patrolling the area. Second, they would be part of forces trying to control the Baltic Approaches, e.g. by disrupting Danish mine laying in Storebælt (East German MTBs and Missile FPBs)

---

4 Capabilities of Baltic Satellite Naval Forces to Conduct Independent Operations and Their Likely Employment in Support of Soviet Naval Operations. HEM. Forsvarsstaben n.d. 1964, 203.155, presented at NATO Naval and Naval Air Intelligence Conference 1964.

and in Øresund (Polish MTBs). If a landing operation was conducted, Polish and East German landing craft would be important, their patrol boats could perform escorting duties and their mine sweepers could clear the mines at the landing areas, being given air superiority. The small landing craft would also be suitable for landing smaller parties anywhere in the Baltic and Danish waters.

A polish plan for attacking the Baltic Approaches

Did the Danish assessments square with WAPA plans? We do not know for sure, but various sources[5] and a Polish exercise plan from 1970 indicates what they would have liked to do at that time, if not what they would actually do. The exercises *Priliv*, *Taifun* and *Baltik* were examples in the period 1963–70. The purposes were the same regarding naval actions: to conquer the territories at the Baltic Approaches and the Kiel Canal to secure free access to the North Sea and the Atlantic. Storebælt and Lillebælt were to be taken by East German forces, Øresund by Soviet forces.

The plans always started with a NATO attack eastwards; this was brought to a halt, and a counter offensive set in. All three WAPA navies took part in landing forces on Danish soil; in addition, paratroopers were landed. The East German navy landed forces on Fehmarn and in the Bay of Kiel to support WAPA land forces moving westwards. NATO submarines were attacked in the eastern Baltic. Missile units were used in the Bay of Kiel and the entrances to the Danish Straits to hit mine layers and NATO missile units. NATO FPBs and larger units were attacked by WAPA naval arm fighter-bombers in the German Bay, Kattegat and Skagerrak. If the attacks went well, the Kiel Canal would be conquered and used for passage to the North Sea.

In preparation for the attacks against the islands, the forces were to be gathered in the harbours of the South-East Baltic, to be sailed to the landing areas by night. First, the Poles were to neutralise the airfield of Bornholm, the communication centre on the island and the listening station on the Southern part by fighter-bombers. Other WAPA air forces were to crush a number of Danish and West

---

5 Gemzell, Carl-Axel. "Warszawapakten, DDR och Danmark. Kampen för en maritim operationsplan." *Historisk Tidsskrift* 16, no. 5 (1996): 32–84; Jensen, Frede P. "The Warsaw Pact's Special Target. Planning the Seizure of Denmark." In *War Plans and Alliances in the Cold War. Threat Perceptions in the East and West.*, eds Vojtech Mastny, Sven G. Holtsmark, and Andreas Wenger, 95–117. London: Routledge, 2006; Diedrich, Torsten. "Die DDR-Marine in den Vereinten Seestreitkräften des Warschauer Paktes und das Operationsgebiet Ostsee." In *OSTSEE. Kriegsschauplatz und Handelsregion. Festschrift für Robert Bohn*, Thomas W. Friis and Michael F Scholz. Gotland: Gotland University Press, 2013.

German airfields together with radar stations and air missile batteries on Zealand and Bornholm. In the subsequent days, NATO ships were to be destroyed up to a line in the Southern Kattegat, and thus sea power would be obtained in the Baltic, and LOCs for own forces be secured.

Now followed the landing of forces; first paratroopers, then amphibious forces in two waves, altogether about 20,000 men, including the seventh Polich marine division, a polish infantry division and a Soviet marine infantry regiment.

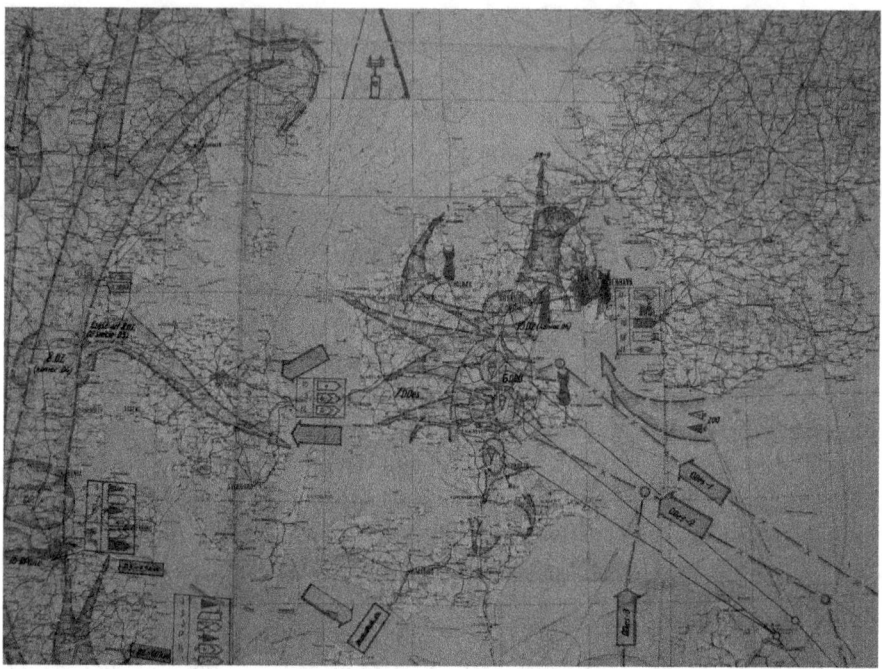

Figure 12.4: This is an excerpt of a major Polish plan for attacking Northern Europe from about 1970. Blue indicates NATO forces, red WAPA forces. Forces were to be landed in the Bays of Køge and Faxe, and paratroopers were to land on southern and mid-Zealand. The German navy was to be locked in by means of a minefield in the Strait of Fehmarn. The contents of the red bombs are not difficult to guess. Source: http://www.imagebam.com/image/1d97f288581520.

The East German navy had a particular role on the southern Danish islands: to take the Harbour of Gedser and secure the bridge connecting the two islands. They would start out from Warnemünde and sail in different directions to avoid detection, and a mock manoeuvre would indicate a landing on the eastern coast of Falster. Instead, they would use the ferry to Gedser: at 03.00 frogmen would be landed from an amphibious craft to neutralise the radar station at Gedser and to disarm the minefields at the harbour; at 04.45 a group of FPBs would enter the harbour to take the ferry terminal, and at 05.00 the ferry would call and its troops sent ashore. At the same time four helicopters were to land commando forces at the bridge, and then the forces could take the whole area, starting from Gedser.

In some plans Bornholm was excluded apart from a bombing of the military key points. In 1967, Polish forces did an exercise with paratroopers (simulated to land mid-island), followed by amphibious landing of forces at four beaches on the south–eastern island.

The islands would be conquered after 10 days, and the ports of Copenhagen, Helsingør and Korsør could now be used by WAPA ships. Jutland would be taken after 11 days, its southern border crossed after control had been achieved over the Kiel Canal and military key points. Fyn would be taken by crossing the bridge to Jutland or by amphibious landings performed by the East German navy. The coastal fort would be taken by East German special forces.

Nuclear weapons were part of WAPA exercises on the premise that NATO would be first user. In the exercise Woge (1964) the East German forces had 2 x 50 KT, 2 x 30 KT, 2 x 20 KT and 3 x 10 KT – all in all nine bombs – for taking Lolland, Falster and for defending Rügen. But one should realise that first all nuclear weapons were under Soviet command and control, and it seems that use would be in response, not as first mover.[6] The illustrative Polish plan above therefore presupposes Soviet approval, and we do not know whether this was the case.

Status 1962: Annual review and combat effectiveness

By the early 1960s, the procedure to be followed for the Annual Review had become quite cumbersome. Too complicated, and seeking to address too many questions in detail, the Annual Review no longer fully met the goal assigned it. So new ways were sought. The 1962 Combat Effectiveness Report, on the other hand, had reached a format that was repeated year after year, measuring the ability of each unit to perform its assigned role within the Emergency Defence Plan of the region.

---

6 Dansk Institut for Internationale Studier. *Danmark under den kolde krig. Den sikkerhedspolitiske situation 1945–1991. Bind 2: 1963–1978*, 601. København: Dansk Institut for Internationale Studier, 2005b.

Annual review

The Review had proved inadequate as a means of pressure in the case of serious divergence between the requirements of NATO military authorities and the actual force contributions of member states. Beginning in 1959, some nations questioned its effectiveness. In January 1960, the Council tasked a Steering Group (AC/159) to make the Annual Review both simpler and more effective. The Group proposed that the Review be carried out every three years to reassess the defence programmes of the nations in the light of NATO's overall requirements. Because of various circumstances, this triennial procedure was never fully implemented. Under the new procedure, instead of focusing on the situation in each country, a horizontal approach to the consideration of problems was adopted. The Annual Review Committee was replaced by the Defence Review Committee in 1967.

The 1962 Triennial Review (MC 19/14) was rather brief. It lacked the previous quite detailed analyses and mainly contained, first, shortcomings of the defence and, second, recommendations for improvement. These ideas, then, were unsubstantiated by data.

The general conclusion of the Triennial Review was that

> ... the military posture of the Alliance in general will remain inadequate to ensure fulfilment of the Major NATO Commanders' missions. Thus, the contribution of NATO forces to the whole spectrum of deterrence cannot be considered fully effective.

For the Northern part of Europe and the Baltic Approaches the forces would only have "limited capability of carrying out their mission" because of shortages in units, personnel, obsolescent equipment and delays in modernisation. Support for ground forces was also inadequate.

The Review made it clear that unless the member countries increased their defence efforts considerably, the most serious deficiencies could not be overcome, and the NATO strategy would come into jeopardy.

Denmark

The main Danish shortcomings were (SGM 564–62):
- vulnerability of the air force to surprise attacks (aircraft were concentrated on three airfields), low rates of crew and aircraft readiness and shortfall in fighter bombers and recce aircraft;
- lack of arrangements for nuclear weapons;
- disregard of SACEUR's recommendations for deployment of forces;
- low manning and lack of technicians and regulars in air force and navy;

- shortfall of ships allocated to SACEUR and inadequate ASW capabilities;
- shortage of ammunition in army and navy units

In short, the Danish armed forces would have a limited capability to carry out their assigned missions. The recommendations were logical: get equipment and supplies as necessary; hire the necessary qualified personnel; provide better training for air crews; re-allocate units as SACEUR wished. And not least: introduce nuclear weapons in the army and air force.

The nuclear recommendation, of course, was impossible to follow due to the policy of the Danish government, and the other recommendations required a boost of the Danish defence budget that was quite unlikely.

West Germany
The German shortcomings were (SGM 606–62):
- vulnerability of air force units and their command and control systems by surprise attack;
- critical shortage of personnel of all kinds but conscripts;
- delays in providing strike units and low flying times for air crews;
- inadequate training areas for the army and some shortage of equipment and supplies.

So the army and air force had only moderate, and the navy limited, capability to carry our their assigned missions. The recommendations for the defence were to secure the air force's survivability, increase flying hours and improve maintenance systems; acquire nuclear strike capability according to plans; fulfil plans for 12 divisions and four brigades; expedite building of ships, aircraft and helicopters for the navy; improve overall manning levels; and increase stocks of all kinds.

Combat effectiveness

The report graded the countries according to quality.

The main army components were: personnel composition, equipment quality, ability to react, and training level. In 1957 the grades were A to D, in 1962 they were (Roman figures) I to IV, I being effective, IV being non-operational.

Navy components were the various types of ships: destroyers, escorts, submarines etc., graded (I to IV) as an evaluation of their effectiveness in factors like personnel, training, logistics and material.

Air force component descriptions were very comprehensive, probably reflecting the weight put by SACEUR on air force defence in Europe. Aircraft squadrons were graded on ten factors like manning, aircrew/aircraft ration, flying hours, aircraft capability and unit equipment. Missile units (three kinds: SSM, IRBM and SAM) were graded on seven factors like manning, missiles being operational and launch crews being operational. Finally the control systems were evaluated (grades I to IV) on material, hours of operation, operational capability and more.

Denmark

The tables (SHAPE 43/63 17–8–63) for the army's groups indicated their effectiveness in 1961 and 1962, most of them in category III, a few in category IV. Interestingly, the table lists "Ground nuclear delivery units" – they were in category II in 1961, but in category in IV in 1962 due to the Danish ban on nuclear war heads. Apparently SACEUR still believed that they might become operational in 1961.

It was estimated that the two brigades were required to be ready by mobilisation day, and that two further brigades would be ready one day after. But distance between their peacetime location and operational deployment areas in Jutland would result in a considerable time lag before they were ready for battle. Support organisation was adequate, but some needed more training to become operational. One nuclear battery was on Zealand and two in Jutland. Material required for mobilisation was adequate, but reserves were unbalanced with some serious deficiencies. There was a lack of large training areas. Army organisation was under change to meet NATO standards.

In conclusion, there was a lack of modern equipment, particularly in signal services, lack of nuclear capability, shortage of specialists and NCOs, lack of suitable training areas and too long a distance from peacetime locations to planned war positions. In sum, the Danish land forces were only moderately effective (grade III).

The tables for the Danish navy showed the units ready by mobilisation day, and those to be mobilised later. The actual numbers were low (e.g. one coastal escort where the 1962 goals were two and the 1966 goals three). The one operational was in category II. The active units were in categories II and III, but the units to be mobilised were but one (a submarine) in the non-operational category.

The problems for the Danish navy were: shortage of regular personnel, lack of personnel to man units to be mobilised, short conscript service time and lack of an immediate modernisation programme. Things would change after 1964, though. In 1962, there were fewer units in service than stipulated.

In sum, the capability of the Danish navy was very limited.

The Danish air force did not fare much better, two squadrons were placed in category II, two in III, and three in IV. SAM was category II.

A significant improvement in early warning had been achieved during the year by the activation of the high powered NATO early warning radar at Bornholm. The rest of the warning system in Denmark was voice manual and relied on a relatively obsolete radar system. Therefore, only limited effectiveness could be expected in the control of fighters. A new command and control site had been set up in Vedbæk. There was, however, a shortage of controllers, and the system was put in category III.

The overall manning of aircraft was 80 per cent with shortage in officers, NCOs and technicians. The air force had taken over the SAM system from the army and had a shortage of personnel. Aircraft readiness had been below standards due to shortage of supplies and maintenance. Aircrew combat readiness was low due to lacking training facilities for gunnery and too few flying hours for pilots. Survival by surprise attack was at risk due to concentration of aircraft on three airfields although three more were ready to take over. Finally, no nuclear capacity was present due to national defence policy principles.

All in all, the war capacity of the Danish air force was limited.

Germany

The combat effectiveness of the German army was a mix of grade II and III. Since only one out of 12 divisions was placed in the Baltic Approaches and since that division cannot be distinguished from the tables, we shall not go into detail with its effectiveness. In general, there was a shortage of specialists and NCOs. The major combat formations were close to their war positions. Some equipment was still inadequate. In particular, the division in the Baltic Approaches lacked supplies. Large training areas were lacking. There was a lack of nuclear capability in the greater part of the ground nuclear delivery units. A modernisation programme was being prepared. In sum, the German army was moderately effective.

The effectiveness of the German navy (SHAPE 43/63 17–8–63) was discussed with the knowledge that the navy was under development, and many units were planned, but not yet built – new destroyers, submarines, mine layers, amphibious vessels etc. A number of older ships were bought from other countries. The effectiveness was very uneven, from II to IV.

The crews were satisfactory in general, but there was a lack of junior officers, NCOs and technical specialists. NATO training had reached acceptable levels. Most material effectiveness in group A was low, seriously affecting the combat effectiveness. There was a serious lack of mine layers, forcing other units to lay mines when they could be more useful in their assigned roles.

In sum, the capability of the German Navy to perform its assigned missions remained limited.

The German air force was also under development. The forces relevant for the Baltic Approaches were on airfields in Husum and Leck, and those were categorised individually: Husum's fighter-bomber squadron in category III and Lecks interceptor fighters in category IV. All were lacking in manning, technicians, aircrew combat readiness, flying hours; Leck also in aircraft capability and combat readiness.

The SAM system was based on NIKE in 1962, and none of those batteries were located in Schleswig-Holstein.

The control system was part of the 2. ATAF with two control centres which were in the process of getting three-dimensional radars; however, there was a lack of personnel.

The overall score of the German air force was moderate, but as indicated above, those stationed in the Baltic Approaches only had limited capacity. In addition, they were vulnerable to a surprise attack and nuclear capability was low.

The Northern command

SACEUR set up the status of the sub-commands, and below we quote the report for the Northern Region which included the Baltic Approaches and Norway.

For the land forces, the main problem was shortage of qualified personnel and brief conscription time; nuclear warheads were available only in the German forces. M-day units could react promptly, but at a distance from their wartime locations. Those units were generally trained to an acceptable standard, but the subsequent echelons needed more training. In general equipment needed modernisation. All in all, the army forces had moderate capacity for their tasks.

Regarding the navies, the summary tables are difficult to interpret, but apparently a maximum of 50 per cent of the Danish naval forces had full or high combat potential, while 75 per cent of the German forces had so.

The air forces were based on the figures for Norway and Denmark, while Northern Germany, in spite of being part of the Northern Command, was not included. The Northern command had zero per cent category I, 17 per cent in category II, and 41 per cent in category III as well as in IV. To compare: in the Centre Region, Category I was 28 per cent, 24 per cent category II, 21 per cent category III and 10 per cent category IV. Some 17 per cent was in reserve. All in all, the Baltic Approaches did not have a high standard of its air forces.

Organizing BALTAP

BALTAP became operational in the summer of 1962. The C-in-C, COMBALTAP, always had to be Danish with a German deputy and a Danish chief of staff. The tasks for the new BALTAP command were the same as for any other command:[7] preparation of war by analysing intelligence information, making operational analyses and planning for action; analysing the state of preparedness of the forces, initiating exercises and drawing lessons learned from them; and testing doctrines for military action – all of the above in communication with the national ministries of defence and the flag officers commanding the forces.

The initiation of a new, international command took time. The first chief of staff, S. Thostrup, has told how he experienced the process.[8] The staff was located in Karup, and it was quite difficult to get suitable offices; the staff took over a building on the airfield with a promise to get war HQ in a bunker. Step by step officers were allocated from national service to the international command, and directives for the working procedures were set up together with an activity calendar. Now the task was to get acquainted with the organisations and units under the command and establish the necessary personal relations among the top officers.

The main task was to set up a war plan, the *Emergency Defence Plan* (EDP), describing what the military units were to do when necessary. The first draft plan was presented to the chief of staff by a German army officer, but the plan contained next to nothing about the defence tasks for the navies. and the tasks on land mainly concerned Schleswig-Holstein. Zealand was not considered of importance.[9] The plans were improved, but several years later the commanding general on Zealand complained that he was neglected in the distribution of forces.[10] Apparently the national way of thinking was difficult to erase.

A Danish officer has given us some examples from the planning tasks of this EDP.[11] A first example was taken from the planning of a counter attack on the WAPA forces. The staff officers thought that the enemy would move 50 kilometres forward each day through Holstein. The roads and railroads were in bad conditions, so stores

---

7 Helms, Adam. "Min tid som Commander Allied Forces Baltic Approaches 1970–75. Første del 1970–72." *Tidsskrift for Søvæsen* 176, no. 1 (2005a): 3–25.
8 Thostrup, S. S. "Chief of Staff from 9th January 1962 to 31st March 1965." In *Safeguarding Security in the Baltic Approaches 1962–2002*, Ove Høegh-Guldberg Hoff, 11–38. Viborg: Public Information Office Joint Headquarters NORTHEAST, 2002.
9 Ibid., 20–21.
10 Ibid., 35.
11 Rodholm, Immanuel Benedict. *Mine 48 År i Forsvaret*, 86–87. København: Marinens Bibliotek, 2009.

would probably come by ship to the harbour of Rostock which was a good harbour. Therefore, NATO had to destroy the cranes on the harbour by frogmen delivered by the amphibious forces of the German navy or, preferably, by low-altitude aircraft attacks from the German navy's air force. Its dedication to the navy was important because such capacity might be difficult to get from the German air force proper.

Another example was the deployment of troops in Denmark with its many islands. The army had no capacity, and the amphibious craft of the navy had other tasks. The army had to rely on ferries and merchant ships, using ordinary harbours for loading. An American lieutenant commander in the BALTAP staff had experience with amphibious warfare and set up a document for Waterborne Movements which became a standing NAVBALTAP order for procedures of moving troops from one part of Denmark to another.

A third example was about reconnaissance. The West Germans had a number of BREGUET ATLANTIC recce aircraft which could transmit radar images from e.g. the Baltic to another station. This system was English. But the German Ministry of Defence was inflexible and would not allocate aircraft for such tasks because they were bought for use in the Atlantic. Such transmitting from the Baltic was not possible until 10 years later with the AWACS system.

That example indicates the presence of politics in the staff work. Another comes from vice admiral Wegener (COMNAVBALTAP) who wanted the fighter bombers of the German navy to work for the navy only. But SHAPE wanted them put into particular roles from the outset, not reserved for German navy tactics. CINCNORTH agreed with SHAPE that the aircraft might be split between several roles, but Wegener maintained his policy vis-a-vis SHAPE. He did mention that his boss probably did not quite agree with him, but the chief of staff in BALTAP thought that Wegener had no solidarity with the obligations of his command.[12]

The activities of COMBALTAP during an exercise

BALTAP was to prepare for the task of handling the commanding of forces assigned to NATO's. An important element in these endeavours was to prepare for receiving reinforcements, and therefore much travel was needed to meet with the commanders and staffs of the assigned forces and prepare for receiving them in harbours and airfields. And in order to become familiar with their future roles, the assigned forces had to participate in exercises in the area they were slated to assist.

In November 1973 a comprehensive exercise, ABSALON EXPRESS, took place in Denmark. It concerned the reinforcements from NATO and therefore involved forces of many nations. The following is the day-to-day diary of the involvement of the COMBALTAP, admiral Helms:[13]

---

12 Thostrup, op. cit., p. 29.
13 Helms, Adam. "Min tid som Commander Allied Forces Baltic Approaches 1970–75. Anden del 1973–75." *Tidsskrift for Søvæsen* 176, no. 2 (2005b): 73–103.

Day one: received C-in-Cs for AFNORTH and AFCENT at the airfield in Værløse. Briefed journalists. Visited General Groven, commanding the AMF, in his HQ at Gisselfeldt Manor.

Day two: Helicopter to airfield Tirstrup. Visited US element (18 Phantom fighters). Helicopter to Karup Airfield, visiting Dutch squadron (18 F-4 Freedom fighters). Moving on to Vandel Airfield, visiting 10 British Harrier fighters. Back to Værløse to receive NATO's Secretary General and send him on with his liason officer.

Day three: Lunch with the NATO Secretary General and the Minister of Defence; a number of high office holders partaking. The minister had to leave for a vote in the parliament, there was "election in the air". Evening: cocktail party and dinner; the Secretary General was in good spirits and told stories.

Day four: Visiting the HQ of the AMF, on to the HQ of the American troops and then the Luxembourg Battalion for lunch. Moving on to the HQ of the British Battalion and then back to Værløse to visit the Air Lift Control Centre.

Day five: Visiting the journalist centre, on to first tank battalion and fourth reconnaissance squadron. Then participate in the Danish C-in-C's lunch for the Secretary General, moving on in a US helicopter to Hovercraft Squadron, sailing for 20 minutes. Moving on to the Belgians and later the Italian participants.

Day six: Saying goodbye at Værløse Airfield to the Secretary General, then visiting Home Guard District no. 92, moving on to Bregentved Manor to visit "Royal Anglians" and their 105 mm battery; then more Brits and Italians, followed by a visit to the Royal Guard Battalion and finally the HQ of the Zealand Brigade.

Day seven: Receiving first CINCNORTH and then SACEUR in Værløse Airport; followed the latter in helicopter to Næstved for a briefing by the Directing Staff. Then to the Ministry for the lunch for SACEUR, followed by a visit with SACEUR at the HQ of the AMF. On to the first Zealand Brigade and then back to Værløse Airfield together with the minister to say goodbye to SACEUR.

Day eight: Meeting with the Queen close to Næstved, presented the various commanders for her Majesty, followed by a short briefing and free manoeuvre. Visited Royal Scots and then had a meeting with the members of the parliamentary committee for defence. Lunch with her Majesty, followed by a visit to the Italians, second Zealand Brigade and the Bornholm contingent.

Day nine: Meeting with the Joint Chiefs of Staff. In the evening reception at the CINCNORTH office in Copenhagen.

Day ten: Debriefing in Næstved followed by drinks and lunch for about 35 officers from the exercise.

Strategy

At a meeting in Copenhagen early December 1961, CINCNORTH Pyman drew a picture of the situation in AFNORTH after the expected establishment of the BALTAP command in the following summer.[14] At his level of command, nuclear weapons were a possibility, but much of the planning went on with conventional weapons.

---

14 Notat om General Pyman's foredrag 2. december 1961. HEM Forsvarsministeriet 11. kontor 22-1-62 26-25/62.

There was no way the enemy could circumvent the defending NATO forces, so any attack had to be head-on, and the NATO tactics had to be to make the enemy concentrate their forces and become a target for the air- and nuclear forces of NATO. The main tasks for Pyman were to maintain command communication lines and the airfields; to block the Danish Narrows and to defend the Schleswig-Holstein territory. On Zealand, one brigade more than the planned one was desirable, this reinforcement was to be brought in by aircraft, and equipment and supplies had to be stocked there in peacetime. The Danish and German naval forces were "not extravagant". In Schleswig-Holstein, two German divisions were planned, but only two thirds of the planned brigades were available; their tanks and equipment were outmoded and had to be replaced. The first and strongest defence line would be the Elbe-Trave Canal, the second the Kiel Canal. The air defence of Schleswig-Holstein was the responsibility of AFCENT, not AFNORTH, and Pyman intended to discuss this issue with the supreme commander.

Four months later, CINCNORTH took the opportunity – opening the exercise VIKING SHIELD – to outline the military tasks for the future BALTAP command in the light of the new emergency plan from SACEUR.[15] Again, he preferred to discuss limited war. NATO had its shield (local) forces set up on the ground and the sea, supported by local air forces. NATO also had the strategic retaliatory forces (the sword, PB) to perform a massive nuclear air attack force. And there were the air defence forces without which NATO could hardly perform in a war. But atomic war aside, the general wanted to stress that limited war was important in the situation where hostilities had begun, and the nuclear threshold had not been overstepped. This would be the situation where a military commander still could make a difference with conventional forces, and VIKING SHIELD would test such a situation.

AFNORTH had two areas of particular interest for the Soviet Union: Northern Norway and the Baltic Approaches. Possessing those two areas would give the Soviets access to the Atlantic which was a main Line of Communication for NATO, and the ships of the Soviet Northern Fleet would get access to the important repair and replenishment facilities in the Baltic.

As to the Baltic Approaches, the most important areas would be the area north of the river Elbe and the channel to Lübeck, and the Baltic leading to the Danish narrows. Since they were adjacent, both those areas had to be held, and if they were lost, Southern Norway would be threatened. SACEUR's new defence plan put more emphasis on the shield than previously, and therefore, this year's

---

15 General Pymans indledning den 12. april 1962. HEM. Forsvarsministeriet 11. kontor 101 24/62, 28-3-62.

exercise VIKING SHIELD was set up to test the NATO shield forces in their forward defence role: meeting the enemy at the border of the region.

The exercise started out in a situation where NATO's council had instructed the supreme commander to halt the attack of the enemy in order to create time for re-thinking before the next step which would be using nuclear weapons, probably in an all-destroying exchange. This possibility of nuclear attacks was the decisive difference from World War II, and it was the situation where much power was left to the military leaders because their decisions would determine the consequences in terms of (avoiding a) nuclear war.

So the first tasks of a commander was to determine the command structure, set up communication systems and get the right intelligence about the situation. The second tasks were to assess the time available for getting one's own forces in the right positions and getting the forces ready for action.

In this exercise, it was assumed that the Soviet commander had been instructed by the Soviet Premier not to use nuclear weapons unless NATO used them against him. He was allocated two airborne army divisions and the necessary air transport and air cover for their operations. He was, however, to avoid any major air battle and keep losses of transport aircraft to a minimum. So, an hour before dawn on D-day the Soviets air dropped one division on Zealand, and one brigade on Bornholm, Karup and Kiel, respectively. The last two were to destroy the two NATO HQs located there.

Four divisions would attack across the Trave-Elbe Canal, supported by adequate air forces, and from each division one brigade would set out to get to the Kiel Canal.

The Soviet navy would attack any maritime forces in the narrows, establish contact with the landed airborne troops and set up a transport link between East Germany and Zealand. The aim would be to have control of the narrows after seven days and then set up a HQ on Zealand.

For the defence, then, two things were critical. One was getting the correct intelligence so that one could see what pattern was developing within the attacking forces. The second was to slow down the attacker as much as possible. In Schleswig–Holstein, the pattern indicated that the attacker wanted to cross the Kiel Canal by conquering the bridges across; consequently, the defence had to demolish the bridges and thus force him to either build new bridges or get barges to cross the water. But before doing that one tried to stop the three brigades by intense bombing from the air.

In the Baltic, the defence intended to stop the enemy by finishing the minefields; this was done with strong support from the air. Once they were ready, the navies could proceed, sending ships deeper into the Baltic to attack the enemy as close as possible to their base. They needed aircraft for recce and for destroying some of the targets. The enemy had to be prevented from linking the airborne forces, landed in Zealand, with the naval forces, and the defence had to prevent a line of communication being established between Northern Germany and Zealand so the provisions would not come to the army.

To fight the enemy on Zealand, the defence needed highly trained, very mobile battle groups with tanks and armoured transport vehicles – somewhat like the American or British marines, but supported by tanks. With support from the home guard the defence would quickly make the enemy quite ineffective. In Jutland everything had to be done to protect the HQs at Karup and Kiel.

As to air forces, they would be active in several aspects. First, at the NATO perimeter to stop enemy progress; second to protect navy and operate in conjunction with ships to attack the enemy; third to protect ground forces and support them in attacks; and fourth to attack as necessary when situations arose.

Sweden

Sweden changed its strategy in 1958, so we shall first go back a few years from 1962 for a general overview. Then we will analyse the Germans' perceptions of Sweden in 1962 as a possible NATO partner.

The changes in 1958

AFNORTH's first war plans included the possibility of Sweden being attacked simultaneously with Denmark and Norway. In 1958, this option still was open and CINCNORTH noted in a paper preparing the establishment of BALTAP that according to the Emergency Plan 1958 (SACEUR EDP 1–58), one had to keep preparations open for including Sweden in the command system.[16] But there was no operational, war-ready organisation for including the Swedes, and Sweden's war plans had no NATO-case laid bare. But in the case of strong tensions and subsequently war, Sweden had prepared for seven groups of officers (68 in all), each commanded by a flag officer, to be sent to seven countries, including Denmark, to maintain contacts with the top military and NATO commands, to collect intelli-

---

16 Holmström, Mikael. *Den dolda alliansen. Sveriges hemliga NATO-förbindelser*, 125. Stockholm: Atlantis, 2011.

gence, to buy military equipment, to secure convoys and, close to home, to cooperate with forces in the Baltic and Øresund etc.[17]

As NATO and the Warsaw Pact developed their strategies in the second half of the 1950, the Swedish C-in-C followed suit – concluding that the two alliances had to bind so many forces to fight each other that the threat against Sweden was reduced.[18] The Swedish parliament used this analysis to cut down the defence spending, deciding that quality had to supplant quantity. The air force would be a major player, and in the south the navy still had a role, but the air force took over the tasks of the large ships, most of which were scrapped in the years to come. Thus the navy got the relatively largest part of the cuts. The army got a cut of ten per cent and lost five brigades. The air force lost ten per cent of its fighters, but a new Swedish fighter and a modernised command system were meant to counterbalance the loss.

The war plan had a clear emphasis on defending the south and the Swedish part of the Baltic Approaches from a Soviet amphibious attack. The concept was in many ways in accordance with the ideas of littoral warfare, taking maximum advantage of the capabilities of the air force which was always close to the sea, and using the protection of naval FPB strike groups behind the many islands. Comprehensive mining was used in connection with coastal batteries. The army was modernized with mobile artillery, and the number of armoured brigades was expanded.

The navy now had two roles related to the Baltic Approaches.[19] The major role was – together with the Air Force – to prevent an amphibious invasion from the east with FPBs, submarines, an elaborate system of minefields and a number of fortresses and mobile coastal batteries. Raids against enemy convoys were also possible. A secondary role was to provide escort for ships bringing in supplies from the west to Gothenburg and other harbours on the west coast; the force in the west also had the role to attack enemy ships that had passed the Baltic Approaches.

In 1960 the navy had two attack groups, each with a cruiser, three destroyers and six FPBs.[20] There were two additional destroyer groups, each with three destroyers. These core forces were stationed in two bases north and south of Stockholm, respectively. Some 18 submarines in four groups were mainly stationed south of Stockholm. Thus the main thrust of the navy was to be found in the mid-baltic, but, of course, the forces were easy to move further to the south. The cruisers, however, soon were scrapped, as well as the attack groups now based on de-

---

17 Ibid., 375.
18 Wallerfelt, Bengt. *Den hemliga svenska krigsplanen*, 126–28. Stockholm: Medströms Bokforlag, 2016.
19 Larsson, Bengt. "Marinens Sjöoperativa Doktrin 1958–1961." *Forum Navale*, no. 67 (2011): 73–74.
20 Ibid., 83–87.

stroyers with FPBs. Twelve more submarines were located in the base of Karlskrona in South-Eastern Sweden, together with six frigates. Some 20 FPBs in two divisions were in smaller bases in South-Eastern Sweden. About ten frigates were stationed on the west coast, primarily for escort duties and submarine hunting; in addition there were two "help cruisers". The navy was also organised for action in the Northern Baltic with six submarines, 12 FPBs and some "help cruisers". Mine sweepers were spread all over Sweden.

The coastal artillery had 24 heavy batteries and about double so many light batteries spread over the coast, but with emphasis on the southern part of the country; most of the minefields were maintained by its battalions.[21]

In 1960, the air force still had about 1,000 airplanes; the bombers were replaced by fighter-bombers in 1958. About 65 per cent were fighters, 25 per cent fighter-bombers and eight per cent recce planes. The rest were for transport etc. About 60 per cent were ready to operate, the rest were reserves, some of which might be operated by recalled pilots – the air force expected to lose 10–15 per cent of its airplanes for each 24 hours of war.[22] Sweden was an early bird in developing missiles, and from 1961 an air-sea missile was operational – the air force now was ready to replace the large ships of the navy.

An advanced warning and command system for air fighters was developed from 1960. The most advanced systems were installed in the southern part of the country. Fighters were on stand-by in various airfields and could be airborne in less than one minute. The control system determined from where the response should be launched, directed the fighters towards the target and determined whether it should be attacked head-on or from another angle. The pilot could overrule such decisions, depending on the situation.[23]

The 1958-plan also included ground-to-air missiles; 12 sites were planned, all along the coast of the Baltic, with none in the northern part of Sweden.[24]

Coordinating air defence
A particular issue came up with the introduction of surface-to-air missiles which became operational about 1960. The Danish NIKE batteries were able to fire against targets over Southern Sweden. If a "sector" was given free, it was up to the battery commander which targets to attack. If the target was handed down by the Danish Air Control System, the permission to fire was controlled by that centre.

---

21 Pettersson, Tommy. *Med invasionen i sikte. Flygvapnets krigsplanläggning och luftoperative doktrin 1958–1966*, 53. Stockholm: Försvarshögskolan, 2009.
22 Ibid., 55–56.
23 Ibid., 71–74.
24 Ibid., 83.

This issue was discussed with the Swedes early 1961 by the Danish chief of the Air Force,[25] but the outcomes are not known. The missile control systems in all three countries were set up to prevent interference between flight control and missile control so that no target would be allocated to both missile and fighter, and one's own fighters would not be attacked by one's own missiles. In the case of war one might presume that the control systems would be able to work across borders and prevent attacks on the same targets and protect one's own airplanes from attack from friends – the Danish and Norwegian archives indicate such ideas, but they are absent from the Swedish archives.[26]

In the air control centre of Copenhagen, there was permission to fire over Skaane if the code word "Udgaardsloke" (name of an ancient Nordic god, PB) was given,[27] but the affiliated plans, communications and authorities are not known.

The main immediate role in protecting the Baltic Approaches was assigned to the Swedish navy in two commands. The commander for Southern Sweden had to lay out minefields in Øresund (cooperating with the Danish navy, depending on the situation), and prevent enemy naval forces from operating there and along the Swedish coast and in the waters between Bornholm and Sweden. He had to prevent enemy forces from approaching and entering Swedish harbours, and escort his own sea transport from there. He could attack enemy transport along the Polish and East German coastline. Finally, but only by direct order, he was to cooperate with allied forces and prepare bases for them. The commander of West Sweden had to protect imports to harbours and patrol the seaways. When possible, he was to attack enemy ships after passage of the Danish narrows. By direct order he was to cooperate with allied forces and prepare bases for them.[28]

The Swedish air force had an important role in reconnaissance over the Baltic and in attacking amphibious invasion vessels if they approached Sweden. The army's role was to fight any troops landing, including paratroopers, and 40 per cent of the army resources were in Southern Sweden to accomplish this task.

The Bundesmarine analysed the Swedish changes in 1963,[29] noting that the Swedish political stance was neutrality. But if some of its territory was attacked, if its transport corridors were blocked and if the WAPA attacked adjacent NATO countries – Denmark and Norway – the Swedish government might join NATO in the fight against the Warsaw Pact. It was highly unlikely that the Swedes would support the Pact in any way.

---

25 Görtz, Hans-Ove. *Skandinavisk försvarsutredning 1948–1949 – uppstarten och dess inverkan under kalla kriget*, 63. Försvarets Historiska Telesamlingar Flygvapnet, 2020b.
26 Ibid., 119.
27 Personal communication to the author from Martin Jespersen by email 8-2-21.
28 Larsson, op. cit., pp. 73–74.
29 Studie. Schwedens strategische Lage zwischen den NATO und dem Waschauer Pakt. Geheim. März 1963. Führungsakademie der Bundeswehr TgbNr. 53/63. BM 1/1020e.

For NATO, a neutral Sweden (and Finland) was a buffer behind which NATO could prepare its actions. Swedish air defence would prevent WAPA air attacks against NATO across Swedish territory. But of course, the very same air defence was an obstacle for NATO strike attacks. And NATO would have a strong interest in Sweden joining NATO: the demand for WAPA forces to prepare for battling Sweden would alone change the whole military pattern in the Baltic to NATO's advantage. WAPA LOCs would be severely threatened, and the risk for amphibious landing forces crossing the Baltic would be strongly reduced.

In order to facilitate a pro-NATO Swedish stance, the German note recommended that NATO and the Bundesmarine demonstrated a willingness to operate in the Baltic. A sort of stepping stone might be Bornholm (not unlike Malta during WWII in the Mediterranean), and one of SACLANT's carrier groups might visit the Baltic, comparable to the sixth US Navy fleet, also in the Mediterranean, to demonstrate NATO's resolve. On the other hand, exercises were to be held with restraint in order to not provoke the Soviets.

Contacts withering away

One form of cooperation has been public since 1960, the SVENORDA cooperative network between Denmark, Sweden and Norway, intended to aid aircraft in distress. It prescribes procedures for landing in another country; radio channels for communication; procedures for saving crews landed on water etc.[30] The network was originally secret and a possible first step towards joint control of the air space in wartime,[31] but it seems that no such development ever took place; the system still exists.

In the 1960s some activities to prepare Swedish cooperation with Denmark, Norway and certain other NATO countries continued.[32] Several activities concerning "assistance from outside" took place in the Swedish military HQ in 1962–63. A study listed a number of situations where assistance could be desirable, and the prime minister was informed about the following issues:
- Contacts for setting up communication channels were discussed, and links for mutual warnings of attack were established to a NATO-HQ in Wiesbaden.

---

30 Utrikesdepartementet. *Fred och Säkerhet*, 697–98. Stockholm: SOU 2002:108. Utrikesdepartementet, 2002.
31 Görtz, Hans-Ove. *SVENORDA. Flygsäkerhetssamarbete mellan Sverige, Norge och Danmark – en del av krigsförberedelserna*, 9. Försvarets Historiska Telesamlingar Flygvapnet, 2020a.
32 Görtz, *Skandinavisk försvarsutredning 1948–1949 – uppstarten och dess inverkan under kalla kriget*, 64–67.

- Plans for NATO-recce flights in the Baltic were systematically given to Sweden in order to avoid misunderstandings; in addition, this knowledge enabled Swedish intelligence to follow Soviet reactions to recce aviation.
- Sending groups liason officers to the HQs of other countries was being planned, but only the heads of each delegation were informed.
- The chiefs of staff of the three Scandinavian countries had plans for how to communicate in case of war in order to avoid mutual disturbances.
- A system for avoiding "friendly fire" by surface-to-air missiles had been set up, and a plan for how to avoid sinking friendly submarines, for knowing the positions of minefields and securing convoys in Skagerrak and Kattegat had been made.

The communication systems were developed and reinforced until 1968. There was no information about cooperation with other countries in the Swedish defence archive after 1968.[33]

Magnus Haglund mentions a series of "tactical discussions" over many years among the Scandinavian military chiefs.[34] The Swedish top ministers saw them as a sort of technical exchanges of information and therefore approved, but the discussions were kept top secret even within one's own organisation and were mainly kept oral by personal meetings when an opportunity came up.

Holmström[35] quotes the Danish vice admiral Bork for information about two booklets indicating the positions of mine fields and procedures for exchanging information between the two navies in war time. Bork's autobiography tells us that he had written some documents with Swedish colleagues about naval movements in case of war or crisis, but there were no operational details; however, common communication channels were determined.[36]

Secret Danish communication link to Sweden
In the Danish air force control centre in Vedbæk there was a phone line to the Swedish defence.[37] It had been set up as part of the Sea and Air Rescue system, connecting to the Ängelholm air force control centre in Sweden. The phone was red, and carried the petname "Jönsson" (a very common name in Sweden, corresponding to "Smith" in England). Only the officer in charge was allowed to use the phone. Of course the line might be used for other purposes, so the personnel also called it "the secret line".

---

33 Ibid., 70.
34 Haglund, Magnus. *Flottan och det kallla kriget*. Stockholm: Kungl. Örlogsmannasällskabet, 2009.
35 Holmström, op. cit.
36 Bork, Jørgen F. *Åbent hav. Mit liv i Søværnet 1945–1990*, 97. København: Gyldendal, 2010.
37 Personal communication from Iben Björnsson.

In a communication centre for the naval district of Øresund at the coastal battery on Stevns there also were connections to Sweden – two phone lines called "Hemmelige Jönsson I" and "Hemmelige Jönsson II" – hemmelig means secret in Danish. So at Stevns one had similar possibilities to call the Swedish counterpart in SAR operations – and for other purposes.

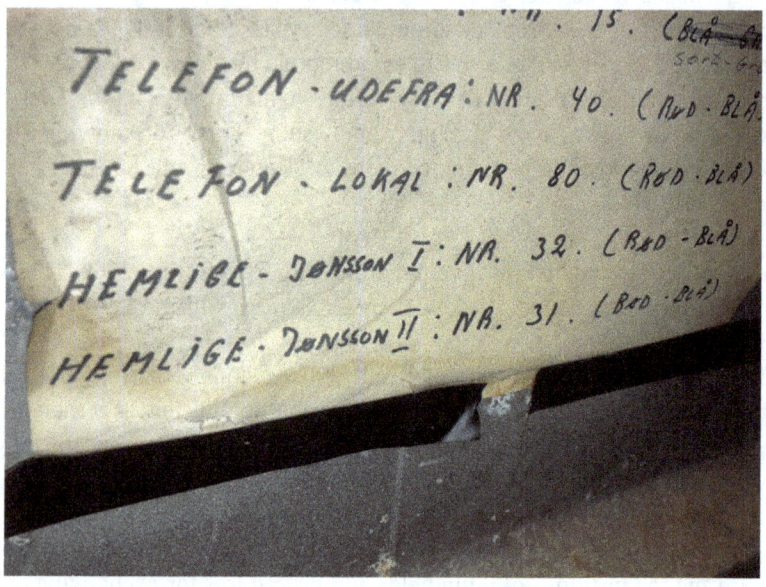

Figure 12.5: Telephone list in a control bunker at the Stevns Battery – Secret Jönsson I and II. Source: private photo.

As time went by, the contacts to other countries were reduced in number and the remaining contacts reserved to a few high-ranking officers. The Swedish C-in-C from 1978 to 1986 actively worked to reduce the connections, thus mirroring the declarations by the cabinet; he ordered the chief of the Navy to stop cooperation and had a series of documents relating to cooperative activities destroyed because "they were now irrelevant".[38]

The reduction in intensity was confirmed by a Danish former brigadier who during his years from young to senior officer consistently found that the common belief among Danish officers was that Sweden was well defended and would be able to keep its status of neutrality, and he never experienced any military coop-

---

[38] Gustafsson, Bengt. *Det kalla kriget – några reflexioner*, 40. Stockholm: Försvarshögskolan, 2006.

erative activities with the Swedes. On the contrary, when he once prepared a staff war game involving Danish forces helping the Swedes in Southern Sweden, he was ordered to change the circumstances to "S-country", and the Swedish maps were changed into generic exercise maps, albeit with an astonishing similarity to a Swedish county.[39]

Summing up: Protecting the Baltic Approaches by 1962

The Warsaw Pact had considerable forces available by 1962: 55 army divisions, 24 large navy units, 70 submarines and about 200 FPBs, as well as a large fleet of auxiliary units to fight submarines and sweep mines. About 100 amphibious units were on hand to land forces on the Danish and German coasts. The number of aircraft was staggering: 900 various types of bombers, 1,500 fighters and 300 recce planes. But most of them were reserved for other purposes.

The Danes analysed their coastal areas to second-guess where WAPA landings might take place. Using knowledge about how such landings took place, one could rule out a number of smaller areas. Several scenarios for an amphibious landing were played out. It seemed likely that the Polish forces would play an important role, but significant Soviet forces were likely to play a part. In all cases, the growing naval forces of Poland and East Germany would be important in an operation. In exercises and plans nuclear warheads were available, but the Soviet military top was the only decision-making body for such use.

The Danish defence was not in a good state by 1962. Sizewise, it was inadequate, and the combat effectiveness was at level three or four in a scale from one to four, four being lowest quality. There was a general lack of equipment and technical personnel. The time to mobilise conscripts was criticised, and there were not enough professional soldiers. The German defence was being developed and therefore not of a high standard – but improving. All in all, the defence of the Baltic Approaches did not have a high standard.

The BALTAP command got organised and war plans were written. It took time to get officers from many countries cooperating well, particularly across the three forces. Exercises began already in the spring of 1962, and the use of nuclear weapons was not included, based on the proposition that the WAPA forces would not take the initiative to use them. The main NATO task on the ground was to slow down WAPA forces to make time for reinforcements from the west. At sea,

---

39 Clemmesen, Michael H. "The Danish View." In *Cold War Views on Sweden*, eds Gunnar Artéus and Kent Zetterberg, 13–29. Stockholm: Medströms Bokförlag, 2018.

laying mines was highest priority to stop WAPA units from passing through the Danish straits. The air forces were to support these activities as best they could, and to attack WAPA forces at the perimeter of NATO territories.

Sweden was still considered a possible allied partner, but the defence was re-organised. In particular the navy took a blow and lost most of the large units, but the changes might be seen as corresponding to some ground rules in littoral warfare. A FPB-heavy coastal defence with many coastal batteries was prioritised with the air force as the main instrument to fight WAPA units at sea in the Baltic. Missiles were developed for this purpose. Cooperation with NATO countries continued at a reduced scale, and war activities at staff level were prepared, but after the 1960s most contacts withered away.

Chapter 13
Making BALTAP operational: Naval tactics in the 1960s

BALTAP was an integrated command, formed to expedite the coordination of the three forces in the Baltic Approaches. The ground forces were under two commands – one for Zealand and the eastern islands (located on Zealand), one for the Cimbric Peninsula (located in Schleswig-Holstein). The C-in-C was located in Jutland (Karup) together with the naval and air commands. In peacetime, the naval command was located in Schleswig-Holstein.

Seen from a German perspective, the territory of Schleswig-Holstein was a core element of the BALTAP command. It was the stepping stone to Denmark for ground forces; it protected the left flank of AFCENT forces, it held several airfields and it had the German naval bases. The main German force was the sixth armoured grenadier division, and there was a local home guard brigade (not under NATO command). The Danish army's Jutland brigades were to join the grenadiers at the East German border. The Luftwaffe had fighter-bombers, the navy fighter-bombers, recce and ASW aircraft. The navy was divided into the North Sea and the Baltic groups and operated under their own operational command, as did the Danish navy; all, however, under the command of BALTAP.

Seen from a Danish perspective, the sea had more immediate interest. At sea, the main area was the waters between Zealand/Fehmarn and Bornholm. This was the route to an amphibious invasion of the Danish islands as well as Schleswig-Holstein. In conditions less than war, Fehmarn and Lolland were obvious targets for a limited invasion creating control over one entrance to the Baltic Approaches. The Danish army was partly in Jutland, partly on Zealand (and a small force on Bornholm), in Jutland ready to move south to Schleswig-Holstein, on Zealand and islands close by and ready to move to those shores that would be invaded by WAPA forces. The air force was concentrating its aircraft on airfields in Jutland, at a distance from the air forces of the WAPA. The navy prepared to block the waters for WAPA ships.

We shall in this chapter focus on the perspectives of the two navies as core forces against the first amphibious moves of the Warsaw Pact. After the creation of BALTAP, the two navies were in war times to act under one command, COM-NAVBALTAP, but in practice, each navy was operating under its separate command, the Danish FOD (Flag Officer Denmark) and the German FOG (Flag officer Germany). So let us sketch out the tactical perspectives of those two navies at the start of the integrated command.

First a caveat. The early military policy papers mostly do not discuss a particular vulnerability of the main instrument in the Baltic Approaches: the minefields. Once laid, they were a very strong weapon, but everything depended on that they were laid in time and that they could be defended afterwards. Since much of the Approaches was international waters, early mine laying would be a breach of international law. Consequently, the politicians had to approve the mine laying in a time of strong tension or even early war, and the mostly unspoken issue was whether that decision would be taken early enough to permit the mine layers to do their job in full. We shall not pursue this theme in depth since it is part of politics and hence out of bounds for the book, but it must be a memento in the mind of the reader. And in the 1970s, the theme of mining international waters came up; we shall return to that in a later chapter.

The general NAVBALTAP perspective

The general mission given from CINCNORTH was that NAVBALTAP should operate in the Baltic to maintain control over the Approaches as choke points, deny the enemy the use of those waters and deny access to invade Danish and German territory. This was a defensive tactic – with some offensive possibilities – which however led the two navies to draw somewhat different consequences in the early 1960s. The German navy strived for a more offensive approach while the Danes with a nearly obsolete navy stayed defensive. However, both navies hoped for improvements later in the 1960s that would sustain more offensive NATO tactics.

There was a division of labour between the two navies in the NAVBALTAP area. The primary area of operation for the Danish navy was the Sound north of a line Møn-Smygehuk, the two Belts, Kattegat and Skagerrak. The German primary area was Gedser Strait west of a line Møn-Arkona, Fehmarn Belt, Bay of Kiel and the German Bay up to 55 latitude. Common areas were the Baltic east of a line Smygehuk-Møn-Arkona, and parts of Skagerrak and the North Sea.

We shall take a look at the major points of view of the two navies after joining BALTAP.

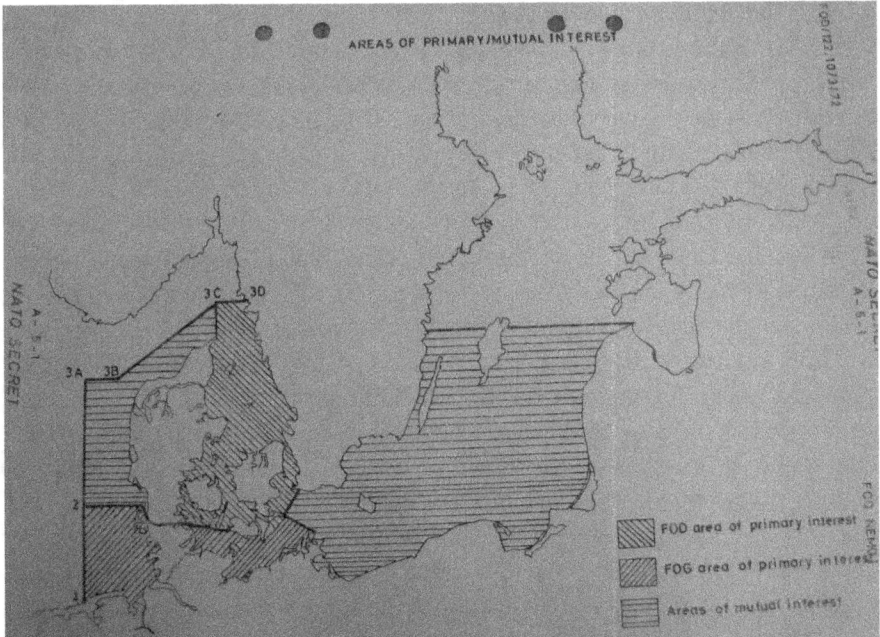

Figure 13.1: Map of interest areas for FOD and FOG. Figure from Danish Fighting Instructions.

Denmark

In a series of papers[1] from 1962 to 63, the Danish FOD analysed the future tasks and the need for building new ships for the Danish navy, but in reality it was an analysis of the role of NAVBALTAP until 1970.

First, the enemy: until 1970, the WAPA naval forces were supposed to have an upper hand because of the missile destroyers and FPBs. Regarding other types of craft one was closer to a balance; WAPA mine sweepers and ASW units were not seen as effective, but they were better armed. WAPA submarines were considered to be mainly defensive and anyway not able to navigate in most of the BALTAP waters.

WAPA air forces were large, but the number of aircraft actually planned for use in the Baltic was debatable, for instance because of special demands to pilot skills in some types of operation (low level attacks and use of missiles). AIRBAL-

---

[1] "Målsætning" for flåden. HEM. Søværnets operative Kommando 5-1-63. Nr. 690.1, U.1/63. 2 Bilag HEM: "Estimate" af 1-11-62 og "Stabsstudie over 'Betænkning af 14 jun 1962'". Marinestaben: V. Diverse (1962–1975) 1: "D" Historiske sager 1962–1963.

TAP evaluated that an all-out war would demand involvement of all forces to prevent NATO from getting air supremacy, but at the same time, NATO's counter air strikes would reduce the number of WAPA aircraft. If so, the priorities of WAPA aircraft commanders would hardly include single or small groups of NATO warships. But bases would get high priority, even with nuclear warheads. NATO would expect that only the German naval air arm would support naval actions in the Baltic, and possibly some aircraft for counter air strikes might be rescheduled for naval operations e.g. in case of threats of invasion. In any case, the southern Danish waters and the western Baltic would be areas for air attacks in day time, and during the night aircraft might attack with missiles.

In littoral warfare, air supremacy was important. With sufficient warning time (one week), NATO would be able to maintain air supremacy in the western Baltic. This would also be the case in limited war. Shorter or no notice would give WAPA an upper hand. The whole territory of Denmark was well suited for landing paratroopers. As to amphibious operations, bays on the south eastern coasts of Zealand, the southern coast of Møn, the south eastern coast of Falster and the south eastern coast of Jutland were well suited for beach landings.

Regarding BALTAP, NATO naval forces in the area would initially only be Danish and German, grouped in their own national areas and bases, because Danish defence policy did not permit stationing of foreign forces in peacetime, and Norwegian, British, Dutch and Belgian forces would anyway be preoccupied with local tasks. Rapid help from American forces was not expected. Sweden and Finland were expected to stay neutral, but their military presence would bind some Soviet forces to secure that especially Swedish forces stayed put. The Soviets would probably designate a force corresponding to the size of the Swedish navy for this purpose. NATO forces in the Baltic could not expect to be able to use nuclear weapons in the short run.

NATO ground forces would fight enemy troops which were not stopped at sea by naval and air NATO forces, and they might be of use in protecting base areas.

Air recce based on radar would be provided by the US Air Force for the first 72 hours up to 57 degrees north in the eastern Baltic. Other air forces could not initially support naval operations, but their counter air offensives were expected to reduce the enemy aircraft pressure on NATO forces. NATO air forces from strategic commands or a SACLANT strike force might operate with nuclear warheads in the Baltic. Conventional air forces might come from the UK Light Bomber Force or SACLANT Strike Force.

As a consequence of the above, NAVBALTAP had a defensive role and would have to define a border line for actions in *war* drawn between the East German island of Rügen and the reef of Falsterbo in Southern Øresund, within the territory of Sweden. West of the border line, the Danish narrows would be blocked by sea mines at Langeland, Gedser Rev, along the coast of Falster and across the Sound from Stevns to Falsterbo Light Vessel. Surface units would initiate battles with WAPA units between Rügen and Falsterbo, and along the East German coast until Fehmarn. East of the border line, submarines would operate for recce and for attacks. In effect, Bornholm would only be defended by forces already deployed to the island.

FOD Denmark found that the following operations would make this possible:
- surveillance of the enemy's movements in the Baltic;
- defensive operations – including mine laying – against enemy operations (including submarines) in those waters;
- submarine operations in the Baltic; and
- securing their own LOCs in the area.

These tasks were defensive, but they could be turned into offensive operations when feasible, and transgress the border defined above to the east, particularly when the German navy had developed use of destroyers and FPBs. Operations should be coordinated with BALTAP's land and air commands, and in particular air operations would have great importance.

The main defensive weapon of BALTAP was sea mines creating choke points and sea denial, supported by coastal batteries and naval units. All Danish waters were suited for sea mine laying. The NATO defence plan was dependent on mine laying in the Danish narrows and at the coastal areas suited for amphibious landing. It would take some time to lay all mines, and enemy counter actions were foreseen. Mines were to preferably be laid during night time, but the time factor might prevent this. Support from destroyers and FPBs was necessary at a distance, preventing enemy destroyers from opening fire or FPBs firing torpedoes. Even farther away one's own FPBs were to patrol to prevent enemy FPBs attacking the destroyer screen, and to attack enemy missile destroyers. Air cover was not guaranteed but had to be requested.

Laying mines in Danish and International waters
Already in 1962, the Danes and the Germans finished a coordination of their mining plans for the Baltic Approaches, aiming at making them operational from 1965 when the four new large Danish mine layers were ready.[2] Nine fields were planned with 5,755 mines at Gedser, The Strait of Fehmarn, Storebælt, Lillebælt, Bay of Faxe, Bay of Faxe and Køge (anti-invasion mines) and the area between Møn and Falsterbo Light Vessel (Sweden).

---

2 Forsvarsstaben: KC. YHM-skrivelser (afklass.) (1956–1969) notat reg nr. 0.3.215.11-62 af 10. januar 1962 til Ad hoc mixed NATO working group AC/197.

Eighty per cent of the mines would be set to the highest sensitivity to explode against almost anything, and 65 per cent at first contact. The mines would be delivered from six Danish depots, and seven harbours were named for on-board receipt of delivery.

The exercise NORTHERN LIGHT was carried out in 1967,[3] illustrating the sequences in mobilisation and mine laying.

Day one. At 18.59 NATO declared reinforced peace alert, and mines could be taken on board the mine layers.

Day two. 09.55. Danish naval forces were deployed according to the plans of FOD. 11.12. Planned controlled mine fields in Øresund were laid. 15.00 SACEUR declared Simple Alert, and one hour later planned not-controlled minefields were laid in Danish territorial waters in the Øresund area. 17.05 controlled minefields at Drogden (approach to Copenhagen harbour) were laid. 22.45. Planned controlled minefields in Storebælt were laid. 22.55. Permission was granted to German units laying minefields in Danish territorial waters in the Strait of Fehmarn.

Day three. 09.59. Non-controlled minefields in the Bays of Faxe and Køge were laid. 11.59. NATO Reinforced Alert, and one hour later non-controlled minefields were laid in international waters in the Øresund area. 22.00 CINCNORTH was authorised to lay mines in Storebælt if Denmark was attacked. 23.40 Two thirds of the minefields in Southern Øresund were laid. 23.50 Anti-invasion mining in the Øresund area was complete.

Day four. 02.45 Hostilities were started by Stevns Fort engaging enemy mine sweepers in the Bay of Køge. 03.28 Alarm Scarlet. 04.05 State of war. 06.05 SACEUR General Alert. 16.00 Controlled minefield Storebælt completed.

Critical comments after the exercise: first, time was wasted because of unclear competences between top commanders. Second, orange forces with civilian ships could harass NATO's mine laying and initiate a mine sweeping process. The were no instructions on how to manage such a situation. Third, political restrictions were curbing efficient naval action against amphibious craft. The enemy could exploit the right of free movement in international waters before the actual attack.

In pauses of mine laying one's own larger units were withdrawn and positioned north of Zealand, and smaller craft would deploy to predetermined waiting positions, e.g. in Grønsund for replenishment. The northern parts of Danish waters would be more safe due to WAPA flying distance and NATO air defence – by missiles to the east, and by a NATO denial zone against low flying aircraft across Southern Jutland and Fyn; this would prevent attacks against naval targets further to the north.

When the mining was concluded, surviving BALTAP units would defend the blockades and perform offensive operations in the Baltic, depending on the air situation. Recce was provided by the German naval air arm and submarines which would also attack WAPA ships in accordance with policy. Air forces might

---

3 Marinestaben: KC. Hemmelig kopibog (afklassificeret) (1946–1975). Rapport udsendt 22. januar 1968.

be ready for strikes against enemy surface units which could not be attacked by naval task forces.

Logistics in Denmark was crucial, particularly for smaller units. POL, torpedoes and ammunition were available nearly all over the country while spare parts and general supplies were concentrated at the naval bases. Replenishment could only take place during daytime and would mostly depend on sea transport. Twelve MTBs would daily use 120 tons oil, 10 tons of water, 48 torpedoes and 6,000 ammunition rounds. Since there was only one depot ship and few other vessels suited for this, there was doubt that all 12 could be fully supplied at all times. Therefore, FOG's Mobile Logistic Support was also to be used for supplies for Danish units, and Danish supplies were to be transported to harbours suitably located for the operations.

Due to wind conditions, FPBs might only operate 20 days per month in the winter and 26 days per month in the summer. This restrained both parties, but the NATO FPBs were larger and more used to operating in those waters.

Finally, there were the submarines. Sonar conditions in the narrows and the western Baltic were poor; this was an advantage for both parties. However, enemy submarines were unlikely to operate west of Bornholm. If operation safety demanded 40 meters depth, submarine operations were not plausible west of 13 degrees east until 57 degrees north in Kattegat. If 20 meters was the limit, none of the Danish narrows might be passed submerged, and only few areas were accessible in the Baltic around Bornholm. If 15 meters was the limit, the Sound might not be passed submerged, even if the other narrows might. In any case, navigation was difficult and currents might be strong in the narrows.

Danish Submarines in the Baltic
Submarines had very good operation conditions east of Bornholm. They could operate where the enemy had sea power, and they could come very close before firing their torpedoes and thus enhance the probability for hitting and exploit the surprise element. The variations in the Baltic regarding water salinity were efficient protections against detection from sonar; therefore, the submarine could come very close to its targets. However, there were limits to their mobility:[4]
- in practice, their operational areas were limited to 30 x 30 miles in a number of pre-defined areas where NATO's surface units would not operate in order to avoid mistakes. Deployment to these areas had to go through particular submarine safety lanes with a fixed speed of six knots, preferably submerged (in between snorkeling at 10 knots). If one had to surface, a NATO unit had to escort them to avoid attacks from their own forces. In the operation area the submarine would go slow, at three knots, in order to avoid making noise. In each operation area only one submarine would be present because safe cooperation was difficult to establish under water.

---

4 Søværnets Operative Kommando, Undervandsbådseskadren: K. Klassificeret arkiv (02.12.1947-31.12.1982). Foredrag FTR sendt til SOK 26. januar 1966.

- Depth in the area was to preferably be more than 35–40 meters and, if possible, close to even greater depths for hiding. Therefore, the operation areas were east of Kriegers Flak (between Rügen and Ystad) and mostly north and east of Bornholm with water depths of 70–80 meters.
- The submarine was, by and large, banned from using its active sensors: radio, radar and sonar. But hydrophones were used all the time together with brief uses of the periscope. When snorkeling, the ESM system was used for warning against anti-submarine aircraft and possible enemy ships in the area. Radar was only used to determine distance to an already identified target, and that was done with a particular antenna in the periscope; it only took a very short time.

The submarine was informed of the enemy situation by long wave frequency radio messages from the naval HQ which could be received until a depth of about 30 meters. Submerged it could also use Decca signals for navigation – surfaced it could use (the military) GPS.

Submarines could manage by themselves for three weeks or until all torpedoes were fired. Unless they got supplies from a depot ship, submarines might therefore be a one time feature in the Baltic Sea. NATO had surveyed "lanes" of at least 15 meters depth for bringing its own submarines submerged from Bornholm to Kattegat.

In summary, fulfilling the mission of FOD within BALTAP would include the following specific tasks for FOD, to be solved in cooperation with FOG, when feasible:

1. Lay, protect and strengthen defensive minefields in the narrows and Kattegat and at conceivable invasion coasts.
2. Perform offensive operations against enemy naval and amphibious forces threatening AFNORTH's area in the Baltic.
3. Surveillance of Danish coastal waters to detect and prevent enemy raids and infiltrations.
4. According to common demands to recce: perform sea recce of the Baltic and enemy harbours feasible for preparing attacks.
5. Perform offensive operations, including sea mining, in the Baltic against enemy bases, harbours and LOCs within operational reach.
6. Perform offensive and recce operations by submarines in the Baltic, and
7. perform operations against enemy submarines when feasible.
8. Secure allied LOCs in the area of primary interest.
9. Organise reception and forwarding of ships destined for Denmark or passage of Danish waters, and yield protection of such vessels.
10. Yield cover from the sea in coastal waters as an integrating part of the territorial defence, if the situation in Denmark should demand this.
11. Sweep enemy sea mines.

The above plan was risky, especially with little warning time. The main enemy forces were expected to be Soviet, East German and Polish navies with their naval air arms and supported by air forces from those countries. The offensive parts were not likely to be carried out.

Germany

The German perspective of naval tactics differed on several points, and they were brought to discussion in AFNORTH. We analysed the German rearmament in chapter 8, showing that the leadership of the German navy was quite keen on a forward strategy in the Baltic, demanding offensive action by the navy, including amphibious landing of forces in East Germany. We also saw that a number of analyses cast doubt on the feasibility of several tactics. The discussions continued in the early 1960s.

Towards a more offensive approach?
The target numbers for the navy in MC 70 were changed in 1960–61 by the introduction of a new order, MC 26/4. In effect, the a new type – a missile destroyer – was introduced with a target number of 13, the destroyers/frigates were six, and a new type of submarine, the chaser, was introduced with six (ordinary subs reduced to 25). These changes would be costly, and the German minister had some numbers reduced: missile destroyers to six (but ordinary destroyers/frigates increased to ten). A new type of patrol craft was introduced as a future project, armed with antiaircraft missiles, later named the TARTAR-corvette. Furthermore, the number of fighter-bombers (F-104 STARFIGHTER) was increased from 72 to 90 while ASW aircraft was reduced from 24 to 12. All together, however, the new target numbers meant a significantly larger and more offensive navy with a potent attack air arm; in addition, there was the new missile-armed corvette (to be designed) to protect the navy in the Baltic against Soviet aircraft and missiles.

The possibilities for this more offensive and well-protected navy spurred the ministry to challenge NATO's plans for the Baltic Approaches. In October 1962, after the creation of BALTAP, the German ministry of defence presented its views on the AFNORTH war plans for the Baltic Approaches at a seminar in AFNORTH in Oslo.[5]

---

[5] Note: Which Strategy should NATO select in the Baltic? NATO SECRET. Fü M II 7 – Az 31-02-02. TgbNr 52/62. 8-10-62. BW 3/1899.

It was a quite strong critique of NATO's defensive tactics, based on mining the Approaches. The Germans found that when one went into detail with the defence plan, there was only the mining left, and not a word about offensive action. This might have been wise under the conditions up to now (the creation of BALTAP) with rather weak naval NATO forces, but for the future it was inadequate.

The Germans maintained that the Soviets would be very interested in getting sea power in the Baltic Approaches, and their navy together with the satellite navies would be strong enough to get control of the western Baltic and conquer the Danish isles. But intelligence information indicated that no major amphibious operation against the Approaches was planned. The main role of the Soviet navy rather was to prevent NATO forces from penetrating the eastern Baltic and to support the operations of the Soviet army (historically, the main role for the navy). If the Soviets were to attack westwards, it would probably be done by army forces entering the Cimbric Peninsula. Of course, one could not completely rule out a surprise landing as a "local hostile action" (the Germans thus pointed indirectly to the possibilities in MC 14 of non-massive retaliation) on one or more Danish islands by provisional landing craft, in cooperation with paratroopers. Bornholm might also be at risk as an isolated hostile action.

The Germans found that the present NATO plan for mining would leave the waters south east of Øresund open for the operations of the enemy and only permit NATO operations as occasional thrusts. If the enemy kept a defensive stance and remained in the Baltic, the mines in the narrows were dispensable. And if the enemy chose to break out into the Atlantic before war, they would be useless. Maybe the mines were useful as an additional security if the enemy turned to an offensive attitude. But if the NATO naval forces got stronger, NATO could maintain sea power in the Western Baltic and keep the enemy at bay, and then the minefields would be an obstacle for own movements. And if the territory linked to the minefields was conquered, the mines would quickly be swept.

So minefields would be desirable now (1962), but only until the NATO naval forces got stronger, and then the role of the navies – step by step – would be to keep the sea clear of the enemy as far to the east as possible. Then the minefields in Kattegat and Storebælt could be cancelled and used for offensive mining operations; in addition one was to keep a reserve for mining their own harbours and inlets if NATO had to evacuate Denmark militarily.

An offensive NATO naval tactics, then, would involve
- maintaining full control over the Western Baltic (East German harbours were located in the south western part). The enemy would probably try to mine the area south of Gedser, which had to be prevented. The harbours of the enemy had to be mined by NATO and remaining enemy ships destroyed.

- challenging the enemy's naval control of the Central Baltic (south east of Øresund, including Bornholm). Easily accessible from southern Denmark and Gedser Strait, NATO was to detect and fight every movement of the enemy in that area. Enemy mining was to be prevented, and enemy sea transport be halted. Offensive NATO mining was to start by German FPBs the night before D-day at the nearest East German harbours and inlets and then continue eastwards, in effect blocking all coastal traffic including the route along Pomerania until Gdansk. The enemy would then be forced to go north of Bornholm, risking attacks from the Danish navy.
- inflicting as much damage as possible to the enemy's naval movements in the eastern and northern Baltic, primarily by submarines and the German navy's air arm.

These plans were maybe daunting, but they would be possible from the start of 1967 when the German navy and its air arm would reach the target force of MC 26/4. The offensive principles would give the initiative to NATO instead of having to wait passively – behind a mine blockade – for the enemy to take action and let them work undisturbed in the Baltic waters.

Offensive mining in the Baltic?
One particular aspect of naval offensives in the Baltic was the prospects for mining, making the operations of the WAPA navies difficult. The German ministry therefore made a list of the harbours and the ships normally based there and asked for an analysis of the possibilities for blocking them from free access westwards,[6] attaching a map of the Baltic and its relevant base areas.

The Marinewaffenkommando did the analysis;[7] we shall only refer to parts of the document. The paper stated that the most efficient way forward would be to lay minefields close the harbours, but this also was difficult and risky, and the desirable maintenance was even more risky. It was recommended to, first, protect one's own coasts with minefields; second, to mine the closest enemy ports; third, to establish fields north and south of Bornholm; fourth, to lay a minefield between Mittel and Stolpe Banks east of Bornholm; and fifth, to block ports further to the north in the Baltic.

The document pointed to 50 (!) FPBs armed with wire guided torpedoes as the most efficient means to carry out the laying of non-controlled mines (since airplanes were not available); other ships were to carry out the laying of controlled mines and minefields north and east of Bornholm. The minefields should, if at all possible, be laid at the same time and just in time when war broke out. Therefore, it was "unavoidable" that about 30 per cent of the FPBs had their mines on board and were close to their operation areas. These were to lay the easternmost fields. The other FPBs were to meet specially dedicated mine transport ships at sea and load their mines from them. Other types of mine layers were to load their mines from barges or land bases with depots.

---

6 Fü M II 3: Studienaufgabe. Geheim. Az 32-01-11-72, 24-2-60. BM 10/23.
7 Marinewaffenkommando: Offensive Minenkriegsführung in der ostlichen Ostsee in den ersten 14 Tagen eines Krieges. Geheim. TgbBr 1986/60 16-12-60. BM 10/23.

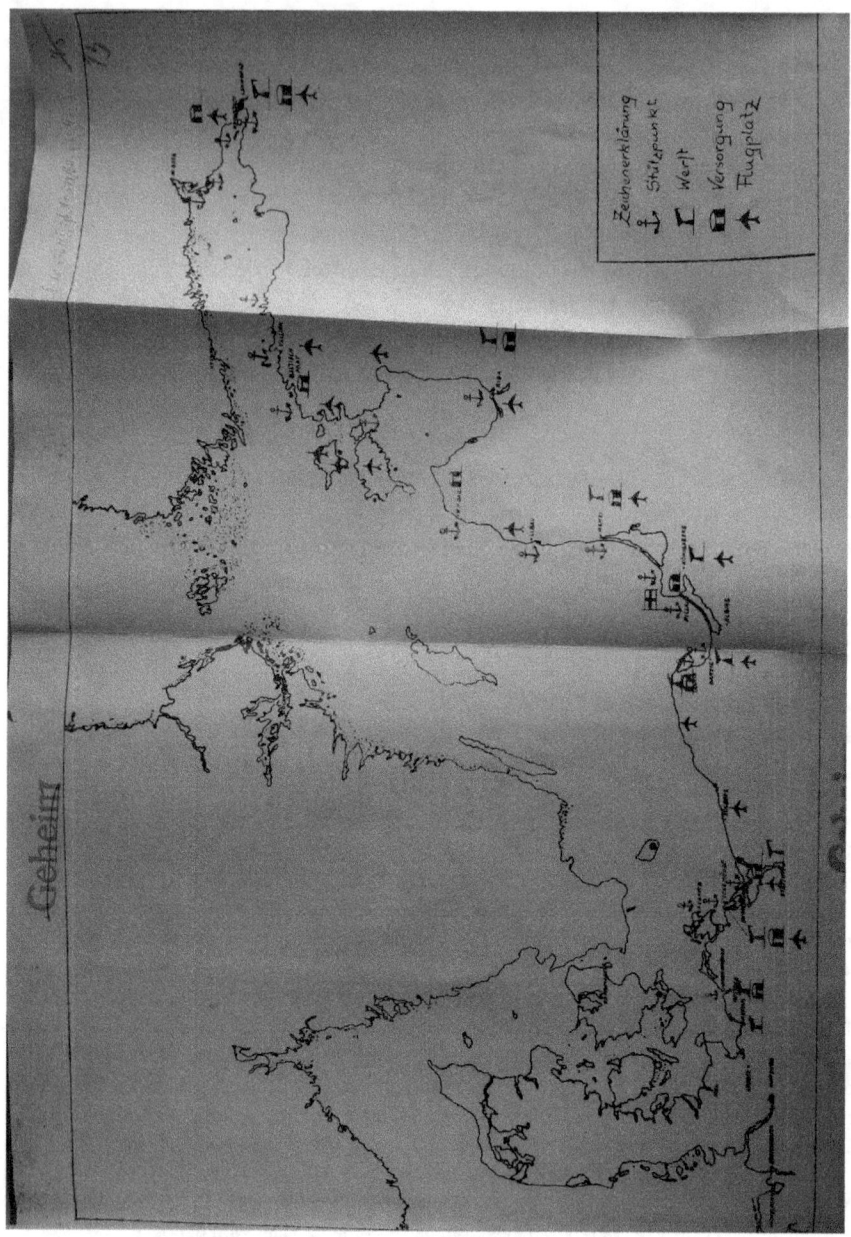

Figure 13.2: Ports to be mined in the Baltic. Source: Archiv für Bundeswehr.

The project was never implemented. The main role of mining remained defensive.

The German ministry stressed that of course, the present (1962) war plans were to the point. But another future should be planned, and the Germans asked NATO to prepare this by letting a working group analyse a move from "bottle up the Baltic Approaches" to "hold them wide open" in order to make NATO sea power felt, also in the Baltic.

The above offensive approach was a continuation of Admiral Ruge's ideas which were presented in chapter 8. In a series of analyses, warnings had been voiced about the threats against NATO naval operations from Soviet aircraft. Captain Wegener, now a commodore (and later COMNAVBALTAP as vice admiral) continued the analytical work on the conception.

Another aspect was introduced in December 1961 in a series of papers analysing the possibilities of naval NATO operations against the Soviet Baltic forces.[8] The starting point was that the Soviet air forces in 1960 had been reorganised so that the previous naval air arm was dissolved and integrated into the joint air defence. The most feared aircraft, the fighter-bombers trained to attack NATO vessels, were retrained to fight NATO strike-aircraft. In effect, the Soviet navy no longer had fighters and light bombers under its command. They only had aircraft for recce, ASW and transport. The consequences were far-reaching, in effect limiting the navy to a defensive role in the eastern Baltic (to some degree supported by aircraft from the air force), some offensive mining by submarines and limited offensive missile attacks by FPBs and/or destroyers in the area west of Bornholm and south of Øresund. The navy was dependent on the air force for support, and intelligence reports had no observations of offensive cooperation between air force and navy, but protective screens could not be ruled out; the pilots, however, did not have the training and understanding of naval actions which the former navy air arm pilots had.

This was a major change in littoral warfare in the Baltics, and the conclusions weighed in when the conception presented for NATO in Oslo the year after was being written by the ministry: The Soviet navy mainly worked as a defensive, not an offensive force, and this permitted a more offensive tactic by NATO.

A position paper from August 1962[9] concluded that the new organisation of the Soviet navy indicated the lack of offensive tactics. The ships were now linked to local commands in each sea district, they had weak anti-aircraft weaponry and the air arm was dissolved (minus TU-16 bombers which were, however, thought to operate in the North Sea and British coast). Offensive measures would be reduced to attacks by missile-FPBs and offensive mining by submarines. Instead, defensive operations to protect one's own LOCs and keep NATO ships out of the eastern Baltic

---

8 Sander-Nagashima, Johannes Berthold. *Die Bundesmarine 1950 bis 1972*, 209–24. München: Oldenbourg Wissenschaftsverlag, 2006.
9 Note "Ostseelage Marine", Geheim Anlage zu FÜ M II – TgbNr 3183/62 010862. BM 1/730.

were prioritised. Larger units were kept in the eastern Baltic to keep the Swedish navy at bay and to be prepared for raid-like attacks north and west of Bornholm to challenge NATO's sea power, maybe supported by aircraft.

Still, a Soviet capability for offensive action should not be ignored. Since Bornholm was so weakly defended, one might suppose that it would be taken by paratroopers even before D-day. It could then become a stronghold for new operations against the western Baltic. The size of the Soviet amphibious craft group did not point to an immediate operation against the islands in the Danish narrows; such an operation would rather start when army forces had taken the Cimbric Peninsula. However, one could not rule out a surprise amphibious attack against the islands on day one. This would require involvement of most of the ships of the Baltic navy, and it would be difficult to hide the intentions in the days before the attack because of the many ships and troop concentration in harbours. In addition, there would be increased recce by aircraft.

The foundation for an offensive approach withering away

Not everybody agreed with the above evaluation of the defence of the Approaches. The Danish Intelligence Office read a draft version and commented (to the Danish navy command)[10] that it saw the Soviet navy as capable of quite offensive actions; yes, part of it was organised locally, but another part was organised for offensive operations. On the other hand, missile destroyers were mainly deployed outside the Baltic – and their AA-weaponry was not that poor. Finally, the Danes did not see Bornholm having any importance for the Soviets, once its radars were taken out (i.e. annihilated by WAPA forces).

From Summer 1962 to Summer 1963 a more negative mood gradually took over in the German navy's top, to some degree fed by commodore Gerlach who was key official in the preparations for a new bill for the navy to the parliament. In a note from June 1962[11] he pointed out that the Soviets could attack the Danish islands as soon as D-day plus one, and the idea that they should wait till later was not credible, in particular if they had control of the Approaches as a high priority. In Gerlach's opinion, they did. Therefore, in June 1963 he concluded that the assessment of the Soviet navy's tactics as rather passive was inaccurate.[12] The Soviet

---

10 FSTE's kommentarer til det med SVK's skr. lb. nr. 5419 O.2/204 af 19-9-62 tilsendte af Führungsstab Marine udarbejdede "Zur Feindlage in der Ostsee". HEM. Forsvarets Efterretningstjeneste: KC. Kopibog med bilag (afklass.) (1947–1967) 12: 1962 901–2114.
11 "Bemerkungen zur Ostseelage 1962. Geheim. 19-6-62. BW 8/I 528c.
12 "Die Vorwärtsverteidigung auf der Ostsee". Geheim. Speech to the "Kommandeurtagung" 6./7. Juni 1963. BM 10/37.

navy had gained a technological lead which it would take many years for NATO to match. The threat from missile destroyers and FPBs could not be denied. Their electronic systems were of high class. And their light bomber TU-16 BADGER could hit NATO vessels from far away – NATO had no ship-bound weapon to counter such an attack. Finally, earlier thoughts that the navy could not expect support from the air force were not correct.

Therefore, the most dangerous case was that the Soviets attacked the Approaches from day one. Such a determined attack could only be planned with comprehensive support from the Soviet air force. If so, NATO could not resist the amphibious landings on Zealand, and at the same time, the Cimbric Peninsula would be conquered by the Soviet army. The Soviets would gain sea control even in the western Baltic. The NATO navies would be pushed back to Skagerrak and the North Sea.

There was hope, however. If the Soviets did not attack the Approaches immediately, there would be time for NATO to lay out mines as planned in the middle Baltic. Still, Bornholm could not be held, and one was to expect attacks by missile-armed units in the middle Baltic. In the western Baltic, the German navy could maintain sea power. NATO would, however, not be able to attack forward east of Bornholm.

However, although this was the situation in the Summer of 1963, such a development would not proceed inevitably. Following NATO's plan, Gerlach made the case for a future destroyer with both sea and air missiles which could operate under almost all conditions. When the German navy got missile destroyers and in addition missiles for FPBs, and when the F-104 STARFIGHTERs became operational in the air arm, the scales might tip for offensive NATO operations into the Baltic east of Bornholm. And if the navy could get ten TARTAR-corvettes, they could protect all naval movements west of Bornholm. Until then, any idea of forward defence in the Baltic was out of the question.

The pessimistic scenario for the defence of the Baltic Approaches thus became dominant: until the mid 1970s, the German navy would not be armed to efficiently counter an amphibious attack in the middle Baltic. The destroyers were not allowed to operate there, the missile corvettes were not built and the first missile FPBs were not ready until 1972. Until then the navy believed that it could attack the LOCs of landed Soviet forces, but hardly prevent the invasion itself in the waters east of Gedser. In the western Baltic the navy could maintain sea power, supported by its own air arm and anti-aircraft missiles.

So in the 1960s, the destroyers and frigates of the German navy were taken out of littoral warfare; their main operations were changed to the North Sea where they would protect LOCs from England and the USA and counter WAPA ships breaking out of the Baltic or trying to enter the Baltic. The only men of war able to operate east of Bornholm were submarines which were to attack Soviet LOCs and invasion forces.

Danish-German cooperation in Denmark: Exercise DALGAS

Danish-German cooperation in war time was tested in exercise DALGAS in 1962.[13] The excerpts below concern the plan for the exercise, not the actual implementation, but they illustrate the stakes.

The situation before day one was that NATO minefields were being laid in the Baltic Approaches under constant fights with enemy groups. A force of enemy merchant ships and amphibious craft with strong escort was closing in on the Copenhagen area in spite of heavy losses. Danish losses also were serious: one frigate, one mine layer, four MTB and one coastal defence craft had been sunk. By dawn an enemy brigade had landed on Amager (southern part of Copenhagen) and at the oil harbour of Copenhagen. The enemy was laying mines from the air outside Fredericia harbour in Lillebælt.

Day one. Signal received from the German navy that the bases Neustadt and Kiel were to be evacuated to Jutland. Needed was:
- 300 meters quay with four meters depth;
- anchorage for six coasters and 2 600-tons tankers;
- 1,000 m^2 storage room within 10 kilometres from the harbour;
- accommodation and catering for 600 reservists within 25 kilometres
- space for 200 trucks within 25 kilometres; and
- buildings with water, electricity, sanitary installations and room for 120 beds for a field hospital within 50 kilometres.

The Danish navy got a political approval of using the harbours in Grenå and Ebeltoft for bases, and the Danish Board of Shipping was requested to remove all ships except the ferries. Seaward transport was to be taken care of by the NCS-authority. The naval base in Frederikshavn was requested to assist in establishing the two emergency bases; transport on land was to be taken care of by two groups of 100 trucks and 400 men, crossing the border at 02.00 and 10.00 next day (this was a time of border control! PB).

13.00. Signal from a patrol craft that had taken up one wounded and one killed crew member from Soviet aircraft that crashed north of Æbelø; arrival in Juelsminde Harbour at 15.00.

14.00 Signal from Esbjerg that a Finnish merchant ship ANA KARELEN had called with 40 trucks and 30 tractors destined for Leningrad. The local naval station asked for orders.

---

[13] Marinestaben: KC. Hemmelig kopibog (afklassificeret) (1946–1975). Brev nr 5849 HEM af 10. oktober 1962.

During the afternoon conventional air strikes against Frederikshavn, Århus, Esbjerg og Fredericia. A power station, several oil depots and the NATO-pipe line in Frederikshavn were destroyed.

15.45. The FPB flotilla wanted a torpedo depot on the Harbour of Grenå for 40 torpedoes, compression gear and technical personnel for readying the torpedoes; all relocated from Torpedo base Kongsøre (on Zealand).

16.00 The workers on the yard Århus Flydedok go on strike – the Danish corvette DIANA was there and lacked eight hours' repair time on its main engines.

16.30 A Danish mine sweeper flotilla calls at Fredericia harbour wirh 8 dead and 3 wounded. Requested POL, food, 20 mm ammunition.

20.00 Eight German mine sweepers request access to Esbjerg Harbour to sweep mines from the following day at 04.00. No mother ship was available.

23.00 German frigate GNEISNAU requests 200 tons oil to be delivered in Mårup Vig.

During the night to day two the Danish navy laid mines in Northern Øresund, and they were enhanced during day two. Counter attacks against the enemy's LOCs South of Copenhagen resulted in losses. Scattered actions between German and enemy groups in the Strait of Fehmarn. An attempt to break through the Strait of Fehmarn was stopped by joined air force and FPB groups, but enemy mines were laid at Langeland and Lillebælt, and enemy FPBs landed enemy special forces in Gedser, Rødbyhavn and Mommark.

Day two. 08.00 Conventional air attack on Frederikshavn – two ammunition depots totally destroyed. Civilian ship sunk in the outer harbour, blocking entry of the whole harbour.

08.15. Signal from Danish patrol craft HUITFELDT requesting repair of superstructure (aluminium), hull, turbines and radar in Århus, arrival at 16.00.

08.30. East German patrol craft calls at Kolding, the crew wants to join the NATO forces. Local commander requests orders.

09.00. Signal from patrol craft Y 338 that it approaches Hvide Sande with two slightly wounded Soviet sailors saved in the North Sea.

10.00. American destroyer USS GEARING calls at Esbjerg Harbour with 15 woulded and five dead. Requests catholic priest.

11.15. Transfer of ammunition from Gribskov (Zealand) to Djursland (Jutland): 700 105 mm, 2,000 102 mm, 40,000 40 mm and 20,000 20 mm. FPB's Mobile Base will assist in taking these on board in Hundested and Gilleleje.

Midday severe damages from conventional air strikes at Frederikshavn Yard and FOD HQ outside Århus. FOD's staff transferred to Frederikshavn.

14.00 15 mechanics and seven electricians needed in Grenå Harbour.

16.00 Danish MTB requests repair in Vejle Harbour of hull, machinery and guns.

20.00 Mine layer VINDHUNDEN requests 58 mines Mk 25 delivered in Århus together with 40 mm ammunition, POL and food.

23.15. German destroyer Z1 seriously damaged, sinking after air attack in the Western Baltic. Requests tug and salvage assistance.

During the night to day three enemy forces are concentrated in the Strait of Fehmarn, and enemy destroyers and FPBs succeed in getting through to the Bay of Kiel and Lillebælt, followed by an amphibious group which is landed during the day in the Bay of Genner. Enemy FPBs break through to the Bay of Århus.

Day three. More of the types of episodes seen above. Exercise ends at 12.00

The exercise showed how various, some quite mundane, requests came to the naval HQ which had to respond by ordering various naval branches to react and/or ask/negotiate with other civilian or military authorities to create a solution to the problem at hand.

Defending Fehmarn

The German island Fehmarn was close to East Germany and deemed a possible target for amphibious landings, making possible a strong enemy influence on the traffic in the Strait of Fehmarn between Denmark and Germany. And vice versa: the island was the north eastern foremost point of Germany and an important base for radar and other systems of observation, in particular sub-sea electronic devices for detecting submarines. It was also base for the protection of minefields in the Sound and for artillery supporting radars.

A German analysis from 1958[14] pointed out how the defence of Fehmarn was dependent on the ability of the defensive forces on the mainland to keep their positions and thus protect Fehmarn from an attack on the beaches on the southern part of the island.

In the case of a surprise attack e.g. in the dark or in foggy weather, the island was defenceless, and a number of ways to block physical access from the sea were discussed. But even then a landing process from the air was still a possibility. In 1967, another report[15] was written, once again describing the need for defence systems. It seems, however, that the main defence remained a system of mines along the coast. In addition mobile army forces, to be delivered where necessary by the German army in the area, were supported by Danish forces moving south from Jutland. Helicopters were to be used for recce to reveal upcoming attacks on the eastern coast of Fehmarn.[16]

---

14 Wehrbereichskommando 1-III: Studie über die Verteidigung von Fehmarn. Geheim. Az 10-01-00 10-6-58. BM 10/22.

15 " Die Bedeutung der Insel Fehmarn für die Sicherung und Verteidigung der linken Flanke der NATO-Streitkräfte im Raum der westlichen Ostsee." Streng Geheim. Blatt 3 zu StabStudÜbBw – AZ 31-05-00-51 – TgbNr 31/67 – 01-12-67. BM 1/2970.

16 Gerd Bolik. *NATO-Planungen für die Verteidigung der Bundesrepublik Deutschland im Kalten Krieg*, 31. Berlin: Miles-Verlag, 2021.

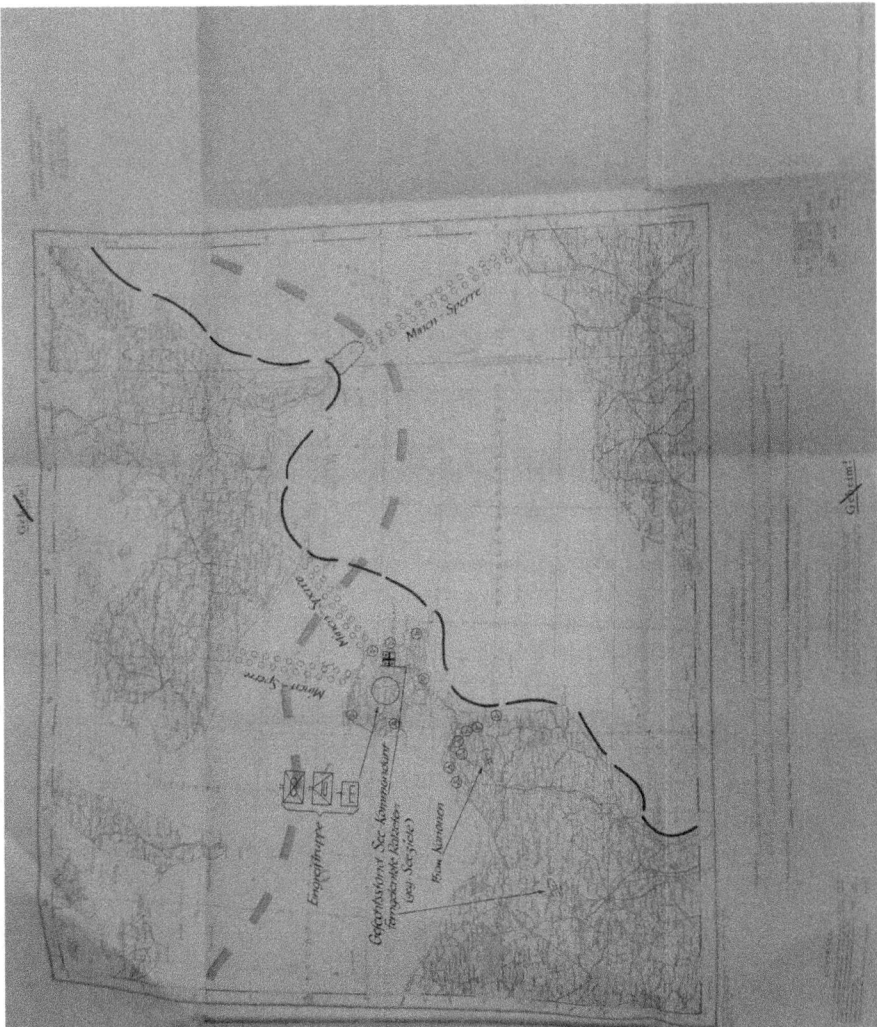

Figure 13.3: Map of Fehmarn and the desired defence positions on the island and on the mainland. Three mine fields are indicated. Source: Bundeswehr Archiv Freiburg.

Modernisation of the two navies

In spite of the somewhat different views of naval tactics in the Baltic, the two navies agreed about the need for modernisation. Most of the ships were from or based on principles from WWII, and the technological development demanded comprehensive changes.

Self-evaluation of the Danish navy 1962

The Danish navy was in a poor condition in 1962. Most ships were outdated, and the crews lacked professional hands. Most of the second half of the 1950s had seen endless and fruitless negotiations in a negative spirit among the political parties to reach a level of military defence suitable for present-day challenges (see chapter 5). The political compromise was reached in 1960, and the navy got a quite comprehensive programme for building new ships.

Were conditions really so bad? The Danish navy wrote an annual report about the state of the navy: material, personnel etc. The 1962 report[17] from FOD Denmark hardly pleased the chief of the navy:

> All together, FOD must say that with present available means it will not be possible to solve in any acceptable way the tasks of the present plans for the command. On the contrary, it can be predicted at even with the utmost dedication from all hands only very modest results can be obtained when we face a conscious and determined opponent with modern material, and with potent forces.

- The three frigates (ex HUNT-class) were worn out and outmoded; their main armament was not usable with radar control; their anti-aircraft guns were poor, their speed was too low.
- Two patrol frigates (for northern waters and fishery inspection) were outdated.
- The four relatively new corvettes were under rearmament. When completed, the ships should operate satisfactorily, but their speed was too low. All of the above had no atomic, biological or chemical defence worth mentioning.
- The two ex-coastal destroyers were outmoded and they could not stay at sea for long without replenishment. To be used for fast mine laying if escorted by other ships.

---

17 "Rapport om tilstanden indenfor Søværnet," HEM. 24-4-62. 269 – HEM u 30/62. Marinestaben: KV Varia, klassificeret (1962–2004) 1: Øvelser 1962.

- Six MTBs were relatively new and well-functioning as MTBs, but not usable for MGB roles and patrol. The remaining four old German WWII MTBs were worn out.
- The fighting value of the four (new!) submarines was modest, lacking modern torpedoes and fighting control instruments. Their submerged manoeuvring abilities were poor.
- Two mine layers operated well in all kinds of weather, but AA-guns were outmoded. Four old mine layers had poor AA-gunnery; one was completely outmoded, three small ones did well in protected waters but were too slow and their capacity was low.
- The various mine sweepers could do their job, but were slow and poorly armed.

In 1962, the navy was in the process of building many new ships (see below). So there was hope, but the forces available in 1962 were without doubt next to worthless.

Ships of the Danish Navy 1962

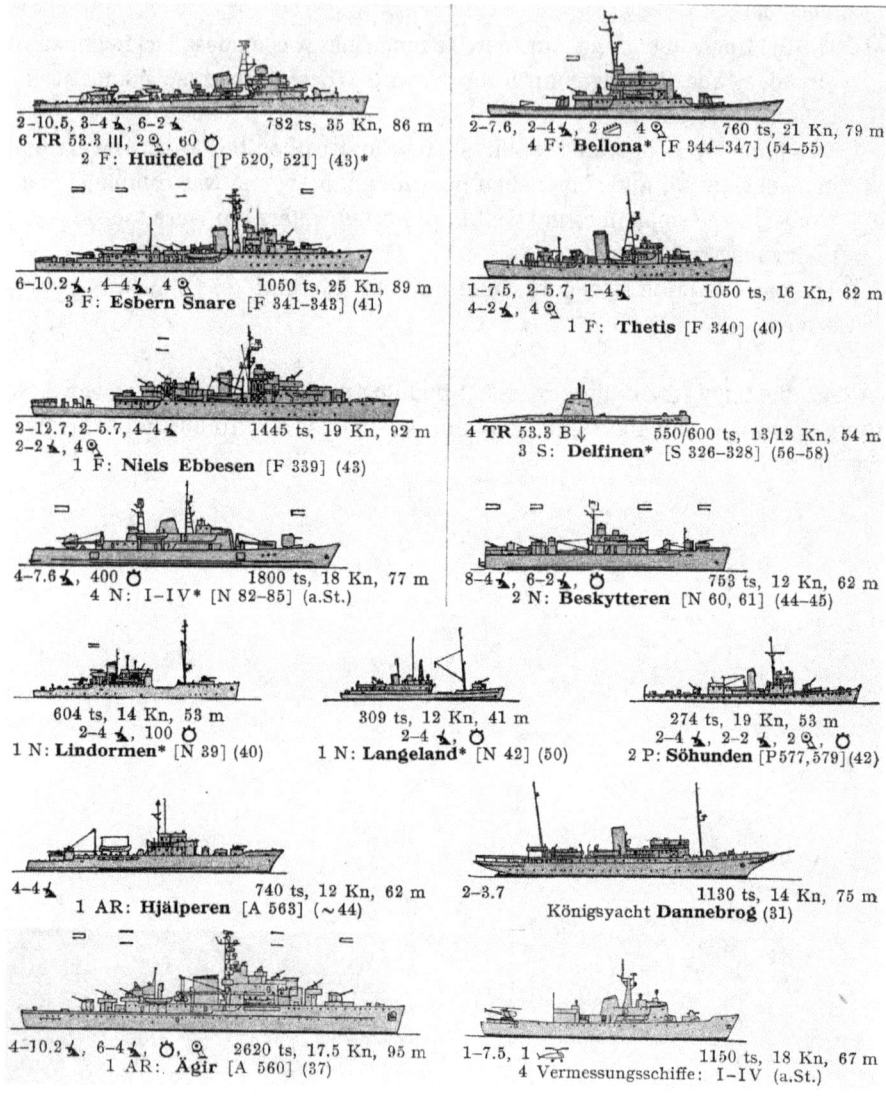

Figure 13.4: Source: *Weyers Flottentaschenbuch* 1962.

18 MTBs and 12 mine sweepers are not included above.

A modernised Danish navy

The political compromise of 1960 specified the size and composition of the future navy: eight "larger units", four frigates (for northern waters), six submarines, eight mine layers, nine small patrol craft, 18 FPBs, 12 mine sweepers and various auxiliary vessels. Two coastal forts, three naval bases.

A building programme of two "patrol" destroyers, four light frigates for the Faroe Islands and Greenland, ten MTBs and GTBs, one submarine, nine patrol craft, four large mine layers and four shallow water mine sweepers was carried though 1961–66, partly financed by the USA. The obsolete ships were scrapped.

Figure 13.5: "Patrol" destroyer (from 1966 frigate) PEDER SKRAM. 2,250 tons, 112 meters, 32 knots, 2 x 2 127 mm guns, 4 40 mm guns, torpedoes. Source: Forsvarsgalleriet.

Several technological advances characterised the new navy. First, gas turbines were used for the destroyers and six GTBs, making them fast with less weight to the machinery, and giving them possibility to leave harbour within minutes. The six GTBs were supposed to get a special role in chasing WAPA missile FPBs; for this their 40 mm guns were adequate, but they never got the radar firing control system that would make them able to operate with more precision day and night.

Second, wire guided torpedoes were introduced; they were controlled by a radar based system and could run for 15 miles (in 1971), depending on their speed. These torpedoes would typically be fired at a distance of eight miles; the previous firing distance was about two miles.

A third technological step was communication which in 1962 was expected to become teletyper-based soon. The whole communication system was expected to be reorganised based on automation as much as possible, leaving out the rather slow

Figure 13.6: GTB SØLØVEN. 75 tons, 55 knots, four torpedoes with 1 40 mm, two torpedoes with two 40 mm. Source: Forsvarsgalleriet.

Figure 13.7: Mine layer FALSTER. 77 meters, 1,900 tons, 17 knots, 2 x 2 76 mm guns, up to 400 mines. Source: Forsvarsgalleriet.

human factor in coding, decoding, writing and moving signals to the receiver. ECM (electronic countermeasures) and ECCM (electronic counter-countermeasures) were also expected to be developed more.

The mine layers were large; they increased the mine capacity of the navy three to four times. The patrol craft did not reach the planned speed of 25 knots, 20 was more likely on a good day. They were supposed to act as sub chasers, working in pairs; for many years they mainly had the task of sea patrol and recce.

A final technological step was desired, but not attained until in the mid-1970s: sea and air missiles. Against aircraft, most ships in the Danish navy had to make do with 40 and 20 mm AA guns, not enough in day time and useless at night. The automated and radar controlled 76 mm guns on the mine layers and the corvettes could do more, but the increased speed of aircraft and their use of missiles created a need for AA missiles on ships. Against ships, the need for missiles was also felt in the light of the Soviet missile destroyers and FPBs.

By 1966, the Danish navy had gone through a necessary change and had more than 30 new warships built within five years. But there still was a lack of destroyers. The defence law of 1960 spoke of eight "larger" vessels; by 1966, two new ships of destroyer size – but classified as frigates – had been built, and the four small corvettes had been redefined as "larger". So as a minimum, two more destroyers/frigates were to be built, and the navy worked on getting an additional two identical ships, but a change of government in 1968 killed the hopes for getting those two. Furthermore, two submarines, one mine layer and two FPBs were missing to fulfil the frame. Only the two subs (German type 205 built in Denmark) became reality.

The Danish navy by 1969
At the end of 1969, the Danish navy had the following ships:
    2 frigates of the PEDER SKRAM-class
    4 light frigates of the HVIDBJØRNEN class with ALOUETTE helicopters for Greenland and Faroe Islands
    4 corvettes of the TRITON-class
    6 submarines of the DELFINEN and NARHVALEN-classes
    16 FPBs of the FLYVEFISKEN, FALKEN and SØ-classes,
    9 patrol craft of the DAPHNE-class
    7 mine layers of the SJÆLLAND-class, LAALAND-class and the LINDORMEN
    12 mine sweepers of the SUND- and VIG-classes
    2 Mother ships
    2 small tankers
    10 small patrol/recce craft
The navy thus fell short of the 1960 political decision by two frigates, and two FPBs.

Modernisation problems in the German navy

The principles for expanding the German navy were to be found in NATO's MC 26/4, but it required money from the German parliament, and such means did not just come readily. The parliament demanded an analysis and a proposal for expanding the navy. The points of view we saw above came out of the preparatory work for the parliamentary bill. Vice Admiral Zenker, inspector general for the navy (after Ruge) from August 1961, was responsible for this work and came up with a modified concept for the navy in 1963, partly based on Gerlach's analyses mentioned above. He pointed out to the parliament[18] that the defence of the Approaches was not only a naval affair; it was an important building stone for the defence of the northern flank in Germany and hence weighty for the entire NATO defence concept in Europe. His presentation was centred on the need for technological modernisation of the navy with missiles: changing the weaponry of 10 FPBs and building 10 new FPBs for sea missiles; building six new destroyers with sea and air missiles, and building ten new corvettes with air missiles. The missiles were the American TARTARs which were being developed for sea as well as air targets (time would show that the sea version never materialised, PB). In addition, the F-104 STARFIGHTER would be armed with sea missiles. The defence of the Baltic Approaches and hence the northern flank in Europe was dangerously weak until the modernisation of the navy was completed.

West German navy 1962

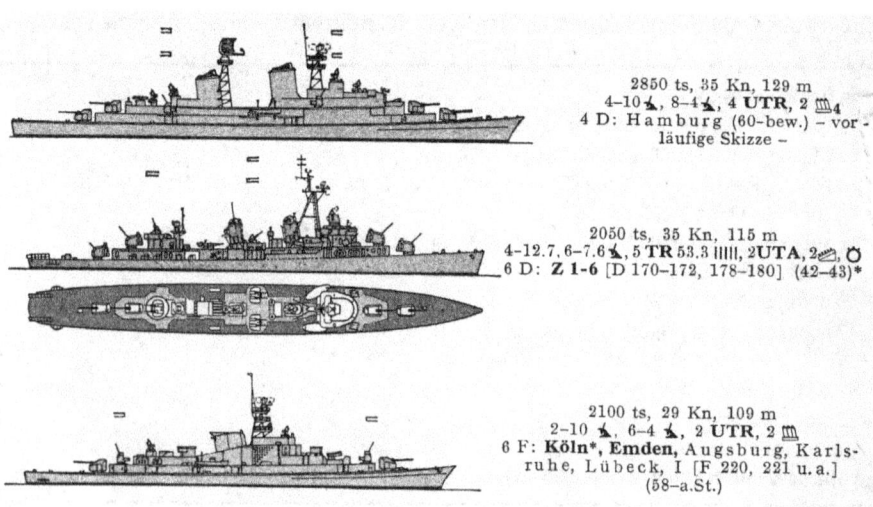

Figure 13.8: German navy 1962. Source: *Weyer's Flottentasch* 1962.

---

18 "Konzeption und Aufbau der Marine" 16-10-63. Geheim. BM 1/285.

Modernisation of the two navies — 427

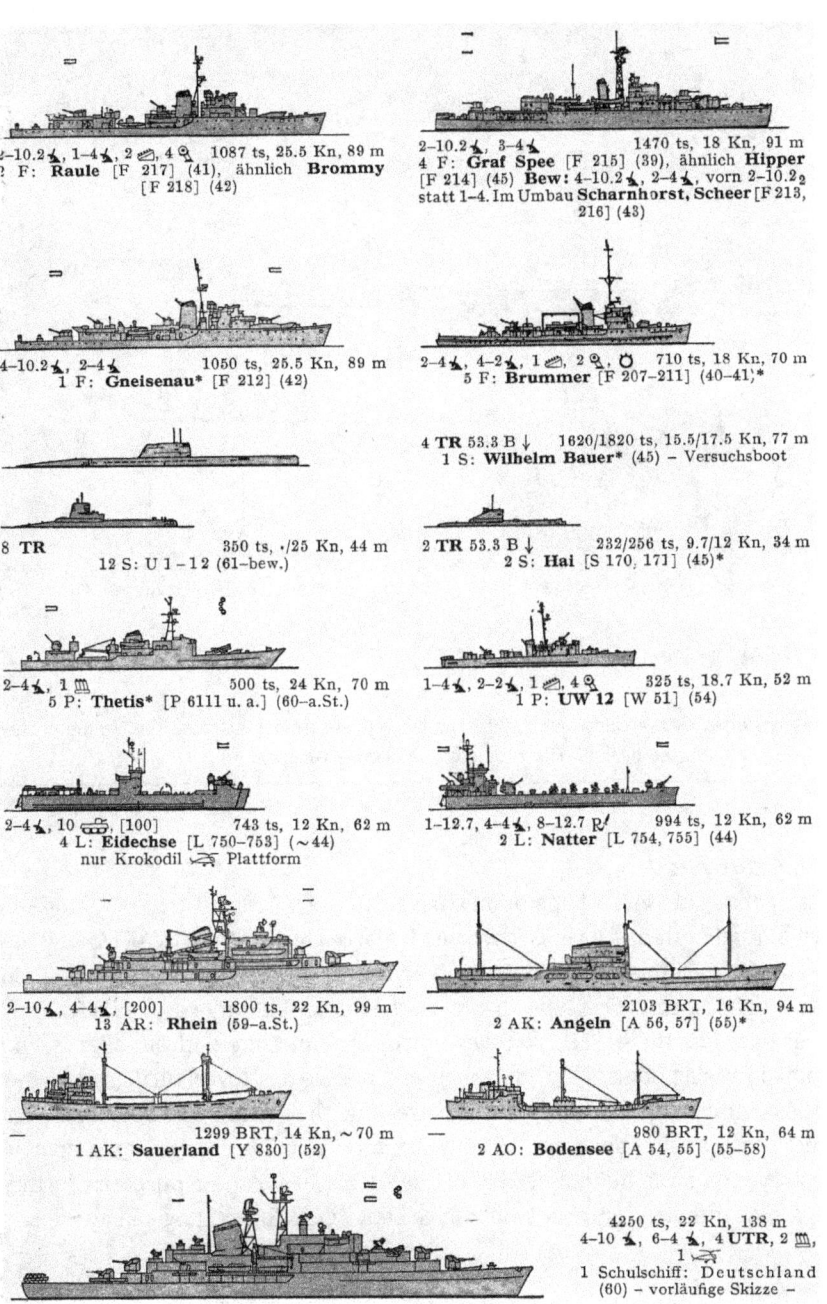

2-10.2⚓, 1-4⚓, 2⚓, 4⚓ 1087 ts, 25.5 Kn, 89 m
? F: **Raule** [F 217] (41), ähnlich **Brommy** [F 218] (42)

2-10.2⚓, 3-4⚓ 1470 ts, 18 Kn, 91 m
4 F: **Graf Spee** [F 215] (39), ähnlich **Hipper** [F 214] (45) **Bew:** 4-10.2⚓, 2-4⚓, vorn 2-10.2₂ statt 1-4. Im Umbau **Scharnhorst, Scheer** [F 213, 216] (43)

4-10.2⚓, 2-4⚓ 1050 ts, 25.5 Kn, 89 m
1 F: **Gneisenau*** [F 212] (42)

2-4⚓, 4-2⚓, 1⚓, 2⚓, ☉ 710 ts, 18 Kn, 70 m
5 F: **Brummer** [F 207–211] (40–41)*

4 TR 53.3 B ↓ 1620/1820 ts, 15.5/17.5 Kn, 77 m
1 S: **Wilhelm Bauer*** (45) – Versuchsboot

8 TR 350 ts, ·/25 Kn, 44 m
12 S: **U 1–12** (61–bew.)

2 TR 53.3 B ↓ 232/256 ts, 9.7/12 Kn, 34 m
2 S: **Hai** [S 170, 171] (45)*

2-4⚓, 1 ▒ 500 ts, 24 Kn, 70 m
5 P: **Thetis*** [P 6111 u. a.] (60–a.St.)

1-4⚓, 2-2⚓, 1⚓, 4⚓ 325 ts, 18.7 Kn, 52 m
1 P: **UW 12** [W 51] (54)

2-4⚓, 10 ⚓, [100] 743 ts, 12 Kn, 62 m
4 L: **Eidechse** [L 750–753] (~44) nur Krokodil ⚓ Plattform

1-12.7, 4-4⚓, 8-12.7 R⚓ 994 ts, 12 Kn, 62 m
2 L: **Natter** [L 754, 755] (44)

2-10⚓, 4-4⚓, [200] 1800 ts, 22 Kn, 99 m
13 AR: **Rhein** (59–a.St.)

2103 BRT, 16 Kn, 94 m
2 AK: **Angeln** [A 56, 57] (55)*

1299 BRT, 14 Kn, ~70 m
1 AK: **Sauerland** [Y 830] (52)

980 BRT, 12 Kn, 64 m
2 AO: **Bodensee** [A 54, 55] (55–58)

4250 ts, 22 Kn, 138 m
4-10 ⚓, 6-4 ⚓, 4 UTR, 2 ▒, 1 ⚓
1 Schulschiff: **Deutschland** (60) – vorläufige Skizze –

Figure 13.8 (continued)

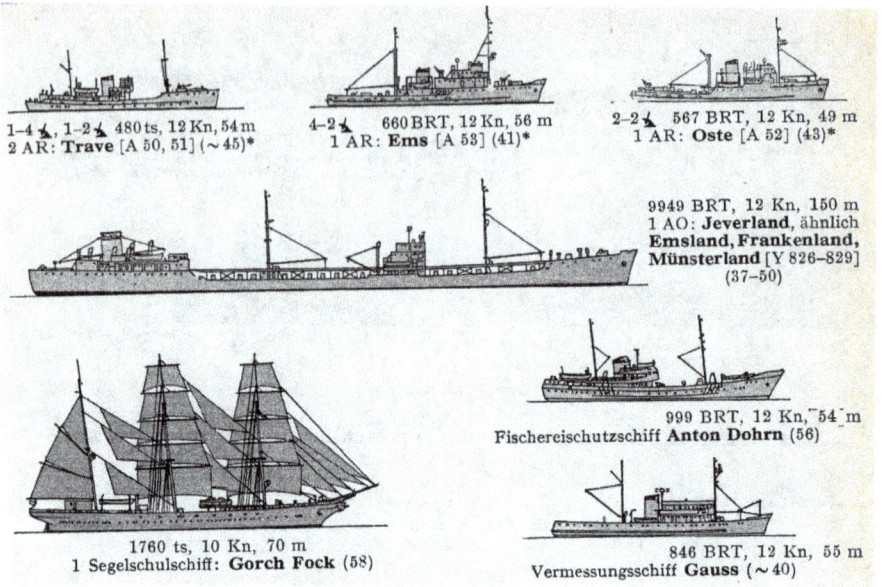

Figure 13.8 (continued)

40 MTBs, designed for the Baltic, and about 70 mine sweepers are not included. The 13 mother ships (Rhein) were mainly used by the MTBs, submarines and mine sweepers.

Missile destroyers

The Germans made several operation analyses of the missile destroyers.[19] One concerned a number of destroyers, supported by large corvettes with TARTAR-missiles and FPBs with sea missiles. They were to operate by night in separate groups with common fighting control systems based on data-links. But large groups were not a must. If one took three FPBs, two with torpedoes and one with missiles, such a group had fighting powers the equivalent of a missile destroyer; furthermore, they were less vulnerable because of their size. But they could not operate in bad weather. They might gain from the anti-aircraft capabilities and radar support of an destroyer, but one did not need a missile destroyer for those purposes; furthermore, a conventional destroyer would have better guns for fighting enemy FPBs.

---

19 Sander-Nagashima, op. cit., pp. 292–327.

The navy analysed Soviet doctrines for missile destroyers in 1964.[20] The basic tenet was that the ships with long range missiles were primarily to be used outside the Baltic, but as more units were built, they could be stationed there. They had good ASW equipment which made them independent of an ASW screening force. The capabilities of radars on ships to detect other vessels were limited; they could use radar data relayed from an airplane or helicopter flying between the firing ship and the target up to a distance of 100–150 miles. Still, the accuracy was quite limited; this might be abated by using nuclear warheads. In the Baltic radar data from other ships ("pickets") or land stations might be relayed, in reality reducing the distance to 40 miles if the target was a destroyer. By large distances the missile had to fly in rather high altitude, this made the missile vulnerable. In the terminal phase the missile used its own radar system which was considered frail. Some terminal systems might make use of the electronic signals from the target. The Soviet destroyers appeared to have a system to illuminate the target in waters like the Baltic, giving data on direction and range to the missile. But if the Soviets would be sure to hit the target with conventional warheads, four missiles had to be fired; with a nuclear warhead only one.

The new FPBs armed with STYX missiles were also analysed. The missile would be programmed for the initial flight (10–15 miles), in the terminal phase (five miles) it would have its own search capability. The KOMAR FPB class was small (75 tons) and believed to have limited at-sea qualities. The OSA FPB was larger (200 tons) and able to operate in circumstances comparable to the NATO FPBs in the Baltic. They only had 25 mm guns, but if they got better radar, they could operate them by night. But they needed escort protection against aircraft.

Since the German destroyers had a maximum gun range of eight to nine miles and the Soviet FPBs a missile range against destroyers of 10–15 miles, the NATO ships were at a disadvantage.[21] The Soviets would probably attack in groups and each fire one missile, together forming a salvo to enhance the probability of hitting the target. The highest number of FPBs in a group was five. If they were commanded by a destroyer, they could fire at 25 miles distance, more or less in a surprise attack safe from enemy fire.

---

20 Die mögliche Feuerdoktrin der russischen See- und Seeluftstritkräfte mit Flugkörpern. Geheim. Studie 19-6-64 and Stellungnahme 30-11-64 in BM 1/1244.
21 BM 1/25109.

Expendable?

The OSA FPBs might operate in groups without escort. This was the case for the East German groups. A comment from a former seaman from the Volksmarine told us why:[22] "They were expendable". He explained that the OSAs were only needed in a short while for asymmetric warfare, lying in an inlet somewhere at the Baltic, waiting for a command to attack NATO units at sea. They were "one way" boats, to go fast forward with a *gung ho*, fire missiles and then it was over. Nobody in the military top cared whether they came back. Accordingly, the training was minimal – you could use a cowboy or a lumber jack for these purposes, seamanship did not matter – they only operated 150 hours per year and the equipment was cheap.

The "states of the art" above for destroyers and FPBs would mean that NATO mother ships and destroyers in the Baltic were very much at risk, possibly from whole series of missiles fired at a large distance – this would threaten NATO traffic in the Baltic west of Bornholm. Attacks on enemy amphibious craft would become more difficult if they were escorted by missile destroyers and missile FPBs. Small NATO craft were hardly at risk due to the poor precision of the missile steering systems. So apart from this the NATO tactics in the middle Baltic were weakened. NATO had to develop gun (or missile) tactics to hit the relatively slow-flying missiles, use chaff and produce electronic means to disturb the steering systems and ways to destroy the various radar pickets for long-flying missiles.

Another possibility would be to attack the missile carriers with NATO aircraft, particularly with the new AS-34 KORMORAN air-to-sea missiles (hoped to be ready by 1968, but was not until 1973). Some of the Soviet destroyers had anti-aircraft missiles, but most could only direct one missile at a time. The sea-target destroyers were carrying relatively light (most 57 mm) anti-aircraft guns and therefore were most vulnerable if several aircraft attacked. The FPBs were likewise, but one might presume that air cover would be in place.

Finally, submarines could attack the destroyers, but hardly the FPBs. In any case, submarines were the only NATO naval units that could operate in the Baltic no matter which sea missiles the Soviets had.

Consequently, German destroyers of any kind could not operate in the middle Baltic until their own air force or submarines had dealt with the larger Soviet sea missiles entities. Therefore, the planned missile destroyers were reduced from six to three, all built in the USA as a modification of the Charles F. Adams class. The main weapons were the TARTAR ship-to-air missile, 127 mm guns and ASROC ASW launchers. The first destroyer, LÜTJENS, was ready for sea trial in 1969.

---

22 2M3. *Wie war die Situation Warschauer Pakt-Nato im Hinblick auf die Ostseeausgänge?* http://www.forum-marinearchiv.de/smf/index.php/topic,19302, 2013a.

Figure 13.9: Missile destroyer LÜTJENS. 4,700 tons, 33 knots, 2 127 mm, 2 20 mm, TARTAR missiles, torpedoes, ASW missiles. Source: Forsvarsgalleriet.

The new destroyers soon became operational but were only allowed into the Baltic if they were escorted by F-104 fighters. Therefore they were mainly used for operations in the North Sea and as members of STANAVFORLANT in the Atlantic.

Missile corvettes

The original idea was to yield protection against air attacks by ten corvettes no larger than 1,500 tons, carrying TARTAR air missiles. For their own protection against enemy FPBs they were to carry 100 mm guns, but they were not supposed to engage destroyers, so high speed was not an issue. They were to operate in groups of three with an advanced joint fighting control system which distributed targets among them. Their area of operation would be the middle Baltic, east of Gedser, serving as an additional feature of the NIKE and HAWK missiles on Zealand and in Schleswig-Holstein (Der Spiegel 1966: 18, 78). The Germans wanted to develop these corvettes together with other NATO partners, e.g. the Dutch.

However, cut-backs in the Bundeswehr in 1964 hit the TARTAR-corvettes which were reduced to four, and so the main idea of a quite widespread air protection yielded by six missile destroyers (which were reduced to three) and ten corvettes had to be put on hold.[23] The focus changed to building replacements for the six FLETCHER destroyers which were becoming obsolete. The project was renamed *Fregatte 70* with four large frigates to be delivered to the navy by 1974. The tasks were to operate against enemy surface-, air- and landing craft with wired torpe-

---

[23] EG-Shiff. Taktische Forderung. VS nur für den Dienstbrauch. Anlage zu BMVtdg Fü M II 1 – Az 10-71-10-023. 8-10-68. BM 10/3792.

does, artillery and if possible with SSM missiles; to protect itself and other, lighter units against air attacks and missiles in the operation theatre with artillery or SAM missiles; to protect itself against submarines with ASW torpedoes; and to carry out surveillance. Additional tasks were to protect reinforcements against air threats and to direct and control operations by own aircraft and helicopters.

These demands required modern electronic equipment to detect, identify, follow and fight targets at sea, under the sea and in the air. All kinds of ECM protection had to be available. Comprehensive electronic interaction with other ships and land stations was a must. The 30-knots, less-than-4000-tons frigate had to be able to operate in all kinds of weather and stay at sea for three weeks, at a range of 2,500 miles at 15 knots. In order to make operations in Danish waters and inlets possible the draught was not to exceed six meters.

But constructing ships takes its time, and the capabilities of the TARTAR missiles were increasingly questioned because of a short operation range. In addition, the various participants in the project wanted the ships to take on more and more tasks. In the end the 250-man frigate was planned with 40 missiles, four 76 mm guns, four torpedo launchers, two firing control systems for missiles and two for guns, sonar, long range air radar and gas turbines. The price followed upwards, and in 1970 the project had become so expensive that it was abandoned (Der Spiegel 1970, 23, 105).

Missile FPBs

The first FPBs of the JAGUAR class were about to be worn out by the end of the 1960s. The ZOBEL class, however, could last longer. The navy wanted to modernise them by installing a new radar-based fighting direction system for the 40 mm guns and add TARTAR missiles. The tests as such were successful: the missiles hit their targets, and the homing radar of the missiles did not get disturbed by radar images from waves.[24] This had been a problem in American tests, maybe because the waves were larger in the open sea. The German tests were carried out close to land at the island Sylt in the North Sea.

But the trial-firing of missiles showed that the hulls of the boats were not robust enough for the shock coming from the launch. In addition, the target had to be illuminated by radar during all the missile's flying time, taking "power" from the fighting control system (a small FPB only had one) until the missile had run its route; then a new target could be illuminated by the system.

The ZOBEL class therefore had to be modernised without missiles; instead they could get wire-controlled torpedoes. But were the boats worth the investment? See the box below for more on this.

---

24 Brinkmann, Rainer, ed. *Die Ära der Schnellboote*, 28. Rostock: Marinekommando, 2020.

Figure 13.10: FPB NERZ of the ZOBEL class testing a TARTAR missile. Source: www.s-boot.net.

Modernising the FPBs

A naval group was asked to analyse the operations of the ZOBEL class FPBs with and without modernisation.[25] They set up a situation with a flotilla of eight ZOBEL FPBs attacking a Soviet replenishment convoy in the mid-Baltic. The observed Soviet convoy pattern from the exercise BAIKAL in 1966 was used.

The situation was that a limited conventional war had broken out; the Soviets had landed forces from the air and from the sea in the Stevns area of Zealand. The two forces had been joined successfully. NATO forces in the area were hard pressed. NATO air forces had successfully bombed harbours, coastal radars and ships along the Baltic coast and were now attacking the enemy on Zealand.

During the night an enemy replenishment convoy had been formed at Swinoujscie by four ALLIGATOR landing craft, two conventional KOTLIN destroyers, and nine FPBs; now it was *en route* towards Zealand, probably to reinforce the landed forces in Rødvig by reaching the coast in the early morning.

It was spotted heading North West, at a speed of 12 knots, with the FPBs 15 miles ahead; one group SHERSHEN was ready to meet NATO ships approaching from Øresund, one OSA group was watching the Grønsund approach and one SHERSHEN was taking care of Gedser. The two destroyers were at close support 60 degrees to the starboard and port of the convoy which was progressing in a square formation.

---

25 Führungsakademie der Bundeswehr, Abteilung Marine: Betr. repräsentative Schnellbootlage. Geheim. 12-6-67. BM 1/1021c. The game has been reproduced at https://steamcommunity.com/sharedfiles/filedetails/?id=1908827637.

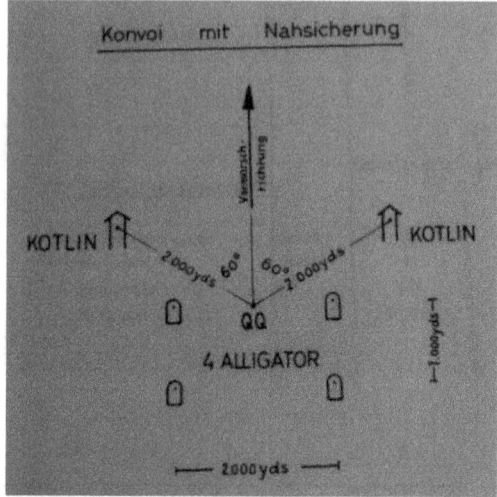

Figure 13.11: Convoy formation.

Three enemy coastal radar stations had been destroyed by the NATO aircraft attacks; therefore the enemy ships supposedly would use own radar for orientation, with one FPB in each group having radar on, and the destroyers having air detection radar on.

The German force was in waiting position in the southern part of Storebælt. It consisted of eight ZOBEL class FPBs; a mobile radar station was available on the NE part of Fehmarn. The Gedser radar station had been destroyed.

When signal was received about the convoy, the ZOBELs left their waiting position and headed east, sailing south of Lolland, passing Gedser Rev and after one hour's sailing towards Møn turning east and then south east to meet the convoy. They had radio and radar silence and used passive ECM: two boats checking for aircraft on X-band, two checking missile frequencies, three S-band for surface craft, and one boat checking IFF (L-band).

They split into three groups: two with three boats, one with two. Each sub-group leader would make a short radar sweep at certain intervals.

During operation the reactions of the ZOBELs would depend on whether they were modernissed or not. If attacked by aircraft the old ZOBELs would fire their 40 mm in concert in the direction of the spotted (visual or radar) aircraft (not unlike a barrage firing from WWII, PB). The modernized ZOBELs would use their radar directed systems to fight airplanes individually.

Destroyers had to be avoided if possible. Enemy FPBs were also as a general rule to be avoided because the main target for NATO was the amphibious craft. If it could not be avoided, the old ZOBELs would have to get on effective artillery range based on visual sight as fast as possible; the modernised units could use their radar systems at a larger distance. If meeting OSAs old ZOBELs had to approach them with maximum speed to undercut the effective missile range; listen with ECM to realise firing and then use chaff to distract the missile. Modernised ZOBELs would fight the missiles with their radar directed guns, but also by firing chaff.

When attacking the amphibious craft, maximum firing range for the torpedoes would be used: for the old ZOBELs less than three miles; for modernised ZOBELs with new torpedoes and a fire direction system ten miles distance in a timed sequence.

The conclusion from the analysis was that the modernisation of the ZOBEL boats was desirable. They remained in service until 1982.

An operational analysis in 1964 had shown that a FPB meeting a KOTLIN class destroyer would need one 76 mm gun, two guided torpedoes and two sea missiles. Against Soviet FPBs it would benefit from a 76 mm. But operations would only be feasible at night because of a lack of air power.

In 1967 it was decided to develop a new FPB of about 300 tons, much larger that the previous two classes. It would have four TARTAR missiles, two launchers for wire-controlled torpedoes, two 76 mm guns and a fight directing system M20 for all these weapons and an information system AEGIS for communicating with the other FPBs and the headquarters. Its speed was 38 knots.[26]

The commander of the FPBs saw tactical possibilities like these: the new FPBs would be a potent artillery adversary for enemy FPBs, and the missiles and torpedoes would endanger larger ships within the range of its radar system and out of reach for the enemy's artillery. Several torpedoes could be guided at the same time, but only one of the missiles. Its electronic system would jam that of the enemy. They could operate in groups of two or three, but it would also be possible to set up groups mixing two old FPBs with a new one, producing a more versatile FPB system, strong on torpedoes but protected with artillery and missiles. The enemy would not be able to distinguish the two types on his radar. The wire controlled torpedoes would put an end to the old mass-attack tactic, allowing for the picking of targets at long distances.

Between the lines of his report it was rather clear that the commander of the FPBs had some reservations against the TARTAR missile ("only one under control at a time"). He was to be right; we shall return to this later.

---

26 Commander of the FPBs: Unterlagen für Arbeitsbesprechung am 4-4-67 bei Fü M II. Geheim. BM 1/933q.

Mines – a new tactical procedure?

All thoughts of an offensive mine campaign were gone by 1968: mines could only be used defensively at this time.[27] The waters of Wismar and Warnemünde might be closed by NATO mines, but it was a very risky endeavour. Actions farther to the east were not possible due to lack of suitable transport platforms, and submarines did not have the right gear to their torpedo launchers.

But mines formed an excellent and economic weapon in the waters of the Baltic Approaches. The fields to be laid were determined by the BALTAP EDP, and a large number were to be laid by FPBs which were able to act quickly and have the job done in a short while – large mine layers took more time and were due to their size quite vulnerable – and once lost, the consequences for all mine laying plans by the navy would be severe. Two or three FPBs lost were relatively easier to replace.

Once laid, the minefields in the Approaches had to be defended against enemy mine sweeping – by one's own ships or shore batteries. But there were other possibilities for mines. Tactical use of minefields would be possible, e.g. in front of an enemy naval force moving west; even if the enemy detected the mines, they were efficient by forcing them to consider alternative actions: halting the operation and sweeping the mines, sailing around the field and running the risk of running into the arms of a NATO group, or going through the field and risking severe losses. The advantage for NATO forces would be that the mines might be programmed to go neutral after a predetermined time span, and then NATO could operate freely in that area, disregarding the mines. The main problem with tactical mining was that the preparation of the mines took time because it could only be carried out in a mine depot ashore, and the capacity was limited.

Anyway, NATO did not have such tactical actions as part of operation procedures for ships; the British had procedures for laying tactical mines by aircraft. The commander of the German mine forces recommended introducing a system of "standardised packages" of tactical mines to be laid by FPBs. Each package had to be programmed with average settings beforehand and thus easy to transport from a depot to a harbour, taken on board and dropped at the right place within a short time. This procedure would be a compromise among several factors, but at least usable in praxis.

The navy reviewed the NATO tasks of mining international waters in 1969.[28]
- The primary goals were those essential for fulfilling the NATO strategy at or before General Alert; these were the Baltic Straits to prevent the enemy to

---

27 Flotille der Minenstreitkräfte: Fakten – Analysen – Vorschläge. Geheim. 16-07-68. BM 1/1408b.
28 Fü M II 1 Az 31-05-14-00. Vermerk. TgbNr 6880/69. Verschlusssache. 5-3-69. BM 1/939e.

land forces on NATO territory. Minefields were to be laid to the west and north of the line Falsterbo-Darsser Ort and Fehmarn (including Fehmarn Belt), and – as tactics required it – mine the approaches to enemy harbours in Mecklenburg Bay. Anti-invasion mine fields were planned to the south east of Zealand. Surface operations were to support the laying of these fields.
- The secondary goals were additional mining after the primary goals; these were Kattegat and the harbours of the WAPA countries in the Baltic.

However, mining in international waters could only take place after a positive decision by the government; such fields had to be watched and neutral commercial vessels were to be guided through. The German navy's top feared that the discrepancy between military and political points of view might lead to mines being laid too late to stop the enemy. Accordingly, there was no one-to-one connection between states of alert and a fulfilled mine plan.

Electronic warfare
A war in 1962 would be heavily dependent on electronic information build-up and communication. A task group analysed status of electronic warfare in 1962 in the Baltic for BALTAP as well as the Warsaw Pact.[29] It was a comprehensive analysis; we shall only deal with the electronic warning and situation system determining the physical presence and movements of one's own and enemy forces. The sources for this information were reports by radio or teletypewriter from various units: situation maps and movement tracks from fixed and mobile radar stations and reports or relays of information from diverse units at sea or in the air. The overarching task for the navy was to integrate those sources into a comprehensive reporting system.

The land-based radars covered the middle and western Baltic, as shown on the map.

Both parties had holes in their radar coverage. It was supposed that the WAPA would use recce aircraft in an altitude of 3,000 meters to cover the western Baltic and the Danish narrows. BALTAP had no such aircraft available. Furthermore, the WAPA had coastal missile batteries whose radar might be attainable. For both parties, information was obtainable by passive ECM, using listening and triangulating devices to track enemy transmissions.

---

29 Elektronische Kampfführung in der mittleren und westlichen Ostsee. Geheim. Anlage zu TgbNr 139/78 FüAkBw. BM 11/82a.

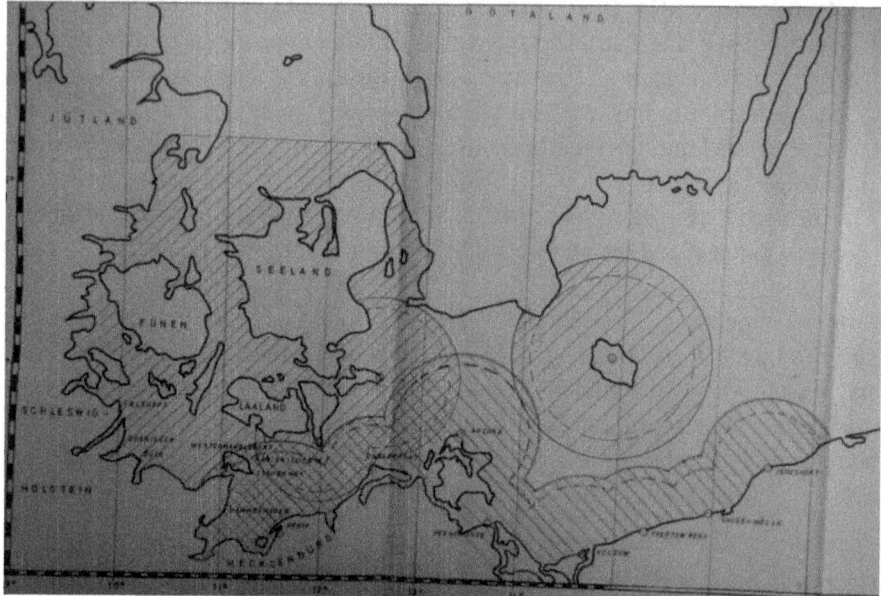

Figure 13.12: The land-based radar coverage in 1962 for NATO (blue) and the Warsaw Pact (red). The fixed perimeter indicates when a destroyer is spotted, the broken perimeter the limit for FPBs. Source: Bundeswehr Archiv.

An important question was how fast new information could get to the decision-makers on staffs. Electronic activities during the Cuba-crisis indicated that the information sharing in the WAPA was efficient, and it was supposed that all stations needing basic situation information could get it. BALTAP had two systems, one for the Danes and one for the Germans, both creating situation reports for their respective staffs. Both were based on communication going to nodes which filtered incoming signals before they were relayed to the next node in the command chain. Most flash reports would go unfiltered so that all units would have them within 10 to 30 minutes.

The report concluded that the WAPA had a very good information coverage of the middle and western Baltic and it could quickly send a low flying aircraft to uncover unknown features. The broad coverage gave excellent conditions for directing missiles from coastal batteries or FPBs. BALTAP had poorer coverage; no aircraft and ships sent out to get information were under observation by the enemy. The German and Danish communication systems did not fit one another, so it was difficult for units in operations to be fully informed. The report had suggestions of how to better the technical side of this, and it appeared that in a not too distant future, recce aircraft (BREGUET) would be available.

Logistics abroad

The German navy planned a large number of support and mother ships which were to be placed at anchor in predetermined places in Danish and Norwegian waters as soon as the threat of war became imminent.[30] In addition, stores were to be placed on the ground in those two countries, and the use of bases prepared. In Denmark, 12,080 tons ammunition, 4,000 tons material and 46,245 m³ POL were to be placed in Frederikshavn, Ebeltoft and Korsør for the navy; 11,500 tons ammunition, 12,435 tons material and 7,500 m³ POL for the army and the air force in locations in Jutland. In Norway, 8,000 tons ammunition, 6,250 tons material and 99,850 m³ POL were to be located in eight locations for the navy. Furthermore, mobile hospitals were prepared in both countries.

Together with the Danes, a system of transferring shipments from large vessels (coming from west) to smaller ships (to enter the smaller German and Danish harbours) was established.

Figure 13.13: Depot Jerup from 1962 in Northern Jutland. Ten buildings each having 470m³ storage, used for naval spare parts and a field hospital.[31]

---

30 Notitz "Betr. Lpg Vorhaben der Bundeswehr in Dänemark und Norwegen". Geheim. BW 2/50054.
31 Kulturministeriet. *Kold krig. 33 fortællinger om den kolde krigs bygninger og anlæg i Danmark, Færøerne og Grønland*, 93. København: Kulturministeriet, 2013.

A very important addition to the NATO infrastructure was the completion in 1962–63 of two naval bases in Korsør (Zealand) and Frederikshavn (Jutland). They were important for the German navy. The base in Frederikshavn had 1.3 kilometres of quay, day-to-day storage, cafeteria, accommodation for crews, repair shops, office buildings etc.

Figure 13.14: The West German navy visiting the NATO base in Frederikshavn during exercise KEY STONE in August 1963.[32]

German Emergency Base in Denmark for FPBs

In the Danish Bay of Ebeltoft, the pier LYNGSBÆK, paid by NATO, had been established to let NATO naval units replenish oil and water. In 1965, the German navy, supported by SACEUR and CINCNORTH, initiated a discussion with the Danes about having this pier expanded into an emergency base for FPBs stationed in Neustadt.[33] This city was so close to East Germany that it was in danger of falling into enemy hands soon after outbreak of war. So the idea was that at NATO simple alert, the FPB squadron would be deployed to Ebeltoft Bay.

The navy needed the following:
- A jetty 120 m. long with 4–5 m. water depth,
- Outlets for water, electric power and telephones,
- Lavatories, showers and toilets for 350 men,
- Mess hall with kitchen capacity for 350 men,
- Accommodation for approx. 200 men (permanent staff of 80 plus temporary accommodation for FPB crew members with no berths),
- Offices for about 30 men,
- Dispensary.

---

32 Ibid., 67.
33 This section is based on a series of documents in BM 1/928s.

Negotiations with Denmark were not very positive; the Danish government had problems – as before – with stationing German personnel (80 men) on Danish soil in peace time. But with the advent of flexible response in 1967 the German navy decided that the imminent danger under the massive retaliation scheme was reduced, and if necessary, a deployment might be handed by mother ship(s) at anchor in Ebeltoft Bay. The resources of the pier would be available under all circumstances.

The plan was abandoned in 1968.

New naval aircraft

The German navy decided to buy the American F-104G STARFIGHTER to supplant the British SEA HAWK. It was a potent aircraft, useful for several purposes. We shall first take a look at its recce qualities which NATO analysed[34] as follows. Four types of attacks were under consideration:

- A WAPA naval strike force made up of up to six cruisers, three missile and 37 conventional destroyers: they might be able to fire missiles at a distance of 100 miles and therefore had to be stopped before 16 degrees east, only five hours (speed 30 knots) from their home bases. A STARFIGHTER could strike them one and a half hours after the recce report was received by a Flag Officer.
- Amphibious forces in the whole of the Baltic numbered 310 vessels of various types, based between 12 and 19 degrees east. A number of those would start their operation between 12 degrees east and 13.50 degrees east, having to sail between four and 18 hours to their destination. They might be detected while in harbours at least four hours before departure. A STARFIGHTER could strike them one hour after the recce report was received by a Flag Officer.
- FPBs, probably controlled by a RIGA class destroyer and maybe coming from Poland or East Germany, raiding the Danish narrows. Some of them were one hour away, so warning time was near nil. If so, only air attacks would be effective, or else they could only be dealt effectively at source.
- Offensive mining which could be carried out by almost any naval vessel and would be difficult to spot. They might be traced by the ordinary recce system.

With an operation range of 500 miles, the STARFIGHTER would make recce possible at far larger distances than before. And its weaponry was larger and more versatile, including nuclear warheads. Its foul weather and night capabilities, however, were limited due to a weak radar system.

To warn against large-ship strikes and amphibious operations, and using the STARFIGHTER, the Baltic was to be divided into three sections for reconnaissance:

---

[34] Enclosure NATO Secret to HQ NAVNORCENT ltr. No. 3320 10-7-61. BM 1/85.

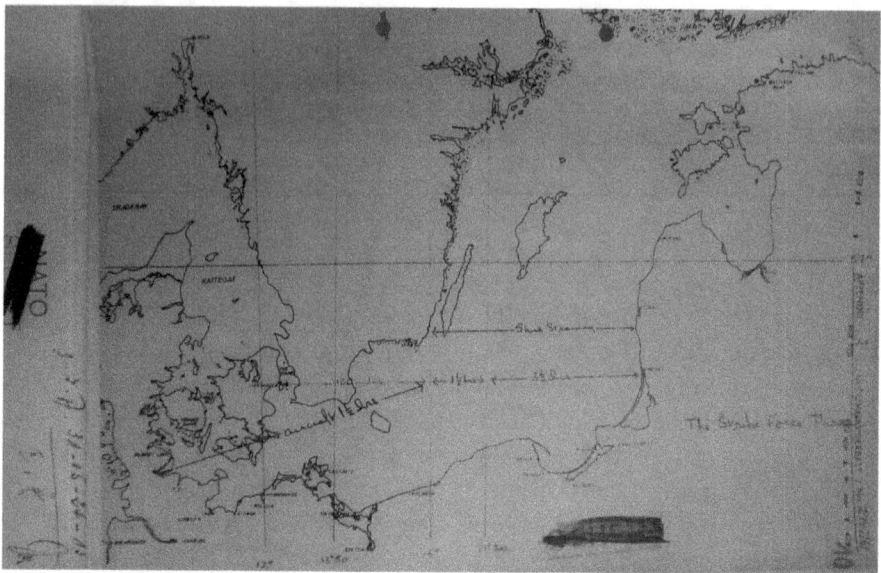

Figure 13.15: Time limits for operations by STARFIGHTERs against WAPA strike force coming from the eastern Baltic. Source: Bundeswehr Archiv.

east of 17.30 degrees east, between 15 and 17.30 degree east and west of 15 degrees east (Bornholm). The easternmost area required recce every three and a half hours to detect strike vessels on their way; the middle area every 12 hours to spot amphibious vessels *en route* west; and the westernmost area every six hours to cover amphibious threats. FPBs could not be "caught" in time, but if the STARFIGHTER was suitably armed, it could deal with them on the spot.

Naval Air Arm dealing with an amphibious landing force
At a seminar in January 1965, the Naval Air Arm described a possible use of aircraft during an amphibious attack on "13. November 1970".[35] The situation time 00.01 was NATO Alarm, Level Scarlet, and armed confrontation was imminent. A BREGUET 1150 recce plane with transferable radar signals was allocated to support the Danish coastal radar stations at Møn and Bornholm – or take over, if they were destroyed. The airplane would circle over Zealand at low altitude, protected by Danish air defence, and with various intervals it would increase altitude to 1,000 meters and use its radar for five minutes.

The day after, two Soviet cruisers and three missile destroyers were detected on patrol, in column formation, between Møn and Rügen. Southwest of those five ships were three Soviet destroyers, presumably as radar pickets. Two cruisers and three destroyers were positioned west of the Bornholm

---

35 "Einsatz der Seeluftstreitkräfte nach der gegebenen Lage". Geheim. Beilage VIII zu Anlage FüAkBw Abt M StudGrp. 26-1-65. BM 1/1244.

Gat, and two missile destroyers and two destroyers were present somewhere in that area, too. The sea was rough because of strong winds and FPBs could not operate; they were anchored in inlets behind Fehmarn. There were four groups of amphibious craft: 14 miles north west of Arcona, 14 miles south of Ystad (Sweden); 14 miles east of Arcona and 16 miles north of Sassnitz. The first two groups had 16 amphibious craft, the last two 22 and 24, respectively. All had about ten mine sweepers and between eight and 11 escorts.

At 0600 on the fifteenth the Soviet government asked for safe passage in Øresund of two cruisers and six destroyers. This was by NATO perceived as a way of access, concealing the real aim – to get close enough to attack the Danish ground-to-air missile batteries around Copenhagen and to block Øresund from the south, and to protect the amphibious groups from north and give artillery support to their landing process.

On the Schleswig-Holstein airfields of the Naval Air Arm, 36 F-104 STARFIGHTERs were ready for conventional attacks. Now the tasks was to determine ship movements east of Bornholm and get a better idea of where the amphibious groups probably were headed. The Breguet 1150 would continue its operations over Zealand, and the F-104 were to be armed with AS-34 and AS-37 missiles; they were on 30 minutes' call.

Later on the fifteenth the enemy forces initiated landings in Faxe and Køge bays. F-104s could get radar screens relayed from the Breguet 1150 which continued operations over Zealand. The Soviet covering forces stayed south of Møn, in the southern part of Øresund and at a position between the two attacking forces, to the east. The two first covering forces yielded good radar images and therefore were attacked with AS-37. The landing forces were attacked from south west in order to make use of the "radar shadow" of the island Møn. The STARFIGHTERs attacked with AS-34, starting with an interval of one and a half minutes from the airfield. But first a group of six attacked the covering force south of Møn and in the southern part of Øresund with AS-37 missiles.

The upcoming quite versatile STARFIGHTER had SACEUR's attention, and he had special tasks for it up his sleeve. This became clear when AFNORTH did a study of its possible roles in the German navy's air arm.[36]

> First, they would in part be used for the supreme commander's scheduled Atomic Strike Programme and CINCNORTH's regional ASP in the overall defence of the Baltic Exits, but particularly attacking the threats against the naval commander's tasks. Such might be part of the regional plan, but in addition, other targets (like ships having left their base) might be hit, following the "seek and kill" procedure within designated areas. SACEUR or CINCNORTH would exercise the overriding control for those purposes and later release the aircraft for the naval commander.
>
> Second, the STARFIGHTER would be used for recce of vital sea areas and harbours.

---

[36] Preliminary study by COMNAVNORTH on the employment of the German naval air arm when re-equipped with the F.104 G. NATO secret. Enclosure to AFNE 2800/3 dated 2-11-61. BM 1/85.

Third, its conventional all-weather capability would be used to its maximum extent, possibly in tandem with the recce task.

Fourth, they might be used in a general air defence capacity, if such demand unexpectedly should arise.

The airfields and air space in Schleswig-Holstein for the Naval Air Arm were under 2. ATAF command while the operations of the aircraft would take place under COMTAFDEN command; it was suggested to establish "corridors" in Schleswig-Holstein to minimise the demand for active coordination when operations were initiated.

The German navy rejected this plan at a meeting in Oslo in December 1961.[37] As to SACEUR, the navy said that other aircraft were slated for his ASP (this was the role for the Luftwaffe, not the navy), and the naval air arm planned other roles for the STARFIGHTER. Following those plans, the navy did not have capacity for the ASP. The same would be the case for use by CINCNORTH, except if the targets obviously were within the naval commander's responsibility. As to the all-weather capability, there were limits e.g. to the ability to fire against targets which were not in sight, i.e. in foul weather and in the night. And finally, under no circumstances would the navy go into general air defence; this was the task of the air force.

A year-long process of disagreements followed. The navy time and again stressed that given the strength of the Soviet navy based on missiles, the STARFIGHTER was indispensable in the planned offensive role of the German navy with attacks on ships *en route* to the middle Baltic; as detailed above, this had to be done quite deep into the eastern Baltic. This forward plan sat the aircraft aside in fixed groups for different roles in recce and attacks.

SACEUR's plan prevented this plan from being executed. If the naval aircraft were made part of an atomic strike plan, they would be held inactive on the ground in times of tension, during limited war and during conventional war – all in preparation for their role in the supreme commander's QRA (Quick Reaction Alert system, see chapter 7) if general war broke out – and thus remain unavailable for the original plans of the navy. More specifically,[38] a squadron of 18 aircraft (and three in reserve) would permanently have four aircraft loaded and ready to take off within 15 minutes. Seventy per cent (12 aircraft) of the squadron had be airborne and on their way towards their targets with nuclear warheads

---

37 Besprechungspunkte für NAVNORTH 5-12-61. Geheim. Fü M II 6. BM 1/86.
38 Fü M II 6: Vermerk Betr. Strike-planung Luftwaffe. Geheim. Az 90-15-10. TgbNr 1178/62. 27-6-62. BM 1/66.

after three hours. These bindings, however, gave too few aircraft available for the routine training and exercises for the 27 pilots in the wing, among other reasons because each STARFIGHTER only was allowed to be airborne 20 hours per month: the demand for 27 pilots would be 6,500 hours/year, with "supply" (due to various bindings) only 2,900 hours.

The recce squadrons within the QRA had the same rules but they were not to carry nuclear warheads. QRA would in effect bind one wing, with two thirds of it locked to the atomic plan, and in any case locked to SACEUR with no possibility for the navy to use them for other purposes.

Time passed, and prospects deteriorated for the navy. By 1962, SACEUR increased his demand to two squadrons for QRA from the navy, leaving only one squadron for the navy's own priorities. However, the number of aircraft to be planned for was increased to 72, and from summer 1962 to summer 1963 various discussions took place to organise for the supreme commander's demands and the navy's stated needs.[39]

What to do? First, the navy pondered to use "bureaucratic politics" by using specific regulations to rule out certain actions.[40] The stores for nuclear warheads were constructed for a specific type of bomb. The navy planned to use nuclear weapons of "type B" which were versatile in that they could be used against submarines under water as well as burst in the air over bases. SACEUR's QRA programme, however, used a "Type C" warhead which were stored in another type of bunker. NATO planned to build bunkers at two of the navy's airfields, and the navy then opted for getting bunker "type B" in both places, thus preventing that the airfield could be used for the supreme commander's QRA with type C. With type B the navy could become part of AFNORTH regional nuclear plans and thus be closer to influencing the plans for use.

The Inspector General of the German defence supported the view of the navy. However, the NATO top commanders – CINCNORTH and SACEUR – had to be persuaded to accept the protests of the navy because the decision was not to be done by the nation (Germany) but by the international system (NATO).[41]

In January 1963, a working group at a seminar in Oslo wrote a proposal for solving the problems of distributing the navy's aircraft. The navy had to accept NATO's demands: two squadrons would be reserved for nuclear strikes, two for the navy – one recce, one fighter-bomber. However, the strike squadrons would

---

39 Various papers "back and forth" are found in BM 1/66.
40 Fü M II 6: Aktenvermerk Betr. Nuklearer Einsatz der Seeluftstreikkräfte: hier: VAP-Flugzeuge. Geheim. 4-4-62. Az 31-05-24-02. TgbNr 1582/62.
41 Besprechung bei dem Herrn Generalinspekteur am 4-6-62. Geheim. Fü M II 7 N872^{II}/62. BM 1/66.

be part of CINCNORTH plans, not SACEUR's. The regional commander could not delegate his authority to a naval commander,[42] but the navy commander could make recommendations for future plans, so targets like a new (non-planned) amphibious enemy group could be taken up in the plan. However, aircraft for the nuclear warheads could not be used in-between for conventional weapons.

The German navy was not pleased with this proposal.[43] First, a role in nuclear strategic strikes had until now been reserved for the German air force. Second, the navy needed 90 aircraft (which were planned at a certain time, but then cut back again) for its tasks to fight the Soviet navy and only had 72. If half of those were taken away, the navy would be seriously weakened, and one could foresee a demand for more destroyers and FPBs to make up for the loss. Third, the navy needed nuclear weapons to fulfil its tasks, and in a foreseeable future only aircraft could provide the platform for such weapons. Such were then planned, and given the number of possible targets; one squadron was perceived to match the task. Fourth, ideas that the strike aircraft later could return to normal service were without foundation in war realities: a large number might be lost, and others might be transferred to SNOWCAT-like operations (see chapter 5). Finally, the strike tasks were waste of money seen from the perspective of the budget: money for naval tasks, not air war, even more so in the light of upcoming budgetary cut-backs.

Nonetheless, the 50–50 per cent division between the navy and CINCNORTH was maintained in 1963. For the navy, one remaining squadron was planned for recce, and the other one for fighter-bombing.

Reality, however, became what the navy wanted. The STARFIGHTERs were all included in the roles that were specific for the navy. Nothing operational happened regarding an implementation of the SACEUR strike roles except that a depot for nuclear warheads was built at the navy's airfield in Jagel. But the navy took no further action: no designation for the strikes took place, no warheads were distributed and the pilots were not trained for the strike role.

Five years later, in 1967, it turned out that in the plans specifying the roles of airplanes, a surplus capacity for the supreme commander's strike roles had been created and, in turn, airplanes for conventional roles were lacking. And – contrary to 1962 – it was now up to the German government to decide the distribu-

---

[42] Fü M II 7: Bericht über ein Gespräch mit Cpt GIBBS über den nuklearen Einsatz der Seeluftstritkräfte am 14.6.62 in Kolsaas. Geheim. 19-6-62. App 4527. BM 1/66.
[43] Kommando der Flotte: Atomare Bewaffnung der F 104. Geheim. 9-4-63. TgbNr 3-0194/6. BM 1/66.

tion of aircraft to these roles within the figures determined by SACEUR.[44] The navy therefore repeated its comprehensive series of arguments against the strike role which we saw above, updated to 1967.[45] In addition, the change in NATO strategy towards the possibility of limited war gave the navy more intense roles in times of tension, first of all in recce and support to ships demonstrating NATO's naval presence in the Baltic.

A series of negotiations among the three German forces followed, ending in an agreement between the navy and the air force that the air force would take upon it all the SACEUR aircraft strike roles, leaving the naval air arm to do what was planned by the navy: perform sea war from the air. This was announced during a perfectly orchestrated presentation in a meeting for the military top preparing the German Inspector General's annual budget conferral to the minister in February 1968.[46] Nothing was left to chance, and the agreement was approved.

This decision came at one cost: CINCNORTH no longer had access to own nuclear forces, all were with AFCENT or SACLANT's strike forces; on the other hand, no strikes were planned in the AFNORTH area (but many strikes were planned along the Baltic coast, as we saw in chapter 7). The navy had pointed out that it did not expect to use nuclear warheads against sea targets because the impact at sea was not much better than attacks with conventional means. But for reasons of deterrence the navy stated that nuclear warheads should be present in Schleswig-Holstein. However, the air force refused to base any of its airplanes in that area, referring to costs, problems with relocating personnel and the problems arising if an AFNORTH commander from Denmark or Norway had the role of commanding the use of nuclear warheads. In principle there also was a risk for the enemy taking over the nuclear depot during a surprise attack. If approved by the supreme commander, the 2. ATAF would be able to deliver nuclear strikes for AFNORTH on demand from airfields close to Schleswig-Holstein. But one should also take note that there were other possibilities for external assistance to AFNORTH.[47] The navy commented that nuclear presence might be implemented by the army and its stance only regarded the participation in strikes, not other nuclear tasks.

---

44 M II 1 – Az 31-02-01 LbNr 24/67 Aktenvermerk ... betreffend die STRIKE-rolle der Marineflieger. Streng Geheim 17-5-67. BM 1/2967.
45 "STRIKE-Rolle der Marineflieger" Fü M II 1 – Az 31-02-01 Streng Geheim 7-6-67. BM 1/2967.
46 Fü M II 1. Vermerk über die nukleare Komponente der Bundeswehr. Geheim. App: 4729. 1-2-68. BM 1-938a.
47 Letter to the Inspector General Fü M 11 1 Az 31-02-01 App 4729 Streng Geheim 28-11-67. BM 1/296.

The tasks in times of war of the Naval Air Arm, then, by 1969, were:[48]
- to perform armed reconnaissance and surveillance, particularly over the central and eastern Baltic, by detecting, identifying and shadowing all enemy forces threatening NATO areas and naval forces;
- to take the offensive by destroying enemy radar stations and then destroying enemy naval units and amphibious forces, and missile sites threatening allied control of the Baltic Approaches,
- participate in NATO naval operations in support of surface forces

It appears that previous roles of supporting one's own amphibious forces by providing close ground support were now removed.

The SACEUR strike roles were taken out, but CINCNORTH maintained a right to let Naval Air Arm aircraft participate in counter air strikes. The Luftwaffe also had demands within activities such as recce, counter air and interdiction tasks. They would make the command of the navy difficult because of conflicting interests in using a relatively low number of aircraft; this would run counter to the basic idea of BALTAP, to integrate the use of all three forces.

1966: Cut-backs

By the mid-1960s, the national German economic conditions led to cuts in the defence budget. This implied a revision of the naval plans for modernisation, and the revised Marine Program 1966–76 was set up.[49] It reflected the general understanding in the Bundeswehr that massive retaliation (which formed the starting point of the previous plans) was out of the question and limited war with flexible response and controlled escalation was what one had to prepare for. This required flexibility in the organisation. But modernisation of the navy was necessary. The destroyers and frigates could not operate against WAPA missile units and would only operate in the North Sea in ASW roles. The torpedoes and artillery of the FPBs were outdated. The mine sweepers were modern, but lacked air protection. Submarines and amphibious units were operable. The F-104Gs already were outdated because they had to come within firing range of the targets to use their weapons. ASW aircraft and helicopters, however, were operable.

The document sums up a modernisation program whose parts we have touched upon above: it involved TARTAR missiles for air and sea targets, SEACAT missiles for air targets, KORMORAN air-ship missiles, wire-controlled torpedoes

---

48 Fü M II 1 Az 31-05-14-00. Vermerk. TgbNr 6880/69. Verschlusssache. 5-3-69. BM 1/939e.
49 Fü M II 1: Das revidierte Schiffsbauprogramm der Marine. Geheim. Az 10-70-00 TgbNr 2670/66. 29-9-66, and several other follow-up papers in BM 1/895.

and new ASW torpedoes. These were in different stages of development to be in use within a not too distant future together with new electronic systems for detection and control.

New ships: missile destroyers. TARTAR-corvettes and missile FPBs would form a core together with new submarines and new two-seated fighter-bombers (the missile tasks were too complicated for one pilot).

Compared with the previous plan, the reduction in ships was not large, but new categories of readiness for operation were introduced (see table 13.1). Earlier on, a number of ships had been in reserve or under repair; now such decisions were made explicit by categories A, B and C where only category A was ready for service within 48 hours. Between 20 and 40 per cent were in category B or C. This had implications for the logistical system and the need for personnel, and a number of bases were downgraded or closed, taking the brunt of the reductions. Organisational changes also helped. In turn, a more complicated system of calling up personnel during mobilisation had to be set up.

Table 13.1: German shipbuilding programme.

Type/ Year	1963	1966	Cat. A	Cat. B/C
Missile destroyer	6	6	5	1
Destroyer	10	4	3	1
Frigate		6	4	2
Missile patrol/ frigate	10	10	8	2
Submarine	31	30	24	6
FPB	50	50	32	18
Landing craft	7	18	12	6
Mine layers	4			
Mine Sweepers	54	54	33	21
Coastal defence		20	10	10
Various other		25	15	10
Fighter-bomber	90	72	72	
ASW–aircraft	12	12	12	
Helicopter	36	36	18	18

The German navy by 1969
By the end of the 1960s the German navy had about 200 ships (of which two thirds were in the Baltic Approaches) and 200 airplanes:[50]

---

50 Arendt, Rudolf. "Die Marine der Bundesrepublik Deutschland im Wandel der Zeit (1956–2005)." In *Die Bundesmarine 1950 bis 1972*, Johannes Berthold Sander-Nagashima, 457. München: Oldenbourg, 2006.

- 12 destroyers of the LÜTJENS, HAMBURG and FLETCHER-classes
- 6 frigates of the KÖLN-class and 2 older frigates in reserve
- 4 FPB-squadrons each with 10 MTBs
- 11 submarines
- 24 amphibious craft of which most in reserve
- 5 gunboats of the THETIS-class
- 2 mine layers
- 74 mine sweepers and mine hunters of the LINDAU, VEGESACK, ADRIANE and SCHÜTZE-classes
- 12 mother ships of the RHEIN- and LAHN-classes
- 115 various support ships

The Naval Air Arm had 135 fighter-bombers F-104 G, and a squadron BREGUET ATLANTIQUE recce and ASW planes. In addition helicopters for Sea-And-Rescue operations.

One consequence of the cutbacks was that the navy had to re-think its strategic and tactical setup. We shall return to this in a later chapter.

Summing up: Caution in the Baltic

When BALTAP was set up, hopes were high for an active role in the Baltic. The commanders of both navies – FOD and FOG – wanted an offensive approach, but both had to adapt to the realities and choose a more defensive part. The Danish navy did not get the eight "patrol" destroyers promised in 1960; it had to make do with two new frigates and four corvettes, and two FPBs less than promised. Four new, large mine layers, however, were efficient but only supported a defensive approach.

The German navy initially continued Ruge's offensive tactics and wanted more action within the new BALTAP command and analysed possibilities for more offensive mining. In particular, they saw changes in the air command system as beneficial for NATO in the Baltic. However, they had to realise that the Soviets had a technologically advanced navy coming up with missiles capable of fighting NATO ships long before their guns could be brought to bear, and until NATO produced missiles to be launched by ships, one had to temper the offensive desires. Of course, this also was the reality for the Danes, but they had not aired such ideas for an offensive tactics as the Germans had. Furthermore, there was a fear in the German naval top that decisions on mining the waters might be drawn out by the politicians and thus come too late.

The cooperation between the two navies was tested in various exercises, particularly regarding the German use of Danish territory for stores and base facilities as well as anchoring mother ships in one of the many inlets. This would be a core element of littoral warfare where small units would make brief attack actions during night time or in weather with limited sight and then return to base – for which the Germans would be deployed northwards.

The Germans integrated the operations of their FPBs with the fighter-bombers of their naval air arm and thus did not need any coordination staff with the air force. The Danes had to ask the Danish air force (or the German naval arm) for support every time it was needed. The Danes therefore had a long lead time, unfortunate in littoral warfare with WAPA airfields close by.

From the perspective of NATO, the new STARFIGHTER aircraft (planned to replace the navy's SEA HAWKs) became of special interest because of its capabilities for nuclear warfare. Probably because of a shortage of such airplanes, the supreme commander decided to include part of the navy's new aircraft in the nuclear strike plan. In effect, many airplanes were denied for use by the navy. This created a strong reaction from the navy, but not to much avail: in the end, CINCNORTH got two squadrons for use in his nuclear plans. It turned out, however, that this was only on paper – the aircraft and their pilots were never trained for a strike role and remained in training for offensive and defensive tasks for the navy.

Both navies were in a relatively poor state in the start of the 1960s with outmoded ships, much technique with roots in WWII and a lack of missiles to match the WAPA navies. Both navies got comprehensive modernisation programs, but both also experienced cut-backs, particularly on larger ships. The Germans had to give up the concept of the TARTAR corvette, meant to protect naval forces operating in the Baltic; the costs became prohibitive. The Danes got modern, wire guided torpedoes about 1965, the Germans had to wait to the 1970s, and they waited so long with modernising the FPBs that their tactics came close to suicide. This was changed in the 1970s, as we shall see.

Chapter 14
Towards flexible response and new NATO bodies

As we saw above (chapter 7), NATO's massive retaliation policy stood out in its pure form for only a few years, and was then weakened by allowing non-nuclear responses to military provocations. Over the ensuing years, it was changed step by step in actual content, if not in formal form until 1967.

This author's maybe daring condensation of flexible response would sound like: get all emerging crises under control and, if necessary, restrict military actions to non-nuclear limited war. The military consequence was comprehensive modernisation of conventional forces.

We shall not go into detail with the forth-and-back changes and the NATO-political processes leading to those changes, and no archive search has been made regarding those political processes. The literature discusses a series of factors in the process, and we shall point to the following:[1]

First, the Kennedy administration took over the US government in January 1961, and soon changes in the US nuclear policy were aired. The new Secretary of Defence, Robert McNamara, strengthened the conventional line for the army and vastly expanded its overseas mobility, and continued the navy's submarine program with nuclear missiles.

Second, the Berlin crisis of the Summer 1961 pushed towards changes in NATO tactics as an eye opener regarding a need for flexibility in the concrete use of military means: who would initiate a devastating nuclear war because of the desire to maintain the status of one single city in Europe?

Third, SACEUR had initiated the process towards creating the AMF before the Kennedy administration (see chapter 15), a military force shaped for giving political signals by its deployment to areas threatened by Soviet military force build-up, thus prolonging the phase of mutual watching-out.

Fourth, defence secretary McNamara in his speech in Athens demanded a redesign of NATO's response. The strategic forces should retaliate in a flexible, measured way. Tactical nuclear weapons should also have a controlled response, exercising restraint in the scope and nature of the targeting. In conventional weapon use, NATO should aspire to conduct a full-fledged forward defence against a major attack, containing it and preferably defeating it.

---

1 Kugler, Richard L. *Commitment to Purpose: How Alliance Partnership Won the Cold War*, chap. 5–6. Santa Monica, CA: RAND, 1993; Palmer, Diego A. Ruiz. *A Strategic Odyssey: Constancy of Purpose and Strategy-Making in NATO, 1949–2019*, chap. 2. Rome: NATO defence college, 2019.

Fifth, the Cuban missile crisis – which strictly speaking was not a NATO affair – created a general sentiment that nuclear exchange should be avoided. However, the French vetoed the proposal (MC 100/1, see below for details), advocating for the massive retaliation system and blocking for further analysis along the flexible lines indicated.

Three years later France left the integrated NATO defence system, and thus made possible a renewed discussion of flexible response, leading to agreement in December 1967.

In the following sections, we shall take a closer look at some of the changes in NATO in the 1960s; first in the organisation and review processes, then in the substantive changes following the approval of flexible response. As briefly noted, a Defence Planning Committee was created in 1963 by the NATO Council[2] as a senior decision-making body on matters relating to the integrated military structure of the Alliance. The members were the same as the council, and thus it relieved the formal NATO Council of some responsibilities. The Standing Group under the Military Committee was abolished in 1966, and in 1967 the Military Committee moved to Brussels from Washington, DC. Finally, a Nuclear Planning Group was formed in 1967 to do the preparatory work for NATO policy decisions in the field.

Military planning of, and political involvement in the use of, nuclear warheads became core themes for the NPG; the committee stated that it should:[3]

> ... consider and recommend possible modifications in organisation and procedure to enable a greater degree of participation in nuclear planning by non-nuclear nations, including participation in selection, deployment, targeting, and conditions of use across the whole spectrum of nuclear weapons, and to make possible consultations in the event their use is considered.

This statement went quite far beyond the initial idea by the Americans and British of creating a body to consider "technical" matters, but it did formulate the basis for fulfilling the promises of the Athens meeting.

Strategy under stress

As we have seen above, the massive retaliation in the shape of MC 14 and MC 48 was under pressure to become less massive nearly from day one, resulting in MC 14/2, MC 48/2 and MC 70 in 1957–58 with a few valves for conventional and adapted

---

2 Unless otherwise stated, the section on institutional change is based on documents in Forsvarsministeriet 11. kontor 795/65 and Legge, J. Michael. *Theatre Nuclear Weapons and the NATO Strategy of Flexible Response*. Santa Monica, CA: Rand Corporation, 1983.
3 PO/66/215 NATO SECRET.

measured responses to Soviet threats. They were thus open to new interpretations in the years to follow. Thus in his "Basic Strategic Guidance for Allied Command Europe" of 13 December 1960, Norstad interpreted NATO strategy in a way that favoured a flexible response:[4] while NATO frequently trained for all-out nuclear war, it was a serious misinterpretation to suggest that this was the only type of warfare NATO should be prepared for. Therefore, NATO's forces had to be equipped, trained and deployed so that they used conventional weapons "when they were adequate to the military situation" and "atomic weapons only when the use of such weapons was necessary". Thus there might be situations limited to conventional exchanges alone, and selective use of limited atomic firepower would not necessarily result in total war, although it might heighten the degree of risk. Norstad was clearly expressing a conception of limited nuclear war.

So did the Americans, and they wanted a much more flexible response system. The French opposed it staunchly, and the Germans wanted stronger assurance for British and American conventional forces in Germany, if the immediate massive retaliation was to be given up.

The Military Committee set up a working group to examine the general strategy. The Germans now were ready to discuss flexibility; their wish for stronger forward defence was fulfilled, and there was hope that Europe could get a stronger say in nuclear warfare.[5] But after several attempts from the rest of the working group, the French vetoed the proposal.

This veto stopped the concrete planning process until the French left the military integrated system two years later, but that did not stop activities in various settings. Thus, the C-in-C of the German Bundeswehr in 1964 declared that the only acceptable NATO strategy would be Flexible Response by step-by-step deterrence activities[6] and, as we saw in the previous chapter, the Germans now planned accordingly. The massive response by any aggression simply was not credible anymore. NATO would remain a whole, reacting in unison, but varied across the area, depending on local circumstances, with maximum response where the danger was greatest. Only immediate, determined and measured responses could guarantee NATO's integrity.

In 1968 NATO decided to set up a system, using each country's force plans as the Minimum NATO Force Plans.[7] These plans were to be based on an enhancement of SACEUR's military capability within the framework of available means.

---

4 Davis, op. cit., pp. 175–76.
5 Haftendorn, Helga. *NATO and the Nuclear Revolution: A Crisis of Credibility 1966–67*, 51. Oxford: Oxford University Press, 1996.
6 Fü B III 1: Deutscher strategischer Standpunkt. TgbNr 7221/64 Geheim. 8-12-64. BM 1/103a.
7 Notat HEM om Natos forsvarsplanlægning. Forsvarsministeriet 7. kontor marts 1968.

This decision was made in the light of knowledge that the means could not be expected to be larger, and more likely smaller. Therefore, the member countries were asked to review their force plans and, if at all possible, amend them along the following lines:[8]
a) reallocate personnel between forces available for NATO and other national forces, so that the NATO component would be increased;
b) increase quality of preparedness and the quality of M-day units;
c) move certain navy units to category A (immediately ready on M-day);
d) improve possibilities for defending the flanks, e.g. by SACEUR mobile forces and maximum use of naval units;
e) correction of SACEUR mobile forces' location;
f) other steps to enhance use of forces.

Furthermore, the members were asked to make fast decision-making possible regarding allocating forces to the supreme commander and permission to use nuclear warheads.

One may be tempted to comment that most of these enhancements (moving forces among categories) were more cosmetic than real, but such was the reality in an era of budgetary cut-backs.

Flexible response elements

After the French withdrawal from the integrated military NATO system, discussions between Germany, Great Britain and the USA were resumed, and they reached a common understanding of balancing conventional forces, tactical nuclear weapons and strategic deterrence weapons – which were in principle reserved for surprise attacks, leaving no time to make conventional and local defence work.[9]

Quite intense work by various committees was resumed, and a conceptual basis became ready for decision-making. The most important element was the adoption of three steps of possible warfare, creating a flexibility in answers to a Soviet attack: direct defence, deliberate escalation and general nuclear response. The two first steps required – as something new – conventional forces, supported by tactical nuclear weapons available to the Major National Commanders, and the third step – as before – strategic nuclear forces. The Defence Planning Com-

---

8 Notat om NATO's forsvarsplanlægning. HEM Forsvarsministeriet 7-12-66 11. kontor 717/67.
9 Ibid., 52.

mittee decided in May 1967 to go ahead based on these steps and change the strategy of massive retaliation to flexible response by asking the Military Committee to start a revising process. The work was based on a quite comprehensive situation document, which we shall not detail here[10] since it is by and large reflected in the documents referred to below. It took more than two years to finish all the desired documents.

The elements of flexible response are not easy to digest in brief form, with the documents somewhat repetitive and the logic of the order not always easy to discern – probably mirroring the fact that most formulations had come about as compromises among the main actors, USA, Great Britain and Germany.

Objectives
In a bird's eye view the objectives of flexible response were:[11]
- Deterrence to keep the adversary from starting a military conflict;
- Direct defence by responding on the spot to any aggression and not relying on remote strategic weapons for a response;
- Crisis stability by acting so that any military response would be measured in scope in order to maintain control over the situation;
- Escalation control by directing any escalation in military response so that the enemy realised that the response was not to initiate global war;
- Arms control and nonproliferation of nuclear warheads;
- Cost control, meaning exactly that – military equipment was expensive and spending on such had to be reined in; and finally
- maintaining Alliance unity so that the members of the alliance were supporting one another rather than undermining the actions of the neighbours.

Types of WAPA aggression
In the following sections the first four objectives are in focus, based on MC 14-3, MC 48-3 and MCM 23-68. Together these documents specified in more and more detail – from MC 14-3 to MCM 23-68 – in a sort of continuum what Soviet aggression could be about, from covert actions in the locality to strategic nuclear war (MC 14-3 16-18, 22-23):

---

[10] Ministerial Guidance to the NATO Military Authorities, DPC/D (67) 23, 9-5-67. The process towards the decision is analyzed by Haftendorn, op. cit.
[11] Kugler, Richard L. *The Great Strategy Debate: NATO's Evolution in the 1960s.* Rand Corporation, 1991.

- Covert actions were actions used to initiate unrest locally and create uncertainty about what was going on in order to create favourable conditions for subsequent limited aggression against NATO and/or interfere with free use of air space and sea. So covert action might and might not involve Soviet military forces and could be met by national internal security forces or military forces.
- Limited aggression had three forms: incursions were small-scale raids, frontier violations or comparable Soviet harassments on the ground, in air space or at sea. Infiltrations were covert penetrations by individuals or small groups to execute various harassments like sabotage, ambushes, establishment of hidden depots etc. Hostile local actions were military actions that were conducted so that it would be clear that the actions and the duration of the operation were limited. One might call it "quick and dirty" and with restricted risk for NATO forces. Limited aggression should be met by the ground, sea and air forces of the alliance. They must be mobile, have adequate fire-power, communications and logistics to provide for a forward defence. But especially in the flanks one should be prepared to get supporting reinforcement forces because of the risk of superior enemy conventional forces.
- Major aggression could be nuclear or non-nuclear attacks against NATO forces or territory, air space or sea area, bringing national freedom or military force integrity into immediate danger. The ultimate response would be strategic nuclear forces, but conventional forces might suffice. Maritime forces should be ready to protect shipping and conduct offensive operations against submarines and surface craft. In addition to counter amphibious operations there would be support of the land battle, to assist in the safe evacuation and dispersal of Allied shipping and in the essential supply of NATO nations.

NATO responses

The MC-14 explained that flexibility (p. 10) would prevent the potential aggressor from predicting with confidence NATO's specific response to aggression; this should lead him to conclude that an unacceptable degree of risk would be involved regardless of the nature of his attack.

The main deterrence to Soviet aggression (p. 14) would be the threat of escalation which would lead the Warsaw Pact to conclude that the risks involved were not commensurate with their objectives. Should an aggression be initiated, short of a major nuclear attack, NATO should respond immediately with a direct defence. The first objective would be to counter the aggression without escalation and preserve or restore the integrity and security of the North Atlantic area. However, NATO must be manifestly prepared at all times to escalate the conflict, using nuclear weapons if necessary. But this would depend on the enemy's actions, on their own preparedness due to available warning, on the effectiveness of the military forces-in-being and reinforcements, and their conventional capability to defend forward.

Should aggression occur, the flexibility of the Alliance permitted reaction in three steps (p. 19) by initially meeting any aggression short of a major nuclear attack with the available direct defence, but with nuclear tactical response not ruled out; then conducting a deliberate escalation of the conflict locally or even to another area or by demonstration explosion of a nuclear warhead, if the aggression could not be held and the situation was restored by direct defence; or initiating the appropriate major nuclear response if the aggression were a major nuclear attack.

Tasks in the Baltic Approaches

The implementation document, the MC 48-3, dealt with the various regions of NATO. We shall restrict the discussion to the Baltic Approaches.

The task of BALTAP was the usual: to get control of the Baltic entrances, the Western Baltic and the adjacent areas of the Central Baltic. A number of possible roles for the three types of military force were listed:

a. Land Forces
(1) To defend NATO's territories as far forward as possible.
(2) To ensure the integrity of land lines of communication.
(3) To control the land borders of the Baltic Straits.
. . .
(5) To implement plans for defensive works, barriers, and demolitions in order to increase the defensive capabilities of combat forces and support the defence in depth.

b. Naval Forces
(1) To provide, in order to discourage and counter Soviet maritime activities that appear to threaten the political, economic or military interest of the Alliance, a continuous and visible evidence of the solidarity and unit of NATO by upholding the principles of freedom of the sea and international laws.
(2) To conduct maritime operations, as necessary, in order to maintain firm control of the sea areas, . . . keep open sea lines of communication, destroy or

disrupt enemy merchant shipping, and protect Allied shipping . . . and defending sea lines of communication . . .

(3) To conduct all appropriate types of naval operations in . . . the Western Baltic Sea and adjacent areas of the Central Baltic Sea . . . In the Eastern and Northern Baltic Sea, to conduct air and submarine operations.
(4) To support the land/air campaign with all types of naval, naval air and amphibious operations.
(5) To contain and destroy enemy naval forces in the enclosed sea areas where possible and to prevent the passage of these forces to the open seas by conducting anti-transit operations, particularly in the Baltic . . .
(6) To implement defensive operations in connection with merchant shipping, by:
   (a) Dispersal and re-routing to safe areas;
   (b) Establishment of Naval Control of Shipping;
   (c) Sailing in groups or convoys; and
   (d) Providing the maximum protection practicable.
(7) To conduct mine countermeasures to provide for the safe passage of NATO shipping in established routes through shallow waters and approaches to ports and anchorages.
(8) To defend NATO territories and island bases against seaborne attacks and to provide air defence from seaward.
(9) To conduct amphibious operations in order to secure or re-capture positions of military importance.
(10) To respond to Warsaw Pact harassment by applying pressures at sea against WAPA merchant ships, fishing fleets or oceanographic ships, as appropriate, within NATO established political guidelines, and to resist similar actions by the Warsaw Pact.
(11) To provide sea-based logistic support and an administrative lift capability for land-based forces to areas where other means are inadequate.

c. Air Forces
(1) To gain and maintain air superiority.
(2) To provide air defence capabilities and operations for the protection of forces, facilities and of the civilian population; and to defend their respective Air Defence Regions, coordinating the air defence requirements and capabilities of land and naval forces and of adjacent and national commands, and organising, operating and coordinating early warning facilities and communications.
(3) To conduct strategic and tactical air operations in support of the overall land, sea and air battle for Europe; and to coordinate or control, as appropriate,

such sorties as may be made available by naval forces, adjacent commands, or external air forces.
(4) To provide, through coordination with national meteorological services, as necessary, meteorological services to support land, sea and air operations.
(5) To coordinate search and rescue services.
(6) To conduct aerial mine laying.
(7) To carry out operations against enemy forces, lines of communication, and ports in and around the Baltic . . .

Political and Military decision powers
A flexible response had consequences for the distinction between peace and war. Before, NATO had an alert level system that soon led to general war, and that was what the national politicians had to consider: join the defence or give up. Flexible response had a step-by-step movement from no aggression to more aggression to war. But the "more aggression" was a sliding scale, where each step was difficult to distinguish from the next. So when would national politics come into consideration?

We shall return to these problems later. Here we shall just exemplify the issues by sketching out the problems of laying minefields,[12] Fehmarn Belt was narrow, about 10 miles, and therefore comprised both national (German, Danish) waters and international waters. For national waters, military plans approved by national authorities could determine when and how mines could be laid. But for international waters only national states could be held accountable, and therefore mine laying had to be approved by national politicians.

Various levels of alert would determine where mine fields were to be laid, but according to the German navy it was not possible to lay mines in Fehmarn Belt stepwise. All mines had to be laid at the same time. This, however, made the military distinction between levels of alert useless. One could not follow the logic. So, were the politicians to be involved (both in Denmark and Germany) at an earlier stage to permit mine laying in international waters? Would that be "legal" according to international law (probably not, PB)?

It soon became obvious that the relations between military commanders and the political systems became more complex; in the future military plans were to be closely analysed before the politicians could approve them.

The increased importance of surveillance

The flexible concept meant that any military reaction by NATO had to balance WAPA provocations. But when could one talk of a provocation? The flexible response strategy required intimate knowledge of the daily pattern of WAPA activities so that one could be forewarned about military actions, meaning hence a stronger need for constant surveillance of the WAPA military.

---

12 Fü M II 1 Az 31-05-14-00. Vermerk. TgbNr 6880/69. Verschlusssache. 5-3-69. BM 1/939e.

Therefore, the German Inspector General of the Bundeswehr in 1976 asked for analyses of the concept: what would it mean for the forces? The navy responded with a 50-page memorandum from which we shall take a few excerpts.[13]

Surveillance of the WAPA had the purposes to collect, analyse, assess and distribute information about the type, strength and location of military units, their equipment including electronic systems; their apparent tactics and behaviour; and their intentions and ways of operation. Much of the memorandum dealt with the general aspects of creating such information in the Baltic and the North Sea, how to group data for various decision-makers etc.; we shall not go into such detail.

Actively, the navy collected data by surveying the sea space to map the activities of the enemy at sea in order to create a picture of the number and composition of enemy forces – their location, course and speed, their formation and their performance, particularly activities linked to exercises.

Such information could only be of use if there was background knowledge about the forces: the technical capabilities and limitations of their weapons and electronic equipment, the training of crews, their tactical ways of operation and their readiness for action. This required data collection over many years, e.g. by observing exercises, collecting electronic data and interviewing people with relevant knowledge.

By continuing observation of WAPA military activities a "normal picture" could be created, and observations of changes from this picture could be used to alert decision-makers about the preparation of possible military aggressions and put them in a position to decide about counter measures.

Many military activities were part of the normal picture: exercises in national waters and in the Baltic, test shooting, hunting submarines, training various ship formations etc. – all these could be carried out nationally or in cooperation among the WAPA countries.

The following activities would indicate a break from the normal situation:
- Higher levels of alert. Fifty per cent of all units normally were ready for action; of these eight per cent in alarm state. Twenty per cent were ready after some days, and the remaining 30 per cent were in reserve.
- Stop for training and return to home base.
- Reduction of mercantile shipping and fishing.
- Abandoning of NATO harbours and installation of weaponry on mercantile ships.

---

13 Fü M VI 1: Aufklärungskonzeption der Marine (Entwurf). Geheim. Az. 31-05-05. TgbNr 520/76. 29-4-76. BM 1/3769.

- Larger naval units leaving the Baltic.
- Unusual manoeuvres after completion of planned activities at sea.

The following activities might point to preparation for military attacks:
- Increased surveillance by naval and aircraft, changes in the normal four permanent recce units at anchor in international waters close to Denmark and Germany.
- Relocations of forces to transport harbours.
- Preparation of amphibious units and mercantile ships in harbours close to Denmark and Germany.
- Increased activity of surface units in the Baltic; reactivation of units in the reserve.
- Indications coming from deciphering electronic traffic.
- Increasing contacts with submarines in the North Sea.
- Electronic jamming activities.
- Unusual passage of WAPA units in the Danish straits.
- Comprehensive changes in mercantile shipping.
- Changes of mercantile ships (weapons, electronic devices)
- Changes in training rhythms and training activities
- Landing of sabotage groups.
- Recall of merchant ships from NATO harbours
- Deployment of WAPA naval units westwards
- Activation of mobile HQs.
- Changes in deployment to Polish and East German airfields.

Of course, these observations by the Germans were also valid for the Danish Intelligence Office. In addition, the Danes had the advantage of controlling Bornholm with its radar stations that could monitor activities in the Eastern Baltic, Poland and East Germany.

The Danish Intellligence Office listed the following activities for recce in peace and times of tension (see table 14.1):[14]

Some of the activities seem unlikely to be carried out daily in peace time. In addition, there were demands for patrolling Kattegat and the North Sea for recce of WAPA ships passing through or anchoring.

---

14 Letter HEM Forsvarets efterretningstjeneste 384/69, 28-2-69. Forsvarets Efterretningstjeneste: KC. Kopibog med bilag (afklass.) (1947–1990) 29.

Table 14.1: Recce activities air force and navy.

	Peace	Times of tension
Air force		
Photo–recce Polish/East German coast	Quarterly, 3–4 sorties	Ad hoc
Photo-recce of certain objects and areas	Monthly or ad-hoc, 2 sorties	Ad-hoc 6 sorties/day
Photo and visual recce of special activities	Ad-hoc 100 sorties/year	Ad-hoc
Visual recce of Eastern Baltic		3 times/day, 9 sorties
Navy		
Patrol south of Bornholm to supplement ground radar	Daily by corvette	Daily by corvette
Patrol along Baltic coast patrol	Bimonthly by patrol craft	Daily by two patrol crafts
Patrol for identifying radar tracks on ground radar	Ad-hoc patrol craft	Ad-hoc patrol craft
Special one-week electronic recce along Baltic coast	Monthly	Ad-hoc
Special recce of WAPA units in Danish waters	Ad-hoc patrol craft/FPB 50 missions/year	Ad-hoc patrol craft or FPB

Danish considerations

Flexible response came into focus gradually. In February 1963, the chief of the navy aired his opinion that nuclear weapons were too dangerous if the two super powers collided, hence one had to ponder the possibilities for limited war.[15]

If Denmark were attacked under flexible response (Bornholm might be one example), a probable response from NATO would be limited to the area attacked and its surroundings, and restraint would be called for in the choice of military means. Therefore, the chiefs of the forces were asked to make plans for such limited responses. The challenge was to translate NATO's steps of escalation (see above) into military reality. For the navy, a starting point could be demonstration of military presence if foreign warships closed in on Danish waters or if apparently civilian ships were placed at unusual spots. The next step would be the de-

---

15 Bogason, *Søværnet under den kolde krig – politik, strategi og taktik*, 161–62.

nial of access for such ships, if necessary by boarding them, investigating them and demanding that they be removed from the area. One step of further escalation might be that foreign men-of-war escorted fishing boats or other vessels into Danish territorial waters; this must be met by military presence and demands of leaving the area. A foreign power might then hold exercises close to or in Danish waters; this must be met with protests. Now a military confrontation was close; however, it must be kept at a low level, in effect initiating a limited war comprising reactions to WAPA assaults against Danish ships or occupation of Danish territory like islands or peninsulas in contested areas.

A case might be that the Soviets started out with a series of complaints over NATO exercises. If NATO MTBs during rough weather called at a harbour on Bornholm, the Soviets might respond with fifth column agents blowing up a radar station on the island, and when those agents were arrested landed groups of special forces might take the Danish military chiefs hostage and subsequently occupy the island. What would a NATO measured response be like?

The primary task under a flexible response for the Danish defence was surveillance of the Warsaw Pact in order to get an early warning from changes in the "normal picture".[16] The waters between the islands of Møn and Bornholm would be essential for forward recce, identification and shadowing with frigates or FPBs or submarines. At the same time, the narrows were under surveillance by radar, loop stations and patrol craft. The surface craft was supposed to stop infringements of sovereignty and prevent foreign forces from dominating or establishing control over areas within a Danish sphere of interest. And of course they were meant to detect any surprise attack before it could develop into an accomplished fact.

German consequences

Under flexible response, three general situations were spelled out by the Germans: peace time, tensions and war. For the German navy the consequences were an allocation of more tasks explicitly linked to the two first situations, making surveillance even more necessary, and occasioning new options: crisis management and limited actions that earlier on were considered less likely.

In February 1965 – following the lead of the Bundeswehr C-in-C in December 1964 – the chief of the navy gave the first orders encompassing a flexible response,

---

[16] Thostrup, S. S. "Søværnets styrkemål." *Tidsskrift for Søvæsen* 144 (1973): 111.

even though it was not official NATO policy.[17] If the aggressor had attacked a NATO-unit on German territory, it would force the German navy into immediate action with full force with a move from strategic-defensive to tactic-offensive operations. Taking such an initiative would show the opponent the resolve to meet any aggression with tough means. Such action might develop in the waters between Bornholm and Rügen, and in the Western Baltic NATO's freedom to operate must be secured with all available means. In particular:

- conventional attacks by naval aircraft on any enemy ship in the Baltic;
- attacking enemy ships in the Eastern and Northern Baltic by submarines;
- laying minefields as far to the east as possible by fast mine layers;
- operations by FPBs against expected enemy mine layers as well as naval transports along the Pommoranian and Mecklenburger coasts;
- any large amphibious activity must be met immediately with destroyers or other large units, at the discretion of the operational chief in the area.

Various actions might be considered steps in an escalation within limited war in the Baltic. By 1966, the year after the order above, the leadership of the navy had the following thoughts – initially strictly only for the eyes of the naval top, but in reality what soon became the leading thoughts – about what the WAPA might do under limited warfare:[18]

- Paralysing Western merchant traffic in the Eastern and Middle Baltic and disturbing it in the Western Baltic;
- Laying mines in the Middle and Western Baltic to reduce the freedom of manoeuvre of the NATO naval forces;
- Conventional attacks on a limited number of territorial bases of the NATO navies;
- Performing geographically limited amphibious operations against islands and inlets in Germany and Denmark to take away important defence positions of the West;
- Supporting geographically limited army operations at the Eastern coast of Holstein, possibly supported by limited amphibious operations.
- If such limited attacks came about, the top of the navy would not expect the whole of the WAPA Baltic Fleet to become involved, and only selected parts of the NATO depots, support bases, training facilities and airfields would be

---

17 Fü M II 1: Deutsches strategisches Konzeept. Geheim. Az 31-02-01-01. TgbNr 6463/65. 15-2-65. BM 1/103a.
18 Fü M II 1: Strategische Planungsvorstellungen der Marine für den "Begrentzen Krieg". Geheim. Az 31-02-02, TgbNr 2380/66. 3-8-66. BM 1/938e.

destroyed. The tasks of the German navy would under such limited war conditions comprise:
- Securing freedom of operation for NATO forces in the Baltic Approaches, particularly the Middle and Western Baltic;
- Stopping enemy sea traffic, particularly supplies for army units;
- Protecting their own sea traffic.

To do this, comprehensive surveillance of enemy forces would be necessary to determine the beginning, art, and scope of naval preparations and their probable aim. Their own sea traffic should be protected by fighting enemy surface craft, submarines and aircraft. In the war theatre, enemy ships, amphibious craft, shore missile batteries and other supporting places should be attacked. Their own army forces might get artillery and fighter-bomber support. Army groups and equipment could be landed on and taken away from beaches. Minefields could be laid in the area, and enemy mines should be swept. The navy must be prepared to get replenishment at sea and on bases.

Therefore, the navy and its equipment must constantly be prepared for action; the command system must be ready with all communication channels open; and it must be flexible and mobile. In other words: be prepared. This would be the way to make deterrence believable and thus keep the WAPA forces from attempts to conquer even small portions of NATO territory. But apart from deterrence, the preparedness was an aim in itself to make the navy able to counter surprise attacks.

Six years later, the navy had revised its conceptual basis and reached these conclusions:[19]

Until simple alert (war) the navy still was under national command rather than NATO command, and consequently the navy must have forces that are suited to counter surprise attacks at sea and from the sea during limited war in cooperation with other allied forces and/or the army and air force. It must fulfil naval tasks in general, in planned escalations and in general war, and it must take part in general defence measures and secure national sovereignty.

To do this, the navy must in peace time maintain a preparedness and perform surveillance of possible enemies from land as well as sea. In times of tension the navy must make ready all forces and increase surveillance of the possible enemy. In war, comprehensive surveillance must be carried out, enemy forces and sea traffic must be fought and one's own traffic must be protected. Amphibious actions must be carried out

---

19 Sander-Nagashima, op. cit., p. 406.

Examples of future war activities leading to flexible response were concealed fights (ambush?) and infiltration, attacks on ships, occupation of islands or peninsulas and limited aggression. Specific examples could be WAPA harassing of German ships, occupation of threatening islands (Bornholm), occupation of Schleswig-Holstein or areas important for the Baltic Approaches. The German leadership did not consider those examples probable – except if the Soviet military top miscalculated a specific situation or NATO showed signs of hesitation – because ultimately, the nuclear threat was there. If they decided to attack, it would be a surprise coming out of an ordinary exercise, or a comprehensive take out of NATO naval and air forces, followed by an amphibious operation in the Baltic Approaches.[20]

The navy foresaw a pattern of WAPA attack groups, each with eight units of amphibious vessels and support ships. Consequently, the German planners analysed various response forms. One would be to change the tactical setup of the navy into attack groups, each with a corvette, three FPBs and two attack helicopters with missiles. A WAPA amphibious group would be met with two of the new attack groups, resulting in a WAPA loss of 40 per cent; this would destroy the fighting capability of the landing force. An attack would be met with up to three waves of counter-attacks: first with fighter-bombers, then with the naval attack groups and finally again with fighter-bombers.

These considerations, however, constituted a rather high level of confrontation, and the steps indicated above would have to be contemplated first.

Solidarity in BALTAP?

There is no doubt that the Danes originally were very sceptical towards the creation of BALTAP; this also was obvious at the Oslo conference in November 1961 when the final BALTAP organisation was drafted. The Danes got most of the chief posts and the C-in-C was to remain Danish for ever. So the final outcome was a bonus to Danish officers who got better chances for promotion to the flag officer level.

In general, the Germans appeared to be satisfied with BALTAP, but the issue of the border between AFNORTH and AFCENT had not been solved the way most Germans wanted it to, and the problem of that border was most apparent for the air commands. Previously in this book we have a few times spotted some dissatisfaction with the agreement on the ground, e.g. Germans complaining that the Danish Division did not meet its task of being present in Schleswig-Holstein with 90 per cent strength within 96 hours.

In 1976, a German Fregattenkapitän (stationed in AFNORTH) wrote a thesis, accusing the Danes of being nationalistic and selfish within NATO, particularly BALTAP.[21] He accused Denmark (as a nation) for working solely for a reduction of military spending (NATO as well as WAPA), prioritising localised

---

20 Ibid., 407.
21 Karl Friedrich Schinkel: Die Zukunft des integrierten Vorbehalte oder Dänemark und die Bundesrepublik Deutschland als NATO-Partner. Eine Untersuchung nach Notwendigkeit und Interesse. Vertraulich. No date (1976). BW 2/8621.

rather than NATO-level defence (this was a few years after the Danish Social Democratic defence proposal of 1971 which certainly was local in scope). But worse, he saw Danish military staff behaviour within BALTAP as neglecting the common bonds and perspectives of NATO and instead promoting the defence of Danish soil. This concerned Schleswig-Holstein in that the Danish Division did not meet its challenge of moving south in time to defend it together with the Germans. It also concerned the air force whose BALTAP air command only covered Danish territory. Furthermore, the Danes were now in the process of abandoning the fighter-bombers which could serve NATO purposes in early combat along the Baltic coast – instead they were about to buy F-16 jets in a fighter, not a fighter-bomber version (this was a mis-interpretation, PB). If so, they would only be able to defend Danish territory, they could not counter-attack. Finally there was the Danish navy which was developing a communication system (CEPLO/DEPLO) which could not communicate properly with the German Navy through the common NATO system Link-11, in effect shutting the Germans out from common operations.

The solution to these problems was relatively simple: since the Danes were trying to separate Denmark from Germany in defence matters, the consequence would be to separate the countries in the NATO command (BALTAP) and set up two national commands. The details, however, were not discussed in the paper which was read by a higher command, and no consequences followed.

Tactical nuclear weapons

The Danish and German policies towards the use of nuclear warheads differed radically. In spite of Denmark's negative reponse to nuclear warheads, there were certain possibilities for Denmark to enjoy the benefits of the nuclear threat umbrella.

The flexible response concept was implemented in various ways. Within nuclear policy, the concept of Selective Employment Plans (SEPs) was introduced to give NATO commanders the possibility to respond with nuclear weapons without resorting to all-out retaliation. The concept also had a political element built into it – meaning that NATO commanders had the possibility to warn the enemy that a nuclear limited response would take place unless the perceived imminent attack was called off. In that sense, the enemy would trigger the nuclear response, if they attacked. So the SEP was regarded as an instrument of crisis control.

Denmark

In the 1950s, the Danish defence used nuclear weapons during exercises, but the public Danish policy was not to use nuclear weapons in peace time and consequently nuclear warheads could not be stored on Danish territory.

In July 1974 a Danish military planning group wrote a note on the use of tactical nuclear weapons. The starting point was that the Americans had command, the weapons were stored under American control and could be handed over to NATO forces in a NATO defined crisis to troops that had been authorised earlier on after training. In addition, a formal agreement between the USA and the state in question had to be in place (see chapter 7).

Until 1973 the Danish army had HONEST JOHN and 203 mm howitzers which could carry nuclear warheads, but no formal treaty and therefore no authorisation of Danish forces. The procedure of transferring nuclear warheads had taken 48 hours, but in 1974, a new procedure had been introduced. The core element was the SEP mentioned above – authorised by SACEUR and released by the principal sub-commanders (e.g. COMBALTAP) which described the preconditions for the use of tactical weapons in a local area: what weapons were to be used, what targets were relevant, how the area was to be delineated and what civilian damages might follow. A SEP was a "contingency plan", meaning that the final use was dependent on the situation; the process now was reduced to 24 hours.

In 1974, two SEPs for the Baltic Approaches were in the process of being written.[22] It appears from various other sources that SEPs were not ready until 1977, so the paper quoted here is ahead of the actual development.

A SEP BARD EPOS (F) was for use in Schleswig-Holstein, supporting COMLANDJUT and based on delivery systems of the German Bundesheer. The nuclear warheads were to be delivered by aircraft linked to the sixth German division. The evaluation by the Danish analytical group was that this solution was militarily good and justifiable.

For the eastern part of Denmark the situation was quite different because only Danish forces were to operate on land, and the main force at sea was also Danish, both to be supported by the Danish air force. None of these had capabilities for nuclear weapons, but since the initial defence was likely to be carried out in international waters, the rules of the Danish government did not apply. Therefore, a Selective Employment Plan, SEP BARD BELL (E), was planned against the amphibious threat against Zealand, based on nuclear weapons delivered by aircraft. The use of nuclear warheads would eliminate the amphibious threat, without civilian losses, and it could be combined with political warnings before actual use, thereby leaving the final initiative for provocation to the enemy. The risk of scaling up would be minimal because the BALTAP area was separated from AFCENT (which was a politically and militarily "loaded" flank). Retaliation against Zealand was not likely for military reasons when the amphibious group had been

---

22 Danmarks strategi – atompolitiske aspekter, en analyse. Forsvarskommandoen, Planlægningsgruppen: KA. Sagsakter fortrolig/hemmelig (afklassificerede) (1970–1978). Sag 419 31-7-75.

eliminated. Consequently, BALTAP saw this SEP as one leaving the final initiative with the enemy and hence it was a means of controlling a crisis situation.

Negotiations were in progress, and it was foreseen that a primary and secondary strike unit would be ready in the Fall of 1975 with two aircraft from 2. ATAF (i.e. from AFCENT, not AFNORTH). In so far as this agreement was valid, Denmark did not need its own systems of delivery. But the note underscored that a Danish delivery system would increase the military credibility of Danish defence and make Denmark less susceptible to threats and pressure and reduce the dependency on remote conventional reinforcements.

We can conclude that in the Summer of 1974, the principles for using nuclear weapons close to Danish territory were being formulated, but the final version and an organisation were not operational yet.

Germany

The NATO forward defence policy was strongly supported by the German minister of defence, Strauss. In spite of his support to arming the German defence with nuclear warheads, he wanted to make sure that there were no loopholes in the conventional defence, allowing for a local fight which the West Germans could not control and hence make the local fight global with its devastating consequences. Within the military top, he thereby supported the army branch which was in constant bureaucratic infighting with the air force which leaned towards the American understanding that a war would be decided by the air force and its nuclear weapons and hence the tactics of the army was of less importance.

Anyway, the West German army's leadership was very hesitant towards the use of nuclear warheads. The difference between the mindsets of German and other NATO generals was laid bare during an exercise in Northern Germany in 1960.[23] The British chief of the engineer forces asked for nuclear warheads in all three situations that were being played out: slowing down the enemy between the border and the river Weser; defence using the river as a barrier for the enemy; and preparing for a counter offensive. The rationale was that the enemy outnumbered the NATO defenders. The German chief, on the contrary, and to the amazement of his NATO colleagues, withheld nuclear warheads as long as each fighting theatre could be held without them. His point was that he would use nuclear warheads only if absolutely no other military action could do the job – be-

---

23 Thoss, *NATO-strategie und nationale Verteidigungsplanung. Planung und Aufbau der Bundeswehr unter den Bedingungen atomaren Vergeltungsstrategie 1952–1960*, 540–41.

cause of the radioactive catastrophic consequences. The other NATO generals saw the use as a technical means of sparing other areas for damage.

Nuclear warheads before and behind the Iron Curtain
In Schleswig-Holstein, the following elements for NATO-led nuclear warfare were found:[24]
    Albersdorf: West German Army nuclear-certified 203 mm artillery
    Boostedt: West German Army nuclear-certified 155 mm artillery
    Flensburg-Meys: storage of nuclear weapons for 294th artillery Group supporting West German lance and artillery units
    Flensburg-Weiche: HQ 294th unit & West German Lance unit. Nuclear warhead custodian for West German Lance and 203 mm artillery units
    Hamburg-Rahlstadt: nuclear-certified West German 155 mm artillery unit
    Kellinghusen: nuclear warhead custodian for West German units
    Wentorf: nuclear-certified West German 155 mm artillery unit
    The weapons: Honest John max range 38 km; M109G 155 mm self-propelled gun range 14–30 km; M110 203 mm gun range 16–29 km
    In WAPA planning, the following examples for use of nuclear weapons against NATO forces in Schleswig-Holstein were found:[25]
    Brekendorf: 1x30 kt
    FlaRakBtl 38: 4x20 kt, 2x40 kt
    Flugplatz: 1x100 kt
    Leck: 1x50 kt
    6. Panzergrenadierdivision: 1x20 kt, 2x40 kt, 3x100 kt, 2x3 kt; 4x10 kt, 2x20 kt
    Raketenartilleribattalion 650: 1x20 kt, 1x40 kt, 2x30 kt.
    Jutland division: 1x3 kt, 2x10 kt, 2x20 kt, 2x30 kt, 5x50 kt

Termed otherwise, the following types of targets have been found in an area including Jutland:
    11 airfields first class; three airfields second class; eight navy bases; four important harbours; four AA batteries; one command center (Karup); 13 radio/radar stations for naval surveillance; seven radio stations; one depot, probably for nuclear weapons; one fort (Bangsbo); three large POL in Esbjerg, Frederikshavn and Aarhus; seven large munition depots: Klosterhede, Dejbjerg, Oksbøl, Søndermark, Todendorf, Putlos, Forst Segeberg; and one torpedo factory in Kiel-Holtenau.
    In addition 21 other airfields, the NATO oil delivery system and three POL depots in Plön, Heide and Brunsbüttelkoog.

One should take note that the East German navy and air force had no weapon platforms for nuclear warheads. The army got tactical land-land rockets FROG-3/5 (two per division) and SCUD-A (six per division) ready in launchers 1962. In 1966, three divisions got FROG-7 launchers with a 65 km reach. But no East German unit had its own nuclear warheads; they were not part of the nuclear WAPA plan-

---

24 Steinkopff, op. cit., pp. 109–10.
25 Ibid., 106.

ning system. In that sense, the situation was the same as in NATO where the American custodians determined when and how to use warheads.

The Warsaw-treaty had plans for use and non-use of nuclear warheads. In plans for attacking Denmark the use of nuclear weapons was foreseen if the forces were to land in the Bays of Køge and Faxe on Zealand. An alternative plan had the forces land on the Island of Falster south of Zealand, and since the defence was expected to be rather weak there, no use of nuclear weapons was presumed. From the late 1960s the WAPA tended towards less use of nuclear weapons, corresponding to the flexible response of NATO.[26]

An overall assessment by Steinkopff[27] is that the WAPA forces had so many options regarding an attack through Schleswig-Holstein that they were unlikely to resort to nuclear weapons unless NATO forces – under strong pressure to withdraw – used them. A staff exercise in 1982 used the 3rd Front – an army group – in an motorised attack, supported by artillery.[28] The attackers were to break through the NATO defence north of Helmstedt with three waves of tanks in a three kilometre wide front, tracking a rolling barrage ("for every five meters") from the artillery.

Summing up: Flexible response complexity

Flexible response was a complex system and correspondingly difficult to handle for the military chiefs. It is impossible to write any short version of it and it resembles in many ways a bureaucratic system that has great difficulties in specifying into detail what its over-arching goal is about. Therefore, more and more rules are written to fill in the blanks that will always come about as the lower echelons of the organisation work with their clients and find that this and that activity may and may not be covered by the organisation. The top then responds by yet another rule.

Likewise, NATO specified in more and more paragraphs activities that were covered by flexible response, but seen from this observer, many were either more than obvious or therefore not necessary, while others were formulated in ways that gave several possible interpretations.

---

26 Gemzell, Carl-Axel. "Die DDR, der Warschauer Pakt und Dänemark im kalten Krieg." In *Deutsch-skandinavische Beziehungen nach 1945*, eds Hohnm Robert, Jürgen Elvert, and Karl Christian Lammers, 53. Stuttgart: Franz Steiner Verlag, 2000.
27 Steinkopff, op. cit., p. 110.
28 Sager, Wilhelm. *Heere zwischen den Meeren. Heeres- und Kriegsgeschichte Schleswig-Holsteins*, 180. Husum: Husum Druck- und Verlagsgesellschaft, 2003.

Basically, the idea was to keep the WAPA chiefs in the dark as to what a NATO reaction would be to an aggression. But one may ask whether NATO commanders themselves were very clear of what to do in those situations?

An example is the mining of national waters which in some areas could not be done without also mining the international section of the strait, *in casu* the Strait of Fehmarn. So what would the political and military decision-makers do? Risk an attack or ignore international law? The same problem would of course come up when a "suspicious" group of WAPA ships was closing in on a beach or harbour suitable for landing forces. What kind of flexibility was to be used?

One may say that if the risk of any one using nuclear weapons was strongly reduced, the basic principles of littoral warfare came to the fore, particularly regarding reconnaissance. It was more necessary than ever to keep tally and position of all the WAPA military units so that one could foresee any aggressive action or at least prepare for counter measures before the fact. Having air supremacy was more important than ever – both for recce purposes and for being able to operate without interference and with maximum exploitation of the geography – islands and inlets as well as shallow waters.

Chapter 15
NATO-reinforcements

NATO's defence was in many areas based on support coming from other countries. We have seen how Denmark and Norway got offers of air force reinforcements in the early 1950s, but the proposals for permanent stationing were turned down. However, some airfields were prepared for receiving reinforcements in war time.

Exercise MAINBRACE in 1952 was an indication of how external support could be implemented in Denmark by landing infantry on the beach and sending airplanes to attack targets from aircraft carriers. Landing on the beach is hardly the most efficient way of getting help, but at that time it was "core business" for the US Marine Corps. It has remained so, but of course, the Corps may also land by calling at a harbour, and another option is landing by aircraft, particularly helicopters.

Transfer is key to a reinforcement plan. For the navies, the task is to move a ship from one area to another, and that task is in principle simple, but when the vessel sails in waters far from home, issues of replenishment soon arise. Oil and water are standard anywhere and may be transferred at sea from tankers or in almost any harbour. Food can also be supplied in most harbours. But ammunition, mines and torpedoes and repair services require special supplies, adapted to the technical systems of the ship. Therefore, many services can only be delivered if a depot is prepared beforehand – or if a supply ship from one's own navy calls at that very harbour.

For aircraft the issues are about the same. They are easier and quicker to move to a foreign airfield, but the various types of aircraft have differing technical systems, and the demand for checkups and mechanical services is high. Therefore, aircraft reinforcements presuppose depots of relevant supplies located close to the receiving airfields. Many countries have had the same type of aircraft, weapons and electronic equipment, but still there may have been national differences demanding special personnel.

Army personnel and their equipment are much more difficult to move. First, it is mostly an issue of many thousand individuals who have to board an airplane or a ship to get to the country they are slated to assist. When they arrive at an airfield or a harbour, they need land transport for transfer to the destination area, and they must have their weapons, other types of equipment and means of transportation delivered. When they go into action, all kinds of supplies must be available. Therefore, pre-planned depots of relevant supplies will make the transfer much easier.

In other words, meticulous planning of any transfer of military forces will enhance the actual delivery. But given the differences among various types and nationalities of forces, decisions must be made beforehand – if at all possible – as to which forces to move and where to so that they are earmarked for the task and well exercised for it when the demand arises. Depots must be built, personnel trained, supplies maintained and actual use exercised, if the future transfer is to become a success.

We have seen some aspects of this when it was planned for the British mine layer APOLLO to lay mine fields in Kattegat: when the Danish airfields were prepared for receiving aircraft and when German Bundeswehr and BALTAP were to be set up. In all cases, depots were built or existing depots reserved for the incomers' needs.

What to do if tension arises?

What steps could NATO forces take if one suspected a Soviet attack being built up from nearby areas? The actions below pertained to AFNORTH's Northern part, in a case of the Soviets appearing to use Finnish territory for an attack, but the steps would probably by and large be the same if Soviet forces were built up near the Baltic Approaches. The following activities stem from a note on "NATO Counter and Precautionary Measures" in certain areas:[1]

Measures which might be taken in NATO areas – near to the contingency area:
A. Declare selected measures of military vigilance in the northern region of ACE:
   (1) Man war HQ with skeleton staffs.
   (2) Implement progressively emergency communications plans.
   (3) Intensify collection and reporting of intelligence.
   (4) Review mobilisation plans.
   (5) Review alert procedures and operations plans and make discreet preparations for possible implementation of alerts.
   (6) Intensify the reporting of naval and maritime air forces.
   (7) Increase the readiness of earmarked forces and their logistic support forces.
   (8) Make discreet preparations for the deployment and change of operational command/control of certain earmarked forces.
   (9) Increase maritime air reconnaissance.
   (10) Conduct readiness exercises.
   (11) Increase duty personnel to assure coverage of essential positions.

---

1 MCM-102-68 (draft) 18-12-68. HEM.

B. In the event of the situation deteriorating further, declare the full state of military vigilance in the Northern Region of ACE plus selected measures of simple alert:
   (1)   Partial manning of NATO Headquarters on a continuous basis.
   (2)   Increase communications facilities.
   (3)   Pre-stock, man and provide maintenance of airfields used, or to be used, by NATO forces.
   (4)   Prepare for supporting guest forces by host nations. Establish necessary logistic support.
   (5)   Alert assigned and/or certain earmarked forces and bring to full strength
   (6)   Bring Allied integrated and national air defence systems to full strength.
   (7)   Prepare for assignment of certain naval and maritime air forces.
   (8)   Prepare for the defence of ports, harbours, anchorage areas and coastal waters.
   (9)   Increase measures to prevent sabotage.
   (10) Conduct reconnaissance of land and sea areas.
   (11) Send National Liaison Detachments to NATO Headquarters.
   (12) Increase the readiness of earmarked forces and their logistic support.
   (13) Make initial preparations for denial measures.
   (14) Prepare for naval control of shipping.
   (15) Implement full intelligence collection plans.
   (16) Establish tighter control of frontiers and refugee screening.
   (17) Intensify control of known or suspected enemy agents.
   (18) Intensify control of frontiers, including civil airports and ports.
   (19) Request pertinent activities to provide counterintelligence information.
C. Authorize appropriate pre-planned exercises to be employed as advanced precautionary measures.
D. Alert the AMF for possible deployment.
E. Exercise major units close to their EDP positions.
F. Increase the flow of intelligence from border patrols and reconnaissance.
G. Reinforce the naval and air forces.
H. Visibly increase air activity.
I. Alert redeployed and dual-based UK and US forces, and the assigned UK forces, for deployment to ACE.
J. Alert the SACEUR strategic reserve for deployment to ACE.
K. Improve and speed the exchange of national and military intelligence between nations, and provide such information to the NATO Military Authorities in a timely manner.
L. . . .
Q. Specific to Northern Norway.

R. Prepare for implementation of defensive operations in connection with merchant shipping.
S. Cancel naval port visits.
T. Consider the withdrawal of merchant ships of NATO nations from Warsaw Pact nation harbours.
U. Consider the closure of ports and airports to Soviet and Warsaw Pact nation ships and aircraft.

These activities could be relevant anywhere: step by step the NATO-commander prepared for military action according to the existing plans for the area, but being careful not to provoke the other side to military steps.

AMF: SACEUR's task force reinforcements

The political directive from 1956 (see chapter 7) asked SACEUR to analyze the minimal needs for military forces in Europe if one wanted a more forward defence line and to open the possibility of conflicts short of general war. In 1958 the supreme commander presented an analysis which pointed to the need for a multi-nation mobile task force, the size of up to a division, to be set anywhere in Europe, but primarily on the flanks.[2] The task force had to be based on a number of national infantry battalions located in Central Europe, airborne and required special plans in relation to national support systems. A preliminary study from 1957 showed that It would be necessary for equipment and vehicles to be pre-stocked at planned war concentration areas: support for 90 days should be at hand.[3]

The issue of this Allied Command Mobile Force (AMF) was presented to the NATO members by SACEUR on the 5 December 1959.[4] He asked for permission to start planning a task force, pointing to the need for a multi-national NATO surface and air force which in a tense situation could show resolve and solidarity within NATO by reacting against any form of aggression, and timely deployment could prevent the outbreak of a major war. The force could be up to five battalions of infantry and three squadron aircraft, composed by forces from USA, France, Belgium, Germany and Great Britain, with a HQ formed under AFCENT.

---

2 SHAPE. *SHAPE History 1958*, 72–74. Mons: SHAPE, 1967b.
3 SHAPE. *History 1957*, 180. Mons: SHAPE, 1967a.
4 Notat om opstilling af mobil NATO-styrke, HEM Forsvarsministeriet 11. kontor 11-4-60 711-A/60.

NATO set up a working group to create the operational groundwork for the Allied Command Mobile Force (AMF).[5] One major issue was that only the British and the Americans had air transport capacity for the AMF, and they demanded their costs to be covered. It took five years to reach a compromise which roughly meant that the costs were shared among the NATO countries.[6]

It took some time before the AMF became operational for the Baltic Approaches. The first exercise involving actual troops took place in Greece in 1961, the second in Northern Norway in 1964. In 1966, a draft plan was ready. AMF now was planned to be embodied by six infantry battalions and six fighter squadrons. For practical purposes, they were divided into two groups, one for action in the Northern flank, one for the Southern. Three British, Italian and Canadian battalions and three Dutch, British and American fighter squadrons were set up for deployment to BALTAP/Zealand or Northern Norway.

In 1966, the NATO Council agreed that in the light of the present plans, particular focus should be placed on the defence of the Northern and Southern Flanks. Over the subsequent two years, a concept for the defence of the flanks was developed, and the AMF was integrated in the concept, details of which will be presented below when we return to the AMF. First, we shall take a look at other reinforcement possibilities.

Reinforcements by surface vessels and aircraft carriers

NATO established two standing naval forces of relevance for the Baltic Approaches. None of them had the area as their primary operation field, but both could and did visit the Baltic and had Danish participants now and then.

In late 1967, NATO decided to create a standing force of up to eight vessels of destroyer-size, STANAVFORLANT, mainly intended for deployment in the Atlantic with a special interest in the sea outside Northern Norway, but there also was a possibility to deploy the force to the Baltic.[7] It could be sent to areas where Soviet forces appeared to threaten NATO shipping. The first option was to pass through with non-threatening posture, and under more severe conditions with weapons ready to respond promptly if attacked. If necessary, it would demand freedom of passage for all shipping by show of force, and if denial of passage was sustained, it would escort NATO shipping through denied waterway. It there was a sudden

---

5 Lemke, Bernd. *Die Allied Mobile Force*, 197–203. München: De Gruyter, 2011.
6 A detailed report of the difficult NATO-process and the AMF planned organisation is found in MCM 14–65 with attachments.
7 MCM-45-67 revised 8-12-67.

reinforcement of Soviet ground forces and deployment of a substantial naval force in the North or in the Baltic, the first move would be to deploy to the area to quietly signal NATO determination; then to coordinate operations with NATO forces in the area, closing the coast as necessary, to demonstrate support. If possible, other NATO naval forces in the area would supplement the actions.

Figure 15.1: STANAVFORLANT in 1971. Danish frigate HERLUF TROLLE is number two, German destroyer HESSEN number six. The other ships are Portuguese, Dutch, British and American. Source: Forsvarsgalleriet.

STANAVFORLANT was an implementation of NATO's flexible response.[8] It would be the first option for NATO naval forces to operate across nations with a large group for a prolonged time. In peace time it would do exercises and show the flag in various NATO countries, demonstrating solidarity. In tension time it could move to threatened areas relatively obscurely and stay out of sight until action became necessary. Any move under tension had to be approved by the NATO top. A ship's

---

8 Notat HEM vedrørende forslag til oprettelse af en Standing Naval Force Atlantic. Forsvarsministeriet 7. kontor december 1967, 12-44/68, 11-1-68.

turn with STANAVFORLANT normally took no less than four months, and permanent Danish participation was originally not foreseen except in specific exercises, but over the years the Danish frigates PEDER SKRAM and HERLUF TROLLE participated as full members now and then.[9] The German destroyers of the HAMBURG class likewise. In 1972 the submarine DELFINEN took part, much to the chagrin of its chief who did not consider this small and old u-boat suited for operating in the Atlantic; his squadron commander, however, disagreed, and off he went.[10] Other submarines participated later, playing the role of attackers on the surface force.

In 1973, a mine-sweeping mobile force, STANAVFORCHAN, with British, Dutch and Belgian mine sweepers, was set up to operate primarily in the Channel and coasts to the North Sea, but there was a possibility for it to operate in the Baltic, too.[11] It was supposed that the force would often cooperate with West German mine sweepers. Danish mine sweepers participated now and then.

As we saw in chapter 3, aircraft carriers in the 1950s several times operated in the North Sea to support operations in the Baltic Approaches, but for some years, not much happened in that vein. However, in 1968 Britain gave up its naval presence east of Suez, and consequently more carrier resources became available for NATO. For instance, HMS BULWARK, a commando carrier, was sent to participate in the exercise POLAR EXPRESS.[12] In later exercises, the strength of the 1950s was back – NATO now operated with two British and four American carriers. Exercise STRONG EXPRESS involved two carrier strike groups: one made up by HMS ARK ROYAL escorted by cruisers, destroyers and frigates, covered an Anglo-Dutch amphibious group including HMS ALBION, HMS FEARLESS and RFA SIR GERAINT operating in Norwegian waters. Two days later another carrier strike group, made up of USS JOHN F. KENNEDY and an amphibious group with the command ship USS MOUNT WHITNEY, arrived and staged two landings of US Marines near Tromsø.[13] In the 1970s, however, the strength was reduced. Britain scrapped HMS ARK ROYAL, their last strike carrier, and after the Vietnam war the Americans reduced their carrier capacity in favour of smaller ASW carriers. Exercises focused more on the GIUK gap and ASW activities to fend off Russian submarines, and activities further to the North in the Norwegian Sea were reduced.

In the early 1970s COMBALTAP had several discussions with various commanders of carrier (strike) forces about how reinforcements could be brought about by

---

9 Bork, Jørgen F. *Åbent hav. Mit liv i Søværnet 1945–1990*, 177–86. København: Gyldendal, 2010.
10 Nørby, Søren. "Sandheden om ubåden Delfinens deltagelse i STANAVFORLANT 1972." *Marinehistorisk Tidsskrift* 43, no. 4 (2010): 3–17.
11 Notat HEM om oprettelse af STANAVFORCHAN. Forsvarsministeriet 7. kontor 23-4-73 711-11/73.
12 Grove, Eric. *Battle for the Fiørds*, 14. London: Ian Allan Ltd, 1991.
13 Ibid., 14–15.

carriers.[14] The concept had changed from the 1950s with emphasis on large vessels carrying bombers to lighter vessels carrying fighter bombers, fighters and helicopters – and some units simply were changed into commando carriers able to land infantry, using helicopters or landing craft. The discussions ranged from the traditional (from the 1950s) fighter–bomber and fighter support from an American strike carrier, supporting the flank of Europe, to "Amphibious Support Planning" from a team of Royal Marines and the needs a British landing force with helicopters would have in terms of command and control, logistics, liasons and communication. The discussions also included its role in a deterrence phase where the mere presence of a carrier group would indicate resolve, not unlike the role of the AMF.

Flexible response for the flanks and the UKMF

In 1968, NATO, pursuing the flexible response strategy analyzed above (chapter 14), redefined in the document MCM 23–68 its reinforcement schemes for the flanks into two types:[15]
- Immediate Reaction Forces to demonstrate NATO's solidarity and resolve. These would be multi-national and very mobile; AMF and an upcoming STANAVFORLANT naval force would belong to this category.
- Reinforcement Forces to yield effective military reinforcement of local forces, wherever demanded. These must be strong entities and each therefore was to be set up by a national sizeable force.

The original planning papers from 1966–67 did not include the Baltic Approaches as part of the Northern flank,[16] but this was remedied in the ensuing process. The final conceptual paper for external reinforcements of the flanks[17] stated that the objectives of the Soviets in the Baltic Approaches would be (well known): to control the exits of the Baltic and gain access to the Atlantic; to obtain naval bases in the area; to secure their flanks and split the NATO front; and to move their early warning and air defence system to the West. The Baltic Approaches with the many isolated sub-areas would require forces with a high degree of self-sufficiency, emphasising

---

14 Helms, Adam. "Min tid som Commander Allied Forces Baltic Approaches 1970–75. Første del 1970–72." *Tidsskrift for Søvæsen* 176, no. 1 (2005a): 3–25.
15 Note HEM Forsvarsministeriet 7. kontor May 1968. Forstærkning til flankerne (Dok. DFC/D(68) 15). 711A/68. See also NATO MCM-23-68 of 16-4-68.
16 Note HEM Notat vedrørende spørgsmålet om mulige forbedringer af forsvaret af NATO's flanker i en krisesituation. Forsvarsministeriet 11. kontor 15-2-67 717 67.
17 MCM 23-68, 16-4-68.

firepower and mobility for the defence against either a possible overland attack or combined airborne and amphibious attacks. The local Danish and German forces might withstand low-scaled aggression, but not a Warsaw Pact determined assault. Many of the areas were suited for amphibious operations, and control of the straits would be essential to prevent the Soviet Baltic Fleet from getting access to the Atlantic. Full control of the straits was only possible if the NATO territory bordering them was in NATO's possession.

The paper took note that Denmark did not allow permanent stationing foreign forces in peace time, and that nuclear warheads were not allowed under the "present conditions". SACEUR and his sub-commanders would make plans for military action under various circumstances: the militarily most useful force types; possible reinforcements; transportation facilities' need for outside logistical support; and the best ways of coordinating local and reinforcing forces. Once the plans were drafted, one had to analyze the needs for local and NATO contributions to the reinforcing forces.

In January 1969, when the NATO defence ministers discussed possible improvements of NATO plans after the Soviet intervention in Czechoslovakia, the British suggested support to the Northern Flank by the United Kingdom Mobile Force (UKMF) consisting of an infantry division (three brigades infantry, one air drop brigade and various support entities) and an aircraft group (five squadrons fighter bombers, helicopters and transport aircraft).[18] By December 1969, AFNORTH had a plan for its activities ready: UKMF could be used in a period of tension or limited aggression in continuance of the AMF being set in. Action would be subject to approval by the relevant governments which supposedly at this time had assigned forces to NATO command. There were two priorities for deployment.

- The first would involve a brigade (without tanks): either in a defensive role at the Kiel Canal, or North of the Canal to fight paratroopers or amphibious forces, or on the Zealand islands to prepare for fighting enemy amphibious- and paratrooper landings. Parts of the mentioned air force group would support this. Transfer time was eight days, with supplies 14 to 18 days.
- The second would involve all of UKMF including the air force group with one brigade in a defensive role at the Kiel Canal, and the rest of the division deployed north of the Kiel Canal for action against amphibious and paratrooper landings. None would be deployed to the Zealand area. Transfer time was 14 days, 20 days with supplies for 30 days.

---

[18] Note HEM Notat om planerne for anvendelse af United Kingdom Mobile Force i det baltiske område. Forsvarsministeriet 7. kontor 711-5/50, February and 15-3-70.

The British paratrooper section would not participate in any of the two alternatives, but it could be deployed anywhere within the Baltic Approaches, if necessary.

The Danish Ministry of Defence did not agree with the prerequisite of Denmark having assigned forces to NATO, nor did it think that the AMF had to be employed first, and it suggested amendments saying so, but several years later the ministry could take note that these wishes were not fulfilled in the AFNORTH plans.[19]

The plans for the UKMF were not ready for implementation until late in the 1970s and we shall return to them below.

Reinforcement options in the 1970s

In 1975 the Danish C-in-C wrote a "sketch" for the future development of the defence.[20] He also dealt with reinforcement forces and concluded that it would be possible to receive them, but in periods of tension or limited aggression the politicians had to agree to such reception. So there was no guarantee for political support. In the ensuing years NATO financed an expansion of the harbour of Esbjerg – strengthening the quays for tanks and building two large warehouses – so that it could meet the task.[21]

The options for the Baltic Approaches in the year 1975 were three types of support: flag-waving forces, reinforcements and forces for general war (see table 15.1).

Flag-waving forces were used to indicate NATO's resolve to allocate forces in cases where a member stats was under threat. The name stems from the naval tradition of "sending a gunboat" to areas deemed problematic. The forces were limited in size and they were not strong enough in and by themselves to wage war, but they could be allocated in a very short time and they indicated a warning to the potential aggressor that NATO would do business if an attack was started. They would bring along all necessary supplies for a limited period of time.

Reinforcements were sizeable and intended to deter. They were to add such strength to the existing forces in the area that the potential aggressor would have to plan accordingly in order to avoid losses – and hopefully give up a planned attack. If not, the reinforcements would at least make it possible – together with

---

19 Notat vedrørende britiske forstærkninger til BALTAP-området. HEM Forsvarsministeriet 7. kontor 20-3-72 711-5/72.
20 Forsvarskommandoen. "Forsvarschefsskitse 1975." Vedbæk: Forsvarskommandoen, 1975.
21 Kulturministeriet. *Kold krig. 33 fortællinger om den kolde krigs bygninger og anlæg i Danmark, Færøerne og Grønland*, 95. København: Kulturministeriet, 2013.

local forces – to hold significant military key points. More reinforcements could then come to assistance. Most of the reinforcements that had been planned in detail would be supported from supplies stored in advance, i.e. in peace time.

Finally, large-size reinforcements were possible, typically from the USA, but it would take a long time to make them ready and transfer them.

Table 15.1: Options for NATO-reinforcements in 1975.[22]

Name	Size	Area/transfer time	Landing location
A. Flag Waving Forces			
AMF land	5–6,000 men	Zealand 6 days	Værløse/Korsør
AMF air	66 planes	BALTAP 48 hours	Jutland
STANAVFORLANT	6–8 destroyers	BALTAP	
B. Reinforcements			
UKMF	29,000 men 45 tanks 52 planes	Schleswig 11 days BALTAP 4 days	Esbjerg/Karup Jutland
UKMF reduced	10,000 men 15 tanks 36 planes	Zealand 8 days (or Schleswig 6 d. BALTAP 3 days	Kastrup/Korsør Skrydstrup/Esbjerg) Jutland
UKJATFOR	2 battalions	BALTAP 3 days	Paratroopers
CASTOG	6,000 men 54 planes	Schles/Zeal 30 d. BALTAP 5 days	Karup/Værløse Esbjerg/Kalundborg Skrydstrup
US Marines AMPF	10,000 men 60 planes	Jutl/Schles 15 days	West coast/Esbjerg
UK Royal Marines	4,000 men	Zeal/Jutl 10 days	West Coast/Esbjerg
C. Forces for "General War"			
US Marines AMPF	46,000 men 320–400 planes	Jyll/Schles 30 days	Vestkyst/Esbjerg
General air support	130 fly-sorties/day	BALTAP	By aircraft carriers

---

22 Forsvarskommandoen, Planlægningsgruppen: KA.Sagsakter fortrolig/hemmelig (afklassificerede) (1970–1978) 2: Middelstudier 1974–1977. The textual descriptions following the Box are mainly based on Lindhardt, Bjarne F. *Allierede forstærkninger til Danmark*, 79–95. København: Samfundsvidenskabeligt Forlag, 1981.

AMF is dealt with in more detail below.

STANAVFORLANT (Standing Naval Force Atlantic) had vessels from up to eight countries; it was planned for use in the Atlantic, but could and did operate in the Baltic.

UKMF (United Kingdom Mobile Force) was the British sixth Field Force with logistical support and air lift transport allocated. It also had one squadron JAGUAR fighters and two squadrons PUMA helicopters, able to lift 600 men at a time.

UKJATFOR (United Kingdom's Joint Airborne Task Force) was severely reduced in the 1970s because their air transport was cut, but a paratrooper element was kept.

US Marine Corps was organised for amphibious landing and had its own logistic system, independent of where they were operating. They would have aircraft and helicopters for support, but no tanks.

The UK Marines were organised as a very light infantry unit with light artillery.

The general air support with aircraft carriers came from the Atlantic Strike Force under SACLANT. As we have seen elsewhere, this Force had many task options and support and therefore was not easy to predict. There were, in principle, other air forces available, particularly from the USA, but such were not planned for.

None of these options were planned for concrete action by 1975, so there were no supplies stored for any of them. "Where and how" would be decided when the situation had arisen, but then COMBALTAP was competing with COMAFCENT for allocation, and within AFNORTH the BALTAP command was competing with Norway commands.

The Danish airfields within the COB programme were Tirstrup and Vandel in Jutland; they were to receive five fighter squadrons – subject to approval by the Danish parliament, however.

In 1976 the Denmark made an agreement with the USA about possible stationing of aircraft within the Collocated Operations Bases (COB) programme. Collocated bases were more than 70 active allied military air-fields from which U.S. aircraft would also operate during wartime, in addition to the main American airfields in Germany and Britain.[23] The contracts determined what types of aircraft could operate from which bases, and which squadrons were to be deployed, if necessary. Types of equipment, fuel, droptanks, weapons etc. to be kept in depots were specified for each airfield. The assigned squadrons were to exercise the use at least every four years. Across Europe, the airfields varied in peacetime activity from fully active fighter aircraft bases to joint civilian and military aircraft installations with limited activity. Generally, the facilities and support available to U.S. forces at these bases

---

23 https://snl.no/COB-avtalen; GAO: NATO Air Defences, 18-11-88.

were considerably less than those available at the main operating bases. Over 60 per cent of all U.S. aircraft scheduled to deploy to Europe would use such bases. The programme was one element in the changes in American policy towards a flexible response, giving more room for conventional responses to Russian military challenges by deploying American aircraft to Europe already in periods of tension.

The Vandel Airfield and reinforcements

The Vandel Airfield is located in Southern Jutland and was built by the Germans during WWII. During most of the Cold War it was a minor airfield, stationing artillery observance aircraft for the Army and functioning on and off as deployment airfield for the Air Force, first fighter squadron 724 with Hawker Hunters (general air defence and bomber escort), later F-100 fighter bombers from squadron 730 (supporting the army in Zealand in fighting Soviet forces landing on the beach).[24]

From 1973, Vandel received as deployment during AMF exercises the British Harrier Gr. Mk. 3 of the No 1 (F) Squadron, the only operational jet in NATO that could start and land vertically. It was part of the British UKMF force, and Vandel was selected because of its many spots suited to hide the planes, and in addition its required 1000-foot-"runway" (necessary with full payload on the Harrier) even if the proper runways were destroyed.[25] The role of the squadron was to attack landing craft and tanks on the beaches of Zealand.

Figure 15.2: The A-10 Thunderbolt fighter-bomber.
Source: Forsvarsgalleriet.

---

24 Schaiffel-Nielsen, N. M. *De tog vore hjem II*, 277. Randbøl: Randbøl Sogns Lokalarkiv og Museumdforenings forlag, n.d.
25 Schaiffel-Nielsen, N. M. "Deployeringsflyvestation Vandel." *Luft- og Rumfartsårbogen 1992–93* (1993), 65.

From 1982, Vandel became a deployment station for the 926th Tactical Fighter Group which was part of the United States Air Force Reserves.[26] About 75 per cent of its personnel were reservists, by contract obliged to serve one weekend per month and to participate in a 15-day exercise per year. Pilots had to have 140 hours flying time per year. The 926th was stationed in Naval Air Station in Louisiana, USA, a 4890 kilometre flight – 10 hours to the Azores and then six and a half hours to Vandel. KC-130 air tankers secured new petrol in the air over the Atlantic, and an EC-130 made sure that the navigation was right. Equipment and stores for the 926th were flown to Denmark by C-141 or C-5A transport planes.

During exercises, the 926th provided the BALTAP defence with 40 sorties per day from Vandel Airfield. Their planes were the A-10 Thunderbolt, a new construction which entered service in 1978:[27] a single-seat, twin engine, straight wing jet aircraft developed by Fairchild-Republic and designed for close air support of ground troops, attacking vehicles and tanks, and providing quick-action support against enemy ground forces. Its main weapon was a 30mm gatling gun, AGM-65 air-to-surface missiles and various types of bombs. It carried Sidewinder missiles for self-defence.

So this aircraft was apt to support Danish ground troops against enemy forces which landed on the Zealand beaches, and to support NATO forces in Schleswig-Holstein. The last exercise was carried out in 1989.

The AMF

Reinforcements for the Baltic Approaches – in actual fact for COMZEALAND – by the AMF could take place if the Danish government asked for it and at the same time put Danish earmarked forces under SACEUR; the supreme commander would at the same time call for a simple alert in the BALTAP area to let CINC-NORTH take command over all forces in the BALTAP area.[28] All national authorities must permit transit and the use of necessary base facilities for the AMF force whose vanguard forces according to schedule would arrive in Zealand three days later, and the rest after seven days. Receiving airfields would be Værløse or Kastup, and the forces would relocate to Southern Zealand. The fighter planes would arrive within 24 hours in airfields in Jutland.

Already in 1963, the Danish C-in-C wanted an exercise to take place as soon as possible, and the ministry supported this, but the Ministry of Foreign Affairs wanted to postpone any such exercise till 1970 or later, and SACEUR demanded that a plan for the use of the AMF was ready before he would allow any exercise. The

---

26 Ibid., 67–72.
27 https://en.wikipedia.org/wiki/Fairchild_Republic_A-10_Thunderbolt_II.
28 Notat om indsættelse af ACE Mobile Force (AMF) i BALTAP's område og om dansk styrkebidrag til AMF. HEM. Forsvarsministeriets 11. kontor 3-11-66. 711 A/66.

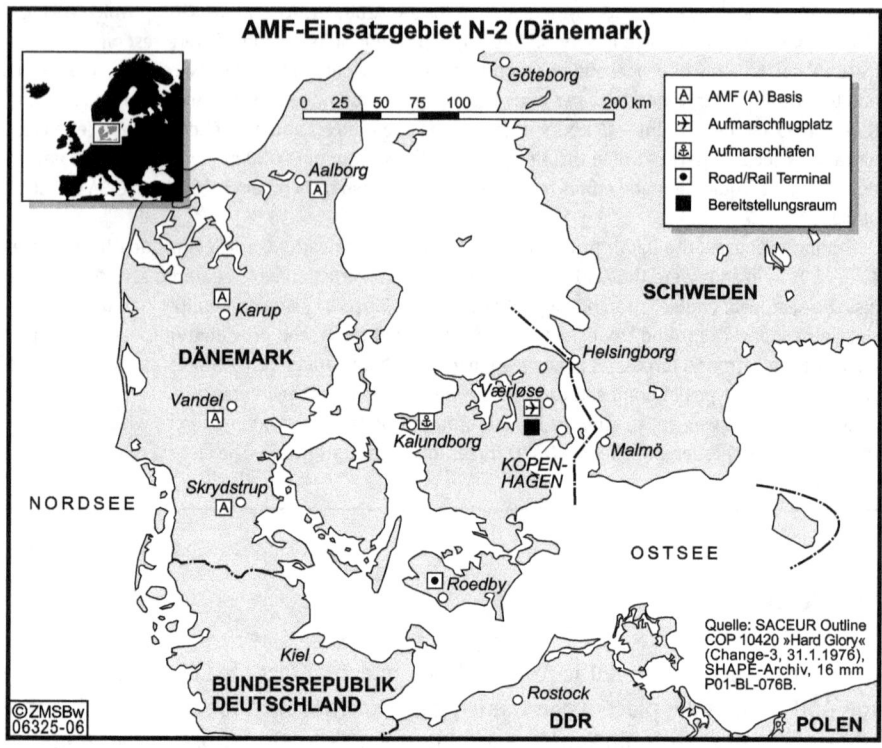

Figure 15.3: Map of AMF locations in Denmark – airplanes in Jutland, ground forces on Zealand.[29] Copyright ZMSBW.

draft plan was ready in April 1968,[30] involving three infantry battalions (deployed to Zealand) and three fighter squadrons (to reinforce AIRBALTAP's forces).

AMF's first exercise in the Baltic Approaches, GREEN EXPRESS, came about in 1969. The principles of operation for the AMF follow below;[31] it is a theoretical case, published by the Danish Defence where the Soviet Union has demanded passage through the Baltic Approaches and wants to station some Soviet forces on the ground around the passages to secure the actions. The Danish government opposes this and calls for AMF support. The NATO council grants this (without

---

29 Lemke, op. cit., p. 225.
30 Note HEM Allied Command Mobile Force (AMF), om planen for dens indsættelse i BALTAP's område og om dansk styrkebidrag til AMF. Forsvarsministeriet 7. kontor 18-4-68. 711A/68.
31 Nielsen, Flemming Schroll. *AMF – NATO's krisestyrke*. København: Forsvarets oplysnings- og velfærdstjeneste, 1981.

the air force fighter squadrons). The decision is made public to notify the Soviets of NATO's resolve.

Day one: SACEUR orders the AMF to move its 6,000 men to Denmark (the island of Zealand) and orders AFCENT to set up an airplane force to transport AMF segments to Denmark. Transport planes are relocated to airfields near to the barracks of the AMF in Central Europe and Britain. AMF HQ prepares for relocation and within a few hours the HQ planning group is on its way to Denmark to contact relevant Danish military authorities. AMF's flight control team relocates with vehicles and electronic equipment to Denmark and moves to the relevant (reserve) air fields in the area. They prepare the sequence of flights from the various member groups in Europe, get supplies for the airplanes and plan their flight back. Since this happens in peace time, all flights must be coordinated with civilian traffic.

Day two: an advance force from each AMF battalion arrives and gets initial orders related to their area of operation. The group relocates and prepares for quarters, vehicles for transport of the main force, connections to Danish military authorities etc. A patrol group, company-size, also lands, bringing their own vehicles along, and gets instructions for initiating patrols in the area of operation in a sort of preliminary flag-waving role.

Day three to six: the remaining men of the battalions arrive, most of them by plane, some by their own vehicles or train. Each company is allocated an area of operation and organises patrols and interaction with Danish forces. The support units – an anti-tank company, sappers, a field hospital, supply forces and the helicopter group arrive – and make formation as required by the situation.

By day seven: the AMF is ready for "expanded flag-waving" to persuade the Soviets to abstain from their goal of landing forces on Danish territory.

These were the principles for the AMF in theory. Seen from the observer's perspectives, it would be tempting to say that while the AMF in several other areas could "watch the border" by patrols along it and demonstrate that the enemy should not cross, the island of Zealand was somewhat different. Of course, the Soviets might try to land small forces for special operations. But apart from that, the most obvious threat was a large-scale landing operation, in other words an obvious crossing of the border. In that case, the AMF would look more like a general reinforcement than an emergency demonstration patrol. But of course, such deployment would make NATO's resolve clear to a potential aggressor.

The above indicates the generic AMF procedure. Of course, problems could arise. It was a comprehensive transport task: one Italian battalion with artillery and about 1,600 men required transport of about 2,300 tons; of these, only about four per cent could be moved by Italian transport airplanes, the rest was to be moved by alliance partners. One may suspect that such capacity would not be available in a real world situation of tension.[32] One Hercules C-130 airplane can carry about 20 tons, so a battalion needed more than 100 flights to be moved if ground or sea transportation was not possible.

Reinforcements in the 1980s

Above we saw the theoretical possibilities for reinforcement to BALTAP. In the 1980s the Danish commanders gave priority to the following options:
- AMF which also had Norway, Italy, Greece and Turkey as possible areas; its value was primarily symbolic.[33] There were 5–6,000 men for deployment to Zealand, it would take them six days to land in Værløse or Korsør.
- STANAVFORLANT, with six to eight destroyers or frigates. Their primary field of action was the Atlantic, but they could be deployed to the Baltic if air security was available.
- UKMF had high Danish priority. It had 29,000 men and 45 tanks, slated to land in Esbjerg in 11 days. In addition, 52 airplanes which would land in Karup after four days. In the 1980s the Danes negotiated a reduced force (10,000 men, 15 tanks and 36 airplanes) for Zealand; supply depots were planned and at least partly implemented. Furthermore, American forces were asked for as a reserve, even if it would take several months to get them.[34]

Let us take a look at the role of the UKMF. In the 1980s, the UK Government became increasingly concerned with the limited forces provided by Denmark for the Baltic Approaches.[35] There was considerable wrangling among Danish politicians about the need for British reinforcement. Concern was raised about the political impact of weapons and equipment stocks being stored in Denmark, but on the military side there was no evidence that Denmark would fail to meet its host nation commitments. Later cuts made by the Danish Defence Ministry caused turmoil in the British ministry of defence. This reduction included fewer regular Danish troops and cancellation of some modernisation plans. The UKMF was by now over-committed and had several different reinforcement plans, including

---

32 Lemke, op. cit., pp. 223–24.
33 Forsvarskommandoen. *Ved forenede kræfter. Forsvarets øverste militære ledelse. Forsvarschefsembedet og forsvarets udvikling 1950–2000*, 153. Vedbæk: Forsvarskommandoen, 2000.
34 Ibid., 171.
35 White, Kenton. *British Defence Planning and Britain's NATO Commitment, 1979–1985*, 89–90. Reading: University of Reading, 2016.

the defence of Zealand and Jutland. The Danish Government dedicated only two mechanised brigades, made up of 80 per cent of reservists, for this purpose. The British ministry felt that the Danish government was using the NATO reinforcement plans as an excuse to reduce their national defences.

This mistrust was pointedly expressed by Jonathan Alford, British colonel and deputy director of the International Institute for Strategic Studies at a conference in 1986:

> ... The Danish problem raises in acute form the issue of how much (or how little) a small country needs to do to be assured of external assistance. The Danish assumption – not wholly incorrect, as it turns out – is that the rest of us cannot afford to allow Denmark to be overrun. Thus whatever Denmark does or does not do, others will move. ... Those of us who commit forces to the defence of Denmark ... do expect some minimum of cover from Denmark if we are to expose our forces. The hope is, of course, that we can somehow stiffen Danish resolve and encourage Denmark to provide a reasonable minimum of defence to cover that reinforcement. ... I happen to believe that Denmark, being where it is, has no option. That is its misfortune but Danes do have a remarkable capacity for self-delusion and I see this tension continuing.[36]

Colonel Alford surely was not a product of a diplomatic career in the British Foreign Service!

Calling upon the UKMF

The sixth Field Force was the land element of UK Mobile Force, consisting of 13,500 troops; it was the strategic reserve for SACEUR and would have been deployed to the Baltic Approaches as its primary destination. The troops were to leave England by the airports at Lyneham and Brize Norton. To deploy this single formation involved the movement of 11,000 troops, 3,600 vehicles, trailers and artillery pieces, 14,500 tons of freight and 38 aircraft.

The group had some organisation problems.[37] The unit needed logistics, but sudden deployment in a crisis would have entailed substantial difficulty, as most of the units within the Logistic Support Group (LSG), the sixth Field Force's logistic support, were at cadre strength in peace time, and would be filled out by reservist reinforcements and individual regular Shadow Postings. Only then would they be operational. In a note to the Director of Military Operations the warning was made clear: "The effect of this situation is that the Regular element of the LSG cannot support the Regular combat element of the 6th Field Force prior to call out of the Reserves."

This meant that a regular force, equivalent to an infantry brigade, would be incapable of supporting itself in a sudden crisis if it were called upon to fight. The same note continues: "To deploy the Regular element of the 6th Field Force before Callout or at least before a guarantee that Callout will take place, would therefore, involve considerable risk."

---

36 Alford, Jonathan. "A Change in British Priorities?" In *Britain and NATO's Northern Flank*, edited by Geoffrey Till, 80–81. London: Macmillan, 1988.
37 White, op. cit., pp. 258–59.

The units of the UKMF were kept at a seven days' notice at all times, and this was reduced in times of tension, normally to 72 hours. The advance and key groups were kept at 24 hours' notice.[38] So the question was whether the general system of alert was initiated at such a time to make the call-up of reservists' work as desired.

By 1987, the Annual Report of the Danish Forces revealed that the planning of BALTAP land and air reinforcements had made progress:
Aircraft: SACEUR would muster seven squadrons with 138 planes (24 British JAGUAR and 114 various American planes). This would release some aircraft of the Danish Air Force for TASMO (Tactical Air Support for Maritime Operations) for the navy.
Ground forces: the deployment of the reduced UKMF force of 15,000 men was planned, and supplies would be in place in depots by 1988. The re-deployment would take 10 days using Danish ferry boats across the North Sea. In addition, the ninth American infantry division (27,000 men) would get status as "dedicated reinforcement" to the BALTAP area, landing in Esbjerg and Billund. Their need for support was now being analysed, and a draft support plan would be ready by 1988.

The processes of receiving infantry reinforcements would tie a large part of the Danish air defence, local ground defence forces, escorts and mine sweepers from the navy. But after war had broken out, the possibilities for receiving reinforcements would be in jeopardy – especially if one took the general endurance of the defence forces into consideration. Therefore, early decision-making was a key to success; this, however, was the responsibility of the political system, not the military.

Summing up: Reinforce management taking its time

During the Cold War, NATO was dependent on reinforcements to the weaker areas. The principles were there all the time, and stores were created e.g. close to airfields and naval bases, but detailed planning, particularly for moving ground forces, did not really start until the AMF was created. Until then, the reinforcement forces were mostly tested by exercises.

The first standing reinforcement force, the AMF, took five years to set up and make operational, and it did not visit the Baltic Approaches until 1966, in spite of

---

38 Ibid., 168.

invitations from the Danish C-in-C. But from then the AMF was reserved to function with forces on the flanks.

At sea, the STANAVFORLANT destroyer force started out in 1967, and Danish and German units regularly participated. But the force was not under AFNORTH, it was commanded by EAST SACLANT, and founded to operate on the high seas, not in the Baltic narrows. Nonetheless, it did exercises in the Baltic, provided that adequate air support was at hand.

AFNORTH on occasions had access to the Carrier Strike Groups (destined for the Norwegian Sea) to use them in the North Sea, supporting various bombing tasks in the Baltic Approaches. But such support could not be planned with any certainty. In some periods, carriers from the Royal Navy participated, creating such capacity, but nothing was certain.

Several other ground forces became available over the years. The AMF was a sort of police force with 5–6,000 men, meant to indicate to the Soviets that a threshold was about to be crossed. But other forces were substantial: the UKMF with up to 29,000 men; the US Marines with up to 46,000 men. Both forces would also deliver air support.

Receiving such forces required the host nation to set up bases (e.g. Vandel Airfield) and stores in the areas where they were supposed to operate. Exercises made sure that the systems worked.

By 1987, 138 British and American aircraft, 15.000 British infantry and 27,000 American infantry were planned for reinforcement, if the situation required it.

Chapter 16
Crises in the 1960s

This chapter deals with two crises of the 1960s: the Cuban missile crisis and the Chech "Spring of Prague" crisis in August 1968. The first crisis brought the participants to the brink of nuclear war, testing the nerves of top decision-makers. The second crisis was in fact more a crisis internal to the Warsaw Pact with NATO as a somewhat worried observer, but it was never a real threat to the West.

Both crises are supposedly known in general terms to the reader. In this book, we are only interested in the way Denmark and Germany dealt with them.

The Cuban missile crisis

In the second half of October 1962, the USA and the USSR confronted one another on the brink of war over the installation of Russian missile launchers in Cuba. In many ways, the Cuban Missile Crisis was a super power confrontation rather than a NATO-WAPA face-off because the decision-makers involved were the heads of state of the Soviet Union and the USA, not NATO's top. But of course, the crisis was felt in NATO as well as in the Warsaw Pact. Below we shall monitor what happened in West Germany's and Denmark's military systems in so far as there is declassified material available. Among these was a signal from the Danish Intelligence Office that the blockade was effective because a Russian merchant ship with military equipment was returning to the Baltic.

Briefly sketched, the crisis started on October 14, 1962, when an American recce plane found indications of Soviet missile launchers being constructed in Cuba. The American government demanded that these and other offensive weapons be removed immediately. President Kennedy asked his chiefs of staff to prepare an attack on Cuba on short notice and initiated a naval blockade of Cuba on 21 October. The day after he announced to America and the World that he would consider any nuclear missile launched from Cuba against any Western nation as an attack by the USSR against the USA, requiring a full retaliatory response by the USA upon the Soviet Union. The naval blockade served the purpose to turn back any ship having a cargo of offensive weapons.

On 24 October, the Soviet leader Khruschev responded that the USSR saw the blockade as an aggression. On 25 October, the Security Council of the United Nations took the matter under consideration with the American and Soviet ambassadors confronting one another. American nuclear bombers were put on 15 minutes' notice. On 26 October, the Soviets started backing down on the premise that the USA pledged not to invade Cuba, and on 27 October, an agreement was reached after a series of informal discussions through third parties; it was announced on 28 October by Khrushchev. The offensive weapons left Cuba and everything was gone by 9 November.

As one can see from the above, the crisis became known to every one by 22 October. The world feared a nuclear war, and the general public was very concerned. As we shall see, the reactions among the military decision-makers in Denmark and Germany were quite composed. On 22 October, SACEUR sent out a message urging military leaders not to take steps that might be considered provocative or might disclose operational plans. Actions should be taken without public notice if possible.[1] They might include intensification of intelligence collection, increased security and anti-sabotage measures, review of alert procedures and plans, manning of certain operational centres and checks of equipment and supplies.

Four days later, SACEUR suggested that each country took his recent evaluation of the Triannual Review 1962 under consideration to remedy major deficiencies. Furthermore, that the countries would strengthen existing combat units and make more combat units available to SACEUR; to increase combat and service support units and improve the status of reserves and reinforcements.[2]

In stark contrast to this pussy-footing, the East Germans put all forces on high alarm on 22 October, with pilots ready to take off within 10 minutes, army soldiers fully ready to leave their barracks and ships of the navy leaving harbour for their battle stations at sea or hiding in inlets.[3]

Denmark

The Danish Joint Chiefs of Staff had a meeting on 23 October.[4] The point of departure was SACEUR's request from the day before that NATO not take any steps that could raise concern in the general public or seem provocative. The chiefs agreed. Therefore, the level of alert was not changed, but certain precautions were taken.

The American forces outside NATO were on higher alert. The status for the Danish defence was that all of the army was in Denmark, the air force had a

---

1 Signal 222305 from SACEUR. NATO Secret. Shoc 233/62. BM 1/731.
2 Signal 260800 from SACEUR. NATO Secret. Sh 38359. BM 1/731.
3 Uhl, Matthias. "'Jederzeit gefechtsbereit' – Die NVA während der Kubakrise." In *Vor dem Abgrund. Die Streitkräfte der USA und der UdSSR sowie ihrer deutschen Bündnispartner in der Kubakrise*, eds Dimitrij Filippovych and Matthias Uhl, 99–119. München: Oldenbourg Wissenschaftsverlag, 2004.
4 Unless stated otherwise, all quotes from the Danish Chiefs of Staff come from the protocols of the staff which are secret and kept by the Danish HQ. All quotes in this book have been approved as unclassified.

squadron abroad and the navy had one frigate at the Faroe Islands and two submarines en route to Denmark in the North Sea. The intelligence office had intensified its work, but there was no reason to formally increase other security- and anti-sabotage measures; the chiefs presumed that the local chiefs were aware of their responsibilities in that respect.

The coastal radars of the navy were functioning normally, i.e. during daylight, and on special request by the intelligence system. The stations did not have personnel for a 24/7 function for an extended period of time, but as long as the cooperation with the intelligence office functioned, everything was well. A naval patrol craft was planned for routine recce the day after along the Baltic coast of Eastern Germany and Poland.

The air force had poor capacity within the recce squadron, and the planned activities would only be changed on demand from the Intelligence Office.

The staffs of the army, navy and air force worked on a normal schedule. The Joint Chiefs of Staff would prepare for moving to the HQ defence bunker in Vedbæk, but many of the rooms there were occupied by various training centres of the air force, preventing the navy from setting up a plotting system. But if necessary, that could be changed within a few hours.

The supreme commander had called attention to stores. There was oil for about 200 days, but the army lacked in ammunition for machine guns and tanks.

Bornholm was a particular issue in the light of the possibilities for limited war if an opportunity for isolated aggression came up. Everything was prepared for a general mobilisation, but an isolated call-up of a battalion to Bornholm required a special run-over of the mobilisation orders and it would take no less that 24 hours. In addition, one would have to fly in officers and NCOs to the island. Moving forces on Zealand to Bornholm would weaken the preparedness there. Facing those facts, the C-in-C said that "I suppose that on Bornholm everything has to be prepared, but it must not happen at the cost of preparedness in other parts of the country." This is understood as Bornholm was on its own, for now. But if the situation got worse, one had to consider reinforcements to the island.

Recce in Danish waters on Soviet merchant ships in 1962
The following is from a biographic novel by a former first lieutenant of a Danish patrol craft, but the story[5] corresponds quite exactly to what actually happened.

> In 1962 I was daily officer of the watch in charge of the Combat Operation Centre of the naval district comprising Kattegat, located in Frederikshavn. In April, 1962, we got a first impression of something in the offing when the chief of operations summoned the three officers of the watch and the skipper

---

5 Lundholm, Kurt. *Søridderne*. Brunlynget Bogforlag, 2011.

of the small patrol boat Y 339 to a meeting. We were told that the Intelligence Office of the navy wanted more details about Russian merchant ships leaving the Baltic with cargo on the deck – like cars, tanks, aircraft parts or boxes. For boxes: length, width, height.

This request was to be kept secret at all costs. The skipper asked for a better camera and hoped that he could do as wished with his maximum speed of seven knots. In August, four months later, several Russian merchant ships were observed leaving the Baltic at the lightship of Læsø Trindel. Most of them had already been observed at Bornholm and at Langeland, but a few got through unobserved during night or foul weather and therefore were not observed until our area. None of us had any idea that those ships were *en route* to Cuba with missiles. They were all photographed by the patrol craft and the pictures sent to the Intelligence Office. By early September, rumours had it that the Russians regularly sent military equipment to Cuba.

On 23 October I was officer on duty and at four in the morning I received a telephone message that a secret signal would be sent and had to be decrypted immediately. The signal told that USA had declared blockage of transport of military equipment for Cuba. The Danish navy immediately would increase surveillance of all ships from the Warsaw Pact. The state of preparedness was not changed, but more naval units would be sent to sea, and surveillance from land-based stations had to be intensified. One hour later all hands were on site, and our chief gave us a briefing. The watch system was changed into 12 hours on, 12 hours off duty.

Figure 16.1: Danish patrol boat Y 343, same type as Y 339 in story.[6]

---

6 Olsen, Gunnar, and Svenn Storgaard. *Flådens Skibe og Fartøjer 1945–1995*, 158. København: Marinehistorisk Selskab, 1998.

> Later that day every one off duty watched Kennedy speaking on TV, and some officers talked about moving their families away from the neighbouring town because this station and the adjacent fort were sure to receive a nuclear bomb if war broke out. Next day we were all quite nervy, and nothing indicated that the ships would stop, They continued until October 24 in the evening when one lightship observed a ship that had passed westbound earlier that day now returned, apparently bound for Russia. The following days more ships returned, and the crisis was over.

It appears that the first indication that the Soviets had actually decided to give up the Cuban missile project was an observation by the Danish naval intelligence system: a merchant vessel observed to be northbound on 22 October was observed southbound on 24 October, and another one did the same the day after.[7] This means that at a rather early stage in the crisis, the Soviet leadership had already begun giving in to the American pressure by returning ships so that they did not face the blockade; the American political top must have been aware of this indication already in the morning (Eastern American time) of 24 October since the signal is sent 0920 hours mid-European time (Zulu).

Germany

According to Thoss, the German military did not immediately follow up upon SACEUR's recommendation.[8] For one, they did not think that a military confrontation was likely. Second, the German military-political top, the Verteidigungsrat, was not to meet until 24 October in the morning, so the military top wanted to wait.

This is not quite correct for the navy. Referring to the supreme commander's recommendation, the navy was ordered on 23 October to intensify reporting on enemy actions; strengthen the security- and sabotage abatement; test the alarms for mobilisation; secure military leadership outside working hours; and test various equipment stores, all to be done without making any "provocations" of the public.[9] But it took up to two days before the order was implemented locally.

---

7 Hansen, Peer Henrik. "The Cuba Crisis 1962 – As Seen Through Danish Intelligence Sources." In *The Global Cuban Missile Crisis at 50*, eds James G Hershberg and Christian F Ostermann, 710. Washington, DC: The Wilson Center, 2012.
8 Thoss, Bruno. "'Bedingt abwehrbereit'. Auftrag und Rolle der Bundeswehr als NATO-Mitglied während der Kuba–Krise." In *Vor dem Abgrund. Die Streitkräfte der USA und der UdSSR sowie ihrer deutschen Bündnispartner in der Kubakrise*, eds Dimitrij Filippovych and Matthias Uhl, 72–75. München: Oldenbourg Wissenschaftsverlag, 2004.
9 Signal akh163 to the Command of the Navy, sent 23-10-62 at 1932 hours. Geheim. BM 13/5.

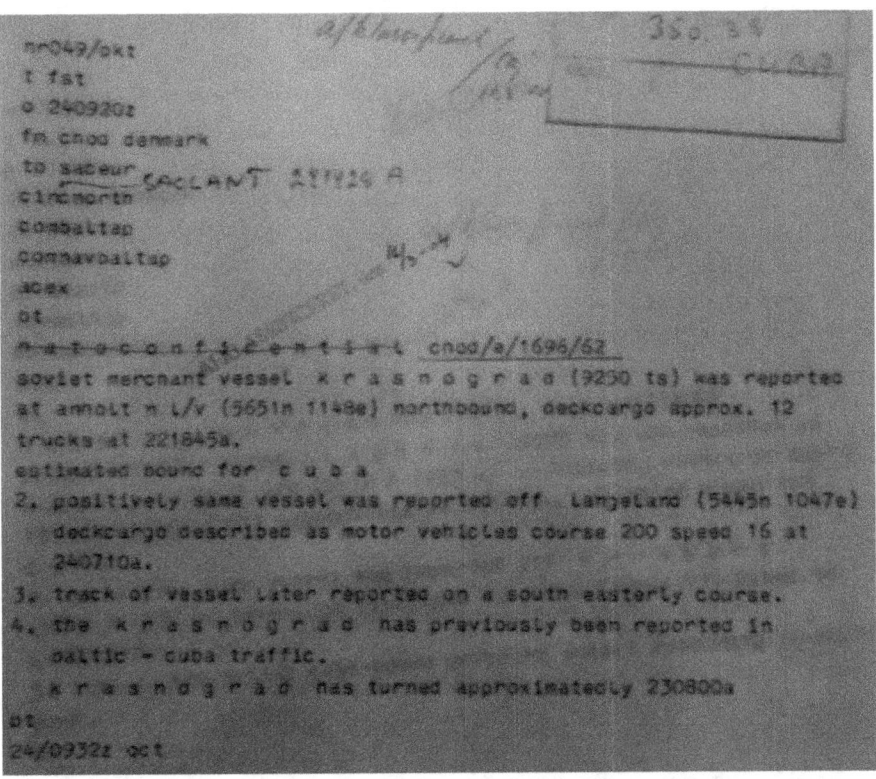

Figure 16.2: Signal from Danish Intelligence Office to NATO HQs that the Soviet merchant ship KRASNOGRAD with motor vehicles as deck cargo has been reported to turn back to the Baltic. Source: Rigsarkivet.

There are not (public) files that tell what happened during this first meeting of the crisis on 24 October, but after the meeting the Ministry established a crisis management, effective the next day, to asses the situations as they arose.[10] Officers on duty could be at home outside normal office hours. But there was not much to be done without a general higher NATO alert (this would allow the German government to initiate a number of actions), and this was not in preparation. So only a few things could be done: in the forces, units abroad or on exercises were to be called home, and specialists were to be called up for service, and furlough in general cancelled. The air defence was to be readied.

---

10 Fü B III note to Kommando der Territorialen Verteidigung 24-10-62 AZ 11-08-05, Tgb Nr 5021/62. BM 1/731.

Consequently, the lower commands were not able to make any far-reaching decisions; they were told to become prepared, but without publicity. After the crisis was over, reports showed that the command system did not function adequately.[11] The signal from 23 October mentioned above was late in getting through to the lower levels. Furthermore, some teletypewriters were out of function. A later order for more presence of the local commanding officers was only in force for two days and when recalled confusion was created; some ministerial offices gave orders to the opposite. Presence by home phone was often not possible, and priorities in orders were not always followed.

On 24 October, the Verteidigungsrat decided that if the situation became more threatening, Germany would assign its forces to SACEUR as if Simple Alert had been established. This, however, was more or less a case of symbolic politics, for in actual fact the German forces would need a month-long preparation phase to be ready for action.

A case in point: the navy was not quite ready for action.[12] The following could be ready within 48 hours:

- Two destroyers, which were as of now heading towards Brest, France.
- One frigate, two other frigates within two to 30 (!) days.
- Five squadrons of MTBs, all of which had two war torpedoes on board and were capable of mining.
- 48 mine sweepers, but many were not yet ready for acoustic mine sweeping.
- Two submarines (the building program was only in preparation)
- About half of the naval air arm.

There was a lack of various equipment and stores. All in all, the paper stated that the conditions of the navy were not satisfactory. In the following days the archives show that step by step, military guarding and control of various key points were increased, but care was taken not to alarm ordinary people. As various aspects of mobilisation were tested, weak points – e.g. a lack of medical doctors for the army and problems of making public administration offices work properly – were identified.

Taken together, one can say that the hierarchical organisation did not work as desired. Some roles were unclear, some limitations on free movement were taken in doubt, and some communication channels simply did not work.

A particular problem came when mines were to be loaded. It turned out that the 1,000 mines for the Baltic could not become operational because there were

---

11 Signal KdoFLB to Fü M II 3. Geheim msg 829 30-10-62. BM 13/5.
12 Fü M IV – Az 10–70–00, TgbNr 2070 Geheim 24–10–62. BM 1/731.

no batteries for them.[13] Thus the entire German mine defence in the Baltic was not available during the crisis.

MTBs on the loose
In October, many German MTBs were participating in exercises in Danish waters, training torpedo firing in Kattegat and tactical training in the Baltic, calling at the Køge Harbour.[14] Because of the lack of decision power in the military top (as we saw above), they had no indication of what to do from the navy HQ, so most carried on the planned tactical surveillance activities. On 24 October, the chief of the Third Squadron, however, decided to return to Flensburg and ordered war preparedness, taking the necessary equipment on board. On Sunday 28 October the MTBs again sailed eastwards, the families of the crews assembled on the quay and waving good-bye. En route east the torpedo specialists re-read the manuals of the war pistols of the torpedoes. They went back to Køge Bay, mooring along the tanker CLAIRE JUNG, and continued the tactical training. Thoughts were of course bound to the threatening war, and the chief had many considerations of what to do with the tanker; on the one hand, it should move north and hide in some Danish inlet to be protected against WAPA attacks, on the other hand he needed it if the MTBs had to go into action. The problems were solved on 29 October when Khruschev announced his decision. Four days later, a KYNDA cruiser and a KOTLIN destroyer passed the Baltic Approaches, and the German MTBs had a special joy in finding them and photoing their missile equipment. The destroyer – in vain – tried to fence them off and nearly caused a collision.

Figure 16.3: MTB PANTHER "chasing" a KOTLIN destroyer on 2 November 1962. Source: http://www.schnellboot-leopard.de.htm.

---

13 Der Befehlshaber der Flotte: Tagung 21-22/2 1963. Beispiele. TgbNr. 7-0288/63. Vertraulich. 6-5-63. BM 1/1691.
14 Hess, Sigurd. "'Eine klare und gegenwärtige Gefahr' oder 'Bedingte Abwehrbereitschaft' am Beispiel des 3. Schnellbootgeschwaders während der Kubakrise 1962." In *Vor dem Abgrund. Die Streitkräfte der USA und der UdSSR Sowie Ihrer Deutschen Bündnispartner in der Kubakrise*, eds Dimitrij Filippovych and Matthias Uhl, 94–95. München: Oldenbourg Wissenschaftsverlag, 2004.

After the crisis, the German military top concluded that the present system was not able to perform as military command. Therefore, military planning had to involve the following: a civilian/military coordinated leadership organised for action; minimum requirements for operational capabilities of those military forces that were to be first defenders; a logistical system that guaranteed equipment for said forces; and finally much improved protection of all forces and population against nuclear attacks.[15]

For the navy, several conclusions were drawn.[16] The meetings of the leadership went well, but the ministry was not organised for work under pressure. Some offices in the ministry gave orders that did not correspond with the actions of other parts of the ministry, so better coordination was required. Furthermore, the mobility of the organisation was questionable, and some competences were unclear, leading to unnecessary involvement of the minister. The whole alarm system had to be thought over, especially for the relations between the ministry and military command organisations. Finally, some equipment was not available because of budgetary restrictions; these had to be reconsidered for situations like the crisis.

The 1968 Czech crisis

On the night between 20 and 21 August, Russian forces moved to occupy Czechoslovakia and stop the liberalisation of politics and the economy together with freedom of speech and organisation, which the government under prime minister Dubcek had initiated. That story is told elsewhere; in this book we are concerned with the short-term consequences within NATO.

Confusion in the NATO HQ

On the night of 20–21 August, the first public information about the invasion came from Radio Prague around 0200, and 0209 Associated Press relayed the message.[17] In NATO's situation centre there was only one teleprinter available, and it did not function. Nobody had realised this because the officer on duty had retired for the night at 0120 – in accordance with his instructions. The officer on duty in

---

15 Thoss, op. cit., p. 81.
16 Fü M II 3 – Az 31-01-01, TgbNr 4663 + 4566 Geheim 09-11-62. BM 1/731.
17 Forsvarsministeriet 11. kontor, j.nr. 906-5/68, a series of notes from 21–30 august 1968.

SHAPE telephoned this officer at 0315, calling the AP-news message to his attention. He then alerted the staff officers who arrived to the situation centre around 0415. The NATO-delegations were informed around 0500.

Three countries – the USA, France and Britain – had been informed about the invasion by the Soviet ambassadors before it actually took place, and they did nothing to inform NATO until later, so for about 12 hours the NATO situation centre only had press releases as information, and after that the amount of information – much of it redundant – grew so much that it was difficult to keep up an acceptable information level. Furthermore, the NATO-wide information system linking the NATO Headquarters with the defence ministries or foreign offices of the member countries then broke down, and information had to be spread by other channels, adding to the time used solely for information relaying.

The report concluded that NATO had perceived correctly that there were no signs of an attack on NATO being prepared. Furthermore, SHAPE had on 19 August noted that the Russian forces were in positions that would allow them to take control in a short time. Given this, the report recommended that in future comparable situations, the NATO situation centre should be manned up, and each NATO country should be asked to immediately inform about the developments they could watch.

Disagreements at the Danish top level

The then Danish Minister of Defence of the three-party government, Erik Ninn-Hansen, told his story in a book on Danish politics in 1974.

> Our intelligence had kept me informed during the Summer months that something was cooking, and mid-August it was clear that Russian troops moved towards Czechoslovakia. What was the situation now? My phone rang at 03.45 in the morning of the 21 august.[18] It ought to have been a military authority, but it was not. It was the prime minister: "Ninn, the Russians have invaded Czechoslovakia". No further comment was necessary, and we agreed to meet in the prime minister's office as fast as possible together with the minister of foreign affairs.
>
> I asked the officer on duty in my ministry to call the Chiefs of Staff for a meeting when I was done in the prime minister's office. In my own ministry I first met with the permanent secretary and two heads of office. After that, I met with the Chiefs of Staff and the chief of intelligence to discuss my main concern: the state of alert. My military advisors did not see the invasion as a threat against NATO, but I thought that nonetheless, the situation was not without risk. Was it possible that the Russians had plans of invading other countries in the East? Romania? Yugoslavia? If so, what would such a conflict mean for the rest of Europe?

---

[18] Ninn-Hansen, Erik. *Syv år for VKR*, 106. København: Det Schønbergske Forlag, 1974.

And, if Russian troops came into a confrontation in Czechoslovakia, would there be a spill-over to West Germany?

I agreed with the Chiefs about a set of actions in the navy and the air force, but for the army, there was not much that could be done. Next step of alert would mean that the forces left barracks to take up stations for imminent threat, and such a step might cause alarm in the population. We agreed to postpone a decision until after a meeting in the Cabinet.[19]

The Ministry of Defence has kept a journal[20] of all meetings involving the minister, giving time for and participants in meetings the first days, plus a relatively detailed story about who said what.

0430. Minister present in the Prime Minister's office. Minister asks C-in-C to call Joint Chiefs of Staff for a meeting and be prepared for a later meeting with the minister.

0450. C-in-C arrives at his Headquarters and meets with the chief of intelligence.

0515. C-in-C calls Minister and recommends to postpone a meeting with the Joint Chiefs.

0720. Minister meets with C-in-C and head of military intelligence, permanent secretary and two heads of offices are also present. C-in-C tells that he has not called for a meeting with the Joint Chiefs of Staff, they are present in their respective headquarters. The minister responded that in his opinion, they should be called for a meeting. The minister then complained over the procedures followed for waking up key actors. The chief of intelligence explained that he had initiated a series of call to wake up, apparently some mistakes had been made. The Foreign Office had called the Staff of the Army to ask for news about the invasion (since they apparently had heard nothing). The minister found this all wrong and asked for an investigation of the process.

0915. Meeting with the Joint Chiefs of Staff. The minister explained how his morning had been and how he saw the situation. Early in the morning, he had asked for a meeting with the Joint Chiefs of Staff, but the C-in-C had the opinion that they should be at their command posts. The press had asked the minister about any special alerts, he had answered that there were none, but he would like the opinion of the Joint Chiefs . . . The C-in-C again said that he saw no need for special alerts, no intelligence indicated any threats, on the contrary. The three Chiefs all agreed . . .

At 10 o'clock the cabinet was called into a meeting, and based on the recommendation of the minister of defence the cabinet ordered all military personnel to stay in barracks or at their service station.

---

19 Ibid., 110.
20 Forsvarsministeriet 11. kontor, j.nr. 906-5/68, a series of notes from 21–30 august 1968.

The following day: the Joint Chiefs of Staff met with the minister at 14.30. The minister indicated that he found his and the Cabinet's order the previous day within the parameters that the Joints Chiefs had accepted at their meeting in the morning. The C-in-C in a polite, but direct way informed the minister that he disagreed: First, there existed a system for alert which accommodated the special conditions within the three forces and therefore was the system to use; if the minister wanted changes, he should give the general order, and the military system would adapt as feasible in the forces. Second, the order of yesterday had several disadvantages for the navy and the air force. The minister's order meant that many specialists had been kept back for no purpose whatsoever, and at a considerable cost because they were not conscripts and therefore had to be compensated for 24-hour watch. The army mainly had conscripts, and the order had been followed.

These notes leave no doubt that the minister was deeply annoyed and felt betrayed by his top officers because he did not get the information about the attack first. On their side, the officers had no understanding of the sentiments of an elected politician.

HAVMANDEN on Patrol

Early in the morning on 21 August, the Danish navy sent a patrol craft, HAVMANDEN, stationed on Bornholm, to check on the situation in the Baltic. A signalman has told about his experiences that morning:[21]

> We set course south west towards the East German island Rügen. We were aware that the reason for our alert was an invasion of Czechoslovakia, but for the first hour we did not know what the reactions of the western world would be. We kept radio silence all the way to Rügen.
>
> As soon as we had left the harbour, the crew started readying the ship for defence in case we were attacked. The 40 mm gun was cleaned for tectyl which in daily order protected the gun against salt water and rust. Ammunition was taken on deck from stores, and the cartridges (sets of four) were put in the racks on the gun. The papers of the ship and keys for coding/decoding telegrams were put into a couple of heavy iron cases and placed so that they could be kicked over board and sink if the ship were boarded by an enemy.

On the radar we saw many ships along the coast of Rügen, and we had no doubt that they were men-of-war, probably from the local naval base. At six o'clock the news from Radio Denmark told us that there was no military response from NATO. After a couple of hours we were close to the territorial border of East Germany, and we could see the East German naval vessels. Probably all ships had been sent to sea in order not to be caught in the harbour in case of a NATO attack. As we got closer, two East German frigates set course towards us. We turned east to a course parallel with the coast, and the two East Germans followed suit parallel to us at a distance of a couple of hundred meters.

---

21 Bogason, Peter. *Søværnet under den kolde krig – politik, strategi og taktik*, 208–9. København: Snorres Forlag, 2015.

Figure 16.4: Danish patrol craft HAVMANDEN. 35 m 170 tons, 20 knots, 1 40 mm AA gun, depth charges. Source: Forsvarsgalleriet.

Their guns were much more powerful than ours, they were manned, and they pointed at us. Their level of alert and manning of the guns indicated that they were ready if the invasion should provoke an answer from the West. The East German greeting had to be interpreted as "We have seen you. Don't mess with our internal affairs. Get Out!"

After a while the ships increased their distances. We went a little more to the north and stayed in those waters for the rest of the day to observe. As time passed, we realized that the situation would not provoke a military action from the West. We stayed for another 24 hours and then returned to Bornholm

Figure 16.5: East German frigate RIGA-class. 3 100 mm and 2 37 mm guns. Source: Forsvarsgalleriet.

Summing up: Crises with little alarm

The Cuban missile crisis and the end of the Czechoslovakian Spring both are major crisis in the history books, and not without reason; in particular the Cuban crisis had the world on the brink of nuclear war.

But in the military headquarters, there were no signs of panic at any time. In both cases, it was obvious that not much could be done because neither Denmark nor Germany were visibly at risk for attacks at any time.

In particular, the Czechoslovakian crisis took the military by surprise and the German military top realised that a number of procedures had to be changed.

The stories about the Danish minister and his military advisors are illustrative in that respect with the minister acting like a fly caught in a bottle: flying against the glass wall time and again, and in effect giving the wrong order.

Chapter 17
Towards NATO missiles in the 1970s

The 1970s saw important changes in the NATO defence of the Baltic Approaches. First of all, NATO could finally implement its own missiles in the tactics in the Baltic Approaches, first with three German destroyers (air missiles), soon followed by FPBs with sea missiles; the Danish navy likewise got missiles for its large ships and FPBs. Second, a general overhaul was necessary to modernise both navies and prepare them for the 1980s. Budgetary restraints, however, formed a Bed of Procrustes which did not allow the admirals to get all their wishes for expansion fulfilled.

In this chapter, we first take stock of the naval situation at the entrance to the 1970s. The perspective is that of a German destroyer commander who concluded that NATO destroyers without sea missiles were in serious danger in the Baltic due to WAPA missiles – unless operated under NATO air supremacy, which was unlikely.

What were the WAPA intentions? The next section goes through the details of a WAPA amphibious landing operation, constructed by German intelligence. We get the probable naval operations at sea and the Soviet doctrines and tactics for the landing army forces.

The third section deals with the WAPA missile threat and NATO's (slow) response, detailing the reactions in both navies. They chose to follow different courses in integrating sea missiles, but agreed on using the SEA SPARROW air missiles.

Section four and five deal with the modernisation processes in the two navies; Denmark had a major defence policy change, reducing the scope of the defence and in reality leaving the navy's role to the defence of Zealand. The German navy decided to focus on FPBs and fighter-bombers working in unison in the Western and Middle Baltic; East of Bornholm submarines would be the main weapon.

Status 1969: A German "head count"

Ever since the German navy was re-installed, the leadership had called for more destroyers because they were versatile, they were assets as flotilla leaders of FPBs and insurance in case of bad weather. When SACEUR in 1964 cut back the planned missile destroyers listed in MC-70 from six to three, the German naval C-in-C reacted quite strongly, but to no avail.[1,2] General cut-backs on military budgets in the subsequent years, however, would have had to postpone new destroyers anyway, and as we saw above, there were several reasons for not sending destroyers into the Baltic Sea.

These reasons were tested again in 1969 when a note was written by the commander of the destroyers on the prospects of using destroyers in the Middle Baltic,[3] i.e. the waters between Gedser and Bornholm. In many ways it depicts quite clearly what the general military situation in the Middle Baltic was like as an area for littoral warfare. Submarines were not included in the analysis – they were mainly reserved for operations in the Baltic east of Bornholm.

The Middle Baltic was not large – 80 miles east-west, 40 miles north-south. In the eastern part of the area NATO had Bornholm, loaded with electronic equipment to gather information about activities at sea and on land to the north-east, east and south of the island. In the northern part, the Danes had a comprehensive system of minefields, blocking the southern part of Øresund (except for the Swedish national waters) and the beaches of the area. On Zealand, there was a coastal fort on Stevns and a system of NIKE and HAWK air defence missiles. There were radar stations on Stevns, Møn and Gedser. The Germans had a radar station and a submarine detecting station on Fehmarn and blocked the Fehmarn Belt with mine fields. German depot ships would have been deployed to Kattegat to service (by day) the units fighting in the Baltic (mostly by night). Fighter-bombers stationed on Zealand (if any) were about 10 minutes away, from Jutland 20 minutes; the same from Schleswig-Holstein (the Naval Air Arm).

In the south, the Warsaw Pact had a series of radar stations along the Baltic coast. On the Rügen and Darss there were SSM batteries, ranging about eight miles, but with relay radars ranging 28 miles. Enemy aircraft was never more than ten minutes away.

The middle Baltic was only about 60 miles from Kiel, but destroyers in deployment could not pass the Mecklenburg Bay because of the dangers from coastal batteries and aircraft. Therefore, if coming from Kiel, German destroyers would rather sail north, around Zealand in order to go south through Øresund – but most likely they would already have been deployed to Kattegat when hostilities were imminent.

---

1 Sander-Nagashima, Johannes Berthold. *Die Bundesmarine 1950 bis 1972*, 334–37. München: Oldenbourg Wissenschaftsverlag, 2006.
2 A series of papers on the topic from the C-in-C are found in BM 1/926h.
3 Kommandeur Zerstörerflotille: Einsatzgrundsätze für Zerstörer in der OSTSEE. Geheim. Führungsakademie der Bundeswehr Abt. Marine. TgbNr. 26/69. BM 1/1360c.

The naval order of battle in the area would – reducing the sizes for reserves, decommissioned ships and other tasks, and excepting submarines – be something like:

Table 17.1: WAPA and NATO order of battle.

	Cruisers	Miss.D.	Dest.	Frig.	Miss FP	FPBs.	Fight-B	Recce
WAPA	4	4	10	15	45	90	90	13
GE/DK		2 (1971)	5	5		36	24	13

In addition, WAPA would have 72 amphibious craft. All in all, the ratio was about 3:1 in favour of the Warsaw Pact. This was a numerical list. But a closer look at the capabilities of the forces did not improve the standing of NATO. The range of the enemy missiles was larger than that of the guns of NATO; the 130 mm guns of WAPA had a larger range than the old 127 and 100 mm guns of NATO, but the new 127 mm guns of the LÜTJENS class would equal the WAPA guns in range but excel in firing rapidity. The missiles of NATO and WAPA were to some degree equal in quality, but the WAPA warheads were much larger and therefore it took fewer missiles to sink an enemy.

WAPA probably would have air superiority and hence better conditions for recce and therefore they could early on detail their tactics. The navies had no fighters, but the German fighter-bombers would prompt interception from the WAPA aircraft. WAPA could set up two fighting groups, each stronger than the only NATO group, and WAPA would have reserves, NATO none – this could only be ameliorated by early counter attacks by NATO bombers against the Baltic bases. Large WAPA amphibious operations would be escorted by combat air fighters, making NATO attacks difficult.

These operations would be expected from the WAPA forces: disturbing NATO mine laying; covering WAPA mine laying; attacking with missiles the coastal fort Stevns and the NIKE batteries on Zealand; deployment of relay ships (or aircraft) for SAMLET coastal missiles; recce advances for their own forces; preparation and execution of amphibious operations. When the NATO forces (especially FPBs) had been reduced (or kept back in bad weather), WAPA cruisers could come into play.

NATO's primary tasks would comprise: mine laying in enemy waters; covering their own mine operations; attacking WAPA amphibious forces.

Given the above, what could German destroyers (and frigates) do? In general, the WAPA units could fire their missiles in a time slot of about half an hour before approaching NATO guns could even be brought to bear. Good WAPA manoeuvring could keep them outside the reach of the NATO guns. Since the enemy was dependent on electronic direction, the main counter weapon would be jamming. But if the upcoming LÜTJENS destroyers and the planned Frigate 121 had new 100 mm guns (35 rounds per minute) and the SM-1a missile (to replace the TARTAR), a balanced scorecard would be more likely, but that was yet to be seen (and the LÜTJENS class was planned with 127 mm, not 100 mm guns, PB). And even with new missile destroyers and frigates NATO might be at a disadvantage because of the small warheads of the missiles.

The worst confrontation would come up by daylight and light wind and sea. OSA FPBs in groups of four could fire their missiles in a joint salvo without being within reach of the NATO guns. With a hit probability of 20% three to four of them would reach their target which would be destroyed. In foul weather the OSAs could not operate, but the destroyers still had missile capabilities.

The situation by night was ambiguous because not enough was known about the possibilities to jam various enemy electronic systems. If OSAs were in operation, they could fire their missiles by day. If OSAs were not at sea, the situation would probably also favour the enemy. Use of the Naval Air Arm at night would not be possible until new KORMORAN missiles were available.

A special case might come about during the first nights of hostilities. One might suppose that the command and control systems of the enemy were not quite operational yet, so a number of hit-and-run operations (using electronic jamming) might succeed, resulting in the destruction of a number of enemy ships.

The main danger, however, would come from a large amphibious attack against the Danish islands. All available NATO forces would be used against such a fleet, even at the risk of comprehensive losses. Such a fleet would probably be detected so early that it could be met in the open sea between Bornholm and Møn. The escorts of the main amphibious fleet had to be attacked by submarines and (mainly) aircraft the night before in order to make it possible for NATO's ships to attack the transport ships. The NATO destroyers would then late at night approach the fleet from Øresund (i.e. after deployment from Germany to waiting position north of Zealand), but the passing by Danish minefields in Southern Øresund at reduced speed would take about 40 minutes with no possibilities to deviate from the course; this would give the WAPA units 40 minutes to fire on a "steadfast" target if a large number of OSA packs were in place further to the south, waiting for the opportunity to fire their missile salvos.

The overall conclusion of the analysis was that the operation of NATO destroyers in the Baltic was very risky. The FLETCHER-class destroyers could only operate if OSAs were not at sea. Operations by the KÖLN-class frigates were hopeless.

Destroyers, then, could only operate with tactical support from aircraft and FPBs. The FPBs would have to use chaff to jam the WAPA missiles and then initiate (wired) torpedo attacks. Aircraft were by day planned to simultaneously attack. By night the destroyers were to attack, but due to the small-calibre shells and warheads they were not likely to be able to sink the enemy destroyers.

What was needed to improve the situation for destroyers operating in the Baltic? Development of:
- active and passive counter measures against the direction systems of the WAPA missiles, based on more knowledge about them;
- weapon systems to meet the missiles *en route* to the targets;
- a FPB with radar directed 76 mm gun to fight OSA FPBs. The FPB must be too small to create a target for the missile target seeker;
- a missile against OSAs, launched from helicopters;
- a larger warhead for the future standard missile against sea targets, capable of sinking a destroyer;
- a common German/Danish firing doctrine and training of destroyers and FPBs in night fighting.

The technological development in the Warsaw Pact had exceeded NATO by 1960. By the mid-1970s operations with destroyers in the Baltic would become suicidal if the technological standing of the German navy did not reach a higher level.

This was the view of a destroyer captain. The German navy's top took strategic stock in December 1971; the report was not encouraging.[4] While it was unlikely that the WAPA would engage in a worldwide conflict, the military-political pressure on the Baltic Approaches was increasing. An attack was more likely if the present military balance in the Baltic worsened and the NATO deterrence lost credibility.
- The threat from aircraft and missiles was particularly great in the Baltic. The enemy had about 340 launchers for missiles on ships and along the coast. The Soviet Naval Air Arm had about 160 conventional bombers and at least 36 fighter-bombers. Other attack aircraft might come from other sources. Attacks were bolstered by in-time recce, short distances and lack of NATO-fighters. The German navy only had light guns for defence and lacked in radar capability, especially against low-flying missiles and aircraft.
- The enemy would be able to land forces in several areas in the Baltic Approaches. The German navy had 45 F 104 G fighter-bombers (ready for action), 40 FPBs, about 400 mines and six submarines (for attacking supply

---

[4] Fü M III 4: Beitrag zur militärstrategischen Beurteilung der Lage. Stand 31-12-71. Az 31-02-03 TgbNr 1653/71 24-11-71. Geheim. BM 1/2850b.

ships). The F-104s were the most efficient units; 30 of the 40 FPBs were outdated. Therefore, the landing of forces would be difficult to prevent, particularly if the enemy could dominate in the air. Nonetheless, partial success might be obtained that would threaten the whole landing operation.
- In the Danish straits and in Kattegat one's own naval forces were helped by the geographical circumstances, and the air threat reduced because of the distances and own air force. Missiles were only of limited use.
- Electronic warfare was favouring the enemy who could disturb all frequencies and paralyse NATO operation direction as well as the use of weapons. Germany did not have comparable jamming systems.

The conclusion was rather obvious; we have seen it in various versions in previous chapters, and in 1973 the minister was told so.[5] The naval concept was this: destroyers and frigates could operate in the Baltic in peace time. They were all-weather men-of-war perfect to show the flag and do recce, protect civilian ships and solve minor skirmishes. In times of tension they could contribute to crisis management. But in wartime the threat from missiles in the Baltic would indicate to keep them away. So in war frigates were to operate in the North Sea, the destroyers in Kattegat and the North Sea.

Hence, seen from the east, the following system of deterrence was set up against WAPA forces: in the Eastern Baltic they would be met by submarines, in the Middle Baltic by Fighter-Bombers and FPBs (by night), in the Western Baltic by FPBs, in the Danish waters by comprehensive minefields and the Danish navy, and in Kattegat and the North Sea destroyers.

This formulation was new: it extended the defence of the Baltic Approaches from primarily East- and Mid-Baltic plus minefields in the Danish Straits to having destroyers ready in Kattegat. Previously their tasks had been formulated for the North Sea. As we shall see in the next chapter, the Germans widened the concept further a few years later.

We shall in this chapter see how the two navies fulfilled this vision and what they wanted to do in the 1970s to get more even with the navies of the Warsaw Pact.

---

5 Fü M VI 1: Betr. Bw-Struktur, hier: Fragen des Ministers. Vertraulich. 16-7-73. App 4729. BM 1/3936.

SACEUR's assessment in 1973

The most recent declassified and hence accessible Combat Effectiveness Report by SACEUR is from 1973. We only include the descriptions of the Northern Region, which goes beyond the Baltic Approaches northwards.[6]

In general, there was a lack of nuclear capability in the region – this, of course, was nothing new and due to the political systems of Denmark and Norway.

Land forces were considerably below the established ACE standards, there was a shortage of officers and NCOs, and one country had reduced conscription time to nine months. The defence of the area was heavily dependent on mobilisation and external reinforcements, and a lack of reserves to back up the standing forces – and those lacked in mobility, firepower, modern communication and logistical support; equipment in stocks was obsolete and deficient. Additional new equipment was on order, but the overall assessment was that the forces were vulnerable when compared with the threat.

Naval forces were improving because of new surface-to-surface missiles being implemented on FPBs which also got wired torpedoes and new fire control systems, and new coastal submarines were being introduced. SAM missiles were being implemented. Furthermore, ten new mine sweepers were being included. But there were not enough large units, there was a shortage of officers and NCOs, quite a few ships were obsolete, and communication systems were out of date. Given the large naval capacity of the WAPA, CINCNORTH's capability to accomplish wartime missions were severely limited.

The existing air forces were efficient as such (well trained etc.), but basically suffering limits pointed to previously (1972: limited number of aircraft, few technicians, lack of modern weapons, lack of ECM capability, lack of night and all-weather capability, and vulnerability of aircraft on the ground), but some flexibility had been added by giving three squadrons a secondary role as interceptors, and recce capabilities had been improved – but still were insufficient. The air defence forces had had no significant changes from 1972 – not enough missiles and aircraft, lack of personnel, lack of electronic equipment and high vulnerability to conventional attacks.

All in all, the supreme commander had strong criticisms of the defence status of the Northern Region and hence the Baltic Approaches.

The tactical operations of an amphibious WAPA assault

What were NATO up against if the WAPA attacked with amphibious vessels? This, of course, was analysed time and again by the two navies. Below we draw upon two German analyses.

---

[6] 1973 Annual Supplement to SACEUR's 1972 Combat Effectiveness Report, 6-7-74, Annex A, Appendix 1, 1101/14-4-4/550/74.

Closing in on the landing areas

In 1968 the German navy initiated an operational research study of the optimal combination of German sea and naval air forces under a supposed major attack in the Baltic from the WAPA under a "new moon period in September,"[7] as part of a general WAPA attack in Central Europe. We do not have the answers available, but the parameters of the study were defined by the navy and they give us an overview of what the leadership of the navy thought about the capacities of the enemy.

It was supposed that most of the Soviet missile cruisers/destroyers and most submarines had left the Baltic before outbreak of war; their roles were to operate in the Atlantic and the North Sea. Some missile destroyers would remain to operate with the other ships of the navy, particularly missile FPBs, ASW ships and amphibious craft. These remaining forces would initiate a comprehensive amphibious attack on the Danish islands and Fehmarn. The two following maps indicate the positions of the forces X-12, 12 hours before general attack in Central Europe.

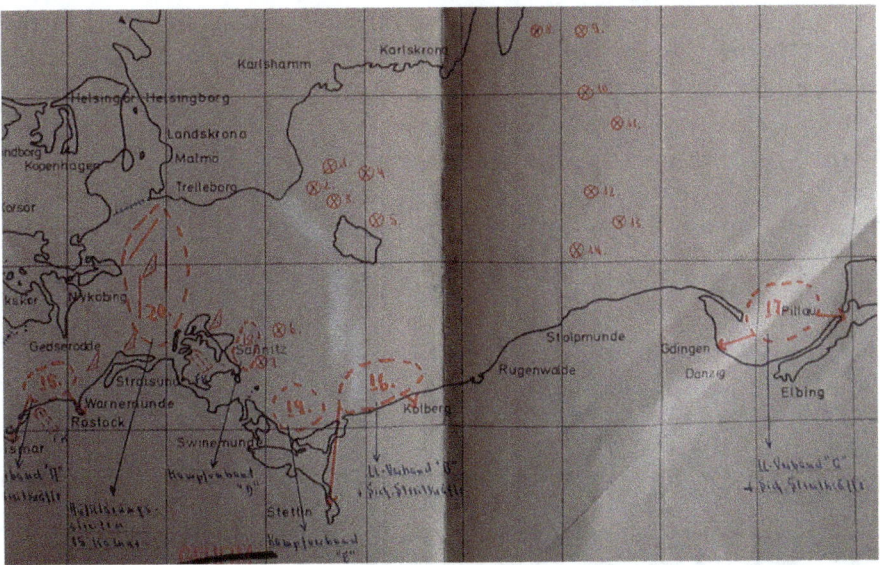

Figure 17.1: Positions of WAPA forces X-12 hours. Source: Bundeswehr Archiv Freiburg.

---

7 Fü M II 13: Annahmekonzept für die Studie "Optimale Zusammensetzung der See und Seeluftstreitkräfte." Geheim. Az 71-04-01-12. TgbNr. 12235/68. 14-11-68. BM 1/1022a.

The X-12 situation had, starting in the southern part, four amphibious forces (15, 16, 17 and 19) in sheltered waters in various inlets along the Baltic coast. North of Bornholm there were five groups of destroyers/frigates each with a fast ASW boat, and at Rügen two groups with Patrol Boats. They kept the NATO submarines away. Between Swedish Øland and the Baltic coast were seven fighting groups: four destroyers and three frigates each with one or two ASW patrol boats to attack NATO submarines that might have come through the blockade to the west. Groups 18 and 19 were fighting groups with up to 33 units – destroyers, frigates and FPBs. Group 20 along the Danish islands had 15 KOMAR class missile FPBs for surveillance and detection. They were to attack NATO mine layers and other ships. Finally, there were two missile coastal batteries, on Rügen and at Rostock, respectively, ranging up to 40 miles (20 for small targets).

Before time X most ships of the German navy had left their home bases and deployed to Kattegat, Skagerrak and various waiting positions in Danish waters. Mine laying in one's own waters had started and increased by time X (2,000 mines).

The Soviet navy had about 60 bombers and a similar number of recce aircraft. At time X WAPA aircraft would attack NATO airfields in Jagel, Eggebek, Leck, Værløse, Tystrup and Karup together with various radar and listening posts, in addition to attacks on ships at sea and stores in harbours.

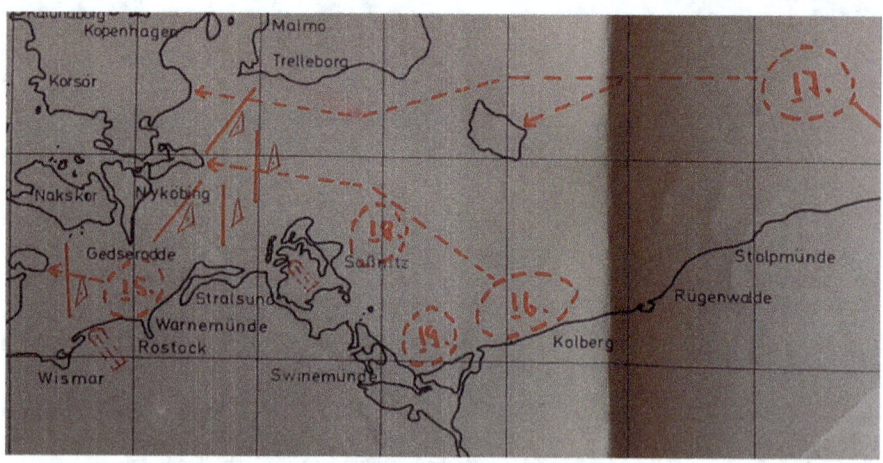

Figure 17.2: Formation of attacking amphibious WAPA forces X hour. Source: Bundeswehr Archiv Freiburg.

The amphibious landings would take place at Bornholm, Stevns, Møn and Fehmarn at time X + 18. Sixty-six amphibious craft would be distributed among the three groups (15, 16 and 17): the largest group to the Stevns landing beach, protected by a large number of destroyers, frigates, patrol boats, mine sweepers and FPBs with and without missiles. For instance for the Stevns group with 47 amphibious craft: Destroyers: three SKORY, Frigates: two PETTA, four RIGA, Patrol craft: nine POTI, 20 KRONSTADT, Mine sweepers: 15 SO-1, 20 T-43 and FPBs: 10 OSA.

The landing process

Four years later the German navy did an analysis of the tactical operations of an amphibious WAPA attack, based on observations of seven previous exercises.[8]

The embarkation of troops could take place in harbours, but for amphibious craft, the Soviets preferred embarkation at beaches, spread widely to ensure concealment of the planned operation and to avoid mass, reducing the threat of NATO nuclear weapons. If the operation was planned as attacks on several beaches, task groups of a battalion size would proceed towards NATO territory. If a large-scale operation was planned, the various groups would proceed from the Baltic coast to a designated rendezvous position, selected so that the final deployment to the landing area could take place in one night. When the formation for the sea lift was organised it would be identical to the final assault formation; if several nations were involved, each nation would have its own group, and they would land at disparate beaches.

Two basic multi-national formations had been seen in these exercises over time: a column formation with each nation in one column, spreading in the last phase to each of their destination beaches; and a line-abreast formation with each nation forming up to three rows after one another. The former was preferred at narrow beaches, the latter for broader landing areas, but it was more complicated to carry out.

Soviet doctrine, however, specified that each task group would not exceed brigade size, and the interval between two groups landing was to be wide enough to avoid both being knocked out by one nuclear strike but still close enough to maintain communication and cooperation. Thus the landing of a whole division would require an area 15–20 kilometres wide with the participating battalions having each a "box" up to six kilometres wide.

The Germans presumed that a large-scale amphibious attack would only take place if the NATO forces had been severely reduced by a surprise attack, hence

---

[8] Amphibious Tactics by Warsaw Pact Navies in the Baltic. Geheim. Fü M VI. TgbNr. 968/72. 6-9-72. BM 1/3936.

no large screening force would be necessary. Anyway, the amphibious force would for as long a time as possible proceed in inshore waters, avoiding NATO submarines, having air cover from land-based fighters and sea cover from land-based missile batteries, and only having to care about light surface forces which could be screened in seaward direction.

Far ahead, larger surface units and groups of FPBs would operate to scare off NATO missile units. One would expect to see screening forces – ASW, hit-and-run FPB groups and mine sweeping groups – off the coast and ahead of the main force. In the last phase *en route* towards the NATO area, the hit-and-run FPBs would protect against NATO surface units, and a forward screening ASW force might be used, operating three miles ahead in a semicircle, possibly also with helicopters. The helicopters might even operate three miles further ahead of the main screen and in addition an ASW aircraft could circle about five miles ahead of the main screen at an altitude of 300 meters.

Mine sweepers would be part of the whole force. When entering an expected mine field area, the mine sweepers would proceed three to four miles ahead of the force in one or more lines abreast and initiate the sweeping procedure to create a channel for passage. The main force would adapt its formation to the passage.

Until 1968, nuclear weapons had been used against the defence forces at the landing area, but no longer (1972) so. The amphibious assault would be preceded by bombing by light bombers and fighter-bombers, and paratroopers and/or forces brought in by helicopters should have landed to neutralise NATO land forces by the beach area(s) and possibly the rear area. Furthermore, mine sweepers would execute search-sweep operations to sweep channels at the landing points. Frogmen landed by helicopters or FPBs would breach barriers and other underwater obstacles.

The landing process itself would be supported by naval gunfire from larger units stationed five miles from the coast, and from the amphibious units with such guns. The sequence would be something like:
- disembarkation of the beach master, assault troops and demolition teams from large ships to amphibious craft;
- massive shore bombardment from escorts;
- after passage of amphibious task forces across a "tactical line" approximately 12 miles at sea the attack had reached the point of no return;
- mine sweepers sweep the appropriate channels while the amphibious craft close in at low speed and those equipped to do so fire their guns and missiles;
- amphibious tanks and floatable mechanised infantry combat vehicles leave the landing craft as the first wave (approximately one mile off shore) and approach the coast, opening fire as they come closer;

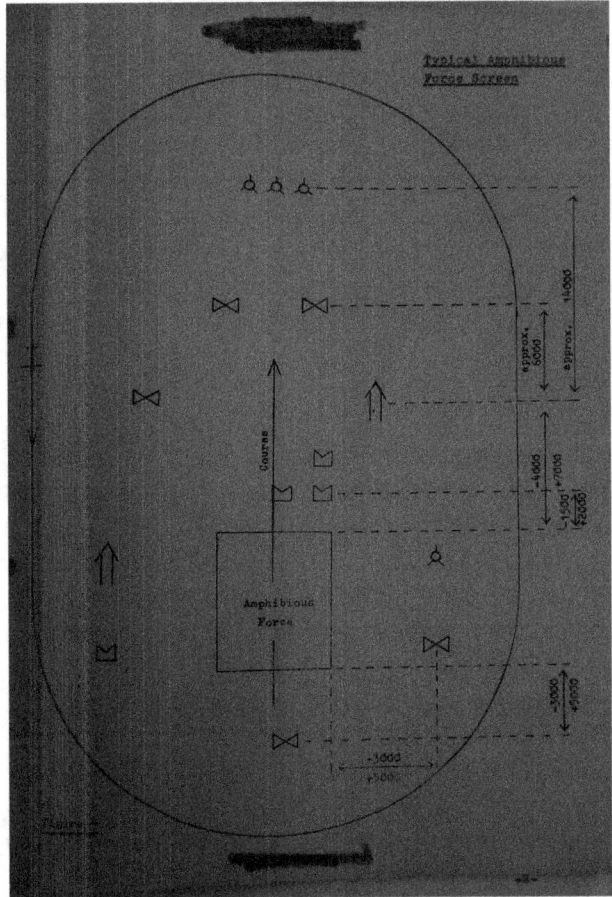

Figure 17.3: Example of an amphibious force and its screen. Source: Bundeswehr Archiv Freiburg.

- they do so following a coordinated sequence to land the beach master and his support, then tanks etc.;
- the subsequent waves of landing craft carrying the first echelon of combat troops follow the amphibious tanks and land their troops which then organise for combat and push in depth to stabilise the beachhead;
- the landing craft withdraws to stand by for other tasks.

So after debarkation, the landing ships would remain in the area to be used for medical evacuation and for landing a second echelon which had been sea-lifted by transporters. This would happen approximately four hours after the first landing team.

The missile threat in the Baltic and NATO's response

As documented above, NATO had one serious deficiency in the Baltic Approaches (but also in general): the lack of ship-based missiles against ships and against airplanes. The Soviet Union had missiles against ships from about 1958, and this – together with a fear of losing air supremacy – led the German naval chiefs to keep their destroyers out of the Baltic. The Danes did not share this fear, or maybe they rather could not afford to because their tactics needed destroyer-size ships to protect their mine layers.

WAPA missiles

There were several types of Soviet anti-ship missiles.[9] The first, the SS-N-1 SCRUBBER, had a range of 42 miles, it was installed on the KILDIN and KANIN class destroyers and was retired in 1977. It was soon followed by the SS-N-2 STYX missile with an original range of 25 and later 50 miles, mounted on destroyers and FPBs from around 1960. It featured a cylindrical body, a rounded nose, two delta wings in the centre and three controls in the tail. It was cheap, but at the same time capable of giving an ordinary FPB the equivalent of a battleship salvo. The built-in control system was based on a simple analog design, with a homing radar sensor.

The STYX missile was the main threat for NATO's ships in the Baltic in the 1960s and most of the 1970s, but the powers of the missile were probaby overestimated by NATO's intelligence officers in the first years. Still, it took many years before NATO weapon developers were able to match this missile.

The German Internet-debate forum *Forum-marinearchiv* has discussions from former WAPA as well as NATO crews. The pseudonym *Der Erste* had this story in 2013:[10]

> The first time I took part in launching a STYX missile – in 1979 – was from an OSA FPB. Just when the commander pressed the firing button, a circuit fuse on the bridge burned over, so nothing happened. That connection was the last thing to secure before being ready for action, so the fuse box was easy to get to. The missile officer of the flotilla was present, and he jumped to the fuse box, opened it and connected the two circuits with two fingers. The missile went off. I did not believe my own eyes . . .

---

9 Most of he data below on missiles are drawn from Wikipedia. They are only intended to give a rough picture.
10 Der Erste. *Wie war die Situation Warschauer Pakt-Nato im Hinblick auf die Ostseeausgänge?* http://www.forum-marinearchiv.de/smf/index.php/topic,19302, 2013a.

Figure 17.4: East German OSA FPB launching a STYX missile. Source: Forsvarsgalleriet.

In 1973 the Israelis proved that their GABRIEL-missile-armed FPBs could outsmart the Syrian STYX-armed FPBs, at least if the right tactics were applied. STYX had the double range of GABRIEL, but in a nightly battle at Latakia in Syria the Israelis succeeded in diverting the STYX of the Syrians with ECM and chaff which misguided the homing radar of the missiles. No missile hit the Israelis who on the other hand were very successful with their missiles when they came within launching range. During an operation against Egyptian OSA-FPBs shortly after the pattern was the same: STYX could be misled by chaff.[11]

The S-2 SOPKA coastal defence system with the NATO nickname SAMLET was a variant of the air-to-surface KSS-1 KOMET short range missile developed to be used against ships from aircraft. In the ground version, the missile would be attached to a rocket to be kicked off from fixed launchers. The rocket would be fired and discharged when a certain speed had been reached, and the SAMLET missile could proceed on its own, using its search radar. The SAMLET systems were found along the coast of the Baltic Sea.

---

[11] Hornhaver, H. "Yom Kippur krigen." *Tidsskrift for Søvæsen* 145 (1974): 82–87.

The Soviet air missiles were a little slower in development. The M-1 VOLNA (SA-N-1) was developed from 1956, and first installed on a rebuilt KOTLIN class destroyer BRAVYI and tested in 1962. The basic missile had a range from two to eight miles, altitude: from 0.1 to 10 km. Fire control and guidance could only engage one target at a time. VOLNA could also be used against naval targets, due to a short response time. Its launcher had a magazine for 16 missiles, and by 1963 improved to a two-missile launcher with 32 missiles.

The OSA-M was a naval Soviet SAM system, operational from 1972. It was developed to act as defence against aircraft and inbound anti-ship missiles. Over time it was upgraded to have more effectiveness against low flying targets. When the system was not in use the launcher was retracted below deck and covered by a large round door. Targets were identified by the ship's main air surveillance radar. The guidance section consisted of a tracking radar and a fire control radar. One single target was engaged at a time. The launcher had two missiles ready to launch. Forty additional missiles were in a magazine below deck. The maximum range was about five miles and targets might be engaged to altitudes of over 3.5 km. The minimum size of ships for this missile was 500 tons.

NATO's expectations to the improvement of Soviet missiles in the 1970s were that the missiles and their warheads would get smaller and thus increase the number carried by each ship.[12] The tactics of firing many missiles to saturate the opponent's electronic systems would continue. The Soviets would probably develop sea-skimming capabilities but also develop a steeper attack angle in the final phase (most radar systems had problems in fetching targets above the ship). They would improve the control- and jamming systems of the missiles and make zig-zagging possible to disturb the radar systems of the targeted ship. The capabilities in foul weather would be improved, and the search heads would get more than one system.

Developing NATO missiles

Several NATO countries were developing missiles in the 1960s: the USA, Norway and France. Sweden also developed its own system. As can be seen from the pictures below, several of the first generation missiles had the same features as the STYX: a set of small wings on the body and steering fins at the aft end. They also had about the same range – 25–35 – miles but were solid fuel driven. But NATO

---

12 Wahrscheinlige Entwicklung der FK-Bedrohung in den späten 70er Jahren. Geheim. 5. Anl. zu InMFü B Nr. 4-1401/71. BM 1-1841a.

countries also developed missiles against sea targets, to be fired by airplanes, e.g. in the German Air Arm. We will explore them in chronological order.

The American TARTAR surface-to-air missile, ready for use in 1962, was supposed to fill the need for a lightweight system for smaller ships, to engage targets at close range. The range was only 10 miles, later 18 miles. The TARTAR was used on ships of a variety of sizes. Early versions proved to be unreliable; its homing radar got disturbed when facing waves of a certain size. As to fighting control systems, that of a destroyer could only link to two incoming sea missiles, so a larger salvo could be catastrophic if fired at close distance. An improved TARTAR upgraded the missile. Further development was cancelled, but many ships still used the TARTAR fire control system. The Americans tried to develop the TARTAR into a sea target version, but it never became operational.

The American MAULER system was developed for the army to combat low-flying high-performance tactical fighters and short-range ballistic missiles. For the navy, a SEA MAULER was put on the drawing board. But in 1965 it became clear that the missile would not become operational, and it was scrapped.

The American SEA SPARROW sea-to-air missile was developed in the early 1960s as a lightweight weapon that could be fitted on existing ships, replacing existing gun-based anti-aircraft weapons. It was initially a very simple system guided by a manually aimed radar illuminator. It soon went through significant developments into an automated system, ready in the mid-1970s, but it still needed electronic contact with the launching ship. Its range was about 15 miles.

The Norwegian PENGUIN sea target missile, fire-and-forget, was developed from the early 1960s with an infrared seeker instead of the commonly used active radar seeker. It was fully developed by 1972, with a range of 18 miles. Initial installation was in 500 kg deck-mounted box launchers allowing them to be fitted on existing small ships like FPBs in the Norwegian Navy. The first airborne installations were on F-104Gs of the Norwegian Air Force, the missiles being fitted to standard Bullpup rails on the two underwing hardpoints. The Penguin could be fired singly or in coordinated-arrival salvos.

TERNE was a Norwegian anti-submarine weapon system using missile-carried depth charges. It was ready for service in 1962. A TERNE weapon system consisted of a search and track sonar, a fire-control system and the rocket launchers, which could store six salvos of six rockets each. The depth charge had multiple fusing modes (preset time after water entry, proximity, or contact); it was propelled through the air by a solid-fuel rocket motor. The fire-control system could fire a rocket salvo to place a string of depth charges 18 meters apart, perpendicular to the target's course.

The KORMORAN air-to-sea missile was developed by the Germans for its fighter-bombers to take over from an earlier AS 30 missile. The KORMORAN missile

Figure 17.5: SEA SPARROW launched from Danish corvette OLFERT FISCHER.
Source: Forsvarsgalleriet.

had a search head which took over the control in the terminal phase. It was in 1973 operational for the F-104 G fighter-bomber and later the TORNADO aircraft.

The EXOCET MM38 was an anti-ship missile which originally was based on a cooperation between Germany and France; Germany supplied the French with details from their development of the KORMORAN air-to-sea missile. Britain joined the cooperation in order to develop a submarine version, but stopped the project in 1970.[13] The sea-launched version was finalised by the French, and MM38 entered service in 1975. The missile was designed for attacking warships like frigates, corvettes and destroyers. It turned on active radar homing late in its flight to find and hit its target. It maintained a very low altitude while inbound, staying just one to two meters above the sea surface. This meant that the target might not detect an incoming attack until the missile was only 6,000 m from impact, leaving little time for counter measures. The EXOCET had a maximum range of 25 miles. It saw its first wartime launch during the Falklands War.

The HARPOON was an American all-weather, over-the-horizon, anti-ship, sea-skimming, fire-and-forget missile. In 1965 the United States Navy began studies

---

[13] Fü M I 15: Notiz über Flugkörper entwicklung SM 38. VS. Az 95-07-72-08. App 5948. 25-11-70. BM 1/25109.

Figure 17.6: EXOCET MM-38 launched from a German ALBATROSS-class FPB.
Source: Forsvarsgalleriet.

for the use of the missile against surfaced submarines. After the Egyptian sinking of the Israeli EILAT with STYX-missiles in 1967, the development of HARPOON was accelerated. The first HARPOON was delivered in 1977. The HARPOON has also been adapted for carriage on several aircraft. Its original range was 60 miles. At a pre-determined distance from the target the radar of the missile was turned on, and it would search for the target whose position had been programmed before launch. Since the target probably had moved since launch, and since the precision of a naval radar decreased with distance, it was clear that the precision of the missile also decreased with distance.

Missiles in the Danish navy

By 1968, the Danish navy took part in developing the SEA SPARROW for anti-aircraft purposes. But the leadership still was undecided regarding anti-ship missiles for its frigates and upcoming FPBs. Obviously, such were there imperative after the EILAT was sunk by STYX missiles in 1967.

Figure 17.7: HARPOON missile launched from Danish FPB WILLEMOES. Source: Forsvarsgalleriet.

The navy ordered an operational analysis of the issue.[14] A war in the Baltic was supposedly dominated by small groups of Soviet missile-armed FPBs operating together with torpedo-armed FPBs, all functioning with electronic data from other sources – larger units, land stations or aircraft. The options for a frigate of the PEDER SKRAM type operating as cover for mine layers in the southern Øresund was analysed. The main issue was that Soviet FPBs of the OSA and KOMAR classes could fire their missiles at a distance beyond the range (for catching FPB-size targets) of the target's radar system, about 15 miles. At that distance, the FPBs could fire the missile in "dumb" mode. The STYX would have a speed of mach. 0.9, flying in an altitude of 100–300 meters. Its homing radar would be started when about halfway to the target, becoming efficient at a distance of about six miles. At a distance of 12 miles, the FPB could catch the target on radar and program the missile before firing it and turning round. In both cases the radar of the frigate could detect the FPB and the missiles *en route* and prepare chaff. At a distance of eight miles the frigate could launch SEA SPARROW missiles against the flying STYX; at five miles its 127 mm guns could be brought to bear.

---

14 Marinestaben: KC. Hemmelig kopibog (afklassificeret) (1946–1975). Tillæg til skrivelse 29-5-69 til NATO om "interception tables".

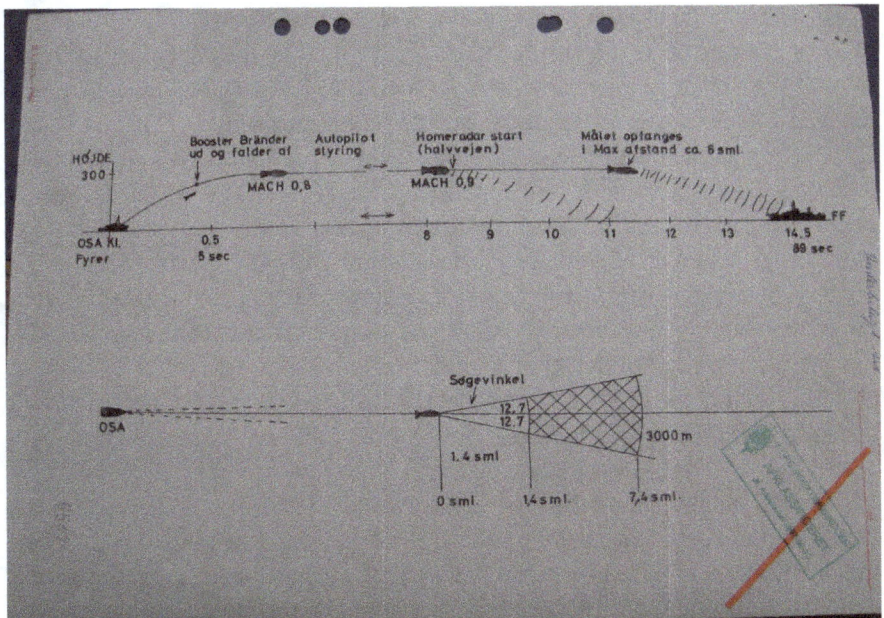

Figure 17.8: Modelling the naval defence: STYX missiles trajectory with activation of homing radar. Source: Rigsarkivet.

In order to protect the mine layers, the frigate would have to engage the attacking FPBs immediately upon detection. It would have to attack at full speed, zig-zagging (to distress the enemy's radar control systems) and engaging the FPBs to prevent or make difficult the processes of target determination and missile launching. The frigate would use decoys, chaff and flares to mislead the incoming missiles. The mine layers could use balloons with radar reflectors and radiant heat to cheat the homing radars of the STYX, and the missile would pass over the ship. Small patrol craft could be used for more balloons, and old merchant ships could be towed to create even more radar echoes. All in all, the enemy's radar scoop of the activities at the minefield would be saturated.

Unfortunately, the WAPA appeared to use a saturation attack tactic with a large number of missiles being fired simultaneously to saturate the radar of the NATO ships. This might be countered by jamming, chaff or decoy tactics.

The Danish navy demanded that its new sea target missile had the same range as the STYX. The navy had considered TARTAR, PENGUIN and the israeli GABRIEL. All had too short a range. EXOCET would be worth considering since the German navy was planning to use it on their new FPBs and frigates and invited the Danes to do the same.

In 1969, the Danish navy postponed a decision but was in favour of PENGUIN or EXOCET, but not as the only weapon. Guns would be necessary e.g. for firing shots of warning in a period of tension. The new OTO MELARA 76 mm was a probable candidate for the new FPBs and it would be efficient against sea missiles.

Four years later a decision had to be taken for the planned new FPBs. The following issues were analysed for PENGUIN, OTOMAT, SEA KILLER MK III, ROBOT 11, EXOCET and HARPOON:[15] distance flown when motor stopped; maximum range; number of missiles on board; time passing between launches in salvo; the possibilities for the enemy to detect the missile; reaction time for guiding system; ballistic dispersal of missiles; the geometric form of the search field of the missile; and effect of the missile on various types of targets.

The result of the evaluation was that the HARPOON was a distinct leader, followed by ROBOT 11 and OTOMAT, then EXOCET and SEA KILLER III, and lastly PENGUIN.

Several models simulating use in the Baltic were analysed. There were two main types of dangerous enemies: destroyers and FPBs. The starting points were that a Soviet 130 mm destroyer gun had a range of 21,000 meters, but it probably would not open fire until 16,000 meters to get a more than two per cent probability of hitting. Therefore, the NATO missile had to have a range of more than 16,000 meters, low probability of being hit by the enemy during the attack and high probability of hitting the target and a strong explosive impact.

The OSA FPBs with missiles were another matter. A NATO attack had to either be at a larger distance than the range of their missiles, or one had be able to jam their radar control systems. Danish FPB radars could detect OSAs at a distance of 25,200 metres. The OSA radars would detect Danish FPBs at 21,500 metres. Therefore, Danish FPBs had to try to engage OSAs within their radar lead.

The planners modelled a case with a Danish PEDER SKRAM-class frigate, four missile FPBs and four to six other torpedo boats attacking an invasion fleet which was escorted by destroyers, frigates, corvettes and missile FPBs. The Danish FPB missiles were planned for use against the escorts which were attacked first, then other weapons were used against the amphibious vessels. There were two alternatives for attacking. The first one made the FPBs attack with missiles to fight the escorts. The second one made the FPBs launch missiles to pass over the escorts to attack the amphibious vessels directly. This required a missile range of 36–40,000 meters, but the main problem would be a lack of radar coverage and therefore

---

15 Søværnets Materielkommando: KC. Hemmelig kopibog (afklassificeret) (1968–1985). Brev 644/3851 10-12-73.

data from other sources were required. Helicopters would be one option in that respect.

The final decision was to use the HARPOON surface missile and the SEA SPARROW air missile. The HARPOON was to be fitted on the two frigates, three new corvettes and ten FPBs. SEA SPARROW was to be mounted on the frigates and the corvettes.

Missiles in the German navy

The leadership of the navy initially wanted to develop a German missile destroyer, built on German shipyards, but soon realised that the relatively easy task was to plan a new ship, but quite another thing was the integration of a missile system with the command and direction system – there was no knowledge of those factors within the navy.[16] Therefore, the American offer of building an improved version of the CHARLES F. ADAMS class destroyer with TARTAR missiles was accepted. The German navy started a group of officers to develop knowledge about systems of control.[17]

The Germans had prepared themselves for a TARTAR sea target missile in various working groups analysing the pros and cons. A discussion on such a version took place in 1964 based on a working paper.[18] By semi-active steering, the limit for firing would be the radar horizon of the ship: for destroyers about 15 miles, for FPBs 10 miles against sea targets. The range of a Soviet 130 mm gun was about 12 miles. The TARTAR missile would need a larger warhead (like the Bullpup warhead) against sea targets, but then the missile would not fit in the present launcher system. The Americans were testing the missile against a large ship and FPBs. Thus the TARTAR anti-aircraft missile was introduced in the German navy, but a sea target version never became operational.

An analysis of the sea target missiles fired by destroyers and FPBs[19] discussed the possibilities of defence against them, supposing that they might be fired far away, directed by airplanes or other radars on land or at sea. First, the electronic systems of the defender had to be active, and its guns had to be radar directed. Second, between 50 and 120 seconds were necessary for the defender to illumi-

---

16 Jeschonnek, Gert. *Bundesmarine 1955 bis heute*, 79–84. Koblenz/Bonn: Wehr und Wissen, 1975.
17 Hess, Sigurd. "Als die Computer lernten zur See zu fahren – die Entwicklung von Führungs- und Waffeneinsatzsystemen in der deutschen Marine 1963 bis 1969." In *Die Bundesmarine 1950 bis 1972*, Johannes Berthold Sander-Nagashima, 433–45. München: Oldenbourg, 2006.
18 Anlage 4 zu FüAkBw – Abt M – StdGrp Az 31-05-14 TgbNr 222/64 Geheim 2-9-64. BM 11/82b.
19 Anlage 3 zu FüAkBw – Abt M – StdGrp Az 31-05-14 TgbNr 222/64 Geheim 2-9-64. BM 11/82b.

nate the incoming missile and its firing direction system. Third, depending on the search system of the missile, decoys, jamming and other means had to be ready for action. Finally, at an earlier phase and if the missiles were not fired at their maximum range but closer, e.g. by a group of FPBs led by a destroyer, the ship directing the missiles would be jammed and attacked e.g. by NATO FPBs.

These findings were probably not very helpful, and the group was asked to analyse more situations. The commander of the Naval Air Arm – clearly perceiving a special advantage for his aircraft – therefore recommended[20] that until further notice only submarines and F-104 airplanes should operate against missile-carrying destroyers, airfields and radar installations. One's own destroyers were not to be used unless one could be sure that no ships carrying missiles would operate in the area.

Realising that after the EILAT affair in 1967 it would take time to get such NATO missiles, the Germans now developed a set of tactical recommendations for the navy to counter missile attacks from enemy ships (as well as aircraft attacks).[21] They concerned the organisation of various groups on board (electronic systems, weapon systems, communication etc.) and the use of the various electronic systems, particularly jamming combined with chaff systems. The Danish test with a frigate above had many similar configurations; for a German case, see the box.

Destroyer tactics for dodging a STYX missile

The Germans analysed various ways of defending the ships against the Soviet sea missiles. In 1968, the commander of the second destroyer flotilla discussed various ways that a destroyer might evade a STYX missile from an OSA FPB.[22]

From the British navy the doctrine for self-defence was as follows:
- as long as no danger had been observed: sail zig-zag
- when danger was imminent: sail short leg zig-zag (change course every two minutes because it would take the enemy's operator three minutes to prepare and launch missile)
- direct your jamming system towards the enemy
- fire your chaff and try to get close to the enemy (minimum firing distance for STYX was four and a half miles).
- If a STYX had been fired (in praxis when it was detected on the radar):
- immediately stop jamming (or the missile might seek the jamming antenna)
- fire chaff continuously

---

20 Kommando der Marineflieger: Beitrag zur Studie . . . Geheim. Az 31-05014 Tgb.Nr. 255/65. 29-3-65. BM 11/82b.
21 Taktische Richtlinien für FK– und Flugzeugsabwehr. Geheim. 1. anlage zu InMFü B Nr. 4-1401/71. BM 1/1841a.
22 Note OSA – KOMAR Bekämpfung. Geheim 21-3-68 to Flottenkommando. 2. Zerstörergeschwader. BM 1/1600. Also in BM 1/943a.

- manoeuvre so that chaff remains in the bearing to the enemy and get ready to shoot with all guns/launchers
- when possible, open fire with all guns/launchers

The German commander found some dangers in this doctrine:
- a jammer would only work within two to four degrees in the bearing; so it might jam one boat, but since Soviet FPBs always worked in groups, another FPB might relay the necessary data to the jammed boat. Furthermore, since the jammer would work at distances of 20 miles or more while the radar of the FPBs hardly had a range of more than 15 miles, the jamming signals would unveil the presence of the destroyer.
- closing in on the enemy looked like suicide when several FPBs were present and one's own ship did not have surplus speed
- success from chaff and firing guns was dubious; success would rather depend on increasing the distance to the enemy and thus reducing the size of one's radar echo in his system. So – "show stern" with the highest speed and fire the chaff and aft guns as appropriate. One might develop a decoy for this purpose, e.g. a balloon fastened to some floating device.

The commander recommended the navy to develop tactics with helicopters against Soviet missile FPBs.

There were, however, other systems under development. The Royal Navy was testing various ways for defence against Soviet FPBs with helicopters; one helicopter would do radar recce and point out targets, and in order not to lose the tactical overview, other helicopter(s) would get the role of hitting the target. Radar systems for helicopters were improving, from an altitude of 50 meters new radars could detect a FPB at 20 miles' distance in fair weather – while the radars of FPBs only detected the helicopter at two to three miles distance, if at all. The 37 mm guns of the Soviet FPBs could hit a target at two miles distance, a helicopter at 3.75 miles with wire-guided AS-12 missiles.[23]

However, a helicopter needed guidance from stronger radar systems to find their targets; it was desirable to get radar signals from Danish territory, preferably by setting up German systems, but that seemed problematic; instead one would have to use Danish information sent e.g. from Møn.[24] The German navy had monitored the British tests and found them satisfactory, noting that the AS-12 missile needed eyeballing sight, so during night action the target had to be illuminated. The American original version of the SEA KING did not have sufficiently sophisticated radar equipment to fulfil such a role, but the British were working on a modified version that appeared to be promising and make the helicopter

---

23 Note OSA – KOMAR Bekämpfung. Geheim 21-3-68 to Flottenkommando. 2. Zerstörergeschwader. BM 1/1600. Also in BM 1/943a.
24 Fü M II 1: Betr. Einsatz von Hubschraubern gegen OSA/KOMAR-Schnellboote. AZ 31-05-24 Geheim 8-5-67 App 4477. BM 1/1600.

less dependent on radar from other platforms. However, it would not be ready for actual use until 1972.

The German navy wrote a paper on the possibilities of using SEA KING helicopters as a flexible instrument in the middle Baltic against missile FPBs, destroyers, frigates and amphibious forces with and without escorts.[25] This preliminary study pointed to the possibilities of setting up groups of four helicopters with missiles (possibly KORMORAN), supported on land by a series of trucks for the commander, radio and radar systems, petrol, repairs and transport of diverse weaponry and materials. They would be flexible by not being tied to an airfield and they could be moved by amphibious craft, even to Danish territory.

The navy did order the SEA KING, but they were planned to be used for SAR and transport purposes. The attack helicopter in the above sense therefore never materialised. The navy got the SEA LYNX later, but for ASW purposes together with new frigates.

Like the Danish navy, the German navy analysed alternative sea target missiles: the PENGUIN, the EXOCET and the GABRIEL, and compared them with the STYX.[26] The PENGUIN was considered to have relatively poor search capabilities in foul weather; it was relatively slow and its range was only eight miles. But it had better promise if fired from a helicopter. The GABRIEL's seek radar could be jammed at an early phase, and the firing controller was bound to the missile during the whole operation. The EXOCET was autonomous as soon as it was fired; it could not be jammed and it had a sophisticated weapon control system with very short reaction time. It was expensive and the launcher required much space. It was still under development, but appeared to be promising.

As we shall see later in this chapter, the Germans in 1971 had to order 20 French produced missile FPBs because there were hardly any alternatives. They were armed with the EXOCET which therefore became the first missile solution for the German FPBs.

Danish defence policy under review

As we saw earlier, the Danish navy did not get the eight large vessels planned in 1960; two new frigates were ready in 1969, but the four corvettes which quite misleadingly had been categorised as "large" were from the mid-1950s and therefore

---

25 Fü M II 1: Studie über die zukünftige Verwendung von Hubschraubers . . . Az 31-04-01-04 App 4477. 29-8-69. BM 1/1600.
26 Zerstörereinsatz in Abhängigkeit von Kriegsbild und Einsatzraum.BM 1/25109.

approaching a condition to be decommissioned and scrapped. Furthermore, six MTBs from 1955 were outmoded together with three mine layers and a depot ship. In 1968, a change of government brought the Radical Party into a coalition cabinet, and, as a consequence, the defence was cut back.

The apparently somewhat bleak future was debated by several naval officers. First, one questioned the demand for a balanced navy which had been the hallmark of the chiefs.[27] One important change was the new German navy which could be seen as an offer for a division of labour:

- Danish mine sweepers were not necessarily used until the enemy actually had laid mines, and that probably would take some time. So that task might be taken care of by ships "from the outside".
- Submarines could be used for surveillance east of Bornholm before war broke out, but other units could do the same, and if an amphibious force had passed the line of submarines before war time they were not very useful any more.
- Mine layers could be replaced by other types of vessels, if mines at all could be seen as instruments preventing war. Larger and faster units could have capacity for mines and lay them as desired in any particular situation, and after that they could participate in defending areas threatened for invasion.
- FPBs were very dependent on the weather and they could not last long. The enemy could put together a force that had few units suited for being targets for torpedoes.
- Larger units were defined by the author as ships larger than FPBs with a speed between 30 and 40 knots and efficient weaponry against surface targets as well as aircraft. Some 1,000 tons would probably be about right – the new frigates were too large.
- Patrol craft also would be a necessity so that the larger units could be held free from patrol, SAR etc.
- Finally, larger units would be necessary for fishery inspection and other tasks up north in the Atlantic (outside the scope of this book).

All in all, and cutting to the bone because of the government's cut-backs and budgetary limits, there was only a need for smaller, well armed frigates and patrol craft plus special auxiliary vessels. The large ships would probably prevent war by their sheer number and strength, and they would be able to lay mines. At the same time, a comprehensive standardisation of weapon systems etc. was warranted.

---

27 Pranov, J. B. "Betragtninger vedrørende flådens sammensætning af egentlige krigsskibe under ændrede vilkår." *Tidsskrift for Søvæsen* 139 (1968): 313–23.

This scheme did not square well with one of the main ideas of littoral warfare because the small units were taken out, and doubt was cast on the use of mines to create choke points. Of course, more traditional views were voiced by other officers, each making points of the necessity of large mine layers, FPBs with missiles, smaller submarines etc. The officer who had started the debate changed his radical view three years later, stressing that his ideas were propelled by the political demands for cut-back (see below).[28] The non-controlled mine fields were part of the (now gone) massive retaliation and were best replaced by controlled minefields which would fit the concept of flexible response, particularly in a period of escalation. Submarines still were superfluous. The navy needed 12 corvettes (capable of mine laying) operating in groups of two at Bornholm, two in the Danish Narrows and two in Kattegat. Helicopters were to replace FPBs as fast weapon platforms and operate with the corvette groups. In addition there were four cable mine layers and 24 mine sweepers/hunters, also capable of operating as patrol craft. His critics maintained that the suggestions led to too weak a navy.

In April 1970 the Danish Social Democrats published a paper debating the future of Danish defence.[29] It may be read as an interpretation of NATOs *flexible response*, leading to a professionalised defence, and probably inspired by the changes in the Swedish defence.

- The army was to be reduced to an emergency professional force of 7,000 soldiers with two thirds stationed on Zealand, and local conscripted forces in groups of 500 men. Thus the forces for Schleswig-Holstein were scrapped.
- The navy would have to scrap the frigates and corvettes and possibly the submarines. The main force would be missile armed FPBs and less vulnerable systems for mine laying. The coastal fixed forts were to be replaced by mobile missile batteries.
- The air force was to have its fighters and bomber-fighters reduced by 50 percent, maintaining its reconnaissance aircraft. Multi-purpose aircraft (Swedish DRAKEN) were to make up for the reduction of each type. There were to be no conscripts in the future, as well as reduction of air bases and more use of small reserve stations.

The pamphlet was based on the preconceptions that, first, a surprise attack was unlikely and, if so, it would concern several countries; therefore NATO as such would be involved. Second, an invasion on Zealand could be foreseen, and there-

---

28 Pranov, J. B. "Forslag til flådeplan 1990." *Tidsskrift for Søvæsen* 142 (1971): 210–29.
29 Forsvarsministeriet. *Beretning fra Forsvarskommissionen af 1969*, 383–93. København: Forsvarsministeriet, 1972.

fore mobilisation would be possible. Third, an attack on Jutland would have to first fight the Germans in Schleswig-Holstein, and such an attack probably would trigger a nuclear confrontation.

In some ways, the proposal was following the ideas of littoral warfare, e.g. by reducing the number of larger units. On the other hand, the possibilities for action under windy conditions (which were frequent) would be nil, and the reductions in forces were considerable, creating a force vacuum.

The proposal was strongly criticised by CINCNORTH.[30] His general conclusion was that the proposal would invalidate the defence of the nation, would reduce the ability to deter and would therefore increase the risk of nuclear war. The Danish C-in-C agreed.[31] The proposal remained a proposal and was not carried through, but the Social Democrats remained critical towards the large units of the navy.

Modernising the navies in the Baltic Approaches

In the 1970s both navies got modernised with the long awaited missiles for sea as well as air targets, but the hopes for larger ships were not fulfilled. It should be noted, however, that the American navy indicated a possible future influx by larger ships in times of tension by initiating the exercise series BALTOPS.[32] The first incidence in May 1971 was purely American when the navy sent the anti-submarine carrier INTREPID and three destroyers into the Baltic, conducting flight operations and sailing as close to the Soviet coast as 20 miles. From 1972, annual BALTOPS exercises took place with participants from the United States, Denmark, the Netherlands, the United Kingdom and Germany. Exercises focused on anti-air, anti-submarine and electronic warfare and anti-FPB operations. In 1977, the exercise objectives were training, intelligence collection on observing Warsaw Pact naval forces, information sharing, communications tests, low flyer detection and surface gunnery. BALTOPS exercises continued for the entire Cold War, and a battle ship, the IOWA, even participated. Care was taken to avoid provoking a miscalculation by the Soviet Union, maintaining a 25 miles distance from the Soviet coastline, and many manoeuvres were held in Skagerrak and Kattegat.

---

30 Marinestaben: V. Sager vedr. Forsvarskommissionen af 1969 (1969–1972). Brev 18-8-70 til Forsvarsministeren, AFNORTH OR 2500.2a and b, NATO Restricted.
31 Ibid., 415–25.
32 French, Ryan W, and Peter Dombrowski. "Exercise BALTOPS: Reassurance and Deterrence in a Contested Littoral." In *Ilitary Exercises: Political Messaging and Strategic Impact*, eds Beatrice Heuser, Tormod Heier, and Guillaume Lasconjarias, 187.211. Rome: NATO Defense College. Forum Paper 26., 2018.

The Danish navy: Plan "1982"

In June 1972 the chief of the navy had prepared a plan for "the navy of 1982", based on the three roles of the navy: preventing war and securing as much time of warning as possible; safeguarding sovereignty, and counter surprise attacking as "forward" as possible. In particular, the navy should maintain control of the approaches and safeguard the LOCs between the various parts of the country. Having such control also meant that the navy could prevent WAPA ships from breaking through the approaches and getting to the North Sea and the Atlantic.

In a period of tension the WAPA might step by step undermine Danish sovereignty by gathering naval forces, jamming Danish warning systems, blocking by grounding vessels in harbours and inlets, harassing vessels, hijacking civilian ships, blocking certain waters for military exercises, and even mine laying in Danish waters.

The first Danish counter measure would be close surveillance of all activities to find changes in the "normal picture". If the NATO alert system was invoked, the waters between Møn and Bornholm would get priority. Submarines would be moved to their operational areas east of Bornholm. If deemed necessary, mines would be taken on board in order to facilitate quick establishment of minefields in Danish waters. Frigates, corvettes and FPBs would be ready to protect mine laying together with the forts and Danish air force.

If war broke out, the last minefields (in international waters) would be laid, and then the mine layers would lay other mine fields further to the north, and the mine sweepers would prepare for action (presumably supported by German mine sweepers). They would be protected by larger units and FPBs which at the same time would prevent enemy infiltration through the approaches. If the enemy gained air power, and if missile attacks were imminent, submarines and the air force would assume a main role.

The plan of the navy for the future would comprise:
- six corvettes, a new type of about 1,000 tons (2 before 1982);
- 24 new missile FPBs (eight before 1982);
- six submarines of the NARHVALEN (Type 205) class (two before 1982);
- 12 helicopters of e.g. WG-13 type (six before 1982);
- two small mine layers for controlled minefields (before 1982);
- three mine hunters;
- 14 patrol craft;
- five (fishery) inspection frigates;
- an unspecified number of auxiliary vessels (existing mine layers to be converted into depot ships but still usable for mines); and

- two mobile missile coastal batteries, if feasible after closer analysis.
- Ideally, the number of ships was to be 33 per cent higher, but the economic situation would not permit that.

The wishing list reflected a change in naval tactics. First, by forming three fighting groups, each with one corvette, six FPBs and two helicopters. Initially they could lay non-controlled sea mines and then be used for fighting WAPA amphibious operations. Forming groups was not a new tactic, but using the helicopters this way was.

Second, the mine tactics were to be changed towards more controlled minefields and fewer large uncontrolled fields. Controlled minefields were closer to the rules of international law and they offered political flexibility.

Third, the mine sweeping concept was to be changed towards more emphasis on mine hunters (against pressure mines). They were, however, expensive, so the tasks would have to be reduced in scope, but still favouring vital traffic routes.

Fourth, the system of surveillance was to be changed with fewer fast patrol craft (which were expensive in running costs) and more small patrol craft and helicopters.

Fifth, the navy had understood the political wish to close the fixed forts and introduce mobile coastal missile batteries; their cost effectiveness, their vulnerability and their ability to identify the enemy correctly would be a theme for further investigation.

These steps would improve the navy's prospects in littoral warfare; particularly controlled mines, increased integration of helicopters and mobile batteries may have seemed promising. But the outcome of the political debates and the political decision was somewhat meagre, seen with the eyes of the navy: three missile corvettes, ten (large) missile FPBs, two mine layers and some years later a completely new type of patrol craft, the 450 tons STANDARD FLEX type, which could carry HARPOON missiles and have interchanging roles of patrol, mine laying and mine sweeping. The type did not become operational during the Cold War and therefore we shall not go into its details.

The two existing large frigates were modernised with HARPOON sea missiles (replacing 127 mm "B" turret) and SEA SPARROW air missiles. This made the frigates able to operate both as escorts for mine layers and as forward defence ships in the Baltic, if possible operating together with new missile FPBs.

The main changes were the introduction of two new types: three missile corvette of the NIELS JUEL- class and ten FPBs of the WILLEMOES-class.

The 1,320-tons, gas-turbine driven corvettes replaced the four old corvettes; the navy thus ended up with five "larger entities" instead of the eight promised in 1960. They were a compromise between many issues: they were faster than the old corvettes, but not fast enough to serve as flotilla leaders for FPBs (the frigates could);

Figure 17.9: Danish corvette OLFERT FISCHER. 84 meters, 28 knots, 1 76 mm, HARPOON and SEA SPARROW missiles. Source: Forsvarsgalleriet.

the crew had to work in a two-watch system which tired people out; they could operate for seven days only; and they were not well suited for sailing in the Atlantic (STANAVFORLANT); still, they were considered quite successful constructs.

The 260 tons, gas-turbine driven FPBs replaced the old German type MTBs; the six British type fast GTBs were kept for the rest of the Cold War to chase WAPA FPBs. The new FPBs were inspired by the Swedish SPICA-class, but had more powerful missiles and a larger gun. They had wire guided torpedoes as well and in many ways were as powerful as the corvettes, but lacked the ability to remain at sea for long and could not operate in strong winds. They were dependent on the mobile base for replenishment; the mother ship HJÆLPEREN was scrapped.

The navy also got two new small mine layers for controlled minefields, very necessary under flexible response, but the controlled mines were somewhat outdated and were not replaced until after the Cold War was over.

Figure 17.10: Danish Missile FPB RODSTEEN. 46 meters, 40 knots, 1 76 mm, torpedoes and HARPOON missiles. Source: Forsvarsgalleriet.

Plans for the German navy

By 1970, work on a new general conception of the navy was on its way to completion.[33] Destroyers and frigates were in wartime only to operate in the North Sea together with the ASW units of the Naval Air Arm. In the future, on-board helicopters were planned for new ships, but that might not be implemented until the 1980s. For now (1970 and the years to follow) the Baltic was the main theme, and given the strength of the WAPA forces, the aim was deterrence and survival rather than obtaining sea power. The key concept was mobility: the navy would have coastal batteries and minefields in fixed positions, but the enemy had to know that the German navy could strike anywhere. The navy was completing studies on how to operate with fighting groups of FPBs and helicopters. In general, submarines would operate submerged east of Bornholm to do recce and fight enemy ships. In the air over the sea the Naval Air Arm was planning to operate with a new missile, the KORMORAN, and the F-104 STARFIGHTERs were to be replaced with more versatile fighter-bombers. At sea, missiles, new long-range guns and wire guided torpedoes based on the new mobile and fast reacting (e.g. from Danish waters) fighting groups would challenge the enemy. The groups should include new, French-built FPBs under 200 tons with EXOCET missiles, a

---

33 Fü M I: Vortrag UAL Fü M I vor dem Militärischen Führungsrat am 24.9.1970. 22-9-70. App 4718. BM 1/25109.

new large flotilla leader, missile FPB type with torpedoes and a 76 mm gun, and land-based (also using Denmark) SEA KING helicopters with KORMORAN missiles. Hydrofoil FPBs were under consideration in the longer run. The navy no longer planned amphibious attacks, but the army wanted the navy to keep some units for its purposes.

The attack helicopters did not materialise, but we shall discuss the other tasks in more detail below, emphasising the building programme for the Baltic.

Destroyers and frigates

The American FLETCHER destroyers were decommissioned in the 1970s. As we have seen in other chapters, the navy needed missiles on its ships. The missiles of the three destroyers of the LÜTJENS class had their limitations, but were modernised and HARPOON sea missiles launchers were installed. The four destroyers of the HAMBURG class from the early 1960s were the only German-built destroyers in the Bundesmarine. They were modernised in the late 1970s with two double EXOCET launchers for sea missiles (replacing one 100 mm gun), chaff and two additional ASW torpedo tubes. The class lasted till after the Cold War and were then replaced by large frigates.

The KÖLN class frigates from the early 1960s did not have their armament modernised to missiles. As we saw above, the frigate (originally corvette) modernisation project (Fregatte 121) never materialised, but another frigate project – Fregatte 122 – was initiated in the mid-1970s, and eight ships, named the BREMEN-class, were built and commissioned in the 1980s, replacing the FLETCHER- and KÖLN-classes. We shall return to those in the ensuing chapter.

FPBs

The first generation of missile FPBs (type 148, 20 boats) were constructed in France, followed by a German type (143, 10 boats) later in the 1970s and early 1980s (143a, 10 boats). These 40 missile FPBs, together with fighter-bombers from the Naval Air Arm, were to be the major surface force in the Baltic.

The torpedoes of the FPBs were outdated. They had to be fired at a maximum range of three miles, well within the range of most enemy guns. The final phase of an attack might therefore well come close to suicide. Furthermore, a coordinated attack among several boats had to be performed if hits were to be more likely, but organising a coordinated attack on an amphibious group of ships escorted by destroyers was a demanding task. In 1970, an electric driven wire guided torpedo (DM2) was ready for service. It had a range of six to seven miles at high speed and up to 15 miles at lower speed. It had a passive acoustic homing system for the terminal phase. This torpedo meant a radical change in tactics; the firing distance was much larger, and the need for torpedo salvos to enhance the probability of hitting the target was eliminated. Therefore, more targets could be addressed one by one, giving the FPB the possibility to operate longer without having to go to base for replenishment.

When the navy started the planning process for retiring the first 40 FPBs built 1958–63, the idea was to replace them with 40 larger FPBs with missiles (type 143). But the German navy planners took a very long time to work out a German solution and the costs of the planned boat increased so much that it was decided to reduce their number to 10.[34] The Germans "tested the market" and found that the French had been successful in developing a somewhat smaller, but quite potent version with another missile, so it was decided to order 20 of those to replace the oldest of the original FPBs.

The TIGER-class (based on the French LA COMBATTANTE II version) became operational in 1972–75, armed with four EXOCET sea missiles, a 76 and a 40 mm gun – but no torpedoes. They got an integrated fighting control system (AEGIS) which coordinated data for guns and missiles across up to ten FPBs operating together in attack formation. They were also capable of operating with the German missile destroyers with a SATIR system.[35]

Figure 17.11: FUCHS of the TIGER class (Class 148) FPB. 165 tons, length 47 m, 38 knots.
Source: Forsvarsgalleriet.

---

34 Fü M I 1: Beschaffungsvorhaben Sboote. AZ 10-71-10-058, no date (Entwurf), App 5948. BM 1/25109.
35 Hess, op. cit.

The FPB class 143 had its principles decided in 1967, but took time to develop. Initially the idea was to use the TARTAR sea target version, but since it was given up, another immediate solution had to be found, and the navy therefore bought the TIGER Class to replace the JAGUARs. Work on Class 143 continued, but the boat had become so expensive that the original number of 20 had to be reduced to 10.

The ALBATROSS (143) class was ready for commissioning in 1976. It was large, double the size of other FPBs, could operate with a two-watch crew system, and was well armed so it could serve as division leader in fighting groups. Such a task required advanced electronic equipment and space for a staff at work in the operation room. Ten more units of the GEPARD class (143A) were a development of the 143 class with an anti-air missile launcher, but there were no torpedoes. They were commissioned in 1982–1984, so by then the modernisation of the FPB fleet came to an end. German hydrofoil boats were analysed, but not built during the Cold War.

Figure 17.12: KONDOR of the 143-class missile FPB. 390 tons, 57 meters, 40 knots, two 76 mm guns, four EXOCET and two torpedo tubes. Source: Forsvarsgalleriet.

Above we saw the idea of forming fighting groups in the Baltic. The Danes operated with fighting groups of fast frigates and FPBs. The Warsaw Pact also used this concept with missile destroyers and missile FPBs, but those groups were the reasons why the German destroyers were in reality banned from the Baltic in wartime.

The only reliable German counter weapon now (1970) was the fighter-bombers of the Naval Air Arm, but since their airfields were relatively far away from the Middle Baltic one could not count on unplanned support in time. The navy therefore had to organise the operations of the FPBs differently.

For many years, the FPBs had operated in flotillas of up to ten FPBs, subdivided in two to three groups. Directed by one commander, they could attack the enemy in sectors from three sides, making the direction of gun or missile defence difficult, especially if only one ship was the target. More ships could of course divide the roles between them. When the JAGUAR class FPBs were to be replaced, the German planners wanted larger FPBs to serve as flotilla (group) leaders, and therefore started the planning of Type 143 which was to be about double the size of the ordinary FPBs; it could then have more electronic sensors, better room for a group staff and stronger armament (76 mm guns and missiles).

So the following concept was desirable.[36] Given that the WAPA would probably operate with destroyers and task groups having one missile corvette and several missile FPBs and torpedo FPBs, the German navy would have to establish task groups with one large FPB (leader), three smaller FPBs and two helicopters. The upcoming type 143 together with – over time – more FPBs with missiles and helicopters would create a potent opponent to the WAPA forces; it would fire its missiles at the maximum range and have helicopters relay steering signals while the missiles were airborne. Torpedoes likewise would be fired at a maximum range. But one must realise that the tactical situation could force the fight to take place at a much shorter distance, hence the need for mid-size guns.

A tactical situation could be played out as follows. Two groups would lie in waiting positions in Danish waters, close to the coast so that WAPA radars could not distinguish them from land, and missiles would have their search radars mislead. Having received a signal from HQ about a target, the groups would start out, and about 30 minutes before they got to an attack position the helicopters would be ordered to a meeting point; the helicopters would find the enemy, attack with missiles and return to land, and then the FPBs would attack and possibly call for assistance from fighter-bombers.

---

36 Fü M I 1: Kleines Kampfboot 162. Vertraulich. Az 10-71-10-058. 28-8-70. App 5948. BM 1/29109.

Paper Exercise with missile FPBs and Helicopters

In 1971–72, a number of combat situations for the new FPBs were tested in operational analyses with various organisations of the fighting groups.[37] In the case retold below, a fighting group was set up of two divisions (each three boats) of the S-148 class (under construction) with their EXOCET missiles, and one helicopter group of three with KORMORAN missiles. In other tests groups of two boats each had a helicopter as third partner.

In this case the FPBs were deployed to Køge Bay and Faxe Bay, respectively, and the helicopters had a war station on Møn. A WAPA amphibious group of ten POLNOCHY landing craft and two T-43 were secured by two groups: one with a destroyer (KANIN) and three OSA FPBS, one with a destroyer (KANIN), two MIRKA and one SHERSHEN class FPBs. They were north of Rügen, heading WNW, at a speed of 12 knots.

It was a night operation, starting 23.00 when helicopters were alerted that a group of ships was approaching their area. The group commander was in Helicopter I. The moved east, at a speed of 120 knots and had radar contact 23.06, identifying the convoy 23.08. A ship, possibly a destroyer, cut out from the formation heading NE. The helicopters crossed the coastal missile range and got permission to attack the convoy 23.19. Helicopter I fired the first missile at the "loose" destroyer 23.21, and fired the second missile 30 seconds later. 23.23 two more ships left the convoy. Helicopter II and III attacked the convoy with missiles and returned to Møn to reload. Helicopter I (with group commander) stayed close to the convoy which was heading west and detected on Møn Station radar 23.30.

23.37 the FPBs in Køge Bay were ordered to proceed south east and would be joined by Helicopter III at 23.50, in order to direct FPB missiles. The FPBs in Faxe Bay were ordered to be ready at 24.00 with Helicopter II as missile director.

23.45 the northernmost FPBs prepared to attack the two destroyers that had left the convoy. Helicopter I directed a first salvo and was preparing a new task when (23.54) the firing FPB was hit and set out of action. 23.57 Helicopter II was cleared for (its own) attack on convoy from north. 00.01 Helicopter III was ordered to direct missile attack on convoy. A WAPA destroyer was so close that it might be attacked without helicopter direction. Helicopter II was ordered NOT to attack from the north because WAPA forces are closing in there, instead to attack from the south east. Executed 00.17, one ship hit.

At 00.15 one FPB had been lost in southern group, 4 missiles had been fired at destroyer, got order to attack the convoy. Northern group was ordered to attack convoy with Helicopter II as director.

00.19 Exercise end.

The papers did not sum up the casualties on either side.

---

37 Seetaktische Lehrgruppe: Untersuchung von operartiven und taktischen Probleme der Kampfgruppe Ostsee. Geheim. Az 31-02-02 TgbNr 22/72. 20-1-72. BM 1/2366.

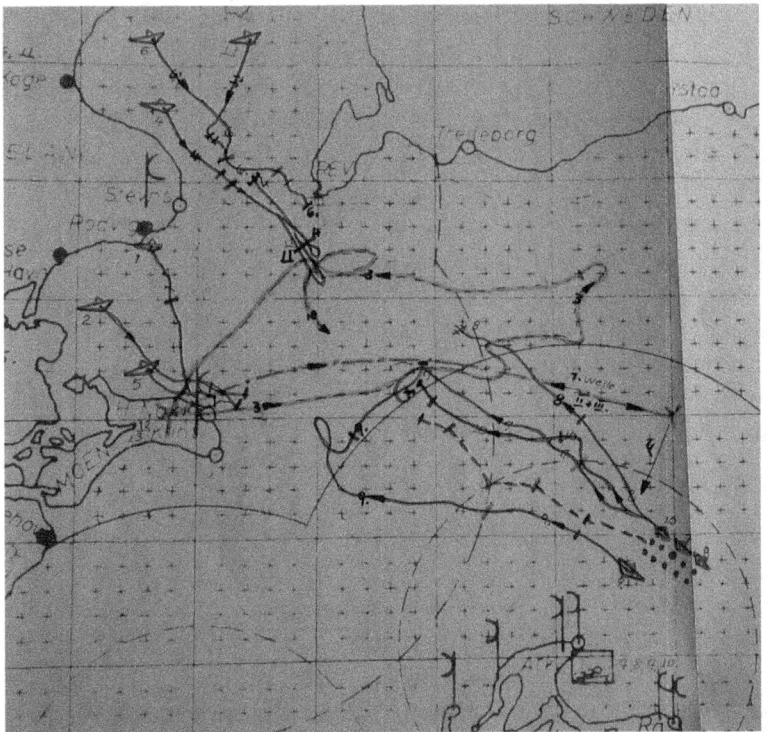

Figure 17.13: The plot map shows the waters between Rügen and Stevns. The circles with centre south indicate the range of WAPA coastal missiles and radars (dottet); the circles with centre west indicate radar range from Danish stations. Movements over one hour and 20 minutes' operations are indicated by red lines for WAPA escorts, yellow lines for NATO helicopters (first one group, then Helicopter II and III in north and south respectively), blue unbroken lines for NATO FPBs. Time sequence: the lines are "cross-marked" three times: red mark at 2320, yellow mark 23.33 and green mark 0010. Source: Bundeswehr Archiv Freiburg.

If helicopters were to operate together with FPBs in the Middle Baltic (see box), it would be advantageous to base them on Danish territory because of the proximity to expected battle areas and hence shorter flying time after alert. At a meeting on 25–26 November 1971 between the Danish and German navies, the Germans presented the issues of using land-based, missile-carrying helicopters together with FPBs in a tactical group.[38] The helicopters should in times of tension be

---

38 Fü M VI 26: Problems concerning employment and support of land based helicopters. Vertraulich. Az 90-15-20-(06), TgbNr 6026/71. 25-11-71. BM 1/1591.

moved to forward bases, i.e. areas large enough to accommodate four helicopters with ground crew and stores.

The helicopters should operate with radio links to relevant HQs and operate independently or together with surface craft. Their roles would be:
- to attack surface units up to destroyer size with missiles. These would be PENGUIN or EXOCET adapted to helicopter use, and using a fire control system to be developed.
- to locate and identify surface forces by radar and ECM. The enemy was assumed to have been detected by earlier recce, and the helicopters must yield more precise data. In order not to endanger the helicopters, this had to be done electronically, creating some problems with identification.
- to transmit information and firing data to one's own surface forces so that they could fire their missiles at maximum range. Depending on the quality of the electronic systems, the data transfer might meet difficulties.

At night, the helicopters might have difficulties in finding their home base unless they get more sophisticated navigation systems.

A movable helicopter base should have: one bus-type vehicle for communication centre and a power supplier on a trailer; one truck with a trailer for workshops, two trucks for stores and special equipment; one truck for missile transport and two fuel trucks. Once in operation, they would need more supplies, by trucks, by helicopters, or by landing craft.

Such logistics had to be planned for, and the overarching question anyway was how to get money for the whole system. The German navy did not get the money for helicopters in fighting groups before the Cold War had ended.

Mine laying

By 1973, the German navy was ready to lay the defensive minefields in the straits, but it also took up the challenge of more offensive, tactical mining in the middle Baltic as a way of defending the primary fields.[39] The original NATO goal of containment by keeping the WAPA navies "bottled up" in the Baltic Sea was hardly sustainable as the only goal anymore since they probably would have sailed their submarines out of the area before war broke out and ordered merchant ships to dock in friendly harbours. Furthermore, the Soviet bases in Northern Russia had gained in importance compared with the Baltic. Submarines would enter the Norwegian Sea, the Atlantic and the North Sea from there.

---

39 Anlage BM 28/76.

So in general, in the Baltic containment was expanded by the goal of anti-invasion – to prevent the WAPA from landing forces on NATO territory. If some fields were lost, new fields were to be laid further north- or westwards, to delay the progress of the enemy. But some offensive mining along the Baltic coastal harbours was still meant to contain the WAPA navies on their own turf.

According to the plans, mines – calibrated to ships of 3,000 tons, three to five meters draught and a speed between eight and 20 knots – were to be laid in three sequences or priorities:

First, amphibious landings were to be prevented by mining the entrance to Grønsund (previously mined by the Danes), Fehmarn Belt and Fehmarn Sound (the Danes took care of Øresund) with 1,250 mines (supposedly for each field area), and the navy should be prepared to help the Danes with certain "backup" fields.

Second, enemy harbour approaches in Mecklenburg Bay; areas and approaches to enemy harbours in middle, east and north Baltic (in cooperation with the Danes); and in night campaigns 28 FPBs should drop 1,067 bottom mines as tactical offensive minefields until 17 miles east of Bornholm (17°35′). Further to the east submarines and airplanes were planned to drop 631 bottom mines, but the navy did not implement that part of the plan.

Third, the German navy should be ready to lay mines in Kattegat, if the Danes were not able to (until 1962, the English mine layer APOLLO was slated for the job). Some 361 bottom- and 269 anchor mines were to be laid by destroyers, frigates, FPBs, fast mine sweepers, mine layers and other available units. If for some reason the first priority fields were not laid, the Kattegat fields would become very important, now as a containment activity backed up by mining in the Skagerrak waters.

In addition, there were mines to be laid in the North Sea and its harbours. They are out of scope for this book.

The mining campaign was very dependent on decisions to be taken in time by the parliament, and for attacks on enemy areas, an approval by SACEUR. To secure timely preparations, the surveillance and recce activities by the navy and air force were cores to detect and report WAPA preparations for attacking. A second stumbling stone was a lack of submarines and airplanes for the offensive parts of the plan.

Submarines

Eighteen new 450-tons submarines (class 206) with eight torpedo launchers for wire-controlled torpedoes came into service in 1973–75, and the previous German-built submarines were retired. The roles of the new submarines were the same as for the previous ones: to operate in the Eastern Baltic to do recce and in war to attack enemy naval and merchant ships, amphibious craft and submarines. They were built of non-magnetic steel.

The wire guided, electric motor driven torpedoes DM2 introduced in 1970 were a manifest step forward for the submarines as well as for the FPBs, as we saw above.

Of course there was an intense interest in how the WAPA navies with their large number of submarine chasers would find and attack NATO submarines. In 1977, the German navy wrote a quite comprehensive paper about that theme, based on a number of exercises by the East German navy, observed north of Rügen and between Rügen and Bornholm.[40] The paper analysed the various ships (two RIGA class frigates and 12 HAI class PCs) and helicopters (six), their communication and command systems and their performance in exercises. We shall quote the gist of the performance analysis and give two examples.

The ships mostly operated in groups of six. Initially they would sail in a formation forming a line abreast with about one mile's distance between each ship. When contact with a submarine was established, they changed pattern into an attack sector formation, forming a circle with the submarine in the centre. The circle was divided into six sectors, each of 60 degrees, with one ship in each (if there were six). This formation moved forward, following the course and speed of the submarine.

So the procedure was that once a chaser got a sonar contact and had determined course and speed, the other ships in the group took position according to the sector system with the detecting ship on the port side and the commanding officer in an adjacent sector; the rest of the ships were commanded to their sectors. The detecting ship initiated an attack, always first by firing its MBU-1800 ASW rocket launcher, followed up by depth charges. After the attack the ships paused to observe the consequences of the attack.

If contact to the submarine was lost, they went back into search abreast formation, nearly always 90 degrees relative to the last known course of the submarine.

Sometimes a helicopter could participate, but only for the detecting process, never in an attack. The helicopter would drop a sonar buoy, and if a submarine was detected, a group of ASW craft would be alerted, and when they got contact, the sector formation would be used for the chase.

The sector formation was also used for escorting a submarine, preventing other submarines to get close to one's own forces.

---

40 Fü M II 1: Auswertung Ujagdübung NVA-VM 1975/76. Geheim. Az DDR 04-06-10-03. TgbNr 847/77. 24-2-77. BM 1/7082.

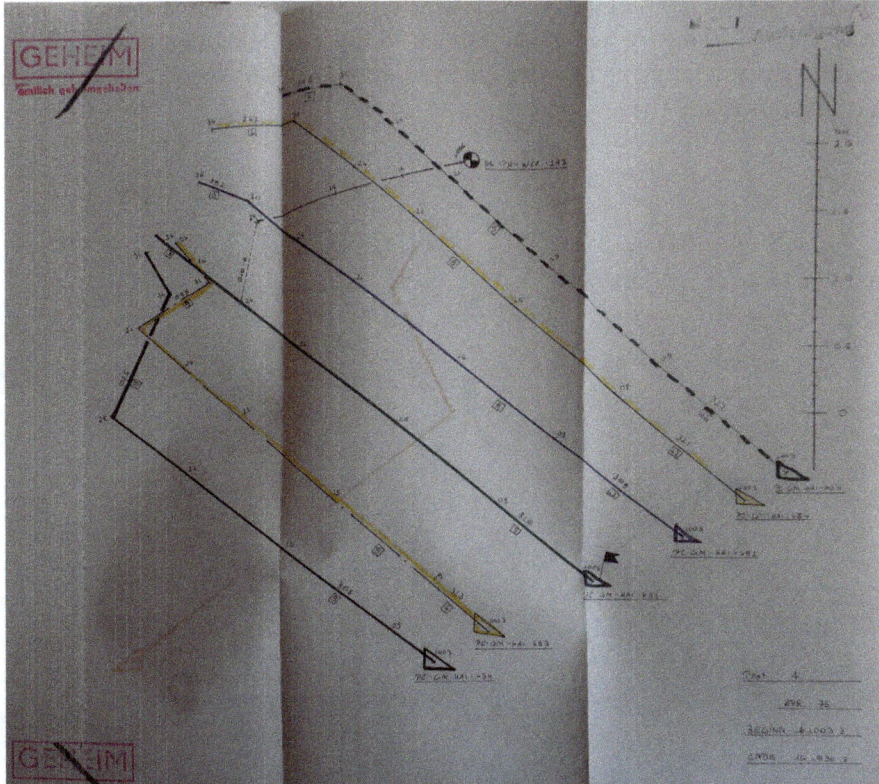

Figure 17.14: Time 10.03–10.36: Search formation with six HAI ASW craft, speed 12 knots. The formation starts in the bottom right in formation line abreast. At the upper left sonar contact is established, and the ships are ordered to take sector formation and close in to one another. Continued in next picture.

Based on observations over time, the German navy supposed that surveillance by the East German navy would take place in the area between the Baltic coast, Bornholm and the Danish coast, particularly in times of tension and war. But even by an intensive formation, the equipment of the WAPA navies probably would only yield a 20 per cent chance of detecting a modern submarine. Furthermore, most of the East German ASW craft were small and only had a small crew working in one watch at sea, tiring them out after 12–15 hours' operation. Finally, the East German navy had many old ships with much equipment in worn out condition, so it was prone to break down. The sonar senders were a case in point – many broke down, a special team would circulate among the ships in the group for repairs, but often the ship had to return to base. Another problem was the main diesel engines on the HAI class, which often broke down. A third problem was the VHF radio system which tended to fall out. Finally, the ASW rocket launchers were not to be trusted – at an exercise between Rügen and Bornholm not one salvo succeeded.

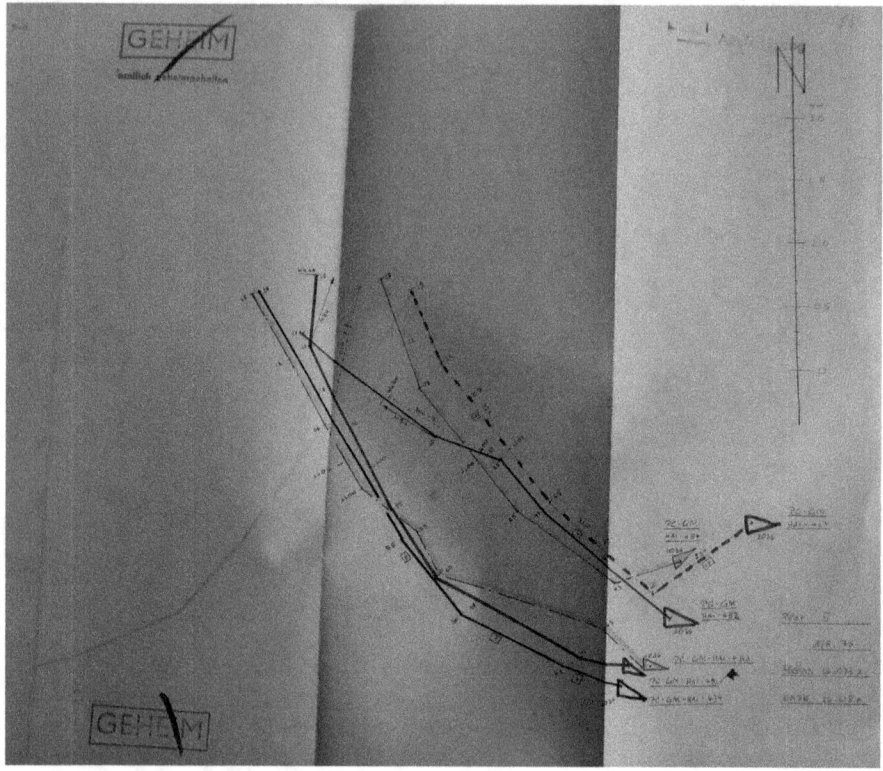

Figure 17.15: Time 10.36–11.18: The six ASW HAI craft moving to sector formation (bottom right), but fail to create it. They rather form two column lines, speed four knots. HAI 452 (blue line) fires ASW rockets and depth charges first. Then HAI 451 (green line) fires ASW rockets followed by depth charges.

Consequently, after about seven days of operation in a period of tension, the ASW capabilities of the navy expectedly would have become considerably lower. Still, the ASW threat might force NATO submarines *en route* to their war stations in the Eastern Baltic to travel submerged. Having thus drained their battery capacity, they would be forced to use their snorkel recharging system when approaching the war station, creating a danger for themselves.

The Naval Air Arm

The Naval Air Arm was able to support the defence of the Baltic Approaches e.g. by escorting naval groups in operation, but its primary strength was defence by detecting enemy formations under development and attacking them further out east in the Baltic, and by attacking coastal bases along the Baltic coast.

SACEUR had given up the idea of having Naval Fighter-bombers participate in STRIKE roles, but early in 1969 CINCNORTH considered some options for his use in counter air and close support (for the army) operations.[41] The German navy responded by writing a document specifying the roles of the Naval Air Arm:[42] beginning in the area east of Bornholm, the fighter-bombers would attack WAPA fighting groups (particularly ships with missiles) and amphibious groups under their deployment westwards. The goal was to weaken the enemy before he reached the Mid- and Western Baltic where the NATO fighting groups were ready for action. West of Bornholm the fighter-bombers were to cooperate with their own forces against enemy ships and to prevent enemy air attacks on NATO ships. Along the Baltic coast enemy traffic, ships in ports, HQs, radar- and missile bases were to be attacked so that their own forces got more freedom of operation. When possible and desirable, the Naval Air Arm were to form a "CAP" around own fighting groups, forming an escort outside the range of their own missiles.

So, regarding CINCNORTH's ideas above, a close air support to army forces was dubious since the navy's pilots had no such training. As to counter air strikes it was the understanding of the navy that such were not part of the NATO defence as long as one was in an escalation phase of flexible response strategy – unless the attacks were relevant locally in the area of confrontation; planned automatic counter strikes were not permissible since they took away the flexibility for politicians to decide how to respond to provocations.

The navy's fighter-bomber was the STARFIGHTER from the early 1960s, but is soon became clear that although it was an efficient weapon platform in itself, the conditions of operating over the sea with its salty air cost much in wear and tear, creating a risk for motor crash. Furthermore, frequent changes in weather conditions – ice, fog, snow, strong winds, many low-flying birds etc. – made the navigation of the aircraft, particularly in low altitude, tiresome for the pilot. The STARFIGHTER was difficult for the pilot to master, and a total of 116 pilots were killed in a crash

---

[41] Signal vv aac356 nr. 44 11-02-69 Vertraulich from Senior German Officer in HQ AFNORTH. BM 1/1497a.
[42] Fü M II 1: Positionen der Marine hinsichtlich der Aufgaben ihrer Jagdbombegeschwader. Vertraulich. Az 31-04-01-01. TgbNr 2468/69. n.d. Entwurf. BM 1/1497a.

(the Bundeswehr had a total of 916 STARFIGHTERs, and 269 crashed, most of them in the first years).

Above, we have seen how the navy planned to use the aircraft for recce and fighter-bomber operations in 1962. Ten years later the combat uses of the airplane were much the same,[43] but the combat challenges greater. The 20 mm gun and the 2,75 inch missiles could only be used within anti-aircraft range of the targets. The AS-30 missile could be fired at a distance of up to 10 km, but had to be controlled by hand, requiring eyesight all the way to the target, and the firing and controlling airplane probably would come as close as three kilometres from the target (another plane could, however, take over control at a larger distance). Some 1,000 lb bombs could be thrown by loft bombing to avoid coming close to the target, but precision would then be poorer.

The electronic equipment was also the same, and did not suffice. The German Naval Air Arm had many tasks in the Baltic Sea and on the Baltic coast. But the WAPA air warning and air defence system along the coast had become comprehensive. The navy analysed it in 1975[44] and found that the whole Baltic coast was continuously covered with Electronic Warfare systems which permitted the enemy to detect airplanes flying in an altitude of 10,000 meters at a distance of 80 miles, aircraft in 300 meters at 40 miles and low-flying aircraft (100 meters) at 20 miles. See map below.

Enemy fighters with guns and air-to-air missiles could be directed from a number of these systems which could be enhanced from radar systems on ships at sea or aircraft with such electronic capability. In addition, a large number of missile launchers as well as A-A guns were located along the coast; these would protect land bases as well as naval fighting groups being deployed along the coast. Finally, ships with missiles could be grouped to form a key point in air defence or to escort convoys with stores.

The navy noted that, seen with WAPA eyes, this system had to be quite satisfying, and therefore a considerable threat for NATO units operating in the Baltic. The system gave the WAPA HQs a comprehensive situation map of all threats.

The STARFIGHTERs were not equipped to withstand the threat from these detection and missile/aircraft control systems. The navy therefore analysed the possibilities for equipping the aircraft with ECCM systems[45] that would weaken the

---

43 Marinefliegerdivision – Fachstab II: Einsatzgrundlagen/Einsatzgrundsätze für das Waffensystem F-104 G (Marine). Geheim. Az 31-05-14, TgbNr F 380/72. 7-4-72. BM 1/3770c.
44 Fü M II: Kurzstudie über Möglichkeiten der USR für die Absicherung des Luftraumes über der Ostsee. Geheim. Anlage zu Fü M II 950/75. 25-2-75. BM 1/3206.
45 Fü M II: Taktische Forderung (Gerät) für P1Begriff: Eloka-Nachrüstsatz F-104 G Marine. Geheim. TgbNr 2804/75, 15-8-75. BM 1/3206.

electronic systems of the enemy in order to prevent their jamming of NATO radar system's capacities to detect targets and incoming missiles, track targets, break enemy lock-on of radars, make decoys and confuse the users of such systems. Furthermore, the aircraft would get chaff systems.

Such a system appears to have been ready by 1978 when the STARFIGHTERs were modernised.

But already in 1970 the navy had started a process to replace the STARFIGHTER with a more modern plane which could fulfil more roles. The STARFIGHTER had a recce (RF 104-G) and a bomber (F-104 G) version. A multi-role – MRCA or Multi Role Combat Aircraft – airplane with a better safety record was desirable. In addition, the navigational challenges in the Baltic and the demands for being in control of new equipment created a demand for a two-seater plane. So the MRCA plane had to be a two-seater and have, first, two engines to promote flying safety over the sea, and second, better electronic equipment which could control missiles without eyesight and block enemy counter measures and, third, also be used for recce operations – also at night.

The navy and the Luftwaffe joined forces in seeking such an aircraft and found a common denominator in the PHANTOM II airplane. But as time and negotiations passed, the commonalities decreased, and the navy decided not to join the Luftwaffe in a procurement of the PHANTOM II. Instead, the navy wanted to await the development of a new MRCA airplane – expected about 1976 – and bought 26 extra STARFIGHTERs to fill the gap in the meantime.[46] They were modernised in 1978 with the KORMORAN missile and better recce equipment.

The development of the new MRCA airplane was a venture involving Germany, Great Britain and Italy. The navy wanted 112 aircraft (including reserve). The tactical demands were quite comprehensive.[47]

The aircraft had to carry out attacks against naval as well as maritime coastal targets within a distance of 360 miles; give naval combat support; do general recce within a range of 420 miles; identify naval target; and carry out post strike recce. It had to yield fighter cover against enemy offensive aircraft and enemy fighters. Thus it would have a combined attack/fighter role. In addition, it had to be prepared for supporting the Luftwaffe in its tasks and give close air support to the army.

---

46 Fü M II 1: Sprechzettel für StvInspM 1-10-1968 im Verteidigungsausschuss. Az 10-70-01-02. 27-9-68. BM 1/999a.
47 Fü M II 1: Vorläufiges operationelles Konzept MRCA Marine. 1. Entwurf. N.d. (August 1969). AZ 31-04-01-01. The 25-page document is very detailed. BM 1/999a.

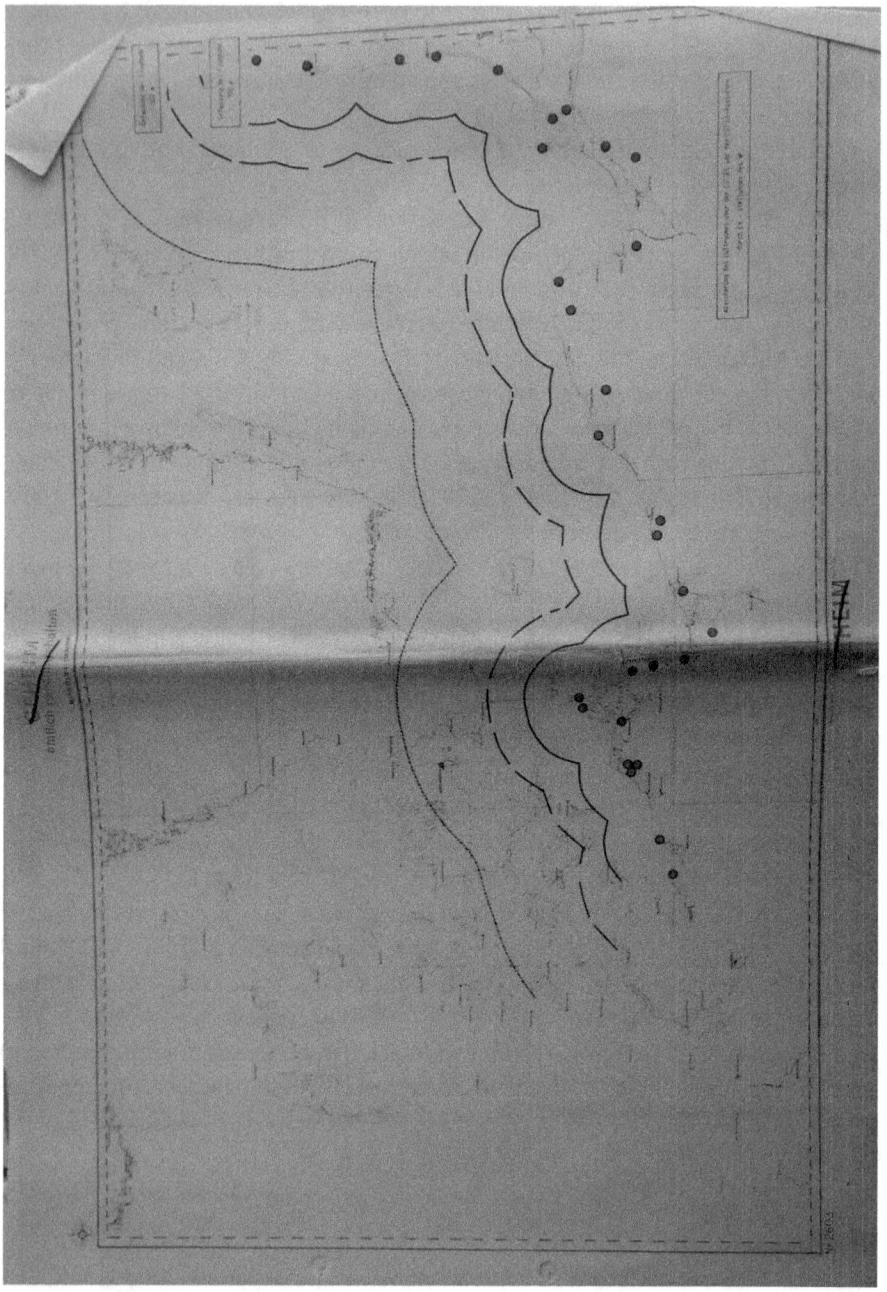

Figure 17.16: Map showing WAPA Baltic EW-systems and their detection ranges for 10,000, 300 and 100 meters. Source: Bundeswehr Archiv.

The aircraft had to always have two 30 mm guns. Depending on its main role by take-off, combinations of bombs, missiles (SIDEWINDER, KORMORAN, AS-30), ECM and recce equipment and reserve gas tanks were to be installed.

The result was the TORNADO aircraft which was ready for service in 1980 and gradually replaced the STARFIGHTER until 1986. We shall return to this in the next chapter.

Summing up: The modernised NATO navies

In 1973, the supreme commander was quite dissatisfied with the military capabilities in NATO's northern region. But the 1970s proved to be the decade for successful modernisation of the two navies and their capabilities for littoral warfare, particularly regarding reconnaissance and sea denial by mission task groups with missiles and new guided torpedo systems. Attack helicopters were desired, but not included.

NATO countries developed various versions of air and sea target missiles, and both navies analysed their pros and cons. They both came to adopt the SEA SPARROW anti air missile, but the Danes chose the HARPOON and the Germans adopted the EXOCET missile as the anti-sea target missile. Thus the Danish frigates, the German-built destroyers and the FPBs of both navies got potent weapons.

In the 1970s conditions still were so that the WAPA countries would have an upper hand in the air and, therefore, the German destroyers and frigates would be withdrawn from the Baltic in case of war, but in times of tension they would still be present in surveillance roles. They also were slated to operate in Kattegat if the Danish straits were compromised by WAPA forces.

The BALTOPS exercises indicated a bolder NATO-posture regarding large ships, but no plans have appeared to release such forces in times of war.

The submarines of both navies were important in surveillance and in attacking all kinds of surface ships in the Eastern Baltic. Most of them got wire guided torpedoes. The Germans got 18 new mid-sized submarines. They were to operate close to the expected LOCs along the Baltic coast, but they also – together with the Danes – watched what was going on in the waters east and north east of Bornholm. They were limited in their roles in that they had to stay within defined "boxes" of operation in order not to mess things up for one another. Particular lanes were defined for the deployment to and from the operation areas.

The missiles for the FPBs meant radical changes in their tactics. The Germans got 40 new FPBs, the Danes 10. The Danes maintained torpedoes with the missiles and thus had a broad range of attack possibilities. Half of the German FPBs (of

French design) only had missiles and 76 mm guns. The other half was larger and kept all three types of weapon.

The Germans wanted to get SEA KING helicopters to create fighting groups with missile FPBs and tested the concept in paper exercises, but that plan did not materialise in the Cold War. Instead, they developed close cooperation tactics between FPBs and the STARFIGHTER when the KORMORAN missiles were ready for action. The STARFIGHTER, however, was slated for retirement when a replacement could be found – the plane was vulnerable because of the flying conditions over the sea, and the complexity of the tasks really required a two-seater. The development of a replacement took longer time than warranted, and the navy had to buy more of an aircraft they really did not want any more. We shall take a closer look at the replacement and the tactics in the next chapter, with a new TORNADO aircraft.

Over time, the intelligence offices collected much and detailed information about the WAPA navies and their ways of operating. Thus the NATO forces were quite well prepared for what to expect and consequently could develop tactics against the WAPA operations.

The Danes had several changes in the defence budgets in a negative direction, and their navy never got the desired eight "larger units"; they had to make do with two relatively large frigates and three new corvettes – all of them got air and sea missiles. The German navy also got limits for an expansion and decided to focus on the FPBs in the 1970s and then get new, modernised frigates in the 1980s.

Chapter 18
NATO and the Baltic Approaches in the 1980s

This chapter discusses the development of the NATO defence of the Baltic Approaches in the final decade of the Cold War. In a way, there were not many changes – the general strategy of NATO was unchanged, the political climates in both Denmark and Germany were unfavourable to military spending and hence not much military growth took place, and the Warsaw Pact stopped its military expansion and aggressive mood from the mid-1980s. By 1989, the Berlin Wall fell and the Cold War petered out.

So the last year observed in this book is 1989. Non-growth, however, does not equal standing still, and within NATO several steps were taken. One was the double-track decision of 1979, which offered the Warsaw Pact a mutual limitation of medium-range ballistic missiles and intermediate-range ballistic missiles, but it was combined with a threat by NATO to deploy more medium-range nuclear weapons in Western Europe. This theme, however, is outside the scope of this book. Another was the initiation of CONMAROPS, a naval comprehensive strategy (which NATO never had before), strongly supported by the Reagan administration's new naval strategy. This had some repercussions for the Baltic Approaches, but mainly because Germany chose to use the concept to support expanded tasks for its navy and prevent quite severe cut-backs.

No growth, but some units were replaced, and NATO's forces got an intensive technological push forward, first by improving the electronic systems guiding the command-and-control features of guns, torpedoes and missiles, second by getting the TORNADO fighter-bombers which doubled the fighting capacity of the German Naval Arm, and third by combining the above into better tactics, especially for FPBs and their air support in the littoral warfare in the Baltics.

The general preparedness of the Danish forces, however, was not satisfactory according to the annual report of the defence from 1987.[1] The logistics had critical deficiencies within "decisive" equipment like weapon systems, ammunition, missiles, mines, tanks and heavy wheel vehicles. Air surveillance was adequate, but the navy could not maintain satisfying recce on and under the sea surface.

In a period of tension all forces would require calling up reserve forces. If war broke out, the army defence of Jutland could only be maintained for a limited period of time due to lack of armoured vehicles, lack of air defence and lack

---

[1] Forsvarets årsrapport 1987 HEM. Forsvarskommandoen KC Klassificeeret kopibog (afklassificeret) 1975–1988 box 131.

of ammunition. Army defence of the islands was satisfactory, and sea control was to be obtained together with the German navy and its air arm. But capacity for mine sweeping and escort was limited. The capabilities of the air force were satisfactory, but a lack of pilots and missiles would challenge endurance. Reinforcement in time was necessary.

In sum, the defence of the Baltic Approaches by Danish forces was heavily dependent on well-timed reinforcements by land and air forces and at sea on a successful cooperation with the German navy. In this chapter, we shall focus on the defence at sea and take a short look at the army defence of the Danish islands.

NATO strategy for the 1980s: CONMAROPS

Until 1981, NATO did not have a comprehensive naval strategy; the organisation had in principle relied on the various navies each to take care of the tasks in their area, coordinated by the relevant NATO command. But in the light of the fast growth of the Soviet navy, now threatening to dominate the seas in large proportions of NATO-waters, a strategy became desirable, and in the fall of 1977 a working group started a process of conceptualising what in 1981 became the *Concept of Maritime Operations*, CONMAROPS,[2] linking naval forces together from the Mediterranean to the Norwegian Sea. As a consequence, the basic roles of naval units were determined as a starting point if Soviet aggression was imminent.

We shall only discuss the parts of CONMAROPS that were relevant for the Baltic Approaches (see also chapter 15), noting in passing that for the German navy better coordination with forces from CINCHAN and SACLANT was a high priority, but outside the scope of this book.

Specifically, a defensive concept within the range of land-based tactical air support should have the aim:[3]
- to keep open the north western approaches to Europe,
- to deny the WAPA exiting or entering the Baltic,
- to maintain coherence of defence between the northern and the central region of SHAPE,
- to repel seaborne attacks against the UK, Norway, Denmark and Schleswig-Holstein, and
- to interfere with WAPA movements from the Barent Sea into the Atlantic.

---

2 Working papers from the group are found in BM 1/6507; the text in following two paragraphs is based on that archive, unless otherwise stated.
3 Note: Tri-MNC Concept of Maritime Operations (CONMAROPS German lead-in). German/Norwegian Staff Talk 6/79. BM 1/25112.

The German navy took the view that these tasks would require that the German destroyers and frigates were allowed to operate north of the sixty-first latitude (20 miles north of Bergen) which until now had been the northern operational border. The perspective included the air space of the area.

In many ways, these thoughts were not new, but the German emphasis on formulating a perspective linking of the areas was novel, and it gave the German navy an opportunity to expand its areas of operation in the North Sea.

This concept, of course, corresponded to what the Germans saw as a strategic goal for the WAPA: getting control over Denmark and Norway and the adjacent waters in order to create a platform for attacking NATO and its LOCs to Central Europe. The perspective also gave the navy a rationale that could be used in the budgetary fights among various interests in the government so that the expansion could be secured financially.

On the strategic level, the German concepts were based on the fact that the carrier strike groups which had been planned to operate in the Norwegian Sea had been reduced by the Americans and the British. The carrier forces now were reserved for service in the Atlantic (the GIUK gap) with a possibility to move forward towards Norway, but this was hardly guaranteed.[4] According to the Germans,[5] the navies in Western Europe no longer could rely on the intervention from such groups if serious problems arose, e.g. in the Baltic Approaches. But the defence of Northern Norway particularly suffered, and this created possibilities for the Soviet forces to take parts of Norway and get sea control in the northernmost waters, hence the necessity of using the strategic perspective of the *Nordflankenraum* so that the joining of WAPA forces from north and south would be made more difficult.

The CONMAROPS would counter the mentioned WAPA movements at the strategic level. CONMAROPS got its final formulations in 1981. There were three basic principles:

a) Containment, preventing Warsaw Pact forces from deploying into open waters (choke points and sea denial);
b) Defence in depth, putting the enemy at risk wherever they were operating, and
c) Keeping the Initiative, positioning forces early in crisis and handling them so that the enemy responded as much as possible to NATO moves rather than vice versa.

---

4 Grove, Eric J. "The Superpowers and Secondary Navies in Northern Waters During the Cold War." In *Navies in Northern Waters 1721–2000*, eds Rolf Hobson and Tom Kristiansen, 211–21. London: Taylor and Francis, 2004.
5 See previous note.

In particular, the containment clause could be used by the Germans in their endeavours to expand the operation areas for their navy. Containment was also important for the Danish navy, but in principle the Danes just had to do what they had always done: mine the straits, creating choke points. The Danish navy had no serious role to play in the North Sea apart from the fact that a Danish frigate or corvette took part in the operations of the STANAVFORLANT now and then.

CONMAROPS, however, did not come to stand alone. The Americans under President Reagen revised their naval strategy quite radically, and the NATO Carrier Striking Fleet was reorganised with the American carriers in a more offensive role, being moved north east towards Norway. A new concept was developed to operate carriers in the Norwegian fjords where geography added to the capabilities of these and supporting surface ships to win the battle against the Northern Fleet's submarines and missile-strike aircraft.[6] Thus the German wishes of a stronger naval presence in the northern waters became real.

WAPA risks

The Danish and the German navies had common general goals for the Baltic, operating for BALTAP, but their tactics had somewhat different aims locally. The Danish navy had focus on the straits and landing beaches; the German navy had a Baltic set of tasks, but expanded the defence concept. Below we shall review some of their thoughts about the risks of attack by the WAPA in the 1980s.

Poland 1981

First, however, a slight aberration. There was one incident that triggered intense naval intelligence gathering, when the Polish solidarity movement gained momentum in the fall of 1981. The Polish military made a coup on 13 December and took control of the government. The Danish government feared that there might come an armed resistance against the military leadership and asked the navy to increase surveillance. If such resistance was quashed, a stream of refugees crossing the Baltic might be expected.

On 13 December a patrol craft was transferred to Bornholm, and the day after an inspection frigate was deployed to the waters around the island. Until 8 January frigates and corvettes took turns in patrolling the area between Swi-

---

6 Ibid., 219.

noujscie and Ustka during the day, and within the range of the Bornholm radar at night. West Germany had a couple of ships patrolling the Eastern Baltic.

In the time period of 19 December to 5 January two mine layers and a LYNX helicopter were on call for 16 hours a day.

In the report to the Ministry of Defence the Danish navy took the opportunity to make a case for its large ships:

> The weather conditions in the Baltic once again made it necessary to resort to large units capable of operating in rough weather in operations around Bornholm. In the last year the navy has had at least one larger unit operating east of Bornholm, checking Russian amphibious exercises and other activities.[7]

This comment may be seen as a point made in the debate on the future of the navy and its frigates in the early 1980s.

Denmark

In the 1980s the Danish Intelligence Office considered the risk of an attack by the WAPA to be relatively low. If it were to take place, comprehensive bombing of Danish airfields, air defence installations, HQs, depots and bases would take place initially.[8] The Baltic navy would become involved step by step. Large units and submarines would have left the Baltic before any attacks to operate in the North Sea and beyond. In the Baltic, the task for the remaining naval units would be to maintain sea power east of Bornholm and then destroy NATO ships in the Western Baltic and the Danish straits and Kattegat, followed by establishing naval power there. Initial operations would use small units like FPBs with missiles and torpedoes and, when the air threat was reduced, with larger units, followed by mine sweepers to make way for the amphibious forces. These would land on the SE side of Zealand, possibly also on Falster. We described the likely landing process in chapter 17.[9]

Around 1980, one could not rule out a limited WAPA operation against Bornholm or Lolland and Falster as an element of a political pressure against the Danish government. In such a case the Danes risked that the aggression was below

---

7 Søværnets Operative Kommando FTR arkiv 350.1-108/82, 12-2 82.
8 Forsvarets Efterretningstjeneste. *Truslen mod Danmark*, M10-M12. Vedbæk: Forsvarskommandoen, 1978.
9 The Danish Intelligence Office has a 73-page description of various options for WAPA landings in its 2000-page HEM treatise "Warszawapagtens Maritime organisation og taktik" written originally in 1971, and updated through the 1980s. Forsvarets Efterretningstjeneste: KC. Kopibog med bilag (afklass.) (1947–1990) 5-11-71, nr. 1813/71.

the threshold for NATO escalation at that time. Alternatively, NATO might be *en route* to dissolution.[10] Such an attack would also be started with air operations followed by naval missions to cut off Danish units from interfering. Then one would expect paratroopers and amphibious operations against the coast of Falster, supported by aircraft. By 1988 the Intelligence Office deemed such an operation unlikely.[11]

In short, then, the Danish navy had as its main task to observe what went on in the Baltic and to prepare for mining the Danish Narrows and some coastal areas to prevent WAPA amphibious forces from landing in Denmark. Nothing new there, but the weapon platforms and electronic systems were changing fast towards more integrated platforms, giving more control over the geographic intricacies of littoral warfare.

How would the WAPA navies operate? The Danish Intelligence office wrote a couple of notes in 1982 and 1984, particularly out of concern for the Danish units armed with the HARPOON missile[12] which supposedly would be the primary targets for WAPA units. This was so much more because the WAPA units were poorly armed against HARPOON missiles because they were sea skimming – so they had to destroy the NATO platforms for those missiles. Consequently, the Danes supposed that the WAPA units would operate in closely knit groups. The Danes did not think that the WAPA naval groups would just attack head-on: they would have to determine the pros and cons of various operations. Important factors might be questioning the necessity for one's own units to operate in Danish waters; one's own capabilities for limiting the movements of NATO-units, e.g. by mining; the number of one's own aircraft for supporting the operations and the size of NATO's air defence. Furthermore the probability of success with own sea missiles.

As to the missile threat, the WAPA lacked in missiles against small units; the existing ones were produced for larger naval units and to some degree targets on land. The missiles were big and had larger war heads; they could carry nuclear war heads, but were not expected to do so in the Baltic. They flew slow (mach. .9), they dived towards the target in a flat curve and hit low, but they were not sea skimmers. They were inexpensive and expected to be used in large quantities.

SS-N-9 was the most modern, it could be used over-the-horizon (60 miles); it had radar as well as infra red homing antenna. STYX was the most common mis-

---

10 Ibid., Section L.
11 Forsvarets Efterretningstjeneste. *Truslen mod Danmark*, 147. Vedbæk: Forsvarskommandoen, 1988.
12 Forsvarets Efterretningstjeneste. HEM Lufttruslen mod Søværnets sejlende enheder, 97/82, 22-1-82. HEM Truslen mod Søværnets HARPOON-bærende enheder, 1331/84, 11-10-84.

sile; some used radar, others infra red homing. Normally they were launched using radar data from the firing unit, but they could also be fired using raw data from other units. STYX could be observed visually or followed on an ordinary air radar. They could be fooled by chaff and by electronic jamming and they could be avoided by vehement manoeuvring in the terminal phase (the Danish FPBs could "brake" from 35 knots to zero in one and a half ship's length).

The Intelligence Office did not expect many aircraft reserved for attacking NATO ships. The Soviet navy had light bombers which threatened NATO's bases, ships in harbours and larger units at sea, and they could lay mines. Soviet fighter-bombers had mainly been observed as support for amphibious operations. Some of them had equipment for jamming NATO systems. The Polish outdated fighter bombers had been seen attacking ships with guns, bombs and non-guided missiles. The East German Fighter-bombers were also used against ships. Those aircraft could not operate in darkness and foul weather.

Only a few larger units in the Baltic had sea missiles (the modern units were in the Northern Fleet in Murmansk). But some had air missiles and ASW missiles which could be fired against surface units. The cruisers and destroyers were outdated and would hardly operate until the air threat was minimised. Their primary use would be support at amphibious landing operations and escorting roles.

WAPA forces had a large number of small units with a primary role to destroy enemy surface ships. The NATO aircraft threat meant that they would probably only operate at night or in weather with poor visibility. Larger units were only expected if small ones could not operate (foul weather).

The OSA FPBs were outdated and to be replaced by larger FPBs and corvettes with larger guns and modern weapon direction systems, and equipped for electronic self-defence. The missile corvettes would use missiles to their full range if they cooperated with helicopters. The torpedo FPBs were also outdated, except for the LIBELLE class which were small, very fast and had flexible armament.

Missiles from coastal batteries could be expected until 45 miles from the coast, but at distances over 20 miles a relaying control unit was a must. The batteries were mobile and could operate from East Germany.

Submarines were deemed only dangerous east of Bornholm, but mini submarines (able to operate in shallow waters) might be in the process of becoming operational. They could come on missions in Danish straits with torpedoes, mines, missiles and frogmen.

Mines could be laid from the air, from LIBELLE FPBs and from merchant vessels. Remote controlled mines were possible. So one could expect mines from the air at harbours, waiting positions and in the narrows.

Submarine routines: Listening to the enemy

Danish submarines frequently patrolled the Eastern Baltic to spy on WAPA activities. Over time certain routines had appeared. The following story comes from submarine NARHVALEN.[13]

Just after leaving its base all watches on board were put on Moscau time because that was the time zone of Soviet navy operations. So life on the submarine was syncronized with Soviet naval operations. The Soviets were prone to follow a rather routinised daily scheme.

The Danes always had two officers of the watch in the operation "room". One manned the periscope and was in command, the other one followed reporting from the sensors and wrote the war diary. These running descriptions of what was observed and the evaluations by the officers were indispensable for the analyses of all tapes which were carried out later by the analysts of the Intelligence Office.

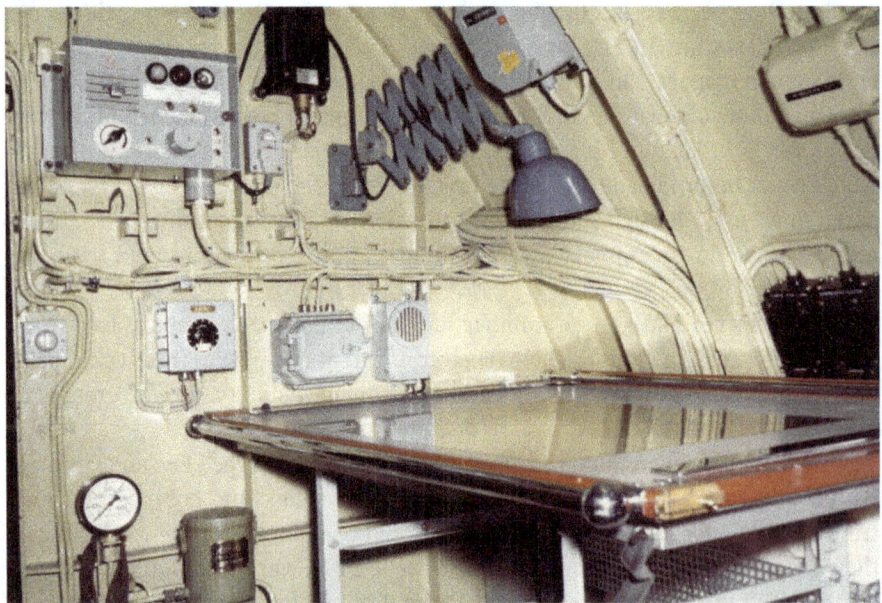

Figure 18.1: Simple plotting table with automatic transfer of own position in the control room of submarine NARHVALEN. Source: Forsvarsgalleriet.

A typical 24-hour sequence would run as follows. Midnight–04: the boat typically would dive deep and carry out routine maintenance, including the extremely important task of baking fresh bread. 4–8: Morning snorkeling before breakfast to get a first impression of what might be in the offing for today. Around 7 many Soviet ships in harbour would start up their radar, and the Danes got an idea of who might go to sea that day, and the submarine could take its position accordingly. After 8

---

[13] Nørby, Søren. *Nordhvalen og Nordkaperen. De sidste danskbyggede ubåde.* København: Statens forsvarshistoriske museum, 2013.

(morning parade) the ships began activities, and around 9 they were at sea to start the exercises of the day. Depending on those exercises they would return between 16 and 18, and the Danes manning the electronic posts could have their dinner in peace and quiet – as opposed to lunch which had to be taken on watch because the crew was too small to have two for each post. After dinner there would be a snorkeling turn and also one "good night" turn before midnight when radio messages were to be received – and then dive deep for the night.

In the early 1980s, the general aims of the Danish navy to meet the WAPA challenges were:[14]
- More units and electronic systems had to support forward defence recce tasks under all weather conditions;
- All surface fighting units needed new air defence systems and better equipment for electronic warfare;
- The mines had to be modernised to make them difficult to sweep, and more minefields should be controlled so that they could be laid early in periods of tension;
- The missiles of small units should be improved so that they could be fired from protected positions e.g. behind small islands;
- Naval helicopters were to be equipped with weapons suited to fighting small naval units;
- Mobile coastal batteries supported by naval helicopters were to supplement the traditional units; and
- the primary base for the navy should in the future be Frederikshavn in Northern Jutland; it would yield a better and more protected support structure than Copenhagen.

Germany

In many ways, the German understanding of the role of its navy in the Baltic was the same as before.[15] The main concept was forward defence, meeting the enemy as far from one's own territory as possible, but first of all maintaining such forces that the enemy would abstain from using military force. The navy was able to do so together with other NATO forces, but the economic conditions demanded that utmost care was taken to get the most out of every budget post.

---

14 Forsvarskommandoen. *Forsvaret år 2000. Perspektivplan 1. del*, 111-12. Vedbæk: Forsvarskommandoen, 1982.
15 Fü M VI 1: Die Marine am Beginn der 80er Jahren. App 4728. April 1979. BM 1/3205.

Defending the German part of the Baltic coast and controlling the Danish Narrows had been the main task and would also be key in the 1980s. However, in the second half of the 1970s, the German navy had started to expand its strategic perspective to what they called the Northern Flank Space (*Nordflankenraum*), and it became operational in the 1980s when NATO created the CONMAROPS strategy (which the Germans eagerly pushed forward towards a decision).

The Germans wanted to link the defence of the Baltic Approaches to the defence of the North Sea and the Norwegian Sea. The task was to prevent the Soviets from merging their two naval sections from the Baltic and the Norwegian Sea – this would create a strong force to threaten the LOCs from the west to Western Europe. The issue of force reinforcements from the USA had become more and more important as the plans for moving forces into West Germany, Norway and Denmark had become more elaborate (see chapter 15), and therefore the Germans now had a stronger interest in maintaining sea power in the North Sea. This also would guarantee the delivery of all sorts of import by the sea. Earlier on, the NATO power of the sea was a fairly sure thing, but the growth of the Soviet Northern Fleet could have changed the balance. The Soviet navy might even be able to attack the Baltic Approaches from the north, passing through Skagerrak and Kattegat from the North Sea. Such an attack was not expected in the war plans, and the Germans repeatedly mentioned the risk in various papers and thus argued for more presence of German frigates and destroyers in the North Sea.

In the Baltic, the Germans foresaw two strategies for the Warsaw Pact: amphibious attacks on NATO territory, particularly in the Danish Narrows, and keeping sea power in the Baltic waters.

The amphibious attacks were prerequisites for getting sea power in the Narrows and from there a breakthrough to the North Sea and the Atlantic, in effect cutting the NATO area in two and blocking LOCs to the Central European forces. WAPA forces were now allowed to get repair services and replenishment in the Baltic ports. The WAPA would have a large number of amphibious craft available for transporting army forces, and likewise a large number of missile-armed corvettes (25) and FPBs (20), and about 40 ASW frigates and corvettes. There were plenty of mine sweepers at hand. Furthermore, there were suitable naval aircraft and air force aircraft available.

The strategy of keeping sea power in the Baltic had as a primary goal securing LOCs along the Baltic coast. Such sea power was a prerequisite for the amphibious operations and breaking through to the Atlantic, and it would secure the transport of stocks to the army forces in North-Central Europe. Widespread use of minefields was expected, and a considerable number of units would be reserved for preventing NATO from laying mines in the area. Intensive surface war would only be expected in connection with amphibious operations. Until then, the WAPA forces would focus on fighting NATO submarines west of Bornholm, deploying to the operation fields in the Middle Baltic, and protecting the harbours and LOCs. East of Bornholm comprehensive ASW operations would take place together with protection of harbours and LOCs. For these tasks there were 15 corvettes and 20 FPBs with missiles, and 40 ASW frigates and corvettes. In addition, East German and Polish naval units, missile coastal batteries and aircraft were available. Furthermore, there were about 120 units for mine sweeping.

Operational plans in the Baltic Approaches

The map below[16] shows the deployment of the German navy in WINTEX 1981 just before the outbreak of hostilities.

Two destroyers and two motherships were in the Baltic; they would be retracted to Kattegat when hostilities started. Other destroyers and the frigates were in the North Sea. The submarines were deployed quite near the WAPA territory, constituting a considerable threat (Danish submarines, not shown, were deployed to the NE of Bornholm). The threat of the Navy Air Arm's fighter-bombers (between Møn and Bornholm) is not depicted.

From the east we see six submarines along the coast and two south of Gotland, then three SE of Bornholm, and one in Fehmarn Belt. A mothership OSTE was north of Sassnitz, another, OKER, was south east of Rügen. One old destroyer was north of Rügen, one missile destroyer NW of Bornholm. Two FPB divisions and a mine sweeper division were ready at Olpenitz. A number of mother ships were at Korsør, one more north of Zealand with a FPB division and a mine sweeper division. Finally, one division FPBs was in Frederikshavn. Destroyers and Frigates in the North Sea are not shown here.

The Danish navy is not on the map. In the war plans it had three submarines north east of Bornholm, one FPB group on Bornholm, three patrol craft between Bornholm and Møn, one frigate between Stevns and Sweden, four mine layers and one FPB group in Øresund, one mine layer in Storebælt and one (reserve) in the Bay of Århus, and one frigate, three corvettes and one FPB group waiting north of Zealand.[17] They clearly were deployed to defend the Zealand islands against an amphibious attack.

---

16 "Einweisung des Stabes in Ausgangslage . . . WINTEX – CIMEX 81" . . . Vertraulich draft version of note in BM 10/4036.
17 Bogason, Peter. *Søværnet under den kolde krig – politik, strategi og taktik*, 277. København: Snorres Forlag, 2015.

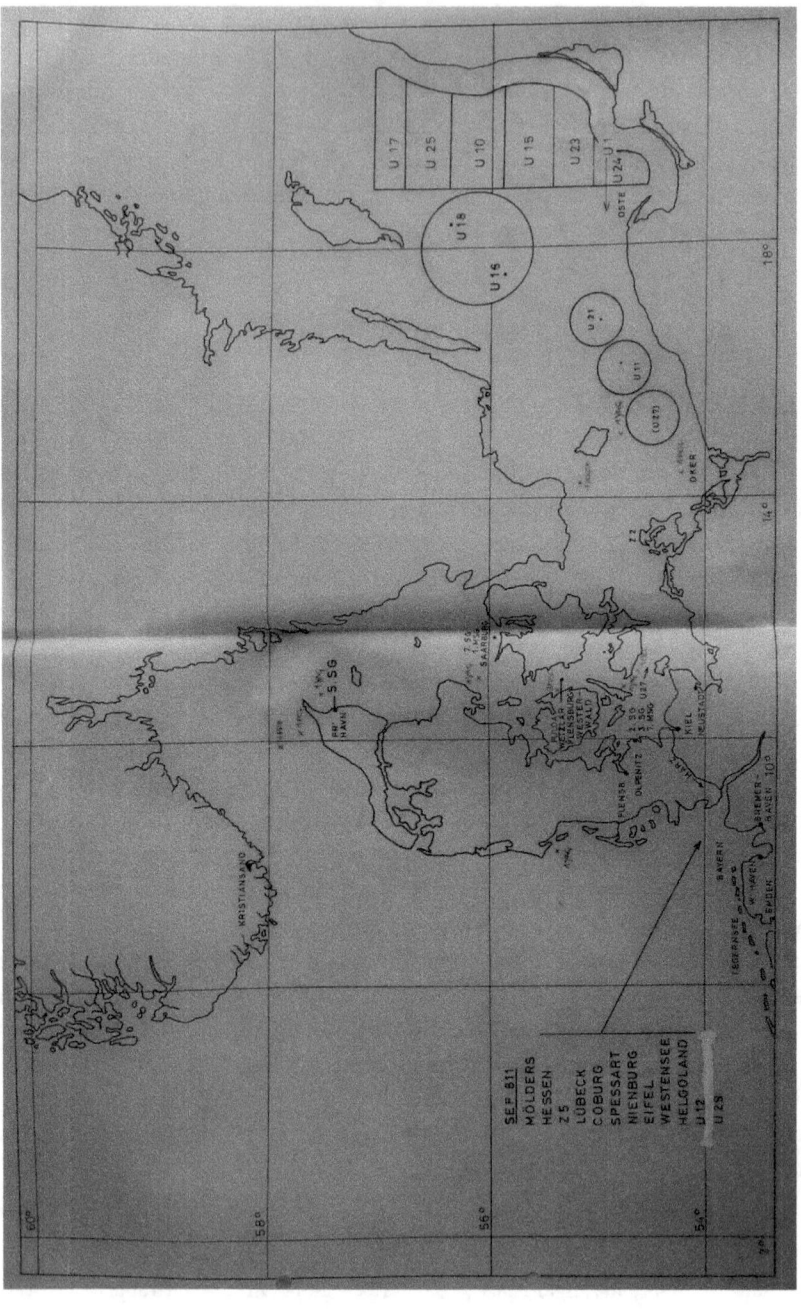

Figure 18.2: Deployment of the German navy in the Baltic Approaches 1981. Source: Bundeswehr Archiv Freiburg.

We shall go through the two naval groups' tasks within the Baltic and the Danish narrows in the 1980s. We include a common major plan for attacking an invasion fleet by both German and Danish forces. But first a brief discussion of the prerequisite for operating together: communication.

NATO and communication

The technological development of weapons has been possible because of the development of computing systems. Originally, the radar was "nice to have" in order to navigate under adverse conditions – darkness and foul weather. And it could be used to project collisions with other ships by giving data over time to a crew member at a plotting table. This was done by verbal communication and hand-drawn lines on the plotting table, but soon one found ways of transferring data electronically to a automatic system which created the desired projections.

From this simple instrument one can go on, creating computers that can treat large masses of data, creating complex images of ships and aircraft on the move, and based on this one can make guiding systems for weapons intended to target them. And as communication has developed, data from these guiding systems have been transferred by first cables (torpedoes and short range missiles) and since radio communication. Or think of guns that are trained in the right direction based on information about the target and its movements, but which also use information about wind speed and other factors of importance for the movement of the projectile from muzzle to target.

So, data creation, data manipulation and correct transfer of the resulting information with great speed are key in modern warfare. Unfortunately, the two navies pursued technological developments that served each navy well, but this did not promote tactical cooperation.

The Danes started out around 1970 with an electronic plotting system, CEPLO, based on a Swedish system for the SPICA torpedo boats.[18] The first version could track 12 targets, updating information every two minutes (later every 30 seconds). Three updates were necessary for a "guaranteed" plot. So it was slow, but miles ahead of the previous plotting by hand. The system was improved and made digital, a new version called CEPLO was installed in frigates and corvettes, and the FPBs became able to electronically draw on the larger systems. Renewal of target data now took place every five seconds. CEPLO could track 199 targets from its own sensors and in addition include 240 targets received from other units by the

---

18 Ibid., 231–35.

Danish-developed data link system. From 1986, the Danish navy was able to track all WAPA units in the Baltic, the Narrows and Kattegat in a system based on recognition of WAPA radars and other electronic systems, "electronic footprints", which the navy had collected over the previous 15 years and stored in a large database. Seven electronic tracking stations from Bornholm to the northern tip of Jutland collected data around the clock, creating a map of the positions of all WAPA and one's own units within reach. Those data could be included in the 240 external tracks in CEPLO, giving the units at sea an until then un-imaginable tactical picture of the operational areas. From 1987, an improved DEPLO-system integrated all data and weapon system on each unit.

The Danes, however, had turned down the idea of joining the NATO communication system, the LINK-11, because the NATO system was considered to be too expensive and, besides, they were developing their own more inexpensive system (as were the British and the Norwegians). In retrospect, this was not a wise decision if one wanted to enhance cooperation, because the Germans did use LINK-11. The system they used (LINK-14) only permitted exchange of raw data on teletypewriters.

The German systems were developed from the mid-1960s.[19] The first system – SATIR – was designed for the three TARTAR missile destroyers in a cooperation with the US Navy. It initially integrated a manual radar- and sonar process and used the LINK-11 data communication system. Furthermore, the German navy started the operations of an HQ that could integrate the systems-to-come in the command system of the navy. The navy developed the PALIS system to feed the LINK-11 communication system with the right data.

The 143 class FPBs got another weapon control system, AEGIS, which was designed to coordinate torpedo- and missile use, even if their operations were based on different fighting dispositions. AEGIS could take command of targeting five enemy units at a time. The system also integrated the operations of several units, using LINK-11 data transfer.

When the BREMEN-class frigates became operational in 1981, they got an improved, fullly automatic SATIR weapon system, integrated with the ships' sensors and data from other units.

---

19 Hess, Sigurd. "Als die Computer lernten zur See zu fahren – die Entwicklung von Führungs- und Waffeneinsatzsystemen in der deutschen Marine 1963 bis 1969." In *Die Bundesmarine 1950 bis 1972*, Johannes Berthold Sander-Nagashima, 433–45. München: Oldenbourg, 2006.

Figure 18.3: Fighting control system on Danish FPB WILLEMOES in 1988, manned by chief, first officer and two technicians. It was placed below deck. From left to right we see a surface plot, then a general overview plot. The third screen is used for an aerial overview or zooming in for torpedo targeting, and the last screen is a tactical system used for torpedo or HARPOON firing. The two screens to the right also were used for "blind navigation". Source: Forsvarsgalleriet.

Danish naval tactics

From 1965, the tactical foundation for the Danish navy was formulated in *Flag Officer Denmark's Naval Emergency Operating Instructions* (FOD NEMOI). It is still (2023) classified SECRET, but the formulations below have been authorised for the author of this book by the Danish Naval Staff in 2015,[20] and they mirror the orders of 1983.

---

20 Bogason, op. cit.

In times of tension the roles of the FOD were to establish recce by corvettes, FPBs and Seaward Defence Craft, prioritising Rügen, the Polish coast and, if feasible, the Hel Peninsula. Mine layers would take on board mines and deploy to waiting positions; defensive mining in national waters would be started when authorised. The navy would provide escorts for the mine layers and assist friendly vessels in passing the fields. Submarines were deployed to Bornholm, and from SIMPLE ALERT they would leave for their war stations.

When war was initiated, NATO would take command, and the submarines would come under the command of FOG in order to coordinate Danish and German submarine manoeuvres. During day NATO aircraft would neutralise enemy units in the Fehmarn Sound (before mine laying) as well as amphibious forces heading west and surface units (particularly those carrying missiles) and coastal missile batteries threatening NATO units.

Air recce was a NATO-issue. In a period of tension COMAIRBALTAP would in daylight do three fixed routine recce flights and three special flights after consultation with the Danish navy. By reinforced alert two air recce operations would be made as far as 17,40 degree east. They could be enhanced by special flights to harbours and concentrations of ships. After BALTAP had taken over command, the main source for recce and tactical support would be the German Naval Air Arm with COMAIRBALTAP's aircraft as a reserve. Airplanes from MARCONFORLANT or STRIKEFLEETATLANT might be able to give air support with the following priorities: to meet air operations, to hamper the enemy from moving forward and to support ground and sea operations directly.

Air defence was taken care of by four HAWK batteries around Copenhagen. Outside that area the Danish air force would defend the country by STARFIGHTERs in high and low altitude, and DRAKEN in low altitudes. If the air force had capacity, the navy could request air defence – also from the German Naval Air Arm with G-91 and STARFIGHTERs.

Mine fields. If war broke out, the Danish controlled mine fields should be ready at nine fixed places: Middelgrundsfortet, Dragørfortet, Mandehoved (Stevns), Hårbølle Batteri (Grønsund), Østerhuse (northern Langeland), Korsør, Frederikshavn, Rønne and Nexø. Non-controlled minefields of highest priority were two fields in the Sound, one field in each of the Bays of Faxe and Køge and at Western Lolland and one or two at Omø. Furthermore, there were anti-invasion mines in the Bays of Køge and Faxe, at Møn and along the coast of Falster. Minefields east of Grønsund, in Fehmarn Belt and in Fehmarn Sound would be laid by the Germans. Decisions about mine laying were to be taken by the government; the navy, however, made preparations at Counter Surprise Alert by taking mines on board and going to waiting positions; by Simple Alert controlled minefields would be laid, first at Drogden and Stevns, and uncontrolled mines would be laid at invasion beaches.

At Reinforced Alert defensive mining would be carried out in the Sound and Storebælt – and in Lillebælt and Kattegat, if deemed necessary.

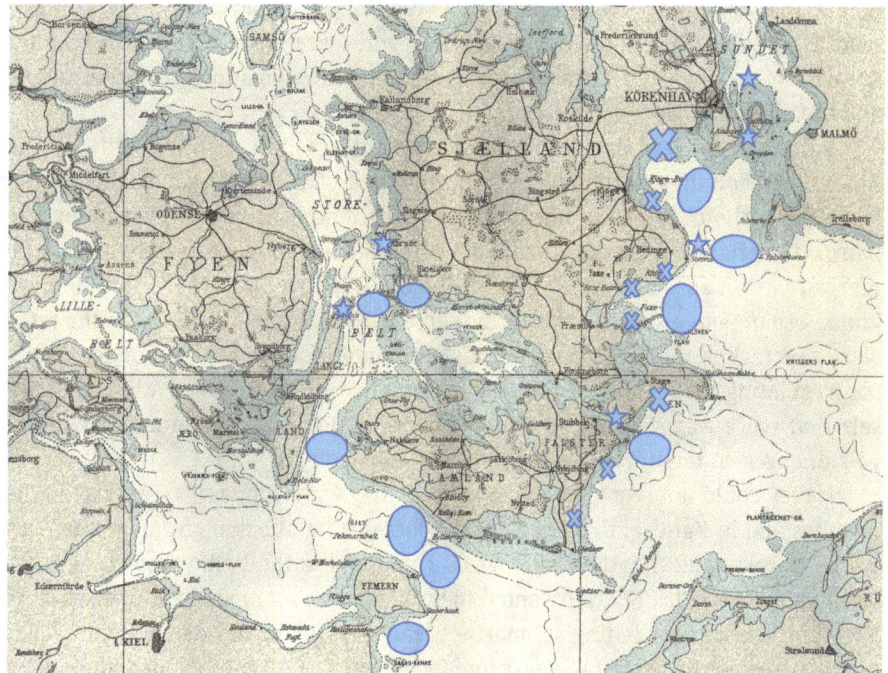

Figure 18.4: Mine fields around 1980. * indicates controlled field, x indicates anti-invasion field and bubble insicates non-controlled field. The fields at Fehmarn and Grønsund would be laid by German forces.

NATO cooperation. German fast, small mine layers and FPBs would carry out mine laying in the south as mentioned above. Larger units might be deployed to Kattegat for recce, to escort mine layers and to fight amphibious forces. Furthermore, they might carry out pre-planned operations against enemy bases and forces.

The immediate tasks for the Danish navy were:

Mine laying. The priorities of minefields were determined beforehand, but alternatives might be chosen, depending on the situation. Mine laying units were to be escorted by frigates, corvettes or FPBs, or covered by the forts on Langeland and Stevns. Escorts were also to prevent infiltration by civilian vessels – fishing boats, ships with motor stops etc.

The large mine layers would take mines on board in Køge, Helsingør and Korsør. One had to be in reserve status at Lyngsbæk Pier (Jutland). The two small mine layers would take mines on board at Skovshoved and Tuborg harbours (north of Copenhagen). The invasion-mine laying mine sweepers would get their mines in Køge. During day time the mine layers were to be deployed and hidden in other harbours, if possible; new moorings should be attempted every 12 hours. If "emergency mining" was necessary, it was to be done as close to the planned field as possible. The following areas, however, were absolutely out of bounds: Areanprth and south of Elsinore (reserved as waiting positions for other units), and the main Danish ferry routes.

Submarines were slated for offensive operations in the Central Baltic; during times of tension they would deploy to Bornholm, by Military Vigilance they would leave the harbour and go to Bornholm or to the mother ship to replenish for war patrol. They had to follow particular NATO-designed submarine safety lanes, submerged with a speed of five knots, if dived out a speed between eight and ten knots. Use of active sensors was forbidden until war broke out. By then the tasks were to attack amphibious forces, LOCs and larger was ships. The London protocol (regulating the legality of military targets) had to be observed. Merchant vessels that were escorted or flew the enemy war flag could be attacked without warning. WAPA territorial waters were not to be entered.

If they could not reach the Baltic in time, they were supposed to operate in the narrows and in Kattegat to prevent WAPA forces from attacking from Denmark towards Norway and the Atlantic. If NATO command in the Baltic proved not to be sustainable, or if CINCNORTH wanted them to operate somewhere else, there were NATO procedures for letting submarines leave the Baltic and deploy to an emergency mooring by Scotland under command of the East Atlantic commander.

Surface Action Group. The main Task Group had frigates, corvettes and FPBs and could be expanded by units from a German Task Force. It was supposed to escort mine laying units, and then protect the minefield and resist enemy amphibious forces targeting the Zealand islands.

Before war times the task was recce, and for that purpose one frigate or corvette was on patrol east of Møn; one division of FPBs would operate from Bornholm, and another from Køge. Three seaward defence craft were patrolling the waters north of Bornholm and east and west of Rügen, possibly supported by helicopters. All other units of the Task Group were in waiting positions in the Sound. MOBA OPS (land-based radar & control unit) was deployed to Møn, and MOBA LOG (repair & service) would be North of Copenhagen. A tanker and torpedo transporter would be at anchor north west of Helsingør.

In war times the tasks were recce, engaging enemies threatening mine laying and preventing mine sweeping. Small amphibious groups were to be fought immediately by aircraft; larger forces were not to be engaged until it was clear whether German naval and air forces would be able to join the group. Fighting amphibious forces was first priority, even if the risk was large. Other tasks were offensive operations and attacks on enemy LOCs east of Bornholm. If the enemy had landed, their LOCs were to be blocked and new minefields laid.

A special document, *Fighting Instructions* (by Commander of the Task Group), supplemented FOD NEMOI. The document stressed the need for offensive, ambitious and daring operations with a concentration of forces – not forgetting to spread them, when feasible.

Fighting Instructions had a map with particular coordinates, subdividing the area to make ordering and reporting easier. It indicated a number of reactions against enemy harassment before war times. It listed the frequencies for communication, had plans for changes in case of jamming and a series of codes for immediate information and/or ordering. It had procedures for cooperating with the Stevns battery and the adjacent HAWK-battery; formations for acting as air defence with SEA SPARROW for the mine layers; and tactical formations of the group when attacking invasion forces, including procedures for pinpointing high value targets.

The **Sea Districts** had many roles to perform in order to make the operations at sea possible. Below follows a summary of a large number of actions for the District of the Sound, covering waters of East Zealand and the Baltic. The main task was to support FODs operations in the area. One Seaward Defence Craft was to do recce along the coast of East Germany; all small craft were to be in local recce operations, possibly supported by a helicopter; and the mobile radar of the district was to be in operation at a convenient location. The Borgsted Battery in Grønsund, the stations for controlled mine fields and all coastal look-outs were to be manned. NCS – Naval Control of Shipping – was to be established in eight locations nationwide, all ships calling in ports were to be controlled and guard ships were to be operating at larger ports. Danish merchant vessels would require a permission with sailing route instructions. A number of depots and military key points were to be guarded, and preparations made for demolishing certain harbours and mine field stations.

German naval tactics

At a meeting among AFNORTH commanders late in the 1970s,[21] a German flag officer summed up the roles for the German navy in the 1980s. The tasks were different in three different theatres of war: East and west of Bornholm, and the North Sea.

---

21 Draft of note in BM 1/25112.

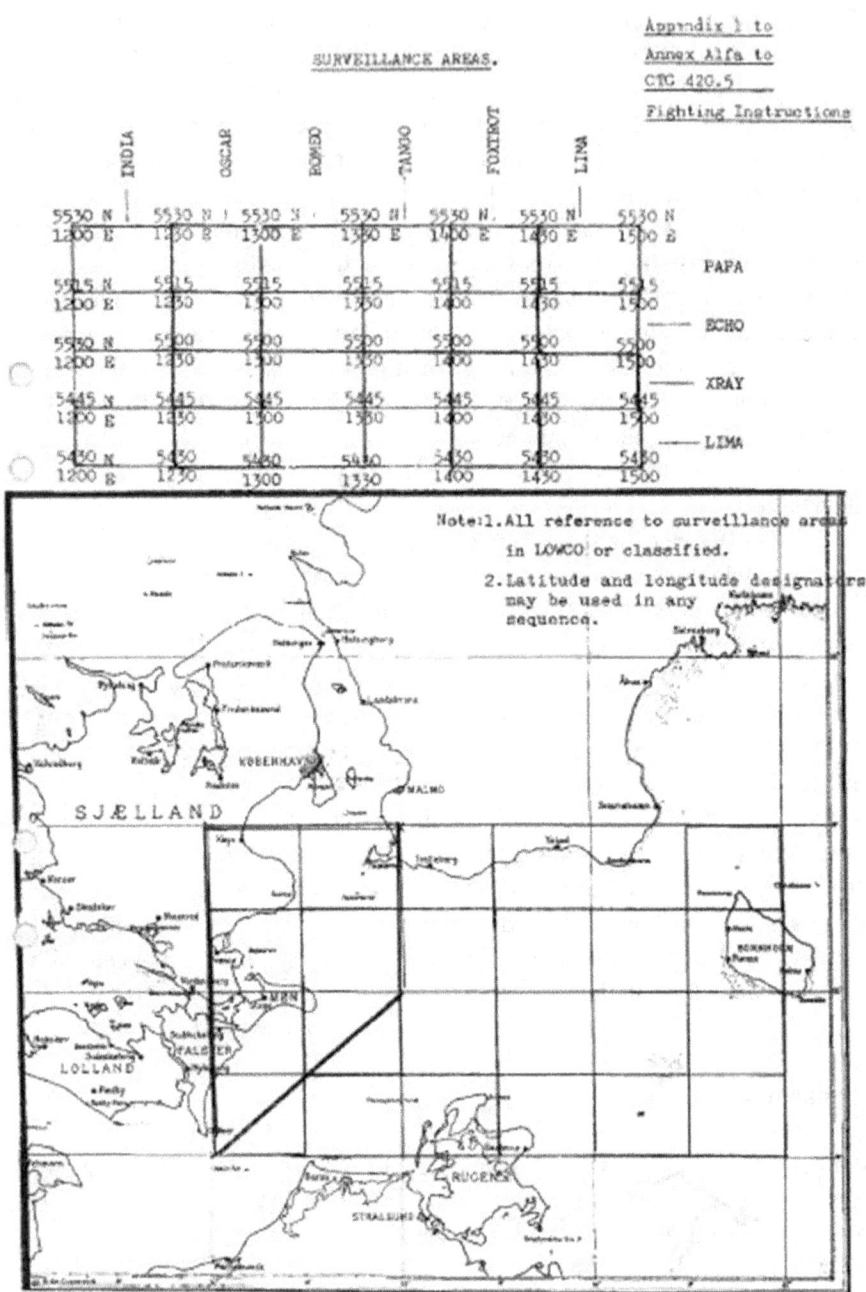

Figure 18.5: FOD Fighting instructions map of operation area.

East of Bornholm, only submarines and fighter bombers would have a reasonable chance of operating undetected (subs) and of penetrating WAPA defence. Therefore,
- 24 coastal (450 tons) submarines (type 205 and 206) had been designed specifically for shallow and confined water conditions. The 206 type subs were extremely quiet and practically unmagnetic. They were armed with wire guided torpedoes and could be fitted with a special belt for offensive mining.
- 72 fighter bombers – STARFIGHTER 104-G – were operating armed with a gun and missiles. They were to be replaced by TORNADO aircraft, armed with KORMORAN missiles in the early 1980s.

West of Bornholm, the main element of the naval concept in the Baltic was a capacity to lay out mines and an extremely flexible use of 40 FPBs with missiles, guns and (some of them) wire-guided torpedoes, in cooperation with STARFIGHTER (later TORNADO) fighter-bombers. The FPBs would initially be used for protecting the mine layers (21 fast mine sweepers and 18 inshore mine sweepers, capable of laying 900 mines simultaneously), and some of them were capable of laying mines themselves. Mining accomplished, they were to operate together with fighter bombers to attack enemy forces.

The fast mine sweepers were supposed to be retired in the 1980s and replaced by new ones with better gun protection. The mines were also up for replacement, but that was a long-term project.

In the *North Sea*, however, the navy aimed at performing a stronger role in the 1980s in order to assist in the defence of the main supply routes to West Europe from the USA and Britain. The German navy could provide forces to operate further north, strengthening NATO's forward defence concept. The navy was in the process of building eight large frigates (type 122, see below) with missiles and ASW-helicopters (LYNX) to replace old frigates and destroyers; the four German-built destroyers from the 1960s had been modernised with EXOCET missiles, and there were three missile TARTAR destroyers available. Furthermore, 12 ASW airplanes were operating, and the STARFIGHTERs – later the TORNADOS – could be assigned to operations in the North Sea. One could consider new, larger submarines. Twelve large mine sweepers would be modernised to mine hunters.

For the Baltic Approaches, the Germans had four levels of plans by 1985.[22] In general, they followed the trend of the 1970s with emphasis on defence rather than offense.

---

22 Jentzsch, Christian. "The Baltic and the Federal German Navy in the Final Stages of the Cold War." In *The Role of Territorial Defense Forces in Peace and War*, Zoltán Jobbágy Szeghy, Viktor Andaházi, Fredrik Erikson, and Peter A. Kiss, 101–18. Budapest: Hungarian Defence Forces Scientific Research Centre, 2020.

1. A massive WAPA attack supposed to precede an amphibious landing would be delayed and attacked with submarines and fighter-bombers as far east as possible. If they moved far enough to the west, they would also be met with minefields – in the Sound laid by the Danish navy, in the Fehmarn Sound and the Bay of Lübeck laid by the Germans. The missile FPBs boats would be held back so that they could attack the landing force supposed to follow. The submarines would remain in their patrol areas or were allowed to use chances on the transit to attack.
2. An amphibious assault force would be met by submarines in the east and defensive minefields as above. FPBs would deliver concentrated attacks west of Bornholm in cooperation with fighter-bombers. Such groups would also attack other kinds of WAPA warships.
3. If no massive attack was initiated, any WAPA units operating in the Baltic would be attacked by submarines, FPB groups with and without fighter-bombers and groups of fighter-bombers. The FPBs, however, were to avoid wear and tear on their crews by maintaining waiting positions in the Kiel Bay and the Danish straits and only attack in "favourable moments". The Naval Air Wing was to carry the brunt of the activities against WAPA units and supply chains.
4. If the Warsaw Pact reacted defensively by not attacking, NATO would resort to offensive mine laying by FPBs at enemy harbours and in enemy LOC routes west of Bornholm. Naval fighter-bombers and submarines would continue to be offensive. The goal would be to expand control beyond Mecklenburg Bay to the east. The Naval Air Arm was to attack enemy ships in harbours – air defence positions and port facilities would be destroyed by aircraft of the Bundesluftwaffe. FPBs could perform selected attacks at night, but only after careful consideration to avoid attrition.

In all cases, mine sweepers would be operating to protect their own LOCs, routes and harbours.

Of course, the plans had been made with the knowledge that the Danish navy would operate with some submarines east of Bornholm, with minefields in the Sound, and after laying mines the navy would start FPB attack groups, supported by frigates or corvettes.

Operation HURRICANE

The two navies had one meticulously common planned operation in case a major WAPA naval attack would take place: Operation HURRICANE. It was a coordinated missile attack; the Danes used HARPOON from its frigates, corvettes and

FPBs, the Germans EXOCET from FPBs and, if feasible, KORMORAN from the TORNADO aircraft. All missiles were in principle supposed to hit at the same time, creating a sort of shock in the enemy force because a large number of ships were struck within seconds, and the invasion force would lose its momentum.

The Danish MOBA OPS was planned to deliver the details of targets and the firing sequence: first HARPOON (longest distance), then EXOCET. Helicopters would assist in the target selection (this was the plan, but neither navy had the equipment to do it until after the Cold War). As soon as the missiles were fired, the participating FPBs would follow up with torpedoes and guns; at this time, many of the enemy's missile units had hopefully been hit and neutralised.

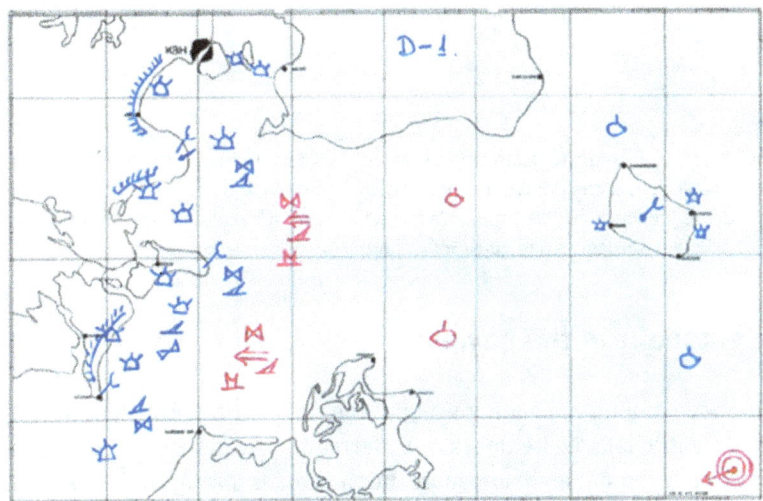

Figure 18.6: Before HURRICANE: Minefields and defending forces in front of them, enemy (red) forces investigating and raiding Danish defence of the minefields. The invasion fleet far to the east. NATO submarines doing recce at Bornholm. Source: http://www.danmarkidenkoldekrig.dk/.

An alternative to operation HURRICANE could be using tactical nuclear weapons; BALTAP had the SEP BARD BELL (E) plan, to be authorised by SACEUR. The attack would take place outside Danish territorial waters and hence not be restricted by the Danish nuclear policy. It was tested against amphibious units in September 1983 with units from US, USA, the NATO Airborne Early Warning system and the German Naval Arm, using STARFIGHTERs.[23]

---

23 Interview with SHAPE Historian Office May 3, 2022.

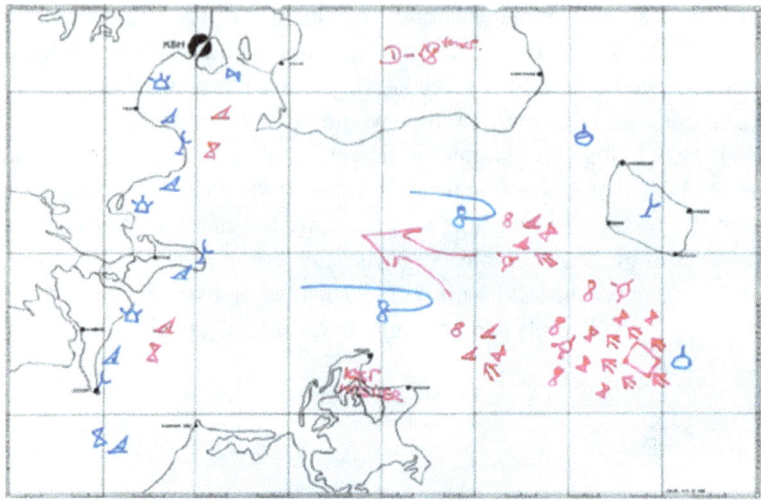

Figure 18.7: HURRICANE initiated after a WAPA invasion fleet has been formed with escorts and is closing in, but not at all close to the Danish landing beaches. Danish naval units are deployed close to the coast in order to fool incoming enemy missiles by creating coastal radar echoes. After missile release, NATO attacks with torpedoes and guns. Source: http://www.danmarkidenkoldekrig.dk/.

Replacement plans in the navies

As indicated above, military spending was not the first thing to consider among the majority of politicians in Denmark and Germany. Denmark had cut-backs, and Germany's navy did not grow any more, but it avoided strong cut-backs.

Denmark

The two frigates of the PEDER SKRAM class were several times targeted for scrap by the Social Democratic Party. The argument was that the frigates were vulnerable in the Baltic – a reasoning that was met with stiff resistance by the navy, but of course the argument had been "proved valid" valid in Germany as well as in Sweden. In the Baltic, both nations relied on FPBs armed with missiles (in cooperation with aircraft, though), and, as we have seen above, the Germans had followed the advice coming from several analyses and kept their destroyers and frigates for war operations in the North Sea. In 1988 the Danish frigates were taken off the naval list; the plan was to use their HARPOON missiles for mobile coastal batteries. PEDER SKRAM was not scrapped; today it is a museum ship in Copenhagen.

The coastal forts were maintained at a minimum level and would only become operational after mobilisation.

The DELFINEN class submarines were to be retired in the 1980s, and in the 1970s, the pros and cons of submarines had been debated in depth.[24] The critique was that a WAPA invasion would probably be started from harbours in East Germany, and since the submarines would have war stations east of Bornholm, they would not be able to attack the invasion fleet. Even if they were west of Bornholm, the waters there were not well suited for submarine operations. The pros were the usual ones: difficult to detect, excellent for recce and with new torpedoes and control systems they were even better to attack the enemy. Some politicians asked for alternatives, but they turned out to be more expensive, and the navy decided to buy three Norwegian, German-built submarines which entered service in 1989.

In the early 1980s the principles for an additional six FPBs were analysed to replace the six British-designed very fast FPBs of the SØLØVEN class from the early 1960s.[25] The hull, machinery and 76 mm gun of the WILLEMOES class was found satisfactory, but torpedoes could be supplanted by short-range missiles like the Norwegian PENGUIN, and a 35 mm gun for close defence was desirable. The electronic systems could be replaced by more modern ones. These ideas, however, became moot because the navy chose to follow a radical alternative (see below). The SØLØVEN class FPBs were sold in 1990.

In 1983, the Danish C-in-C of the navy sent a suggestion for a "Danish Navy 1994" to the ministry. The tasks for the navy were the same as before, but the navy wanted to emphasise some war tasks more: better forward recce with submarines, helicopters and data from offensive air operations, use of helicopters against smaller units, better electronic warfare, better defensive mine laying with larger controlled minefields (replacing uncontrolled ones), better protection of minefields using mobile HARPOON batteries and more efficient mine sweeping using mine hunters.

Therefore, the navy wanted to plan for a navy with these ships:
- six submarines for forward recce,
- six fast frigates or corvettes,
- 18 FPBs,
- four large and three small mine layers (plus certain state owned ships),
- four mine hunting groups (one hunter, one support ship),
- eight fighting helicopters,

---

24 Bogason, op. cit., pp. 255–58.
25 Borck, Niels Chr., and Søren Nørby. *Søheltenes Skibe. Historien om Søværnets torpedomissilbåde af Willemoes-klassen*, 245–47. København: Statens forsvarshistoriske museum, 2007.

- a couple of mobile HARPOON missile batteries,
- three stationary gun batteries (two in the Sound, one in Storebælt) plus local, simple gun positions for controlling larger harbours,
- nine Seaward Defence Craft,
- nine smaller patrol craft
- and in addition five large and five small patrol ships for Greenland and the Faroes plus various special ships.

The tally gave 20 units more than was available that year (1983) with an investment of 13 mia DKK. As no more than six mia would be available, the plan could not be fulfilled. The navy then came up with a plan of constructing a ship that might take different roles by getting different interchangeable weappn system based on containers: one with HARPOON missiles, one with SEA SPARROW missiles, one with torpedo launchers and one with mine hunter equipment: in all cases a 76 mm gun.

Thus the navy could in a few hours in the base harbour change the tasks of these ships – from missile attacks and torpedoes to mine hunting and mine laying. Sixteen such ships could replace 22 ships: three corvettes, one submarine, eight FPBs, nine Seaward Defence Craft and one small mine layer. The speed would be lower than FPBs, but the armament stronger.

The concept was approved with first seven and later 14 units. The first ship was launched in 1989, and since the ships did not become operational in the Cold War, we shall not go into detail with them. A discussion is found in Bogason.[26]

Germany

As foreseen in the 1970s, focus on the new ships in Germany in the 1980s was on replacing old destroyers and frigates for operations in the North Sea and beyond. Ships in the Baltic were, by and large, the same, but the Naval Air Arm got a strong boost from the multi-purpose fighter-bomber TORNADO. But the improvements were decided in the processes of very tight budgeting, making strict prioritising a must.[27] Thus frigates were reduced from 12 to eight, modernisation of old (206) submarines and a series of new submarines had to be postponed, new fast mine layers also were postponed and new potent PUMA helicopters were replaced by cheaper LYNX helicopters.

---

26 Bogason, op. cit.
27 The budgeting papers in BM 1/5213 discuss various alternative, summarised below.

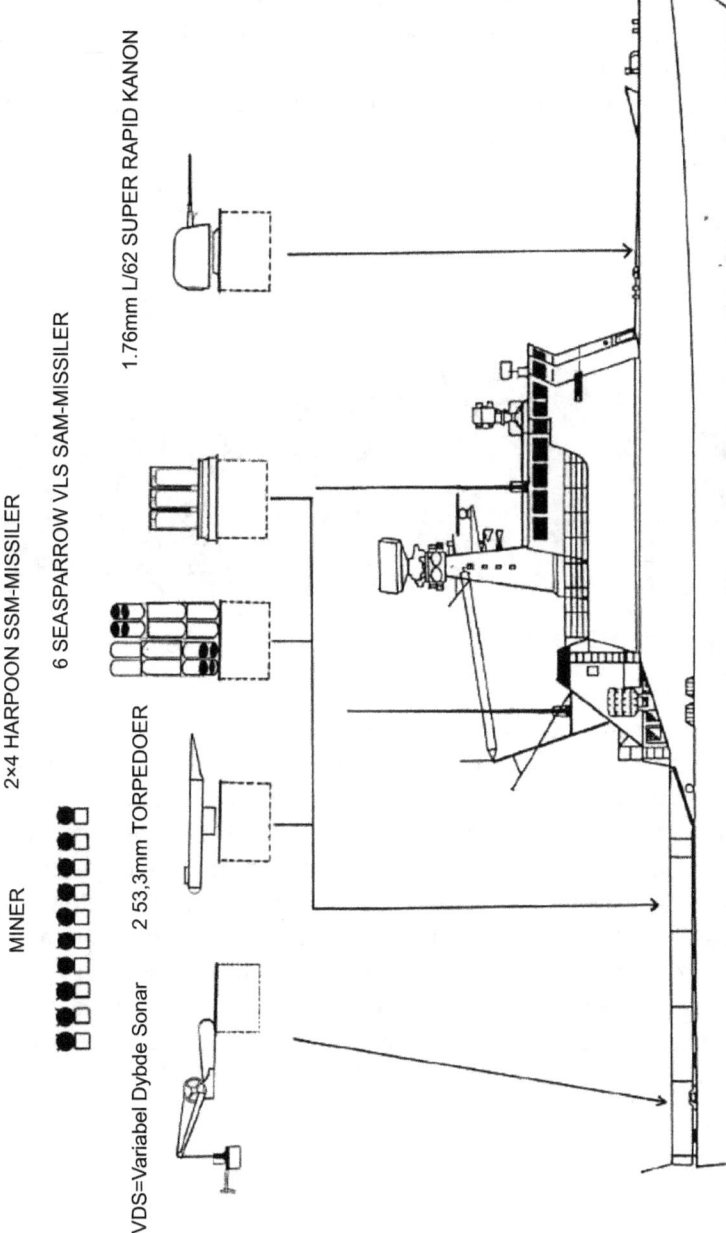

Figure 18.8: STANDARD FLEX 300 hull with alternate containers. From stem to stern: 76 mm gun, 6 SEA SPARROW, 2x4 HARPOON, two torpedo tubes, mines and a variable depth sonar. 450 tons, 30 knots. Source: Rigsarkivet.

Frigates

By 1987, the German navy shelved the project for a new, large (type 211) submarine, and replacements for the 205 subs were not built until after the cold war. So the main extra contribution to the Northern waters became the BREMEN-class frigate with eight units, able to serve all the way from the Norwegian Sea to Kattegat, if necessary. They were developed in a cooperation between Germany and the Netherlands

Figure 18.9: Frigate NIEDERSACHSEN of the BREMEN-class. Length 130 m, 3680 tons, 30 knots, one 76 mm, SSM, SAM, ASW torpedoes, two helicopters. Source: Forsvarsgalleriet.

Due to the budgetary cuts the navy did not plan any replacements until about 1980. Therefore, there was ample time to prepare the building process. By 1974 a study group had completed the work on the tactical demands and the C-in-C of the navy approved the document.[28] The essence of the demands to the frigate was that it must be multi-purpose – i.e. fight surface ships, defend itself against aircraft/missile, and fight submarines; the last task would be its main role. It had to carry guns, missiles (SSM and SAM) and ASW torpedoes. Furthermore, it had to carry helicopters on board for ASW and relayed fire direction purposes; it had be able to operate in the North Sea under all weather conditions for three weeks without replenishment (except oil); it had be able to run 30–32 knots continuously. The ship had to have top modern electronic equipment and be able to per-

---

[28] Inspekteur der Marine: Taktische Forderung Fregatte F 122. Vertraulich. Az 09-01-00-01. TgbNr 20/74. 03-01-74. BM 1/12333.

form all roles in cooperation with German and NATO units. The helicopter had to be able to detect and fight submarines and detect and relay information about surface craft. It had to have a speed of 130 knots and be able to operate for two hours.

The project was presented to a Bundestag Committee in December 1976,[29] specifying that the helicopters were to be SEA LYNX with ASW torpedoes. The capabilities of the frigate for air and sea defence with an integrated fire control system were also detailed. The Frigate followed a number of NATO standards which would save money over time.

The capabilities of the frigate were illustrated for the politicians with overheads, with excerpts following below.

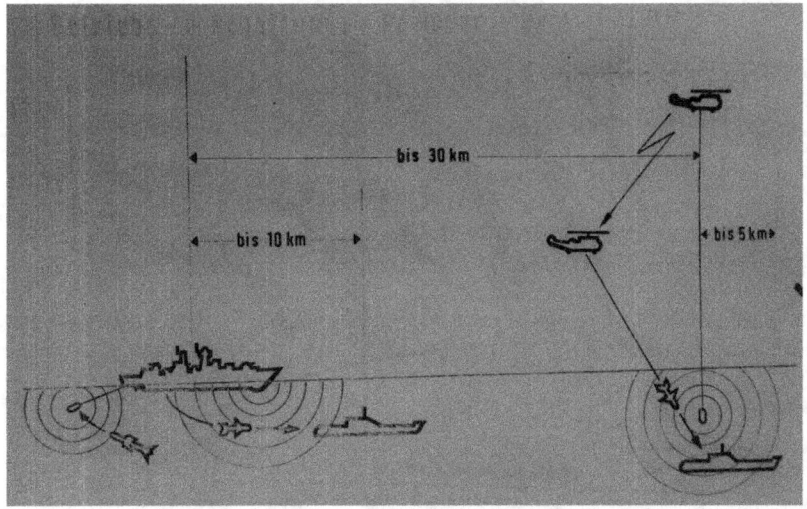

Figure 18.10: Illustration for the politicians: fighting submarines with frigate or helicopter. The frigate tows a decoy to fool torpedoes from the submarine. Source: Bundeswehr Archiv.

Twelve ships and 24 helicopters would be desirable, starting operations in 1979, but as time went by the military budget only permitted eight ships and 16 helicopters; the first ship was ready for operations by 1982.

---

29 Fü M VII 7/SBWS: Das Beschaffungsvorhaben FREGATTE 122. Vertraulich. BM 1/8704.

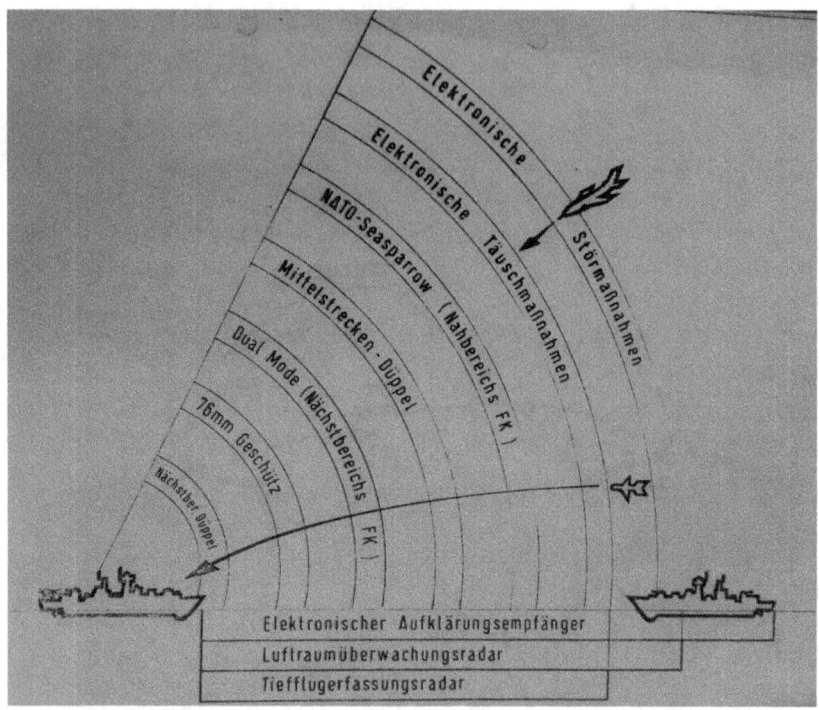

Figure 18.11: Illustration for the politicians: fighting aircraft and missiles – sequence from the right: electronic jamming, electronic fooling; SEA SPARROW missile, chaff, close range missile, 76 mm gun, and chaff. Source: Bundeswehr Archiv.

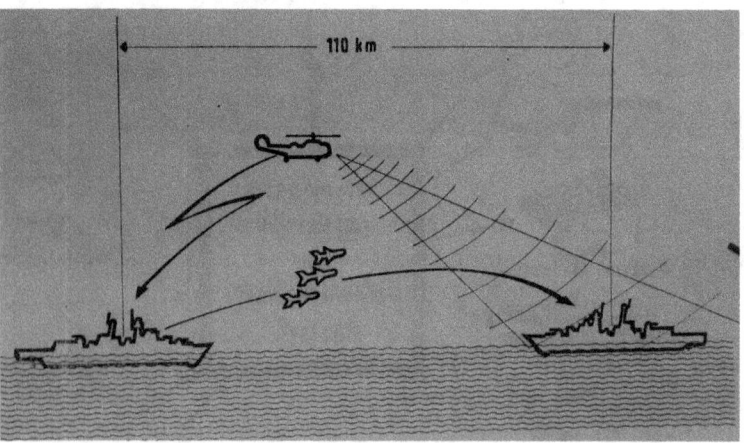

Figure 18.12: Illustration for the politicians: Fighting surface craft with missiles. Helicopter relays radar and control system. Source: Bundeswehr Archiv.

FPBs

The last ten new FPBs, class 143A GEPARD, were incorporated from 1982. The tactics of the FPBs developed step by step.[30] The point of departure for the Bundesmarine in 1956 had been WWII experiences, and they were nearly unchanged by 1970 because the boats had been built for such tactical behaviour. But the changes in technology meant all. First of all, the fighting command system of all class 143 was linked to the other FPBs by NATO's Link 11 system so that other boats could take over e.g. the directing of a missile. Furthermore, it was lightening fast. In the old systems of the frigates and destroyers, the time from detecting an aircraft to having a lock-on was 80 seconds in the German-built ships and 46 seconds in the LÜTJENS-TARTAR class; in Class 143 it took seven seconds. But such systems took time to learn – not so much the technicalities as the principles of tactics. For instance, the German navy had in its own understanding been the best on earth in gunnery zeroing in on the enemy since the Battle of Jutland (1916). This was done by following a special procedure of two short salvos plus, if necessary, a check-salvo. But the new electronic directing system only needed one salvo, then it would correct the gun(s) to hit. But the German School of Artillery maintained the old principles for a long time after.

When operating towards an identified enemy, a new tactics was to operate "at random dynamic". Instead of the traditional high-speed "gung-ho" attack in close formation, the FPBs would operate at low speed, in spread formation, in order to make it difficult for the enemy at a distance to distinguish the FPBs from other vessels. Speed would, of course, be used when the attack was imminent.

As the FPBs grew older in the 1980s, and as the fast mine layers also grew older, it was discussed whether a new, fast and larger *Kampfboot* (a sort of 750-ton corvette) could replace both types, having the capacity for mines and adequate missiles for one's own protection.[31] But the solution was found in the 1990s, so it is outside the scope of this book.

The Naval Air Arm

The German navy had two squadrons with fighter-bombers (Price 1986, 140–147). In the 1980s, the STARFIGHTERs were replaced by the TORNADOs with a two-man

---

30 Brinkmann, Rainer, ed. *Die Ära der Schnellboote*, 34–38. Rostock: Marinekommando, 2020.
31 Fü M VI 1/2/4: Zielvorstellungen Überwasserkriegsführung BALTAP. GEHEIM. TgbNr 199/89. 14-2-89. BM 1/13624c.

crew and armed with the KORMORAN sea target missile which had many features that had been repeated in the EXOCET missile. The KORMORAN was most efficient in the open sea; operating closer to land its homing radar might get confused by land echoes. Therefore, convoys would probably operate close to land for as long a time as possible.

A KORMORAN missile could not sink a large target, but it could make it inoperable, especially by destroying its electronic systems. Thus it might be a "sitting duck" for subsequent attacks with cheap, dumb bombs.

A typical attack group would have six TORNADOS. At night they would close in on the target individually, in daylight they would operate as a group to protect one another and attack escorting fighters with their anti-air missiles. Approaching a convoy, the TORNADOs would split the formation, dive and take individual attack positions in 30–60 meters altitude, based on a specific procedure. This was to saturate and thus block the radar systems of the enemy. The aircraft would stay at a distance of ten miles, if possible to avoid sea-to-air missiles.

Another attack formation would have five TORNADOS, three for attacking, two for escort.[32] The further to the east the operation took place, the higher the risk of WAPA airplanes defending the area. But as long as the satellite systems were not better developed, there was a need for recce operations in the Eastern Baltic because the German submarines only had a limited horizon for observation.

If the air group cooperated with FPBs, the air attack would come first, and then FPBs could yield more precise attacks on the remaining ships with missiles and guns.

Mine sweepers

Technology had made the old ways of sweeping mines moot; mine hunters were now better able to operate with success. They used sonar for detection and divers for neutralising the mines. This was slower than traditional sweeping, but much more efficient. The equipment, however, was very expensive, so only a few mine hunters could be built. Ten new mine sweepers (class 343) were built to replace ten of the old SCHÜTZE class; the first joined the navy in 1989. The Germans planned ten mine hunters (class 332) to be built in the 1990s.

---

32 See previous note.

Figure 18.13: TORNADO aircraft with KORMORAN missiles. Source: Forsvarsgalleriet.

WAPA Tactics

In the 1980s, the WAPA threat in general was reduced, especially after 1985 when the economic stress from military expenses became an issue, and Gorbachev took over the leadership. Still, the NATO partners could do nothing but continue to analyse the threat pattern and get better knowledge about the WAPA tactics.

Units in the Baltic

In 1988 the balance between NATO and WAPA in the Baltic was the following – the figures in brackets are German units which would primarily operate in the North Sea:

The airplanes were those under the command of the navies. From the airforces one might tally 400–550 from the WAPA and 170 from NATO, but they probably would have other tasks to see to.[33]

---

33 Ibid., Bilag 3:50.

Table 18.1: WAPA and NATO Order of Battle 1988.

	WAPA	NATO
Cruisers	5	
Destroyers	9	(7)
Frigates	14	2 (11)
Corvettes	70	8
Torpedo/Missile FPBs	75	56
Strategic missile submarines	4	
Missile submarines	3	
Other submarines	42	29
Mine layers		12
Mine sweepers	195	60
Large amphibious craft	60	
Small amphibious craft	40	22
Various smaller vessels	210	60
Fighter-bombers	75	62
Recce aircraft	19	20
ASW helicopters	70	14[34]

Those were the numbers: the WAPA had more units, more missiles and good logistics with large depots, but many units was relatively old, causing weaknesses due to technical features, lack of renewal and poor training, such as in practical seamanship. The real capacity for mine laying was low, the ASW systems were inadequate, the air defence was lacking, the mine sweeping gear was outdated and the centralised system of command rendered little room to adapt to the tactical situation at sea.

These comments may be seen as a first harbinger of the breakdown of the European communist systems. The economy could not sustain the military build-up, and NATO was getting a technological lead. NATO's airplanes were better, and increasing in number.

NATO had quite good information about the tactics of the WAPA navies. A few examples follow from an analysis of the WAPA threat against the Danish missile armed units.[35]

Missile attacks with FPBs were typically executed in pairs. Two pairs could initiate an attack with a distance between the groups of one to five miles. They had to reduce speed to 10–15 knots when launching missiles, at a distance of 8–12

---

[34] Forsvarsministeriet. *Beretning fra Forsvarskommissionen af 1988*, Bilag 3:43–44. København: Forsvarsministeriet, 1989.
[35] Forsvarets Efterretningstjeneste. HEM Truslen mod Søværnets HARPOON-bærende enheder, 1331/84, 11-10-84.

miles, preferably crossing the course of the target. Joint attacks with torpedoes and missiles had been seen with two to four groups. After recce by a couple of torpedo FPBs they would attack from the same side, the torpedo FPBs closer to the target so that they might be overflown by the missiles. There would be 10–15 minutes between the firing of torpedoes and the missiles. Polish attacks by aircraft had also been seen, but apparently no coordination took place. Soviet FPBs had been seen directing aircraft attacks, but apparently not coordinated with missile attacks. In general, the teamwork between ships and aircraft did not appear to function well in the WAPA. Missile corvettes had been seen working with helicopters distributing chaff; the corvettes then fired their missiles while positioned in the chaff cloud.

WAPA FPB tactics

On the German Internet-debate forum *Forum-marinearchiv* in 2013 there was a discussion among earlier crew members of FPBs from the WAPA as well as NATO about FPB tactics during the Cold War. The Pseudonym *2M3* from the *Volksmarine* wrote as follows:[36]

> We attacked from several angles and our salvoes always depended on the target. Against single units one fired 4–6 missiles against cruisers and missile destroyers, 2–4 against destroyers and frigates, transport vessels etc., and against FPBs 2 missiles. The missiles in the salvo would have different search systems; a TARANTUL FPB would have at least one missile (out of 4) with [an] infra red search head. The distance for firing would depend on the range of the radar and the size of the target: a light cruiser 20 miles, a destroyers 16, a mine sweeper 11, a FPB 8. In the *Volksmarine* we would prefer to use the sensors of other ships or coastal installations to get better coverage.

Urs Hessling (Bundesmarine) commented (partly due to a misunderstanding):[37]

> If the tactics was sending all four missiles from a FPB against a FPB and larger, then we West Germans had a problem because we counted on your firing two at a time; if you fired four, a class 142 FPB did not have enough counter measures. Furthermore, NATO thought that a STYX homing radar would start about 10 miles from the target, but it turned out that the radar did not start until at a short range from the target, so the time for us to shoot down the missile was correspondingly short.

The pseudonym Der Erste (*Volksmarine*) went on commenting:[38]

---

36 2M3. *Wie war die Situation Warschauer Pakt-Nato im Hinblick auf die Ostseeausgänge?* http://www.forum-marinearchiv.de/smf/index.php/topic,19302, 2013a.
37 Hessling, Urs. *Wie war die Situation Warschauer Pakt-Nato im Hinblick auf die Ostseeausgänge?* http://www.forum-marinearchiv.de/smf/index.php/topic,19302, 2013a.
38 Der Erste. *Wie war die Situation Warschauer Pakt-Nato im Hinblick auf die Ostseeausgänge?* http://www.forum-marinearchiv.de/smf/index.php/topic,19302, 2013a.

In Baltysk we have had exercises trying to shoot down a STYX, and we never succeeded with A-A guns. It was very robust. If you hit it, it was disturbed a little, but then went back on course and flew on. So imagine a situation where the enemy does not know from where and at what speed it is coming – and how many. The STYX had chaff to fool the radar of the NATO units, and when they were on target, they went head-on.

He also wrote that the use of relayed radar was not successful until the TARANTUL corvettes were ready; they also had an excellent firing direction system, HARPUN.

Helicopters had been used by the East German navy with thread guided anti-armour missiles. It was not clear whether they could be used against ships, but East German journals had reported them operating together with FPBs. They could not operate in darkness and bad sight. When attacking targets on land, four helicopters would approach in 15 metres' altitude with 500 meters distance between them; guided missiles would be fired at a distance of 3,000 metres, then they rose to 50 metres' altitude to control the missile for about 20 seconds, and then the next helicopter would attack.

Fighter-bombers mostly attacked two at a time, preferably from aft (note that the Danish corvettes of the NIELS JUEL-class could not fire their aft 76 mm gun); they would approach in an altitude of 300–1,500 meters, then dive 5–10 degrees until an altitude of 100 meters, a speed of 6–900 kilometres. Unguided missiles were launched at a distance about 2,300 meters while diving 15–20 degrees, and then terminated in 700 metres' altitude.

Exercises

Exercises were held the year round in the 1980s. Exercise reports, however, are difficult to find, probably because of confidentiality issues. We shall only quote one document from WINTEX 1981.

The WINTEX exercises were held every two years in a command post version involving all levels of government. They reflected the Flexible Response concept and tested the cooperation among military staffs, civil defence units and rescue services at the local level. The exercises built up increasingly challenging events in a process lasting about ten days and ranging from crisis to war: cases spanning from getting replenishment in a non-military harbour to atomic attacks on large cities. The main players were civil servants in various ministries (some playing roles as ministers) and military staff officers. The game schedules were written by NATO officers.

WINTEX 1981 was to take place in the spring, and below we take out the planned activities involving the navy in Germany[39] in two selected days, one early, one late in the process, to illustrate what the themes were like and hence get an idea of what NATO feared might happen in a time of tension and in wartime.

The general background was a general economic crisis and lack of oil in the West. The Soviets try to get more influence in the third world and the Middle East, and follow up their success by trying to influence some member states of NATO: Denmark should give up the control of warships passing the straits, Norway should forbid British and Dutch exercises and Iceland should throw out the Americans from the Keflavik base. More and more WAPA exercises took place close to NATO members, and the LOCs from USA to Europe appeared threatened. As time went by, more forces were congregated in harbours with amphibious capacities, and air and navy patrols got closer to NATO territory.

We start out a more detailed report for day 5 of the exercise, 14 March 1981. The WAPA exercises ended two days previous, but the WAPA military alert level was very high, and alarm procedures were tested. WAPA recce activity was high, with lots of electronic activity with frequent changes of channel. Ten submarines were on patrol in the North Sea. In the Western Baltic, several FPB patrol groups operated, and 21 mine sweepers were west-bound. About ten merchant ships had passed the straits northbound. More and more RO/RO vessels were gathering in East German harbours together with amphibious craft. Three destroyers and one cruiser were operating west of Bornholm.

Within the West German military, it was now obvious that quite a few of the reserve soldiers had not followed the call-up order, and various defence units were therefore not able to operate properly. There were political actions in various units. At sea, several German submarines had reported WAPA ASW units on the hunt, so it was more and more difficult to use the snorkel.

Specifics:

00.30 A group of WAPA mine layers had been spotted east of Rügen.

01.55 Three merchant vessels in line ahead formation with equal distance, 12 knots, observed.

03.00 The number of RO/RO ships in Swinemünde (reported yesterday) was increasing.

07.45 Orange recce aircraft (BEAR) observed over the North Sea.

---

[39] BM 10/4036 contains the parts the navy was involved in, and the examples are taken from there.

08.00 Police in Flensburg reported that an informer has heard a radio amateur speaking thie strange message: "Everybody should come to KORINTH; ARES will bring ice cream, but where is IKARUS?"

08.35 Orange recce aircraft (BACKFIRE) observed over Western Baltic.

09.00 A radio set working on the frequency equal to the abovementioned was captured by the police.

10.00 NATO's LINK-11 radio system was disturbed in the Fehmarn area.

10.05 All HF radios ship-shore were jammed (lasted eight hours, disturbing many important calls by radio).

10.30 Forty per cent of the civilian crews on supply ships in First and Second Supply Flotillas refused to muster. They initiated a work-to-rule action, hurting the replenishment of oil.

11.08 The radio amateur above is reported for this comment: "The ice cream is ready – where is IKAROS?"

11.15 Large number of amphibious craft gathered in Gdansk.

13.00 Recce ship ALSTER reporting: asked to stop. Surrounded by Orange units. Situation threatening. Am destroying all secret material.

13.15 ALSTER not responding to radio calls.

15.10 Tender LAHN reported all oil emulsified. Unusable.

16.20 Destroyer Z1 reported firing director fall-out. Sender defect.

16.25 FPB reports radio sender 100W fall-out. Needed exchange.

23.45 Antenna mast blown up, but not totally destroyed. More guards. Ready for service in two days.

On day 10, 19 March 1981, war had started. There were many air attacks in Schleswig-Holstein and the Danish isles, and the straits had probably been mined by aircraft. In Skagerrak, the earlier reported an attach group with destroyers and one cruiser had escorted 14 merchant vessels towards the Norwegian coast. Mine sweeper groups were operating in several areas in the Baltic. In Gdansk, an amphibious group with nine amphibious craft, five FPBs and one frigate appeared to take troops on board. West of Bornholm, the attack group was now formed by one cruiser, two destroyers, one frigate, two OSA FPBs and one mother ship.

Orange forces had used chemical weapons, and the mood among many NATO soldiers was terse. There was a high number of casualties, with many losses among pilots and ground personnel and many losses in the navy, particularly in the Baltic. Civilians increasingly tried to block their own forces. The unknown destiny of families in the areas, taken by the enemy, worried many soldiers.

Specifics:

02.35 Four fires set off on frigate ROMMEL. The fires were put out in time. Cans with petrol and petrol-soaked laps point to arson.

04.30 In Bay of Faxe 35 amphibious craft, three frigates and three FPBs were reported approaching the coast.
07.00 Ten RO-RO vessels were reported taking forces on board in Swinoujscie.
08.00 Air attacks on Eggebek and Schleswig. Runways destroyed, not usable for two to three days.
08.05 Destroyer HAMBURG called at NATO depot Amoy in Norway to get rest time for the crew. Supplies necessary. Repaired using local workers.
11.30 Supply ship SAARBURG sunk, hit by mine. 73 survivors, 13 injured.
12.20 Destroyer Z4 hit by missile, foremost gun destroyed. Firing director destroyed.
13.05 Destroyer BAYERN reported search radar had fallen out. Munition elevator for foremost gun had fallen out, gun unusable.
13.50 Several returning F-104G had malfunctions in hydraulic systems and computer systems.
14.35 Heavy Orange air attacks had hit the fire brigades and their equipment so much that they were incapable of full service.
17.00 Ten RO/RO vessels reported in Bay of Faxe.
19.18 WAPA paratroopers landed at Flensburg. Must consider to move the naval HQ.

The above incidents were triggers for increasingly serious action; the landing of WAPA paratroopers probably meant that the naval HQ had to be transferred to Karup. And forces were landing on Zealand.

What was actually done is not part of these papers, they are just determining the sequence and contents of incidents, giving us a quite clear picture of what NATO feared would be attempted by the WAPA forces, and what consequences the various authorities – in this case in Germany – had to suffer.

The army forces on Zealand

The WINTEX exercise reported above had amphibious landings as part of the WAPA operations. We saw earlier in this chapter what the navies were supposed to do. In chapter 17 the phases of an amphibious WAPA attack around 1970 were spelled out. In the 1980s the processes were probably about the same, but what would the army forces defending the territory do? We shall briefly review the army's defence plans for the Danish Zealand islands according to a document from 1984.[40]

The general aim of the plan was to stop the enemy's first amphibious landing with relatively light equipment so that a second (follow-up) landing, reinforcing the battalions with tanks etc., was illusory. A dilemma in distributing the NATO forces was that one could expect a paratrooper landing

---

40 Rasmussen, Peter Hertel. "Det landmilitære forsvar af den sjællandske øgruppe og Bornholm under den kolde krigs sidste årtier (1979–1989). Del 2: Perioden fra 1980 til og med 1989." *Fra Krig og Fred* (2023): 55–95.

inland first, and shortly after a sea landing. How were the defending forces to be distributed between these two enemy forces?

The plan operated with three situations: a "coup" defence with no prior warning, a defence with a warning of a few days and a fully mobilised defence (one week or so). All plans aimed to counter and fight amphibious forces from air and sea, prioritising the latter which were to be met as early as possible; certain beaches in the east and south east of Zealand were the most likely ones according to the plan.

The forces to meet a surprise attack were those available in the peace formation of the army. A surprise attack was thought to have paratroopers as the main element, but probably combined with sea landings. The peacetime forces were to counter the attack(s) and make possible the required mobilisation of Danish forces.

An attack a couple of days after D-day (most likely in Central Europe) would make mobilisation of the first reserve possible, and the mobilised forces were to attack all types of landing and destroy them. Meanwhile the home guard and other defence units would be mobilised.

An attack one week after D-day would be met by the fully mobilised Danish defence on the islands; it had two mobile brigades which would divide the Zealand island between them; in addition there would be local forces in four groups available (one of them for the islands south of Zealand), plus the home guard. The four groups which had light artillery and some tanks were to initiate the counterattacks on sea landings within their area immediately; one of the main brigade forces would then deploy to the area and fight the enemy. The main artillery of the defence was deployed to an area from where they could quickly come to the assistance of a brigade fighting an amphibious attack.

After 1984 the Danish defence had cut-backs and the command of Zealand noted that the peace standing force had a size that made immediate counterattack illusory. Some of the equipment was worn out, and many vehicles had to be scrapped. Consequently, mobilisation had to be initiated in time, and reinforcements were crucial. The UK Mobile Force with 15,000 men was first in line with three infantry battalions, an armoured recce regiment, an artillery regiment and an engineering regiment. Five helicopters were part of the force.

The British, however, increasingly had scruples to deploying the corps, because "reinforcement presupposes that there is something to reinforce". This statement was meaningful in the sense that the British had alternative options for using the corps outside Denmark.

WAPA use of nuclear warheads?

The declassified archive material dealing with the use of nuclear weapons is scarce, and most of the other types of documents analyse the WAPA without the use of nuclear warheads. So we shall only quote a few secondary sources analysing the issue.

The Soviet plans for war were based on the premise that a war would be started by NATO.[41] But any time such an attack was foreseen, the Soviet forces

---

41 Nielsen, Harald. *Die DDR und die Kernwaffen – Die nukleare Rolle der National Volksarmee im Warschauer Pakt*, 21–22. Baden-Baden: Nomos Verlagsgesellschaft, 1998.

might act to prevent such aggression. If the Soviets were to wage war, the general tactics – to attack NATO territory rather than defend one's own territory – was based on conventional weapons as long as possible because the military strength of the WAPA lay in conventional, not nuclear weaponry. But if NATO started atomic warfare, the Soviet response would be comprehensive. NATO's Flexible Response strategy had no Soviet counterpart; any nuclear attack by NATO would trigger a massive nuclear response at least until the beginning of the 1980s. Such a response would mean that over one and a half hour, up to nine Megatons would be released against NATO forces in Western Europe in a depth of about 300 kilometres.

Nielsen, contrary to some other authors and to NATO strategic positions, has not found any indication that the WAPA might have attacked NATO out of the blue; any attack would have been triggered by NATO actions (or build-up).[42] From the mid-1980s the attack strategy turned into a more defensive posture on one's own territory and to re-establish a *status quo ante*. Furthermore, several of the exercises within WAPA did no longer entail a nuclear phase and the conventional phase of fighting was prolonged; this may have been an indication of a change of military strategic perspective.[43]

The Soviets declared in 1977 and again in 1982 that they would not be first users of nuclear warheads and it appears that after 1982 the Soviets did open up for a sort of flexible response by controlled escalation and selective strikes.[44] It should be clear, however, that the Soviet military understanding of no first use was so that they were "allowed" to fire nuclear warheads the minute it became clear that NATO was preparing to launch such weapons. The Soviet release, then, was to be interpreted as a preemptive strike in the face of the authorized, but not yet launched, NATO nuclear initiative.

Many analysts have stated that there was no such thing as a limited Soviet nuclear response. But in the WAPA war plans of late 1970s and 1980s Heuser found that the military operated with limited nuclear exchanges, and there appeared to be a hope that follow-on exchanges might be avoidable.[45] Such a first WAPA strike would consist of two consecutive salvos aimed primarily at NATO nuclear command centres and firing stations. The first would be launched when it had become clear that NATO was in a preparation process of striking and that a command of release had been given. The second strike would come some hours

---

42 Ibid., 29–30.
43 Ibid., 22.
44 Heuser, Beatrice. "Warsaw Pact Military Doctrines in the 1970s and 1980s: Findings in the East German Archives." *Comparative Strategy* 12, no. 4 (1993): 437–57.
45 Ibid., 444–46.

later, when reconnaissance had revealed which targets had been incapacitated by the first strike, and which had been missed. The number of nuclear warheads used differed in the East German exercises, but typically 30–35 warheads were used by a segment of the East German force. The army groups using the weapons could be under East German command, but the order to fire had to be given by the Soviet front command. The whole WAPA front had about 840 warheads at its disposition in the exercise, but only 250 were used in the first strike.

The Soviets even exercised attacks on NATO command centres, firing stations, airfields, key logistic points and other important targets with purely conventional forces, the so-called desant operations with special forces being airlifted into enemy territory far behind the front line.[46] Such conventional strikes were to replace nuclear strikes.

It is of course impossible to judge whether these conventional or limited nuclear interventions would result in a comparable limited NATO response. But this was exactly what the flexible NATO doctrine was about. Still, the overall WAPA doctrine seemed to be that if NATO attacked, the response would be to conquer all of Western Europe. One might speculate that the hostilities would cease earlier, given the restrained uses of nuclear weapons.

After the Chernobyl power plant catastrophe, the Soviet strategy became more and more hesitant to use nuclear warheads at all, and around 1989 they disappeared from the plans which at the same time step by step were changed into defence rather than attack plans.[47]

1989 – the end?

In December 1988 the Soviet president, Gorbachev, announced in the United Nations that the USSR would reduce its military forces by 500,000 over the next few years and withdraw 50,000 from the "Satellite" states. He invited the USA to a better and peaceful cooperation.

The Danish Intelligence Office evaluated the situation nine months later, two months before the Berlin wall fell.[48] The Danes felt somewhat suspicious towards any claims of large reductions, because:

---

46 Ibid., 442–43.
47 Ibid., 448–49.
48 Telex 11384/89 19-9-89 HEM to the Danish military attache in Bonn. Forsvarets Efterretningstjeneste: KC. Kopibog med bilag (afklass.) (1947–1990) 109 (box from 1988 in spite of being sent in 1989; PB).

- in the Soviet army, both quantity and quality had improved in the early 1980s. Now quite comprehensive reorganisations were taking place while forces were withdrawn from East Germany and Poland, but the remaining forces were of better quality. Some equipment was left behind, but many of the forces that would be essential for an amphibious attack were gone. Therefore, such an attack would in the future take much more preparation time. The East German and Polish armies also undertook reductions.
- in the Soviet navy a large number of ships, about 100, had been scrapped, and were absolutely outdated. In addition, about 30 newer ships from the Baltic and Black Sea would be scrapped. Outdated submarines were also planned to be scrapped. But in recent years about 20 large ships had been built by Baltic shipyards, so the balance seemed to be upheld.
- in the Soviet air force some reductions had taken place, but the forces for air defence stationed in East Germany had grown slightly, and the offensive powers were more or less maintained.

The office concluded that the offensive capabilities had been reduced, but the quality of remaining forces had increased, and the air defence strengthened.

We have not analysed the perceptions of the WAPA military leadership in past chapters, but it is tempting to briefly review what the chief of the East German navy thought about Gorbachev's doctrine and cuts in military spending and their consequences:[49]

First, the over-arching task of the WAPA defence was now to prevent war. Socialism was now against waging any form of war.

Second, the WAPA defence had to be organised so that security became a joint task with NATO.

Third, defence activities were now to be "adequate" (before the right term was probably "overwhelming", PB).

Born – at that time a rear admiral – commented with some resentment that the NATO doctrine was unaltered and that NATO still perceived the WAPA countries as a threat to security.

One consequence of the new WAPA doctrine was that the alert time for the navy was increased from two to four hours. This meant that most of the professional crew could go home every day after working hours. But, in addition, the capabilities of the armed forces were hollowed out because the many defections of East Germans to the West left the industrial production and agriculture with a

---

49 Born, Hendrik. *Es kommt ALLES ganz ANDERS*, 248–50. Berlin: Mittler, 2018.

lack of labour. The navy was ordered to supply some desired hands, and in the fall of 1989 the ships under Born's command had been reduced by 50 per cent due to lack of personnel. The remaining professional crews were replaced by personnel from the reserve. "What an absurdity", commented admiral Born.

We shall conclude the analysis of the NATO defence of the Baltic approaches with those two accounts, and leave the issues of how NATO perceived the dissolution of the WAPA forces after November 1989 to others.

Summing up: NATO and the WAPA in the 1980s

The Danish Intelligence perceived the risk for a WAPA attack as relatively low in the 1980s, but one could not rule out a local attack on e.g. Bornholm or the islands south of Zealand. As time passed by, the risk of a nuclear exchange also became very low – at least as a direct decision to attack. By the mid-1980s, the Soviet leadership declared that it would never strike first.

The low risk, however, did not permit the military forces to reduce their level of aspiration – because who knew? Political declarations is one thing, but military reality is another – which is "look at what they have, and draw your conclusions". What NATO did know formed quite a comprehensive insight into how the WAPA forces would operate with various types of weapons. They also had a good idea of how an amphibious attack would be played out. But as the 1980s progressed, it became clear that the technological supremacy of the Soviets was being challenged, and by the end of the 1980s some of the naval units and much of their equipment were deteriorating. So in terms of numbers, they had many, but the quality level did not rise much.

On the NATO side, the capabilities to wage littoral warfare got better than ever. Missiles finally were operating on all levels, torpedoes were more precise and long-ranging and the German Naval Air Arm had reached a level of performance never seen before. The communication systems of the individual navies was of high quality, but across countries the systems did not match one another because the NATO standard Link-11 was not used by all countries. Therefore, the Danish and German attack groups in the Baltic could only communicate at a simple data level instead of using the potential for exchanging tactical complex information and ready-to-use missile or gun firing data. Nonetheless, NATO developed a lethal attack system against an amphibious attack, operation HURRICANE, involving Danish larger units and FPBs from both navies, supported by the German Naval Air Arm.

The Danes refined their operations with missiles and developed a new flexible design for patrol craft, but it did not become operational until after the Cold

War. The naval top had high hopes for getting money for more units of corvette size to form attack groups with the FPBs, but the defence budget was not expanded for that purpose. The sea mines needed replacement, particularly in favour of controlled mines, but there was not enough money for this.

The Germans got their last state-of-the-art FPBs and the TORNADO airplane with the efficient KORMORAN missile, but the interests of the naval top were more in expanding activities outside the Baltic (moving northwards in the North Sea), perceived as an interlink to the defence of the Baltic Approaches. Thus eight large frigates were built for blue-water purposes – but strategically, their activities were bound together with the Baltics.

The exercises followed the pattern from the 1970s and were useful for changing the operations on the margins; the exact changes are difficult to analyse due to lack of declassified material.

What still remained to ponder was the role and quality of enemy and one's own air forces. What remained to improve from the inside was the quality of communication among naval units, with air control and aircraft supporting the naval operations. The perfect mission command system, linking all NATO units together and thus making perfect use of the capacities of the BALTAP command, was not yet in place by 1989.

Chapter 19
Conclusions

This book set out to answer five questions about NATO and the Baltic approaches 1949–1989: what were the purposes of the military organisations; what military instruments were they meant to organise; how did they organise cooperation with one another in order to create a military alliance among units from sovereign states; and how did they test the military capabilities of the organisations. All of this was on the basis of the question of how the military leaders perceived the goals of the stated enemy, the Soviet Union and its allies.

It is important to stress the perspective – the perceptions of the actors in this international game. There is no attempt in this book to produce an "objective" depiction of the military threats and capabilities. For the people involved, perception was reality.

The themes have been illustrated and analysed with a focus on how the naval forces of NATO were planned to defend the Baltic Approaches, waging littoral warfare. Covering all three military forces fully has not been possible. One cannot, however, disregard the two other forces because they supplement one another in that defence. Therefore, the analyses of the armies and air forces are more like a skeleton, indicating the interdependence and interplay without telling the whole story.

The short, general answers

Let us start with rather short and general answers to the questions, skipping the details. In the subsequent sections we detail what this meant for the defence of the Baltic Approaches.
- The purpose of NATO and its sub-organisations was to create a credible military force to make the enemy – the Soviet Union and its allies – refrain from a military assault on any of the member countries, and if they nonetheless attacked, to counter the attacks and make the enemy withdraw. If some territory had to be given up, key military points were to be held. Behind this posture was a belief that reinforcements could be brought in, particularly from the USA, but that might take some time.
- The military instruments were, first, nuclear weapons delivered by the USA and later England and France, and second, conventional forces on the ground, at sea and in the air. But the conventional forces were those most of the military leaders focused on by increasing their technological capabilities and train-

ing the personnel for action around the clock. The main role of the NATO commands and sub-commands was to write up war plans and construct exercises which determined how the forces of the member countries were to be of use in times of tension and war: creating systems of intelligence, preparing choke points, planning how to attack the enemy at source and how to counter attack. These plans also detailed how reinforcements could be deployed.
- Cooperation among the military forces of the many countries was organised by setting up trans-nationally staffed headquarters for territorial regions of NATO, with specialised sub-commands for the three forces. Formally, these commands worked as military bureaucracies, as they would if war broke out. But in daily routines, a comprehensive system of working relations arose, involving more or less all military levels in perpetual negotiations about the contents of the documents-to-be-written. Thus various interests of the national states behind the personnel of the staffs were fed into the contents of the final documents which typically took a year or even longer to finalise. At the level of operations, national forces were always under command of own officers, but cross-national task forces were seen e.g. by creating an integrated system of air defence in Europe.
- The military capabilities of the NATO commands were routinely checked by a series of annual exercises which tested the contents of the war plans in situations where the military commanders at all levels were put under stress to meet the enemy with their forces. However, during the 40 years of observation the politicians of the NATO countries time and again did not want to finance the demands of the military leadership for forces, so often the forces available were not deemed adequate by the military top actors to the tasks to be faced. For an extended period of time, the military leaders also had to realise that the enemy was more advanced in military technology than the NATO forces. This changed in the 1980s.

The NATO leaders perceived the leaders of the Soviet Union and its allies with deep mistrust – and vice versa. Neither side tried to hide this. Both sides, however, developed advanced systems of intelligence gathering to assess the military capabilities of the enemy, and from what we know from NATO's intelligence offices, the knowledge was comprehensive and in-depth. Thus NATO intelligence told the military commanders in detail how an amphibious attack would be organised, how enemy aircraft would attack various types of targets and how army units would operate in crossings of rivers. So the perception of possible military operations was probably quite accurate. The perception of the risks for an attack, however, was probably exaggerated; in the 1980s the Danes did not at any time see any imminent risk. But of course the WAPA military top made plans for attacks – just as NATO made quite aggressive plans for its defence. If they had not made such plans, they would not have fulfilled their roles.

A Soviet attack never happened in spite of the NATO-perceived wish of Soviet leaders for worldwide communist domination. But NATO and its military systems were busy preparing their defence against such attacks throughout the period 1949–1989.

Military capabilities in littoral warfare

Defending the Baltic Approaches may be understood as a version of littoral warfare,[1] as opposed to blue water warfare where there are few, if any, geographic obstacles. The Danish Straits were narrow and difficult to navigate, in themselves forming choke points which the Danish navy augmented by minefields, supported by coastal batteries, ships and, if possible, aircraft. A few of the minefields were controlled, as were narrow passages (created for own forces) through the rest which were uncontrolled mines, most of them lying at the bottom of the sea. Large minefields were also to be laid by the beaches, to deny access for enemy amphibious landing craft. As time passed, and particularly after the flexible response strategy became key, the Danish navy wished to change to more controlled mines, but that was not accomplished during the Cold War. The navies had the capabilities for laying the minefields; however, the main issue, however, was political: would the governments decide to lay mines in time before WAPA forces attacked?

The minefields were laid to create choke points and to impede the landing of amphibious troops on the sandy beaches of the Danish islands. The army participated in the total picture by having forces ready to counter-attack forces that had passed the minefields to go ashore. The air force also was ready to attack amphibious forces *en route* or after they had landed. Thus the defence of the Baltic Approaches was requiring cooperation among the three traditional forces, and the BALTAP organisation was from 1962 meant to facilitate such integrated command, and to enhance cooperation between the two navies.

When the Cold War started, the NATO warships – mainly Danish – were hardly in a position to maintain sea control and deny the Soviet forces the sea for long. As time passed, the German navy became a co-player, and hopes were high for a strong navy moving forward and attacking WAPA units in the Baltic. But the changes in missile technology and the strong WAPA air forces prevented the use of the large

---

1 Vego, Milan, "On Littoral Warfare," Naval War College Review 68, no. 2, Article 4 (2015).

units necessary for such actions. Instead, the Germans developed a defence line of submarines in the Eastern Baltic, naval air arm fighter-bombers (TORNADO with KORMORAN missiles) in the Middle Baltic and FPBs operating in mission teams with the air arm in the Mid- to Western Baltic. They could not establish full sea control, but they could prevent the units of the WAPA from getting access for a while. In the 1980s, the Danes and Germans developed operation HURRICANE to stop an amphibious fleet. Both navies wanted to strengthen their attack groups with attack helicopters, but neither succeeded in this during the Cold War due to budgetary constraints. The Germans also had a possibility to use nuclear warheads against such a fleet – but the exercises of the 1970s and 1980s did not include use of nuclear warheads.

The Danish navy maintained the large units – two fast missile frigates – to defend the mine laying units and subsequently to lead FPB missions as recce and communication platform. The Danish politicians, however – to some degree inspired by previous changes in the Swedish navy – ordered the frigates to be scrapped in the last year of the cold war.

What did the military actors know of their enemy? As reconnaissance systems were developed and expanded, the combined knowledge of the intelligence offices became comprehensive and detailed. They knew details of weaponry: range, speed, control systems, warheads etc. The technical capabilities of the weapon platforms – ships and submarines – were known, and their manoeuvres and tactics were observed when displayed in exercises. Thus a description of the operations of amphibious forces took 79 pages of a 2,000-page Danish treatise of the WAPA navies. When the Cold War was ending, the Danish navy could track the electronic footprints of nearly all WAPA ships, and a hydrophone rating could identify all WAPA submarines by their propel noise.

Good communication is a must for successful operations in littoral warfare. The NATO units met some problems in that respect. One issue was the quality of electronic equipment and the training of personnel to carry out tasks of communication. Time and again the communication was slowed down because of tiresome procedures and overload of messages which required special treatment because of security demands. Redundancy was frequent, and staff members did not understood the benefits of frugality in communication in times of tension and war. Until the mid-1960s the Germans had severe problems in getting English-speaking operators, and some staff officers also needed a comprehensive training program. During the entirety of the Cold War, technical problems arose in communication. Signals could be jammed, they could be barred by bad weather and they could be treated wrongly by the signalmen.

In 1954 NATO started the creation of an integrated air defence system across Europe, making the choice of when to use missiles and when to resort to air fighters easier, and making the direction of manned aircraft safer and easier.

Both navies created (nearly) all-encompassing tactical systems linked to firing control systems on the units, giving high-quality information about the theatre of war. But as systems became more sophisticated, the consequences of break-down became more and more serious, and the bans on certain electronic systems in the time preceding an attack caused many problems for weapon operators. When missiles were introduced, new barriers came with them, making the use of other units to relay signals more or less mandatory. Helicopters became popular for that role, but they were themselves vulnerable.

In principle, only one country – Denmark – was "responsible" for defending the Baltic Approaches until 1958. Norway was involved in Schleswig-Holstein until 1953 and participation with FPBs (together with British FPBs) was standard in exercises in the 1950s. Sweden, however, was neighbour with coasts along the Baltic, and particularly important in creating choke points in Øresund because the Swedes controlled the eastern coast. The country had considerable military strengths. It had opted out of joining NATO in 1949 and maintained neutrality throughout the Cold War. Hence, the eternal question was: will Sweden join NATO if the Soviets attacks westwards, or will it keep its neutrality? If so, will Soviet ships be permitted to pass through Swedish territorial waters in Øresund and Kattegat? The question was never answered because the Soviets stayed in the Baltic, but in the 1950s various contacts were made between Sweden and the two NATO neighbours, and NATO seems to have counted on Sweden joining NATO, if necessary. Until late in the 1960s, Sweden was ready to send senior officers to NATO staffs for consultations; in the 1970s and 1980s the contacts withered away – but certain cooperative measures existed regarding the air defence of Copenhagen and Southern Sweden, as did some sea and air rescue procedures.

A recurring issue was the military strength of the NATO members in relation to the perceptions of the strength of the WAPA forces. In 1952, the goals for the NATO forces were decided at the Lisbon meeting in February. But by and large, those goals were never reached. NATO set up its Annual Review to monitor progress, but the annual reports by the member countries to NATO rarely fulfilled the desires by the military top. Denmark, in particular, was a country that did not; the Germans were more willing – at least in the 1960s – to live up to the goals, but many other European countries did not. Therefore, a reading of e.g. SACEUR's comments gives the observer an impression of a NATO that could not fulfil its military obligations. Most ideas from the supreme commander seemed to be uphill with individual countries explaining that this and that goal could not be reached. The reaction from SACEUR typically called attention to the threshold for using nuclear warheads – which was lowered when conventional forces did not live up to the desired level. To make things worse, the NATO reports on the WAPA forces gave the impression that the enemy was very strong and not likely to be kept back without generous use of nuclear warheads.

Even when the flexible response system was decided, the supreme commander was very hesitant to accept it – as opposed to many of the member countries which finally perceived the nuclear scare reduced. But the tasks of the military commanders did not become easier with the flexibility. In the Baltic Approaches there were many possibilities for the enemy to probe NATO's resolve. The WAPA forces might test NATO by attacking Bornholm, Fehmarn or one of the islands south of Zealand. Would that be considered a local skirmish which would not initiate NATO's musketeer oath? Keeping an eye on WAPA forces and second-guessing a possible confrontation-build-up became more important than ever.

We have seen how the British Joint Chiefs of Staff repeatedly criticised the defence of the Baltic Approaches and Denmark's lacklustre policies to use money for military purposes. That criticism continued even in the 1980s when the Brits informally raised doubt about the benefits of sending reinforcements to Zealand – thus undermining the flexible response system.

Negotiating the defence of the Baltic Approaches

We have dealt with a developing system of complex interactions among military leaders and to some degree also their political masters, based on ever broadening and increasingly accurate information about the military adversary, the Warsaw Pact. We have seen how principles of defence were tested in large as well as small exercises, using that information to increase the quality of the defence. By the end of the 1980s, it appears that the defence of the Baltic Approaches had become credible. But it took 40 years, and the opponent – the Warsaw Pact – had a military system that was deteriorating by the end of the cold war.

On the brink of joining NATO in 1949, Denmark and Norway were well prepared for military planning because in the preceding eight months, they had analysed the possibilities for forming a defence alliance with Sweden; in 1949, Sweden pulled out and chose to remain neutral.

The Danish navy had contacts to a former German admiral who sketched out the strategic parameters Denmark should follow in NATO. He hit the nail on the head: the NATO goals for the defence of the Baltic Approaches by and large remained the same for the entirety of the Cold War. The Western Baltic and the Danish straits became a key defence area to keep the Soviet navy in the Baltic, preventing it from entering the Atlantic and the LOCs from USA to NATO countries in Europe. Thus the European dependency on American reinforcements and supplies was upheld, more or less as in WWII. Furthermore, the Northern flank of the NATO forces in Central Europe was to be secured. For this task, NATO should lay out sea mines in the Approaches and attack Soviet forces coming near. NATO furthermore should counter-attack by bombing Soviet bases along the Baltic coast and maintain a credible army force in Schleswig-Holstein, supported by the air forces and navies. Thus important air fields were kept for NATO use – obviously, they would have served the WAPA air forces well, if they had been conquered.

It took some time to get to those goals formulated, but they were too ambitious. NATO established a command – AFNORTH – for the northern region of NATO, and it soon became clear that Denmark and Norway had too few military forces for an appropriate defence. From 1953, Norway followed NATO plans and dedicated most of its forces to the northern part of the country, leaving the Approaches to Denmark. In spite of convincing military arguments, the Danish government – initially positive under a bourgeois cabinet, but later negative when the Social Democrats took over – refused offers from the USA and Great Britain to station air forces the same size as the Danish Air Force on Danish territory. This remained Danish policy for the entire Cold War, as did a ban on having nuclear warheads in Denmark – at least as long as war was not a reality.

Danish and AFNORTH policies were strongly criticised in the 1950s by the British for their military weaknesses, and they drew up a comprehensive counter-attack plan in the Baltics, mainly based on aircraft. The ideas of this plan later were to some degree adapted by SACEUR in its rapid counter-measure plans. By then and throughout the Cold War the defence of the Baltic Approaches was dependent on reinforcements of the native military forces. This was on the mind of most military leaders, but almost neglected by, first and foremost, the majority of the Danish politicians who forcefully denied access for and stationing of foreign forces in peace time.

There is hardly any doubt that until about 1960 the army forces in Schleswig-Holstein were so weak that they would not be able to resist a Soviet attack, and the air force likewise was very weak, making the defence of the territory completely dependent on timely reinforcements. The defence at sea was entirely dependent on minefields being laid in time. It is an open question whether the Danish navy could perform that role before a Soviet naval strike. A proposal from the Danish C-in-C to set up a strong NATO sea and air force, stationed in bases close to the Baltic Approaches and showing the flag in the Baltic, did not win support from the NATO allies.

The Danish military top told the politicians that more forces were desirable, as were nuclear warheads. The military top supported permanent stationing of mainly

American aircraft; they asked for more forces to Schleswig-Holstein to make NATO also allocate more forces; and they pushed for getting storage for NATO-forces, particularly German. The politicians refused the first two and dragged their feet on the third. All three issues were subject to complicated negotiations among the military commands, some of them down to extreme detail. The archives also show disagreements among the military top, particularly between the Danish C-in-C and the chief of the air force.

The criticism from own military top and abroad was to no avail; the Danish military forces remained weak and dependent on assistance from other NATO partners. There is hardly any doubt that in case of war, even the politicians would welcome such forces, but the question remains whether they could arrive in time. Maybe the politicians thought that this was possible, but they neglected or did not understand the size and complexity of such a task. The political "no" created a negative stance towards Denmark in many other NATO countries, particularly in Great Britain. To make up for the deficit, many exercises therefore had an element of forces coming in from abroad, and such units were put on what one might call a list of possible aids, but in was not until the 1980s that more firm plans for reinforcements came into place and the locations of the stores necessary for their operations planned.

In the late 1950s many discussions took place regarding NATO stores for German forces; an issue that took time but was ultimately solved was storage for the German navy using Danish waters in-between operations in the Baltic, and storing mines for use in the Fehmarn Belt.

These military problems of reinforcement had their roots in the Danish constitution which does not allow foreign forces on Danish soil until an attack takes place; ways to circumvent this clause were not politically acceptable or convenient, as the Danish population was dead against such forces with the German occupation during WWII in mind. The constitution also prevented NATO from commanding Danish forces until Denmark was attacked, and in reality Denmark did not offer a solution to this problem until 1967 when it adopted the principle used by other countries: to let a Danish NATO top officer also have a Danish top post, just like SACEUR often held a top American post as chief of American forces in Europe.

The "New Approach" of NATO, initiated in 1953, was an intense system of using atomic warheads from the outset of a war: a massive retaliation. The Danish politicians and general public were opposed, and several other NATO partners were hesitant. Ultimately, the scheme was softened in 1957–58, opening the gate for the later flexible response. Denmark refused to receive nuclear warheads on Danish territory in peace time and in reality made it impossible to do so in war time after 1963 because the Danish units were not trained to do so. Until then, the denial was a sort of Janus Head – maybe yes, maybe no. BALTAP developed procedures to use such ammunition close to Denmark. Nonetheless, it is noticeable how most activities and exercises only operated with nuclear weapons as a theoretical possibility. The navies only had conventional weapons, and that was what they trained. The German air force was ready to use nuclear warheads, the Danish not.

The New Approach, however, changed the role of the Danish air force dramatically, from being a national defence unit to playing a role in the counter-attacks against Warsaw Pact bases along the Baltic coast, at least in the first days of a war, albeit without nuclear warheads on the Danish airplanes. This change of roles is one of the strongest footprints of NATO on Danish defence, but it is also the most secret part; even in 2022 the targets were not declassified whereas it was no longer secret where the German airplanes would have been headed.

The NATO bureaucracy initially was rather ignorant about the specific issues of defending the Baltic Approaches. The top staff did not understand the intricacies of the Danish straits, or they did not believe in the possibilities there – they had a "blue ocean" perspective and therefore rather preferred to block Skagerrak. The Danish military top several times reacted against elements of the proposed plans, in particular the heavy use of airplanes for roles that the Danish navy would have reserved for naval action. Over time, NATO became more receptive, to some degree because Denmark stopped SACEUR initiatives that ignored Danish points of view in the NATO Standing Group.

The NATO system set up several quite bureaucratic processes for controlling national forces. The most comprehensive was the Annual Review which monitored the national forces closely and compared them with the goals set by the supreme commander. Another was the Combat Effectiveness report which dealt with the training of national forces. Both reports indicated that the quantity and quality of AFNORTH forces were inadequate, particularly in Denmark. The reports were subject to intense negotiations between national and NATO staff officers; in the Danish case, the NATO chairman once could not hide his anger against the Danish politicians dragging their feet.

The West German rearmament started in 1956 after joining NATO. Four years of fruitless negotiations to create the West European Union preceded; France did everything to keep the German forces at a minimum but failed to approve the union politically. NATO was less restrictive. It took six year to build up an air force, less to form the necessary army units which took over the defence of Schleswig-Holstein in 1958. The navy also took its time, but when BALTAP was ready, the navy had reached a quite impressive size. However, it lacked in quality, it needed renewal of ships and weapons. The initial high hopes for aggressive destroyer operations in the Baltic had to be put aside in the light of the technologically advanced growth of the WAPA navies with sea missiles and a large WAPA air force. Instead, the German navy relied on submarines operating along the eastern Baltic coast and a large group of FPBs with torpedoes, working together with fighter-bombers. It took several years of analysis and negotiation within the navy to reach this conclusion.

The Danes were very slow in accepting the militarily much desired NATO command that would integrate the German forces with the Danish in defending the Baltic Approaches. The eight-year long process of negotiations on and off is an example of how a military top (SACEUR) had to keep its temper against a political body – the Danish Social Democratic government – with various top officers from Germany and the German defence minister intervening at appropriate and in-between also less appropriate times. Ultimately, however, the supreme commander got his desired integrated command for the Baltic Approaches, the BALTAP, with most top commands going to the weak partner, Denmark. This was the political price Germany had to pay.

The BALTAP command was operating from the summer of 1962. The top posts were dominated by the Danes in spite of their lack of military strength. The tasks had been well prepared for the navies by a group which had worked on war plans since 1957. But disagreements between the Germans and SACEUR had postponed a decision on the roles of the Naval Air Arm, with the supreme commander wanting to be part of the nuclear counter-attack plans. The issue was solved "peacefully" some years later, and the navy kept its airplanes for its own purposes.

NATO saw three serious crises in the 1960s. For the Baltic Approaches, the 1961 Berlin crisis resulted in a rather weak and contended system of harassing WAPA ships in international waters. The Cuban missile crisis in 1962 tested NATO's systems of alarm, and the Germans in particular identified a number of weaknesses when the alarm level was raised. The Czechoslovakian crisis in 1968 revealed problems in the NATO HQ, but not in the forces defending the Baltic Approaches.

Within the Baltic Approaches, the Danish forces under BALTAP would from 1960 concentrate on defending the Zealand islands – as before by mining the straits and the beaches. The Danish air force's fighter bombers and fighters were stationed in Jutland, at a distance from the WAPA air fields, but their first role was to participate in counter-strikes along the Baltic coast and thus thin out the capabilities of the WAPA forces. Thus they were not available immediately for supporting Danish forces directly. The Danish navy, however, became more independent with its missiles (sea and air) and wire guided torpedo systems, and at a later phase there was the possibility that the airplanes might be of assistance for Danish ground and sea forces (TASMO: Tactical Air Support for Maritime Operations).

The German navy had strengthened its submarine forces in the Eastern Baltic. West of Bornholm, it would mine the Fehmarn Belt and other areas and attack amphibious WAPA forces approaching Denmark and Germany – in cooperation with the Danes. For that purpose, the Naval Air Arm came in useful in the attacks coordinated with FPBs, from the early 1970s missile armed. From 1980 the navy got the multi-tasking TORNADO aircraft, armed with KORMORAN missiles. The German army forces were to defend Schleswig-Holstein with a Danish army contingent moving to that area, too. The German air force would be of assistance when possible, but its main roles were in Central Europe.

This division of labour remained in place for the rest of the Cold War. The NATO forces were in a serious deficit regarding missiles until the mid-1970s, but from then on NATO's level of technology rose steadily, and the military balance became better – if not in quantity, then in quality. NATO developed missile tactics in the Baltic, and ultimately a pre-planned nuclear attack against amphibious forces was a possibility outside Danish national waters. The Soviet navy increasingly was deployed to the Kola peninsula and the bases in Murmansk, probably with an aim to get easier access to the Atlantic and the NATO LOCs from the USA to Europe. For the defence of the Baltic Approaches this meant fewer high-class missile destroyers and relatively older naval material. The Poles and East Germans got a larger role, but in particular the air forces seem to have been reduced. Increasingly, Poland as a nation appears to have become less reliable as a Cold War partner, at least as seen by the Soviets.

Perceptions and realities

The whole Cold War was dominated by hard work for the military top to obtain and use the newest technology. The most obvious examples were electronic communication and missiles – the latter being dependent on the former. The intelligence offices were busy collecting information about all military issues and helping to develop more advanced systems of communication to collect even more intelligence. The Danish office developed a sophisticated system of recognising the WAPA electronic footprints and by the end of the Cold War they could map the location and movements of nearly all WAPA ships. This removed the most risky and time-consuming step from the past recce operations: identifying a radar or other electronic signals. Now they knew the identity – of course dependent on the existence of some electronic signal to recognise.

The military intelligence offices had a, if not the, key role in forming the images of the enemy that were the basic elements for creating the minds of the military top. One thing was the classic bad-guys-impression of an adversary whose mind was set on attacking any time it could be convenient and chances for victory were there. But this basic belief had to be supported by more detailed knowledge about what the enemy actually was capable of doing – and what their own forces were able to do. When the Cold War started, the image and knowledge was rather simple because the West had atomic weapons to threaten the East with destruction. As the East improved its capabilities in that regard, the West had to change its perceptions to a less comprehensive and hence less dangerous understanding of military operations based on conventional weapons. Backed up by the atomic scare, yes, but using the bombs became more and more unlikely as time passed. This is not to say that the WAPA military did not make plans for such use, but the political will was waning, both in the east and west.

Regardless, NATO got the flexible response and the intelligence offices became even busier with creating information about the capabilities of the enemy so that measured responses to military challenges could be created and exercised. And the military top therefore needed even more information. The amount of papers created by the German navy for the military and political top and archived in Freiburg is staggering. The Danish counterparts produced less paper, but still they have an impressing archive in Copenhagen and Karup. But as far as an observer can see (because most of the papers are still classified and therefore cannot be accessed), the NATO staffs beat them all. The NATO staffs kept the national staffs and their ministries busy with filling out forms, reacting to drafts for future orders, monitoring the activities of the military forces and analysing their quality. In addition there were many meetings among staff members visiting each other's countries, learning about new military technology and discussing for how long one could trust that the capabilities of the existing military systems would endure.

The military top thus operated within a comprehensive system of information which was constantly changing and whose parts were in a never ending process of negotiations – among the top, with their subordinates and with their political masters. Negotiations typically dealt with principles for distributing resources.

A first item was money, or budgetary distributions. This we have not dealt with in any detail, but was an issue for the military top vis-a-vis their political masters who decided their budget in the parliament; and before that negotiations on the size of the military and the allocation of resources for various types of weapon. It also was an issue within the Ministry of Defence; all had an interest in getting a (larger) share of the cake or deciding how the budget was to be distributed to subordinates within the ministry. Therefore this also was an issue among the military chiefs themselves because they all had ideas of how to expand their activities, but in so far as it was a zero-sum game, a balance had to be kept among them. Ample evidence about these problems are found in the analysis of the Danish military in the 1950s.

A second issue for the military top was the use of resources understood as military units – singularly and/or in cooperation with other forces – in military plans and other documents that preceded future military action. This probably was the core of any military chief's thoughts, and one example is the discussions between the Danish military top and SACEUR and/or CINCNORTH in the 1950s regarding the plans for e.g. mining the approaches. A second example is the disagreements between the German navy and the supreme commander in the early 1960s regarding the use of the German navy's Fleet Arm – for the navy or for SACEUR's nuclear strikes? A third example is the command of aircraft and air defence over the territory of Schleswig-Holstein – was it to be 2. ATAF or the AIRBALTAP command? Regarding the navies of BALTAP, one can say that the distribution of command to two national flag officers – each therefore commanding his own forces – was a solution to avoid skirmishes between the two navies.

This leads to a third item, the system of command where subordinates within the NATO system in most cases in peace time were something like equal partners with their chiefs. At the very least, all plans and systems of orders have been negotiated in detail among all interested parties, and most comments from subordinates were taken seriously indeed. But the Danes experienced being neglected in the first half of the 1950s; the NATO top did not understand the intricacies of the Baltic Approaches. There also were severe skirmishes among SACEUR's deputy Montgomery, CINCNORTH and the Danish military top regarding the border between AFNORTH and AFCENT, and from 1956 the Germans also got involved. The differences in policy were rooted in different perceptions of military security, but there also were interests of power involved.

A fourth issue was the relations to other nations' military forces. Within NATO, this was a complex issue regarding, first, access to national military resources like base areas and space for various activities, and second, placing depots of equipment for future use. In Denmark, this became highly politicised in the 1950s regarding the stationing of foreign aircraft in peace time and later having "German" depots on Danish soil. For the navy, this was to some degree solved by NATO financing most of two naval bases in the 1960s. For the air force a solution became reserving two airfields for foreign aircraft in times of tension. And in the 1980s preparations for reinforcements no longer was a political issue, but still a complex process involving many actors in the preparation phase.

So we have seen that – based on the interpretation of various data on the enemy and own forces – a multitude of perceptions were constantly being formulated, subject to discussion and change through negotiations with other observers before they were made permanent as a reality NATO would use as the basis for its operations. That is, until it was challenged, negotiated and changed again – if only marginally – into a new reality.

Sources and References

The use of archives

The main sources are the original documents from four archives – The Danish National Archive, the German Bundeswehr Archiv, the British Chiefs of Staff (COS) archive and the NATO archives on the internet. I also use quite a few illustrations from those archives; to increase the authenticity they are presented as they looked when I photographed them so they are not redrawn. The papers are referenced with their original classification, but they are all declassified with a few Danish exceptions – the use of those has been read and authorised by the relevant organisation as part of an earlier publication in Danish.

Sources from archives are referenced by footnotes. The archive reference is found last in each note. The reader may find that contrary to tradition.

Files from the German Bundeswehr Archiv are identified by the letters BM, BL and BW, followed by numbers. The date and organisational reference is included. All files used are declassified and original classification is noted. Streng Geheim: Top secret. Geheim: Secret. Vertraulich: Confidential.

Unless commented otherwise, all Danish files quoted in archival notes are from the Danish National Archive. They are identified by the office name for the specific archive and – when possible – a date and journal number. To locate the files, one must then use the index or journal of that office archive if the archive is large. Many of the files are difficult to identify, but mostly the date is helpful because the archives often are organised by date. All files are declassified but many archives nonetheless require permission for access. YHM: Top secret. HEM: Secret. FTR: Confidential.

Minutes from the Danish Joint Chiefs of Staff are identified by FSS or (in the text) by the date quoted. The assembled minutes (archived by the Danish Supreme Command) are classified in their totality, but the minutes used here have been declassified for my purposes and hence are accessible, but only by personal approval by the Command.

Files from the British Joint Chiefs of Staff are identified by C.O.S. They are declassified and available from the internet.

NATO files (on the internet archive) are identified by their title or number. They are declassified. As a researcher, I regret that NATO keeps so many papers classified; it appears to be an unsurmountable task to declassify them. This has had consequences for this book regarding the regional commands, particularly AFNORTH and of course BALTAP. The exact consequences, however, we can only speculate about. Many NATO papers are found or reflected upon in the Danish and German archives, so we are informed to a certain degree.

References

2M3, *Wie war die Situation Warschauer Pakt-Nato im Hinblick auf die Ostseeausgänge?* (http://www.forum-marinearchiv.de/smf/index.php/topic,19302, 2013a).

Agger, Jonathan Søborg and Lasse Wolsgård, "Den størst mulige fleksibilitet: Dansk atomvåbenpolitik 1956–60," *Historisk Tidsskrift* 101, no. 1 (2001): 76–110.

Alford, Jonathan, "A Change in British Priorities?" in *Britain and NATO's Northern Flank*, ed. Geoffrey Till (London: Macmillan, 1988), 74–82.

Allison, Graham T., *Essence of Decision* (Boston: Little, Brown & Co, 1971).

Arendt, Rudolf, "Die Marine der Bundesrepublik Deutschland im Wandel der Zeit (1956–2005)," in *Die Bundesmarine 1950 bis 1972*, Johannes Berthold Sander-Nagashima (München: Oldenbourg, 2006), 447–70.
Aunesluoma, Juhana, *Britain, Sweden and the Cold War, 1945–54* (Oxford: Palgrave Macmillan, 2003).
Berdal, Mats, *British Naval Policy and Norwegian Security. Maritime Power in Transition, 1951–60* (Oslo: Institutt for forsvarsstudier, 1992).
Berdal, Mats, *The United States, Norway and the Cold War, 1954–60* (London: Macmillan, 1997).
Bogason, Peter, *Public Policy and Local Governance: Institutions in Postmodern Society*, New Horizons in Public Policy (Cheltenham: Edward Elgar, 2000).
Bogason, Peter, *Søværnet under den kolde krig – politik, strategi og taktik* (København: Snorres Forlag, 2015).
Bolik, Gerd, *NATO-Planungen für die Verteidigung der Bundesrepublik Deutschland im Kalten Krieg* (Berlin: Miles-Verlag, 2021).
Borck, Niels Chr. and Søren Nørby, *Søheltenes Skibe. Historien om Søværnets torpedomissilbåde af Willemoes-klassen* (København: Statens forsvarshistoriske museum, 2007).
Bork, Jørgen F., *Åbent hav. Mit liv i Søværnet 1945–1990* (København: Gyldendal, 2010).
Born, Hendrik, *Es kommt ALLES ganz ANDERS* (Berlin: Mittler, 2018).
Brinkmann, Rainer, ed., *Die Ära der Schnellboote* (Rostock: Marinekommando, 2020).
Burns, William F., "Tactical Nuclear Weapons and NATO: An Introductory Reminiscence," in *Tactical Nuclear Weapons and NATO*, eds Tom Nichols, Douglas Stuart, and Jeffrey McCausland (US Army College: The Strategic Studies Institute, 2012), xii–xix.
Clemmesen, Michael H., "The Danish View," in *Cold War Views on Sweden*, eds Gunnar Artéus and Kent Zetterberg (Stockholm: Medströms Bokförlag, 2018), 13–29.
Clemmesen, Michael H., "Den massive gengældelses lille ekko. De taktiske atomvåbens rolle i dansk forsvarsplanlægning i 1950erne," in *Danmark, Norden og NATO 1948–1962*, eds Carsten Due Nielsen, Johan Peder Noack, and Nikolaj Petersen (København: Jurist- og Økonomforbundets Forlag, 1990), 121–44.
Clemmesen, Michael H., "Udviklingen i Danmarks forsvarsdoktrin fra 1945 til 1969," *Militært Tidskrift* (1987): 7–81.
Colbourn, Susan, *Euromissiles: The Nuclear Weapons That Nearly Destroyed NATO* (Ithaca: Cornell University Press, 2022).
Dalsjö, Robert, *Sweden's Squandered Life-Line to the West*, Parallel History Project on Cooperative Security (http://www.php.isn.ethz.ch/, 2007).
Dansk Institut for Internationale Studier, *Danmark under den kolde krig. Den sikkerhedspolitiske situation 1945–1991. Bind 2: 1963–1978* (København: Dansk Institut for Internationale Studier, 2005b).
Dansk Institut for Internationale Studier, *Danmark under den kolde krig. Den sikkerhedspolitiske situation 1945–1991. Bind 1: 1945–1962* (København: Dansk Institut for Internationale Studier, 2005a).
David, Francois, "The Doctrine of Massive Retaliation and the Impossible Nuclear Defense of the Atlantic Alliance," in *The Routledge Handbook of Transatlantic Secutiry*, eds Basil Germond and Soutou Hanhimäki, Georges-Henru (Milton Park: Routledge, 2010), 32–44.
Davis, Robert Thomas, *The Dilemma of NATO Strategy, 1949–1968* (Athens, OH: Ohio University, 2008).
Der Erste, *Wie war die Situation Warschauer Pakt-Nato im Hinblick auf die Ostseeausgänge?* (http://www.forum-marinearchiv.de/smf/index.php/topic,19302, 2013a).

Diedrich, Torsten, "Die DDR-Marine in den Vereinten Seestreitkräften des Warschauer Paktes und das Operationsgebiet Ostsee," in *OSTSEE. Kriegsschauplatz und Handelsregion. Festschrift für Robert Bohn*, Thomas W. Friis and Michael F Scholz (Gotland: Gotland University Press, 2013).

Diedrich, Torsten, "Zur Rolle der Nationalen Volksarmee der DDR," in *Die Streitkräfte der DDR und Polens in der Operationsplanung des Warschauer Paktes*, ed. Rüdiger Wenke (Potsdam: Militärgeschichtliches Forschungsamr, 2011), 13–34.

Duffield, John S., *Power Rules. The Evolution of Nato's Conventional Force Posture* (Stanford, CA: Stanford University Press, 1995).

Espenes, Øistein, "'Den dolda alliansen' og svensk Natodebatt," *Kungl Krigsvetenskapsakademiens Handlingar och Tidskrift* 2015, no. 1 (2015): 140–48.

Forsvarets Efterretningstjeneste, *Truslen mod Danmark* (Vedbæk: Forsvarskommandoen, 1978).

Forsvarets Efterretningstjeneste, *Truslen mod Danmark* (Vedbæk: Forsvarskommandoen, 1988).

Forsvarskommandoen, *Forsvaret år 2000. Perspektivplan 1. del* (Vedbæk: Forsvarskommandoen, 1982).

Forsvarskommandoen, "Forsvarschefsskitse 1975" (Vedbæk: Forsvarskommandoen, 1975).

Forsvarskommandoen, *Ved forenede kræfter. Forsvarets øverste militære ledelse. Forsvarschefsembedet og forsvarets udvikling 1950–2000* (Vedbæk: Forsvarskommandoen, 2000).

Forsvarsministeriet, *Beretning fra Forsvarskommissionen af 1969* (København: Forsvarsministeriet, 1972).

Forsvarsministeriet, *Beretning fra Forsvarskommissionen af 1988* (København: Forsvarsministeriet, 1989).

French, Ryan W. and Peter Dombrowski, "Exercise BALTOPS: Reassurance and Deterrence in a Contested Littoral," in *Ilitary Exercises: Political Messaging and Strategic Impact*, eds Beatrice Heuser, Tormod Heier, and Guillaume Lasconjarias (Rome: NATO Defense College. Forum Paper 26., 2018), 187–211.

Frorath, Gerd, Dieter Matthei, and Hans W. Worringer, *Die Crew X/62 im Spiegel der Zeit* (http://www.crewx62.de/Texte/DokuCrewX62+Schlussversion+HP.pdf, n.d.).

Fursdon, Edward, *The European Defence Community: A History* (London: Palgrave Macmillan, 1980).

Gearson, John and Kori Schake, eds, *The Berlin Wall Crisis* (London: Palgrave Macmillan, 2002).

Geckler, Niels and Morten Friis Jørgensen, *Bornholm i krig og fred* (Rønne: Hakon Holm Publishing, 2021).

Gemzell, Carl-Axel, "Die DDR, der Warschauer Pakt und Dänemark im kalten Krieg," in *Deutsch-skandinavische Beziehungen nach 1945*, eds Hohnm Robert, Jürgen Elvert, and Karl Christian Lammers (Stuttgart: Franz Steiner Verlag, 2000), 44–56.

Gemzell, Carl-Axel, "Warszawapakten, DDR och Danmark. Kampen för en maritim operationsplan," *Historisk Tidsskrift* 16, no. 5 (1996): 32–84.

Görtz, Hans-Ove, *Skandinavisk försvarsutredning 1948–1949 – uppstarten och dess inverkan under kalla kriget* (Försvarets Historiska Telesamlingar Flygvapnet, 2020b).

Görtz, Hans-Ove, *SVENORDA. Flygsäkerhetssamarbete mellan Sverige, Norge och Danmark – en del av krigsförberedelserna* (Försvarets Historiska Telesamlingar Flygvapnet, 2020a).

Gregory, Shaun R., *Nuclear Command and Control in NATO* (Hounds, Basinstoke, Hampshire: Macmillan Press Ltd, 1996).

Greiner, Christian, "Die militärische Eingliederung der Bundesrepublik Deutschland in die WEU und die NATO," in *Die NATO-Option*, Hans Ehlert, et al. (München: R. Oldenbourg Verlag, 1993).

Grove, Eric J., *Battle for the Fiørds* (London: Ian Allan Ltd, 1991).

Grove, Eric J., "The Superpowers and Secondary Navies in Northern Waters During the Cold War," in *Navies in Northern Waters 1721–2000*, eds Rolf Hobson and Tom Kristiansen (London: Taylor and Francis, 2004), 211–21.

Gustafsson, Bengt, *Det kalla kriget – några reflexioner* (Stockholm: Försvarshögskolan, 2006).
Haftendorn, Helga, *NATO and the Nuclear Revolution: A Crisis of Credibility 1966-67* (Oxford: Oxford University Press, 1996).
Haglund, Magnus, *Flottan och det kallla kriget* (Stockholm: Kungl. Örlogsmannasällskabet, 2009).
Hammerich, Helmut R., "Fighting for the Heart of Germany: German I Corps and NATO's Plans for the Defence of the North German Plain in the 1960s," in *Blueprints for Battle: Planning for War in Central Europe.*, eds Jan Hoffenaar, Dieter Krüger, and David T Zabecki (Lelxington, KY: University Press of Kentucky, 2012), 155-74.
Hammerich, Helmut R., et al., *Das Heer 1950 Bis 1970. Konzeption, Organisation, Aufstellung* (München: R. Oldenbourg Verlag, 2006).
Hansen, Peer Henrik, "The Cuba Crisis 1962 – As Seen Through Danish Intelligence Sources," in *The Global Cuban Missile Crisis at 50*, eds James G Hershberg and Christian F Ostermann (Washington, DC: The Wilson Center, 2012), 708-25.
Helms, Adam, "Min tid som Commander Allied Forces Baltic Approaches 1970-75. Anden del 1973-75," *Tidsskrift for Søvæsen* 176, no. 2 (2005b): 73-103.
Helms, Adam, "Min tid som Commander Allied Forces Baltic Approaches 1970-75. Første del 1970-72," *Tidsskrift for Søvæsen* 176, no. 1 (2005a): 3-25.
Henriksen, Jesper Thestrup, "Side om side i det kommende Europa," *Sønderjyske Årbøger*, 2016, 95-120.
Henriksen, Jesper Thestrup, "Der Weg zum Einheitskommando," in *Grenzen überwinden – Schleswig-Holstein, Dänemark und die DDR*, eds Aaron Jessen, Elmar Moldenmauer, and Karsten Biermann (Husum: Husum Druck- und Verlagsgesellschaft, 2016), 49-70.
Hess, Sigurd, "Als die Computer lernten zur See zu fahren – die Entwicklung von Führungs- und Waffeneinsatzsystemen in der deutschen Marine 1963 bis 1969," in *Die Bundesmarine 1950 bis 1972*, Johannes Berthold Sander-Nagashima (München: Oldenbourg, 2006), 433-45.
Hess, Sigurd, "'Eine klare und gegenwärtige Gefahr' oder 'Bedingte Abwehrbereitschaft' am Beispiel des 3. Schnellbootgeschwaders während der Kubakrise 1962," in *Vor dem Abgrund. Die Streitkräfte der USA und der UdSSR Sowie Ihrer Deutschen Bündnispartner in der Kubakrise*, eds Dimitrij Filippovych and Matthias Uhl (München: Oldenbourg Wissenschaftsverlag, 2004), 85-97.
Hess, Sigurd, "Die Schnellbootgruppe Klose," in *Die deutschen Schnellboote im Einsatz*, ed. Hans Frank (Hamburg: E S Mittler Verlag, 2007).
Hessling, Urs, *Wie war die Situation Warschauer Pakt-Nato im Hinblick auf die Ostseeausgänge?* (http://www.forum-marinearchiv.de/smf/index.php/topic,19302, 2013a).
Heuser, Beatrice, "The Development of NATO's Nuclear Strategy," *Contemporary European History* 4, no. 1 (1995): 37-66.
Heuser, Beatrice, "Warsaw Pact Military Doctrines in the 1970s and 1980s: Findings in the East German Archives," *Comparative Strategy* 12, no. 4 (1993): 437-57.
Heuser, Beatrice, Tormod Heier, and Guillaume Lasconjarias, eds, *Military Exercises: Political Messaging and Strategic Impact* (Rome: NATO Defense College. Forum Paper 26., 2018).
Holmström, Mikael,*Den dolda alliansen. Sveriges hemliga NATO-förbindelser* (Stockholm: Atlantis, 2011).
Hornemann, Jacob, *Bornholm mellem Øst og Vest. En udenrigspolitisk dokumentation* (Rønne: Bornholms Tidendes Forlag, 2006).
Hornhaver, H., "Yom Kippur krigen," *Tidsskrift for Søvæsen* 145 (1974): 82-87.
Jensen, Bent, *Bornholmske Samlinger III række 9. Bind* (Rønne: Bornholms historiske samfund, 1996).
Jensen, Frede P., "The Warsaw Pact's Special Target. Planning the Seizure of Denmark," in *War Plans and Alliances in the Cold War. Threat Perceptions in the East and West.*, eds Vojtech Mastny, Sven G. Holtsmark, and Andreas Wenger (London: Routledge, 2006), 95-117.

Jentzsch, Christian, "The Baltic and the Federal German Navy in the Final Stages of the Cold War," in *The Role of Territorial Defense Forces in Peace and War*, Zoltán Jobbágy Szeghy, et al. (Budapest: Hungarian Defence Forces Scientific Research Centre, 2020), 101-18.
Jeschonnek, Gert, *Bundesmarine 1955 bis heute* (Koblenz/Bonn: Wehr und Wissen, 1975).
Johnston, Seth, *How NATO Adapts: Strategy and Organization in the Atlantic Alliance Since 1950* (Baltimore: John Hopkins University Press, 2017).
Jordan, Robert S. and Parley W. Newman, "The Secretary-General of NATO and Multinational Political Leadership," *International Journal (Toronto)* 30, no. 4: 732-57.
Kaarsted, Tage, *De danske ministerier 1953-1972* (København: PFA Pension, 1992).
Kesselring, Agilof, "The Nordic Balance and the Realities of Defence in the Baltic Region, 1948-1961," in *Periphery or Contact Zone? The NATO Flanks 1961 to 2013*, ed. Bernd Lemke (Freiburg: Rombach Verlag KG, 2015), 25-41.
Kollmer, Dieter, "Schleswig-Holstein: 'Flugzeug Träger' Im Kalten Krieg," *Militärgeschichte*, no. 3 (2016).
Korstad, Dag Inge, "Luftforsvaret i kald krig," in *Alt henger sammen med alt!* eds Karl Erik Haug, Ole Jørgen Maaø, and Steinar Sanderød (Oslo: Forsvarets Høgskole/Luftkrigsskolen, 2020), 107-24.
Kugler, Richard L., *Commitment to Purpose: How Alliance Partnership Won the Cold War* (Santa Monica, CA: RAND, 1993).
Kugler, Richard L., *The Great Strategy Debate: NATO's Evolution in the 1960s* (Rand Corporation, 1991).
Kulturministeriet, *Kold krig. 33 fortællinger om den kolde krigs bygninger og anlæg i Danmark, Færøerne og Grønland* (København: Kulturministeriet, 2013).
Larsen, Margit Bech, "Vejen til Danmarks sidste kystforter: Stevnsfort og Langelandsfort 1945-1954," *Fra Krig og Fred* 2014/1 (2014): 181-234.
Larsson, Bengt, "Marinens Sjöoperativa Doktrin 1958-1961," *Forum Navale*, no. 67 (2011): 48-91.
Lauridsen, John T., et al., *Den kolde krig og Danmark* (København: Gads Forlag, 2011).
Legge, J. Michael, *Theatre Nuclear Weapons and the NATO Strategy of Flexible Response* (Santa Monica, CA: Rand Corporation, 1983).
Lemke, Bernd, *Die Allied Mobile Force* (München: De Gruyter, 2011).
Lemke, Bernd, et al., *Die Luftwaffe 1950 bis 1970. Konzeption, Aufbau, Integration* (München: R. Oldenbourg Verlag, 2006).
Lindhardt, Bjarne F., *Allierede forstærkninger til Danmark* (København: Samfundsvidenskabeligt Forlag, 1981).
Lundholm, Kurt, *Søridderne* (Brunlynget Bogforlag, 2011).
Mahan, Alfred Thayer, *The Influence of Sea Power Upon History: 1660-1783* (Boston: Little, Brown and Company, 1890).
Maloney, S. M., "Berlin Contingency Planning: Prelude to Flexible Response," *Journal of Strategic Studies* 25, no. 1 (2002): 99-134.
Minow, Fritz, *Die NVA und Volksmarine in den Vereinten Streitkräften. Geheimnisse der Warschauer Vertragsorganisation* (Friedland: Steffen Verlag, 2011).
Monte, Peter, "Die Rolle der Marine der Bundesrepublik Deutschland," in *Deutsche Marinen im Wandel. Vom Symbol nationaler Einheit zum Instrument internationaler Sicherheit*, Werner Rahn (München: R. Oldenbourg Verlag, 2005).
Nes, Harald van, "Crisis Management During the Cold War Illustrated by 'Live Oak'," in *Periphery or Contact Zone? The NATO Flanks 1961 to 2013*, ed. Bernd Lemke (Freiburg: Rombach Verlag KG, 2015), 185-96.
Neutralitetspolitikkommissionen, *Om Kriget Kommit* (Stockholm: Statens Offentliga Utredningar 1994:11, 1994).

Nielsen, Flemming Schroll, *AMF – NATO's krisestyrke* (København: Forsvarets oplysnings- og velfærdstjeneste, 1981).

Nielsen, Harald, *Die DDR und die Kernwaffen – Die nukleare Rolle der National Volksarmee im Warschauer Pakt* (Baden-Baden: Nomos Verlagsgesellschaft, 1998).

Nielsen, Jens Perch, *Socialdemokratiet og enhedskommandoen 1961* (Århus: Institut for Statskundskab, 1987).

Ninn-Hansen, Erik, *Syv år for VKR* (København: Det Schønbergske Forlag, 1974).

Nørby, Søren, *Nordhvalen og Nordkaperen. De sidste danskbyggede ubåde* (København: Statens forsvarshistoriske museum, 2013).

Nørby, Søren, "Sandheden om ubåden Delfinens deltagelse i STANAVFORLANT 1972," *Marinehistorisk Tidsskrift* 43, no. 4 (2010): 3–17.

Olsen, Gunnar and Svenn Storgaard, *Flådens Skibe og Fartøjer 1945–1995* (København: Marinehistorisk Selskab, 1998).

Osborn, Patrick R., *Operation Pike: Britain Versus the Soviet Union, 1939–1941* (London: Greenwood, 2000).

Palmer, Diego A. Ruiz, *A Strategic Odyssey: Constancy of Purpose and Strategy-Making in NATO, 1949–2019* (Rome: NATO defence college, 2019).

Pedlow, Gregory W., *The Evolution of NATO's Command Structure 1951–2009* (Brussels: NATO, n.d.).

Pedlow, Gregory W., "NATO and the Berlin Crisis of 1961: Facing the Soviets While Maintaining Unity" (Supreme Headquarters Allied Powers Europe, 2002).

Pedlow, Gregory W., *NATO Strategy Documents 1949–1969* (Bruxelles: Supreme Headquarters Allied Powers Europe, 1997).

Pedlow, Gregory W., "The Politics of NATO Command, 1950–1962," in *U:S: Miliitary Forces in Europe. The Early Years*, eds Simon W. Duke and Wolfgang Krieger (Boulder, CO: Westview Press, 1993), 15–42.

Peters, B. Guy, *The Politics of Bureaucracy* (London: Routledge, 2000).

Petersen, Jørgen, *Mit liv i Søværnet 1934–80* (Odense: Odense Universitetsforlag, 1985).

Pettersson, Tommy, *Med invasionen i sikte. Flygvapnets krigsplanläggning och luftoperative doktrin 1958–1966* (Stockholm: Försvarshögskolan, 2009).

Pfeifer, Douglas, "Forerunners to the West German Bundesmarine: The Klose Fast Patrol Group, the Naval Historical Team Bremerhaven, and the U.S. Navy's Labor Service Unit (B)," *International Journal of Naval History* 1, no. 1 (2002).

Pranov, J. B., "Betragtninger vedrørende flådens sammensætning af egentlige krigsskibe under ændrede vilkår," *Tidsskrift for Søvæsen* 139 (1968): 313–23.

Pranov, J. B., "Forslag til flådeplan 1990," *Tidsskrift for Søvæsen* 142 (1971): 210–29.

Rasmussen, Peter Hertel, "Det landmilitære forsvar af den sjællandske øgruppe og Bornholm under den kolde krigs sidste årtier (1979 – 1989). Del 2: Perioden fra 1980 til og med 1989," *Fra Krig og Fred* (2023): 55–95.

Rasmussen, Peter Hertel, *Den danske Tysklandsbrigade 1947–1958* (Odense: Syddansk Universitetsforlag, 2019).

Risso, Linda, "'I Am the Servant of the Council': Lord Ismay and the Making of the NATO International Staff," *Contemporary European History* 28 (2019): 342–57.

Rodholm, Immanuel Benedict, *Mine 48 År i Forsvaret* (København: Marinens Bibliotek, 2009).

Ruge, Friedrich, *In vier Marinen. Lebenserinnerungen als Beitrag zur Zeitgeschichte* (München: Bernard & Graefe Verlag, 1979).

Sager, Wilhelm, *Heere zwischen den Meeren. Heeres- und Kriegsgeschichte Schleswig-Holsteins* (Husum: Husum Druck- und Verlagsgesellschaft, 2003).

Sander-Nagashima, Johannes Berthold, *Die Bundesmarine 1950 bis 1972* (München: Oldenbourg Wissenschaftsverlag, 2006).
andnes, Hans Ole, *The 1970-1974 Combat Aircraft Analysis* (Trondheim: Tapir Academic Press, 2010).
ayle, Timothy Andrews, *Enduring Alliance: A History of NATO and the Postwar Global Order* (Ithaca: Cornell University Press, 2019).
chaiffel-Nielsen, N. M., *De tog vore hjem II* (Randbøl: Randbøl Sogns Lokalarkiv og Museumdforenings forlag, n.d.).
chaiffel-Nielsen, N. M., "Deployeringsflyvestation Vandel," *Luft- og Rumfartsårbogen 1992-93* (1993): 50-75.
chrøder, Hans A., *Historien om Flyvevåbnet* (Komiteen til udgivelse af "Historien om Flyvevåbnet," 1990).
chulte, Paul, "Tactical Nuclear Weapons in NATO and Beyond: A Historical and Thematic Examination," in *Tactical Nuclear Weapons and NATO*, eds Tom Nichols, Douglas Stuart, and Jeffrey McCausland (US Army College: The Strategic Studies Institute, 2012), 13-71.
HAPE, *History 1957* (Mons: SHAPE, 1967a).
HAPE, *SHAPE History - The New Approach 1953-1956* (Mons: SHAPE, 1976).
HAPE, *SHAPE History 1958* (Mons: SHAPE, 1967b).
HAPE, *SHAPE History Volume I* (Versailles: SHAPE, 1953).
HAPE, *SHAPE History Volume II* (Versailles: SHAPE, 1959).
teinkopff, Klaus Christoph, *Die geostrategische Bedeutung der Cimbrischen Halbinsel in der westlichen Verteidigungsplanung* (Kiel, 2003).
hoss, Bruno, "'Bedingt abwehrbereit'. Auftrag und Rolle der Bundeswehr als NATO-Mitglied während der Kuba-Krise," in *Vor dem Abgrund. Die Streitkräfte der USA und der UdSSR sowie ihrer deutschen Bündnispartner in der Kubakrise*, eds Dimitrij Filippovych and Matthias Uhl (München: Oldenbourg Wissenschaftsverlag, 2004), 65-84.
hoss, Bruno, *NATO-strategie und nationale Verteidigungsplanung. Planung und Aufbau der Bundeswehr unter den Bedingungen atomaren Vergeltungsstrategie 1952-1960* (München: R. Oldenbourg Verlag, 2006).
hostrup, S. S., "Enhedkommandoen," *Tidsskrift for Søvæsen* 135 (1963): 209-30.
hostrup, S. S., "Chief of Staff from 9th January 1962 to 31st March 1965," in *Safeguarding Security in the Baltic Approaches 1962-2002*, Ove Høegh-Guldberg Hoff (Viborg: Public Information Office Joint Headquiarters NORTHEAST, 2002), 11-38.
hostrup, S. S., "Søværnets styrkemål," *Tidsskrift for Søvæsen* 144 (1973): 97-135.
wigge, Stephen and Len Scott, *Planning Armageddon. Britain, the United States and the Command of Western Nuclear Forces 1945-1964* (Amsterdam: Harwood Academic Publishers, 2000).
Jdenrigsministeriet, *Dansk Sikkerhedspolitik 1948-1966. Bilag* (København: Udenrigsministeriet, 1968b).
Jdenrigsministeriet, *Dansk Sikkerhedspolitik 1948-1966* (København: Udenrigsministeriet, 1968a).
Jhl, Matthias, "'Jederzeit gefechtsbereit' - Die NVA während der Kubakrise," in *Vor dem Abgrund. Die Streitkräfte der USA und der UdSSR sowie ihrer deutschen Bündnispartner in der Kubakrise*, eds Dimitrij Filippovych and Matthias Uhl (München: Oldenbourg Wissenschaftsverlag, 2004), 99-119.
Jhl, Matthias, "Storming on to Paris. The 1961 Buria Exercise and the Planned Solution of the Berlin Crisis," in *War Plans and Alliances in the Cold War. Threat Perceptions in the East and West.*, eds Vojtech Mastny, Sven G. Holtsmark, and Andreas Wenger (London: Routledge, 2006), 46-71.
Jtrikesdepartementet, *Fred och Säkerhet* (Stockholm: SOU 2002: 108. Utrikesdepartementet, 2002).
Vegger, A. C. B., *Slesvig-Holsten fra 1945 til 1962* (Viborg: Det kongelige Garnisonsbibliotek, 1985).

Vego, Milan, "On Littoral Warfare," *Naval War College Review* 68, no. 2, Article 4 (2015).
Vego, Milan, *Operational Warfare at Sea. Theory and Practice*. (New York: Routledge, 2009).
Villaume, Poul, *Allieret med forbehold* (København: Eirene, 1995).
Villaume, Poul, "Amerikanske flybaser på dansk jord i fredstid? En studie i Danmarks base- og stationeringspolitik i NATO 1951-1957," *Historisk Tidsskrift* 15, no. 2 (1987): 238-98.
Villaume, Poul, "Mulig fjende – nødvendig allieret?" in *Danmark, Norden og NATO 1948-1962*, Carsten Due Nielsen, Johan peder Noack, and Nikolaj Petersen (København: Jurist- og Økonomforbundets Forlag, 1991), 147-90.
Wagner, Gerhard, "Die ersten Jahre der Bundesmarine," in *Seemacht un Geschichte*, Deutsches Marine Institut (Bonn: MOV-Verlag, 1975), 229-38.
Wallerfelt, Bengt, *Den hemliga svenska krigsplanen* (Stockholm: Medströms Bokforlag, 2016).
Wennerholm, Bertil, *Fjjärde Flygvapnet i Världen?* (Stockholm: Försvarshögskolan, 2006).
Wenzke, Rüdiger, ed., *Die Streitkräfte der DDR und Polens in der Operationsplanung des Warschauer Paktes* (Berlin: Militärgeschichtliches Forschungsamt, 2010).
White, Kenton, *British Defence Planning and Britain's NATO Commitment, 1979 – 1985* (Reading: University of Reading, 2016).
Wilkinson, P. J., "Offensive Operations – Strike," in *Royal Air Force in Germany*, Royal Air Force Historical Society (Brighton: Royal Air Force Historical Society, 1998), 71-85.

www.ingramcontent.com/pod-product-compliance
Lightning Source LLC
Chambersburg PA
CBHW061702300426
44115CB00014B/2528